Isco Open Channel
Flow Measurement
Handbook

Isco Open Channel Flow Measurement Handbook

Third Edition
First Printing

By Douglas M. Grant

Divisional General Manager
Isco Environmental Division
Lincoln, Nebraska

Table of contents

List of illustrations

List of tables

Chapter

1

Introduction

Overview

The first chapter of the handbook provides a general introduction to both the handbook itself and the subject of open channel flow measurement. Included are sections briefly dealing with the purpose and organization of the handbook, the early history of flow measurement, and the present need for flow measurement.

Purpose and organization

This handbook provides assistance to individuals involved in measuring open channel flow. By assembling flow measurement information from various sources into a single comprehensive volume, it is hoped that the handbook will be of practical value to individuals dealing with the realities of difficult open channel flow measurement problems.

The handbook has been divided into seventeen chapters. The first chapter provides a general introduction to the handbook and to the subject. The second chapter discusses open channel flow measurement in general terms. The third chapter describes in detail the use of weirs. The fourth chapter gives an in-depth look at flumes. The fifth chapter contains methods for selecting primary devices. The sixth chapter discusses the measurement of gravity flow using the Manning formula. The seventh chapter provides practical information on flow measurement system installations.

1

Chapters eight through sixteen provide discharge tables on many commonly used primary measuring devices. The final chapter, seventeen, presents conversion tables used in flow measurement work.

Early history of flow measurement

Since the beginning of civilization, man has recognized the need to quantitize the flow of liquids. His first efforts were probably directed toward survival during floods and to waterborne transportation. As civilization became more advanced, the demands for water supply, irrigation, navigation, and water power all contributed to the development of techniques to measure liquid level, flow rates, and quantities. It is known that the ancient Egyptians and Babylonians used some form of water accounting as a basis for levies to individual land holders for their usage of water from extensive irrigation systems.

The River Nile of Egypt has probably been studied by man longer than any other river in the world. The crop yields in the lower Nile valley are dependent upon the annual flooding of the river, and thus the annual yields are a function of the river's level. Because of this, taxes were based on the maximum level of the river. Mention of the annual rises of the Nile dates back between 3000 and 3500 B.C., and known flood marks extend as far back as 1800 B.C. More than 3000 years ago, the Egyptian Pharaoh Menes developed a flood control system for the Nile River. Part of this system included at least 20 recording stations along the Nile. These stations used a crude form of a staff gauge to measure the level of the river. These levels were recorded daily, and compared with previous year's records to predict the future levels of the river.

One of the earliest and most complete records of an attempt to measure water flow volume is that of Sextus Julius Frontinus, who was the Water Commissioner of Rome in 52 A.D. He attempted to determine the quantity of water delivered to each user in the Roman system by measuring the cross-sectional area of the spouts through which the water was discharged. Since Frontinus ignored the velocity of the flow, his efforts were not entirely successful. However, it presents an interesting record of an early flow measurement system.

The techniques of flow measurement have advanced through the centuries. Much of the theoretical background for the science of hydraulics, which is the basis for modern flow measurement, was developed in the 17th and 18th centuries by researchers such as Torricelli, Pitot, Woltman, and Venturi. Advances in the art and science of liquid flow measurement continued into the 19th and 20th centuries, paralleling the general advancement of technology. However, most methods of open channel flow measurement are simply sophisticated adaptions of the level measurements practiced by the Egyptians on the Nile over 4000 years ago.

Present need for flow measurement

The rapid growth of urban areas in recent times and advances in technology and industry to meet society's ever increasing demands for more goods, energy, etc. have greatly increased the potential for environmental pollution. They have also contributed to an increasing awareness of and concern for the environment. Population density and advanced technology continue to place increasing demands on society to control the quality and conserve the supply of water.

Increasingly stricter legislation and continuing public interest in conservation and environmental matters have emphasized the importance of flow measurement. Uniform and reliable measurement data are needed to identify the resource levels and quality of bodies of water, to determine the results of conservation and quality control efforts, and to enforce water conservation and quality regulatory requirements. The majority of recent interest in flow measurement has centered on water quality regulatory requirements. Federal law states that "...the purpose of self-monitoring and reporting effluent data is to permit Federal and State regulating agencies to follow on a continuing basis, the discharger's effluent quality trends as well as specific variation from established limitations." Local agencies are required by the same legislation to establish a local surcharge on industrial waste to insure that these users pay their "fair share" of the cost of existing and new treatment facilities. Their "fair share" entails the measurement of both the quality and the quantity of industrial discharge. Thus, an economic value has been placed on industrial waste, and it is important for both industrial dischargers and municipalities to be able to measure and record flow data.

Of course, flow measurement still is of great importance in more traditional areas such as irrigation, stream measurement, and sewage treatment plants. It also has other applications, for example, in storm and combined sewer flow studies, in sedimentation work, in runoff studies, and infiltration and inflow isolation.

As Shelley and Kirkpatrick [1] state: "Measurements of quantity of flow, usually in conjunction with sampling for flow quality, are essential to nearly all aspects of water pollution control. Research, planning, design, operation and maintenance, and enforcement of pertinent laws—all are activities which rely on flow measurement for their effective conduct."

Thus in the context of modern society, there is an ever increasing need for simple, accurate, and reliable methods of flow measurement. These needs are usually dictated by legislation, but in a larger sense are dictated by society's desire to reverse the trend of increasing environmental pollution, and to ensure a clean, liveable planet for this and future generations.

References

1. Kirkpatrick, George A., and Shelley, Philip E. *Sewer Flow Measurement—A State-of-the-Art Assessment.* EPA Environmental Protection Technology Series, EPA-600/2-75-027, 1975.

Suggested readings

Kulin, Gershon, and Compton, Philip R. *A Guide to Methods and Standards for the Measurement of Water Flow.* National Technical Information Service, Springfield, Va., 1975.

Stevens Water Resources Data Book. 2nd Edition. Leupold & Stevens, Inc., Beaverton, Ore., 1974.

Chapter

2

Open channel flow measurement

Overview

This chapter provides a general discussion of open channel flow measurement techniques. Included are sections briefly defining open channel flow, discussing methods of open channel flow measurement, primary and secondary measuring devices, and general units of flow measurement.

Types of flow systems

There are two basic types of flow systems: flow in closed channels and flow in open channels. **Closed channel** flow is flow in completely filled pressure conduits (pipes). Pressure conduits are usually used for fresh water lines or for industrial process lines, and flow through them is often measured by some type of device inserted into the line. Common types of closed channel flow measuring devices are venturi meters, ultrasonic meters (both doppler and transit time), flow nozzles, orifice meters, magnetic flow meters, and pitot tube flow meters. A complete discussion of closed channel flow measurement is outside the scope of this handbook; for further information, the reader is directed to reference [1].

Open channel flow is flow in any channel in which the liquid flows with a free surface. Examples are rivers, irrigation ditches, canals, flumes, and other uncovered conduits. Certain closed channels, such as sewers and tunnels when flowing partially full and not under pressure, are also classified as open channels.

Open channels are used in most storm and sanitary sewer systems, sewage treatment plants, many industrial waste applications, and some water treatment plants. Most irrigation water is also distributed in open channels.

Methods of open channel flow measurement

There are many ways to determine the rate of flow in open channels. Kirkpatrick and Shelley [1] presented a comprehensive review of the various techniques available for measuring flow. Some of the more common methods of open channel flow rate measurement are discussed below, making liberal use of Kirkpatrick and Shelley's comments.

Timed gravimetric

In this method, the entire contents of the flow stream are collected in some type of container for a fixed length of time. The weight of the fluid is then determined and the flow rate calculated. If the flow rate was uniform over the period of the collection, the result will be an average flow rate for the period of the collection.

Gravimetric meters include weighers, tilting traps, and weigh dump meters. In its simplest form, a gravimetric meter involves determining the weight of a quantity of fluid in a tank mounted on beam scales, load cells, or some other mass or force measuring device. Weighing the fluid is a primary standard and, since the accuracy of weighing devices is routinely considered to be better than ±0.1%, gravimetric meters are frequently used to calibrate other meters.

In field use, the tipping bucket rain gauge is probably one of the most common meters of this type. Another field application, often used as a calibration method where a scale or some other weighing device is available, is the simple "bucket and stopwatch" technique. Practical considerations limit the use of this technique to fairly low flow rates, and because of the nature of the measurement, it is not suited for continuous measurement.

Dilution

In this method, the flow rate is measured by determining how much the flowing water dilutes an added tracer solution. Although brine tracers have been used, radioactive and fluorescent dye tracers are more commonly used today. The dilution technique produces no pressure loss, requires no drop in hydraulic grade line, offers no obstruction to the flow, and indicates flow rate directly by simple theoretical formulas.

There are two general techniques used in dilution flow measurement: the constant-rate injection method and the total recovery (or slug injection) method. The constant-rate injection method requires the tracer solution to be injected into the flow stream at a constant flow rate for a given period of time. The flow rate is determined by a formula involving the background concentration in the stream (if any), the tracer concentration and injection rate, and the measured plateau of the concentration-time curve at the measuring site. In the total recovery method, a known quantity of the tracer solution is placed in the flow stream, and a continuous sample is removed at a uniform rate during the time needed for the tracer wave to pass, in effect integrating the concentration-time curve. The flow rate is determined from the total quantity of tracer injected and the integral of the concentration-time curve.

Although both of these dilution methods have advantages and limitations, they are basically similar. A fluorometer, Geiger counter, or some other appropriate instrument is required for determining sample concentration, a method of extracting a sample for analysis is needed, and a device to either inject a tracer at a steady, known rate, or withdraw a sample at a steady (but not necessarily known) rate is required. Both methods require complete vertical and lateral mixing at the measurement site. The main disadvantages of dilution techniques are the cost of the instruments required to determine tracer concentrations, the lack of ruggedness of these instruments, and the required training for operator personnel.

Velocity-area

In this method, the flow rate is calculated by determining the mean flow velocity across a cross-section and multiplying this by the flow area at that point. In open channels, this will generally require two separate measurements—one to determine the mean velocity and the other to determine the flow depth. A complication in this simple procedure is that the velocity profile of a flow stream depends on many factors, and frequently a series of velocity measurements will be necessary to arrive at the mean velocity across a section. The following quotation from reference [2] is given to illustrate some of the problems with determining the mean velocity:

The following methods are used to determine mean velocities in a vertical line with a current meter:
1. Two-point method
2. Six-tenths-depth method
3. Vertical velocity-curve method
4. Subsurface method
5. Integration method
6. Two-tenths method
7. Three-point method
8. One-point continuous method

The two-point method consists of measuring the velocity at 0.2 and then at 0.8 of the depth from the water surface, and using the average of the two measurements. The accuracy obtainable with this method is high and its use is recommended. The method should not be used where the depth is less than 2 feet.

The six-tenths-depth method consists of measuring the velocity at 0.6 of the depth from the water surface, and is generally used for shallow flows where the two-point method is not applicable. This method gives fairly satisfactory results. The vertical velocity-curve method consists of measuring the velocities at equal vertical intervals of 0.5 foot or more and calculating their arithmetical mean, or finding the mean value from a curve obtained by plotting the measurements on cross-section paper. This method is very accurate, but is time consuming and costly.

The subsurface method involves measuring the velocity near the water surface and then multiplying it by a coefficient ranging from 0.85 to 0.95, depending on the depth of water, the velocity, and the nature of the stream or canal bed. The difficulty of determining the exact coefficient limits the usefulness and accuracy of this method.

The integration method is performed by observing the velocity along a vertical line by slowly and uniformly lowering and raising the meter throughout the range of water depth two or more times. This method is not accurate and should be used only for comparisons or quick rough checks.

The two-tenths, three-point, and one-point continuous methods are special procedures based on a relationship previously established for the section between the true discharge and the velocities observed by these methods. These methods are generally reliable for sections which undergo no serious changes because of erosion, sedimentation, or other deformation.

Devices used to measure velocity in open channels are commonly known as current meters. There are a number of different types of current meters available; good reviews of velocity measuring devices may be found in references [3] and [4]. Some of the more common types of velocity measuring techniques include floats, tracers, eddyshedding vortex meters, turbine meters, rotating element meters, doppler ultrasonic meters, and electromagnetic probe meters.

2

Hydraulic structure
In this method, some type of hydraulic structure (primary device) is introduced into the flow stream. The function of the hydraulic structure is to produce a flow that is characterized by a known relationship (usually nonlinear) between a liquid level measurement (head) at some location and the flow rate of the stream. This relationship or head-flow rate curve for the particular structure or device is called the rating. The change in liquid level is measured by a secondary device, which may also convert the liquid level to a flow rate automatically.

Slope—hydraulic radius
In this method, measurements of water surface slope, cross-sectional area, and wetted perimeter over a length of uniform section channel are used to determine the flow rate, using a resistance equation such as the Manning formula. The flow channel serves as the primary device. The Manning formula requires a knowledge of the channel cross-section, liquid depth, slope of the water surface, and a roughness factor dependent on the character of the channel.

• • •

The timed gravimetric and dilution techniques are generally not suited to provide a continuous record of flow rate. They are more often used for occasional flow rate measurements at a particular time and place, for calibrating some other type of device, or for developing a liquid level-flow rate curve for a particular location. These techniques have a definite role in open channel flow measurement, but because they are not adaptable to continuous flow rate recording they will not be discussed here. For a complete discussion, see references [1] and [2].

The velocity-area technique is often used like the timed gravimetric and dilution techniques to determine the flow rate in a stream at a particular time for calibration purposes. However, some manufacturers have designed instrument systems combining depth measurement with a point-velocity sensor. The velocity in the flow stream is measured at one point, typically the bottom of

2

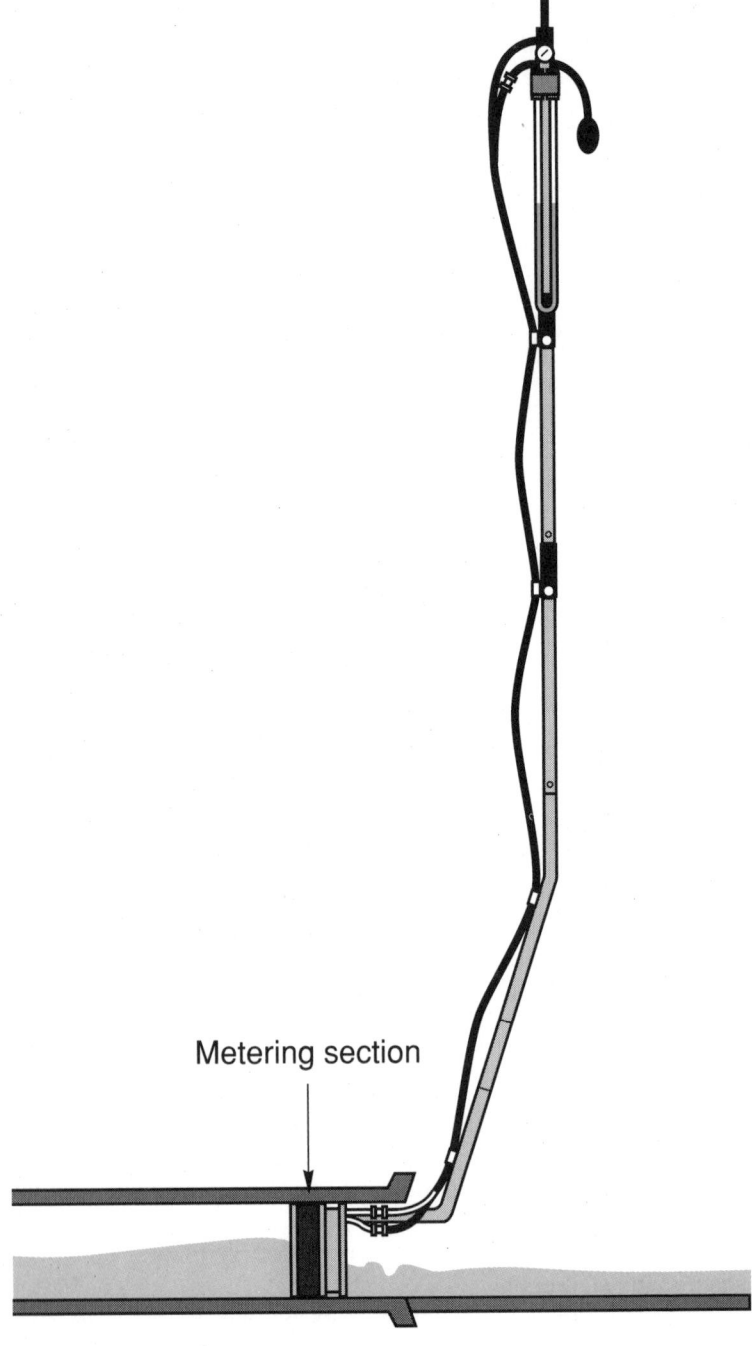

Metering section

Figure 2-1: Isco Flow Poke™

the channel, and the point velocity is converted into an average stream velocity based on stored calibration data. The average velocity is then used with the measured depth to determine the flow rate in the stream. These patented devices typically have been used in temporary situations such as sewer flow measurements for infiltration and inflow. Because of their complexity and expense, these devices are not as widely used as hydraulic structures, and will not be discussed here. For a complete discussion of this technique, see references [4], [5], and [6].

The hydraulic structures technique differs from the first three techniques in that, provided a standard type of structure is used and certain installation and application rules are followed, no field calibrations or measurements other than a continuous measurement of liquid level are required to obtain a continuous record of flow rate. Because of this, the hydraulic structures technique is widely used in open channel flow measurement. This technique is briefly discussed in the following two sections and at length in Chapters 3, 4, and 5.

The slope-hydraulic radius-area technique, using the Manning formula, is applied in a manner similar to the hydraulic structures technique in that only a continuous measurement of liquid level is required to obtain a continuous record of flow rate. Because of uncertainties associated with the Manning formula, the accuracies obtainable are not as good as those achieved with hydraulic structures. The slope-hydraulic radius-area technique is normally used where great accuracy is not required. But, since this technique does not require the installation of an additional structure in the flow stream, it is often used for temporary measurements in sewers, for example, for inflow and infiltration studies. The slope-hydraulic radius-area method is discussed in Chapter 6.

One other method of measuring flow rate in an open channel, not presented by Kirkpatrick and Shelly, will be briefly discussed. This technique, the proprietary, patented Flow Poke™, shown in Figure 2-1, allows reasonably accurate flow rate readings to be quickly obtained from small diameter sewers without the operator entering the sewer environment. Basically a combination of a specially calibrated weir and an orifice plate, the metering section of the Flow Poke is attached to a pole assembly which allows it to be inserted into a sewer pipe from ground level and temporarily secured in the pipe by an inflatable rubber collar. A pneumatic system measures the head upstream from the metering section and provides a visual indication of the instantaneous flow rate in the sewer. The Flow Poke is often used for inflow and infiltration work or for calibrating other flow measuring devices.

™Isco, Inc.

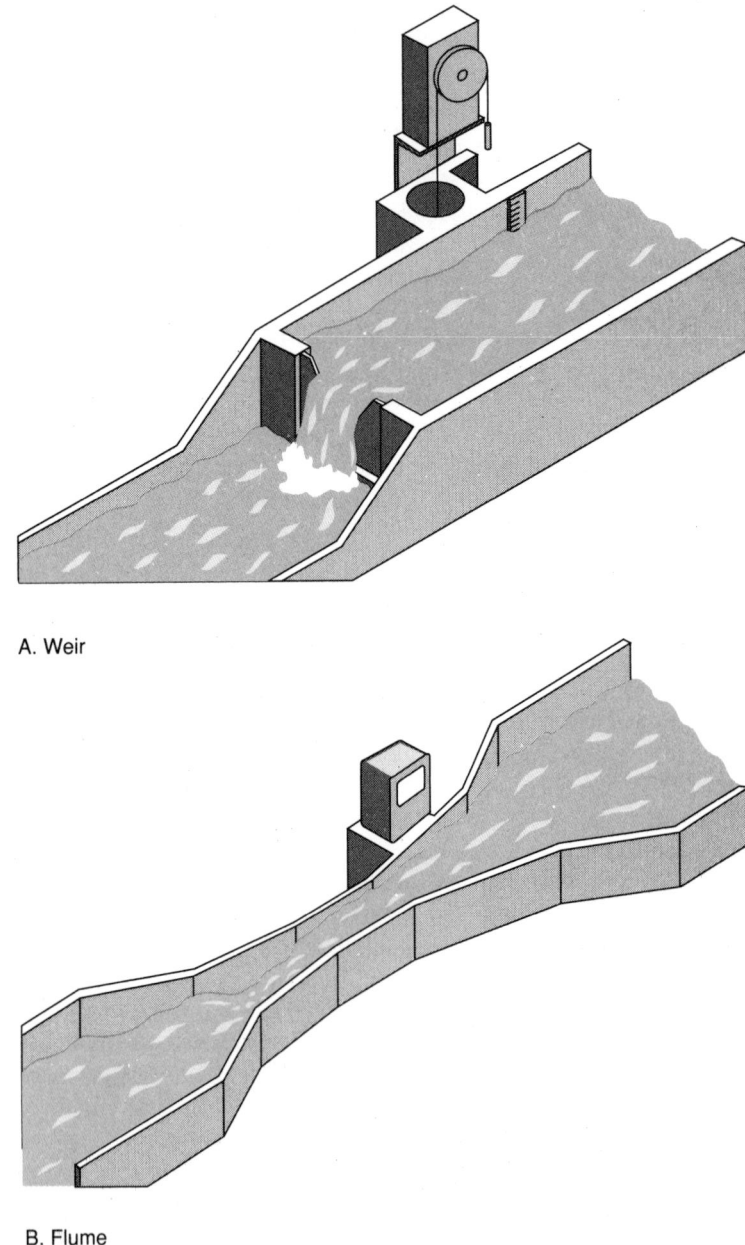

A. Weir

B. Flume

Figure 2-2: Primary measuring devices

Primary measuring devices: weirs and flumes

As discussed in the above section, the most commonly used technique of measuring the rate of flow in an open channel is that of hydraulic structures. In this method, flow in an open channel is measured by inserting a hydraulic structure into the channel, which changes the level of liquid in or near the structure. By selecting the shape and dimensions of the hydraulic structure, the rate of flow through or over the restriction will be related to the liquid level in a known manner. Thus, the flow rate through the open channel can be derived from a single measurement of the liquid level.

The hydraulic structures used in measuring flow in open channels are known as primary measuring devices, and may be divided into two broad categories—**weirs** and **flumes**, shown in Figure 2-2.

A weir is essentially a dam built across an open channel over which the liquid flows, usually through some type of an opening or notch. Weirs are normally classified according to the shape of the notch, the most common types being the rectangular weir, the trapezoidal (or Cipolletti) weir, and the triangular (or V-notch) weir. Each type of weir has an associated equation for determining the flow rate through the weir.

A flume is a specially shaped open channel flow section with an area or slope or both that is different from that of the channel. This results in an increased velocity and change in the level of the liquid flowing through the flume. A flume normally consists of a converging section, a throat section, and a diverging section. The flow rate through the flume is a function of the liquid level at some point or points in the flume. The most commonly used types of flumes are Parshall and Palmer-Bowlus flumes, although there are many other types available.

Secondary measuring devices: open channel flow meters

As discussed above, the flow rate or discharge through a weir or flume is usually a function of the liquid level in or near the primary measuring device. A secondary measuring device (or open channel flow meter) is used in conjunction with a primary measuring device to measure the rate of liquid flow in an open channel. The secondary measuring device has two purposes:

1. To measure the liquid level in the primary measuring device.

2. To convert this liquid level into an appropriate flow rate according to the known liquid level-flow rate relationship of the primary measuring device. This flow rate may then be integrated to obtain a totalized volume, transmitted to a recording device, and/or used to pace an automatic sampler.

Thus, a combination of a weir or flume (primary measuring device) and an open channel flow meter (secondary measuring device) is necessary to measure flow in an open channel. The flow measurement system requires both a primary and secondary measuring device to be complete. A weir or a flume (primary device) restricts the flow in a controlled manner and generates a liquid level which is related to the flow rate through the device. And, an open channel flow meter (secondary device) measures this level, and converts it into a corresponding flow rate according

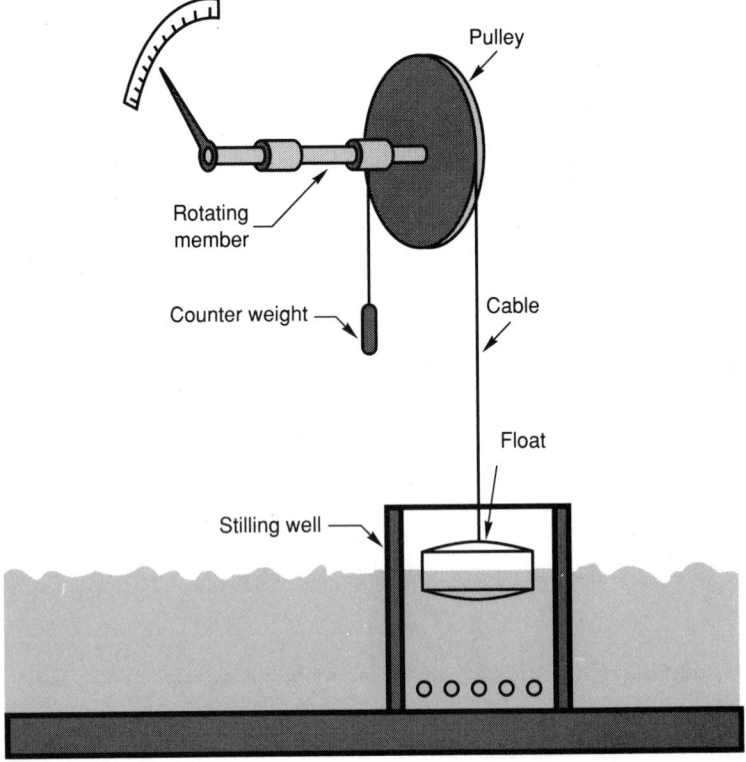

Figure 2-3: Float operated flow meter

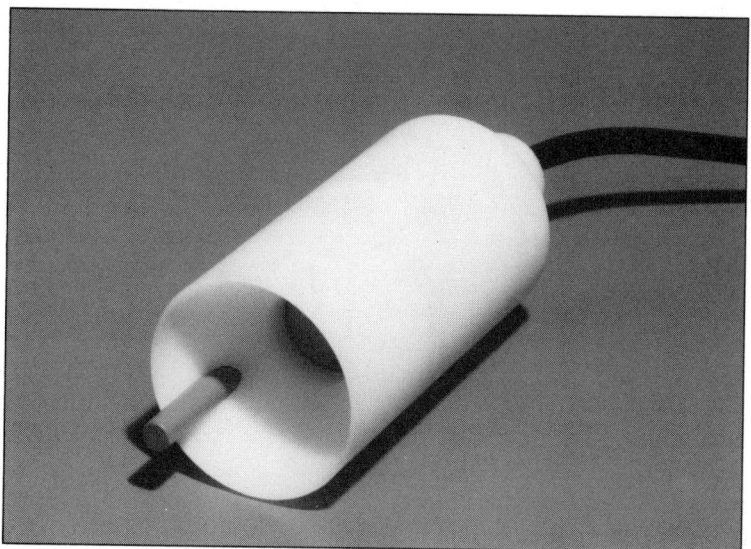

Figure 2-4: Isco ultrasonic sensor

to the known liquid level-flow rate relationship of the primary device.

The **first task** of an open channel flow meter is to measure the liquid level at an appropriate point in or near the primary measuring device. The following are some of the more commonly used methods for liquid level measurement:

Float

A float, in combination with either a cable and pulley or a pivoting arm, converts the liquid level (as measured by the float) into an angular position of a shaft, which is proportional to liquid level. Refer to Figure 2-3 for a view of a float operated flow meter.

Electrical

This type of level measurement system uses some sort of change in an electrical circuit caused by a changing level to indicate the liquid level. Most designs use a capacitive or reactance type probe.

Ultrasonic

The liquid level is measured by determining the time required for an acoustic pulse to travel from a transmitter to the liquid surface (where it is reflected) and returned to a receiver. Refer to Figure 2-4 for a view of an Isco ultrasonic sensor.

2

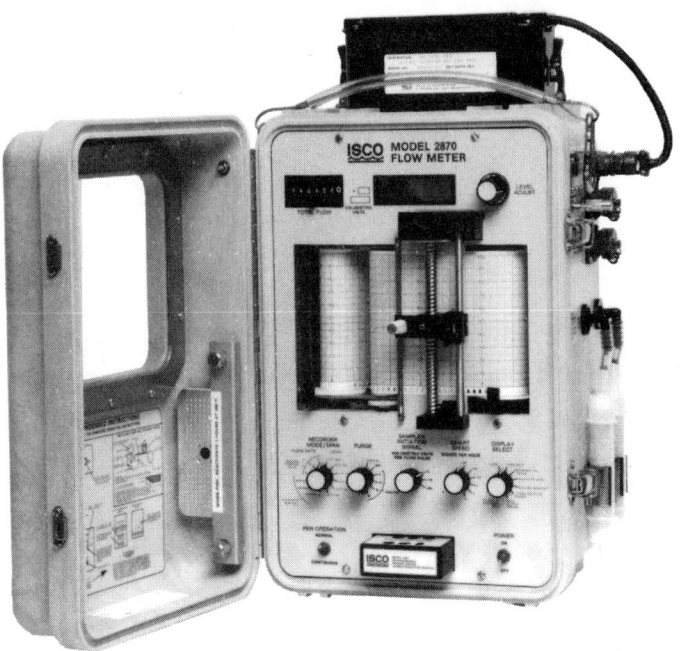

Figure 2-5: Isco 2870 Bubbler Flow Meter

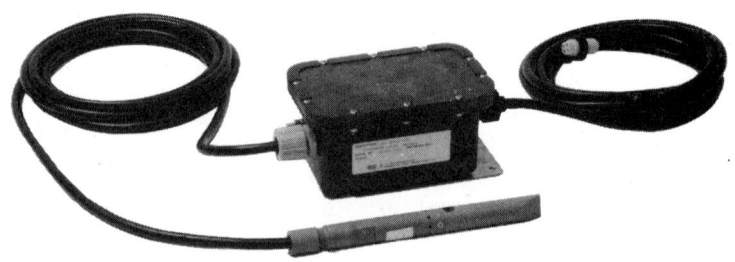

Figure 2-6: Submerged pressure transducer

2

Bubbler

A bubbler tube is anchored in the flow stream at a fixed depth, and the tube supplies a constant bubble rate of pressurized air or other gas. The pressure required to maintain the bubble rate is measured; this pressure is proportional to the liquid level. Refer to Figure 2-5 for a view of the Isco 2870 Bubbler Flow Meter.

Submerged pressure transducer

This system is similar to the bubbler, except that instead of using a bubbler system, a sealed pressure transducer is submerged directly in the flow stream. The pressure measured by the transducer is proportional to the liquid level. Refer to Figure 2-6 for a view of an Isco submerged pressure transducer unit.

• • •

The **second task** of an open channel flow meter is to convert the measured liquid level into a corresponding flow rate according to the level-flow rate relationship for the primary measuring device being used. This conversion can be accomplished by a number of different methods:

Mechanical cam

A mechanical cam, whose profile follows the level-flow rate relationship of the primary measuring device in question, is rotated

Figure 2-7: Isco Field Programmable Primary Device Characterization Module

2

Figure 2-8: Isco Preprogrammed Primary Device
Characterization Module

by the level measuring device. The position of the cam follower is
then proportional to flow rate.

Electronic analog function generator

In this type of conversion system, a solid state analog integrated
circuit device is used to convert an electrical analog of the level
into a flow rate analog, according to a selectable power formula.

Electronic digital function generator

In this method, the measured level is digitally converted into a
flow rate according to a selectable power formula, typically by a
microprocessor-based system. Refer to Figure 2-7 for a view of an
Isco Field Programmable Primary Device Characterization Module.

Electronic memory device

A large scale digital integrated circuit memory device is pro-
grammed such that, for a given level input, the output of the
device is the flow rate corresponding to that level. Refer to Figure
2-8 for a view of an Isco Preprogrammed Primary Device
Characterization Module, using a PROM type electronic memory.

2

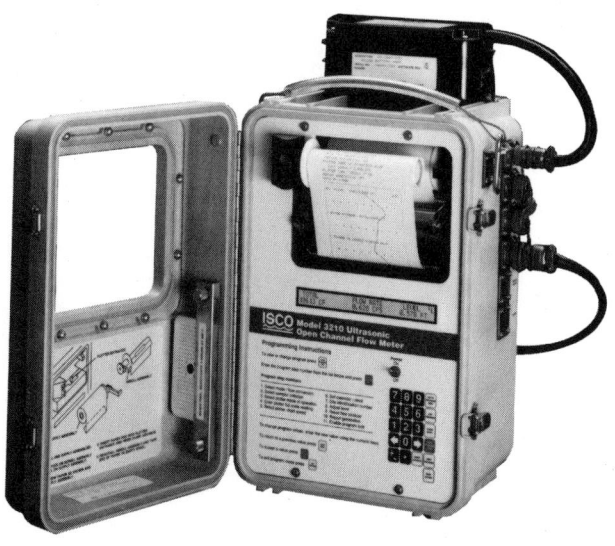

Figure 2-9: Isco 3210 Ultrasonic Flow Meter

Software

The software program in a microprocessor-controlled instrument is used to convert the measured liquid level into a flow rate corresponding to that level. Refer to Figure 2-9 for a view of the Isco 3210 Ultrasonic Flow Meter using microprocessor-based software flow conversion.

The conversion methods listed are just some of the more commonly used methods; there are other techniques available. Any one of the level measurement techniques may be combined with any one of the level-to-flow rate conversion techniques to result in a complete open channel flow meter.

• • •

An exhaustive discussion of the relative merits of the various types of open channel flow meters is beyond the scope of this handbook. However, some general comments on potential problems with the level measurement techniques are listed below.

Floats may be affected by ambient air temperature changes, are subject to build-up of grease and solids, and generally require the use of a stilling well.

Electrical systems may be affected by a coating of grease or solids and may be subject to physical damage from debris in the flow stream.

Ultrasonic systems may be affected by high cross winds and ambient air temperature changes, may have problems in very narrow or irregular channels, and may give inaccurate results in channels with floating debris or foam.

Bubblers may be affected by ambient air temperature changes and may have problems in channels with high concentrations of grease or suspended solids.

Submerged pressure transducers may be affected by changes in the temperature of the flow stream and may be difficult to install in large channels with high flow.

Any one of the level-to-flow rate conversion techniques, when properly designed and applied, will give satisfactory results in most situations. When designing an open channel flow measuring system, the importance of both the primary and secondary measuring devices should be recognized. In a complete open channel flow measurement system, a proper weir or flume installation can be negated through the use of an inaccurate flow meter. Similarly, a very accurate flow meter cannot overcome the inaccuracies of a poorly installed or maintained weir or flume. As with any measurement system, an open channel flow measurement system can be no more accurate than its least accurate component.

General units of measurement

Two types of units are used in measuring liquids: units of discharge (flow rate) and units of volume.

Discharge, or flow rate, is defined as the volume of liquid that passes a particular reference section in a unit of time. The unit of discharge generally used in irrigation practice in the U.S. is the cubic foot per second (cfs) also known as the second-foot (sec.-ft.). In water supply and waste treatment in the U.S., the units of discharge normally used are million gallons per day (mgd) or, in some cases, gallons per minute (gpm). In metric units, discharge is normally expressed in cubic meters per second (cms), less often in liters per second (lps) or cubic meters per day (cmd).

Volume measurements are usually obtained by integrating flow rate over a period of time, which then represents an accumulated total of liquid. The unit of volume commonly used in irrigation work in the U.S. is the acre-foot (ac.-ft.). An acre-foot is defined as the quantity of water required to cover 1 acre of land to a depth of 1 foot, or 43,560 cubic feet. In water supply and waste treatment the unit of volume normally used is the gallon (gal). In metric units, volume is normally expressed in liters (l) or cubic meters (m^3).

2

References

1. Kirkpatrick, George A., and Shelley, Philip E. *Sewer Flow Measurement—A State-of-the-Art Assessment.* EPA Environmental Protection Technology Series, EPA-600/2-75-027, 1975.

2. *Water Measurement Manual.* United States Department of the Interior, Bureau of Reclamation, Denver, Colo., 1967.

3. Smoot, G.F. "A Review of Velocity Measuring Devices." United States Department of the Interior, Geological Survey Open File Report (April 1974).

4. Parr, A. David; Judkins, Joseph F.; and Jones, Thomas E. "Point-Velocity Discharge Measurement Method for Sewers." *Journal Water Pollution Control Federation,* Volume 53, Number 1 (January 1981).

5. Debevoise, N. T., and Fernandez, R. B. "Recent Observations and New Developments in the Calibration of Open Channel Wastewater Monitors." *Journal Water Pollution Control Federation,* Volume 56, Number 11 (November 1984).

6. "Data Systems For Portable Open Channel Flow Measurement." *Pollution Equipment News* (June 1984).

Suggested readings

Mougenot, G. "Measuring Sewage Flow Using Weirs and Flumes." *Water & Sewage Works* (July 1974): 78-81.

Stevens Water Resources Data Book. 2nd Edition. Leupold & Stevens, Inc., Beaverton, Ore., 1974.

Ackers, P.; White, W.R.; Perkins, J.A.; and Harrison, A.J.M. *Weirs and Flumes for Flow Measurement.* John Wiley & Sons, New York, N.Y., 1978.

Chapter

3

Weirs

Overview

This chapter provides detailed information concerning the use of various types of weirs.

Please note that the recommendations presented in this chapter are derived from standard references and are intended to be used as general guidelines only. The details of a particular installation may justify a deviation from these recommendations, based on sound engineering judgement.

Weirs

Weirs are the simplest, least expensive, and probably the most common type of primary measuring device used to measure flow in open channels. A weir, essentially, is an obstruction or dam built across an open channel over which the liquid flows, often through a specially shaped opening or notch. Weirs are normally classified according to the shape of the notch. The most common types of weirs are the rectangular weir, the trapezoidal (or Cipolletti) weir, and the triangular (or V-notch) weir, shown in Figure 3-1. Each type of weir has an associated equation for determining the flow rate through the weir. The equation is based on the depth of the liquid in the pool formed upstream from the weir.

The edge or surface over which the liquid passes is called the **crest** of the weir, as shown in Figure 3-2. (Note that the V-notch weir comes to a point at the bottom, so it has no actual crest length; the point may be thought of as the "crest" of a V-notch weir). Generally, the top edge of the weir is thin or beveled with

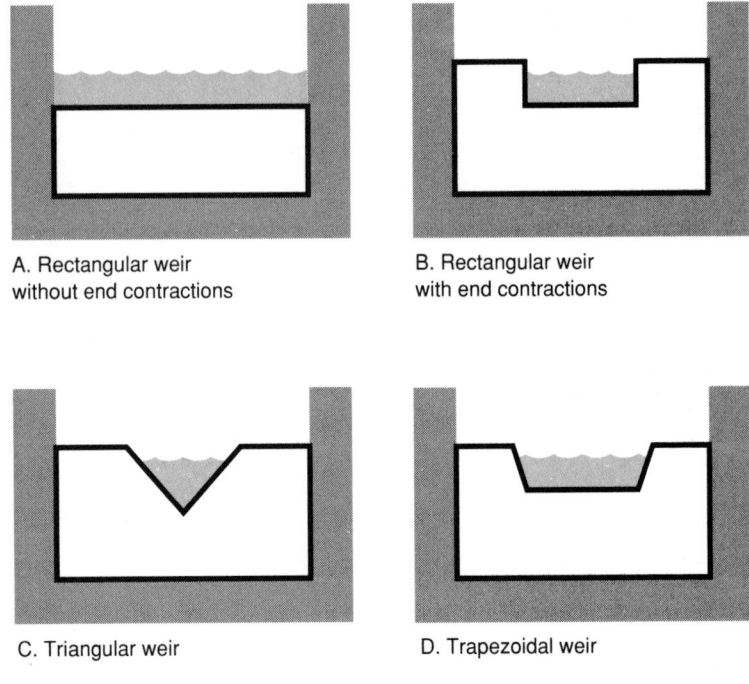

A. Rectangular weir
without end contractions

B. Rectangular weir
with end contractions

C. Triangular weir

D. Trapezoidal weir

Figure 3-1: Various sharp-crested weir profiles

a sharp upstream corner so that the liquid does not contact any part of the weir structure downstream, but rather, springs past it. Weirs of this type are called sharp-crested weirs, and are the only type of weir discussed in this section. Broad-crested weirs are briefly discussed on page 38.

The stream of water leaving the weir crest is called the **nappe**. When the water surface downstream from the weir is far enough below the weir crest so that air flows freely beneath the nappe, the nappe is aerated and the flow is referred to as **free** or **critical.** When the downstream water level rises to the point where air does not flow freely beneath the nappe, the nappe is not ventilated and the discharge rate may be inaccurate because of the low pressure beneath the nappe. When the downstream water level rises above the crest, the flow is referred to as **submerged** or **subcritical.** This can affect the discharge rate to a measurable degree, so dependable measurements should not be expected in this range. To determine the rate of flow under submerged conditions, both the upstream and downstream levels must be measured and reference made to submerged flow tables. Submerged

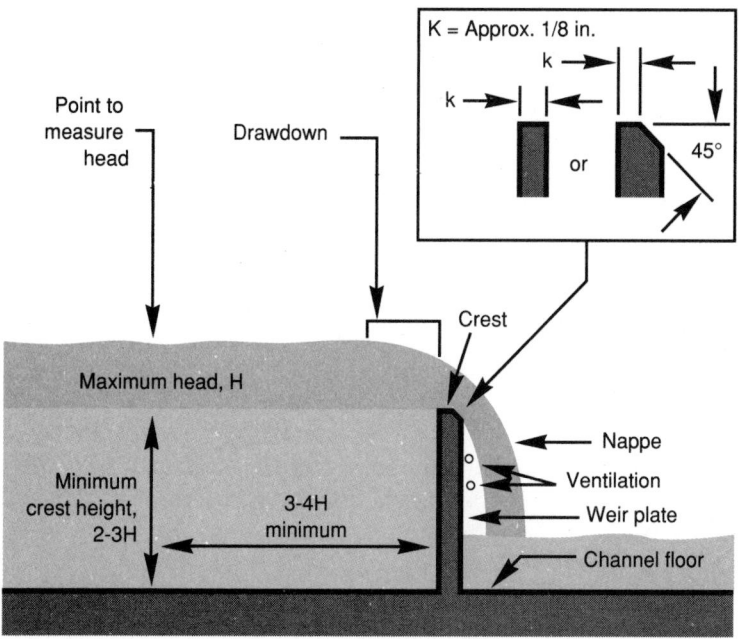

Figure 3-2: Sharp-crested weir

and nonventilated flows are undesirable for standard conditions and, should usually be avoided. In most cases, weirs should be installed and sized to obtain ventilated and free or critical discharge conditions.

The discharge rate of a weir is determined by measuring the vertical distance from the crest of the weir to the liquid surface in the pool upstream from the crest. This liquid depth is called the **head**. As shown in Figure 3-2, a slight drop in the liquid surface begins upstream from the weir. This drop occurs at a distance of at least twice the head on the crest, and is called the surface contraction or drawdown of the weir. To avoid sensing the effects of drawdown, the head measuring point of the weir should be located upstream of the weir crest a distance of at least three, and preferably four times the maximum head expected over the weir, as shown in Figure 3-2. Once the head is known, the flow rate or discharge can be determined using the known head-flow rate relationship of the weir.

Thus, for a weir of a given size and shape with free-flow, steady-state conditions and proper weir-to-pool relationships, only one depth of liquid can exist in the upstream pool for a given discharge. A weir may be thought of as a device for shaping the flow of the liquid to allow a single depth reading that is uniquely related to a discharge rate.

Although weirs are comparatively easy to construct and convenient to use, they are not always suitable. Accurate flow rate measurements cannot be expected unless the proper conditions and dimensions are maintained. Weirs are not suitable for flat-sloped channel installations where head loss must be considered. Weirs are also not suitable for water carrying excessive solid materials or silt, which will deposit in the approach channel behind the weir and destroy the conditions required for accurate discharge measurement. Some silt, sand, or other solid material will inevitably collect in any open channel flow system. To allow the periodic removal of these deposits, it is suggested that the weir bulkhead be constructed with an opening beneath the notch, through which accumulations can be sluiced as required. A metal plate or plank placed across the upstream side of this opening and securely fixed in place will serve as a cover while the weir is in operation.

To assure accurate discharge measurement, there are certain general weir design requirements that apply to all types:

1. The weir should consist of a thin plate $1/8$ to $1/4$ inch thick with a straight edge or a thicker plate with a downstream chamfered edge. The upstream sharp edge prevents the nappe from adhering to the crest. Knife edges should be avoided because they are difficult to maintain. However, the upstream edge of the weir must be sharp with right angle corners, since rounded edges will decrease the head for a given flow rate.

2. The upstream face of the weir should be smooth and perpendicular to the axis of the channel in both horizontal and vertical directions. The crest of the weir should also be exactly level to insure a uniform depth of flow.

3. The connection of the weir to the channel should be waterproof. Therefore, the joint between the weir plate and channel should be packed with chemically inert cement or asphalt type roofing compound.

4. The length of the weir crest or the notch angle must be accurately determined, because the percentage error in measured flow rate will be proportional to the error in determining these dimensions.

5. The weir should be ventilated, if necessary, to prevent a vacuum from forming on the underside of the nappe.

6. The height of the weir from the bottom of the channel to the crest should be at least 2 times the maximum expected head of liquid above the crest. This is necessary to lower the velocity of approach. The weir height should never be less than 1 foot.

7. The approach section should be straight upstream from the weir for a distance of at least 20 times the maximum expected head of liquid, and should have little or no slope.

8. The crest must be set higher than the maximum downstream elevation of the water surface, otherwise a submerged flow condition will occur instead of the free flow condition required for reliable flow measurement.

9. The device for measuring the head (flow meter) should be placed upstream at a distance of at least 3 times the maximum expected head on the weir and should be located in a quiet section of the channel away from all disturbances, preferably in a stilling well. Also, the zero point of the head measuring device must be set exactly level with the weir crest.

10. The crest of the weir must be kept clean. Fibers, stringy materials, and larger particles tend to cling to the crest and should be removed periodically. The upstream side of the weir should also be periodically purged of accumulated silt and solids.

11. The weir size should be selected only after preliminary studies have determined the expected flow rates in the channel in question. The Manning formula, as described in Chapter 6, can sometimes be used to estimate the flow rate in open channels.

12. The cross-sectional area of the approach channel should be at least 8 times that of the nappe at the crest for a distance upstream of 15 to 20 times the head on the crest. This is necessary to minimize the velocity of approach. The approach channel should also permit the liquid to approach the weir in a smooth stream free from turbulence, and the velocity

should be uniformly distributed over the channel; this may be accomplished through the use of baffle plates if necessary.

13. If the weir pool is smaller than defined by the above criteria, the velocity of approach may be too high and the head reading too low. Refer to reference [1] for velocity of approach corrections. Weirs should be installed and maintained to make the velocity of approach negligible, but where this is not possible, appropriate corrections should be made.

Weirs are classified in accordance with the shape of the notch or opening in the weir. The basic types—triangular, rectangular, and trapezoidal—are discussed individually, along with certain other types of weirs.

Triangular (V-notch) weirs

The triangular or V-notch sharp-crested weir (Figure 3-3) consists of an angular notch cut into a bulkhead in the flow channel. The apex of the notch is at the bottom and the sides are set equally on either side of a vertical line from the apex. The angle of the notch

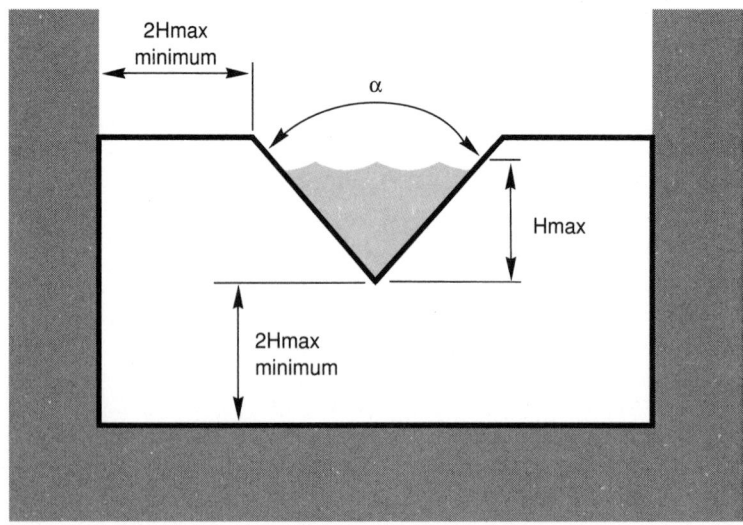

Figure 3-3: V-notch (triangular) sharp-crested weir

Table 3-1: Minimum and maximum recommended flow rates for V-notch weirs

V-notch angle	Min. head, Ft.	Minimum flow rate			Max. head, Ft.	Maximum flow rate		
		CFS	MGD	GPM		CFS	MGD	GPM
22¹/₂°	0.2	0.009	0.006	4.04	2.0	2.81	1.82	1260
30°	0.2	0.012	0.008	5.39	2.0	3.82	2.47	1710
45°	0.2	0.019	0.012	8.53	2.0	5.85	3.78	2630
60°	0.2	0.026	0.017	11.7	2.0	8.16	5.28	3660
90°	0.2	0.045	0.029	20.2	2.0	14.1	9.14	6330
120°	0.2	0.077	0.050	34.8	2.0	24.5	15.8	11,000

(α) most commonly used is 90°, although V-notch weirs with angles of 120°, 60°, 45°, 30°, and 22¹/₂° are also used.

Some problems exist with narrow-angled V-notch weirs. The small included angle of these weirs makes it difficuilt to accurately produce the geometry of the weir at the apex. Also, the capillary effect will restrict flow at a surprisingly high head, causing the head/discharge relationship to be unreliable.

When installing a V-notch weir, the minimum distance of the sides of the weir from the channel banks should be at least twice the maximum expected head on the weir. The minimum distance from the crest to the pool bottom should also be at least twice the maximum expected head.

The V-notch weir is an accurate flow measuring device particularly suited for low flows. Because the V-notch weir has no crest length, the head required for a small flow through it is greater than that required with other types of weirs. This is an advantage for small discharges in that the nappe will spring free of the crest, whereas it would cling to the crest of another type of weir and reduce the accuracy of the measurement.

The V-notch weir is the best weir profile for measuring discharges less than 1 cfs (0.65 mgd/450 gpm) and has reasonable accuracy for flows up to 10 cfs (6.46 mgd/4500 gpm). It is generally recommended that the minimum head on a V-notch weir be at least 0.2 foot to prevent the nappe from clinging to the crest. It is also recommended that the maximum head be limited to 2.0 feet, to assure accuracy of the device head/flow rate relationship. Based on these lower and upper head restrictions, Table 3-1 presents the minimum and maximum recommended flow rates for the most common V-notch weirs.

The discharge (head vs flow rate) equation of a free flowing V-notch weir takes the form:

$$Q = K H^{2.5}$$

where: Q = flow rate
H = head on the weir
K = a constant, dependent on the angle of notch and units of measurement

For flow rate in cubic feet per second (cfs), million gallons per day (mgd), and gallons per minute (gpm), and head in feet, the discharge equations for the common V-notch weirs are as follows:

α	CFS	MGD	GPM
22 1/2°:	$Q = 0.4970\ H^{2.5}$	$Q = .3212\ H^{2.5}$	$Q = 223.1\ H^{2.5}$
30°:	$Q = 0.6760\ H^{2.5}$	$Q = .4369\ H^{2.5}$	$Q = 303.4\ H^{2.5}$
45°:	$Q = 1.035\ H^{2.5}$	$Q = .6689\ H^{2.5}$	$Q = 464.5\ H^{2.5}$
60°:	$Q = 1.443\ H^{2.5}$	$Q = .9326\ H^{2.5}$	$Q = 647.6\ H^{2.5}$
90°:	$Q = 2.500\ H^{2.5}$	$Q = 1.616\ H^{2.5}$	$Q = 1122\ H^{2.5}$
120°:	$Q = 4.330\ H^{2.5}$	$Q = 2.798\ H^{2.5}$	$Q = 1943\ H^{2.5}$

Complete discharge tables for V-notch weirs are found in Chapter 8 of this handbook.

Rectangular (contracted and suppressed) weirs

The rectangular sharp-crested weir (Figure 3-4) may be used in one of two configurations. The first configuration (Figure 3-4 A) consists of a rectangular notch cut into a bulkhead in the flow channel, producing a box-like opening. This configuration is called a **contracted rectangular** weir because a curved flow path or contraction results with the nappe forming a jet narrower than the weir opening. The horizontal distances from the end of the weir crest to the side walls of the channel are called the end contractions. These end contractions reduce the width and accelerate the channel flow as it passes over the weir and provide the needed ventilation. Flow through this type of weir is said to be with end contractions. (Any weir which is narrower than the channel in which it is placed is technically a contracted weir).

In the second configuration of the rectangular weir (Figure 3-4 B), the end contractions are completely suppressed by extending the weir across the entire width of the channel. Thus, the sides of the

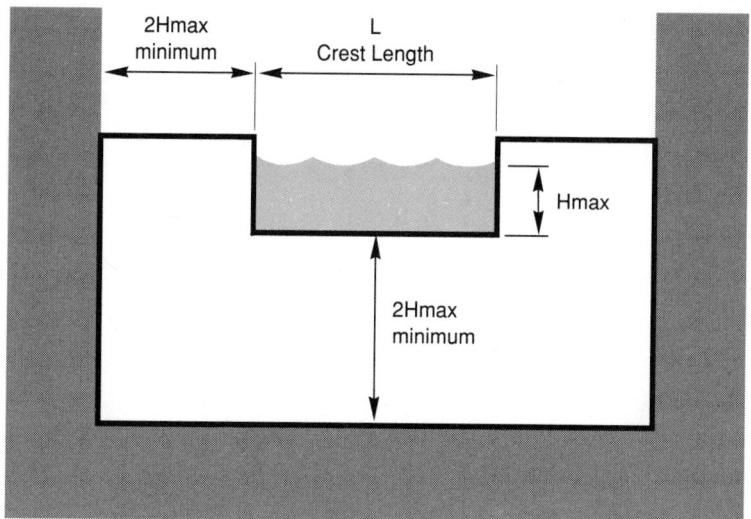

A. Contracted (with end contractions)

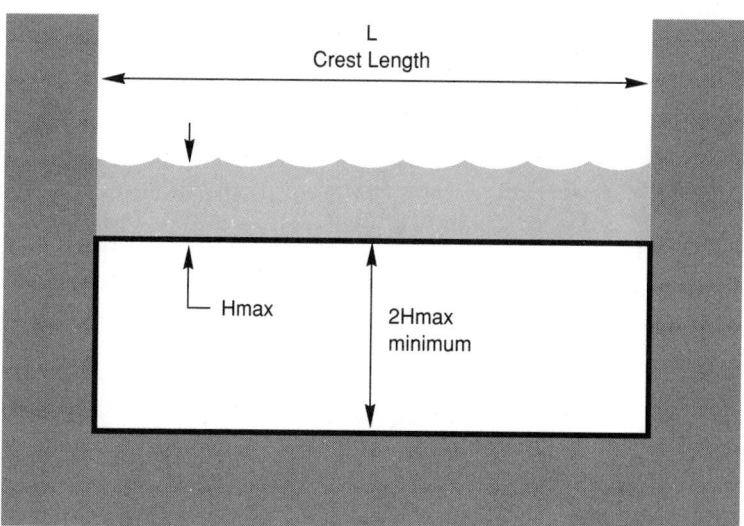

B. Suppressed (without end contractions)

Figure 3-4: Rectangular sharp-crested weirs

Table 3-2: Minimum and maximum recommended flow rates for rectangular weirs with end contractions

Crest length, Ft.	Min. head, Ft.	Minimum flow rate			Max. head, Ft.	Maximum flow rate		
		CFS	MGD	GPM		CFS	MGD	GPM
1	0.2	0.286	0.185	128	0.5	1.06	0.685	476
1 1/2	0.2	0.435	0.281	195	0.75	2.92	1.89	1310
2	0.2	0.584	0.377	262	1.0	5.99	3.87	2690
2 1/2	0.2	0.733	0.474	329	1.25	10.5	6.77	4710
3	0.2	0.882	0.570	396	1.5	16.5	10.7	7410
4	0.2	1.18	0.762	530	2.0	33.9	21.9	15,200
5	0.2	1.48	0.955	664	2.5	59.2	38.3	26,600
6	0.2	1.77	1.15	794	3.0	93.4	60.4	41,900
8	0.2	2.37	1.53	1060	4.0	192	124	86,200
10	0.2	2.97	1.92	1330	5.0	335	217	150,000

channel also act as the sides of the weir, and there are no lateral contractions. This type of weir is called a **suppressed rectangular** weir, and flow through it is said to be without end contractions.

When installing a rectangular weir with end contractions, the distance from the side of the weir notch to the side of the channel should be at least twice the maximum expected head on the weir. This is necessary to allow the liquid in the channel a free, unconstrained lateral approach to the weir crest. Special care must also be taken in the installation of rectangular weirs without end contractions to obtain adequate aeration of the nappe. This is usually accomplished by placing vents on both sides of the weir box under the nappe. For rectangular weirs both with and without end contractions, the minimum distance from the crest to the pool bottom should be at least twice the maximum expected head.

When constructing a rectangular weir, a crest length of 1 foot is the minimum that should be considered, since a V-notch weir can more accurately measure the same flow rates as rectangular weirs smaller than 1 foot. It is conventional practice to increase the crest-length in increments of 6 inches up to 3 feet, and in 1 foot increments beyond 3 feet, to suit the particular installation. Rectangular weir crest-lengths up to 10 feet are common and, theoretically, there is no maximum crest length. However, beyond 6 or 8 feet, a limit is usually set by economic rather than engineering considerations.

In general, it is recommended that the minimum head on a rectangular weir be at least 0.2 foot to prevent the nappe from clinging to the crest. It is generally accepted practice to limit the maximum head to no more than one half the crest length. However, laboratory experiments have shown that the accuracy of measurement is not impaired to a great extent by exceeding this limit, especially for crest lengths of 1 to 4 feet. But, to insure strict conformance to the weir head/flow rate relationship, the maximum head limitation of one half the crest length should usually be adhered to. Based on these lower and upper head restrictions, Table 3-2 presents the minimum and maximum recommended flow rates for common rectangular weirs with end contractions. Table 3-3 presents similar information for rectangular weirs without end contractions.

The discharge (head vs flow rate) equation of a free flowing rectangular weir with end contractions takes the form:

$$Q = K (L - 0.2 H) H^{1.5}$$

where: Q = flow rate
          H = head on the weir
          L = crest length of weir
          K = constant dependent upon units

For flow rate in cubic feet per second, million gallons per day, and gallons per minute, and head in feet, the discharge equation for a rectangular weir with end contractions is as follows:

Table 3-3: Minimum and maximum recommended flow rates for rectangular weirs without end contractions

Crest length, Ft.	Min. head, Ft.	Minimum flow rate			Max. head, Ft.	Maximum flow rate		
		CFS	MGD	GPM		CFS	MGD	GPM
1	0.2	0.298	0.192	134	0.5	1.18	0.761	530
1 1/2	0.2	0.447	0.289	201	0.75	3.24	2.10	1450
2	0.2	0.596	0.385	267	1.0	6.66	4.30	2990
2 1/2	0.2	0.745	0.481	334	1.25	11.6	7.52	5210
3	0.2	0.894	0.577	401	1.5	18.4	11.9	8260
4	0.2	1.19	0.770	534	2.0	37.7	24.3	16,900
5	0.2	1.49	0.962	669	2.5	65.8	42.5	29,500
6	0.2	1.79	1.16	803	3.0	104	67.1	46,700
8	0.2	2.38	1.54	1070	4.0	213	138	95,600
10	0.2	2.98	1.92	1340	5.0	372	241	167,000

CFS: $Q = 3.330 (L - 0.2 H) H^{1.5}$

MGD: $Q = 2.152 (L - 0.2 H) H^{1.5}$

GPM: $Q = 1495 (L - 0.2 H) H^{1.5}$

where: L = crest length of weir in feet

Complete discharge tables for rectangular weirs with end contractions are found in Chapter 9 of this handbook.

The discharge equation of a free flowing rectangular weir without end contractions takes the form:

$$Q = K L H^{1.5}$$

where: Q = flow rate
H = head on the weir
L = crest length of weir
K = constant dependent upon units

For flow rate in cubic feet per second, million gallons per day, and gallons per minute, and head in feet, the discharge equation for a rectangular weir without end contractions is as follows:

CFS: $Q = 3.330 L H^{1.5}$

MGD: $Q = 2.152 L H^{1.5}$

GPM: $Q = 1495 L H^{1.5}$

where: L = crest length of weir in feet

Complete discharge tables for rectangular weirs without end contractions are found in Chapter 10.

Trapezoidal (Cipolletti) weirs

The trapezoidal sharp-crested weir (Figure 3-5) is similar to a rectangular weir with end contractions except that the sides incline outwardly, producing a trapezoidal opening. When the end-inclinations of a trapezoidal weir are in the ratio of 4 vertical to 1 horizontal, the weir is known as a Cipolletti weir—named for the Italian experimenter, Cesare Cipolletti, who first proposed its use. Although the Cipolletti weir is a contracted weir, its discharge occurs essentially as though its end contractions were suppressed.

Thus, no correction is necessary for the crest width as in a rectangular contracted weir, resulting in a simpler discharge equation.

All of the installation conditions stated for rectangular weirs with end contractions also apply to Cipolletti weirs. The Cipolletti weir offers a slightly wider range than the rectangular weir. However, the measurement accuracy with a Cipolletti weir is inherently less than that obtained with the rectangular or a V-notch weir.

The minimum and maximum recommended heads for a Cipolletti weir are the same as rectangular weirs: minimum head of 0.2 foot and maximum head of no more than one half the crest length. Based on these lower and upper head restrictions, Table 3-4 presents the minimum and maximum recommended flow rates for common Cipolletti weirs.

The discharge (head vs flow rate) equation of a free flowing Cipolletti weir takes the form:

$$Q = K L H^{1.5}$$

where: Q = flow rate
H = head on the weir
L = crest length of weir
K = constant dependent upon units

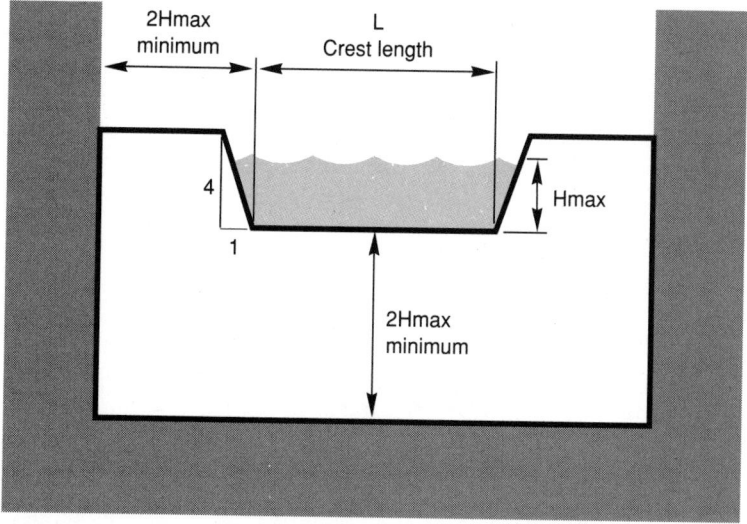

Figure 3-5: Trapezoidal (Cipolletti) sharp-crested weir

Table 3-4: Minimum and maximum recommended flow rates for Cipolletti weirs

Crest length, Ft.	Min. head, Ft.	Minimum flow rate			Max. head, Ft.	Maximum flow rate		
		CFS	MGD	GPM		CFS	MGD	GPM
1	0.2	0.301	0.195	135	0.5	1.19	0.769	534
1 1/2	0.2	0.452	0.292	203	0.75	3.28	2.12	1470
2	0.2	0.602	0.389	270	1.0	6.73	4.35	3020
2 1/2	0.2	0.753	0.487	338	1.25	11.8	7.60	5300
3	0.2	0.903	0.584	405	1.5	18.6	12.0	8350
4	0.2	1.20	0.778	539	2.0	38.1	24.6	17,100
5	0.2	1.51	0.973	678	2.5	66.5	43.0	29,800
6	0.2	1.81	1.17	812	3.0	105	67.8	47,100
8	0.2	2.41	1.56	1080	4.0	214	139	96,000
10	0.2	3.01	1.95	1350	5.0	375	243	168,000

For flow rate in cubic feet per second, million gallons per day, and gallons per minute, and head in feet, the discharge equation for a Cipolletti weir is as follows:

CFS: $\quad Q = 3.367 \, L \, H^{1.5}$

MGD: $\quad Q = 2.176 \, L \, H^{1.5}$

GPM: $\quad Q = 1511 \, L \, H^{1.5}$

where: $\quad$ L = crest length of weir in feet

Complete discharge tables for Cipolletti weirs are found in Chapter 11 of this handbook.

Other weirs

There are certain other types of primary devices classified as weirs which are in use, but are much less common than the sharp-crested weir profiles discussed above. Among these are special profiles of sharp-crested weirs, compound weirs, broad-crested weirs, open flow nozzles, and the California Pipe method. These will be briefly discussed in the following sections.

Special profiles of sharp-crested weirs

Special sharp-crested weir profiles, as shown in Figure 3-6, have been developed to achieve certain head/discharge relationships or

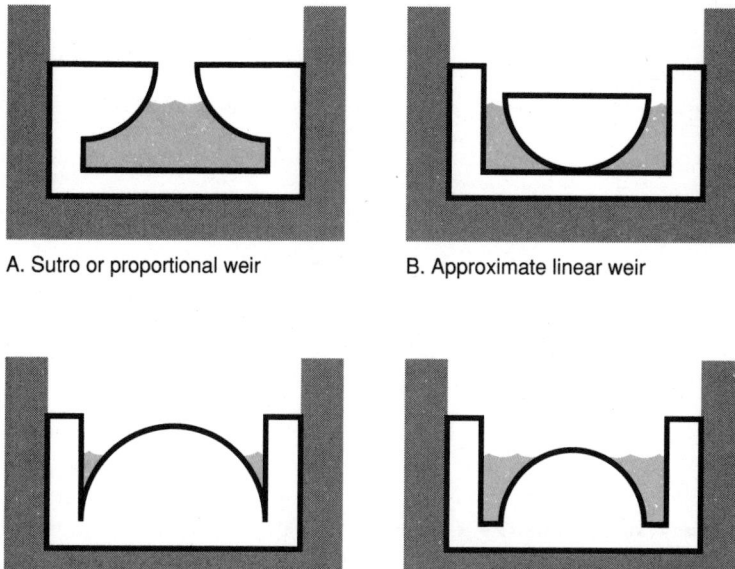

A. Sutro or proportional weir

B. Approximate linear weir

C. Approximate exponential weir

D. Poebing weir

3

Figure 3-6: Various other sharp-crested weir profiles

to achieve some benefit peculiar to a particular type of site. The most common of these special devices is the proportional or Sutro weir [2] [3] (Figure 3-6 A), designed so that the discharge varies directly with the head on the weir. This weir has the obvious advantage of a simple head/discharge relationship, but its shape is complicated and difficult to fabricate. To overcome this disadvantage, the approximate linear weir (Figure 3-6 B) was developed. This weir consists of a semi-circular plate attached to a rectangular weir with end contractions, making it fairly simple to fabricate. However, its head/discharge relationship is only approximately linear, thus introducing a certain amount of error. Other special purpose sharp-crested weir profiles are shown in Figure 3-6 C and D. None of these special weir profiles have been used or investigated nearly as extensively as the triangular, rectangular, and trapezoidal profiles discussed above, and will not be dealt with here.

Compound weirs

For situations where the normal range of discharges at a site might easily be handled by a V-notch weir but occasional larger flows would require, for example, a rectangular weir. The two

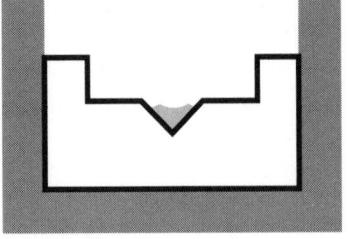

A. Low flow—acts as a
V-notch weir only

B. High flow—acts as a combination
of V-notch and rectangular weir

Figure 3-7: Compound weir (90° v-notch weir with contracted rectangular weir)

profiles may be combined to form what is termed a compound weir, as shown in Figure 3-7. Such a weir has a disadvantage, however. While flows may be measured rather accurately when the weir is behaving as a V-notch weir or as a rectangular weir, there will be a transition zone where accurate readings will be difficult to achieve. When the discharge begins to exceed the capacity of the V-notch, thin sheets of liquid will begin to pass over the wide horizontal crests in a less than predictable fashion, causing an ambiguous discontinuity in the discharge curve. The size of the V-notch and of the rectangular notch should be selected so that the discharge measurements in the transition zone will be of minimum importance. A compound weir may be fabricated from different weir profiles than those mentioned, for example, a combination of a small and large Cipolletti weir.

Quite often, the discharge over a compound weir is calculated by simply applying the standard discharge equation for each segment of the weir to the head on that segment of the weir. The total discharge is then the sum of the discharges of each to the two segments of the weir. Although this technique is commonly used, it apparently has not been fully investigated either in the laboratory or in the field. In fact, it appears as though little research has been performed on compound weirs in general. Thus, to assure accurate flow rate measurement with a compound weir, the structure should be calibrated either in the laboratory or in place.

Broad-crested weirs

If the weir notch is mounted in a wall too thick for the water to spring clear, the weir is called a broad-crested weir. The broad-crested weir can be rectangular, triangular, or trapezoidal in cross-section, and can have either a square or rounded leading edge.

Broad-crested weirs have not been used as extensively as sharp-crested weirs. In practice, they are usually pre-existing structures, such as dams, levees, diversion structures, etc. Discharge coefficients and discharge tables are usually obtained by calibrating the weir in place or by model studies. Reference [4] contains discharge equations for square-edge and rounded-edge broad-crested weirs, along with a fairly extensive discussion of this type of weir.

A broad-crested weir is sometimes used where the sharp-crested weir causes undue maintenance problems. It has a certain structural stability which sharp-crested weirs lack and permits a higher down-stream water level without submergence effects. On the other hand, it also possesses the disadvantages of the sharp-crested weirs—trapping of debris, sensitivity of discharge to edge and crest conditions, and susceptibility to leading-edge damage.

Open flow nozzles

The open flow nozzle will be discussed here, although it is actually a combination of a sharp-crested weir and a flume. Flow nozzles are designed to be attached to the end of a conduit flowing partially full and must discharge to a free fall. As with weirs, the design of a flow nozzle is such that a predetermined relationship exists between the depth of the liquid within the nozzle and the rate of flow. Two designs of flow nozzles are shown in Figure 3-8. In one (the Kennison nozzle), the cross-section is shaped so that this relationship is linear. In the second (the parabolic nozzle), the relationship is a parabola so that each unit increase in the flow produces a smaller incremental increase in head. Open flow nozzles are factory calibrated and offer reasonable accuracy even under rather severe field conditions. Standard sizes are available from 6 to 36 inches, with maximum capacities up to 30 cfs (19.4 mgd/13,500 gpm). Dimensions and approximate capacities for a number of parabolic and Kennison nozzles are listed in Table 3-5. Parabolic nozzle lengths are roughly four times the pipe diameter, while Kennison nozzle lengths are twice the diameter. Flow nozzles require a length of straight pipe immediately upstream of the nozzle, and the slope of the approach pipe must not exceed certain limits or else the calibration will be in error. Unlike the conventional weir, the flow nozzle can handle suspended solids rather effectively, as a self-scouring action exists, and relatively large solids will pass without clogging. Use of flow nozzles for heavy sludge is not recommended because deposits will alter the contour of the nozzle and, hence, its flow characteristics. The flow nozzle does not have the low head loss characteristics of a

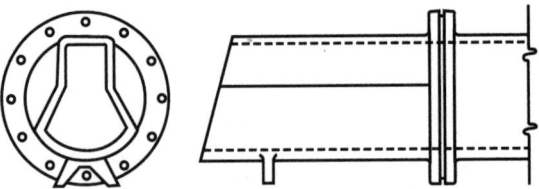

A. Kennison nozzle (Q proportional to H)

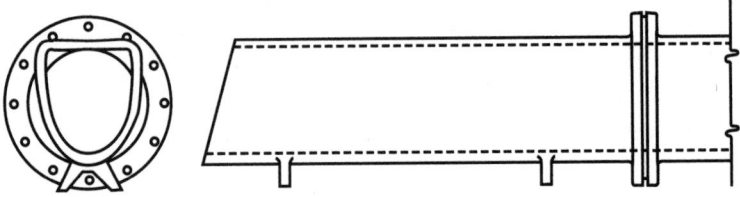

B. Parabolic nozzle (Q proportional to H^2)

Figure 3-8: Open flow nozzles

flume. The loss of head through the device will be at least one pipe diameter, due to the restriction in the pipe cross-sectional area presented by the nozzle.

Table 3-5: Open flow nozzles—dimensions and approximate capacities

Nozzle diameter, Inches	Parabolic				Kennison			
	Nozzle length, Inches	Approximate max. capacity			Nozzle length, Inches	Approximate max. capacity		
		CFS	MGD	GPM		CFS	MGD	GPM
6	28	0.42	0.27	188	12	0.42	0.27	188
8	35	0.88	0.57	395	16	0.70	0.45	314
10	43	1.50	0.97	673	20	1.31	0.84	588
12	50	2.32	1.50	1040	24	1.94	1.25	871
16	66	4.52	2.92	2030	32	4.19	2.71	1880
20	81	7.60	4.91	3410	40	6.97	4.51	3130
24	96	11.6	7.47	5210	48	11.5	7.46	5160
30	119	19.4	12.5	8710	60	17.9	11.6	8030
36	142	30.1	19.4	13,500	72	30.1	19.4	13,500

California pipe method

The two designs of flow nozzles discussed in the previous section are characterized by a cross sectional profile shaped to give a better depth/flow rate relationship than the ordinary circular pipe cross-section. A circular pipe, however, can be used for measuring flow rate, but high accuracies are not normally achieved. Errors of ±10% or worse are typical. The method, developed by Vanleer [5], is commonly referred to as the California pipe method. It is used for determining the flow rate from the open end of a partially filled horizontal pipe discharging freely into the air. The discharge pipe should be level and at least six diameters long. The pipe, which cannot be flowing full, must be located so the liquid falls freely into air. If the pipe is flowing nearly full, there should be an air vent a few diameters back from the outlet to provide for the free circulation of air in the unfilled portion of the discharge pipe. Also, liquid should not enter the discharge pipe with excessive velocity.

The California pipe method is particularly adapted to the measurement of comparatively small flows in pipes. It can also be used to measure flows in small open channels if the liquid can be diverted into a pipe which it does not completely fill and which discharges without any submergence of the outlet.

The empirically-developed rating formula for the California pipe method is as follows (refer to Figure 3-9):

$$Q = 8.69 \, [\, 1 - a \, / \, d \,]^{\,1.88} \, d^{\,2.48}$$

where: Q = flow rate in cubic feet per second
d = pipe diameter in feet
a = distance from the top of the inside surface of the pipe to the liquid surface, measured in the plane of the end of the pipe, in feet.

For flow rate in gallons per minute, the formula is:

$$Q = 3900 \, [\, 1 - a \, / \, d \,]^{\,1.88} \, d^{\,2.48}$$

For flow rate in million gallons per day, the formula is:

$$Q = 5.62 \, [\, 1 - a \, / \, d \,]^{\,1.88} \, d^{\,2.48}$$

If the California pipe method is to be used with liquid depth measuring instrumentation (for example, an open channel flow

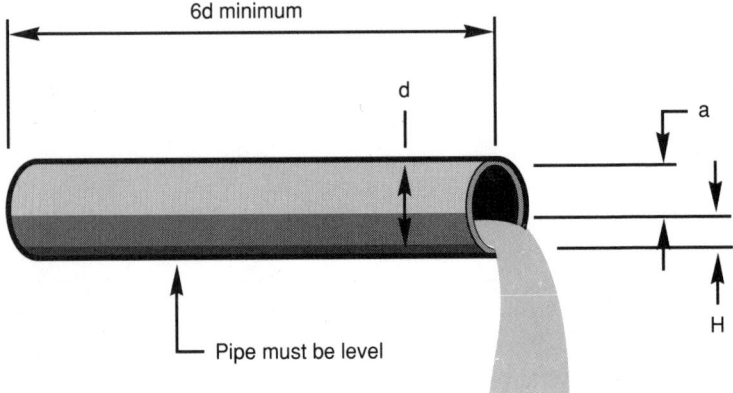

Figure 3-9: California pipe method

meter), the formula may be rewritten as follows:

$$Q = 8.69 [1 - (d - H) / d]^{1.88} d^{2.48}$$
$$= 8.69 d^{0.60} H^{1.88}$$

where: H = depth of liquid at the pipe outlet, in feet.
         Q = Flow rate in CFS

For flow rate in gallons per minute, the formula is:

$$Q = 3900 [1 - (d - H) / d]^{1.88} d^{2.48}$$
$$= 3900 d^{0.60} H^{1.88}$$

For flow rate in million gallons per day, the formula is:

$$Q = 5.62 [1 - (d - H) / d]^{1.88} d^{2.48}$$
$$= 5.62 d^{0.60} H^{1.88}$$

The above formulas are based on experimental data for pipes 3 to 10 inches in diameter, and they are accurate within these limits. The formulas have also been successfully used on pipes up to 3 feet in diameter.

References

1. *Water Measurement Manual*. United States Department of the Interior, Bureau of Reclamation, Denver, Colo., 1967.

2. Pratt, E.A. "Another Proportional-Flow Weir: Sutro Weir." *Engineering News*, 72, No. 9 (August 27, 1914): 462-463.

3. Mavis, F.T.; Soucek, E.; and Howe, H.E. "Sutro Weir Investigations Furnish Discharge Coefficients." *Engineering News Record*, 117, No. 20 (November 12, 1936): 679-680.

4. Kulin, Gershon, and Compton, Philip R. *A Guide to Methods and Standards for the Measurement of Water Flow.* National Technical Information Service, Springfield, Va., 1975.

5. Vanleer, B.R. "The California Pipe Method of Water Measurement." *Engineering News Record* (August 3, 1922, August 21, 1924).

Suggested readings

Associated Water & Air Resources Engineers. *Handbook For Monitoring Industrial Wastewater.* Environmental Protection Agency Technology Transfer Publication (August 1973).

Chow, Ven Te. *Open-Channel Hydraulics.* McGraw-Hill Book Company, New York, 1959.

Harris, James P.; Kacman, Stephen A.; Grant, Forest; and Tomcik, John. "Flow Monitoring Techniques in Sanitary Sewers." *Deeds & Data*, Water Pollution Control Federation, Washington, D.C. (July 1974).

Stevens Water Resources Data Book. 2nd Edition, Leupold & Stevens, Inc., Beaverton, Ore., 1974.

Vennard, John K. *Elementary Fluid Mechanics.* John Wiley & Sons, Inc., New York, 1961.

Chapter

4

Flumes

Overview

This chapter provides detailed information concerning the use of various types of flumes.

Please note that the recommendations presented in this chapter are derived from standard references and are intended to be used only as general guidelines. The details of a particular installation may justify a deviation from these recommendations based on sound engineering judgement.

Flumes

The second major class of commonly used primary measuring devices is the flume. A flume is a specially shaped open channel flow section that restricts the channel area and/or changes the channel slope, resulting in an increased velocity and a change in the level of the liquid flowing through the flume. Normally, a flume (Figure 4-1) consists of a converging section to restrict the flow, a throat section, and a diverging section to assure that the downstream level is less than the level in the converging section. The flume restricts the flow then expands it again in a definite fashion. The flow rate through the flume may be determined by measuring the head on the flume at a single point, usually at some distance downstream from the inlet. The head-flow rate relationship of a flume may be defined by either test data (calibration curves) or by an empirically derived formula.

In general, a flume is used to measure flow in an open channel where the use of a weir is not feasible. A flume can measure a higher flow rate than a comparably sized weir. It can also operate

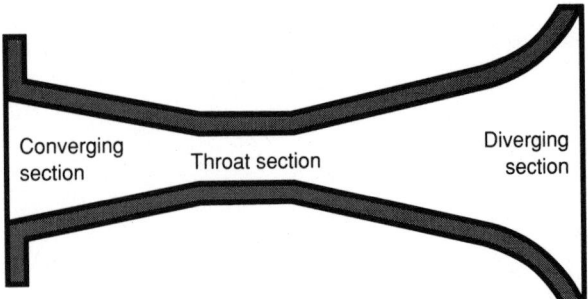

Figure 4-1: General flume configuration

with a much smaller loss of head than a weir, an advantage for many existing open channel flow applications where the available head is limited. Finally, a flume is better suited to the measurement of flows containing sediment or solids because high velocity of flow through the flume tends to make it self-cleaning, reducing deposits of solids. The major disadvantage is that a flume installation is typically more expensive than a weir.

Flumes can be categorized as belonging to one of three general families, depending upon the state of flow induced—subcritical, critical, or supercritical. By definition, the **critical flow** state is that for which the Froude number (the ratio of the inertia force to the force of gravity) is unity; this is the state of flow at which the specific energy is minimum for a given discharge. If the Froude number is less than unity (inertial forces less than gravitational forces), the flow is **subcritical**. In this state the gravitational forces are predominant, and the flow has a low velocity which is often described as tranquil and streaming. If the Froude number is greater than unity (inertial forces greater than gravitational forces), the flow is **supercritical**. In this state the inertial forces become dominant and the flow has a high velocity which is usually described as rapid, shooting, and torrential.

For a given discharge through a given channel, the critical depth in the channel is the depth at which critical flow occurs, and similarly, the critical velocity in the channel is the velocity at which critical flow occurs. When the depth of flow is greater than the critical depth, the velocity of flow is less than the critical velocity for the given discharge and hence, the flow is subcritical. When the depth of flow is less than the critical depth, the velocity of flow is greater than the critical velocity for the given discharge and hence, the flow is supercritical.

In a flume designed to induce critical flow, some means is provided (for example, an increase in the channel slope) to increase the velocity of the flow to a value greater than the critical velocity for the discharge(s) of interest. An increased velocity (due to the increased slope) results in a lower depth of flow, since the same quantity of liquid is being discharged with a higher velocity, and therefore the depth must decrease if the continuity equation is to be satisfied (flow rate = velocity x area). Thus, as a given discharge in a flume passes from subcritical to supercritical, the depth of flow decreases. Note that critical velocity and critical depth are defined for a given discharge through a particular channel. Critical depth cannot be achieved in a channel by simply decreasing the discharge; this new lower discharge would have a new critical depth, lower than the previous critical depth. Critical depth (and critical flow) can only be achieved in a previously subcritical channel through the introduction of some external means (increased slope, width reduction, etc.) which causes the flow to pass into the critical region.

In general, flumes which induce a critical or supercritical state of flow are most commonly used. This is because when critical or supercritical flow occurs in a channel, one head measurement can indicate the discharge rate if it is made far enough upstream so that the flow depth is not affected by the drawdown of the water surface as it achieves or passes through a critical state of flow. For channels in which critical depth is not achieved, it is necessary to measure the head in both the approach section and in the throat in order to determine the discharge rate. For critical or supercritical states of flow, a definitive head-discharge relationship can be established and measured based on a single head reading. Thus, most commonly encountered flumes are designed to pass the flow from subcritical through critical at or near the point of measurement.

Kilpatrick [1] has identified six approaches used in various flume designs. Of these six, four achieve critical or supercritical flow, and are briefly described, following Kilpatrick's discussion:

Type II, critical-flow large width reduction flumes are shown in Figure 4-2 A. Subcritical flow enters the flume, and the side contractions reduce the width to the extent that critical flow is achieved in the throat. This gives the advantage of requiring measurement at only one location, which may be either in the immediate approach to the flume or in the throat. Measurement in the approach will yield a more sensitive head-discharge relationship because changes in discharge will result in greater changes in depth in subcritical flow than would like changes in discharges in critical flow. Unfortunately, the head-discharge relationship in the

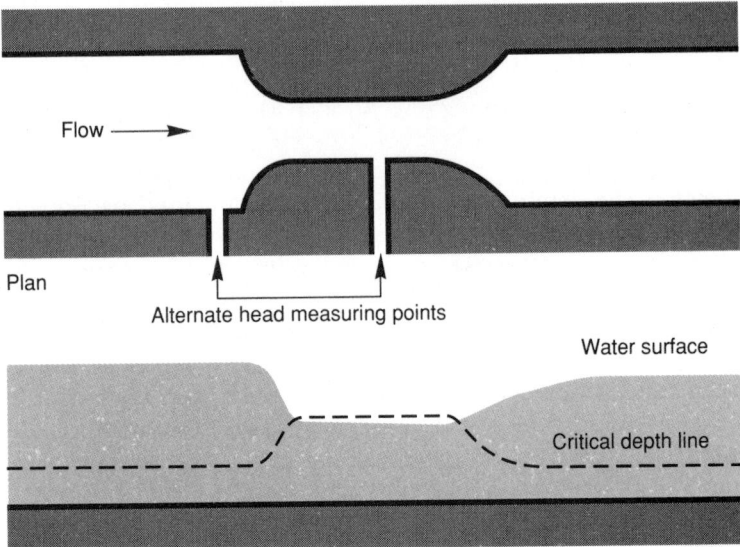

Figure 4-2 A: Type II Flume, critical flow contraction obtained by large width reduction, horizontal bed.

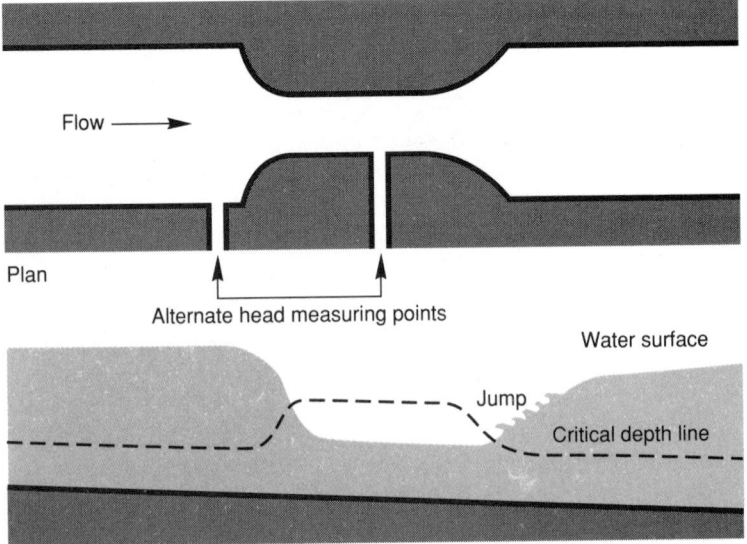

Figure 4-2 B: Type IV Flume, supercritical flow contraction obtained by width reduction and sloping bed

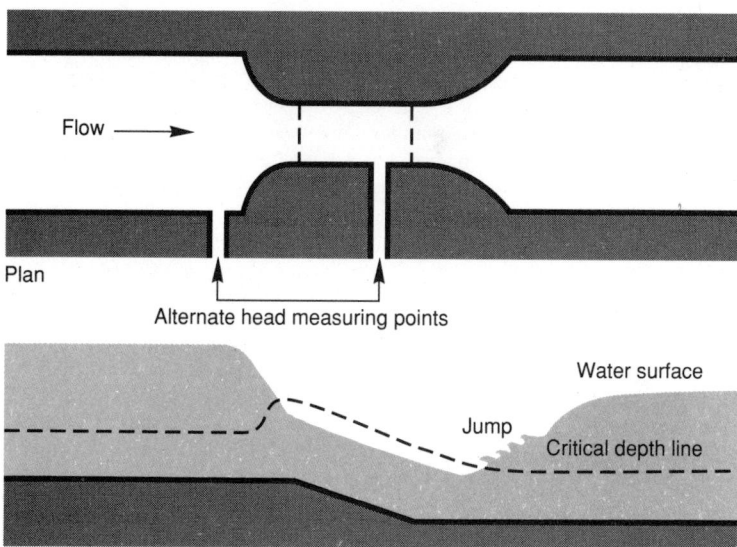

Figure 4-2 C: Type V Flume, supercritical flow contraction obtained by width reduction and drop in bed

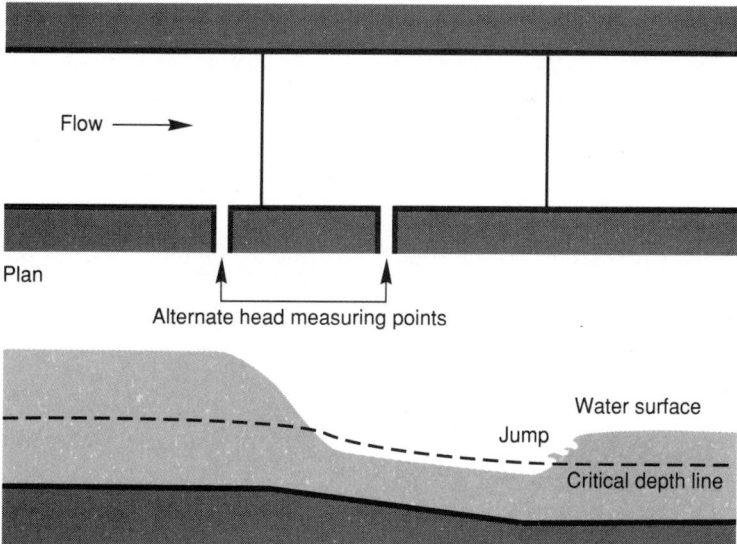

Figure 4-2 D: Type VI Flume, supercritical flow contraction obtained by steepening floor.

approach may be unstable due to approach conditions such as scour and fill. Consequently, the head is usually measured in the throat to alleviate any influences from either upstream or downstream. Approach conditions can have some effect on flow in the throat, but it is generally insignificant. The site at which critical depth is first reached may shift further downstream into the throat as a result of excessive deposition in the approach. For this reason, and to avoid possible flow separations near the entrance, head measurements in the throat should not be too close to the entrance. Flow close to critical is very unstable, constantly attempting to become either subcritical or supercritical. Therefore, this type of flume is seldom encountered in practice.

Type IV, supercritical-flow, width-reduction, steep-slope flumes are shown in Figure 4-2 B. For flumes that have bed slopes of near zero, critical depth is the minimum depth possible in the flume. Further contraction, either at the side or bottom, will not produce supercritical flow. This can be accomplished only by increasing the available specific energy from the approach into the throat. For Type IV flumes, the bed is placed on a slope sufficient to cause the required increase in specific energy to produce supercritical flow in the throat. It may be thought of as a Type II tilted in the downstream direction. Only a single gauging point is required.

Type V, supercritical-flow, width-reduction, drop-in-bed flumes are shown in Figure 4-2 C. Here the increase in specific energy required to achieve supercritical flow is provided by a sudden drop in the bed. Measurement of head is made either in the throat or the approach. A discharge rating based upon measurements in the region of super-critical flow, while not as sensitive as compared with measurements in subcritical flow, is the least influenced by disturbances either upstream or downstream, and hence is apt to be the most stable. Similarly, such flumes are the most capable of stable operation up to high submergences.

Type VI, supercritical-flow, steep slope flumes are shown in Figure 4-2 D. Here there is no contraction, the increase in specific energy necessary for achieving supercritical flow being produced simply by the presence of sufficient downstream slope. Although a slope of one degree is usually sufficient to produce critical depth in the vicinity of the upstream edge of the flume, waves and disturbances are apt to be numerous downstream. For this reason slopes on a flume of this type will more typically range from 2 to 5%.

The preceding paragraphs concerning general flume design were included mainly for reference. The majority of flumes currently in use belong to the critical or supercritical families, and are of one of these four designs. Most of the commonly encountered flumes are designed to pass the flow through a critical state for a specified head range, provided the flume is accurately constructed, properly installed and maintained, and operated within the specified head range.

To assure accurate discharge measurement, there are certain general requirements for the installation of flumes that apply to all types and sizes of flumes:

1. A flume should be located in a straight section of the open channel, without bends immediately upstream.

2. The approaching flow should be well distributed across the channel, and relatively free of turbulence and waves.

3. Generally, a site with high velocity of approach should not be selected for a flume installation. However, if the water surface just upstream is smooth with no surface boils, waves, or high velocity current concentrations, accuracy may not be greatly affected by velocity of approach.

4. Consideration should be given to the height of upstream banks with regard to their ability to sustain the increased depth caused by the flume installation.

5. Although less head is lost through flumes than over weirs, it should be noted that significant losses may occur with large installations.

6. The possibility of submergence of the flume due to backwater from downstream should also be considered, although the effect of submergence upon the accuracy of most flumes is much less than is the case with weirs.

Most flumes in common use today can be traced to one of three early design sources: rectangular English flumes based upon early work in India around 1908–1914 and the writings of F.V.A.E. Engal [2]; the Parshall flume whose forerunner, a venturi flume developed by Cone [3] [4], was extensively modified and tested by Parshall; and flumes of the type first developed by Palmer and Bowlus. The following sections will discuss in detail some of the more popular flume designs currently in use. Included are discussions of the Parshall flume, the Palmer-Bowlus flume, the HS, H, and HL flumes, the Leopold-Lagco® flume, the trapezoidal flume, and certain other types of flumes.

Parshall flumes

The Parshall flume (see Figure 4-3) was developed in the 1920s primarily to measure irrigation water flow, but it is now frequently used in industrial and municipal sewers, and in sewage treatment plants. In 1922, Dr. Ralph L. Parshall of the U.S. Soil Conservation Service made some radical changes to the existing venturi (subcritical) flume design. The essential change introduced by Parshall was a drop in the floor which produced supercritical flow through the throat of the flume (Type V). This perfected device was named the Parshall Measuring Flume by the Irrigation Committee of the American Society of Civil Engineers. The flumes are not patented and the discharge tables are not copyrighted.

The constricted throat of the flume produces a head that is related to discharge. The level converging section followed by the downward sloping floor in the throat gives the Parshall flume its ability to withstand relatively high degrees of submergence without affecting the rate of flow. The converging upstream portion of the flume accelerates the entering flow, helping to eliminate deposits of sediment which would otherwise reduce measurement accuracy. The approaching flow should be relatively free of turbulence, eddies, and waves if accurate measurements are expected.

The principal advantages of the Parshall flume are its capabilities for self-cleaning (particularly when compared with sharp-edged weirs), its relatively low head loss, and its ability to function over a wide operating range while requiring only a single

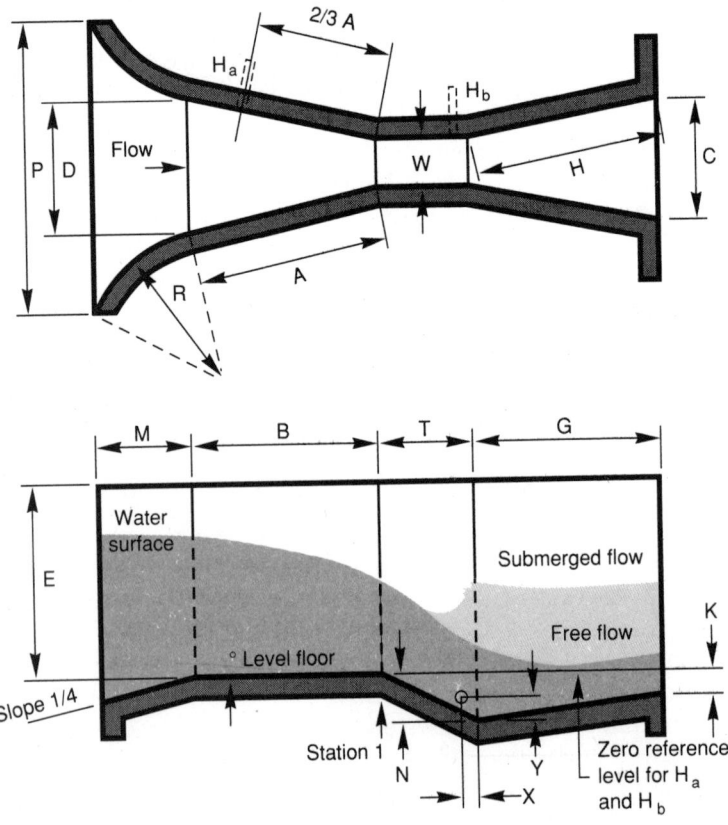

Figure 4-3: Parshall flume

Table 4-1: Parshall flume dimensions for various throat widths, W

W	A	2/3 A	B	C	D	E	T	G	H	K	M	N	P	R	X	Y
1"	1' 2-9/32"	9-17/32"	1' 2"	3-21/32"	6-19/32"	6' to 9"	3"	8"	8-1/8"	3/4"		1-1/8"				1"	1-1/2"
2"	1' 4-5/16"	10-7/8"	1' 4"	5-5/16"	8 13/32"	6 to 10'	4-1/2"	10"	10-1/8"	7/8"		1-11/16"				1"	1"
3"	1' 6-3/8"	1' 1/4"	1' 6"	7"	10-3/16"	1 to 1-1/2'	6"	1'	1' 5/32"	1"		2-1/4"				1"	1-1/2"
6"	2' 7/16"	1' 4-5/16"	2'	1' 3-1/2"	1' 3-5/8"	1'	1'	2'		3"	1'	4-1/2"				2"	3"
9"	2' 10-5/8"	1' 11-1/8"	2' 10"	1' 3"	1' 10-5/8"	1'	1'	1' 6"		3"	1'	4-1/2"				2"	3"
1'	4' 6"	3'	4' 4-7/8"	2'	2' 9-1/4"	2'	2'	3'		3"	1' 3"	9"	2' 11-1/2"	1' 4"	2"	3"	
1' 6"	4' 9"	3' 2"	4' 7-7/8"	2' 6"	3' 4-3/8"	2' 6"	2'	3'		3"	1' 3"	9"	3' 6-1/2"	1' 4"	2"	3"	
2'	5'	3' 4"	4' 10-7/8"	3'	3' 11-1/2"	3'	2'	3'		3"	1' 3"	9"	4' 10-3/4"	1' 8"	2"	3"	
3'	5' 6"	3' 8"	5' 4-3/4"	4'	5' 1-7/8"	3'	2'	3'		3"	1' 3"	9"	5' 6"	1' 8"	2"	3"	
4'	6'	4'	5' 10-5/8"	5'	6' 4-1/4"	3'	2'	3'		3"	1' 6"	9"	6' 1"	1' 8"	2"	3"	
5'	6' 6"	4' 4"	6' 4-1/2"	6'	7' 6-5/8"	3'	2'	3'		3"	1' 6"	9"	7' 3-1/2"	1' 8"	2"	3"	
6'	7'	4' 8"	6' 10-3/8"	7'	8' 9"	3'	2'	3'		3"	1' 6"	9"	8' 10-3/4"	1' 8"	2"	3"	
7'	7' 6"	5'	7' 4-1/4"	8'	9' 11-3/8"	3'	2'	3'		3"	1' 6"	9"	10' 1-1/4"	2'	2"	3"	
8'	8'	5' 4"	7' 10-1/8"	9'	11' 1-3/4"	3'	2'	3'		3"	1' 6"	9"	11' 3-1/2"	2'	3"	3"	
10'		6'	14'	12'	15' 7-1/4"	4'	3'	6'		6"		9"	12' 6"	2'	3"	9"	
12'		6' 8"	16'	14' 8"	18' 4-3/4"	5'	3'	8'		6"		9"	13' 8-1/4"	2'	3"	9"	
15'		7' 8"	25'	18' 4"	25'	6'	4'	10'		9"		1' 6"		2'	3"	9"	
20'		9' 4"	25'	24'	30'	6'	6'	12'		1'		2' 3"		2'	3"	9"	
25'		11'	25'	29' 4"	35'	6'	6'	13'		1'		2' 3"			3"	9"	
30'		12' 8"	26'	34' 8"	40' 4-3/4"	6'	6'	14'		1'		2' 3"			3"	9"	
40'		16'	27'	45' 4"	50' 9-1/2"	6'	6'	16'		1'		2' 3"			1"	9"	
50'		19' 4"	27'	56' 8"	60' 9-1/2"	6'	6'	20'		1'		2' 3"			1"	9"	

head measurement. These characteristics of the Parshall flume make it particularly suitable for flow measurement in irrigation canals, in certain natural channels, and in sewers. Parshall flume sizes are designated by the throat width, W, as shown in Figure 4-3. Dimensions are available for flumes with throat widths ranging from 1 inch to 50 feet. For convenience, Parshall flumes have been somewhat arbitrarily classified into three main groups. The groups are "very small" for 1, 2 and 3 inch flumes, "small" for 6 inch through 8 foot flumes, and "large" for 10 foot through 50 foot flumes. The flumes cover a range of discharges from 0.01 to 3000 cfs (0.006 to 1940 mgd, or 4.49 to 1,350,000 gpm) and have overlapping capacities to provide wide latitude in selecting sizes.

The configuration and standard nomenclature for Parshall flumes is given in Figure 4-3. For a given throat width (W), all other dimensions are rigidly prescribed. Since the discharge tables for Parshall flumes are based upon extensive research, faithful adherence to all dimensions is necessary to achieve accurate flow measurement. The flumes must be constructed according to the dimensions listed in Table 4-1 for each flume, because the flumes are not geometrically similar. For example, it cannot be assumed that a dimension in the 12 foot flume will be three times the corresponding dimension in the 4 foot flumes. The flumes may be built of wood, concrete, galvanized sheet metal, fiberglass, or other materials. Large flumes are usually constructed on-site, but small flumes may be obtained as prefabricated structures to be installed in one piece. Prefabricated flumes, typically constructed of fiberglass, are available from a number of manufacturers.

Discharge through a Parshall flume can occur for two conditions of flow. The first, free flow, occurs when there is insufficient backwater depth to reduce the discharge rate. For free flow, only the head H_a (refer to Figure 4-3) at the upstream gauge location is needed to determine the discharge from a standard table. Under free flow conditions a phenomenon known as the hydraulic jump or "standing wave" occurs downstream from the flume. Formation of this is a certain indication of free flow conditions.

The second condition of flow, submerged flow, occurs when the water surface downstream from the flume is high enough to reduce the discharge. When the discharge is increased above a critical value, the resistance to flow in the downstream channel becomes sufficient to reduce the velocity, increase the flow depth, and cause a backwater effect at the flume. In order to determine the discharge, submerged flow requires the measurement of both an upstream depth H_a and a depth in the throat, H_b (Figure 4-3).

The ratio of the downstream depth to the upstream depth, H_b/H_a, expressed as a percentage, is referred to as the submergence ratio. Calibration tests show that the discharge of a Parshall flume is not reduced (that is, the flume is operating under free flow conditions) until the submergence ratio exceeds the following values:

50 percent for flumes 1, 2, 3 inches wide,
60 percent for flumes 6 and 9 inches wide,
70 percent for flumes 1 to 8 feet wide, and
80 percent for flumes 8 to 50 feet wide.

4

When the submergence ratio exceeds the values listed above, the flume is operating under submerged conditions, and submerged discharge tables will have to be used to calculate the discharge. See references [5] and [6] for a complete discussion of the calculation of discharge under submerged conditions of flow. In general, selecting and installing a Parshall flume so that conditions of free flow exist is desired since submerged conditions greatly complicate the determination of flow rate.

When selecting and installing a Parshall flume, there are a number of factors to be considered to assure an accurate flow measurement system. The first consideration is the size of flume to be installed. Because of considerable overlap in flume discharges, it is possible to pass a given discharge through any one of several different standard size flumes. The choice of the proper size also requires consideration of other factors in addition to capacity. For example, a different throat width, W, will be required if 20 cfs (8980 gpm / 12.9 mgd) is to be discharged with 2.5 feet of depth rather than with 1 foot of depth. In the interests of economy, the smallest practical size should usually be selected.

In selecting a flume size, it is usually necessary to use a "trial-and-error" system on several sizes believed adequate. The final selection is normally made on the basis of the original channel dimensions. Thus, if a 2 foot flume can accommodate the discharge without overrunning the upstream channel banks or flooding other outlets and facilities, it would be preferred over a 3 or 4 foot flume. However when the width of the channel is considered, it may be just as economical to use a 3 or 4 foot flume because longer and more costly wingwalls may be needed to span the channel when using the narrower flume. Reference [5] contains an excellent discussion of the flume size selection process.

When installing a Parshall flume, particularly in the very small sizes, the crest should be used as an index. Careful leveling is necessary in both longitudinal and transverse directions if standard discharge tables are to be used. The flume should be set on a solid foundation to prevent settlement or heaving. Collars should be attached to either or both the upstream and downstream flanges of the flume, and should extend well out into the channel banks and invert to prevent flow from bypassing the structure and eroding the foundation.

4

Table 4-2: Minimum and maximum recommended flow rates for free flow through Parshall flumes

Throat width, W	Min. head, Ft.	Minimum flow rate			Max. head, Ft.	Maximum flow rate		
		CFS	MGD	GPM		CFS	MGD	GPM
1 in.	0.07	0.005	0.003	2.24	0.60	0.153	0.099	68.7
2 in.	0.07	0.011	0.007	4.94	0.60	0.306	0.198	137
3 in.	0.10	0.028	0.018	12.6	1.5	1.86	1.20	835
6 in.	0.10	0.054	0.035	24.2	1.5	3.91	2.53	1750
9 in.	0.10	0.091	0.059	40.8	2.0	8.87	5.73	3980
1 ft.	0.10	0.120	0.078	53.9	2.5	16.1	10.4	7220
1½ ft.	0.10	0.174	0.112	78.1	2.5	24.6	15.9	11,000
2 ft.	0.15	0.423	0.273	190	2.5	33.1	21.4	14,900
3 ft.	0.15	0.615	0.397	276	2.5	50.4	32.6	22,600
4 ft.	0.20	1.26	0.816	565	2.5	67.9	43.9	30,500
5 ft.	0.20	1.55	1.00	696	2.5	85.6	55.3	38,400
6 ft.	0.25	2.63	1.70	1180	2.5	103	66.9	46,200
8 ft.	0.25	3.45	2.23	1550	2.5	139	90.1	62,400
10 ft.	0.30	5.74	3.71	2580	3.5	292	189	131,000
12 ft.	0.33	7.93	5.13	3560	4.5	519	335	233,000

To assure accurate discharge measurement, the approach flow conditions should be considered. The approaching flow should enter the converging section reasonably well distributed across the entrance width, and flowlines should be essentially parallel to the flume centerline. Surges and waves of any appreciable size should be eliminated. Also, the flow at the flume entrance should be free of "white" water and free from turbulence in the form of visible surface boils. Experience has shown that Parshall flumes should not be placed at right angles to flowing streams unless the flow is effectively straightened and uniformly redistributed before it enters the flume.

Although Parshall flumes are usually self-cleaning, large rocks and other debris in the flow may cause problems. Kilpatrick [1] notes that, "....its use on flashy, cobble-strewn streams has been relatively unsuccessful."

The minimum and maximum recommended flow rates for free flow through Parshall flumes have been experimentally determined. Table 4-2 presents the minimum and maximum recommended flow rates for a number of common sizes of Parshall flumes.

The discharge (head vs. flow rate) equation of free flow through a Parshall flume takes the form:

$$Q = KH^n$$

where: Q = flow rate
           H = head measured at point H_a
           K = constant, dependent upon throat width and units
           n = constant power, dependent upon throat width

For flow rate in cubic feet per second, million gallons per day, and gallons per minute, and head in feet, the discharge equations for a number of common Parshall flumes are as follows:

Width	CFS	MGD	GPM
1"	$Q = .3380 \, H^{1.550}$	$Q = .2184 \, H^{1.550}$	$Q = 151.7 \, H^{1.550}$
2"	$Q = .6760 \, H^{1.550}$	$Q = .4369 \, H^{1.550}$	$Q = 303.4 \, H^{1.550}$
3"	$Q = .9920 \, H^{1.547}$	$Q = .6411 \, H^{1.547}$	$Q = 445.2 \, H^{1.547}$
6"	$Q = 2.060 \, H^{1.580}$	$Q = 1.331 \, H^{1.580}$	$Q = 924.5 \, H^{1.580}$
9"	$Q = 3.070 \, H^{1.530}$	$Q = 1.984 \, H^{1.530}$	$Q = 1378 \, H^{1.530}$
1' to 8'	$Q = 4 \, W \, H^{1.522 \, W^{0.026}}$	$Q = 2.585 \, W \, H^{1.522 \, W^{0.026}}$	$Q = 1795 \, W \, H^{1.522 \, W^{0.026}}$
10' to 50'	$Q = (3.69 \, W + 2.5) \, H^{1.6}$	$Q = (2.385 \, W + 1.616) \, H^{1.6}$	$Q = (1656 \, W + 1122) \, H^{1.6}$

where: W = throat width in feet

Complete discharge tables for a number of common Parshall flumes are found in Chapter 12 of this handbook.

Some practitioners have used a simplified version of the Parshall flume, sometimes referred to as the Montana flume [5]. If a Parshall flume is never to be operated above 70 percent submergence, there is no need to construct the portion of the flume downstream from the end of the flat crest section, shown as station 1 in Figure 4-3. This configuration, with only the upstream portion of the flume present, is known as the Montana flume. The crest of a Montana flume should be set above the channel bottom. This will assure that the flow profile over the crest section is not modified by backwater from the downstream channel. As long as the 70 percent submergence limit is not exceeded, the standard discharge equations for Parshall flumes may be applied to similarly sized Montana flumes.

Palmer-Bowlus flumes

The Palmer-Bowlus flume was developed in the mid 1930s by Harold V. Palmer and Fred D. Bowlus [7] of the Los Angeles County Sanitation District as a simple and effective wastewater flow measuring device. Palmer-Bowlus flumes are a form of the Type IV flume, being dependent upon an existing conduit slope and channel contractions (provided by the flume) to produce supercritical flow. This type of flume arose out of a desire to have a primary measuring device that could be inserted into an existing conduit, usually round, with minimal site requirements other than suitable slope.

The Palmer-Bowlus flume is essentially a restriction in the channel designed to produce a higher velocity critical flow in the throat. The flume is most often used in manholes or open round or rectangular bottom channels to measure flow rate. It is useful in temporary installations to provide flow data for determining flume size and equipment requirements for permanent installation. Some of the flume's advantages include accuracy of measurement (comparable to Parshall flumes), low energy loss, and minimal restriction to flow. A principal advantage of the Palmer-Bowlus flume is the comparative ease with which it can be installed in existing conduits, since it does not require a drop in the conduit invert as would be required with a Parshall flume. A disadvantage of Palmer-Bowlus flumes is that they have a smaller useful range of flow rates than a Parshall flume, with a range that seldom exceeds twenty to one. Also, the resolution of the Palmer-Bowlus flume is not as good as that of the Parshall flume. For a given change in flow rate, the Parshall flume produces a greater change in head than does the Palmer-Bowlus flume. Thus, more sensitive head measuring instrumentation may be required with the Palmer-Bowlus flume.

The Palmer-Bowlus flume is a type of venturi flume characterized by a throat of uniform cross section and a length approximately equal to one diameter of the pipe or conduit in which it is

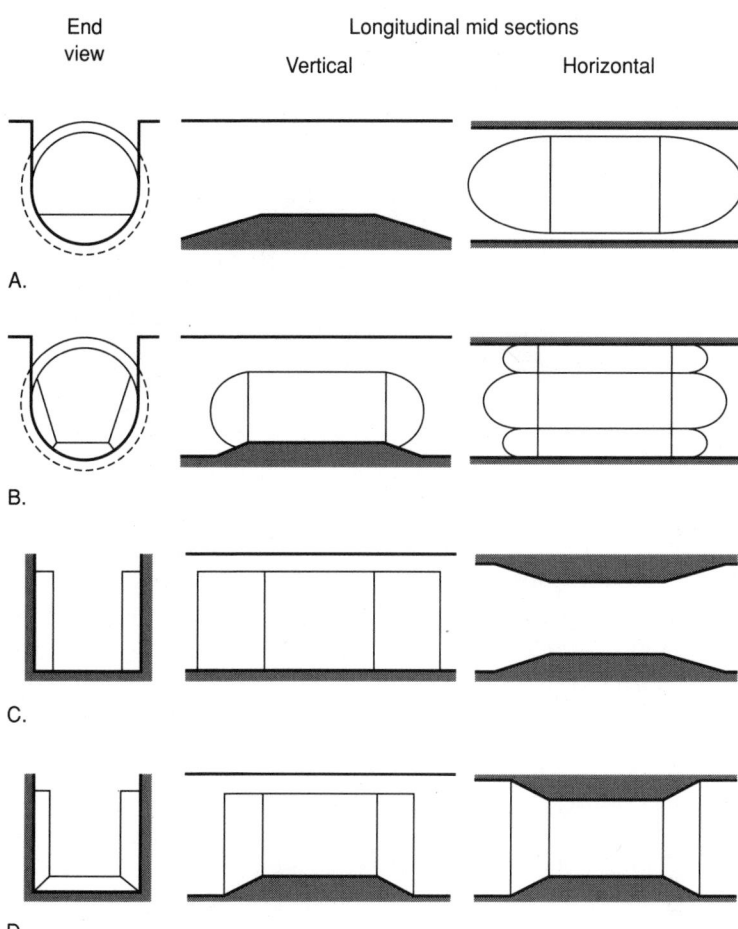

Figure 4-4: Various cross-sectional shapes of
Palmer-Bowlus flumes

to be installed. A number of different cross-sectional shapes have
been proposed, tested, and/or used over the years. Typical
shapes of Palmer-Bowlus flumes for installation in round and rectangular conduits are shown in Figure 4-4.

It is important to note that the term "Palmer-Bowlus flume"
technically refers only to the general class of flumes which have a
form as discussed previously. Unlike the Parshall flume, the
dimensional configuration of a Palmer-Bowlus flume is not rigidly
established for each flume size. Much latitude is possible in both

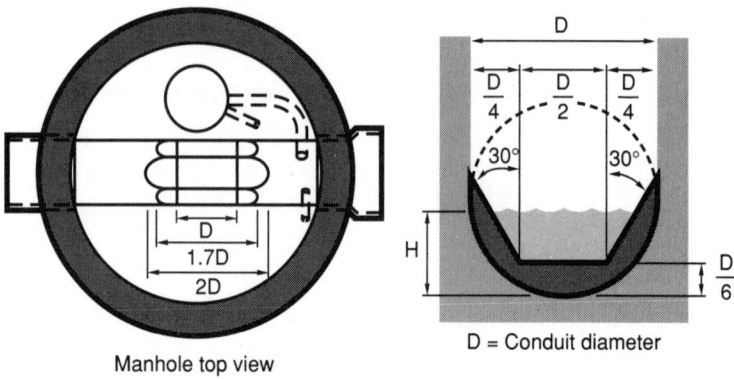

Manhole top view

D = Conduit diameter

Figure 4-5: Dimensional configuration of standardized Palmer-Bowlus flume-trapezoidal throat cross-section.

the design and construction of Palmer-Bowlus flumes. As shown in Figure 4-4, the cross-sectional configuration of a Palmer-Bowlus flume may assume any of several different shapes: rectangular, trapezoidal (with various slopes and base widths and heights), with or without the bottom slab, etc. Thus, without further qualification, the term "Palmer-Bowlus flume" is not fully definitive of flume configuration and dimensions.

However, there appears to have been a standardization among many commercial manufacturers and users of "Palmer-Bowlus flumes" upon a flume with a trapezoidal throat having the configuration shown in Figure 4-5. This trapezoidal section with a flat bottom is considered to be the preferred design for circular conduits and pipes since this shape has the least constriction through the critical flow area and provides for minimum head loss through the conduit. Most flumes currently being marketed with the description "Palmer-Bowlus flume" are this particular trapezoidal configuration with other dimensions as shown in Figure 4-5. Note that all dimensions are proportional to the conduit diameter, D.

Following what appears to be common practice, the term "Palmer-Bowlus flume" will, in the remainder of this chapter, refer to a flume with the configuration shown in Figure 4-5, and the discussion will be limited to flumes of this type. However, it is advisable to remember that the term "Palmer-Bowlus flume" is not definitive, and may be applied to flumes with any number of different throat cross-sectional configurations.

Palmer-Bowlus flume sizes are designated by the size of the pipe or conduit into which they fit, not by the throat width as is the case with Parshall flumes. Thus, an 8 inch Palmer-Bowlus flume is designed to be inserted into an 8 inch diameter pipe. Standard Palmer-Bowlus flumes are available from the various manufacturers to fit pipe sizes ranging from 4 inches to 42 inches. Larger sizes are available by special order. The standard sizes appear to be 4, 6, 8, 10, 12, 15, 18, 21, 24, 27, 30, 36, and 42 inches.

Palmer-Bowlus flumes are usually purchased prefabricated from one of the many flume manufacturers. They are normally made of fiberglass, a reinforced plastic, or stainless steel, and are available in a number of installation configurations. The permanent type flume is intended to be embedded in poured concrete for new construction, and has the same inside radius as the pipe to which it is joined. The permanent type flume is usually available with or without an integral approach section. The approach section is sometimes necessary to assure a smooth approach to reduce the turbulence present in a poorly defined channel. The invert or insert type flume is used for temporary measurements or for permanent installation in an existing pipe. The flume is inserted and seated into the existing half-section of pipe with the outside radius of the flume being the same as the inside radius of the pipe. A final type is the cutback or exit type flume. This special version of the Palmer-Bowlus flume is intended for temporary or permanent installation in the downstream exit pipe of a manhole, allowing space for upstream monitoring and sampling installations.

When choosing the size of Palmer-Bowlus flume to be installed at a particular location, both the diameter of the conduit or pipe in which the flume is to be installed and the range of expected flow rates should be considered. The expedient sizing technique for flumes (such as Palmer-Bowlus flumes) designed to be inserted into the invert of a pipe is to select a flume whose outside diameter matches the existing diameter of the pipe in which flow is to be measured. However, as with any flume, to achieve maximum accuracy the size of the flume should be determined by the expected rate of flow, rather than strictly by the pipe diameter. Many large sewer lines have very low flows and therefore require only small size Palmer-Bowlus flumes. In this case, a flume designed for use in a smaller diameter pipe may be used, and the flow channel gently tapered to provide a gradual transition into bulkheads which can be installed to match the smaller flume to the larger pipe inside diameter; typically, flumes with bulkheads are fabricated with an integral approach section (two to four pipe diameters long) to smooth the flow before it reaches the flume

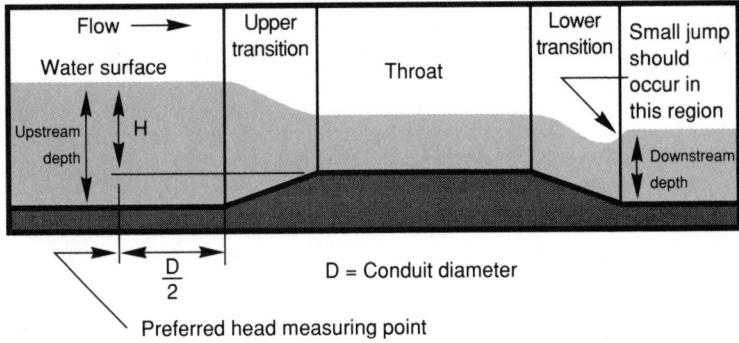

Figure 4-6: Free flowing Palmer-Bowlus flume

section. The user should be cautioned that there appears to be no research to detail the effects of a tapered transition from a larger diameter pipe to a smaller flume or the use of bulkheads to adapt a smaller flume to a larger pipe. Some users have suggested that the use of either of these techniques can lead to some loss in measurement accuracy, particularly at higher flows. Sometimes, a slightly larger than required flume which will provide adequate accuracy without the difficulty of necking down the pipe or installing bulkheads and with the capacity to accommodate possible future increases in flow rates can be economically justified for use.

The depth of the liquid above the throat of the flume (not the bottom of the pipe or conduit) is the index of discharge. As shown in Figure 4-6, the ideal location for the level measuring point is at a distance one-half D (pipe diameter or channel width) upstream from the entrance of the flume. However, this location is not critical, as long as the point of level measurement is located above the upper transition section (Figure 4-6) in a zone where the depth of flow does not change significantly within a range of one pipe diameter.

Tabular data or rating curves are provided by the various manufacturers of Palmer-Bowlus flumes which relate the depth or head of liquid above the flume throat to a corresponding flow rate. Because of the great latitude possible in Palmer-Bowlus flume design mentioned previously, it is important to assure that the rating curve being used is the correct one for the flume in question. The rating curves supplied by two different manufacturers of the same size Palmer-Bowlus flume may have some differences. Therefore, the rating curve used should be the one provided by the manufacturer with the flume.

When installing a Palmer-Bowlus flume it is important to consider the conduit or channel slope. A minimum channel slope (which applies only to the downstream section) is necessary to maintain critical flow through the throat of the flume and prevent the flume from becoming submerged. It has been determined that the required critical flow will occur if the downstream depth of flow is not greater than 85% of the upstream depth (Figure 4-6), that is, if the submergence ratio is less than 85%. This is considered to be the upper limit of submergence allowable for proper flume operation. In new installations, effective operation can be assured by building in a slight drop on the downstream end of the installation. A small jump or rise in the water surface just below the throat of the flume is evidence that the required critical flow is occurring through the flume, as shown in Figure 4-6.

There is also a maximum allowable upstream slope, which is necessary to assure that the upstream flow is subcritical (lower in velocity than the throat of the flume) and is not turbulent. Otherwise, the flow at the point of measurement would be too choppy and rough to make meaningful head determinations. Also, the flow through the flume and at the measuring point above the throat must be straight and parallel. In order to obtain proper head readings, corrective measures must be taken to quiet any turbulence so that the upstream flow is tranquil and the flow is uniformly parallel through the flume. The upper limit of channel conduit slope necessary to maintain subcritical flow in the upstream section is normally on the order of a 2% slope for smaller flume sizes and a lesser slope for larger flume sizes.

When installing a Palmer-Bowlus flume, the downstream outlet pipe slope should be greater than or equal to the upstream pipe slope. The flume itself should be level, although a small slope will not significantly affect the accuracy of the flume. The downstream outlet pipe should be free of obstructions which would contribute to submergence. Upstream turbulence or obstructions to the flow should be avoided. There should be no bends, drop manholes, flow junctions, etc., within 25 pipe diameters (D) upstream of the flume location.

Wells and Gotaas [8] conducted detailed studies on Palmer-Bowlus type flumes. Based on these studies, they summarized the characteristics of a freely discharging (nonsubmerged), properly functioning Palmer-Bowlus flume as follows:

1. Upstream channel: The flow in the upstream channel is smooth and tranquil. There should be no aeration or prominent surface waves, especially at the point of upstream depth measurement.

2. At the flume: The water enters and passes through the flume smoothly and with little turbulence. The surface profile should drop throughout the length of the flume. Streamlines are evident in the flow even after the point of critical depth has been reached.

3. Downstream channel: A shooting flow is evident on the downstream side of the flume, indicating that the free discharge necessary for proper functioning of the flume prevails. In no case should the flow merely "neck down," i.e., show a smooth surface depression at the flume. In some instances, a hydraulic jump may form immediately downstream from the flume. Operation will be satisfactory if the upstream edge of the jump remains below the throat of the flume.

Chapter 13 of this handbook presents discharge tables for a number of Palmer-Bowlus flumes manufactured by Plasti-Fab, Inc. (P.O. Box 227, Tualatin, Oregon 97062). Plasti-Fab is a leading manufacturer of fiberglass reinforced plastic products for the water and wastewater industry, and manufactures a wide variety of flumes. The discharge tables cover Plasti-Fab Palmer-Bowlus flumes ranging in size from 6 inches to 30 inches. These flumes

Table 4-3: Minimum and maximum recommended flow rates for free flow through Plasti-Fab Palmer-Bowlus flumes

Flume size, In.	Max. slope for upstream, percent	Min. head, Ft.	Min. flow rate			Max. head, Ft.	Max. flow rate		
			CFS	MGD	GPM		CFS	MGD	GPM
4	2.2	0.02	0.001	0.001	0.563	0.25	0.121	0.078	54.5
6	2.2	0.03	0.004	0.002	1.68	0.35	0.295	0.190	132
8	2.0	0.03	0.008	0.005	3.43	0.50	0.690	0.445	310
10	1.8	0.05	0.014	0.009	6.17	0.60	1.12	0.722	502
12	1.6	0.05	0.016	0.011	7.35	0.70	1.68	1.08	752
15	1.5	0.06	0.027	0.017	12.1	0.90	3.09	1.99	1385
18	1.4	0.08	0.051	0.033	22.7	1.05	4.61	2.98	2070
21	1.4	0.10	0.081	0.052	36.5	1.25	7.04	4.54	3160
24	1.3	0.10	0.096	0.062	43.0	1.40	9.47	6.11	4250
27	1.3	0.11	0.126	0.081	56.4	1.60	13.1	8.44	5870
30	1.3	0.20	0.346	0.223	155	1.75	16.5	10.7	7410

are of the configuration shown in Figure 4-5. Do not apply these discharge tables to flumes of other manufacture, since discrepancies may exist.

Table 4-3 presents recommended minimum and maximum flow rates through a number of Plasti-Fab Palmer-Bowlus flumes, based on Plasti-Fab's recommendations.

HS, H, and HL flumes

4

The HS, H and HL flumes were developed in the mid 1930s by the U.S. Department of Agriculture (USDA) Soil Conservation Service to measure runoff from small agricultural watersheds and experimental plots. They have served this purpose adequately. Because of their proven performance, H-type flumes are now used to measure runoff from feedlots, runoff from infiltration areas for wastewater disposal, low flows of streams in pollution abatement work, and flow in sewage systems. The H-type flumes are capable of monitoring flow over a wide range with reasonably good accuracy, and have the advantage of simple construction. The wide span makes this primary device particularly suitable for measuring drainage water and for portable applications where a wide range of flow rates may be encountered. Other applications may be at installations having normal high flows and very low flows during off hours.

The H-type flumes, shown in Figure 4-7, differ from the flumes discussed above because they are more weir than flume. They are more properly termed open channel flow nozzles; but are included here because of historical precedent. Their design attempts to combine the sensitivity and accuracy of the sharp-crested weir with the self-cleaning features of a flume. The result is a compromise in both. The flat, unobstructed bottom

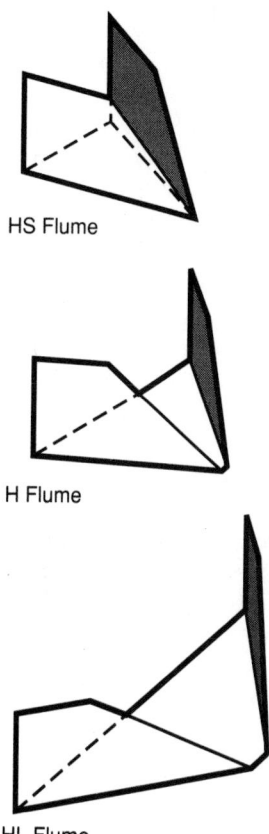

HS Flume

H Flume

HL Flume

Figure 4-7: HS, H, and HF flumes.

allows the passage of silt better than a weir. Like the weir, flow control is achieved by discharging through a sharp-edged opening. However, the flow is contracted gently from the sides only, much like the converging section of ordinary flumes. The plane of the exit tilts backward toward the incoming flow.

The forms of the H-type flumes were dictated by the desire for a simple geometric shape and by the character of the flows from small agricultural watersheds and plots. Because these flows often carry vegetal debris and sediment, the sidewalls of the flumes were made to converge gradually to the control opening, reducing the possibility of debris being caught on the flume and providing an increased velocity through the flume to reduce sediment. Also, these flumes must measure the full range of a flow event, so there was a need to provide both sensitivity for low-flow measurement and maximum capacity, with minimum head loss for the design flow because the available head is usually limited. To meet the requirements for sensitivity and capacity, the tops of the converging vertical sidewalls slope upward from the lip of the outlet. This forms a trapezoidal opening, narrow at the bottom and wide at the top, which acts as the flow control section. The size of the flow-control opening is a function of the convergence angle and the sidewall top slope. Varying these parameters also varies the sensitivity and maximum capacity of the flume.

HS, H, and HL flumes are designated according to the maximum depth attainable in the flume, which is also the depth of the flume at the entrance. Thus, a 1.0 ft H flume has a maximum head of 1.0 foot. Dimensional proportions and maximum capacities of the H-type flumes are shown in Figures 4-8 A, B, and C. Note that the dimensions of each type flume are proportional to the maximum depth, D. The HS flumes were designed to measure relatively small flows, with maximum flow rates ranging from 0.08 to 0.82 cfs (0.05 to 0.53 mgd/36 to 370 gpm). The H flumes were designed to measure medium flows, with maximum flow rates ranging from 0.35 to 31.0 cfs (0.23 to 20 mgd/157 to 14,000 gpm). The HL flumes were designed to measure larger flows, with maximum flow rates ranging from 20.7 to 117.0 cfs (13.4 to 75.6 mgd/9290 to 52,500 gpm). The head measurement section for each of the flumes is shown in Figures 4-8 A, B, and C.

When installing an H-type flume, the preferred configuration of the approach channel is rectangular, having the same depth and width as the flume and a length 3 to 5 times the depth of the flume. An H-type flume is generally installed with a free spill off of the downstream end, as shown in Figure 4-9. Although H-type

Depth D, Ft.	Max Capacity, CFS
0.4	0.085
0.5	0.14
0.6	0.23
0.8	0.47
1.0	0.82

4

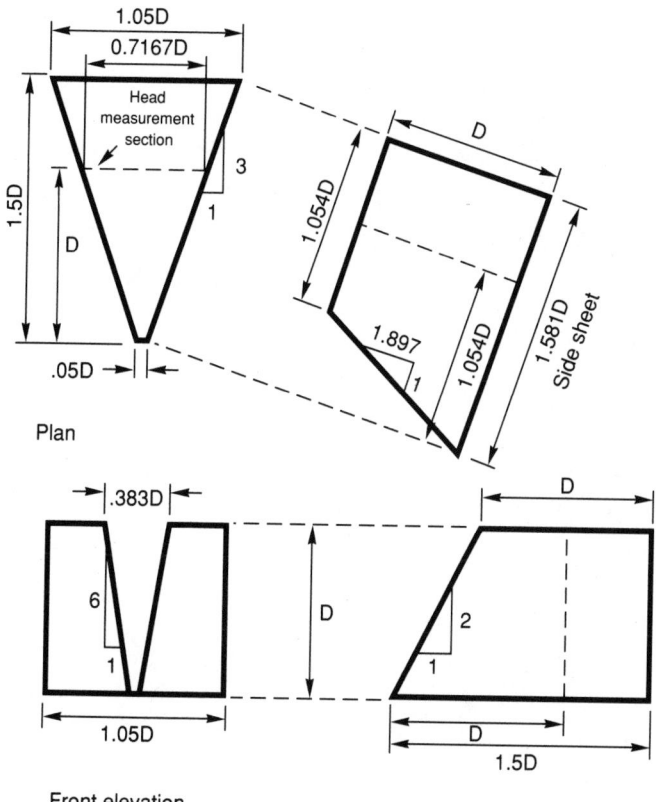

Plan

Front elevation

HS Flume

Figure 4-8 A: Dimensions and capacities of H type flumes

Depth D, Ft.	Max Capacity, CFS
0.5	0.347
0.75	0.957
1.0	1.97
1.5	5.42
2.0	11.1
2.5	19.3
3.0	30.7
4.5	84.5

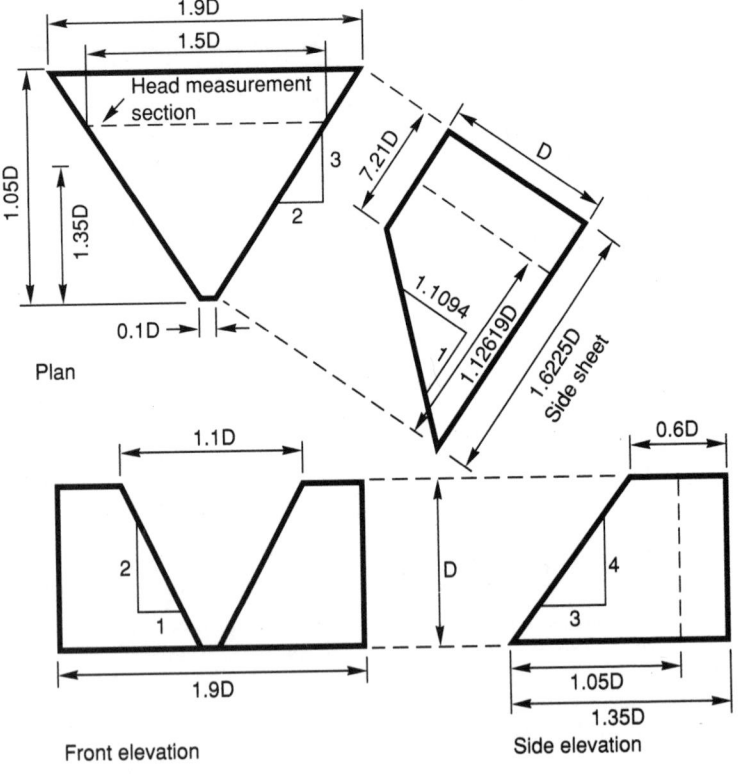

H Flume

Figure 4-8 B: Dimensions and capacities of H type flumes

Depth D, Ft.	Max Capacity, CFS
2.0	20.7
2.5	36.2
3.0	57.0
3.5	83.9
4.0	117.0

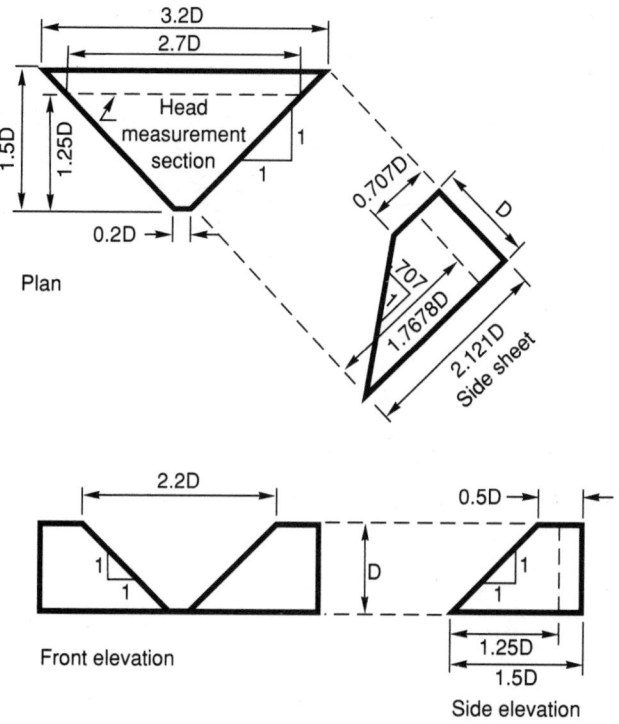

HL Flume

Figure 4-8 C: Dimensions and capacities of H type flumes

Figure 4-9: Discharge from H flumes

flumes were not originally intended to be used with a pipe at either the inlet or outlet end, they can often be installed quite satisfactorily in this manner. An H-type flume may be used in conjunction with an outlet pipe, as long as the water is permitted to flow or spill away from the flume in such a way that it does not slow down the flow through the flume notch. The water must spill from the flume or flow unimpeded in a manner comparable to spilling off of the end.

An H-type flume must be installed so it is level, with the bottom of the flume at the same elevation as the inlet channel. The velocity of the water entering the flume must be subcritical and not turbulent.

Generally, H-type flumes should be installed so there is free discharge, that is, the flume is not operating in a submerged condition. This may require enlargement and/or regrading of the outfall channel. Submergence of an H-type flume is defined as the ratio, expressed as a percentage, of the downstream water depth to the depth in the head measuring section. Tests have shown that submergence of 30 percent has less than a 1 percent effect on the calibration, and a 50 percent submergence has less than a 3 percent effect.

Since H-type flumes, especially the HS flumes, are designed to measure very small flows relatively accurately, it is necessary to construct the flume according to the dimensions shown in Figures 4-8 A, B, and C. It is especially important that the slanted opening be bounded by straight edges, have precisely the dimensions shown on the drawings, and that the opening lies in a plane with an inclination of the exact angle shown. Discharge (head vs. flow rate) equations for free flow through H-type flumes have been developed by Gwinn and Parsons. However, these equations are quite complex, and are not listed here; for further information, the reader is directed to reference [9].

Of the three H-type flumes, the H flumes appear to be the most widely used. Table 4-4 presents the minimum and maximum recommended flow rates for free flow through a number of common sizes of flumes. Complete discharge tables for H flumes are found in Chapter 14. These tables are from reference [10], and are derived from tests made by the Soil Conservation Service at the Hydraulic Laboratory of the National Bureau of Standards using H flumes with a 1-on-8 sloping false floor. The purpose of the sloping floor in the H flume is to concentrate low flows along the sidewall having the stilling well intake. Low flows can scour the sediment from the small channel formed along this wall, thereby permitting water to enter and leave the stilling well. This helps to assure reliable head readings despite heavy sediment loads and the attendant sediment deposition in the flume. The discharges found in Chapter 14 can be used with both flat and sloping floor

Table 4-4: Minimum and maximum recommended flow rates for free flow through H flumes

H flume size, Ft.	Min. head, Ft.	Minimum flow rate			Max. head, Ft.	Maximum flow rate		
		CFS	MGD	GPM		CFS	MGD	GPM
0.50	0.02	0.0004	0.0003	0.180	0.50	0.347	0.224	156
0.75	0.02	0.0006	0.0004	0.269	0.75	0.957	0.619	430
1.0	0.02	0.0007	0.0005	0.314	1.0	1.97	1.27	884
1.5	0.02	0.0011	0.0007	0.494	1.5	5.42	3.50	2430
2.0	0.02	0.0014	0.0009	0.628	2.0	11.1	7.17	4980
2.5	0.02	0.0018	0.0012	0.808	2.5	19.3	12.5	8660
3.0.	0.02	0.0021	0.0014	0.942	3.0	30.7	19.8	13,800
4.5	0.02	0.0031	0.0020	1.39	4.5	84.5	54.6	37,900

flumes, since the difference in calibration of a flume with a flat floor and that with a sloping false floor is less than 1 percent. Thus, these tables are commonly applied to both types of H flumes.

Leopold-Lagco flume

The Leopold-Lagco flume is a proprietary flume manufactured by the F. B. Leopold Company (a subsidiary of the Mueller Company) of Zelienople, Pennsylvania. The Leopold-Lagco Flume (Figure 4-10) is actually a "Palmer-Bowlus" type flume with a rectangular cross-section throat, designed to be installed in circular channels. The manufacturer claims that the flume was "...designed to produce metering heads within 2% of theoretical rating curve for particular physical conditions of installation."

The characteristics and installation of the Leopold-Lagco flume are generally similar to those of the trapezoidal-throated conventional Palmer-Bowlus flume. Leopold-Lagco flume sizes are designated by the size of the pipe into which they fit, not by the throat width as is the case with Parshall flumes. Thus, a 12 inch

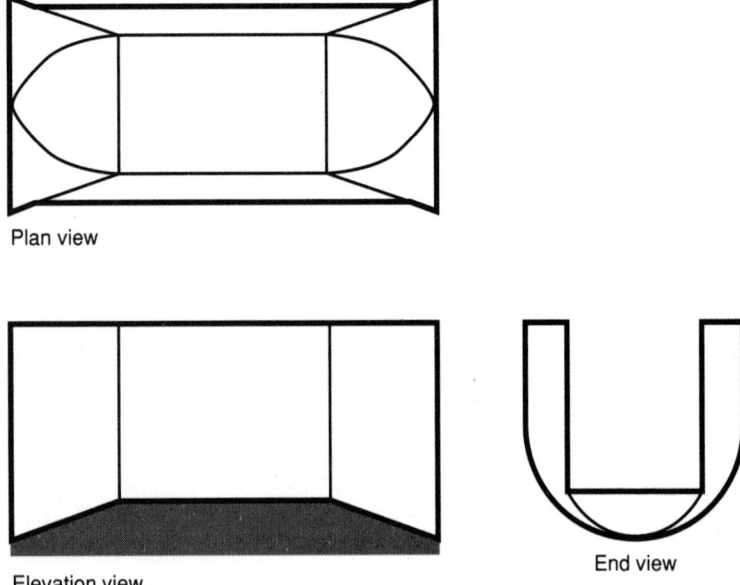

Plan view

Elevation view

End view

Figure 4-10: Leopold-Lagco flume

Leopold-Lagco flume is designed to be inserted into a 12 inch diameter pipe. Leopold-Lagco flumes are available from the F. B. Leopold Company to fit pipe sizes ranging from 4 inches to 72 inches.

Leopold-Lagco flumes are made from Leo-Lite resin reinforced with fiberglass mat. As with Palmer-Bowlus flumes, they are available in three installation configurations. The fixed type is intended for new construction, and has the same inside radius as the pipe to which it is to be joined. The insert type is used for temporary installations or for permanent installation in an existing pipe, and has an outside radius corresponding to the inside radius of the pipe into which it is to be installed. The cutback type is intended for temporary or permanent installation in the downstream exit pipe of a manhole.

When choosing the size of Leopold-Lagco flume to be installed at a particular location, both the diameter of the conduit or pipe in which the flume is to be installed, and the range of expected flow rates should be considered. For maximum accuracy, the size of the flume should be determined by the expected volume of flow, rather than strictly by the pipe diameter.

The manufacturer states that a Leopold-Lagco flume will give accurate flow measurements on minimum grades or on grades up to 2 percent. They also state that the flume will result in no more loss in head than a straight pipe of the same size and length.

The depth of the liquid above the throat of the flume (not the bottom of the pipe) is the index of discharge. As shown in Figure 4-11, the ideal location for the level measuring point is at a distance one-half D (pipe diameter or channel width) upstream from the entrance of the flume. However, this location is not critical, as long as the point of level measurement is located in a zone where the depth of flow does not change significantly within a range of one pipe diameter.

The manufacturer does not specify minimum recommended flow rates for Leopold-Lagco flumes. However, there are recommendations for maximum flow rates for free flow, as shown in Table 4-5, for a number of common sizes of Leopold-Lagco flumes.

The F. B. Leopold Company publishes copywritten curves and tabular data detailing the discharge (head vs. flow rate) relationship of Leopold-Lagco flumes. However, it has been determined that the discharge relationship of Leopold-Lagco flumes may also be represented by an equation. The discharge equation for free

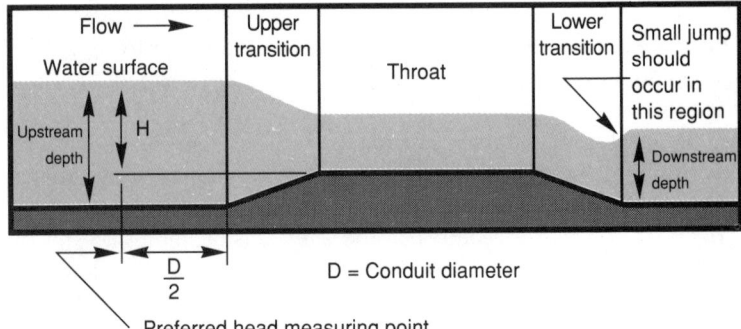

Figure 4-11: Leopold-Lagco flume preferred head measuring point

flow through a Leopold-Lagco flume takes the form:

$$Q = K D^{0.953} H^{1.547}$$

where: Q = flow rate

Table 4-5: Maximum recommended flow rates for Leopold-Lagco flumes

Flume size, In.	Maximum head, Ft.	Maximum flow rate		
		CFS	GPM	MGD
4	0.24	0.093	41.7	0.060
6	0.35	0.245	110	0.158
8	0.45	0.475	213	0.307
10	0.60	0.918	412	0.593
12	0.70	1.39	622	0.896
15	0.90	2.53	1140	1.63
18	1.05	3.82	1710	2.47
21	1.25	5.79	2600	3.74
24	1.40	7.84	3520	5.07
30	1.75	13.7	6150	8.85
36	2.10	21.6	9700	14.0
42	2.45	31.8	14,300	20.5
48	2.80	44.4	19,900	28.7
54	3.15	59.6	26,700	38.5
60	3.50	77.5	34,800	50.1
66	3.90	100	45,000	64.8
72	4.10	118	52,900	76.1

H = head measured at D/2 upstream from the flume
entrance with the floor of the throat as a zero index

K = constant, dependent upon units (for cfs,
K = 2.407; for mgd, K = 1.556; and for gpm,
K = 1080)

D = diameter of flume, in feet

For flow rate in cubic feet per second, million gallons per day, and gallons per minute, and head in feet the discharge equations for a number of common Leopold-Lagco flumes are as follows: Complete discharge tables for a number of common Leopold-

Size	CFS	GPM	MGD
4 inch	$Q = 0.8448\, H^{1.547}$	$Q = 379.1\, H^{1.547}$	$Q = 0.5462\, H^{1.547}$
6 inch	$Q = 1.243\, H^{1.547}$	$Q = 557.9\, H^{1.547}$	$Q = 0.8038\, H^{1.547}$
8 inch	$Q = 1.636\, H^{1.547}$	$Q = 733.8\, H^{1.547}$	$Q = 1.057\, H^{1.547}$
10 inch	$Q = 2.023\, H^{1.547}$	$Q = 907.9\, H^{1.547}$	$Q = 1.307\, H^{1.547}$
12 inch	$Q = 2.407\, H^{1.547}$	$Q = 1080\, H^{1.547}$	$Q = 1.556\, H^{1.547}$
15 inch	$Q = 2.977\, H^{1.547}$	$Q = 1336\, H^{1.547}$	$Q = 1.924\, H^{1.547}$
18 inch	$Q = 3.542\, H^{1.547}$	$Q = 1590\, H^{1.547}$	$Q = 2.289\, H^{1.547}$
21 inch	$Q = 4.103\, H^{1.547}$	$Q = 1841\, H^{1.547}$	$Q = 2.652\, H^{1.547}$
24 inch	$Q = 4.660\, H^{1.547}$	$Q = 2091\, H^{1.547}$	$Q = 3.012\, H^{1.547}$
30 inch	$Q = 5.764\, H^{1.547}$	$Q = 2587\, H^{1.547}$	$Q = 3.725\, H^{1.547}$

Lagco flumes are found in Chapter 15 of this handbook.

Trapezoidal flumes

In attempt to obtain wider ranges of discharge than those available with Parshall flumes, several investigators have considered supercritical trapezoidal flumes. These generally operate as Type IV flumes, and a typical configuration is shown in Figure 4-12. The outward sloping of the flume walls provides increased sensitivity to low discharge rates for a given size and, hence, increased range.

The trapezoidal flume was developed primarily to measure flow in irrigation channels and has been used for many years by the Agricultural Research Service, U.S. Department of Agriculture. For agricultural applications it is superior to Parshall-type flumes for a number of reasons, particularly for measuring smaller flows. The trapezoidal shape conforms to the normal shape of ditches, especially those that are lined. This minimizes the amount of transition section needed as compared to that required when changing from a trapezoidal shape to a rectangular one and back to the

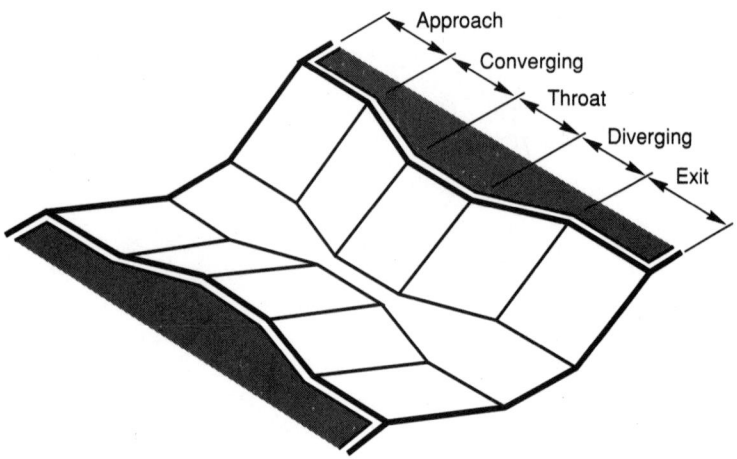

Figure 4-12: Elements of a trapezoidal supercritical flow flume

trapezoidal. The trapezoidal shape is also desirable since the side-walls expand as the depth increases. This means that a given trapezoidal flume rates since an incremental increase in flow produces a relatively small increase in depth because of the trapezoidal shape. The trapezoidal flume can operate under a higher degree of submergence than the Parshall flume without the need for corrections. Also, the straight through bottom of the flume permits the flume to pass trash quite readily, and reduces the problem of silt build-up upstream of the flume.

A trapezoidal flume need not include all of the elements shown in Figure 4-12. In some designs, the throat section is absent. Other designs eliminate the diverging and exit sections where channel erosion is not a problem. In yet another variation, the floor slopes slightly towards the center to form a very shallow "V". There are so many variations that no attempt will be made here to describe them all. Various trapezoidal flumes have been constructed to measure maximum flow rates ranging from 0.01 to 26,000 cfs (0.006 to 16,800 mgd/4.49 to 11,670,000 gpm).

Probably the most widely used trapezoidal flumes are those of the various configurations designed and extensively evaluated by Robinson and Chamberlain [11] and [12]. These are similar to the flume shown in Figure 4-12, and feature a flat floor throughout the flume that conforms to the general slope of the channel. Two of these flumes are shown in Figure 4-13. Flume No. 1 was designed for use in a 1 foot irrigation channel and has a maxi-

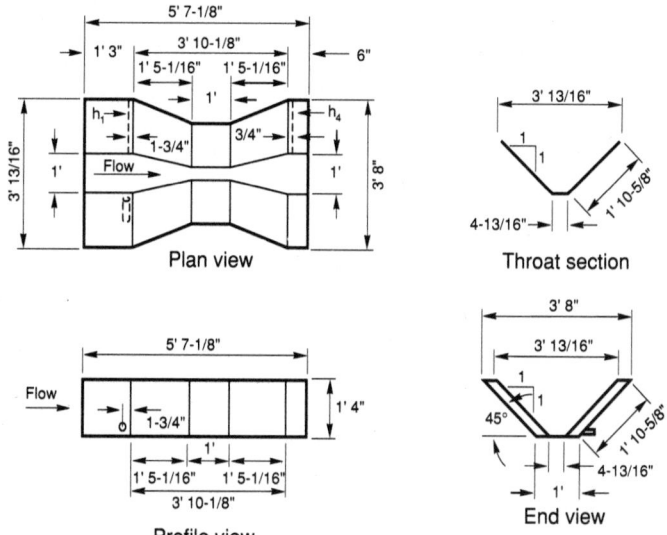

Plan view Throat section

Profile view End view

A. Flume No. 1 (for 1 foot irrigation channel)

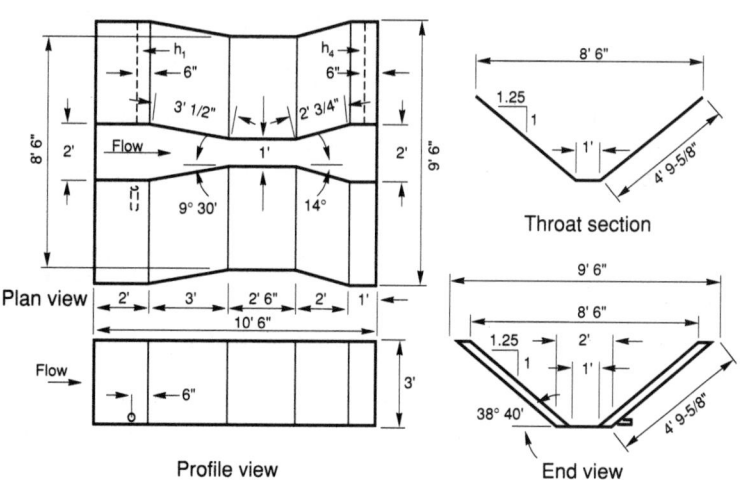

Throat section

Plan view Profile view End view

B. Flume No. 2 (for 2 foot irrigation channel)

Figure 4-13: Trapezoidal flumes for 1 and 2 foot irrigation channels

mum flow rate of approximately 7 cfs (4.5 mgd/3100 gpm). Flume No. 2 was designed for use in a 2 foot irrigation channel and has a maximum flow rate of approximately 50 cfs (32 mgd/22,000 gpm). The discharge (head vs. flow rate) equations for free flow through these two trapezoidal flumes are given by the following equations:

Flume No. 1

CFS: $Q = 3.23 H^{2.5} + 0.63 H^{1.5} + 0.05$ (h_1 range $0.20 - 1.30$ ft.)

GPM: $Q = 1450H^{2.5} + 283H^{1.5} + 22$

MGD: $Q = 2.09H^{2.5} + 0.407H^{1.5} + 0.03$

Flume No. 2

CFS: $Q = 4.27H^{2.5} + 1.67H^{1.5} + 0.19$ (h_1 range $0.30 - 2.60$ ft.)

GPM: $Q = 1920H^{2.5} + 749H^{1.5} + 85$

MGD: $Q = 2.76H^{2.5} + 1.08H^{1.5} + 0.12$

where: Q = flow rate in units indicated
H = head in feet measured at h_1

Robinson and Chamberlain also evaluated seven other configurations of trapezoidal flumes, smaller than the two flumes discussed above. These flumes, shown in Figure 4-14, were developed primarily for agricultural and stream flow measurement use. However, the flumes are now being used in wastewater and industrial applications. Discharge curves for these flumes are shown in Figure 4-15. For a further discussion, consult reference [12].

As with most flumes, it is preferred that these trapezoidal flumes be installed so the flow through them is critical, not submerged. Submergence is defined as the ratio, expressed as a percent, of the downstream depth, h_4 or h_2 (as shown in Figures 4-13 and 4-14) to the upstream depth h_1. Test results have shown that corrections for submerged flow will have to be made for submergence ratios of greater than 80 percent. When operating at free flow, there is a high velocity jet pattern as the water passes through the throat, but as the flow becomes submerged, the velocity in the throat decreases appreciably and the head increases at h_1. By reading the head at both h_1 and h_4 or h_2, the flow rate may

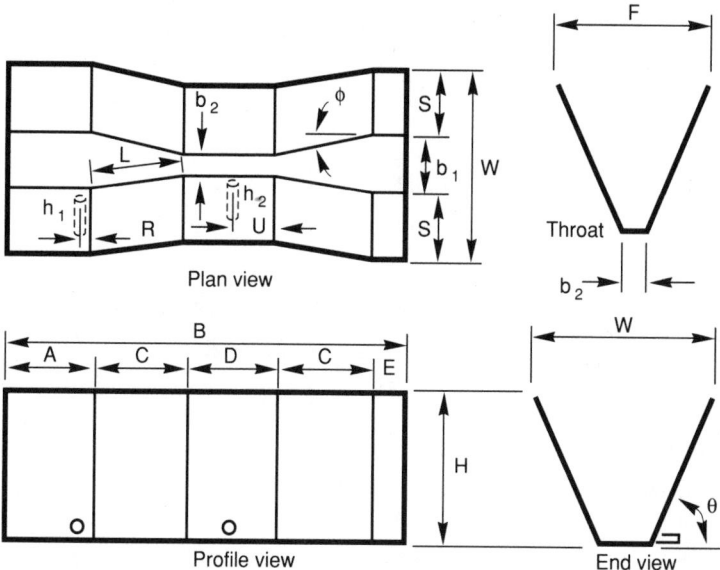

Flume No.	Description	b_1	b_2	A	L	C	D	E	F
3	Large 60°-V	2	0	7	7	6 15/16	7	3	8
4	Small 60°-V	2	0	5	4 1/8	4 3/64	5	2	4 3/4
5	2" 60° WSC	4 7/8	2	8	8 1/2	8 13/32	8 1/2	3	14
6	2" 45° WSC	4 7/8	2	8	8 1/2	8 3/8	8 1/2	3	22 13/16
7	2" 30° WSC	4 7/8	2	8	8 1/2	8 3/8	8 1/2	3	36 41/64
8	4" 60° WSC	8	4	9	10	9 13/16	10	3	20
9	2" 30° CSU	10	2	10	10 3/4	10	10	3	35 1/2

Flume No.	H	B	R	S	U	W	θ	ϕ
3	6 3/4	30 7/8	1 1/2	4	3 1/2	10	60°	8.25°
4	4	20 3/32	1	2 3/8	2 1/2	6 1/4	60°	11.20°
5	13 1/2	36 5/16	1 1/2	6	4 1/4	16 7/8	60°	9.22°
6	10 19/32	36 1/4	1 1/2	10 19/32	4 1/4	26 1/16	45°	9.91°
7	10	36 1/4	1 1/2	17 5/16	4 1/4	39 33/64	30°	9.80°
8	13 7/8	41 5/8	1 1/2	8	5	24	60°	11.20°
9	9 21/32	43	1 1/2	16 3/4	5	43 1/2	30°	21.80°

Note: Dimensions in inches except as shown

Figure 4-14: Dimensions of various other trapezoidal flumes

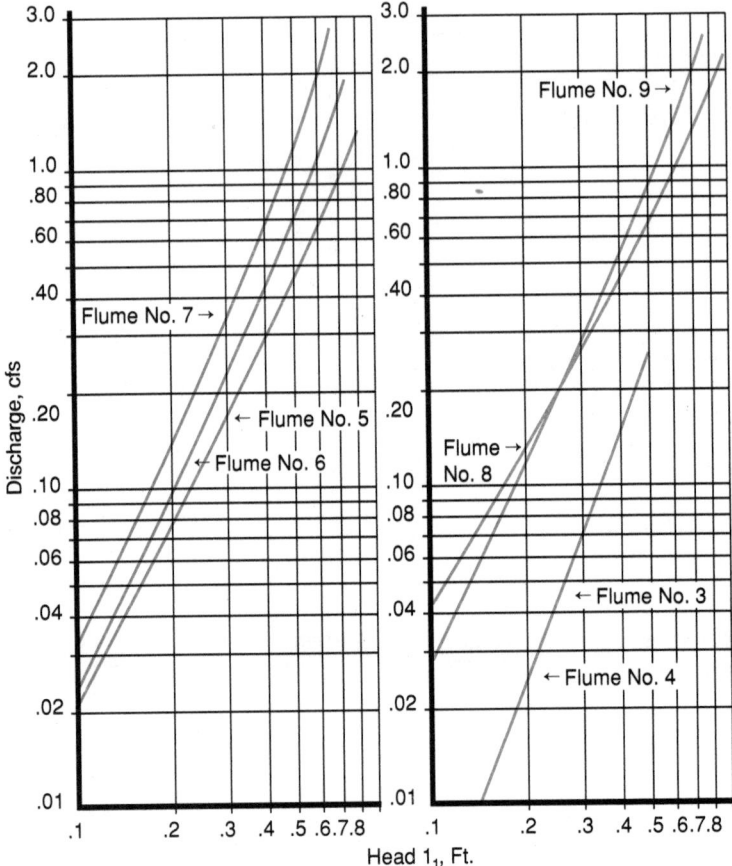

Figure 4-15: Calibration curves for trapezoidal flumes

be determined under submerged conditions by using the depth at h_1 and making corrections as shown on a submergence flow correction curve or chart. See references [11] and [12] for submerged flow corrections.

Trapezoidal flumes should generally be installed level. Occasionally flumes are installed with a slight slope, which necessitates the adjustment of the head gauges so that the zero level is at the same elevation as the flume throat. If a trapezoidal flume is installed in an earth ditch, the flume bottom should always be placed higher than the ditch bottom. If the flume is installed in a concrete ditch having a flat slope that may cause submergence, then the flume should also be raised above the bottom.

Table 4-6: Minimum and maximum recommended flow rates for trapezoidal flumes (Manufactured by Plasti-Fab, Inc.)

Flume type	Minimum head, Ft.	Minimum flow rate			Maximum head, Ft.	Maximum flow rate		
		CFS	MGD	GPM		CFS	MGD	GPM
Large 60° V	0.14	0.010	0.006	4.37	0.45	0.198	0.128	88.8
2" 45° WSC	0.10	0.023	0.015	10.3	0.77	1.82	1.18	817
12" 45° SRCRC	0.20	0.160	0.103	71.8	1.29	7.08	4.58	3180

4

Of the nine trapezoidal flumes discussed above, three have been most widely used because they have been made commercially available by Plasti-Fab, Inc. These are Flume No. 1 (12-inch 45° SRCRC), Flume No. 3 (Large 60° V), and Flume No. 6 (2-inch 45° WSC). The 12-inch 45° SRCRC flume has a capacity range of 0.16 to 7.1 cfs (0.10 to 4.6 mgd / 72 to 3200 gpm). The Large 60° V flume has a capacity range of 0.01 to 0.2 cfs (0.006 to 0.13 mgd/4.5 to 90 gpm). The 2-inch 45° WSC flume has a capacity range of 0.025 to 1.8 cfs (0.016 to 1.2 mgd / 11 to 810 gpm). Complete discharge tables for these three trapezoidal flumes are found in Chapter 16 of this handbook. Table 4-6 presents the minimum and maximum recommended flow rates for free flow through the same three commonly used trapezoidal flumes.

Other flumes

A number of other types of flumes have been developed to meet special design criteria or to solve a specific problem. As a general rule, these flumes have not been as widely used or as extensively investigated as the flumes previously discussed. As representatives of these types of flumes, the cutthroat flume and the San Dimas flume are briefly described in the following sections.

Cutthroat flume

The cutthroat flume was developed at the Utah State University Water Research Laboratory in the mid 1960s. It derives its name from the absence of a parallel-wall throat section, as shown in Figure 4-16. The cutthroat flume is a flat-bottomed device whose main advantage is extreme simplicity of form and construction, since fabrication is facilitated by the flat bottom and removal of the throat section. The level flume floor also permits placing the device directly on an existing channel bed, without further excavation.

The cutthroat flume was developed for use in flat gradient

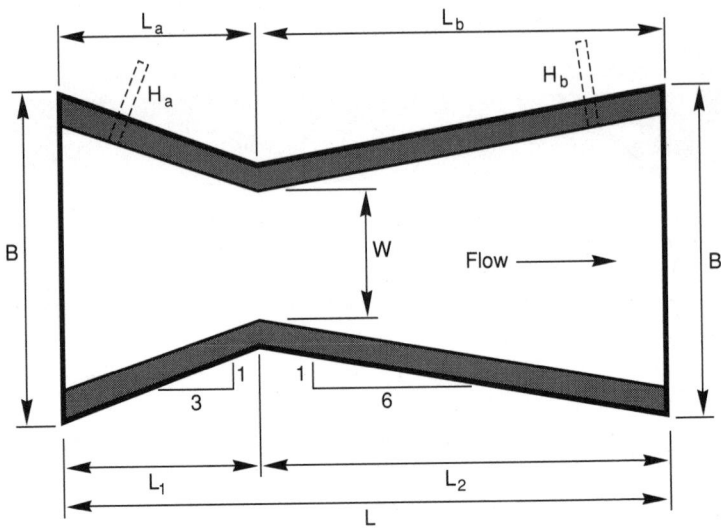

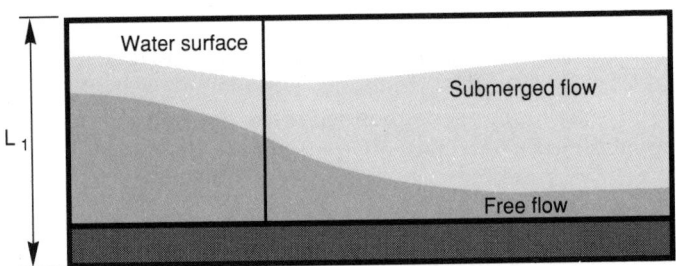

$$B = W + 2L_1 / 3 = W + L_2 / 3$$
$$L_a = 2L / 9 \qquad L_b = 5L / 9$$

Figure 4-16: Dimensional configuration of rectangular cutthroat flume

channels where a flume which could operate satisfactorily under both free (critical) flow and submerged flow conditions might be desired. Under free flow conditions, the cutthroat flume operates as a Type II flume. The transition from critical (free) to subcritical (submerged) flow occurs for submergence ratios of 79 to 88%, depending upon the size of the flume. The submergence ratio is defined as the ratio of downstream depth to upstream depth (H_b/H_a, as shown in Figure 4-16), expressed as a percentage.

The rectangular cutthroat flume, shown in Figure 4-16, is

Table 4-7: Coefficients and exponents for cutthroat flumes

Length, L, Ft.	Width, W , Ft.	Free flow		
		C	n_1	K
9.00	1.000	3.50	1.560	3.500
9.00	2.000	7.11	1.560	3.500
9.00	4.000	14.49	1.560	3.500
9.00	6.000	22.0	1.560	3.500
4.50	0.250	0.96	1.720	3.980
4.50	0.500	1.96	1.720	3.980
4.50	1.000	3.98	1.720	3.980
4.50	2.000	8.01	1.720	3.980
3.00	0.167	0.719	1.840	4.500
3.00	0.333	1.459	1.840	4.500
3.00	0.667	2.970	1.840	4.500
3.00	1.333	6.040	1.840	4.500
1.50	0.083	0.501	2.000	6.400
1.50	0.167	1.020	2.000	6.400
1.50	0.333	2.076	2.000	6.400
1.50	0.667	4.224	2.000	6.400

4

dimensionally defined by a characteristic length, L, and by the throat width, W. All other flume dimensions can be derived from these two dimensions, as shown. Common sizes of cutthroat flumes are listed in Table 4-7. For free flow conditions, only the head H_a (shown in Figure 4-16) at the upstream gauge location is needed to determine the discharge. For submerged flow conditions, both the upstream head and the downstream head (H_b) are required to determine the discharge. For this reason, a free flow condition is normally preferred.

The discharge (head vs. flow rate) equation of free flow through a cutthroat flume takes the form:

$$Q = K W^{1.025} H^{n_1} = C H^{n_1}$$

where: Q = flow rate
        K = free-flow coefficient
        C = free-flow coefficient
        W = throat width
        H = head measured at point H_a
        n_1 = free flow exponent

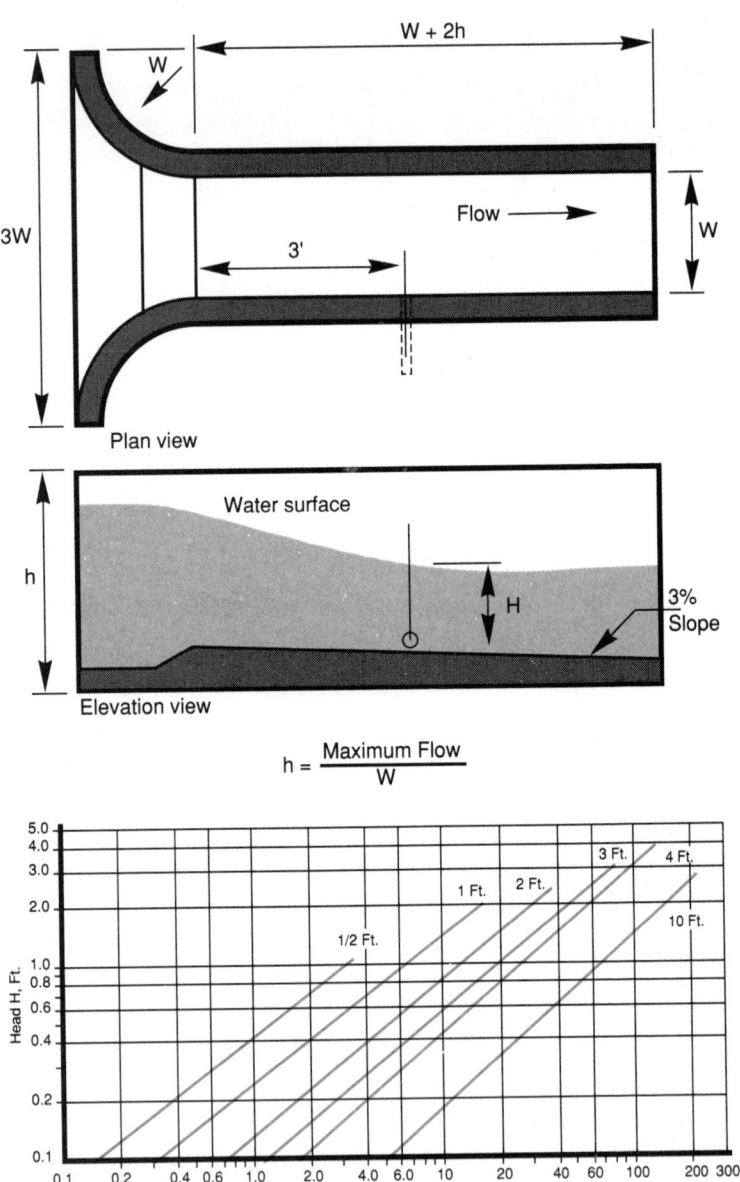

$$h = \frac{\text{Maximum Flow}}{W}$$

Based on general equation for free flow:

$$Q = 6.35\, W^{1.04}\, H^{1.5-n}$$

Where: $n = 0.179\, W^{0.32}$ $Q = \text{cfs}$ $H = \text{Ft.}$

Figure 4-17: Original San Dimas flume

For flow rate in cubic feet per second, and gallons per minute and head and width in feet, Table 4-7 lists free flow values for several families of flumes. Since K and n_1 depend only upon flume length, interpolations can be made for coefficients of intermediate size flumes which are proportioned according to Figure 4-16. For submerged flow discharge equations, see reference [13].

San Dimas flume

The San Dimas flume was developed to measure sediment and debris-laden flows in the San Dimas Experimental Forest in 1938. It is a modified Type IV flume in that it uses lateral contraction plus a 3% slope in its floor to create a supercritical flow. In the entry, the floor rises quickly to the crest, after which it falls as indicated in Figure 4-17. Because head measurements are made in supercritical flow in the throat and critical depth occurs upstream, the discharge ratings should be independent of upstream and downstream disturbances. Variation in approach conditions also should have little effect on the ratings. Because of its rectangular cross-section, the San Dimas flume is not sensitive or accurate at low flows.

The dimensional configuration and rating curves for San Dimas flumes ranging in size from 0.5 foot to 10 feet are also shown in Figure 4-17.

References

1. Kilpatrick, F.A. "Use of Flumes in Measuring Discharges at Gaging Stations." *Surface Water Techniques*, Book 1, Chapter 16, U.S. Geological Survey, United States Department of the Interior, Washington, D.C., 1965.

2. Engal, F.V.A.E. "Non-Uniform Flow of Water: Problems and Phenomena in Open Channels with Side Contractions." *The Engineer*, 155 (1933): 392-394, 429-30, 456-57.

3. Cone, V.M. "28th Annual Report." Colorado Agricultural Experiment Station, 1915.

4. Cone, V.M. "The Venturi Flume." *Journal of Agricultural Research*, Vol. 9, No. 4 (April 12, 1917):115-129.

5. *Water Measurement Manual.* United States Department of the Interior, Bureau of Reclamation, Denver, Colo., 1967.

6. Parshall, R.L. "Measuring Water in Irrigation Channels with Parshall Flumes and Small Weirs." U.S. Soil Conservation Service, Circular 843, (May 1950).

7. Palmer, Harold K., and Bowlus, Fred D. "Adaptation of Venturi Flumes to Flow Measurements in Conduits." *Transactions, American Society of Civil Engineers,* Vol. 101, (1936): 1195-1216.

8. Wells, Edwin A., Jr., and Gotaas, Harold B. "Design of Venturi Flumes in Circular Conduits." *Transactions, American Society of Civil Engineers,* Vol. 123 (1958): 749-771.

9. Gwinn, E. R., and Parson, D.A. "Discharge Equations for HS, H, and HL Flumes." *Journal of the Hydraulics Division, ASCE,* Vol. 102 (January 1976), No. HY1, Proc. Paper 11874: 73-88.

10. *Field Manual for Research in Agricultural Hydrology,* Agricultural Handbook No. 224, Agricultural Research Service, Soil and Water Conservation Research Division, U.S. Department of Agriculture, Washington, D.C., 1962.

11. Robinson, A.R. "Trapezoidal Flumes for Measuring Flow in Irrigation Channels." ARS 41-140, Agricultural Research Service, U.S. Department of Agriculture (March 1968).

12. Robinson, A.R., and Chamberlain, A.R. "Trapezoidal Flumes for Open-Channel Flow Measurement." *Transactions of The American Society of Agricultural Engineers,* Vol. 3, No. 2, (1960): 120-128.

13. Skogerboe, Gaylord V.; Bennett, Ray S.; and Walker, Wynne R. "Generalized Discharge Relations For Cutthroat Flumes." *Journal of the Irrigation and Drainage Division, ASCE,* Vol. 98, No. IR4 (December 1974): 569-583.

Suggested readings

Associated Water & Air Resources Engineers. *Handbook For Monitoring Industrial Wastewater.* Environmental Protection Agency Technology Transfer Publication (August 1973).

Chow, Ven Te. *Open-Channel Hydraulics.* McGraw-Hill Book Company, New York, 1959.

Harris, James P.; Kacman, Stephen A.; Grant, Forest; and Tomcik, John. "Flow Monitoring Techniques in Sanitary Sewers." *Deeds & Data,* Water Pollution Control Federation, Washington, D.C. (July 1974).

Kulin, Gershon, and Compton, Philip R. *A Guide to Methods and Standards for the Measurement of Water Flow.* National Technical Information Service, Springfield, Va., 1975.

Ludwig, John L., and Ludwig, Russell G., "Design of Palmer-Bowlus Flumes." *Sewage and Industrial Wastes,* Vol. 23, No. 9 (September 1951): 1096-1107.

Ludwig, Russell G., and Parkhurst, John D. "Simplified Application of Palmer-Bowlus Flow Meters." *Journal, Water Pollution Control Federation,* Vol. 46, No. 12 (December 1974): 2764-2769.

Robinson, A.R. "Water Measurement in Small Irrigation Channels Using Trapezoidal Flumes." *Transactions of the American Society of Agricultural Engineers,* Vol. 9, No. 3 (1966): 382-385.

Stevens Water Resources Data Book. 2nd Edition, Leupold & Stevens, Inc., Beaverton, Ore., 1974.

Vennard, John K. *Elementary Fluid Mechanics.* John Wiley & Sons, Inc., New York, 1961.

4

Chapter

5

Selecting a
primary
measuring
device

Overview

*This chapter provides information on
methods for selecting primary measuring
devices. It also provides advantages and
disadvantages of the various types of weirs
and flumes.*

Selecting a primary measuring device

The selection of a primary measuring device for a particular flow measurement installation usually involves a series of three decisions. The first decision concerns which general type of primary measuring device to use: a weir or a flume. Once the general type of primary device has been selected, the second decision involves which specific type of device to use. That is, if a weir has been chosen as the general type of device, the specific type such as V-notch, rectangular, Cipolletti, etc., must be selected. When the specific type of primary device has been chosen, the third and final decision involves the exact size of the primary device to be installed at the location in question. The factors involved in these three decisions are discussed at length in the following paragraphs.

The first decision involved in the selection of a primary measuring device is whether to use a weir or a flume. Weirs and flumes each have decided advantages and disadvantages. A weir is the simplest device that can be used to measure flow in open channels. A weir is low in cost, relatively easy to install, and quite accurate when properly used. However, a weir normally operates with a rather significant loss in the head of the flow stream, and its accuracy can be affected by variations in the approach velocity of the liquid in the flow channel. A weir must also be periodically cleaned to prevent deposits of sediment or solids in the upstream side of the weir, which will adversely affect its accuracy.

A flume tends to be self-cleaning since the velocity of flow through it is high and there is no actual "dam" across the channel. It can also operate with a much smaller loss of head than a weir, which can be important for many applications where the available head is limited. A flume is also not affected nearly as much as a weir by varying approach velocities. However, a flume is much more costly than a weir, and the installation is more difficult and time consuming. Flumes are also generally less accurate than weirs.

A very important factor here is the cost involved with the installation and use of the primary device. Weirs are generally much less expensive to fabricate than flumes, due to simpler design and the type of materials required. Weirs are also generally easier and less costly to install than flumes, although the flumes designed to fit inside of a round pipe (such as Palmer-Bowlus and Leopold-Lagco flumes) are usually fairly simple to install. Parshall flumes are generally the most difficult and expensive to install.

It should be noted that the initial installation cost is not the only expense that should be considered when choosing a primary device. As mentioned earlier, flumes tend to be self-cleaning whereas weirs must be periodically cleaned to prevent build-up on the weir. Lower maintenance costs associated with a flume may eventually outweigh the higher initial costs. Therefore, the maintenance and upkeep costs associated with a primary device, along with the acquisition and installation costs, should be considered, when choosing the type of primary device to be installed at a particular location.

Another factor which is often considered in the selection of a primary measuring device is the accuracy required of the flow rate measurement. A review of the literature on the subject of accuracy of primary devices reveals few positive statements and those statements that are made are extremely cautious. However, weirs are generally recognized as being more accurate than flumes. Mougenot [1] rates the basic error in the head/flow rate relationship of V-notch weirs as ±3 to 6%. ASTM Standards D2034-68 (weirs) and D1941-67 (Parshall flumes) [2] list similar inaccuracies.

It should be noted, that primary measuring device head/flow rate errors of much greater magnitudes than those mentioned above can be developed from the improper installation or maintenance of a primary device. A silted weir or an inaccurately constructed flume can have associated errors of ±5 to 10% or more.

The main point of this discussion is that, assuming a properly installed and maintained primary measuring device, most types of weirs and flumes fall well within the ±10% accuracy requirement proposed by Shelley and Kirkpatrick [3]. Thus for most installations, the question of accuracy in choosing between a particular type of weir or flume can be relegated to a relatively minor position, with other factors weighing much more heavily.

The second decision in the primary measuring device selection process involves the choice of the specific type of device to be used. Once the general type of primary measuring device has been selected (for example, a flume), then the specific type of device within this general type must be chosen (for example, a Parshall flume). This choice is normally based on the existing site configuration, the nature of the flow stream, and the range of expected flow rates. For example, a Palmer-Bowlus flume would normally be chosen over a Parshall flume for use in a round pipe based on its ease of installation in a pipe. Similarly, a rectangular weir would be chosen over a V-notch weir for an application where high flow rates are to be encountered because it is better suited than a V-notch weir to measure high flow rates. The choice between a rectangular weir with or without end contractions for a flow channel of a given width and flow rate range would be limited because the crest length of a rectangular weir without end contractions must correspond to the channel width. If the flow rate range of the rectangular weir without end contractions were not consistent with the range of flow rates in the channel, a rectangular weir with end contractions would be chosen.

The third and final decision in the selection of a primary measuring device concerns the exact size of the specific type of primary device to be installed at the location in question (for example, a contracted rectangular weir with a crest length of 2 feet). The basic consideration for any primary measuring device is that the minimum and maximum expected flow rates through the open channel in which the device is installed should lie within the useful range of flow rates of the primary device. All types and sizes of primary measuring devices have a minimum flow rate below which their accuracy is questionable, and a maximum flow rate above which their accuracy is again questionable or the

Table 5-1: Selection of a primary device —weirs

Advantages of weirs

1. Low cost.
2. Easy to install.

Disadvantages of weirs

1. Fairly high head loss.
2. Must be periodically cleaned—not suitable for channels carrying excessive solids.
3. Accuracy affected by excessive approach velocities.

Type of flume	Comments
A. Triangular (V-notch) weir	Accurate device particularly suited to measuring low flows. Best weir profile for discharges of less than 1 cfs and may be used for flows up to 10 cfs. Discussed on pages 28-30. For discharge tables see Ch. 8.
B. Rectangular (contracted) weir with end contractions	Able to measure much higher flows than V-notch weir. Discharge equation more complicated than other types of weirs. Widely used for measuring high flow rates in channels suited to weirs. Discussed on pages 30-34. For discharge tables see Ch. 9.
C. Rectangular (supressed) weir without end contractions	Able to measure same range of flows as contracted rectangular weir, but easier to construct and has simpler discharge equation. However, width of weir crest must correspond to width of channel so use is restricted. May have problems obtaining adequate aeration of nappe. Discussed on pages 30-34. For discharge tables see Ch. 10.
D. Trapezoidal (Cipolletti) weir	Similar to rectangular contracted weir except that inclined ends result in simplified discharge equation. Less accurate than rectangular or V-notch weir, and therefore less often used. Discussed on pages 34-36. For discharge tables see Ch. 11.
E. Compound weir	Combination of any two types or sizes of above weirs to provide wide range of flows. Ambigious discharge curve in transition zone between two weirs. Discussed on pages 37-38.

Table 5-2: Selection of a primary device—flumes

Advantages of flumes

1. Self-cleaning to a certain degree.
2. Relatively low head loss.
3. Accuracy less affected by approach velocity than weirs.

Disadvantages of flumes

1. High cost.
2. Difficult to install.

Type of flume	Comments
A. Parshall flumes	Most widely known and used flume for permanent installations. Available in throat widths ranging from 1 inch to 50 feet to cover most flows. Fairly difficult installation requiring a drop in the conduit invert. Discussed on pages 51-58. For discharge tables see Ch. 12.
B. Palmer-Bowlus flumes	Flume designed to be easily installed in existing conduit. Good for portable or temporary installations, as no drop in conduit invert required. Widely used in sanitary field for measuring flows in manholes. Discussed on pages 58-65. For discharge tables see Ch. 13.
C. H, HS, & HL flumes	Developed to measure agricultural runoff. Principle advantage is ability to measure wide range of flows with reasonable accuracy. Construction is fairly simple and flume is easily installed. Discussed on pages 65-72. For discharge tables see Ch. 14.
D. Leopold-Lagco flumes	Flume designed to be easily installed in existing conduit. Good for portable or temporary installations, as no drop in conduit invert required. Widely used in sanitary field for measuring flows in manholes. Discussed on pages 72-75. For discharge tables see Ch. 15
E. Trapezoidal flumes	Developed to measure flow in irrigation channels. Principle advantage is ability to measure wide range of flows and also maintain good accuracy at low flows. Discussed on pages 75-81. For discharge tables see Ch. 16.
F. Cutthroat flumes	Similar to Parshall, except that flat bottom does not require drop in conduit invert. Can function well with high degree of submergence. Flat bottom passes solids better than Parshall. Discussed on pages 81-85.

5

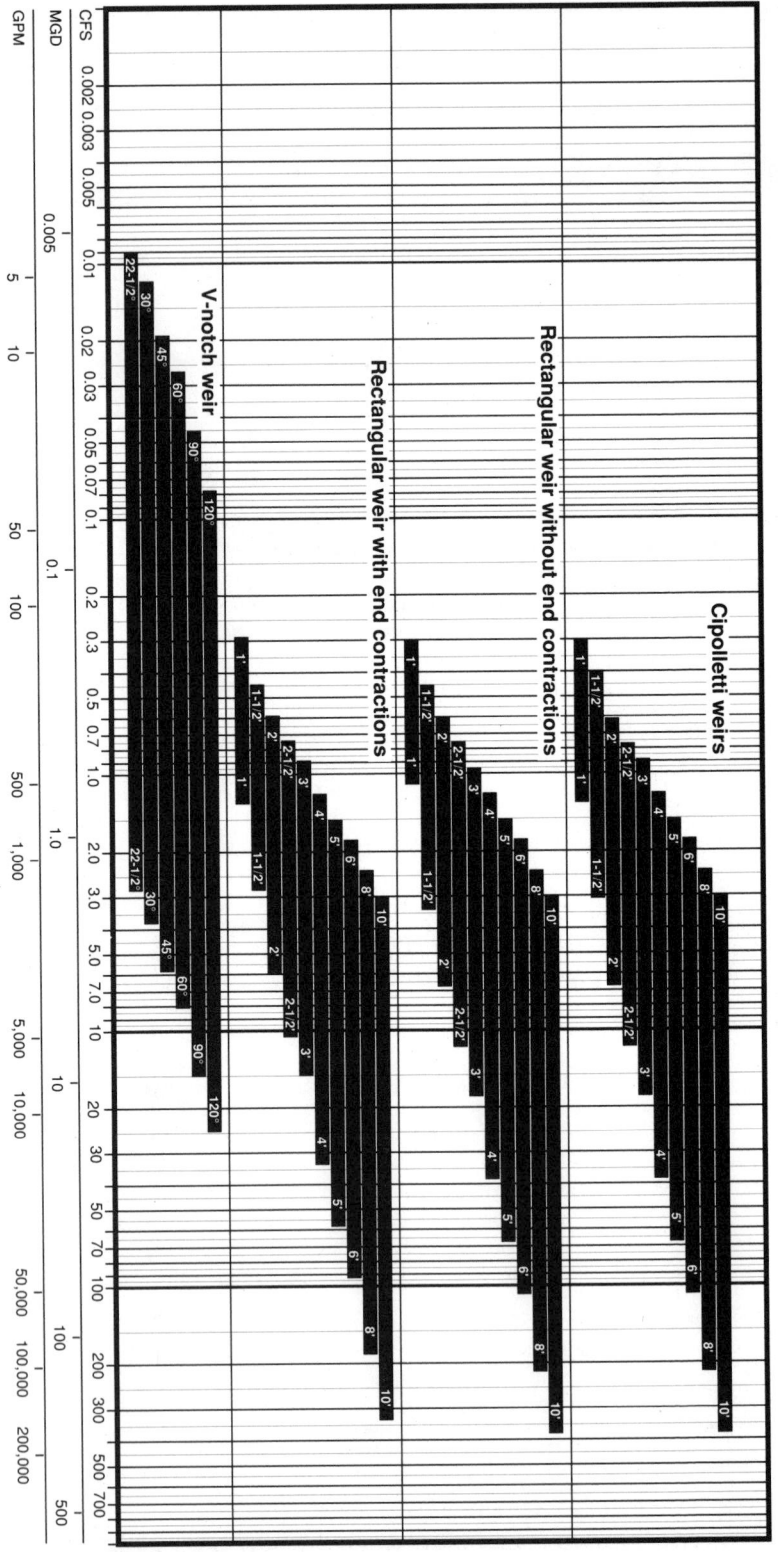

Table 5-3: Useful flow rate range of various types of weirs

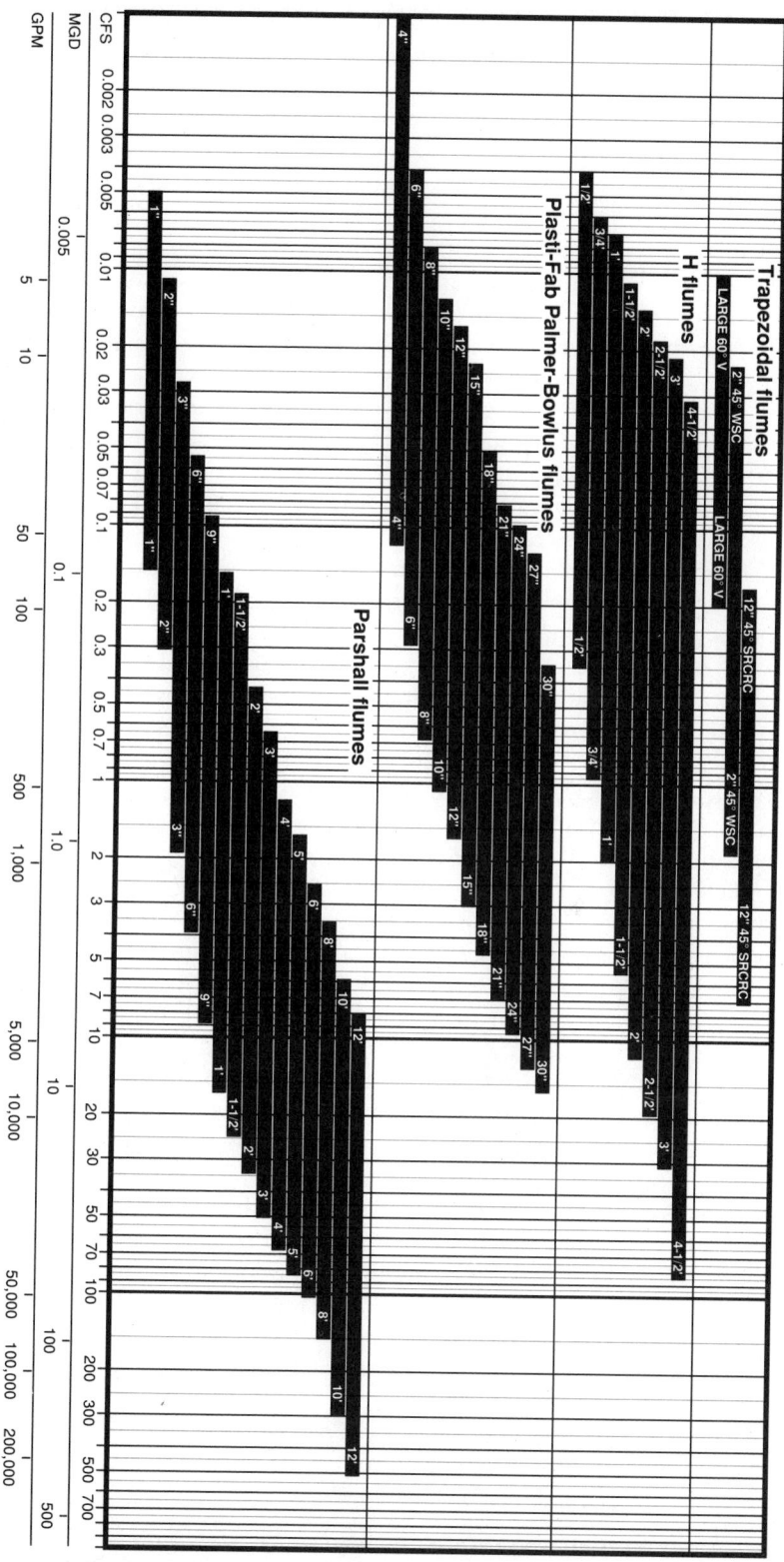

Table 5-4: Useful flow rate range of various types of flumes

5

device overflows. To select the appropriate size of primary device for a particular application, it is necessary to obtain a reasonable estimate of the minimum and maximum flow rates expected for the location. The primary measuring device chosen to be installed at this location should then have a useful flow rate range which includes the minimum and maximum expected flow rates. Also, the primary device should be sized such that an appreciable change in liquid level occurs for the transition from minimum to maximum flow; a minimum change of 0.5 foot is recommended.

Chapters 3 and 4 described in detail many of the commonly used types of primary measuring devices. However, as a quick guide in selecting the type and size of primary device to be used for a particular application, Tables 5-1, 5-2, 5-3, and 5-4 may be used. Table 5-1 describes the application of many types of weirs. Table 5-2 similarly describes flume applications. Tables 5-3 and 5-4 show the minimum and maximum flow rates for various sizes of some of these primary devices.

As an example of the primary measuring device selection process, consider the following hypothetical flow stream: The flow channel is an existing 18 inch diameter sanitary sewer line. Consequently, the flow contains a relatively high degree of suspended solids and floating materials. Based on rough measurements, the normal minimum flow rate is approximately 0.75 cfs and the normal maximum flow rate is approximately 3.0 cfs.

Referring to Tables 5-1 and 5-2, it may be seen that flumes are generally more suitable than weirs for a channel of this type which carries a high degree of solid materials, and that their relatively low head loss is an asset in a sewer line where the available head may be limited. Also, because weirs require a minimum crest elevation of 1 foot from the bottom of the channel, they are generally unsuitable for smaller pipes. Referring to Tables 5-1 and 5-2, it may be seen that of the commonly available types of flumes, the Palmer-Bowlus flume is probably most suitable for this type of application, because of its ease of installation in an existing conduit invert. This, of course, assumes that a suitable manhole can be located which has a "U" channel section in which the flume may be installed. Thus, the first two decisions in the primary device selection process have been made with the aid of Table 3-11. The general type of primary device was selected, the flume, and then the specific type of device within the general type was chosen, the Palmer-Bowlus flume.

The final decision in the selection process concerns the exact size of primary device to be installed. The logical size of Palmer-

Bowlus flume to be installed in an 18 inch sewer line is, of course, an 18 inch flume. Referring to Table 5-4, it may be seen that the minimum and maximum flow rates of the site in question fall within the useful flow rate range of an 18 inch Palmer-Bowlus flume. Thus, following the three step selection process, an 18 inch Palmer-Bowlus flume was chosen to be installed in the hypothetical flow stream.

References

1. Mougenot, G. "Measuring Sewage Flow Using Weirs and Flumes." *Water & Sewage Works* (July 1974): 78-81.

2. *Annual Book of ASTM Standards, Part 31, Water.* American Society for Testing and Materials, Philadelphia, Pa., 1974.

3. Kirkpatrick, George A., and Shelley, Philip E. *Sewer Flow Measurement—A State-of-the-Art-Assessment.* EPA Environmental Protection Technology Series, EPA-600/2-75-027, 1975.

Chapter

6

Gravity flow in
open channels:
the Manning
formula

Overview

*This chapter provides an introduction to
the use of the Manning formula for
measuring gravity flow in open channels.
Included are sections describing the
general use of the formula, and its use to
estimate flows in circular conduits.*

The Manning formula

Theree is a method by which, under certain circumstances,
the rate of flow in an open channel can be determined
without the benefit of a separate primary measuring
device. In this technique the flow conduit itself serves as the
primary device. If the cross section of the conduit is uniform, the
slope and roughness of the conduit are known, and the flow is
moved by the force of gravity only (not under pressure), the rate
of flow, in the conduit may be calculated using the Manning
formula (refer to Figure 6-1):

$$Q = \frac{1.49 \, A \, R^{2/3} \, S^{1/2}}{n}$$

where: Q = quantity of flow in cubic feet per second
n = Manning coefficient of roughness dependent upon
material of conduit
A = cross sectional area of flow in square feet

R = hydraulic radius in feet (cross sectional area divided by the wetted perimeter).

S = slope of the hydraulic gradient

For flow rate in million gallons per day, the Manning formula is:

$$Q = \frac{0.963 \; A \; R^{2/3} \; S^{1/2}}{n}$$

For flow rate in gallons per minute, the formula is:

$$Q = \frac{669 \; A \; R^{2/3} \; S^{1/2}}{n}$$

A version of this formula was presented in 1889 by the Irish engineer Robert Manning at a meeting of the Institute of Civil Engineers of Ireland [1]. The formula was later modified to the form shown above and was recommended for international use in 1936 by the Third World Power Conference. Because of its simple form and generally satisfactory results, the Manning formula has become the most widely used of all gravity flow formulas for open channel flow computations.

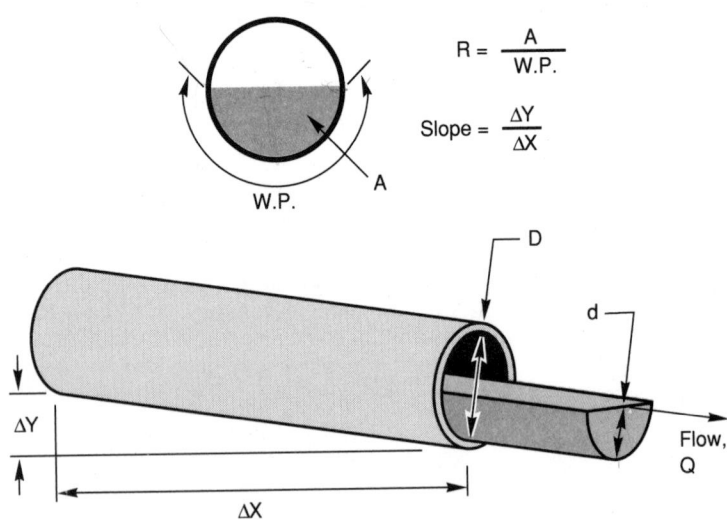

Figure 6-1: Gravity flow in open channel (round pipe)

From the formula shown above, it can be seen that the quantities n and S are assumed to be constants for a given conduit, and that the quantities A and R are variables which can be geometrically derived from a single measurement of the depth of the liquid in the conduit. Thus, the flow rate in the conduit can also be calculated from this single depth measurement. The Manning formula can be used in two ways. First, the depth can be measured and the flow rate calculated using the Manning formula; this use is further discussed in the following section. Alternatively, a secondary measuring device can be used to measure the liquid level in the conduit, and automatically convert this level into an appropriate flow rate using the Manning formula.

For best results with the Manning formula, a straight course of channel of at least 200 feet (and preferably up to 1000 feet) in length upstream from the point of depth measurement is desired. The conduit channel should be nearly uniform in slope, cross section, and roughness, and free of rapids, abrupt falls (dips), sudden contractions or expansions and tributary inflows. There should also be no downstream backup or submerged flow.

Quite often the Manning formula is used to measure flow through round pipes in manholes. Poor results will be obtained if any of the following conditions exist in the manhole:

1. The channel in the middle of the manhole does not approximate the shape of a round pipe.

2. There is an abrupt change of the flow in the manhole, such as that caused by the inlet pipe being located at a different height than the exit pipe.

3. There are two or more streams entering the manhole.

4. The flow is not straight, but enters at a different angle than it exits.

Use of the Manning formula requires knowledge of the channel cross section and liquid depth so that the flow cross section and hydraulic radius can be calculated. Note that although the conduit configuration most often encountered is a round pipe, the conduit may be of any cross section: round, rectangular, trapezoidal, semi-circular, etc. The use of the Manning formula also requires a knowledge of the slope of the water surface or the conduit invert (hydraulic gradient line). This slope is often difficult to measure under actual field operating conditions. In one method, the slope may be determined by dividing the difference in the water surface elevations at the two ends of the course, as determined by secondary devices carefully referenced to a common datum level, by the length of the course. The slope of the conduit invert as shown on design drawings may also be used, although this slope should be verified. The significance of errors in the determination of the water surface slope is diminished by the fact that the slope is a square root function in the formula. The use of the Manning formula also requires the determination of the Manning roughness coefficient, n, for the conduit in question. This coefficient is basically an index of the frictional resistance to flow offered by the conduit. In applying the Manning formula, the greatest difficulty lies in the determination of the roughness coefficient n, for there is no exact method for selecting the n value. At the present state of knowledge, the selection of a value for n is in reality an estimate of the resistance to flow in a given channel, which is actually a matter of intangibles. For veteran engineers, this means the exercise of sound engineering judgement and experience; for beginners, this can only be a guess, and different individuals will obtain different results.

Values for the Manning roughness coefficient n are usually determined from tabular data. Table 6-1 lists the coefficient n for channels of various configurations and materials. For each kind of channel the minimum, normal, and maximum values on n are shown. The normal values for artificial channels given in the table are recommended only for channels with good maintenance.

There are numerous factors that affect the value of the roughness coefficient, n. Chow [2] lists ten such factors: surface roughness, vegetation, channel irregularity, channel alignment, silting and scouring, obstruction, size and shape of channel, seasonal change, suspended material and bed load, and stage (depth of flow) and discharge. The latter factor, stage and discharge, is both interesting and distressing. The Manning formula assumes that the roughness coefficient n is a constant. For most channels, however, the value of n is believed to vary with the depth of flow. Figure 6-2 illustrates the variability of the coefficient n for various flow depths in a round pipe. Maynes [3] has reported a similar, (although differently shaped) curve from experiments performed on a 24 inch reinforced concrete sewer pipe. In practice, this means that the n coefficient selected for use in the Manning formula is actually an average value for the channel in question. The actual n value varies with the flow depth, leading to certain inaccuracies in the flow rate determination. It should also be noted that the value of n can increase

Table 6-1: Manning roughness coefficient "n" for various channel configurations and conditions

Description of channel	Min.	Norm.	Max.
I. Closed conduit—Partly full			
A. Metal			
1. Steel			
a. Lockbar and welded	0.010	0.012	0.014
b. Riveted and spiral	0.013	0.016	0.017
2. Cast Iron			
a. Coated	0.010	0.013	0.014
b. Uncoated	0.011	0.014	0.016
3. Wrought Iron			
a. Black	0.012	0.014	0.015
b. Galvanized	0.013	0.016	0.017
4. Corrugated			
a. Subdrain	0.017	0.019	0.021
b. Storm drain	0.021	0.024	0.030
B. Nonmetal			
1. Acrylic	0.008	0.009	0.010
2. Glass	0.009	0.010	0.013
3. Wood			
a. Stave	0.010	0.012	0.014
b. Laminated, treated	0.015	0.017	0.020
4. Clay			
a. Common drainage tile	0.011	0.013	0.017
b. Vitrified sewer	0.011	0.014	0.017
c. Vitrified sewer with manholes, inlets, etc.	0.013	0.015	0.017
5. Brick			
a. Glazed	0.011	0.013	0.015
b. Lined with cement	0.012	0.015	0.017
6. Concrete			
a. Culvert, straight and free of debris	0.010	0.011	0.013
b. Culvert with bends, connections, and some debris	0.011	0.013	0.014
c. Sewer with manholes, inlet, etc., straight	0.013	0.015	0.017
d. Unfinished, steel form	0.012	0.013	0.014
e. Unfinished, smooth wood form	0.012	0.014	0.016

6

Table 6-1: Manning roughness coefficient "n" for various channel configurations and conditions (*Continued*)

Description of channel	Min.	Norm.	Max.
6. Concrete			
f. Unfinished, rough			
wood form	0.015	0.017	0.020
7. Sanitary sewers coated			
with sewage slimes	0.012	0.013	0.016
8. Paved invert, sewer,			
smooth bottom	0.016	0.019	0.020
9. Rubble masonry, cemented	0.018	0.025	0.030
II. Lined or built-up channels			
A. Metal			
1. Smooth steel surface			
a. Painted	0.011	0.012	0.014
b. Unpainted	0.012	0.013	0.017
2. Corrugated	0.021	0.025	0.030
B. Nonmetal			
1. Cement			
a. Neat surface	0.010	0.011	0.013
b. Mortar	0.011	0.013	0.015
2. Concrete			
a. Trowel finish	0.011	0.013	0.015
b. Float finish	0.013	0.015	0.016
c. Finished, with gravel			
on bottom	0.015	0.017	0.020
d. Unfinished	0.014	0.017	0.020
3. Wood			
a. Planed, untreated	0.010	0.012	0.014
b. Planed, creosoted	0.011	0.012	0.015
c. Unplaned	0.011	0.013	0.015
d. Plank with battens	0.012	0.015	0.018
4. Brick			
a. Glazed	0.011	0.013	0.015
b. In cement mortar	0.012	0.015	0.018
5. Masonry			
a. Cemented rubble	0.017	0.025	0.030
b. Dry rubble	0.023	0.032	0.035
6. Asphalt			
a. Smooth	0.013	0.013	•••
b. Rough	0.016	0.016	•••
7. Vegetal lining	0.030	•••	0.500

6

Table 6-1: Manning roughness coefficient "n" for various channel configurations and conditions (*Continued*)

Description of channel	Min.	Norm.	Max.
III. Excavated or dredged			
A. Earth, straight and uniform	0.016	0.022	0.035
B. Earth, winding and sluggish	0.023	0.030	0.040
C. Rock cuts	0.030	0.040	0.050
D. Unmaintained channels	0.040	0.070	0.140
IV. Natural channels (Minor streams,			
top width at flood 100 ft.)			
A. Fairly regular section	0.030	0.050	0.070
B. Irregular section with pools	0.040	0.070	0.100

6

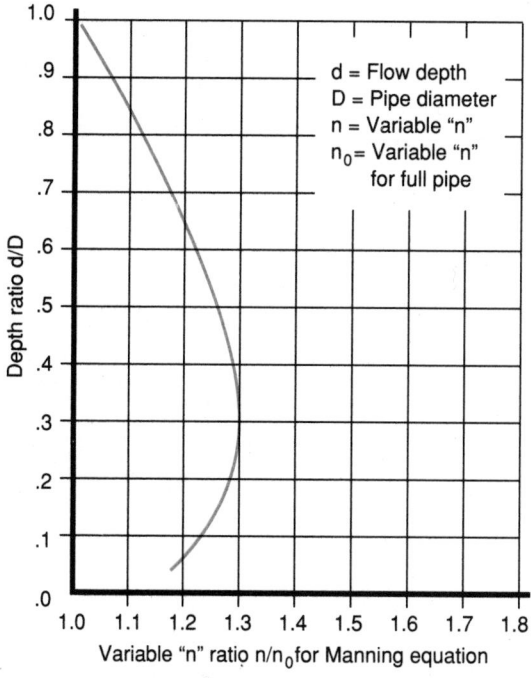

Figure 6-2: Variable "n" coefficient ratio for circular pipes

with time, due to erosion, settled solids, corrosion, etc. Thus, the value of the roughness coefficient selected should be periodically reevaluated if the interior surface condition of the channel is subject to change.

Because of the difficulties associated with determining the slope of the hydraulic gradient, and because the selection of a roughness coefficient is at best an estimate (which probably varies with the depth), the flow rate calculated using the Manning formula can only be considered an approximation, and the formula should be used only where accuracy requirements are relatively low. The Manning formula should be applied with caution and with a full knowledge of the uncertainties involved. However, within the limitations imposed by these uncertainties, the formula can produce useful flow data, and at worst an indexing of the flow can be accomplished. In a field situation, a careful use of the Manning formula can result in the determination of a flow rate which is accurate to within 10 to 20%. Less careful use may result in errors of 20 to 50% or more.

In an attempt to improve upon these accuracies, Lanfear and Coll [4] have suggested the use of a "fitted" Manning formula. In this method, the flow rate through the channel in question is determined (by means other than the Manning formula) for a particular depth. The Manning formula is then "fitted" to this data. This is done by rearranging the Manning formula as follows:

$$Q = K A R^{2/3}$$

where: Q = quantity of flow in cubic feet per second

$$K = \frac{1.49 \, S^{1/2}}{n}$$

Thus, the slope, Manning roughness coefficient, and the Manning formula constant (1.49) have been combined into a single, new constant, K. Knowing a single flow rate Q_1 from, for example, a velocity measurement, and the hydraulic radius, R_1^2, from the corresponding depth measurement, K can be calculated as follows:

$$K = Q_1/(A_1 R_1^{2/3})$$

This calculated value of K would then be used in the first equation above, resulting in a Manning formula "fitted" to the particular channel. Calculating K in this manner not only avoids the problems associated with determining the Manning roughness coefficient n, but also eliminates the need for slope measurement. Furthermore, if K is measured near the flow rate of most interest (for example, late at night for infiltration, high flows for inflow, etc.), much of the error caused by a variable roughness coefficient can be eliminated. Lanfear and Coll reported very good results using this technique.

The required flow rate measurement can be accomplished by a number of methods. A fast, simple, and accurate method is to take velocity measurements with a current meter. For greatest accuracy, the velocity should be determined at several depths, averaged, and then multiplied by the cross sectional area (as calculated from a depth measurement), resulting in a flow rate. Other methods of flow measurement include dye dilution (adding a known quantity of dye to the flow stream and measuring the concentration downstream), temporary weir or flume installations, or the simple "bucket and stopwatch" approach. Each of these techniques is applicable under certain circumstances. Refer to page 6 in Chapter 2 for a general discussion of the above-mentioned methods of open channel flow measurement.

The use of the Lanfear-Coll "fitted" Manning formula has been demonstrated to be a useful technique in the field application of the Manning formula. However, it does not directly address one of the major problems associated with the Manning formula, namely that of the variation of the roughness coefficient, n, with the depth of flow.

In order to compensate for a Manning roughness coefficient, n, which varies with the depth of flow, it is necessary to "calibrate" the flow stream in question. The calibration involves determining the flow rate in the stream for several different depths of flow, usually requiring measurements at several different times of day. The flow rates may be determined as described above and in Chapter 2. The result is a set of level-flow rate data points.

This empirically derived level-flow rate data for the flow stream may then be used in one of two ways. In the first method, the level-flow rate data is used to calculate a series of roughness coefficients for various zones of level or flow rate. The roughness coefficient appropriate to the level in question is then used in the Manning formula to calculate the flow rate. Thus, the variation in the roughness coefficient with level is accounted for by using different coefficients for different depths of flow.

In the second method, if sufficient level / flow rate data points have been collected, a graphical or mathematical relationship between the level and the flow rate may be established. This level / flow rate relationship may be established by simply plotting the level / flow rate data points on graph paper, or may be established by mathematically fitting the data to an equation by a technique such as the least squares method [5]. Thus, the variation in the roughness coefficient with level (and in fact, the entire use of the Manning formula) is bypassed by directly establishing a level / flow rate relationship for the flow stream in question.

Use of the Manning Formula to calculate flow rates in circular conduits

6

The Manning formula is commonly used to calculate the rate of flow in circular conduits or round sewer pipes. In such cases, the formula is often used to estimate the range of flow rates in order to properly size a primary measuring device to be subsequently installed. The following paragraphs discuss the use of the Manning formula for calculating the rate of flow in round pipes. A similar procedure can be used for a conduit of any cross section; however, because circular conduits are most commonly encountered, only they will be discussed.

Figure 6-3 is a plot of the quantity of flow in a circular pipe calculated using the Manning formula at various depths of flow. The vertical axis of Figure 6-3 represents the ratio of the depth of flow to the full diameter of the pipe, while the horizontal axis represents the ratio of the flow rate for the depth in question to the flow rate at the pipe full condition. Figure 6-3 illustrates the fact that, for a circular pipe, the greatest quantity of flow occurs when the pipe is flowing at about 94% of full depth. The reason for this phenomenon is that as the pipe approaches full flow, the additional frictional resistance caused by the crown of the pipe has a greater affect than the added cross sectional area.

To calculate the rate of flow in a circular pipe of a given diameter, the first step is to determine the best values to use for the slope of the hydraulic gradient, S, and the Manning roughness coefficient, n. This can be done (using Table 6-1) as described in the first section of this chapter. After these values have been determined, it is necessary to measure the depth of flow. This can be done with a head meter, ruler, hook gauge, or any other convenient depth measuring procedure. After the depth of flow has been determined, the area of flow, A, and the hydraulic

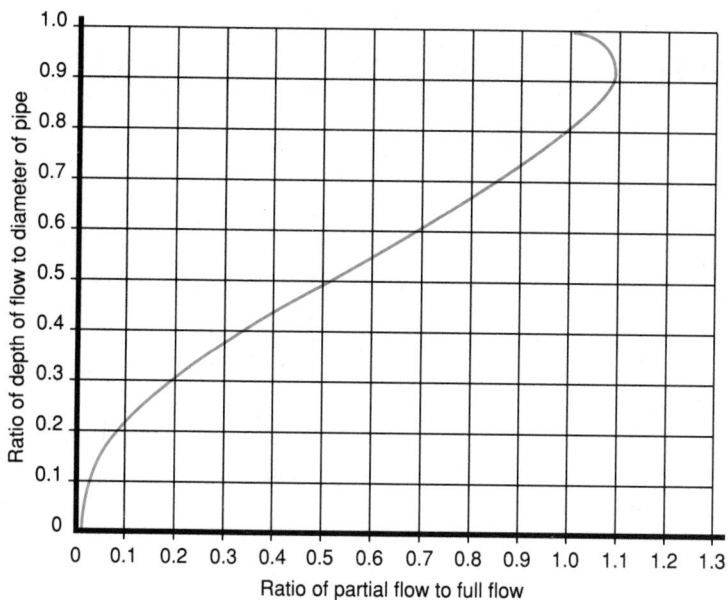

Figure 6-2: Quantity of flow in a circular pipe according to Manning formula

radius, R, for the measured depth of flow need to be calculated. Table 6-2 lists the area of flow and hydraulic radius for various flow depths. All three quantities are listed as ratios based on the diameter of the pipe in question. Thus, Table 6-2 can be used to determine the area of flow and hydraulic radius for any flow depth in any diameter pipe.

To use Table 6-2, the ratio d / D (the ratio of the actual depth of flow to the pipe diameter) must be calculated. Then, for the calculated d / D ratio, the ratio of the flow area to square of the pipe diameter (A / D^2) and the ratio of the hydraulic radius to the pipe diameter (R / D) can be found in the table. The actual values of these two quantities for the pipe diameter in question can then be calculated by multiplying the tabular values by D^2 and D respectively. Intermediate values may be determined by interpolation.

After the values of A and R have been determined, the final step is to "plug" the values into the Manning formula and calculate the flow rate for a given depth. Note that the resulting flow rate will be in cubic feet per second. To calculate the flow

Table 6-2: Area and hydraulic radius, for various flow depths

d/D	A/D²	R/D	d/D	A/D²	R/D	d/D	A/D²	R/D
0.01	0.0013	0.0066	0.36	0.2546	0.1978	0.71	0.5964	0.2973
0.02	0.0037	0.0132	0.37	0.2642	0.2020	0.72	0.6054	0.2984
0.03	0.0069	0.0197	0.38	0.2739	0.2061	0.73	0.6143	0.2995
0.04	0.0105	0.0262	0.39	0.2836	0.2102	0.74	0.6231	0.3006
0.05	0.0147	0.0326	0.40	0.2934	0.2142	0.75	0.6318	0.3017
0.06	0.0192	0.0389	0.41	0.3032	0.2181	0.76	0.6404	0.3025
0.07	0.0242	0.0451	0.42	0.3130	0.2220	0.77	0.6489	0.3032
0.08	0.0294	0.0513	0.43	0.3229	0.2257	0.78	0.6573	0.3037
0.09	0.0350	0.0574	0.44	0.3328	0.2294	0.79	0.6655	0.3040
0.10	0.0409	0.0635	0.45	0.3428	0.2331	0.80	0.6736	0.3042
0.11	0.0470	0.0695	0.46	0.3527	0.2366	0.81	0.6815	0.3044
0.12	0.0534	0.0754	0.47	0.3627	0.2400	0.82	0.6893	0.3043
0.13	0.0600	0.0813	0.48	0.3727	0.2434	0.83	0.6969	0.3041
0.14	0.0668	0.0871	0.49	0.3827	0.2467	0.84	0.7043	0.3038
0.15	0.0739	0.0929	0.50	0.3927	0.2500	0.85	0.7115	0.3033
0.16	0.0811	0.0986	0.51	0.4027	0.2531	0.86	0.7186	0.3026
0.17	0.0885	0.1042	0.52	0.4127	0.2561	0.87	0.7254	0.3017
0.18	0.0961	0.1097	0.53	0.4227	0.2591	0.88	0.7320	0.3008
0.19	0.1039	0.1152	0.54	0.4327	0.2620	0.89	0.7384	0.2996
0.20	0.1118	0.1206	0.55	0.4426	0.2649	0.90	0.7445	0.2980
0.21	0.1199	0.1259	0.56	0.4526	0.2676	0.91	0.7504	0.2963
0.22	0.1281	0.1312	0.57	0.4625	0.2703	0.92	0.7560	0.2944
0.23	0.1365	0.1364	0.58	0.4723	0.2728	0.93	0.7612	0.2922
0.24	0.1449	0.1416	0.59	0.4822	0.2753	0.94	0.7662	0.2896
0.25	0.1535	0.1466	0.60	0.4920	0.2776	0.95	0.7707	0.2864
0.26	0.1623	0.1516	0.61	0.5018	0.2797	0.96	0.7749	0.2830
0.27	0.1711	0.1566	0.62	0.5115	0.2818	0.97	0.7785	0.2787
0.28	0.1800	0.1614	0.63	0.5212	0.2839	0.98	0.7816	0.2735
0.29	0.1890	0.1662	0.64	0.5308	0.2860	0.99	0.7841	0.2665
0.30	0.1982	0.1709	0.65	0.5404	0.2881	1.00	0.7854	0.2500
0.31	0.2074	0.1755	0.66	0.5499	0.2899			
0.32	0.2167	0.1801	0.67	0.5594	0.2917			
0.33	0.2260	0.1848	0.68	0.5687	0.2935			
0.34	0.2355	0.1891	0.69	0.5780	0.2950			
0.35	0.2450	0.1935	0.70	0.5872	0.2962			

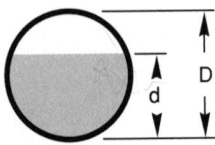

A = Area of flow
R = Hydraulic radius

rate for another depth of flow, appropriate values of A and R will have to be determined from Table 6-2 for the new depth.

Examples:
Suppose water is flowing 1.5 feet deep in a 2 foot diameter concrete pipe. It has been determined that the Manning roughness coefficient of the pipe is 0.013 and that the slope of the hydraulic gradient is 0.7 foot per 100 feet. Thus:

$$n = 0.013$$
$$S = 0.007 \ (\ 0.7 \ / \ 100 \ )$$

The area of flow, A, and hydraulic radius, R, for a depth of flow of 1.5 feet can be determined using Table 6-2. The first step is to calculate the ratio d / D. In this case:

$$d \ / \ D = 1.5 \ / \ 2 = 0.75$$

Then, from Table 6-2, the ratios A / D^2 and R / D can be found for a d / D ratio of 0.75; and the actual values of A and R calculated for a 2 foot diameter pipe.

$$A / D^2 = 0.6318$$
$$A = (\ 0.6318 \ ) \ (\ 2 \ )^2$$
$$A = 2.5272 \ ft.^2$$

$$R / D = 0.3017$$
$$R = (\ 0.3017 \ ) \ (\ 2 \ )$$
$$R = 0.6034 \ ft.$$

Finally, substituting these values into the Manning formula, the flow rate may be calculated.

$$Q = \frac{1.49 \ A \ R^{2/3} \ S^{1/2}}{n}$$

$$Q = \frac{(\ 1.49 \ ) \ (\ 2.5272 \ ) \ (\ 0.6034 \ )^{2/3} \ (\ 0.007 \ )^{1/2}}{0.013}$$

$$Q = 17.3 \ cfs$$

This is the flow rate calculated using the Manning equation for the conditions stated at a depth of 1.5 feet.

Suppose the depth of flow fell to 0.5 foot. Then the flow rate would be calculated as follows:

$$d / D = 0.5/2 = 0.25$$

$$A / D^2 = 0.1535$$
$$A = (0.1535)(2)^2$$
$$A = 0.6140 \text{ ft.}^2$$

$$R / D = 0.1466$$
$$R = (0.1466)(2)$$
$$R = 0.2932 \text{ ft.}$$

$$Q = \frac{(1.49)(0.6140)(0.2932)^{2/3}(0.007)^{1/2}}{0.013}$$

$$Q = 2.59 \text{ cfs}$$

References

1. Manning, Robert. "On the Flow of Water in Open Channels and Pipes." *Transactions of Civil Engineers of Ireland,* Vol. 20 (1891): 161-207; Supplement, Vol. 24 (1895): 179-207.

2. Chow, Te Ven. *Open-Channel Hydraulics.* McGraw-Hill Book Company, New York, 1959.

3. Maynes, John S. "Flow Data Collection for Infiltration—Inflow Analysis." *Journal, Water Pollution Control Federation,* Vol. 28, No. 8 (August 1974): 2055-2061.

4. Lanfear, Kenneth J., and Coll, John J. "Modifying Manning's Equation for Flow Rate Estimates." *Water & Sewage Works* (March 1978): 68-69.

5. Cuthbert, Daniel, and Wood, Fred S. *Fitting Equations to Data.* John Wiley & Sons, New York, 1980.

Suggested readings

Associated Water & Air Resources Engineers. *Handbook for Monitoring Industrial Wastewater.* Environmental Protection Agency Technology Transfer Publication (August 1973).

Kirkpatrick, George A., and Shelley, Phillip E. *Sewer Flow Measurement—A State-of-the Art Assessment.* EPA Environmental Protection Technology Series, EPA-600/2-75-027, 1975.

Hammer, Mark J. *Water and Wastewater Technology.* John Wiley & Sons, Inc., New York, 1975.

Schontzler, Gordon J. "New Electronic Flow Measurement for Wastewater." *Water Resources Engineering,* Ann Arbor Science Publishers, Inc., Ann Arbor, Mich., 1975.

Water Measurement Manual. United States Department of the Interior, Bureau of Reclamation, Denver, Colo., 1967.

6

Chapter

7

Flow
measurement
system
installations

Overview

This chapter provides some general
recommendations regarding primary and
secondary measuring device installation
and set-up. Included are sections
discussing the installation of a stilling well
and staff gauge at the primary device,
instrument shelters, "zero" adjustment
procedures for flow meters, and common
errors in open channel flow measurement
installations.

Stilling well

It is recommended that, where practical, primary measuring device installations include a stilling well. A stilling well is necessary for most types of flow meters using float operated level measuring systems, and may be beneficial to the operation of several of the other level measurement methods. A stilling well (see Figure 7-1) is basically a chamber which is connected to the main flow channel by a small inlet. Waves and surges are often present in a flowing open channel, because of wind, pumps, or high liquid velocities. Since the stilling well is isolated from the main flow stream by the small diameter inlet, the liquid surface in the well will be quiet, but nonetheless will follow all the steady fluctuations of the open channel flow. All the non-flow related oscillations of the open channel will be damped out by the action of the stilling well.

The size of the stilling well depends on the type and configuration of the secondary device to be installed. At a minimum, the inside diameter of the stilling well needs only to be

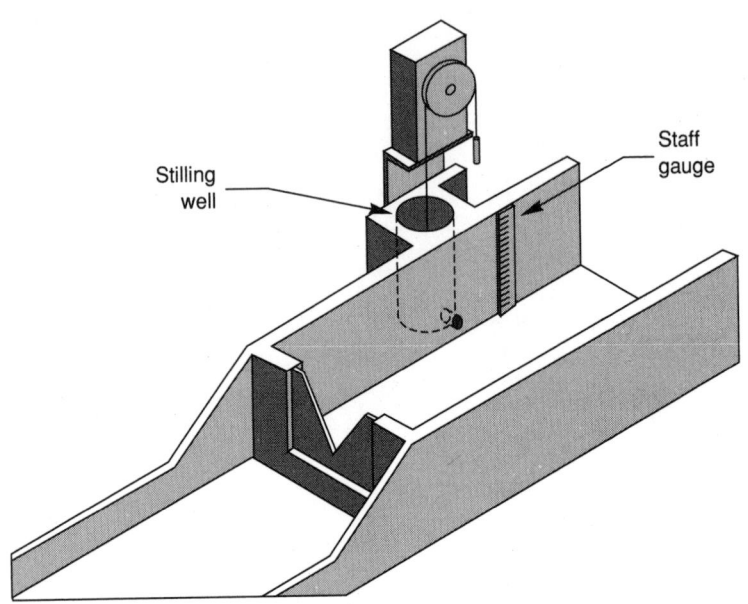

Figure 7-1: Flow measurement system with stilling well and staff gauge

large enough to accommodate the level measuring element, for example, a float. However, it is often advisable to make the stilling well large enough to be easily cleaned, especially if the water carries large amounts of solids. The stilling well must be high enough to accommodate the entire range of expected liquid level plus enough for proper installation of the flow meter.

The inlet to the stilling well should be located at the appropriate head measuring point in the primary measuring device. The area of liquid inlet from the open channel to the well should be approximately 1/1000 the area of the stilling well. If the stilling well is offset from the primary device by some distance, the inlet area may have to be increased. Table 7-1 lists satisfactory port and pipe sizes for stilling well inlets.

The stilling well may be made of wood, reinforced concrete, metal pipe, sewer pipe, corrugated galvanized iron culvert pipe, or other suitable material. The well must have a bottom, and should be as water tight as possible, except for the inlet. The inlet on most stilling wells will require occasional cleaning, especially on channels carrying sediment. When the channel is silty, some type of water flushing system may be necessary. This could be

Table 7-1: Port and pipe sizes for stilling well inserts

Diameter of float well	Diameter of inlet hole	Diameter of inlet pipe 20 to 30 Ft. long
6 inches	3/8 inch	1/2 inch
8 inches	7/16 inch	1/2 inch
10 inches	1/2 inch	1/2 inch
12 inches	1/2 inch	1/2 inch
16 inches	1/2 inch	3/4 inch
20 inches	5/8 inch	3/4 inch
24 inches	3/4 inch	1 inch
30 inches	1 inch	1 1/2 inch
36 inches	1 1/4 inch	2 inch
3 x 3 feet, square	1 1/4 inch	2 inch
3 x 4 feet, rectangular	1 1/2 inch	3 inch
4 x 5 feet, rectangular	1 1/2 inch	4 inch

manually accomplished using a tank and pump where the tank is filled with a hand pump, and a sudden release of the tank water is used to flush out the well and inlet. Alternatively, fresh water could be continuously fed into the well at a slow rate to provide an automatic flushing action.

To provide for continuous flow monitoring during freezing weather, it is often necessary to take certain measures to keep the stilling well free of ice. This is usually accomplished by one of two methods. In the first method, the liquid in the stilling well is heated, either by means of an electric immersion heater, or by a cluster of lights above the well with a reflector directing the heat onto the liquid surface in the well. In a second method, a layer of oil on the top of the liquid in the well is used to prevent freezing. If this method is used, be sure that the flow meter "zero" level is set with respect to the liquid level in the channel, not in the stilling well, as the oil in the well will stand somewhat higher than the liquid in the channel outside. This second method is not recommended for bubbler or submerged pressure transducer type flow meters due to the difference in densities of the two liquids.

Staff gauge

To aid in the zero adjustment of the flow meter, it is strongly recommended that every primary measuring device installation include a staff gauge. A staff gauge (Figure 7-1) is simply a fixed scale, on which the level of liquid in the primary device can be read. Most staff gauges are mounted vertically, but greater accuracy can often be obtained by inclining the staff so the graduations are larger for a given change in liquid level. It is important that the staff gauge be solidly and accurately attached to the primary device. The staff should be placed at the proper head measuring location in the primary device, and the staff gauge zero should be precisely aligned with the primary device zero level. Enameled iron gauges are preferred since they resist rust and will last almost indefinitely.

Instrument shelters

Under certain circumstances it may be advantageous to provide an instrument shelter as a part of the flow measurement system installation. The instrument shelter serves to house the flow meter and associated equipment and to protect them from the elements and malicious interference. Shelter sizes range from the small "look-in" type, only large enough to house the flow meter, to the large "walk-in" type, big enough to walk about inside. Choosing the type of shelter to be installed depends on a number of factors, including the permanency of the installation, ambient climactic conditions, accessibility of site, degree of protection required, and the availability of funds. There are a number of manufacturers who supply plastic or metal enclosures suitable for providing a shelter for flow measurement instrumentation.

No matter what type of shelter is selected, they should normally be mounted above the maximum liquid level, and should be provided with locks to prevent vandalism and unauthorized entrance. The shelter should be well ventilated, especially in humid climates, to prevent excessive build-up of moisture. It may also be advisable to equip the shelter with an electric blower, thermostatically controlled heater, etc. to provide for a controlled environment in the shelter.

Flow meter "zero" adjustment

Probably the greatest single controllable source of error associated with an open channel flow measurement system can result from flow meter setup ("zero" errors) [1]. This type of error may originate from improper instrument installation and/or failure to accurately adjust the flow meter's indicated liquid level (or flow rate) with the actual liquid level (or flow rate) in the open channel. It is imperative that the flow meter be properly "zeroed"

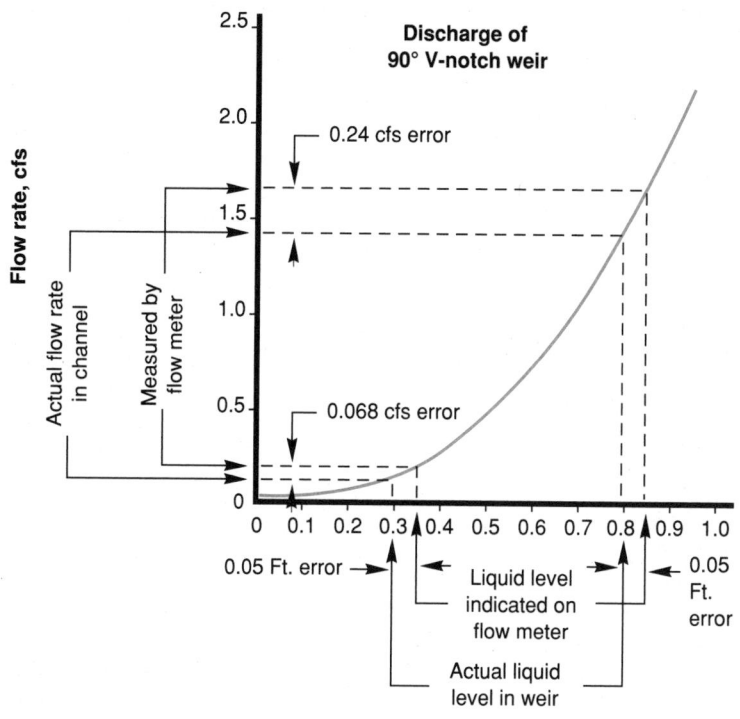

Figure 7-2: Flow meter "zero" errors

with the zero reference level in the primary measuring device. If this is not accurately done, a systematic level offset error will be introduced, resulting from the fact that the liquid level indicated by the flow meter will not correspond to the level actually existing in the primary measuring device. Due to the nonlinear level / flow rate relationship of most primary measuring devices, this will result in a flow rate error whose magnitude becomes increasingly larger at increased liquid levels (Figure 7-2).

A properly constructed flow meter can greatly aid in mini-mizing setup of "zero" errors. The flow meter should have some type of accurate visual indication of the instrument's liquid level reading, and the resolution of this level should be on the same order as the readability of the level in the primary device. Visual indication of liquid level (as opposed to flow rate) is preferred because the level can be directly observed, while the flow rate is a secondary quantity which must be calculated from the observed level. Also, the nonlinear level / flow rate relationship of most primary devices results in a flow rate scale in which a major portion of the level range is compressed into a minor portion of the flow rate range. This causes a consequent decrease in instrument resolution and setability with respect to flow rate at lower liquid level values. The flow meter should have a mechanical or electronic control which easily allows the adjustment of the indicated liquid level. These features are desirable because in most open channel flow measurement situations the flow cannot be stopped and is subject to frequent variation, resulting in a constantly changing, nonzero level setpoint. Thus, any flow meter feature which can ease the task of adjusting the instrument liquid level to match the actual level will aid in decreasing the setup or "zero" errors.

7 Common errors in open channel flow measurement installations

Mort [1] and Thomas [2] discussed sources of errors commonly encountered in open channel flow measurement installations. They identified two classes of errors: 1) avoidable errors which result from carelessness and can be eliminated through supervision and strict attention to details, and 2) unavoidable errors, which are errors of degree, and although they cannot be completely eliminated, they can, by exercise of extreme care and knowledge of their nature and magnitude be reduced to such a degree as to ensure satisfactory overall results. The errors identified by Mort and Thomas are briefly summarized below:

Faulty fabrication or construction of the primary device

There are numerous possibilities for the introduction of errors in flow measurements resulting from faulty construction of the primary measuring device. Most typical of these are errors in the crest length of contracted weirs, errors in the angle of V-notch weirs, deviation from the standard dimensions of Parshall flumes, etc. Any deviation of a primary device from the standard configuration, dimensions, and geometry will result in an error in flow measurement through the device.

Improper gauge or head measuring location

In most types of primary devices, the head / flow rate relationship has been empirically determined with the head being measured at a specific point in relation to the primary device. Errors will occur if the gauge or head measuring instrumentation is not located at the proper location in the primary device. Most typical installation errors of this type occur in weirs where the gauge location is at a point where drawdown over the weir is measured, for example by mounting a staff gauge on the weir plate instead of at the recommended three to four times the maximum head upstream from the weir. Errors can also occur in flumes if the gauge or head measuring location is not in the specified position.

Incorrect zero setting

These types of errors are basically as discussed on page 118. They may also originate from the lack of knowledge of the proper zero reference level in the primary device. An example of this is the Palmer-Bowlus flume, where the zero level is the floor of the flume throat, not the invert of the pipe as might be suspected.

Improper head measurement

Errors in measuring the head in a primary device will result in flow measurement errors of the same type and magnitude as those resulting from an incorrect zero setting. Improper head measurement may result from an incorrect location of the gauge, from carelessness in not obtaining a good head reading, or from a faulty, improperly installed, or poorly maintained head measuring and recording instrument.

Use of primary device outside its proper range

All types and sizes of primary measuring devices have a recommended range of flow rates, outside of which errors in flow measurement will result. The use of a primary device to measure flow rates outside the recommended range of a particular device (for example, a flow rate resulting in a head of less than 0.2 foot. on a V-notch weir) will result in inaccurate flow measurement.

Improper installation or maintenance of weirs

There are many possibilities for improper installation or maintenance of weirs which can contribute to errors in flow measurement. Included in these are transverse slope of the weir crest, the weir plate sloping upstream or downstream, roughness of the upstream face of the weir plate, rounding of the sharp edge at the weir crest, improper aeration of the downstream nappe of the weir, submergence of the weir, or excessive velocity of approach.

Turbulence and surges in the approach channel

Turbulence and surges may occur in the approach channel to a primary device, caused by a high velocity of approach, gates, valves, pumps, or a sudden change in section. This results in an erratic head measurement and hence inaccurate flow measurement. Corrective measures to quiet the flow provide the best solution, although this may not be an easy task.

References

1. Mort, S.F. "The Practical Gaging of Dirty Water and Its Applications to Sewer Design." *Journal of the Irrigation and Drainage Division,* ASCE, Part 3, No. 1 (1955): 81-113.

2. Thomas, C.W. "Errors in Measurement of Irrigation Water." *Proceedings, American Society of Civil Engineers,* 83, IR3, Proc. Paper 1362 (September 1957): 14.

Suggested readings

Water Measurement Manual. United States Department of the Interior, Bureau of Reclamation, Denver, Colo., 1967.

Stevens Water Resources Data Book. 2nd Edition. Leupold & Stevens, Inc., Beaverton, Ore., 1974.

Chapter

8

V-notch weir discharge tables

- This chapter contains discharge (flow rate
- vs head) tables for V-notch weirs. Note that
- all of the tabular data is for free flow. If the
- flow is submerged, corrections will have to
- be made to determine the discharge, as
- discussed in Chapter 3.
-   Note also that in many cases, discharges
- are listed for heads which are above the
- maximum recommended operating head
- or below the minimum recommended
- operating head of the weir in question.
- Discharge for these heads outside the nor-
- mal operating range are listed for refer-
- ence only; it should not be implied that the
- primary device is intended to be used in
- these regions. Refer to Chapter 3 for mini-
- mum and maximum recommended heads.
-

8

V-notch weir discharge tables

8-1: 22^1/$_2$° V-notch Weir

8-2: 30° V-notch Weir

8-3: 45° V-notch Weir

8-4: 60° V-notch Weir

8-5: 90° V-notch Weir

8-6: 120° V-notch Weir

Note: The discharges of the weirs are listed in four different units:

CFS—cubic feet per second   GPS—gallons per second

GPM—gallons per minute   MGD—million gallons per day.

The equation used to develop each table is listed on the table.

8-1: 22 $^1/2°$ V-notch Weir Discharge Table

Formulas: CFS = $0.4970H^{2.5}$ GPS = CFS x 7.481
GPM = CFS x 448.8 MGD = CFS x 0.6463

Head Feet	CFS	GPS	GPM	MGD	Head Feet	CFS	GPS	GPM	MGD
0.01	0.0000	0.0000	0.0022	0.0000	0.51	0.0923	0.6906	41.43	0.0597
0.02	0.0000	0.0002	0.0126	0.0000	0.52	0.0969	0.7250	43.49	0.0626
0.03	0.0001	0.0006	0.0348	0.0001	0.53	0.1016	0.7603	45.61	0.0657
0.04	0.0002	0.0012	0.0714	0.0001	0.54	0.1065	0.7967	47.80	0.0688
0.05	0.0003	0.0021	0.1247	0.0002	0.55	0.1115	0.8341	50.04	0.0721
0.06	0.0004	0.0033	0.1967	0.0003	0.56	0.1166	0.8725	52.35	0.0754
0.07	0.0006	0.0048	0.2892	0.0004	0.57	0.1219	0.9120	54.71	0.0788
0.08	0.0009	0.0067	0.4038	0.0006	0.58	0.1273	0.9525	57.15	0.0823
0.09	0.0012	0.0090	0.5420	0.0008	0.59	0.1329	0.9941	59.64	0.0859
0.10	0.0016	0.0118	0.7054	0.0010	0.60	0.1386	1.037	62.20	0.0896
0.11	0.0020	0.0149	0.8951	0.0013	0.61	0.1444	1.081	64.82	0.0934
0.12	0.0025	0.0185	1.113	0.0016	0.62	0.1504	1.125	67.51	0.0972
0.13	0.0030	0.0227	1.359	0.0020	0.63	0.1566	1.171	70.27	0.1012
0.14	0.0036	0.0273	1.636	0.0024	0.64	0.1629	1.218	73.09	0.1053
0.15	0.0043	0.0324	1.944	0.0028	0.65	0.1693	1.266	75.98	0.1094
0.16	0.0051	0.0381	2.284	0.0033	0.66	0.1759	1.316	78.93	0.1137
0.17	0.0059	0.0443	2.658	0.0038	0.67	0.1826	1.366	81.96	0.1180
0.18	0.0068	0.0511	3.066	0.0044	0.68	0.1895	1.418	85.05	0.1225
0.19	0.0078	0.0585	3.510	0.0051	0.69	0.1966	1.470	88.21	0.1270
0.20	0.0089	0.0665	3.990	0.0057	0.70	0.2038	1.524	91.44	0.1317
0.21	0.0100	0.0751	4.508	0.0065	0.71	0.2111	1.579	94.74	0.1364
0.22	0.0113	0.0844	5.064	0.0073	0.72	0.2186	1.635	98.12	0.1413
0.23	0.0126	0.0943	5.659	0.0081	0.73	0.2263	1.693	101.6	0.1463
0.24	0.0140	0.1049	6.294	0.0091	0.74	0.2341	1.751	105.1	0.1513
0.25	0.0155	0.1162	6.970	0.0100	0.75	0.2421	1.811	108.7	0.1565
0.26	0.0171	0.1282	7.689	0.0111	0.76	0.2503	1.872	112.3	0.1617
0.27	0.0188	0.1408	8.449	0.0122	0.77	0.2586	1.934	116.0	0.1671
0.28	0.0206	0.1542	9.253	0.0133	0.78	0.2671	1.998	119.9	0.1726
0.29	0.0225	0.1684	10.10	0.0145	0.79	0.2757	2.062	123.7	0.1782
0.30	0.0245	0.1833	11.00	0.0158	0.80	0.2845	2.128	127.7	0.1839
0.31	0.0266	0.1989	11.93	0.0172	0.81	0.2935	2.195	131.7	0.1897
0.32	0.0288	0.2154	12.92	0.0186	0.82	0.3026	2.264	135.8	0.1956
0.33	0.0311	0.2326	13.95	0.0201	0.83	0.3119	2.334	140.0	0.2016
0.34	0.0335	0.2506	15.04	0.0217	0.84	0.3214	2.404	144.2	0.2077
0.35	0.0360	0.2695	16.17	0.0233	0.85	0.3311	2.477	148.6	0.2140
0.36	0.0386	0.2891	17.34	0.0250	0.86	0.3409	2.550	153.0	0.2203
0.37	0.0414	0.3096	18.57	0.0267	0.87	0.3509	2.625	157.5	0.2268
0.38	0.0442	0.3310	19.85	0.0286	0.88	0.3610	2.701	162.0	0.2333
0.39	0.0472	0.3532	21.19	0.0305	0.89	0.3714	2.778	166.7	0.2400
0.40	0.0503	0.3762	22.57	0.0325	0.90	0.3819	2.857	171.4	0.2468
0.41	0.0535	0.4002	24.01	0.0346	0.91	0.3926	2.937	176.2	0.2537
0.42	0.0568	0.4250	25.50	0.0367	0.92	0.4035	3.018	181.1	0.2608
0.43	0.0603	0.4508	27.04	0.0389	0.93	0.4145	3.101	186.0	0.2679
0.44	0.0638	0.4775	28.64	0.0412	0.94	0.4258	3.185	191.1	0.2752
0.45	0.0675	0.5051	30.30	0.0436	0.95	0.4372	3.271	196.2	0.2826
0.46	0.0713	0.5336	32.01	0.0461	0.96	0.4488	3.357	201.4	0.2900
0.47	0.0753	0.5631	33.78	0.0486	0.97	0.4606	3.445	206.7	0.2977
0.48	0.0793	0.5935	35.61	0.0513	0.98	0.4725	3.535	212.1	0.3054
0.49	0.0835	0.6249	37.49	0.0540	0.99	0.4847	3.626	217.5	0.3132
0.50	0.0879	0.6573	39.43	0.0568	1.00	0.4970	3.718	223.1	0.3212

8

8-1: 22 ½° V-notch Weir Discharge Table (Continued)

Formulas: CFS = 0.4970H$^{2.5}$ GPS = CFS x 7.481
GPM = CFS x 448.8   MGD = CFS x 0.6463

Head Feet	CFS	GPS	GPM	MGD	Head Feet	CFS	GPS	GPM	MGD
1.01	0.510	3.812	228.7	0.3293	1.51	1.393	10.42	625.0	0.9000
1.02	0.522	3.907	234.4	0.3375	1.52	1.416	10.59	635.4	0.9150
1.03	0.535	4.003	240.2	0.3458	1.53	1.439	10.77	645.9	0.9301
1.04	0.548	4.101	246.0	0.3543	1.54	1.463	10.94	656.5	0.9453
1.05	0.561	4.200	252.0	0.3629	1.55	1.487	11.12	667.2	0.9608
1.06	0.575	4.301	258.0	0.3716	1.56	1.511	11.30	678.0	0.9763
1.07	0.589	4.403	264.2	0.3804	1.57	1.535	11.48	688.9	0.9921
1.08	0.602	4.507	270.4	0.3894	1.58	1.560	11.67	699.9	1.008
1.09	0.616	4.612	276.7	0.3984	1.59	1.584	11.85	711.1	1.024
1.10	0.631	4.718	283.1	0.4076	1.60	1.609	12.04	722.3	1.040
1.11	0.645	4.826	289.5	0.4170	1.61	1.635	12.23	733.6	1.056
1.12	0.660	4.936	296.1	0.4264	1.62	1.660	12.42	745.1	1.073
1.13	0.675	5.047	302.8	0.4360	1.63	1.686	12.61	756.6	1.090
1.14	0.690	5.159	309.5	0.4457	1.64	1.712	12.81	768.3	1.106
1.15	0.705	5.273	316.3	0.4555	1.65	1.738	13.00	780.0	1.123
1.16	0.720	5.388	323.3	0.4655	1.66	1.765	13.20	791.9	1.140
1.17	0.736	5.505	330.3	0.4756	1.67	1.791	13.40	803.9	1.158
1.18	0.752	5.624	337.4	0.4858	1.68	1.818	13.60	816.0	1.175
1.19	0.768	5.744	344.6	0.4962	1.69	1.845	13.80	828.2	1.193
1.20	0.784	5.865	351.9	0.5067	1.70	1.873	14.01	840.5	1.210
1.21	0.800	5.988	359.2	0.5173	1.71	1.900	14.22	852.9	1.228
1.22	0.817	6.112	366.7	0.5281	1.72	1.928	14.43	865.4	1.246
1.23	0.834	6.238	374.3	0.5390	1.73	1.956	14.64	878.1	1.264
1.24	0.851	6.366	381.9	0.5500	1.74	1.985	14.85	890.8	1.283
1.25	0.868	6.495	389.7	0.5611	1.75	2.013	15.06	903.7	1.301
1.26	0.886	6.626	397.5	0.5724	1.76	2.042	15.28	916.6	1.320
1.27	0.903	6.758	405.4	0.5838	1.77	2.072	15.50	929.7	1.339
1.28	0.921	6.892	413.5	0.5954	1.78	2.101	15.72	942.9	1.358
1.29	0.939	7.027	421.6	0.6071	1.79	2.131	15.94	956.2	1.377
1.30	0.958	7.164	429.8	0.6189	1.80	2.160	16.16	969.6	1.396
1.31	0.976	7.303	438.1	0.6309	1.81	2.191	16.39	983.1	1.416
1.32	0.995	7.443	446.5	0.6430	1.82	2.221	16.61	996.8	1.435
1.33	1.014	7.585	455.0	0.6553	1.83	2.252	16.84	1011	1.455
1.34	1.033	7.728	463.6	0.6677	1.84	2.282	17.07	1024	1.475
1.35	1.052	7.873	472.3	0.6802	1.85	2.314	17.31	1038	1.495
1.36	1.072	8.020	481.1	0.6928	1.86	2.345	17.54	1052	1.516
1.37	1.092	8.168	490.0	0.7057	1.87	2.377	17.78	1067	1.536
1.38	1.112	8.318	499.0	0.7186	1.88	2.409	18.02	1081	1.557
1.39	1.132	8.469	508.1	0.7317	1.89	2.441	18.26	1095	1.577
1.40	1.153	8.623	517.3	0.7449	1.90	2.473	18.50	1110	1.598
1.41	1.173	8.777	526.6	0.7583	1.91	2.506	18.75	1125	1.619
1.42	1.194	8.934	536.0	0.7718	1.92	2.539	18.99	1139	1.641
1.43	1.215	9.092	545.4	0.7855	1.93	2.572	19.24	1154	1.662
1.44	1.237	9.252	555.0	0.7993	1.94	2.605	19.49	1169	1.684
1.45	1.258	9.413	564.7	0.8132	1.95	2.639	19.74	1184	1.706
1.46	1.280	9.576	574.5	0.8273	1.96	2.673	20.00	1200	1.728
1.47	1.302	9.741	584.4	0.8416	1.97	2.707	20.25	1215	1.750
1.48	1.324	9.908	594.4	0.8559	1.98	2.742	20.51	1230	1.772
1.49	1.347	10.08	604.5	0.8705	1.99	2.776	20.77	1246	1.794
1.50	1.370	10.25	614.7	0.8852	2.00	2.811	21.03	1262	1.817

8

Formulas: $CFS = 0.4970H^{2.5}$ $GPS = CFS \times 7.481$
$GPM = CFS \times 448.8$ $MGD = CFS \times 0.6463$

Head Feet	CFS	GPS	GPM	MGD	Head Feet	CFS	GPS	GPM	MGD
2.01	2.847	21.30	1278	1.840	2.51	4.961	37.11	2226	3.206
2.02	2.882	21.56	1294	1.863	2.52	5.010	37.48	2249	3.238
2.03	2.918	21.83	1310	1.886	2.53	5.060	37.85	2271	3.270
2.04	2.954	22.10	1326	1.909	2.54	5.110	38.23	2293	3.303
2.05	2.990	22.37	1342	1.933	2.55	5.161	38.61	2316	3.335
2.06	3.027	22.65	1359	1.956	2.56	5.211	38.99	2339	3.368
2.07	3.064	22.92	1375	1.980	2.57	5.262	39.37	2362	3.401
2.08	3.101	23.20	1392	2.004	2.58	5.314	39.75	2385	3.434
2.09	3.138	23.48	1409	2.028	2.59	5.365	40.14	2408	3.468
2.10	3.176	23.76	1425	2.053	2.60	5.417	40.53	2431	3.501
2.11	3.214	24.04	1442	2.077	2.61	5.470	40.92	2455	3.535
2.12	3.252	24.33	1460	2.102	2.62	5.522	41.31	2478	3.569
2.13	3.291	24.62	1477	2.127	2.63	5.575	41.71	2502	3.603
2.14	3.330	24.91	1494	2.152	2.64	5.628	42.10	2526	3.637
2.15	3.369	25.20	1512	2.177	2.65	5.682	42.50	2550	3.672
2.16	3.408	25.49	1529	2.203	2.66	5.735	42.91	2574	3.707
2.17	3.448	25.79	1547	2.228	2.67	5.789	43.31	2598	3.742
2.18	3.487	26.09	1565	2.254	2.68	5.844	43.72	2623	3.777
2.19	3.527	26.39	1583	2.280	2.69	5.898	44.13	2647	3.812
2.20	3.568	26.69	1601	2.306	2.70	5.953	44.54	2672	3.848
2.21	3.609	27.00	1620	2.332	2.71	6.009	44.95	2697	3.883
2.22	3.650	27.30	1638	2.359	2.72	6.064	45.37	2722	3.919
2.23	3.691	27.61	1656	2.385	2.73	6.120	45.78	2747	3.955
2.24	3.732	27.92	1675	2.412	2.74	6.176	46.21	2772	3.992
2.25	3.774	28.23	1694	2.439	2.75	6.233	46.63	2797	4.028
2.26	3.816	28.55	1713	2.466	2.76	6.290	47.05	2823	4.065
2.27	3.859	28.87	1732	2.494	2.77	6.347	47.48	2848	4.102
2.28	3.901	29.18	1751	2.521	2.78	6.404	47.91	2874	4.139
2.29	3.944	29.51	1770	2.549	2.79	6.462	48.34	2900	4.176
2.30	3.987	29.83	1789	2.577	2.80	6.520	48.78	2926	4.214
2.31	4.031	30.15	1809	2.605	2.81	6.578	49.21	2952	4.252
2.32	4.075	30.48	1829	2.633	2.82	6.637	49.65	2979	4.290
2.33	4.119	30.81	1848	2.662	2.83	6.696	50.09	3005	4.328
2.34	4.163	31.14	1868	2.690	2.84	6.755	50.54	3032	4.366
2.35	4.208	31.48	1888	2.719	2.85	6.815	50.98	3059	4.405
2.36	4.252	31.81	1908	2.748	2.86	6.875	51.43	3085	4.443
2.37	4.298	32.15	1929	2.778	2.87	6.935	51.88	3113	4.482
2.38	4.343	32.49	1949	2.807	2.88	6.996	52.34	3140	4.521
2.39	4.389	32.83	1970	2.837	2.89	7.057	52.79	3167	4.561
2.40	4.435	33.18	1990	2.866	2.90	7.118	53.25	3195	4.600
2.41	4.481	33.52	2011	2.896	2.91	7.179	53.71	3222	4.640
2.42	4.528	33.87	2032	2.926	2.92	7.241	54.17	3250	4.680
2.43	4.575	34.22	2053	2.957	2.93	7.303	54.64	3278	4.720
2.44	4.622	34.58	2074	2.987	2.94	7.366	55.10	3306	4.761
2.45	4.670	34.93	2096	3.018	2.95	7.429	55.57	3334	4.801
2.46	4.717	35.29	2117	3.049	2.96	7.492	56.05	3362	4.842
2.47	4.765	35.65	2139	3.080	2.97	7.555	56.52	3391	4.883
2.48	4.814	36.01	2160	3.111	2.98	7.619	57.00	3419	4.924
2.49	4.862	36.38	2182	3.143	2.99	7.683	57.48	3448	4.966
2.50	4.911	36.74	2204	3.174	3.00	7.747	57.96	3477	5.007

8-2: 30° V-notch Weir Discharge Table

Formulas: CFS = $0.6760H^{2.5}$ GPS = CFS x 7.481
GPM = CFS x 448.8   MGD = CFS x 0.6463

Head Feet	CFS	GPS	GPM	MGD	Head Feet	CFS	GPS	GPM	MGD
0.01	0.0000	0.0001	0.0030	0.0000	0.51	0.1256	0.9394	56.35	0.0812
0.02	0.0000	0.0003	0.0172	0.0000	0.52	0.1318	0.9861	59.16	0.0852
0.03	0.0001	0.0008	0.0473	0.0001	0.53	0.1382	1.034	62.04	0.0893
0.04	0.0002	0.0016	0.0971	0.0001	0.54	0.1449	1.084	65.01	0.0936
0.05	0.0004	0.0028	0.1696	0.0002	0.55	0.1517	1.135	68.06	0.0980
0.06	0.0006	0.0045	0.2675	0.0004	0.56	0.1586	1.187	71.20	0.1025
0.07	0.0009	0.0066	0.3933	0.0006	0.57	0.1658	1.240	74.42	0.1072
0.08	0.0012	0.0092	0.5492	0.0008	0.58	0.1732	1.296	77.73	0.1119
0.09	0.0016	0.0123	0.7372	0.0011	0.59	0.1807	1.352	81.12	0.1168
0.10	0.0021	0.0160	0.9594	0.0014	0.60	0.1885	1.410	84.60	0.1218
0.11	0.0027	0.0203	1.218	0.0018	0.61	0.1965	1.470	88.17	0.1270
0.12	0.0034	0.0252	1.513	0.0022	0.62	0.2046	1.531	91.83	0.1322
0.13	0.0041	0.0308	1.849	0.0027	0.63	0.2130	1.593	95.58	0.1376
0.14	0.0050	0.0371	2.225	0.0032	0.64	0.2215	1.657	99.41	0.1432
0.15	0.0059	0.0441	2.644	0.0038	0.65	0.2303	1.723	103.3	0.1488
0.16	0.0069	0.0518	3.107	0.0045	0.66	0.2392	1.790	107.4	0.1546
0.17	0.0081	0.0603	3.615	0.0052	0.67	0.2484	1.858	111.5	0.1605
0.18	0.0093	0.0695	4.170	0.0060	0.68	0.2578	1.928	115.7	0.1666
0.19	0.0106	0.0796	4.774	0.0069	0.69	0.2673	2.000	120.0	0.1728
0.20	0.0121	0.0905	5.427	0.0078	0.70	0.2771	2.073	124.4	0.1791
0.21	0.0137	0.1022	6.131	0.0088	0.71	0.2871	2.148	128.9	0.1856
0.22	0.0153	0.1148	6.887	0.0099	0.72	0.2974	2.225	133.5	0.1922
0.23	0.0172	0.1283	7.697	0.0111	0.73	0.3078	2.303	138.1	0.1989
0.24	0.0191	0.1427	8.561	0.0123	0.74	0.3184	2.382	142.9	0.2058
0.25	0.0211	0.1580	9.481	0.0137	0.75	0.3293	2.464	147.8	0.2128
0.26	0.0233	0.1743	10.46	0.0151	0.76	0.3404	2.546	152.8	0.2200
0.27	0.0256	0.1916	11.49	0.0165	0.77	0.3517	2.631	157.8	0.2273
0.28	0.0280	0.2098	12.59	0.0181	0.78	0.3632	2.717	163.0	0.2348
0.29	0.0306	0.2290	13.74	0.0198	0.79	0.3750	2.805	168.3	0.2424
0.30	0.0333	0.2493	14.96	0.0215	0.80	0.3870	2.895	173.7	0.2501
0.31	0.0362	0.2706	16.23	0.0234	0.81	0.3992	2.986	179.1	0.2580
0.32	0.0392	0.2929	17.57	0.0253	0.82	0.4116	3.079	184.7	0.2660
0.33	0.0423	0.3164	18.98	0.0273	0.83	0.4243	3.174	190.4	0.2742
0.34	0.0456	0.3409	20.45	0.0294	0.84	0.4372	3.270	196.2	0.2825
0.35	0.0490	0.3665	21.99	0.0317	0.85	0.4503	3.369	202.1	0.2910
0.36	0.0526	0.3932	23.59	0.0340	0.86	0.4637	3.469	208.1	0.3097
0.37	0.0563	0.4211	25.26	0.0364	0.87	0.4772	3.570	214.2	0.3084
0.38	0.0602	0.4502	27.01	0.0389	0.88	0.4911	3.674	220.4	0.3174
0.39	0.0642	0.4804	28.82	0.0415	0.89	0.5052	3.779	226.7	0.3265
0.40	0.0684	0.5117	30.70	0.0442	0.90	0.5195	3.886	233.1	0.3357
0.41	0.0728	0.5443	32.66	0.0470	0.91	0.5340	3.995	239.7	0.3451
0.42	0.0773	0.5781	34.68	0.0499	0.92	0.5488	4.106	246.3	0.3547
0.43	0.0820	0.6132	36.78	0.0530	0.93	0.5638	4.218	253.1	0.3644
0.44	0.0868	0.6494	38.96	0.0561	0.94	0.5791	4.332	259.9	0.3743
0.45	0.0918	0.6870	41.21	0.0593	0.95	0.5946	4.449	266.9	0.3843
0.46	0.0970	0.7258	43.54	0.0627	0.96	0.6104	4.567	274.0	0.3945
0.47	0.1024	0.7659	45.95	0.0662	0.97	0.6264	4.686	281.1	0.4049
0.48	0.1079	0.8073	48.43	0.0697	0.98	0.6427	4.808	288.4	0.4154
0.49	0.1136	0.8500	50.99	0.0734	0.99	0.6592	4.932	295.9	0.4261
0.50	0.1195	0.8940	53.63	0.0772	1.00	0.6760	5.057	303.4	0.4369

8

8-2: 30° V-notch Weir Discharge Table *(Continued)*

Formulas: CFS = $0.6760H^{2.5}$ GPS = CFS x 7.481
           GPM = CFS x 448.8   MGD = CFS x 0.6463

Head Feet	CFS	GPS	GPM	MGD	Head Feet	CFS	GPS	GPM	MGD
1.01	0.6930	5.185	311.0	0.4479	1.51	1.894	14.17	850.0	1.224
1.02	0.7103	5.314	318.8	0.4591	1.52	1.926	14.41	864.2	1.244
1.03	0.7278	5.445	326.7	0.4704	1.53	1.957	14.64	878.5	1.265
1.04	0.7456	5.578	334.6	0.4819	1.54	1.990	14.88	892.9	1.286
1.05	0.7637	5.713	342.7	0.4936	1.55	2.022	15.13	907.5	1.307
1.06	0.7820	5.850	351.0	0.5054	1.56	2.055	15.37	922.2	1.328
1.07	0.8006	5.989	359.3	0.5174	1.57	2.088	15.62	937.0	1.349
1.08	0.8194	6.130	367.8	0.5296	1.58	2.121	15.87	952.0	1.371
1.09	0.8385	6.273	376.3	0.5419	1.59	2.155	16.12	967.1	1.393
1.10	0.8579	6.418	385.0	0.5545	1.60	2.189	16.38	982.4	1.415
1.11	0.8775	6.565	393.8	0.5671	1.61	2.223	16.63	997.8	1.437
1.12	0.8974	6.714	402.8	0.5800	1.62	2.258	16.89	1013	1.459
1.13	0.9176	6.864	411.8	0.5930	1.63	2.293	17.15	1029	1.482
1.14	0.9380	7.017	421.0	0.6062	1.64	2.328	17.42	1045	1.505
1.15	0.9587	7.172	430.3	0.6196	1.65	2.364	17.69	1061	1.528
1.16	0.9797	7.329	439.7	0.6332	1.66	2.400	17.95	1077	1.551
1.17	1.001	7.488	449.2	0.6469	1.67	2.436	18.23	1093	1.575
1.18	1.022	7.649	458.9	0.6608	1.68	2.473	18.50	1110	1.598
1.19	1.044	7.812	468.7	0.6749	1.69	2.510	18.78	1126	1.622
1.20	1.066	7.977	478.6	0.6892	1.70	2.547	19.06	1143	1.646
1.21	1.089	8.145	488.6	0.7036	1.71	2.585	19.34	1160	1.671
1.22	1.111	8.314	498.8	0.7183	1.72	2.623	19.62	1177	1.695
1.23	1.134	8.485	509.1	0.7331	1.73	2.661	19.91	1194	1.720
1.24	1.157	8.659	519.5	0.7481	1.74	2.700	20.20	1212	1.745
1.25	1.181	8.834	530.0	0.7632	1.75	2.739	20.49	1229	1.770
1.26	1.205	9.012	540.7	0.7786	1.76	2.778	20.78	1247	1.795
1.27	1.229	9.192	551.5	0.7941	1.77	2.818	21.08	1265	1.821
1.28	1.253	9.374	562.4	0.8099	1.78	2.858	21.38	1282	1.847
1.29	1.278	9.558	573.4	0.8258	1.79	2.898	21.68	1301	1.873
1.30	1.303	9.745	584.6	0.8419	1.80	2.939	21.98	1319	1.899
1.31	1.328	9.933	595.9	0.8581	1.81	2.979	22.29	1337	1.926
1.32	1.353	10.12	607.3	0.8746	1.82	3.021	22.60	1356	1.952
1.33	1.379	10.32	618.9	0.8913	1.83	3.062	22.91	1374	1.979
1.34	1.405	10.51	630.6	0.9081	1.84	3.104	23.22	1393	2.006
1.35	1.431	10.71	642.4	0.9252	1.85	3.147	23.54	1412	2.034
1.36	1.458	10.91	654.4	0.9424	1.86	3.190	23.86	1431	2.061
1.37	1.485	11.11	666.5	0.9598	1.87	3.233	24.18	1451	2.089
1.38	1.512	11.31	678.7	0.9774	1.88	3.276	24.51	1470	2.117
1.39	1.540	11.52	691.1	0.9952	1.89	3.320	24.83	1490	2.146
1.40	1.568	11.73	703.6	1.013	1.90	3.364	25.16	1510	2.174
1.41	1.596	11.94	716.2	1.031	1.91	3.408	25.50	1530	2.203
1.42	1.624	12.15	729.0	1.050	1.92	3.453	25.83	1550	2.232
1.43	1.653	12.37	741.9	1.068	1.93	3.498	26.17	1570	2.261
1.44	1.682	12.58	754.9	1.087	1.94	3.544	26.51	1590	2.290
1.45	1.711	12.80	768.1	1.106	1.95	3.589	26.85	1611	2.320
1.46	1.741	13.03	781.4	1.125	1.96	3.636	27.20	1632	2.350
1.47	1.771	13.25	794.9	1.145	1.97	3.682	27.55	1653	2.380
1.48	1.801	13.48	808.5	1.164	1.98	3.729	27.90	1674	2.410
1.49	1.832	13.70	822.2	1.184	1.99	3.776	28.25	1695	2.441
1.50	1.863	13.94	836.0	1.204	2.00	3.824	28.61	1716	2.471

8

8-2: 30° V-notch Weir Discharge Table *(Continued)*

Formulas: CFS = 0.6760H$^{2.5}$ GPS = CFS x 7.481
GPM = CFS x 448.8   MGD = CFS x 0.6463

Head Feet	CFS	GPS	GPM	MGD	Head Feet	CFS	GPS	GPM	MGD
2.01	3.872	28.97	1738	2.502	2.51	6.747	50.48	3028	4.361
2.02	3.920	29.33	1759	2.534	2.52	6.815	50.98	3058	4.404
2.03	3.969	29.69	1781	2.565	2.53	6.883	51.49	3089	4.448
2.04	4.018	30.06	1803	2.597	2.54	6.951	52.00	3119	4.492
2.05	4.068	30.43	1826	2.629	2.55	7.019	52.51	3150	4.537
2.06	4.117	30.80	1848	2.661	2.56	7.088	53.03	3181	4.581
2.07	4.167	31.18	1870	2.693	2.57	7.158	53.55	3212	4.626
2.08	4.218	31.55	1893	2.726	2.58	7.228	54.07	3244	4.671
2.09	4.269	31.94	1916	2.759	2.59	7.298	54.60	3275	4.717
2.10	4.320	32.32	1939	2.792	2.60	7.369	55.12	3307	4.762
2.11	4.372	32.70	1962	2.825	2.61	7.440	55.66	3339	4.808
2.12	4.424	33.09	1985	2.859	2.62	7.511	56.19	3371	4.854
2.13	4.476	33.49	2009	2.893	2.63	7.583	56.73	3403	4.901
2.14	4.529	33.88	2033	2.927	2.64	7.655	57.27	3436	4.948
2.15	4.582	34.28	2056	2.961	2.65	7.728	57.81	3468	4.995
2.16	4.635	34.68	2080	2.996	2.66	7.801	58.36	3501	5.042
2.17	4.689	35.08	2104	3.031	2.67	7.875	58.91	3534	5.089
2.18	4.743	35.49	2129	3.066	2.68	7.948	59.46	3567	5.137
2.19	4.798	35.89	2153	3.101	2.69	8.023	60.02	3601	5.185
2.20	4.853	36.30	2178	3.136	2.70	8.098	60.58	3634	5.233
2.21	4.908	36.72	2203	3.172	2.71	8.173	61.14	3668	5.282
2.22	4.964	37.14	2228	3.208	2.72	8.248	61.71	3702	5.331
2.23	5.020	37.56	2253	3.244	2.73	8.324	62.27	3736	5.380
2.24	5.077	37.98	2278	3.281	2.74	8.401	62.85	3770	5.429
2.25	5.133	38.40	2304	3.318	2.75	8.478	63.42	3805	5.479
2.26	5.191	38.83	2330	3.355	2.76	8.555	64.00	3839	5.529
2.27	5.248	39.26	2355	3.392	2.77	8.633	64.58	3874	5.579
2.28	5.306	39.70	2381	3.429	2.78	8.711	65.17	3909	5.630
2.29	5.365	40.13	2408	3.467	2.79	8.789	65.75	3945	5.681
2.30	5.423	40.57	2434	3.505	2.80	8.868	66.34	3980	5.732
2.31	5.482	41.01	2461	3.543	2.81	8.948	66.94	4016	5.783
2.32	5.542	41.46	2487	3.582	2.82	9.028	67.54	4052	5.834
2.33	5.602	41.91	2514	3.621	2.83	9.108	68.14	4088	5.886
2.34	5.662	42.36	2541	3.659	2.84	9.188	68.74	4124	5.938
2.35	5.723	42.81	2568	3.699	2.85	9.270	69.35	4160	5.991
2.36	5.784	43.27	2596	3.738	2.86	9.351	69.96	4197	6.044
2.37	5.845	43.73	2623	3.778	2.87	9.433	70.57	4234	6.097
2.38	5.907	44.19	2651	3.818	2.88	9.515	71.18	4271	6.150
2.39	5.970	44.66	2679	3.858	2.89	9.598	71.80	4308	6.203
2.40	6.032	45.13	2707	3.899	2.90	9.681	72.43	4345	6.257
2.41	6.095	45.60	2736	3.939	2.91	9.765	73.05	4383	6.311
2.42	6.159	46.07	2764	3.980	2.92	9.849	73.68	4420	6.366
2.43	6.222	46.55	2793	4.022	2.93	9.934	74.31	4458	6.420
2.44	6.287	47.03	2821	4.063	2.94	10.02	74.95	4496	6.475
2.45	6.351	47.51	2850	4.105	2.95	10.10	75.59	4535	6.530
2.46	6.416	48.00	2880	4.147	2.96	10.19	76.23	4573	6.586
2.47	6.482	48.49	2909	4.189	2.97	10.28	76.88	4612	6.642
2.48	6.548	48.98	2939	4.232	2.98	10.36	77.53	4651	6.698
2.49	6.614	49.48	2968	4.274	2.99	10.45	78.18	4690	6.754
2.50	6.680	49.98	2998	4.317	3.00	10.54	78.83	4729	6.811

8

8-3: 45° V-notch Weir Discharge Table

Formulas: $CFS = 1.035H^{2.5}$ $GPS = CFS \times 7.481$
$GPM = CFS \times 448.8$ $MGD = CFS \times 0.6463$

Head Feet	CFS	GPS	GPM	MGD	Head Feet	CFS	GPS	GPM	MGD
0.01	0.0000	0.0001	0.0046	0.0000	0.51	0.1922	1.438	86.28	0.1243
0.02	0.0001	0.0004	0.0263	0.0000	0.52	0.2018	1.510	90.57	0.1304
0.03	0.0002	0.0012	0.0724	0.0001	0.53	0.2117	1.583	94.99	0.1368
0.04	0.0003	0.0025	0.1486	0.0002	0.54	0.2218	1.659	99.54	0.1433
0.05	0.0006	0.0043	0.2597	0.0004	0.55	0.2322	1.737	104.2	0.1501
0.06	0.0009	0.0068	0.4096	0.0006	0.56	0.2429	1.817	109.0	0.1570
0.07	0.0013	0.0100	0.6022	0.0009	0.57	0.2539	1.899	113.9	0.1641
0.08	0.0019	0.0140	0.8408	0.0012	0.58	0.2652	1.984	119.0	0.1714
0.09	0.0025	0.0188	1.129	0.0016	0.59	0.2767	2.070	124.2	0.1789
0.10	0.0033	0.0245	1.469	0.0021	0.60	0.2886	2.159	129.5	0.1865
0.11	0.0042	0.0311	1.864	0.0027	0.61	0.3008	2.250	135.0	0.1944
0.12	0.0052	0.0386	2.317	0.0033	0.62	0.3133	2.344	140.6	0.2025
0.13	0.0063	0.0472	2.830	0.0041	0.63	0.3261	2.439	146.3	0.2107
0.14	0.0076	0.0568	3.407	0.0049	0.64	0.3391	2.537	152.2	0.2192
0.15	0.0090	0.0675	4.048	0.0058	0.65	0.3526	2.637	158.2	0.2279
0.16	0.0106	0.0793	4.757	0.0068	0.66	0.3663	2.740	164.4	0.2367
0.17	0.0123	0.0923	5.535	0.0080	0.67	0.3803	2.845	170.7	0.2458
0.18	0.0142	0.1064	6.385	0.0092	0.68	0.3947	2.952	177.1	0.2551
0.19	0.0163	0.1218	7.309	0.0105	0.69	0.4093	3.062	183.7	0.2645
0.20	0.0185	0.1385	8.309	0.0120	0.70	0.4243	3.174	190.4	0.2742
0.21	0.0209	0.1565	9.387	0.0135	0.71	0.4396	3.289	197.3	0.2841
0.22	0.0235	0.1758	10.55	0.0152	0.72	0.4553	3.406	204.3	0.2942
0.23	0.0263	0.1964	11.78	0.0170	0.73	0.4712	3.525	211.5	0.3046
0.24	0.0292	0.2185	13.11	0.0189	0.74	0.4876	3.647	218.8	0.3151
0.25	0.0323	0.2420	14.52	0.0209	0.75	0.5042	3.772	226.3	0.3259
0.26	0.0357	0.2669	16.01	0.0231	0.76	0.5212	3.899	233.9	0.3368
0.27	0.0392	0.2933	17.60	0.0253	0.77	0.5385	4.028	241.7	0.3480
0.28	0.0429	0.3212	19.27	0.0278	0.78	0.5561	4.160	249.6	0.3594
0.29	0.0469	0.3507	21.04	0.0303	0.79	0.5741	4.295	257.7	0.3711
0.30	0.0510	0.3817	22.90	0.0330	0.80	0.5925	4.432	265.9	0.3829
0.31	0.0554	0.4143	24.85	0.0358	0.81	0.6112	4.572	274.3	0.3950
0.32	0.0600	0.4485	26.91	0.0387	0.82	0.6302	4.714	282.8	0.4073
0.33	0.0647	0.4844	29.06	0.0418	0.83	0.6496	4.860	291.5	0.4198
0.34	0.0698	0.5219	31.31	0.0451	0.84	0.6693	5.007	300.4	0.4326
0.35	0.0750	0.5611	33.66	0.0485	0.85	0.6894	5.158	309.4	0.4456
0.36	0.0805	0.6021	36.12	0.0520	0.86	0.7099	5.311	318.6	0.4588
0.37	0.0862	0.6448	38.68	0.0557	0.87	0.7307	5.466	327.9	0.4723
0.38	0.0921	0.6892	41.35	0.0595	0.88	0.7519	5.625	337.4	0.4859
0.39	0.0983	0.7355	44.12	0.0635	0.89	0.7734	5.786	347.1	0.4999
0.40	0.1047	0.7835	47.00	0.0677	0.90	0.7953	5.950	356.9	0.5140
0.41	0.1114	0.8334	50.00	0.0720	0.91	0.8176	6.117	366.9	0.5284
0.42	0.1183	0.8852	53.10	0.0765	0.92	0.8403	6.286	377.1	0.5431
0.43	0.1255	0.9388	56.32	0.0811	0.93	0.8633	6.458	387.4	0.5579
0.44	0.1329	0.9943	59.65	0.0859	0.94	0.8867	6.633	397.9	0.5731
0.45	0.1406	1.052	63.10	0.0909	0.95	0.9104	6.811	408.6	0.5884
0.46	0.1485	1.111	66.66	0.0960	0.96	0.9346	6.992	419.4	0.6040
0.47	0.1567	1.173	70.35	0.1013	0.97	0.9591	7.175	430.4	0.6199
0.48	0.1652	1.236	74.15	0.1068	0.98	0.9840	7.361	441.6	0.6360
0.49	0.1740	1.301	78.07	0.1124	0.99	1.009	7.551	453.0	0.6523
0.50	0.1830	1.369	82.11	0.1182	1.00	1.035	7.743	464.5	0.6689

8-3: 45° V-notch Weir Discharge Table (Continued)

Formulas: $CFS = 1.035H^{2.5}$ $GPS = CFS \times 7.481$
$GPM = CFS \times 448.8$ $MGD = CFS \times 0.6463$

Head Feet	CFS	GPS	GPM	MGD	Head Feet	CFS	GPS	GPM	MGD
1.01	1.061	7.938	476.2	0.6858	1.51	2.900	21.69	1301	1.874
1.02	1.088	8.136	488.1	0.7029	1.52	2.948	22.06	1323	1.905
1.03	1.114	8.337	500.1	0.7202	1.53	2.997	22.42	1345	1.937
1.04	1.142	8.541	512.4	0.7378	1.54	3.046	22.79	1367	1.969
1.05	1.169	8.747	524.8	0.7557	1.55	3.096	23.16	1389	2.001
1.06	1.197	8.957	537.4	0.7738	1.56	3.146	23.53	1412	2.033
1.07	1.226	9.170	550.1	0.7922	1.57	3.197	23.91	1435	2.066
1.08	1.255	9.386	563.1	0.8108	1.58	3.248	24.30	1458	2.099
1.09	1.284	9.604	576.2	0.8297	1.59	3.299	24.68	1481	2.132
1.10	1.313	9.826	589.5	0.8489	1.60	3.352	25.07	1504	2.166
1.11	1.344	10.05	603.0	0.8683	1.61	3.404	25.47	1528	2.200
1.12	1.374	10.28	616.6	0.8880	1.62	3.457	25.86	1552	2.234
1.13	1.405	10.51	630.5	0.9080	1.63	3.511	26.26	1576	2.269
1.14	1.436	10.74	644.5	0.9282	1.64	3.565	26.67	1600	2.304
1.15	1.468	10.98	658.8	0.9487	1.65	3.620	27.08	1624	2.339
1.16	1.500	11.22	673.2	0.9694	1.66	3.675	27.49	1649	2.375
1.17	1.533	11.46	687.8	0.9905	1.67	3.730	27.91	1674	2.411
1.18	1.565	11.71	702.6	1.012	1.68	3.786	28.33	1699	2.447
1.19	1.599	11.96	717.6	1.033	1.69	3.843	28.75	1725	2.484
1.20	1.633	12.21	732.7	1.055	1.70	3.900	29.18	1750	2.521
1.21	1.667	12.47	748.1	1.077	1.71	3.958	29.61	1776	2.558
1.22	1.702	12.73	763.6	1.100	1.72	4.016	30.04	1802	2.595
1.23	1.737	12.99	779.4	1.122	1.73	4.074	30.48	1829	2.633
1.24	1.772	13.26	795.3	1.145	1.74	4.133	30.92	1855	2.671
1.25	1.808	13.53	811.5	1.169	1.75	4.193	31.37	1882	2.710
1.26	1.844	13.80	827.8	1.192	1.76	4.253	31.82	1909	2.749
1.27	1.881	14.07	844.3	1.216	1.77	4.314	32.27	1936	2.788
1.28	1.919	14.35	861.0	1.240	1.78	4.375	32.73	1964	2.828
1.29	1.956	14.63	877.9	1.264	1.79	4.437	33.19	1991	2.868
1.30	1.994	14.92	895.1	1.289	1.80	4.499	33.66	2019	2.908
1.31	2.033	15.21	912.4	1.314	1.81	4.562	34.13	2047	2.948
1.32	2.072	15.50	929.9	1.339	1.82	4.625	34.60	2076	2.989
1.33	2.111	15.80	947.6	1.365	1.83	4.689	35.08	2104	3.030
1.34	2.151	16.09	965.5	1.390	1.84	4.753	35.56	2133	3.072
1.35	2.192	16.40	983.6	1.416	1.85	4.818	36.04	2162	3.114
1.36	2.232	16.70	1002	1.443	1.86	4.883	36.53	2192	3.156
1.37	2.274	17.01	1020	1.470	1.87	4.949	37.03	2221	3.199
1.38	2.315	17.32	1039	1.496	1.88	5.016	37.52	2251	3.242
1.39	2.358	17.64	1058	1.524	1.89	5.083	38.02	2281	3.285
1.40	2.400	17.96	1077	1.551	1.90	5.150	38.53	2311	3.329
1.41	2.443	18.28	1097	1.579	1.91	5.218	39.04	2342	3.373
1.42	2.487	18.60	1116	1.607	1.92	5.287	39.55	2373	3.417
1.43	2.531	18.93	1136	1.636	1.93	5.356	40.07	2404	3.462
1.44	2.575	19.27	1156	1.664	1.94	5.426	40.59	2435	3.507
1.45	2.620	19.60	1176	1.694	1.95	5.496	41.11	2466	3.552
1.46	2.666	19.94	1196	1.723	1.96	5.566	41.64	2498	3.598
1.47	2.712	20.29	1217	1.753	1.97	5.638	42.18	2530	3.644
1.48	2.758	20.63	1238	1.782	1.98	5.710	42.71	2562	3.690
1.49	2.805	20.98	1259	1.813	1.99	5.782	43.25	2595	3.737
1.50	2.852	21.34	1280	1.843	2.00	5.855	43.80	2628	3.784

Formulas: CFS $=1.035H^{2.5}$ GPS = CFS x 7.481
           GPM = CFS x 448.8   MGD = CFS x 0.6463

8

Head Feet	CFS	GPS	GPM	MGD	Head Feet	CFS	GPS	GPM	MGD
2.01	5.928	44.35	2661	3.831	2.51	10.33	77.28	4636	6.677
2.02	6.002	44.90	2694	3.879	2.52	10.43	78.06	4683	6.743
2.03	6.077	45.46	2727	3.927	2.53	10.54	78.83	4729	6.810
2.04	6.152	46.02	2761	3.976	2.54	10.64	79.61	4776	6.878
2.05	6.228	46.59	2795	4.025	2.55	10.75	80.40	4823	6.946
2.06	6.304	47.16	2829	4.074	2.56	10.85	81.19	4871	7.014
2.07	6.381	47.73	2864	4.124	2.57	10.96	81.98	4918	7.083
2.08	6.458	48.31	2898	4.174	2.58	11.07	82.78	4966	7.152
2.09	6.536	48.90	2933	4.224	2.59	11.17	83.59	5015	7.221
2.10	6.614	49.48	2969	4.275	2.60	11.28	84.40	5063	7.291
2.11	6.693	50.07	3004	4.326	2.61	11.39	85.21	5112	7.362
2.12	6.773	50.67	3040	4.377	2.62	11.50	86.03	5161	7.432
2.13	6.853	51.27	3076	4.429	2.63	11.61	86.85	5211	7.503
2.14	6.934	51.87	3112	4.481	2.64	11.72	87.68	5260	7.575
2.15	7.015	52.48	3148	4.534	2.65	11.83	88.51	5310	7.647
2.16	7.097	53.09	3185	4.587	2.66	11.94	89.35	5360	7.719
2.17	7.179	53.71	3222	4.640	2.67	12.06	90.19	5411	7.792
2.18	7.262	54.33	3259	4.694	2.68	12.17	91.04	5462	7.865
2.19	7.346	54.96	3297	4.748	2.69	12.28	91.89	5513	7.939
2.20	7.430	55.58	3335	4.802	2.70	12.40	92.75	5564	8.013
2.21	7.515	56.22	3373	4.857	2.71	12.51	93.61	5616	8.087
2.22	7.600	56.86	3411	4.912	2.72	12.63	94.48	5668	8.162
2.23	7.686	57.50	3449	4.967	2.73	12.75	95.35	5720	8.237
2.24	7.772	58.15	3488	5.023	2.74	12.86	96.22	5773	8.313
2.25	7.860	58.80	3527	5.080	2.75	12.98	97.10	5825	8.389
2.26	7.947	59.45	3567	5.136	2.76	13.10	97.99	5878	8.465
2.27	8.035	60.11	3606	5.193	2.77	13.22	98.88	5932	8.542
2.28	8.124	60.78	3646	5.251	2.78	13.34	99.77	5986	8.620
2.29	8.214	61.45	3686	5.308	2.79	13.46	100.7	6040	8.697
2.30	8.303	62.12	3727	5.367	2.80	13.58	101.6	6094	8.775
2.31	8.394	62.80	3767	5.425	2.81	13.70	102.5	6148	8.854
2.32	8.485	63.48	3808	5.484	2.82	13.82	103.4	6203	8.933
2.33	8.577	64.16	3849	5.543	2.83	13.94	104.3	6258	9.012
2.34	8.669	64.85	3891	5.603	2.84	14.07	105.2	6314	9.092
2.35	8.762	65.55	3932	5.663	2.85	14.19	106.2	6370	9.172
2.36	8.856	66.25	3974	5.723	2.86	14.32	107.1	6426	9.253
2.37	8.950	66.95	4017	5.784	2.87	14.44	108.0	6482	9.334
2.38	9.044	67.66	4059	5.845	2.88	14.57	109.0	6538	9.416
2.39	9.140	68.37	4102	5.907	2.89	14.70	109.9	6595	9.498
2.40	9.236	69.09	4145	5.969	2.90	14.82	110.9	6653	9.580
2.41	9.332	69.81	4188	6.031	2.91	14.95	111.8	6710	9.663
2.42	9.429	70.54	4232	6.094	2.92	15.08	112.8	6768	9.746
2.43	9.527	71.27	4276	6.157	2.93	15.21	113.8	6826	9.830
2.44	9.625	72.01	4320	6.221	2.94	15.34	114.8	6884	9.914
2.45	9.724	72.75	4364	6.285	2.95	15.47	115.7	6943	9.998
2.46	9.824	73.49	4409	6.349	2.96	15.60	116.7	7002	10.08
2.47	9.924	74.24	4454	6.414	2.97	15.73	117.7	7061	10.17
2.48	10.03	74.99	4499	6.479	2.98	15.87	118.7	7121	10.25
2.49	10.13	75.75	4545	6.544	2.99	16.00	119.7	7181	10.34
2.50	10.23	76.52	4590	6.610	3.00	16.13	120.7	7241	10.43

8-4: 60° V-notch Weir Discharge Table

Formulas: $CFS = 1.443H^{2.5}$ $\quad GPS = CFS \times 7.481$
$\qquad\quad GPM = CFS \times 448.8$ $\quad MGD = CFS \times 0.6463$

Head Feet	CFS	GPS	GPM	MGD	Head Feet	CFS	GPS	GPM	MGD
0.01	0.0000	0.0001	0.0065	0.0000	0.51	0.2615	1.956	117.4	0.1690
0.02	0.0001	0.0006	0.0362	0.0001	0.51	0.2745	2.054	123.2	0.1774
0.03	0.0002	0.0017	0.0993	0.0001	0.52	0.2879	2.154	129.2	0.1861
0.04	0.0005	0.0034	0.2034	0.0003	0.53	0.3017	2.257	135.4	0.1950
0.05	0.0008	0.0059	0.3548	0.0005	0.54	0.3158	2.363	141.7	0.2041
0.06	0.0012	0.0093	0.5593	0.0008	0.55	0.3304	2.472	148.3	0.2135
0.07	0.0018	0.0137	0.8217	0.0012	0.56	0.3453	2.583	155.0	0.2232
0.08	0.0026	0.0191	1.147	0.0017	0.57	0.3607	2.698	161.9	0.2331
0.09	0.0034	0.0257	1.539	0.0022	0.58	0.3764	2.816	168.9	0.2433
0.10	0.0045	0.0334	2.002	0.0029	0.59	0.3926	2.937	176.2	0.2537
0.11	0.0057	0.0423	2.540	0.0037	0.60	0.4091	3.061	183.6	0.2644
0.12	0.0070	0.0526	3.157	0.0045	0.61	0.4261	3.188	191.2	0.2754
0.13	0.0086	0.0643	3.856	0.0056	0.62	0.4435	3.318	199.0	0.2866
0.14	0.0103	0.0773	4.640	0.0067	0.63	0.4613	3.451	207.0	0.2981
0.15	0.0123	0.0919	5.513	0.0079	0.64	0.4795	3.587	215.2	0.3099
0.16	0.0144	0.1080	6.477	0.0093	0.65	0.4982	3.727	223.6	0.3220
0.17	0.0168	0.1256	7.537	0.0109	0.66	0.5173	3.870	232.1	0.3343
0.18	0.0194	0.1449	8.694	0.0125	0.67	0.5368	4.016	240.9	0.3469
0.19	0.0222	0.1659	9.951	0.0143	0.68	0.5567	4.165	249.9	0.3598
0.20	0.0252	0.1886	11.31	0.0163	0.69	0.5771	4.317	259.0	0.3730
0.21	0.0285	0.2130	12.78	0.0184	0.70	0.5979	4.473	268.4	0.3864
0.22	0.0320	0.2393	14.35	0.0207	0.71	0.6192	4.632	277.9	0.4002
0.23	0.0357	0.2674	16.04	0.0231	0.72	0.6409	4.795	287.7	0.4142
0.24	0.0398	0.2974	17.84	0.0257	0.73	0.6631	4.961	297.6	0.4286
0.25	0.0440	0.3293	19.76	0.0284	0.74	0.6857	5.130	307.8	0.4432
0.26	0.0486	0.3632	21.79	0.0314	0.75	0.7088	5.303	318.1	0.4581
0.27	0.0534	0.3991	23.95	0.0345	0.76	0.7324	5.479	328.7	0.4733
0.28	0.0584	0.4371	26.22	0.0378	0.77	0.7564	5.658	339.5	0.4888
0.29	0.0638	0.4772	28.63	0.0412	0.78	0.7808	5.841	350.4	0.5047
0.30	0.0694	0.5194	31.16	0.0449	0.79	0.8058	6.028	361.6	0.5208
0.31	0.0754	0.5637	33.82	0.0487	0.80	0.8312	6.218	373.0	0.5372
0.32	0.0816	0.6103	36.61	0.0527	0.81	0.8571	6.412	384.7	0.5539
0.33	0.0881	0.6591	39.54	0.0569	0.82	0.8834	6.609	396.5	0.5710
0.34	0.0949	0.7101	42.60	0.0613	0.83	0.9103	6.810	408.5	0.5883
0.35	0.1021	0.7635	45.80	0.0660	0.84	0.9376	7.014	420.8	0.6060
0.36	0.1095	0.8192	49.14	0.0708	0.85	0.9654	7.223	433.3	0.6240
0.37	0.1173	0.8772	52.63	0.0758	0.86	0.9938	7.434	446.0	0.6423
0.38	0.1253	0.9377	56.25	0.0810	0.87	1.023	7.650	458.9	0.6609
0.39	0.1338	1.001	60.03	0.0864	0.88	1.052	7.869	472.1	0.6798
0.40	0.1425	1.066	63.95	0.0921	0.89	1.082	8.092	485.4	0.6991
0.41	0.1516	1.134	68.02	0.0980	0.90	1.112	8.318	499.0	0.7186
0.42	0.1610	1.204	72.24	0.1040	0.91	1.143	8.549	512.9	0.7385
0.43	0.1707	1.277	76.62	0.1103	0.92	1.174	8.783	526.9	0.7588
0.44	0.1808	1.353	81.15	0.1169	0.93	1.206	9.021	541.2	0.7793
0.45	0.1913	1.431	85.84	0.1236	0.94	1.238	9.263	555.7	0.8002
0.46	0.2021	1.512	90.69	0.1306	0.95	1.271	9.508	570.4	0.8214
0.47	0.2132	1.595	95.69	0.1378	0.96	1.304	9.758	585.4	0.8430
0.48	0.2247	1.681	100.9	0.1453	0.97	1.338	10.01	600.6	0.8649
0.49	0.2366	1.770	106.2	0.1529	0.98	1.373	10.27	616.0	0.8871
0.50	0.2489	1.862	111.7	0.1609	1.00	1.443	10.80	647.6	0.9326

8

Formulas: CFS = $1.443H^{2.5}$ GPS = CFS x 7.481
GPM = CFS x 448.8   MGD = CFS x 0.6463

Head Feet	CFS	GPS	GPM	MGD	Head Feet	CFS	GPS	GPM	MGD
1.01	1.479	11.07	663.9	0.9561	1.51	4.043	30.25	1815	2.613
1.02	1.516	11.34	680.5	0.9799	1.52	4.110	30.75	1845	2.656
1.03	1.554	11.62	697.3	1.004	1.53	4.178	31.26	1875	2.700
1.04	1.592	11.91	714.3	1.029	1.54	4.247	31.77	1906	2.745
1.05	1.630	12.20	731.6	1.054	1.55	4.316	32.29	1937	2.790
1.06	1.669	12.49	749.2	1.079	1.56	4.386	32.81	1968	2.835
1.07	1.709	12.78	767.0	1.104	1.57	4.457	33.34	2000	2.880
1.08	1.749	13.09	785.0	1.130	1.58	4.528	33.87	2032	2.926
1.09	1.790	13.39	803.3	1.157	1.59	4.600	34.41	2064	2.973
1.10	1.831	13.70	821.9	1.184	1.60	4.673	34.96	2097	3.020
1.11	1.873	14.01	840.7	1.211	1.61	4.746	35.51	2130	3.067
1.12	1.916	14.33	859.7	1.238	1.62	4.820	36.06	2163	3.115
1.13	1.959	14.65	879.1	1.266	1.63	4.895	36.62	2197	3.164
1.14	2.002	14.98	898.6	1.294	1.64	4.970	37.18	2231	3.212
1.15	2.046	15.31	918.5	1.323	1.65	5.046	37.75	2265	3.261
1.16	2.091	15.64	938.6	1.352	1.66	5.123	38.33	2299	3.311
1.17	2.137	15.98	958.9	1.381	1.67	5.201	38.91	2334	3.361
1.18	2.183	16.33	979.5	1.411	1.68	5.279	39.49	2369	3.412
1.19	2.229	16.68	1000	1.441	1.69	5.358	40.08	2405	3.463
1.20	2.276	17.03	1022	1.471	1.70	5.437	40.68	2440	3.514
1.21	2.324	17.39	1043	1.502	1.71	5.518	41.28	2476	3.566
1.22	2.372	17.75	1065	1.533	1.72	5.599	41.88	2513	3.618
1.23	2.421	18.11	1087	1.565	1.73	5.680	42.50	2549	3.671
1.24	2.471	18.48	1109	1.597	1.74	5.763	43.11	2586	3.725
1.25	2.521	18.86	1131	1.629	1.75	5.846	43.73	2624	3.778
1.26	2.572	19.24	1154	1.662	1.76	5.930	44.36	2661	3.832
1.27	2.623	19.62	1177	1.695	1.77	6.014	44.99	2699	3.887
1.28	2.675	20.01	1200	1.729	1.78	6.100	45.63	2738	3.942
1.29	2.727	20.40	1224	1.763	1.79	6.186	46.28	2776	3.998
1.30	2.781	20.80	1248	1.797	1.80	6.273	46.93	2815	4.054
1.31	2.834	21.20	1272	1.832	1.81	6.360	47.58	2854	4.111
1.32	2.889	21.61	1296	1.867	1.82	6.448	48.24	2894	4.168
1.33	2.944	22.02	1321	1.903	1.83	6.537	48.91	2934	4.225
1.34	2.999	22.44	1346	1.938	1.84	6.627	49.58	2974	4.283
1.35	3.056	22.86	1371	1.975	1.85	6.717	50.25	3015	4.341
1.36	3.113	23.28	1397	2.012	1.86	6.808	50.93	3056	4.400
1.37	3.170	23.72	1423	2.049	1.87	6.900	51.62	3097	4.460
1.38	3.228	24.15	1449	2.086	1.88	6.993	52.31	3138	4.520
1.39	3.287	24.59	1475	2.124	1.89	7.086	53.01	3180	4.580
1.40	3.346	25.03	1502	2.163	1.90	7.180	53.72	3223	4.641
1.41	3.407	25.48	1529	2.202	1.91	7.275	54.43	3265	4.702
1.42	3.467	25.94	1556	2.241	1.92	7.371	55.14	3308	4.764
1.43	3.529	26.40	1584	2.281	1.93	7.467	55.86	3351	4.826
1.44	3.591	26.86	1611	2.321	1.94	7.564	56.59	3395	4.889
1.45	3.653	27.33	1640	2.361	1.95	7.662	57.32	3439	4.952
1.46	3.717	27.80	1668	2.402	1.96	7.761	58.06	3483	5.016
1.47	3.781	28.28	1697	2.443	1.97	7.860	58.80	3528	5.080
1.48	3.845	28.77	1726	2.485	1.98	7.960	59.55	3573	5.145
1.49	3.910	29.25	1755	2.527	1.99	8.061	60.31	3618	5.210
1.50	3.976	29.75	1785	2.570	2.00	8.163	61.07	3663	5.276

Formulas: CFS $=1.443H^{2.5}$ GPS = CFS x 7.481
GPM = CFS x 448.8   MGD = CFS x 0.6463

Head Feet	CFS	GPS	GPM	MGD	Head Feet	CFS	GPS	GPM	MGD
2.01	8.265	61.83	3709	5.342	2.51	14.40	107.7	6464	9.309
2.02	8.368	62.60	3756	5.409	2.52	14.55	108.8	6529	9.402
2.03	8.472	63.38	3802	5.476	2.53	14.69	109.9	6594	9.495
2.04	8.577	64.17	3849	5.543	2.54	14.84	111.0	6659	9.589
2.05	8.683	64.95	3897	5.612	2.55	14.98	112.1	6725	9.684
2.06	8.789	65.75	3944	5.680	2.56	15.13	113.2	6791	9.779
2.07	8.896	66.55	3993	5.749	2.57	15.28	114.3	6857	9.875
2.08	9.004	67.36	4041	5.819	2.58	15.43	115.4	6924	9.971
2.09	9.112	68.17	4090	5.889	2.59	15.58	116.5	6991	10.07
2.10	9.222	68.99	4139	5.960	2.60	15.73	117.7	7059	10.17
2.11	9.332	69.81	4188	6.031	2.61	15.88	118.8	7127	10.26
2.12	9.443	70.64	4238	6.103	2.62	16.03	119.9	7196	10.36
2.13	9.555	71.48	4288	6.175	2.63	16.19	121.1	7265	10.46
2.14	9.667	72.32	4339	6.248	2.64	16.34	122.2	7334	10.56
2.15	9.781	73.17	4390	6.321	2.65	16.50	123.4	7403	10.66
2.16	9.895	74.02	4441	6.395	2.66	16.65	124.6	7473	10.76
2.17	10.01	74.88	4492	6.469	2.67	16.81	125.7	7544	10.86
2.18	10.13	75.75	4544	6.544	2.68	16.97	126.9	7615	10.97
2.19	10.24	76.62	4597	6.619	2.69	17.13	128.1	7686	11.07
2.20	10.36	77.50	4649	6.695	2.70	17.29	129.3	7758	11.17
2.21	10.48	78.38	4702	6.771	2.71	17.45	130.5	7830	11.28
2.22	10.60	79.27	4756	6.848	2.72	17.61	131.7	7902	11.38
2.23	10.72	80.17	4809	6.926	2.73	17.77	132.9	7975	11.48
2.24	10.84	81.07	4863	7.004	2.74	17.93	134.2	8048	11.59
2.25	10.96	81.98	4918	7.082	2.75	18.10	135.4	8122	11.70
2.26	11.08	82.89	4973	7.161	2.76	18.26	136.6	8196	11.80
2.27	11.20	83.81	5028	7.240	2.77	18.43	137.9	8270	11.91
2.28	11.33	84.74	5083	7.320	2.78	18.59	139.1	8345	12.02
2.29	11.45	85.67	5139	7.401	2.79	18.76	140.4	8420	12.13
2.30	11.58	86.61	5196	7.482	2.80	18.93	141.6	8496	12.23
2.31	11.70	87.55	5252	7.564	2.81	19.10	142.9	8572	12.34
2.32	11.83	88.50	5309	7.646	2.82	19.27	144.2	8649	12.45
2.33	11.96	89.46	5367	7.728	2.83	19.44	145.4	8725	12.57
2.34	12.09	90.42	5424	7.812	2.84	19.61	146.7	8803	12.68
2.35	12.22	91.39	5483	7.895	2.85	19.79	148.0	8880	12.79
2.36	12.35	92.36	5541	7.980	2.86	19.96	149.3	8958	12.90
2.37	12.48	93.35	5600	8.064	2.87	20.14	150.6	9037	13.01
2.38	12.61	94.33	5659	8.150	2.88	20.31	152.0	9116	13.13
2.39	12.74	95.33	5719	8.236	2.89	20.49	153.3	9195	13.24
2.40	12.88	96.33	5779	8.322	2.90	20.67	154.6	9275	13.36
2.41	13.01	97.33	5839	8.409	2.91	20.84	155.9	9355	13.47
2.42	13.15	98.35	5900	8.496	2.92	21.02	157.3	9436	13.59
2.43	13.28	99.37	5961	8.585	2.93	21.20	158.6	9517	13.70
2.44	13.42	100.4	6023	8.673	2.94	21.39	160.0	9598	13.82
2.45	13.56	101.4	6085	8.762	2.95	21.57	161.4	9680	13.94
2.46	13.70	102.5	6147	8.852	2.96	21.75	162.7	9762	14.06
2.47	13.84	103.5	6210	8.942	2.97	21.94	164.1	9845	14.18
2.48	13.98	104.6	6273	9.033	2.98	22.12	165.5	9928	14.30
2.49	14.12	105.6	6336	9.124	2.99	22.31	166.9	10010	14.42
2.50	14.26	106.7	6400	9.216	3.00	22.49	168.3	10100	14.54

Formulas: $CFS = 2.500H^{2.5}$ $GPS = CFS \times 7.481$
$GPM = CFS \times 448.8$ $MGD = CFS \times 0.6463$

Head Feet	CFS	GPS	GPM	MGD	Head Feet	CFS	GPS	GPM	MGD
0.01	0.0000	0.0002	0.0112	0.0000	0.51	0.4644	3.474	208.4	0.3001
0.02	0.0001	0.0011	0.0635	0.0001	0.52	0.4875	3.647	218.8	0.3151
0.03	0.0004	0.0029	0.1749	0.0003	0.53	0.5112	3.825	229.4	0.3304
0.04	0.0008	0.0060	0.3590	0.0005	0.54	0.5357	4.008	240.4	0.3462
0.05	0.0014	0.0105	0.6272	0.0009	0.55	0.5609	4.196	251.7	0.3625
0.06	0.0022	0.0165	0.9894	0.0014	0.56	0.5867	4.389	263.3	0.3792
0.07	0.0032	0.0242	1.455	0.0021	0.57	0.6132	4.588	275.2	0.3963
0.08	0.0045	0.0339	2.031	0.0029	0.58	0.6405	4.791	287.5	0.4139
0.09	0.0061	0.0454	2.726	0.0039	0.59	0.6685	5.001	300.0	0.4320
0.10	0.0079	0.0591	3.548	0.0051	0.60	0.6971	5.215	312.9	0.4506
0.11	0.0100	0.0751	4.503	0.0065	0.61	0.7265	5.435	326.1	0.4696
0.12	0.0125	0.0933	5.597	0.0081	0.62	0.7567	5.661	339.6	0.4891
0.13	0.0152	0.1140	6.837	0.0098	0.63	0.7876	5.892	353.5	0.5090
0.14	0.0183	0.1372	8.228	0.0118	0.64	0.8192	6.128	367.7	0.5294
0.15	0.0218	0.1630	9.777	0.0141	0.65	0.8516	6.371	382.2	0.5504
0.16	0.0256	0.1915	11.49	0.0165	0.66	0.8847	6.618	397.1	0.5718
0.17	0.0298	0.2229	13.37	0.0193	0.67	0.9186	6.872	412.3	0.5937
0.18	0.0344	0.2571	15.42	0.0222	0.68	0.9533	7.131	427.8	0.6161
0.19	0.0393	0.2943	17.66	0.0254	0.69	0.9887	7.396	443.7	0.6390
0.20	0.0447	0.3346	20.07	0.0289	0.70	1.025	7.667	460.0	0.6624
0.21	0.0505	0.3780	22.67	0.0327	0.71	1.062	7.944	476.6	0.6863
0.22	0.0568	0.4246	25.47	0.0367	0.72	1.100	8.227	493.5	0.7107
0.23	0.0634	0.4745	28.47	0.0410	0.73	1.138	8.515	510.9	0.7357
0.24	0.0705	0.5277	31.66	0.0456	0.74	1.178	8.810	528.5	0.7611
0.25	0.0781	0.5845	35.06	0.0505	0.75	1.218	9.111	546.6	0.7871
0.26	0.0862	0.6447	38.67	0.0557	0.76	1.259	9.417	565.0	0.8136
0.27	0.0947	0.7084	42.50	0.0612	0.77	1.301	9.730	583.7	0.8406
0.28	0.1037	0.7759	46.55	0.0670	0.78	1.343	10.05	602.9	0.8682
0.29	0.1132	0.8470	50.81	0.0732	0.79	1.387	10.37	622.4	0.8963
0.30	0.1232	0.9219	55.31	0.0796	0.80	1.431	10.71	642.3	0.9249
0.31	0.1338	1.001	60.03	0.0865	0.81	1.476	11.04	662.5	0.9541
0.32	0.1448	1.083	64.99	0.0936	0.82	1.522	11.39	683.2	0.9838
0.33	0.1564	1.170	70.19	0.1011	0.83	1.569	11.74	704.2	1.014
0.34	0.1685	1.261	75.63	0.1089	0.84	1.617	12.09	725.6	1.045
0.35	0.1812	1.355	81.31	0.1171	0.85	1.665	12.46	747.4	1.076
0.36	0.1944	1.454	87.25	0.1256	0.86	1.715	12.83	769.6	1.108
0.37	0.2082	1.557	93.43	0.1345	0.87	1.765	13.20	792.1	1.141
0.38	0.2225	1.665	99.87	0.1438	0.88	1.816	13.59	815.1	1.174
0.39	0.2375	1.776	106.6	0.1535	0.89	1.868	13.98	838.4	1.207
0.40	0.2530	1.893	113.5	0.1635	0.90	1.921	14.37	862.2	1.242
0.41	0.2691	2.013	120.8	0.1739	0.91	1.975	14.77	886.3	1.276
0.42	0.2858	2.138	128.3	0.1847	0.92	2.030	15.18	910.9	1.312
0.43	0.3031	2.268	136.0	0.1959	0.93	2.085	15.60	935.8	1.348
0.44	0.3210	2.402	144.1	0.2075	0.94	2.142	16.02	961.2	1.384
0.45	0.3396	2.541	152.4	0.2195	0.95	2.199	16.45	987.0	1.421
0.46	0.3588	2.684	161.0	0.2319	0.96	2.257	16.89	1013	1.459
0.47	0.3786	2.832	169.9	0.2447	0.97	2.317	17.33	1040	1.497
0.48	0.3991	2.985	179.1	0.2579	0.98	2.377	17.78	1067	1.536
0.49	0.4202	3.143	188.6	0.2716	0.99	2.438	18.24	1094	1.576
0.50	0.4419	3.306	198.3	0.2856	1.00	2.500	18.70	1122	1.616

8-5: 90° V-notch Weir Discharge Table *(Continued)*

Formulas: $CFS = 2.500H^{2.5}$ $GPS = CFS \times 7.481$
$GPM = CFS \times 448.8$ $MGD = CFS \times 0.6463$

Head Feet	CFS	GPS	GPM	MGD	Head Feet	CFS	GPS	GPM	MGD
1.01	2.563	19.17	1150	1.656	1.51	7.005	52.40	3144	4.527
1.02	2.627	19.65	1179	1.698	1.52	7.121	53.27	3196	4.602
1.03	2.692	20.14	1208	1.740	1.53	7.239	54.15	3249	4.678
1.04	2.758	20.63	1238	1.782	1.54	7.358	55.04	3302	4.755
1.05	2.824	21.13	1268	1.825	1.55	7.478	55.94	3356	4.833
1.06	2.892	21.64	1298	1.869	1.56	7.599	56.85	3410	4.911
1.07	2.961	22.15	1329	1.914	1.57	7.721	57.76	3465	4.990
1.08	3.030	22.67	1360	1.959	1.58	7.845	58.69	3521	5.070
1.09	3.101	23.20	1392	2.004	1.59	7.970	59.62	3577	5.151
1.10	3.173	23.73	1424	2.050	1.60	8.095	60.56	3633	5.232
1.11	3.245	24.28	1456	2.097	1.61	8.223	61.51	3690	5.314
1.12	3.319	24.83	1489	2.145	1.62	8.351	62.47	3748	5.397
1.13	3.393	25.39	1523	2.193	1.63	8.480	63.44	3806	5.481
1.14	3.469	25.95	1557	2.242	1.64	8.611	64.42	3865	5.565
1.15	3.546	26.52	1591	2.291	1.65	8.743	65.40	3924	5.650
1.16	3.623	27.10	1626	2.342	1.66	8.876	66.40	3983	5.736
1.17	3.702	27.69	1661	2.392	1.67	9.010	67.40	4044	5.823
1.18	3.781	28.29	1697	2.444	1.68	9.146	68.42	4105	5.911
1.19	3.862	28.89	1733	2.496	1.69	9.282	69.44	4166	5.999
1.20	3.944	29.50	1770	2.549	1.70	9.420	70.47	4228	6.088
1.21	4.026	30.12	1807	2.602	1.71	9.559	71.51	4290	6.178
1.22	4.110	30.75	1845	2.656	1.72	9.700	72.56	4353	6.269
1.23	4.195	31.38	1883	2.711	1.73	9.841	73.62	4417	6.360
1.24	4.280	32.02	1921	2.766	1.74	9.984	74.69	4481	6.453
1.25	4.367	32.67	1960	2.823	1.75	10.13	75.77	4546	6.546
1.26	4.455	33.33	1999	2.879	1.76	10.27	76.86	4611	6.640
1.27	4.544	33.99	2039	2.937	1.77	10.42	77.95	4677	6.735
1.28	4.634	34.67	2080	2.995	1.78	10.57	79.06	4743	6.830
1.29	4.725	35.35	2121	3.054	1.79	10.72	80.17	4810	6.926
1.30	4.817	36.04	2162	3.113	1.80	10.87	81.30	4877	7.024
1.31	4.910	36.73	2204	3.174	1.81	11.02	82.43	4945	7.121
1.32	5.005	37.44	2246	3.235	1.82	11.17	83.58	5014	7.220
1.33	5.100	38.15	2289	3.296	1.83	11.33	84.73	5083	7.320
1.34	5.196	38.87	2332	3.358	1.84	11.48	85.89	5153	7.420
1.35	5.294	39.60	2376	3.421	1.85	11.64	87.06	5223	7.521
1.36	5.392	40.34	2420	3.485	1.86	11.80	88.24	5294	7.624
1.37	5.492	41.09	2465	3.550	1.87	11.95	89.43	5365	7.726
1.38	5.593	41.84	2510	3.615	1.88	12.12	90.63	5437	7.830
1.39	5.695	42.60	2556	3.681	1.89	12.28	91.84	5510	7.935
1.40	5.798	43.37	2602	3.747	1.90	12.44	93.06	5583	8.040
1.41	5.902	44.15	2649	3.814	1.91	12.60	94.29	5657	8.146
1.42	6.007	44.94	2696	3.882	1.92	12.77	95.53	5731	8.253
1.43	6.113	45.73	2744	3.951	1.93	12.94	96.78	5806	8.361
1.44	6.221	46.54	2792	4.021	1.94	13.11	98.04	5882	8.470
1.45	6.329	47.35	2841	4.091	1.95	13.27	99.31	5958	8.579
1.46	6.439	48.17	2890	4.162	1.96	13.45	100.6	6034	8.690
1.47	6.550	49.00	2940	4.233	1.97	13.62	101.9	6112	8.801
1.48	6.662	49.84	2990	4.306	1.98	13.79	103.2	6190	8.913
1.49	6.775	50.68	3041	4.379	1.99	13.97	104.5	6268	9.026
1.50	6.889	51.54	3092	4.452	2.00	14.14	105.8	6347	9.140

Formulas: CFS $= 2.500H^{2.5}$ GPS = CFS x 7.481
GPM = CFS x 448.8   MGD = CFS x 0.6463

Head Feet	CFS	GPS	GPM	MGD	Head Feet	CFS	GPS	GPM	MGD
2.01	14.32	107.1	6427	9.255	2.51	24.95	186.7	11200	16.13
2.02	14.50	108.5	6507	9.370	2.52	25.20	188.5	11310	16.29
2.03	14.68	109.8	6588	9.487	2.53	25.45	190.4	11420	16.45
2.04	14.86	111.2	6669	9.604	2.54	25.71	192.3	11540	16.61
2.05	15.04	112.5	6751	9.722	2.55	25.96	194.2	11650	16.78
2.06	15.23	113.9	6834	9.841	2.56	26.21	196.1	11770	16.94
2.07	15.41	115.3	6917	9.961	2.57	26.47	198.0	11880	17.11
2.08	15.60	116.7	7001	10.08	2.58	26.73	200.0	12000	17.28
2.09	15.79	118.1	7085	10.20	2.59	26.99	201.9	12110	17.44
2.10	15.98	119.5	7170	10.33	2.60	27.25	203.9	12230	17.61
2.11	16.17	120.9	7256	10.45	2.61	27.51	205.8	12350	17.78
2.12	16.36	122.4	7342	10.57	2.62	27.78	207.8	12470	17.95
2.13	16.55	123.8	7429	10.70	2.63	28.04	209.8	12590	18.12
2.14	16.75	125.3	7517	10.82	2.64	28.31	211.8	12710	18.30
2.15	16.94	126.8	7605	10.95	2.65	28.58	213.8	12830	18.47
2.16	17.14	128.2	7694	11.08	2.66	28.85	215.8	12950	18.65
2.17	17.34	129.7	7783	11.21	2.67	29.12	217.9	13070	18.82
2.18	17.54	131.2	7873	11.34	2.68	29.40	219.9	13190	19.00
2.19	17.74	132.7	7963	11.47	2.69	29.67	222.0	13320	19.18
2.20	17.95	134.3	8055	11.60	2.70	29.95	224.0	13440	19.35
2.21	18.15	135.8	8147	11.73	2.71	30.22	226.1	13560	19.53
2.22	18.36	137.3	8239	11.86	2.72	30.50	228.2	13690	19.71
2.23	18.57	138.9	8332	12.00	2.73	30.79	230.3	13820	19.90
2.24	18.77	140.4	8426	12.13	2.74	31.07	232.4	13940	20.08
2.25	18.98	142.0	8520	12.27	2.75	31.35	234.5	14070	20.26
2.26	19.20	143.6	8615	12.41	2.76	31.64	236.7	14200	20.45
2.27	19.41	145.2	8711	12.54	2.77	31.93	238.8	14330	20.63
2.28	19.62	146.8	8807	12.68	2.78	32.21	241.0	14460	20.82
2.29	19.84	148.4	8904	12.82	2.79	32.51	243.2	14590	21.01
2.30	20.06	150.0	9001	12.96	2.80	32.80	245.4	14720	21.20
2.31	20.28	151.7	9100	13.10	2.81	33.09	247.6	14850	21.39
2.32	20.50	153.3	9198	13.25	2.82	33.39	249.8	14980	21.58
2.33	20.72	155.0	9298	13.39	2.83	33.68	252.0	15120	21.77
2.34	20.94	156.7	9398	13.53	2.84	33.98	254.2	15250	21.96
2.35	21.16	158.3	9499	13.68	2.85	34.28	256.5	15390	22.16
2.36	21.39	160.0	9600	13.82	2.86	34.58	258.7	15520	22.35
2.37	21.62	161.7	9702	13.97	2.87	34.89	261.0	15660	22.55
2.38	21.85	163.4	9805	14.12	2.88	35.19	263.3	15790	22.74
2.39	22.08	165.2	9908	14.27	2.89	35.50	265.5	15930	22.94
2.40	22.31	166.9	10010	14.42	2.90	35.80	267.9	16070	23.14
2.41	22.54	168.6	10120	14.57	2.91	36.11	270.2	16210	23.34
2.42	22.78	170.4	10220	14.72	2.92	36.42	272.5	16350	23.54
2.43	23.01	172.2	10330	14.87	2.93	36.74	274.8	16490	23.74
2.44	23.25	173.9	10430	15.03	2.94	37.05	277.2	16630	23.95
2.45	23.49	175.7	10540	15.18	2.95	37.37	279.5	16770	24.15
2.46	23.73	177.5	10650	15.34	2.96	37.69	281.9	16910	24.36
2.47	23.97	179.3	10760	15.49	2.97	38.00	284.3	17060	24.56
2.48	24.21	181.1	10870	15.65	2.98	38.32	286.7	17200	24.77
2.49	24.46	183.0	10980	15.81	2.99	38.65	289.1	17340	24.98
2.50	24.71	184.8	11090	15.97	3.00	38.97	291.5	17490	25.19

8

8-6: 120° V-notch Weir Discharge Table

Formulas: CFS = 4.330H$^{2.5}$ GPS = CFS x 7.481
             GPM = CFS x 448.8   MGD = CFS x 0.6463

Head Feet	CFS	GPS	GPM	MGD	Head Feet	CFS	GPS	GPM	MGD
0.01	0.0000	0.0003	0.0194	0.0000	0.51	0.8043	6.017	361.0	0.5198
0.02	0.0002	0.0018	0.1099	0.0002	0.52	0.8443	6.316	378.9	0.5457
0.03	0.0007	0.0050	0.3029	0.0004	0.53	0.8855	6.624	397.4	0.5723
0.04	0.0014	0.0104	0.6219	0.0009	0.54	0.9278	6.941	416.4	0.5997
0.05	0.0024	0.0181	1.086	0.0016	0.55	0.9714	7.267	436.0	0.6278
0.06	0.0038	0.0286	1.714	0.0025	0.56	1.016	7.602	456.0	0.6567
0.07	0.0056	0.0420	2.519	0.0036	0.57	1.062	7.946	476.7	0.6865
0.08	0.0078	0.0586	3.518	0.0051	0.58	1.109	8.299	497.9	0.7170
0.09	0.0105	0.0787	4.722	0.0068	0.59	1.158	8.661	519.6	0.7483
0.10	0.0137	0.1024	6.145	0.0088	0.60	1.207	9.033	541.9	0.7804
0.11	0.0174	0.1300	7.799	0.0112	0.61	1.258	9.414	564.8	0.8133
0.12	0.0216	0.1616	9.694	0.0140	0.62	1.311	9.805	588.2	0.8470
0.13	0.0264	0.1974	11.84	0.0171	0.63	1.364	10.21	612.2	0.8816
0.14	0.0318	0.2376	14.25	0.0205	0.64	1.419	10.61	636.8	0.9170
0.15	0.0377	0.2823	16.93	0.0244	0.65	1.475	11.03	661.9	0.9532
0.16	0.0443	0.3317	19.90	0.0287	0.66	1.532	11.46	687.7	0.9903
0.17	0.0516	0.3860	23.16	0.0333	0.67	1.591	11.90	714.0	1.028
0.18	0.0595	0.4453	26.71	0.0385	0.68	1.651	12.35	741.0	1.067
0.19	0.0681	0.5097	30.58	0.0440	0.69	1.712	12.81	768.5	1.107
0.20	0.0775	0.5795	34.76	0.0501	0.70	1.775	13.28	796.7	1.147
0.21	0.0875	0.6546	39.27	0.0566	0.71	1.839	13.76	825.4	1.189
0.22	0.0983	0.7354	44.12	0.0635	0.72	1.905	14.25	854.8	1.231
0.23	0.1099	0.8218	49.30	0.0710	0.73	1.971	14.75	884.8	1.274
0.24	0.1222	0.9141	54.84	0.0790	0.74	2.040	15.26	915.4	1.318
0.25	0.1353	1.012	60.73	0.0875	0.75	2.109	15.78	946.7	1.363
0.26	0.1493	1.117	66.98	0.0965	0.76	2.180	16.31	978.5	1.409
0.27	0.1640	1.227	73.61	0.1060	0.77	2.253	16.85	1011	1.456
0.28	0.1796	1.344	80.62	0.1161	0.78	2.327	17.41	1044	1.504
0.29	0.1961	1.467	88.01	0.1267	0.79	2.402	17.97	1078	1.552
0.30	0.2134	1.597	95.80	0.1380	0.80	2.479	18.54	1112	1.602
0.31	0.2317	1.733	104.0	0.1497	0.81	2.557	19.13	1148	1.652
0.32	0.2508	1.876	112.6	0.1621	0.82	2.636	19.72	1183	1.704
0.33	0.2709	2.026	121.6	0.1751	0.83	2.718	20.33	1220	1.756
0.34	0.2919	2.183	131.0	0.1886	0.84	2.800	20.95	1257	1.810
0.35	0.3138	2.348	140.8	0.2028	0.85	2.884	21.58	1294	1.864
0.36	0.3367	2.519	151.1	0.2176	0.86	2.970	22.22	1333	1.919
0.37	0.3606	2.697	161.8	0.2330	0.87	3.057	22.87	1372	1.976
0.38	0.3854	2.883	173.0	0.2491	0.88	3.146	23.53	1412	2.033
0.39	0.4113	3.077	184.6	0.2658	0.89	3.236	24.21	1452	2.091
0.40	0.4382	3.278	196.6	0.2832	0.90	3.327	24.89	1493	2.150
0.41	0.4661	3.487	209.2	0.3012	0.91	3.421	25.59	1535	2.211
0.42	0.4950	3.703	222.2	0.3199	0.92	3.515	26.30	1578	2.272
0.43	0.5250	3.928	235.6	0.3393	0.93	3.612	27.02	1621	2.334
0.44	0.5561	4.160	249.6	0.3594	0.94	3.709	27.75	1665	2.397
0.45	0.5882	4.400	264.0	0.3801	0.95	3.809	28.49	1709	2.462
0.46	0.6214	4.649	278.9	0.4016	0.96	3.910	29.25	1755	2.527
0.47	0.6557	4.906	294.3	0.4238	0.97	4.013	30.02	1801	2.593
0.48	0.6912	5.171	310.2	0.4467	0.98	4.117	30.80	1848	2.661
0.49	0.7277	5.444	326.6	0.4703	0.99	4.223	31.59	1895	2.729
0.50	0.7654	5.726	343.5	0.4947	1.00	4.330	32.39	1943	2.798

8

Formulas: CFS = $4.330H^{2.5}$ GPS = CFS x 7.481
GPM = CFS x 448.8   MGD = CFS x 0.6463

Head Feet	CFS	GPS	GPM	MGD	Head Feet	CFS	GPS	GPM	MGD
1.01	4.439	33.21	1992	2.869	1.51	12.13	90.76	5445	7.841
1.02	4.550	34.04	2042	2.941	1.52	12.33	92.27	5535	7.971
1.03	4.662	34.88	2092	3.013	1.53	12.54	93.79	5627	8.103
1.04	4.776	35.73	2144	3.087	1.54	12.74	95.33	5719	8.236
1.05	4.892	36.59	2195	3.162	1.55	12.95	96.89	5813	8.370
1.06	5.009	37.47	2248	3.237	1.56	13.16	98.46	5907	8.506
1.07	5.128	38.36	2301	3.314	1.57	13.37	100.1	6002	8.643
1.08	5.249	39.27	2356	3.392	1.58	13.59	101.6	6098	8.781
1.09	5.371	40.18	2410	3.471	1.59	13.80	103.3	6195	8.921
1.10	5.495	41.11	2466	3.551	1.60	14.02	104.9	6293	9.062
1.11	5.621	42.05	2523	3.633	1.61	14.24	106.5	6392	9.204
1.12	5.748	43.00	2580	3.715	1.62	14.46	108.2	6491	9.348
1.13	5.877	43.97	2638	3.799	1.63	14.69	109.9	6592	9.493
1.14	6.008	44.95	2697	3.883	1.64	14.91	111.6	6693	9.639
1.15	6.141	45.94	2756	3.969	1.65	15.14	113.3	6796	9.787
1.16	6.275	46.95	2816	4.056	1.66	15.37	115.0	6899	9.936
1.17	6.411	47.96	2877	4.144	1.67	15.61	116.7	7004	10.09
1.18	6.549	49.00	2939	4.233	1.68	15.84	118.5	7109	10.24
1.19	6.689	50.04	3002	4.323	1.69	16.08	120.3	7215	10.39
1.20	6.830	51.10	3065	4.414	1.70	16.32	122.1	7323	10.54
1.21	6.974	52.17	3130	4.507	1.71	16.56	123.9	7431	10.70
1.22	7.118	53.25	3195	4.601	1.72	16.80	125.7	7540	10.86
1.23	7.265	54.35	3261	4.696	1.73	17.05	127.5	7650	11.02
1.24	7.414	55.46	3327	4.792	1.74	17.29	129.4	7761	11.18
1.25	7.564	56.59	3395	4.889	1.75	17.54	131.2	7873	11.34
1.26	7.716	57.73	3463	4.987	1.76	17.79	133.1	7986	11.50
1.27	7.870	58.88	3532	5.087	1.77	18.05	135.0	8100	11.66
1.28	8.026	60.04	3602	5.187	1.78	18.30	136.9	8215	11.83
1.29	8.184	61.22	3673	5.289	1.79	18.56	138.9	8331	12.00
1.30	8.343	62.42	3745	5.392	1.80	18.82	140.8	8447	12.16
1.31	8.505	63.62	3817	5.497	1.81	19.08	142.8	8565	12.33
1.32	8.668	64.85	3890	5.602	1.82	19.35	144.8	8684	12.51
1.33	8.833	66.08	3964	5.709	1.83	19.62	146.7	8804	12.68
1.34	9.000	67.33	4039	5.817	1.84	19.89	148.8	8925	12.85
1.35	9.169	68.59	4115	5.926	1.85	20.16	150.8	9046	13.03
1.36	9.340	69.87	4192	6.036	1.86	20.43	152.8	9169	13.20
1.37	9.512	71.16	4269	6.148	1.87	20.71	154.9	9293	13.38
1.38	9.687	72.47	4347	6.261	1.88	20.98	157.0	9417	13.56
1.39	9.863	73.79	4427	6.375	1.89	21.26	159.1	9543	13.74
1.40	10.04	75.12	4507	6.490	1.90	21.55	161.2	9670	13.93
1.41	10.22	76.47	4588	6.606	1.91	21.83	163.3	9798	14.11
1.42	10.40	77.83	4669	6.724	1.92	22.12	165.5	9926	14.29
1.43	10.59	79.21	4752	6.843	1.93	22.41	167.6	10050	14.48
1.44	10.77	80.60	4836	6.964	1.94	22.70	169.8	10190	14.67
1.45	10.96	82.01	4920	7.085	1.95	22.99	172.0	10320	14.86
1.46	11.15	83.43	5005	7.208	1.96	23.29	174.2	10460	15.05
1.47	11.34	84.87	5091	7.332	1.97	23.59	176.4	10590	15.24
1.48	11.54	86.32	5178	7.457	1.98	23.89	178.7	10720	15.44
1.49	11.73	87.78	5266	7.584	1.99	24.19	181.0	10860	15.63
1.50	11.93	89.26	5355	7.712	2.00	24.49	183.2	10990	15.83

8

8-6: 120° V-notch Weir Discharge Table *(Continued)*

Formulas: CFS = $4.330H^{2.5}$ GPS = CFS x 7.481
           GPM = CFS x 448.8   MGD = CFS x 0.6463

Head Feet	CFS	GPS	GPM	MGD	Head Feet	CFS	GPS	GPM	MGD
2.01	24.80	185.5	11130	16.03	2.51	43.22	323.3	19400	27.93
2.02	25.11	187.9	11270	16.23	2.52	43.65	326.5	19590	28.21
2.03	25.42	190.2	11410	16.43	2.53	44.08	329.8	19790	28.49
2.04	25.74	192.5	11550	16.63	2.54	44.52	333.1	19980	28.77
2.05	26.05	194.9	11690	16.84	2.55	44.96	336.4	20180	29.06
2.06	26.37	197.3	11840	17.04	2.56	45.40	339.7	20380	29.34
2.07	26.69	199.7	11980	17.25	2.57	45.85	343.0	20580	29.63
2.08	27.02	202.1	12130	17.46	2.58	46.30	346.3	20780	29.92
2.09	27.34	204.6	12270	17.67	2.59	46.75	349.7	20980	30.21
2.10	27.67	207.0	12420	17.88	2.60	47.20	353.1	21180	30.50
2.11	28.00	209.5	12570	18.10	2.61	47.65	356.5	21390	30.80
2.12	28.34	212.0	12720	18.31	2.62	48.11	359.9	21590	31.09
2.13	28.67	214.5	12870	18.53	2.63	48.57	363.4	21800	31.39
2.14	29.01	217.0	13020	18.75	2.64	49.03	366.8	22010	31.69
2.15	29.35	219.6	13170	18.97	2.65	49.50	370.3	22220	31.99
2.16	29.69	222.1	13330	19.19	2.66	49.97	373.8	22430	32.29
2.17	30.04	224.7	13480	19.41	2.67	50.44	377.3	22640	32.60
2.18	30.38	227.3	13640	19.64	2.68	50.91	380.9	22850	32.90
2.19	30.73	229.9	13790	19.86	2.69	51.39	384.4	23060	33.21
2.20	31.08	232.5	13950	20.09	2.70	51.87	388.0	23280	33.52
2.21	31.44	235.2	14110	20.32	2.71	52.35	391.6	23490	33.83
2.22	31.80	237.9	14270	20.55	2.72	52.83	395.2	23710	34.15
2.23	32.16	240.6	14430	20.78	2.73	53.32	398.9	23930	34.46
2.24	32.52	243.3	14590	21.02	2.74	53.81	402.6	24150	34.78
2.25	32.88	246.0	14760	21.25	2.75	54.30	406.2	24370	35.10
2.26	33.25	248.7	14920	21.49	2.76	54.80	409.9	24590	35.42
2.27	33.62	251.5	15090	21.73	2.77	55.30	413.7	24820	35.74
2.28	33.99	254.3	15250	21.97	2.78	55.80	417.4	25040	36.06
2.29	34.36	257.1	15420	22.21	2.79	56.30	421.2	25270	36.39
2.30	34.74	259.9	15590	22.45	2.80	56.80	425.0	25490	36.71
2.31	35.12	262.7	15760	22.70	2.81	57.31	428.8	25720	37.04
2.32	35.50	265.6	15930	22.94	2.82	57.82	432.6	25950	37.37
2.33	35.88	268.4	16100	23.19	2.83	58.34	436.4	26180	37.70
2.34	36.27	271.3	16280	23.44	2.84	58.86	440.3	26410	38.04
2.35	36.66	274.2	16450	23.69	2.85	59.37	444.2	26650	38.37
2.36	37.05	277.2	16630	23.94	2.86	59.90	448.1	26880	38.71
2.37	37.44	280.1	16800	24.20	2.87	60.42	452.0	27120	39.05
2.38	37.84	283.1	16980	24.45	2.88	60.95	456.0	27350	39.39
2.39	38.24	286.1	17160	24.71	2.89	61.48	459.9	27590	39.73
2.40	38.64	289.1	17340	24.97	2.90	62.01	463.9	27830	40.08
2.41	39.04	292.1	17520	25.23	2.91	62.55	467.9	28070	40.43
2.42	39.45	295.1	17700	25.50	2.92	63.09	472.0	28310	40.77
2.43	39.86	298.2	17890	25.76	2.93	63.63	476.0	28560	41.12
2.44	40.27	301.2	18070	26.03	2.94	64.17	480.1	28800	41.48
2.45	40.68	304.3	18260	26.29	2.95	64.72	484.2	29050	41.83
2.46	41.10	307.5	18440	26.56	2.96	65.27	488.3	29290	42.18
2.47	41.52	310.6	18630	26.83	2.97	65.82	492.4	29540	42.54
2.48	41.94	313.7	18820	27.11	2.98	66.38	496.6	29790	42.90
2.49	42.36	316.9	19010	27.38	2.99	66.94	500.8	30040	43.26
2.50	42.79	320.1	19200	27.65	3.00	67.50	505.0	30290	43.62

Chapter 9

This chapter contains discharge (flow rate vs head) tables for rectangular weirs with end contractions. Note that all of the tabular data is for free flow. If the flow is submerged, corrections will have to be made to determine the discharge, as discussed in Chapter 3.

Rectangular weir with end contractions discharge tables

Note also that in many cases, discharges are listed for heads which are above the maximum recommended operating head or below the minimum recommended operating head of the weir in question. Discharge for these heads outside the normal operating range are listed for reference only; it should not be implied that the primary device is intended to be used in these regions. Refer to Chapter 3 for minimum and maximum recommended heads.

Rectangular weirs with end contractions

9-1: 1 ft. Crest Length Rectangular Weir with End Contractions

9-2: 1¹/₂ ft. Crest Length Rectangular Weir with End Contractions

9-3: 2 ft. Crest Length Rectangular Weir with End Contractions

9-4: 2¹/₂ ft. Crest Length Rectangular Weir with End Contractions

9-5: 3 ft. Crest Length Rectangular Weir with End Contractions

9-6: 4 ft. Crest Length Rectangular Weir with End Contractions

9-7: 5 ft. Crest Length Rectangular Weir with End Contractions

9-8: 6 ft. Crest Length Rectangular Weir with End Contractions

9-9: 8 ft. Crest Length Rectangular Weir with End Contractions

9-10: 10 ft. Crest Length Rectangular Weir with End Contractions

Note: The discharges of the weirs are listed in four different units:

CFS—cubic feet per second	GPS—gallons per second
GPM—gallons per minute	MGD—million gallons per day.

The equation used to develop each table is listed on the table.

9-1: 1 ft. Rectangular Weir with End Contractions Discharge Table

Formulas: $CFS = 3.330(1.0-0.2H)H^{1.5}$ $GPS = CFS \times 7.481$

$GPM = CFS \times 448.8$ $MGD = CFS \times 0.6463$

Head Feet	CFS	GPS	GPM	MGD	Head Feet	CFS	GPS	GPM	MGD
0.01	0.0033	0.0249	1.492	0.0021	0.51	1.089	8.148	488.8	0.7039
0.02	0.0094	0.0702	4.210	0.0061	0.52	1.119	8.370	502.1	0.7231
0.03	0.0172	0.1287	7.719	0.0111	0.53	1.149	8.593	515.5	0.7424
0.04	0.0264	0.1977	11.86	0.0171	0.54	1.179	8.818	529.0	0.7618
0.05	0.0369	0.2757	16.54	0.0238	0.55	1.209	9.044	542.5	0.7813
0.06	0.0484	0.3617	21.70	0.0313	0.56	1.239	9.270	556.2	0.8009
0.07	0.0608	0.4549	27.29	0.0393	0.57	1.270	9.498	569.8	0.8206
0.08	0.0741	0.5547	33.28	0.0479	0.58	1.300	9.727	583.6	0.8404
0.09	0.0883	0.6605	39.63	0.0571	0.59	1.331	9.958	597.4	0.8603
0.10	0.1032	0.7720	46.32	0.0667	0.60	1.362	10.19	611.2	0.8802
0.11	0.1188	0.8889	53.32	0.0768	0.61	1.393	10.42	625.2	0.9003
0.12	0.1351	1.011	60.63	0.0873	0.62	1.424	10.65	639.1	0.9204
0.13	0.1520	1.137	68.23	0.0983	0.63	1.455	10.89	653.2	0.9406
0.14	0.1696	1.268	76.09	0.1096	0.64	1.487	11.12	667.2	0.9609
0.15	0.1877	1.404	84.22	0.1213	0.65	1.518	11.36	681.4	0.9812
0.16	0.2063	1.543	92.59	0.1333	0.66	1.550	11.59	695.6	1.002
0.17	0.2255	1.687	101.2	0.1457	0.67	1.582	11.83	709.8	1.022
0.18	0.2451	1.834	110.0	0.1584	0.68	1.613	12.07	724.1	1.043
0.19	0.2653	1.985	119.1	0.1715	0.69	1.645	12.31	738.4	1.063
0.20	0.2859	2.139	128.3	0.1848	0.70	1.677	12.55	752.7	1.084
0.21	0.3070	2.297	137.8	0.1984	0.71	1.709	12.79	767.1	1.105
0.22	0.3285	2.458	147.4	0.2123	0.72	1.741	13.03	781.6	1.126
0.23	0.3504	2.621	157.3	0.2265	0.73	1.774	13.27	796.0	1.146
0.24	0.3727	2.788	167.3	0.2409	0.74	1.806	13.51	810.6	1.167
0.25	0.3954	2.958	177.5	0.2556	0.75	1.838	13.75	825.1	1.188
0.26	0.4185	3.131	187.8	0.2705	0.76	1.871	14.00	839.7	1.209
0.27	0.4420	3.306	198.4	0.2856	0.77	1.903	14.24	854.3	1.230
0.28	0.4658	3.484	209.0	0.3010	0.78	1.936	14.48	868.9	1.251
0.29	0.4899	3.665	219.9	0.3166	0.79	1.969	14.73	883.6	1.272
0.30	0.5143	3.848	230.8	0.3324	0.80	2.002	14.97	898.3	1.294
0.31	0.5391	4.033	242.0	0.3484	0.81	2.034	15.22	913.0	1.315
0.32	0.5642	4.221	253.2	0.3647	0.82	2.067	15.46	927.7	1.336
0.33	0.5896	4.411	264.6	0.3811	0.83	2.100	15.71	942.5	1.357
0.34	0.6153	4.603	276.1	0.3977	0.84	2.133	15.96	957.3	1.379
0.35	0.6413	4.797	287.8	0.4144	0.85	2.166	16.20	972.1	1.400
0.36	0.6675	4.994	299.6	0.4314	0.86	2.199	16.45	986.9	1.421
0.37	0.6940	5.192	311.5	0.4485	0.87	2.232	16.70	1002	1.443
0.38	0.7208	5.392	323.5	0.4658	0.88	2.265	16.95	1017	1.464
0.39	0.7478	5.594	335.6	0.4833	0.89	2.298	17.19	1031	1.485
0.40	0.7750	5.798	347.8	0.5009	0.90	2.331	17.44	1046	1.507
0.41	0.8025	6.004	360.2	0.5187	0.91	2.365	17.69	1061	1.528
0.42	0.8303	6.211	372.6	0.5366	0.92	2.398	17.94	1076	1.550
0.43	0.8582	6.420	385.2	0.5547	0.93	2.431	18.19	1091	1.571
0.44	0.8864	6.631	397.8	0.5729	0.94	2.464	18.44	1106	1.593
0.45	0.9148	6.843	410.5	0.5912	0.95	2.498	18.68	1121	1.614
0.46	0.9433	7.057	423.4	0.6097	0.96	2.531	18.93	1136	1.636
0.47	0.9721	7.272	436.3	0.6283	0.97	2.564	19.18	1151	1.657
0.48	1.001	7.489	449.3	0.6470	0.98	2.597	19.43	1166	1.679
0.49	1.030	7.707	462.4	0.6659	0.99	2.631	19.68	1181	1.700
0.50	1.060	7.927	475.5	0.6848	1.00	2.664	19.93	1196	1.722

9

9-1: 1 ft. Rectangular Weir with End Contractions Discharge Table *(Continued)*

Formulas: $CFS = 3.330(1.0-0.2H)H^{1.5}$
$GPM = CFS \times 448.8$
$GPS = CFS \times 7.481$
$MGD = CFS \times 0.6463$

Head Feet	CFS	GPS	GPM	MGD	Head Feet	CFS	GPS	GPM	MGD
1.01	2.697	20.18	1211	1.743	1.51	4.313	32.26	1936	2.787
1.02	2.731	20.43	1225	1.765	1.52	4.343	32.49	1949	2.807
1.03	2.764	20.68	1240	1.786	1.53	4.374	32.72	1963	2.827
1.04	2.797	20.93	1255	1.808	1.54	4.404	32.95	1976	2.846
1.05	2.830	21.17	1270	1.829	1.55	4.434	33.17	1990	2.866
1.06	2.864	21.42	1285	1.851	1.56	4.464	33.39	2003	2.885
1.07	2.897	21.67	1300	1.872	1.57	4.494	33.62	2017	2.904
1.08	2.930	21.92	1315	1.894	1.58	4.524	33.84	2030	2.924
1.09	2.963	22.17	1330	1.915	1.59	4.553	34.06	2044	2.943
1.10	2.997	22.42	1345	1.937	1.60	4.583	34.28	2057	2.962
1.11	3.030	22.67	1360	1.958	1.61	4.612	34.50	2070	2.981
1.12	3.063	22.91	1375	1.980	1.62	4.642	34.72	2083	3.000
1.13	3.096	23.16	1389	2.001	1.63	4.671	34.94	2096	3.019
1.14	3.129	23.41	1404	2.022	1.64	4.700	35.16	2109	3.037
1.15	3.162	23.66	1419	2.044	1.65	4.729	35.38	2122	3.056
1.16	3.195	23.90	1434	2.065	1.66	4.758	35.59	2135	3.075
1.17	3.228	24.15	1449	2.086	1.67	4.786	35.81	2148	3.093
1.18	3.261	24.40	1464	2.108	1.68	4.815	36.02	2161	3.112
1.19	3.294	24.64	1478	2.129	1.69	4.843	36.23	2174	3.130
1.20	3.327	24.89	1493	2.150	1.70	4.871	36.44	2186	3.148
1.21	3.360	25.13	1508	2.171	1.71	4.900	36.65	2199	3.167
1.22	3.392	25.38	1523	2.193	1.72	4.928	36.86	2212	3.185
1.23	3.425	25.62	1537	2.214	1.73	4.956	37.07	2224	3.203
1.24	3.458	25.87	1552	2.235	1.74	4.983	37.28	2236	3.221
1.25	3.490	26.11	1566	2.256	1.75	5.011	37.49	2249	3.239
1.26	3.523	26.35	1581	2.277	1.76	5.038	37.69	2261	3.256
1.27	3.555	26.60	1596	2.298	1.77	5.066	37.90	2273	3.274
1.28	3.588	26.84	1610	2.319	1.78	5.093	38.10	2286	3.292
1.29	3.620	27.08	1625	2.340	1.79	5.120	38.30	2298	3.309
1.30	3.653	27.32	1639	2.361	1.80	5.147	38.50	2310	3.326
1.31	3.685	27.57	1654	2.381	1.81	5.173	38.70	2322	3.344
1.32	3.717	27.81	1668	2.402	1.82	5.200	38.90	2334	3.361
1.33	3.749	28.05	1683	2.423	1.83	5.226	39.10	2346	3.378
1.34	3.781	28.29	1697	2.444	1.84	5.253	39.30	2357	3.395
1.35	3.813	28.53	1711	2.464	1.85	5.279	39.49	2369	3.412
1.36	3.845	28.76	1726	2.485	1.86	5.305	39.69	2381	3.429
1.37	3.877	29.00	1740	2.506	1.87	5.331	39.88	2392	3.445
1.38	3.908	29.24	1754	2.526	1.88	5.356	40.07	2404	3.462
1.39	3.940	29.48	1768	2.546	1.89	5.382	40.26	2415	3.478
1.40	3.972	29.71	1782	2.567	1.90	5.407	40.45	2427	3.495
1.41	4.003	29.95	1797	2.587	1.91	5.432	40.64	2438	3.511
1.42	4.035	30.18	1811	2.607	1.92	5.457	40.83	2449	3.527
1.43	4.066	30.42	1825	2.628	1.93	5.482	41.01	2460	3.543
1.44	4.097	30.65	1839	2.648	1.94	5.507	41.20	2471	3.559
1.45	4.128	30.88	1853	2.668	1.95	5.531	41.38	2482	3.575
1.46	4.159	31.11	1867	2.688	1.96	5.556	41.56	2493	3.591
1.47	4.190	31.35	1881	2.708	1.97	5.580	41.74	2504	3.606
1.48	4.221	31.58	1894	2.728	1.98	5.604	41.92	2515	3.622
1.49	4.252	31.81	1908	2.748	1.99	5.628	42.10	2526	3.637
1.50	4.282	32.04	1922	2.768	2.00	5.651	42.28	2536	3.652

9

9-1: 1 ft. Rectangular Weir with End Contractions Discharge Table (Continued)

Formulas: $CFS = 3.330(1.0-0.2H)H^{1.5}$ $GPS = CFS \times 7.481$
    $GPM = CFS \times 448.8$ $MGD = CFS \times 0.6463$

Head Feet	CFS	GPS	GPM	MGD	Head Feet	CFS	GPS	GPM	MGD
2.01	5.675	42.45	2547	3.668	2.51	6.595	49.33	2960	4.262
2.02	5.698	42.63	2557	3.683	2.52	6.607	49.43	2965	4.270
2.03	5.721	42.80	2568	3.698	2.53	6.620	49.52	2971	4.278
2.04	5.744	42.97	2578	3.712	2.54	6.632	49.62	2977	4.286
2.05	5.767	43.14	2588	3.727	2.55	6.644	49.71	2982	4.294
2.06	5.789	43.31	2598	3.742	2.56	6.656	49.79	2987	4.302
2.07	5.812	43.48	2608	3.756	2.57	6.668	49.88	2992	4.309
2.08	5.834	43.64	2618	3.770	2.58	6.679	49.97	2998	4.317
2.09	5.856	43.81	2628	3.785	2.59	6.690	50.05	3003	4.324
2.10	5.878	43.97	2638	3.799	2.60	6.701	50.13	3007	4.331
2.11	5.899	44.13	2648	3.813	2.61	6.712	50.21	3012	4.338
2.12	5.921	44.29	2657	3.827	2.62	6.722	50.29	3017	4.344
2.13	5.942	44.45	2667	3.840	2.63	6.732	50.36	3021	4.351
2.14	5.963	44.61	2676	3.854	2.64	6.742	50.44	3026	4.357
2.15	5.984	44.76	2686	3.867	2.65	6.752	50.51	3030	4.364
2.16	6.004	44.92	2695	3.881	2.66	6.761	50.58	3034	4.370
2.17	6.025	45.07	2704	3.894	2.67	6.770	50.65	3038	4.376
2.18	6.045	45.22	2713	3.907	2.68	6.779	50.71	3042	4.381
2.19	6.065	45.37	2722	3.920	2.69	6.788	50.78	3046	4.387
2.20	6.085	45.52	2731	3.933	2.70	6.796	50.84	3050	4.392
2.21	6.105	45.67	2740	3.945	2.71	6.804	50.90	3054	4.397
2.22	6.124	45.82	2749	3.958	2.72	6.812	50.96	3057	4.402
2.23	6.143	45.96	2757	3.971	2.73	6.819	51.02	3061	4.407
2.24	6.162	46.10	2766	3.983	2.74	6.827	51.07	3064	4.412
2.25	6.181	46.24	2774	3.995	2.75	6.834	51.12	3067	4.417
2.26	6.200	46.38	2783	4.007	2.76	6.840	51.17	3070	4.421
2.27	6.218	46.52	2791	4.019	2.77	6.847	51.22	3073	4.425
2.28	6.237	46.66	2799	4.031	2.78	6.853	51.27	3076	4.429
2.29	6.255	46.79	2807	4.042	2.79	6.859	51.31	3078	4.433
2.30	6.272	46.92	2815	4.054	2.80	6.865	51.36	3081	4.437
2.31	6.290	47.05	2823	4.065	2.81	6.870	51.40	3083	4.440
2.32	6.307	47.18	2831	4.076	2.82	6.876	51.44	3086	4.444
2.33	6.324	47.31	2838	4.087	2.83	6.880	51.47	3088	4.447
2.34	6.341	47.44	2846	4.098	2.84	6.885	51.51	3090	4.450
2.35	6.358	47.56	2853	4.109	2.85	6.889	51.54	3092	4.453
2.36	6.375	47.69	2861	4.120	2.86	6.893	51.57	3094	4.455
2.37	6.391	47.81	2868	4.130	2.87	6.897	51.60	3095	4.458
2.38	6.407	47.93	2875	4.141	2.88	6.901	51.62	3097	4.460
2.39	6.423	48.05	2882	4.151	2.89	6.904	51.65	3099	4.462
2.40	6.438	48.16	2889	4.161	2.90	6.907	51.67	3100	4.464
2.41	6.454	48.28	2896	4.171	2.91	6.910	51.69	3101	4.466
2.42	6.469	48.39	2903	4.181	2.92	6.912	51.71	3102	4.467
2.43	6.484	48.50	2910	4.190	2.93	6.914	51.73	3103	4.469
2.44	6.498	48.61	2916	4.200	2.94	6.916	51.74	3104	4.470
2.45	6.513	48.72	2923	4.209	2.95	6.918	51.75	3105	4.471
2.46	6.527	48.83	2929	4.218	2.96	6.919	51.76	3105	4.472
2.47	6.541	48.93	2936	4.227	2.97	6.920	51.77	3106	4.472
2.48	6.555	49.04	2942	4.236	2.98	6.921	51.77	3106	4.473
2.49	6.568	49.14	2948	4.245	2.99	6.921	51.78	3106	4.473
2.50	6.581	49.24	2954	4.254	3.00	6.921	51.78	3106	4.473

9-2: 1 ½ ft. Rectangular Weir with End Contractions Discharge Table

Formulas: $CFS = 3.330(1.5-0.2H)H^{1.5}$ $GPS = CFS \times 7.481$
$GPM = CFS \times 448.8$ $MGD = CFS \times 0.6463$

Head Feet	CFS	GPS	GPM	MGD	Head Feet	CFS	GPS	GPM	MGD
0.01	0.0050	0.0373	2.239	0.0032	0.51	1.696	12.68	761.0	1.096
0.02	0.0141	0.1054	6.324	0.0091	0.52	1.743	13.04	782.3	1.127
0.03	0.0259	0.1934	11.60	0.0167	0.53	1.791	13.40	803.8	1.158
0.04	0.0397	0.2973	17.84	0.0257	0.54	1.839	13.76	825.5	1.189
0.05	0.0555	0.4150	24.90	0.0359	0.55	1.888	14.12	847.3	1.220
0.06	0.0728	0.5448	32.68	0.0471	0.56	1.937	14.49	869.3	1.252
0.07	0.0916	0.6856	41.13	0.0592	0.57	1.986	14.86	891.4	1.284
0.08	0.1118	0.8365	50.18	0.0723	0.58	2.036	15.23	913.6	1.316
0.09	0.1332	0.9968	59.80	0.0861	0.59	2.086	15.60	936.0	1.348
0.10	0.1558	1.166	69.95	0.1007	0.60	2.136	15.98	958.5	1.380
0.11	0.1796	1.343	80.59	0.1160	0.61	2.186	16.35	981.2	1.413
0.12	0.2043	1.528	91.70	0.1320	0.62	2.237	16.73	1003	1.446
0.13	0.2301	1.721	103.3	0.1487	0.63	2.288	17.12	1027	1.479
0.14	0.2568	1.921	115.2	0.1660	0.64	2.339	17.50	1050	1.512
0.15	0.2844	2.127	127.6	0.1838	0.65	2.391	17.89	1073	1.545
0.16	0.3129	2.341	140.4	0.2022	0.66	2.443	18.27	1096	1.579
0.17	0.3422	2.560	153.6	0.2211	0.67	2.495	18.66	1120	1.612
0.18	0.3723	2.785	167.1	0.2406	0.68	2.547	19.05	1143	1.646
0.19	0.4032	3.016	181.0	0.2606	0.69	2.600	19.45	1167	1.680
0.20	0.4349	3.253	195.2	0.2810	0.70	2.652	19.84	1190	1.714
0.21	0.4672	3.495	209.7	0.3020	0.71	2.705	20.24	1214	1.749
0.22	0.5003	3.743	224.5	0.3234	0.72	2.759	20.64	1238	1.783
0.23	0.5341	3.995	239.7	0.3452	0.73	2.812	21.04	1262	1.818
0.24	0.5685	4.253	255.1	0.3674	0.74	2.866	21.44	1286	1.852
0.25	0.6036	4.515	270.9	0.3901	0.75	2.920	21.84	1310	1.887
0.26	0.6393	4.782	286.9	0.4131	0.76	2.974	22.25	1335	1.922
0.27	0.6756	5.054	303.2	0.4366	0.77	3.028	22.66	1359	1.957
0.28	0.7124	5.330	319.7	0.4605	0.78	3.083	23.06	1384	1.993
0.29	0.7499	5.610	336.6	0.4847	0.79	3.138	23.47	1408	2.028
0.30	0.7879	5.895	353.6	0.5092	0.80	3.193	23.89	1433	2.064
0.31	0.8265	6.183	370.9	0.5342	0.81	3.248	24.30	1458	2.099
0.32	0.8656	6.476	388.5	0.5594	0.82	3.303	24.71	1483	2.135
0.33	0.9052	6.772	406.3	0.5851	0.83	3.359	25.13	1508	2.171
0.34	0.9454	7.072	424.3	0.6110	0.84	3.415	25.55	1533	2.207
0.35	0.9860	7.376	442.5	0.6373	0.85	3.471	25.96	1558	2.243
0.36	1.027	7.684	461.0	0.6638	0.86	3.527	26.38	1583	2.279
0.37	1.069	7.995	479.6	0.6907	0.87	3.583	26.81	1608	2.316
0.38	1.111	8.310	498.5	0.7179	0.88	3.640	27.23	1633	2.352
0.39	1.153	8.628	517.6	0.7454	0.89	3.696	27.65	1659	2.389
0.40	1.196	8.949	536.9	0.7731	0.90	3.753	28.08	1684	2.426
0.41	1.240	9.274	556.4	0.8012	0.91	3.810	28.50	1710	2.462
0.42	1.283	9.602	576.0	0.8295	0.92	3.867	28.93	1736	2.499
0.43	1.328	9.932	595.9	0.8581	0.93	3.924	29.36	1761	2.536
0.44	1.372	10.27	615.9	0.8869	0.94	3.982	29.79	1787	2.573
0.45	1.417	10.60	636.1	0.9160	0.95	4.039	30.22	1813	2.611
0.46	1.463	10.94	656.5	0.9454	0.96	4.097	30.65	1839	2.648
0.47	1.509	11.29	677.1	0.9750	0.97	4.155	31.08	1865	2.685
0.48	1.555	11.63	697.8	1.005	0.98	4.213	31.52	1891	2.723
0.49	1.601	11.98	718.7	1.035	0.99	4.271	31.95	1917	2.760
0.50	1.648	12.33	739.7	1.065	1.00	4.329	32.39	1943	2.798

Formulas: CFS = 3.330(1.5-0.2H)H$^{1.5}$ GPS = CFS x 7.481

GPM = CFS x 448.8   MGD = CFS x 0.6463

Head Feet	CFS	GPS	GPM	MGD	Head Feet	CFS	GPS	GPM	MGD
1.01	4.387	32.82	1969	2.836	1.51	7.402	55.38	3322	4.784
1.02	4.446	33.26	1995	2.873	1.52	7.463	55.83	3350	4.824
1.03	4.504	33.70	2022	2.911	1.53	7.525	56.29	3377	4.863
1.04	4.563	34.14	2048	2.949	1.54	7.586	56.75	3405	4.903
1.05	4.622	34.58	2074	2.987	1.55	7.647	57.21	3432	4.942
1.06	4.681	35.02	2101	3.025	1.56	7.708	57.66	3459	4.982
1.07	4.740	35.46	2127	3.063	1.57	7.769	58.12	3487	5.021
1.08	4.799	35.90	2154	3.102	1.58	7.830	58.58	3514	5.061
1.09	4.858	36.34	2180	3.140	1.59	7.891	59.04	3542	5.100
1.10	4.917	36.79	2207	3.178	1.60	7.953	59.49	3569	5.140
1.11	4.977	37.23	2234	3.217	1.61	8.014	59.95	3597	5.179
1.12	5.036	37.68	2260	3.255	1.62	8.075	60.41	3624	5.219
1.13	5.096	38.12	2287	3.294	1.63	8.136	60.86	3651	5.258
1.14	5.156	38.57	2314	3.332	1.64	8.197	61.32	3679	5.298
1.15	5.215	39.02	2341	3.371	1.65	8.258	61.78	3706	5.337
1.16	5.275	39.46	2368	3.409	1.66	8.319	62.23	3733	5.376
1.17	5.335	39.91	2394	3.448	1.67	8.379	62.69	3761	5.416
1.18	5.395	40.36	2421	3.487	1.68	8.440	63.14	3788	5.455
1.19	5.455	40.81	2448	3.526	1.69	8.501	63.60	3815	5.494
1.20	5.516	41.26	2475	3.565	1.70	8.562	64.05	3843	5.534
1.21	5.576	41.71	2502	3.604	1.71	8.623	64.51	3870	5.573
1.22	5.636	42.16	2529	3.643	1.72	8.683	64.96	3897	5.612
1.23	5.696	42.61	2557	3.682	1.73	8.744	65.42	3924	5.651
1.24	5.757	43.07	2584	3.721	1.74	8.805	65.87	3952	5.691
1.25	5.817	43.52	2611	3.760	1.75	8.865	66.32	3979	5.730
1.26	5.878	43.97	2638	3.799	1.76	8.926	66.78	4006	5.769
1.27	5.938	44.43	2665	3.838	1.77	8.986	67.23	4033	5.808
1.28	5.999	44.88	2692	3.877	1.78	9.047	67.68	4060	5.847
1.29	6.060	45.33	2720	3.916	1.79	9.107	68.13	4087	5.886
1.30	6.120	45.79	2747	3.956	1.80	9.168	68.58	4114	5.925
1.31	6.181	46.24	2774	3.995	1.81	9.228	69.03	4141	5.964
1.32	6.242	46.70	2801	4.034	1.82	9.288	69.48	4169	6.003
1.33	6.303	47.15	2829	4.074	1.83	9.348	69.93	4196	6.042
1.34	6.364	47.61	2856	4.113	1.84	9.408	70.38	4223	6.081
1.35	6.425	48.06	2883	4.152	1.85	9.468	70.83	4249	6.119
1.36	6.486	48.52	2911	4.192	1.86	9.528	71.28	4276	6.158
1.37	6.547	48.98	2938	4.231	1.87	9.588	71.73	4303	6.197
1.38	6.608	49.43	2965	4.270	1.88	9.648	72.18	4330	6.236
1.39	6.669	49.89	2993	4.310	1.89	9.708	72.63	4357	6.274
1.40	6.730	50.34	3020	4.349	1.90	9.768	73.07	4384	6.313
1.41	6.791	50.80	3048	4.389	1.91	9.827	73.52	4411	6.351
1.42	6.852	51.26	3075	4.428	1.92	9.887	73.96	4437	6.390
1.43	6.913	51.72	3103	4.468	1.93	9.946	74.41	4464	6.428
1.44	6.974	52.17	3130	4.507	1.94	10.01	74.85	4491	6.467
1.45	7.035	52.63	3157	4.547	1.95	10.07	75.30	4517	6.505
1.46	7.096	53.09	3185	4.586	1.96	10.12	75.74	4544	6.543
1.47	7.158	53.55	3212	4.626	1.97	10.18	76.18	4570	6.582
1.48	7.219	54.00	3240	4.665	1.98	10.24	76.63	4597	6.620
1.49	7.280	54.46	3267	4.705	1.99	10.30	77.07	4623	6.658
1.50	7.341	54.92	3295	4.745	2.00	10.36	77.51	4650	6.696

9-2: 1 ½ ft. Rectangular Weir with End Contractions Discharge Table *(Continued)*

Formulas: CFS $= 3.330(1.5-0.2H)H^{1.5}$ GPS = CFS x 7.481
GPM = CFS x 448.8   MGD = CFS x 0.6463

Head Feet	CFS	GPS	GPM	MGD	Head Feet	CFS	GPS	GPM	MGD
2.01	10.42	77.95	4676	6.734	2.51	13.22	98.87	5931	8.541
2.02	10.48	78.39	4703	6.772	2.52	13.27	99.26	5955	8.575
2.03	10.54	78.83	4729	6.810	2.53	13.32	99.65	5978	8.609
2.04	10.60	79.26	4755	6.848	2.54	13.37	100.0	6001	8.643
2.05	10.65	79.70	4781	6.886	2.55	13.42	100.4	6025	8.676
2.06	10.71	80.14	4808	6.923	2.56	13.48	100.8	6048	8.710
2.07	10.77	80.57	4834	6.961	2.57	13.53	101.2	6071	8.743
2.08	10.83	81.01	4860	6.998	2.58	13.58	101.6	6094	8.776
2.09	10.89	81.44	4886	7.036	2.59	13.63	102.0	6117	8.809
2.10	10.94	81.88	4912	7.073	2.60	13.68	102.4	6140	8.842
2.11	11.00	82.31	4938	7.111	2.61	13.73	102.7	6163	8.875
2.12	11.06	82.74	4964	7.148	2.62	13.78	103.1	6186	8.908
2.13	11.12	83.17	4990	7.185	2.63	13.83	103.5	6209	8.941
2.14	11.18	83.60	5015	7.223	2.64	13.88	103.9	6231	8.973
2.15	11.23	84.03	5041	7.260	2.65	13.93	104.2	6254	9.006
2.16	11.29	84.46	5067	7.297	2.66	13.98	104.6	6276	9.038
2.17	11.35	84.89	5093	7.334	2.67	14.03	105.0	6299	9.070
2.18	11.40	85.32	5118	7.371	2.68	14.08	105.4	6321	9.102
2.19	11.46	85.74	5144	7.407	2.69	14.13	105.7	6343	9.134
2.20	11.52	86.17	5169	7.444	2.70	14.18	106.1	6365	9.166
2.21	11.57	86.59	5195	7.481	2.71	14.23	106.5	6387	9.198
2.22	11.63	87.02	5220	7.517	2.72	14.28	106.8	6409	9.230
2.23	11.69	87.44	5246	7.554	2.73	14.33	107.2	6431	9.261
2.24	11.74	87.86	5271	7.590	2.74	14.38	107.6	6453	9.293
2.25	11.80	88.28	5296	7.627	2.75	14.43	107.9	6475	9.324
2.26	11.86	88.70	5321	7.663	2.76	14.47	108.3	6496	9.355
2.27	11.91	89.12	5346	7.699	2.77	14.52	108.6	6518	9.386
2.28	11.97	89.54	5372	7.735	2.78	14.57	109.0	6539	9.417
2.29	12.02	89.95	5397	7.771	2.79	14.62	109.4	6561	9.448
2.30	12.08	90.37	5422	7.807	2.80	14.67	109.7	6582	9.479
2.31	12.14	90.79	5446	7.843	2.81	14.71	110.1	6603	9.509
2.32	12.19	91.20	5471	7.879	2.82	14.76	110.4	6624	9.540
2.33	12.25	91.61	5496	7.915	2.83	14.81	110.8	6645	9.570
2.34	12.30	92.03	5521	7.950	2.84	14.85	111.1	6666	9.600
2.35	12.36	92.44	5545	7.986	2.85	14.90	111.5	6687	9.630
2.36	12.41	92.85	5570	8.021	2.86	14.95	111.8	6708	9.660
2.37	12.47	93.26	5595	8.057	2.87	14.99	112.2	6729	9.690
2.38	12.52	93.66	5619	8.092	2.88	15.04	112.5	6749	9.719
2.39	12.57	94.07	5643	8.127	2.89	15.08	112.8	6770	9.749
2.40	12.63	94.48	5668	8.162	2.90	15.13	113.2	6790	9.778
2.41	12.68	94.88	5692	8.197	2.91	15.17	113.5	6811	9.808
2.42	12.74	95.28	5716	8.232	2.92	15.22	113.9	6831	9.837
2.43	12.79	95.69	5740	8.267	2.93	15.26	114.2	6851	9.866
2.44	12.84	96.09	5765	8.301	2.94	15.31	114.5	6871	9.895
2.45	12.90	96.49	5789	8.336	2.95	15.35	114.9	6891	9.923
2.46	12.95	96.89	5812	8.370	2.96	15.40	115.2	6911	9.952
2.47	13.00	97.29	5836	8.405	2.97	15.44	115.5	6930	9.980
2.48	13.06	97.68	5860	8.439	2.98	15.49	115.9	6950	10.01
2.49	13.11	98.08	5884	8.473	2.99	15.53	116.2	6970	10.04
2.50	13.16	98.47	5908	8.507	3.00	15.57	116.5	6989	10.06

9

9-3: 2 ft. Rectangular Weir with End Contractions Discharge Table

Formulas: $CFS = 3.330(2.0-0.2H)H^{1.5}$ $GPS = CFS \times 7.481$
$GPM = CFS \times 448.8$ $MGD = CFS \times 0.6463$

Head Feet	CFS	GPS	GPM	MGD	Head Feet	CFS	GPS	GPM	MGD
0.01	0.0067	0.0498	2.986	0.0043	0.51	2.302	17.22	1033	1.488
0.02	0.0188	0.1406	8.437	0.0122	0.52	2.367	17.71	1063	1.530
0.03	0.0345	0.2581	15.48	0.0223	0.53	2.434	18.21	1092	1.573
0.04	0.0531	0.3970	23.82	0.0343	0.54	2.500	18.70	1122	1.616
0.05	0.0741	0.5543	33.25	0.0479	0.55	2.567	19.20	1152	1.659
0.06	0.0973	0.7279	43.67	0.0629	0.56	2.635	19.71	1182	1.703
0.07	0.1225	0.9163	54.97	0.0792	0.57	2.703	20.22	1213	1.747
0.08	0.1495	1.118	67.09	0.0966	0.58	2.771	20.73	1244	1.791
0.09	0.1782	1.333	79.98	0.1152	0.59	2.840	21.25	1275	1.836
0.10	0.2085	1.560	93.58	0.1348	0.60	2.910	21.77	1306	1.880
0.11	0.2403	1.798	107.8	0.1553	0.61	2.979	22.29	1337	1.926
0.12	0.2735	2.046	122.8	0.1768	0.62	3.050	22.82	1369	1.971
0.13	0.3081	2.305	138.3	0.1991	0.63	3.121	23.34	1400	2.017
0.14	0.3440	2.573	154.4	0.2223	0.64	3.192	23.88	1432	2.063
0.15	0.3811	2.851	171.0	0.2463	0.65	3.263	24.41	1465	2.109
0.16	0.4194	3.138	188.2	0.2711	0.66	3.335	24.95	1497	2.156
0.17	0.4589	3.433	205.9	0.2966	0.67	3.408	25.49	1529	2.202
0.18	0.4995	3.736	224.2	0.3228	0.68	3.481	26.04	1562	2.250
0.19	0.5411	4.048	242.8	0.3497	0.69	3.554	26.59	1595	2.297
0.20	0.5838	4.367	262.0	0.3773	0.70	3.627	27.14	1628	2.344
0.21	0.6275	4.694	281.6	0.4055	0.71	3.701	27.69	1661	2.392
0.22	0.6721	5.028	301.6	0.4344	0.72	3.776	28.25	1695	2.440
0.23	0.7177	5.369	322.1	0.4639	0.73	3.851	28.81	1728	2.489
0.24	0.7643	5.717	343.0	0.4939	0.74	3.926	29.37	1762	2.537
0.25	0.8117	6.072	364.3	0.5246	0.75	4.001	29.93	1796	2.586
0.26	0.8600	6.434	386.0	0.5558	0.76	4.077	30.50	1830	2.635
0.27	0.9091	6.801	408.0	0.5876	0.77	4.153	31.07	1864	2.684
0.28	0.9591	7.175	430.5	0.6199	0.78	4.230	31.65	1898	2.734
0.29	1.010	7.555	453.3	0.6527	0.79	4.307	32.22	1933	2.784
0.30	1.062	7.941	476.4	0.6861	0.80	4.384	32.80	1968	2.834
0.31	1.114	8.333	499.9	0.7199	0.81	4.462	33.38	2002	2.884
0.32	1.167	8.730	523.8	0.7542	0.82	4.540	33.96	2037	2.934
0.33	1.221	9.133	547.9	0.7891	0.83	4.618	34.55	2073	2.985
0.34	1.275	9.542	572.4	0.8243	0.84	4.697	35.14	2108	3.035
0.35	1.331	9.956	597.3	0.8601	0.85	4.776	35.73	2143	3.086
0.36	1.387	10.37	622.4	0.8963	0.86	4.855	36.32	2179	3.138
0.37	1.443	10.80	647.8	0.9329	0.87	4.934	36.91	2215	3.189
0.38	1.501	11.23	673.6	0.9700	0.88	5.014	37.51	2250	3.241
0.39	1.559	11.66	699.6	1.007	0.89	5.094	38.11	2286	3.292
0.40	1.617	12.10	725.9	1.045	0.90	5.175	38.71	2322	3.344
0.41	1.677	12.54	752.5	1.084	0.91	5.255	39.32	2359	3.397
0.42	1.737	12.99	779.4	1.122	0.92	5.336	39.92	2395	3.449
0.43	1.797	13.44	806.6	1.162	0.93	5.418	40.53	2431	3.501
0.44	1.858	13.90	834.0	1.201	0.94	5.499	41.14	2468	3.554
0.45	1.920	14.36	861.7	1.241	0.95	5.581	41.75	2505	3.607
0.46	1.982	14.83	889.6	1.281	0.96	5.663	42.37	2542	3.660
0.47	2.045	15.30	917.8	1.322	0.97	5.745	42.98	2579	3.713
0.48	2.108	15.77	946.3	1.363	0.98	5.828	43.60	2616	3.767
0.49	2.172	16.25	975.0	1.404	0.99	5.911	44.22	2653	3.820
0.50	2.237	16.73	1004	1.446	1.00	5.994	44.84	2690	3.874

9

9-3: 2 ft. Rectangular Weir with End Contractions Discharge Table *(Continued)*

Formulas: $CFS = 3.330(2.0-0.2H)H^{1.5}$ $GPS = CFS \times 7.481$
$GPM = CFS \times 448.8$ $MGD = CFS \times 0.6463$

Head Feet	CFS	GPS	GPM	MGD	Head Feet	CFS	GPS	GPM	MGD
1.01	6.077	45.46	2728	3.928	1.51	10.49	78.49	4709	6.781
1.02	6.161	46.09	2765	3.982	1.52	10.58	79.18	4750	6.840
1.03	6.245	46.72	2803	4.036	1.53	10.68	79.86	4791	6.900
1.04	6.329	47.35	2840	4.090	1.54	10.77	80.55	4833	6.959
1.05	6.413	47.98	2878	4.145	1.55	10.86	81.24	4874	7.019
1.06	6.498	48.61	2916	4.200	1.56	10.95	81.93	4915	7.078
1.07	6.583	49.24	2954	4.254	1.57	11.04	82.62	4957	7.138
1.08	6.668	49.88	2992	4.309	1.58	11.14	83.32	4998	7.198
1.09	6.753	50.52	3031	4.364	1.59	11.23	84.01	5040	7.258
1.10	6.838	51.16	3069	4.420	1.60	11.32	84.70	5081	7.318
1.11	6.924	51.80	3108	4.475	1.61	11.41	85.40	5123	7.377
1.12	7.010	52.44	3146	4.531	1.62	11.51	86.09	5165	7.437
1.13	7.096	53.09	3185	4.586	1.63	11.60	86.78	5206	7.497
1.14	7.182	53.73	3223	4.642	1.64	11.69	87.48	5248	7.558
1.15	7.269	54.38	3262	4.698	1.65	11.79	88.18	5290	7.618
1.16	7.356	55.03	3301	4.754	1.66	11.88	88.87	5332	7.678
1.17	7.442	55.68	3340	4.810	1.67	11.97	89.57	5373	7.738
1.18	7.529	56.33	3379	4.866	1.68	12.07	90.27	5415	7.798
1.19	7.617	56.98	3418	4.923	1.69	12.16	90.96	5457	7.858
1.20	7.704	57.64	3458	4.979	1.70	12.25	91.66	5499	7.919
1.21	7.792	58.29	3497	5.036	1.71	12.35	92.36	5541	7.979
1.22	7.880	58.95	3536	5.093	1.72	12.44	93.06	5583	8.040
1.23	7.968	59.61	3576	5.150	1.73	12.53	93.76	5625	8.100
1.24	8.056	60.27	3615	5.206	1.74	12.63	94.46	5667	8.160
1.25	8.144	60.93	3655	5.264	1.75	12.72	95.16	5709	8.221
1.26	8.233	61.59	3695	5.321	1.76	12.81	95.86	5751	8.281
1.27	8.321	62.25	3735	5.378	1.77	12.91	96.56	5793	8.342
1.28	8.410	62.92	3774	5.436	1.78	13.00	97.26	5835	8.403
1.29	8.499	63.58	3814	5.493	1.79	13.09	97.96	5877	8.463
1.30	8.588	64.25	3854	5.551	1.80	13.19	98.66	5919	8.524
1.31	8.678	64.92	3895	5.608	1.81	13.28	99.37	5961	8.584
1.32	8.767	65.59	3935	5.666	1.82	13.38	100.1	6003	8.645
1.33	8.857	66.26	3975	5.724	1.83	13.47	100.8	6045	8.706
1.34	8.946	66.93	4015	5.782	1.84	13.56	101.5	6088	8.766
1.35	9.036	67.60	4055	5.840	1.85	13.66	102.2	6130	8.827
1.36	9.126	68.27	4096	5.898	1.86	13.75	102.9	6172	8.888
1.37	9.216	68.95	4136	5.957	1.87	13.85	103.6	6214	8.949
1.38	9.307	69.62	4177	6.015	1.88	13.94	104.3	6256	9.010
1.39	9.397	70.30	4217	6.073	1.89	14.03	105.0	6299	9.070
1.40	9.488	70.98	4258	6.132	1.90	14.13	105.7	6341	9.131
1.41	9.578	71.66	4299	6.191	1.91	14.22	106.4	6383	9.192
1.42	9.669	72.34	4340	6.249	1.92	14.32	107.1	6425	9.253
1.43	9.760	73.02	4380	6.308	1.93	14.41	107.8	6468	9.314
1.44	9.851	73.70	4421	6.367	1.94	14.50	108.5	6510	9.374
1.45	9.942	74.38	4462	6.426	1.95	14.60	109.2	6552	9.435
1.46	10.03	75.06	4503	6.485	1.96	14.69	109.9	6594	9.496
1.47	10.13	75.75	4544	6.544	1.97	14.79	110.6	6637	9.557
1.48	10.22	76.43	4585	6.603	1.98	14.88	111.3	6679	9.618
1.49	10.31	77.12	4626	6.662	1.99	14.98	112.0	6721	9.679
1.50	10.40	77.80	4667	6.721	2.00	15.07	112.7	6763	9.740

9

9-3: 2 ft. Rectangular Weir with End Contractions Discharge Table (Continued)

Formulas: $CFS = 3.330(2.0-0.2H)H^{1.5}$ $GPS = CFS \times 7.481$
$GPM = CFS \times 448.8$ $MGD = CFS \times 0.6463$

Head Feet	CFS	GPS	GPM	MGD	Head Feet	CFS	GPS	GPM	MGD
2.01	15.16	113.4	6806	9.801	2.51	19.84	148.4	8903	12.82
2.02	15.26	114.1	6848	9.861	2.52	19.93	149.1	8944	12.88
2.03	15.35	114.9	6890	9.922	2.53	20.02	149.8	8985	12.94
2.04	15.45	115.6	6932	9.983	2.54	20.11	150.5	9026	13.00
2.05	15.54	116.3	6975	10.04	2.55	20.20	151.1	9068	13.06
2.06	15.63	117.0	7017	10.10	2.56	20.30	151.8	9109	13.12
2.07	15.73	117.7	7059	10.17	2.57	20.39	152.5	9150	13.18
2.08	15.82	118.4	7101	10.23	2.58	20.48	153.2	9191	13.24
2.09	15.92	119.1	7144	10.29	2.59	20.57	153.9	9232	13.29
2.10	16.01	119.8	7186	10.35	2.60	20.66	154.6	9273	13.35
2.11	16.11	120.5	7228	10.41	2.61	20.75	155.3	9314	13.41
2.12	16.20	121.2	7270	10.47	2.62	20.84	155.9	9355	13.47
2.13	16.29	121.9	7313	10.53	2.63	20.94	156.6	9396	13.53
2.14	16.39	122.6	7355	10.59	2.64	21.03	157.3	9436	13.59
2.15	16.48	123.3	7397	10.65	2.65	21.12	158.0	9477	13.65
2.16	16.58	124.0	7439	10.71	2.66	21.21	158.7	9518	13.71
2.17	16.67	124.7	7481	10.77	2.67	21.30	159.3	9559	13.77
2.18	16.76	125.4	7523	10.83	2.68	21.39	160.0	9599	13.82
2.19	16.86	126.1	7566	10.89	2.69	21.48	160.7	9640	13.88
2.20	16.95	126.8	7608	10.96	2.70	21.57	161.4	9680	13.94
2.21	17.05	127.5	7650	11.02	2.71	21.66	162.0	9721	14.00
2.22	17.14	128.2	7692	11.08	2.72	21.75	162.7	9761	14.06
2.23	17.23	128.9	7734	11.14	2.73	21.84	163.4	9802	14.12
2.24	17.33	129.6	7776	11.20	2.74	21.93	164.1	9842	14.17
2.25	17.42	130.3	7818	11.26	2.75	22.02	164.7	9882	14.23
2.26	17.51	131.0	7860	11.32	2.76	22.11	165.4	9923	14.29
2.27	17.61	131.7	7902	11.38	2.77	22.20	166.1	9963	14.35
2.28	17.70	132.4	7944	11.44	2.78	22.29	166.7	10000	14.40
2.29	17.79	133.1	7986	11.50	2.79	22.38	167.4	10040	14.46
2.30	17.89	133.8	8028	11.56	2.80	22.47	168.1	10080	14.52
2.31	17.98	134.5	8070	11.62	2.81	22.56	168.7	10120	14.58
2.32	18.07	135.2	8112	11.68	2.82	22.65	169.4	10160	14.64
2.33	18.17	135.9	8154	11.74	2.83	22.73	170.1	10200	14.69
2.34	18.26	136.6	8196	11.80	2.84	22.82	170.7	10240	14.75
2.35	18.35	137.3	8237	11.86	2.85	22.91	171.4	10280	14.81
2.36	18.45	138.0	8279	11.92	2.86	23.00	172.1	10320	14.86
2.37	18.54	138.7	8321	11.98	2.87	23.09	172.7	10360	14.92
2.38	18.63	139.4	8363	12.04	2.88	23.18	173.4	10400	14.98
2.39	18.73	140.1	8404	12.10	2.89	23.26	174.0	10440	15.04
2.40	18.82	140.8	8446	12.16	2.90	23.35	174.7	10480	15.09
2.41	18.91	141.5	8488	12.22	2.91	23.44	175.4	10520	15.15
2.42	19.00	142.2	8529	12.28	2.92	23.53	176.0	10560	15.21
2.43	19.10	142.9	8571	12.34	2.93	23.62	176.7	10600	15.26
2.44	19.19	143.6	8613	12.40	2.94	23.70	177.3	10640	15.32
2.45	19.28	144.3	8654	12.46	2.95	23.79	178.0	10680	15.38
2.46	19.38	144.9	8696	12.52	2.96	23.88	178.6	10720	15.43
2.47	19.47	145.6	8737	12.58	2.97	23.96	179.3	10760	15.49
2.48	19.56	146.3	8779	12.64	2.98	24.05	179.9	10790	15.54
2.49	19.65	147.0	8820	12.70	2.99	24.14	180.6	10830	15.60
2.50	19.74	147.7	8861	12.76	3.00	24.22	181.2	10870	15.66

9-4: 2 ½ ft. Rectangular Weir with End Contractions Discharge Table

Formulas: CFS = $3.330(2.5-0.2H)H^{1.5}$
GPM = CFS x 448.8

GPS = CFS x 7.481
MGD = CFS x 0.6463

Head Feet	CFS	GPS	GPM	MGD	Head Feet	CFS	GPS	GPM	MGD
0.01	0.0083	0.0622	3.733	0.0054	0.51	2.908	21.76	1305	1.880
0.02	0.0235	0.1759	10.55	0.0152	0.52	2.992	22.38	1343	1.934
0.03	0.0432	0.3228	19.37	0.0279	0.53	3.076	23.01	1380	1.988
0.04	0.0664	0.4966	29.79	0.0429	0.54	3.161	23.65	1419	2.043
0.05	0.0927	0.6935	41.61	0.0599	0.55	3.246	24.29	1457	2.098
0.06	0.1218	0.9109	54.65	0.0787	0.56	3.332	24.93	1496	2.154
0.07	0.1533	1.147	68.81	0.0991	0.57	3.419	25.58	1535	2.210
0.08	0.1872	1.400	84.00	0.1210	0.58	3.507	26.23	1574	2.266
0.09	0.2232	1.669	100.2	0.1442	0.59	3.595	26.89	1613	2.323
0.10	0.2612	1.954	117.2	0.1688	0.60	3.683	27.56	1653	2.381
0.11	0.3010	2.252	135.1	0.1946	0.61	3.773	28.22	1693	2.438
0.12	0.3427	2.564	153.8	0.2215	0.62	3.863	28.90	1734	2.496
0.13	0.3862	2.889	173.3	0.2496	0.63	3.953	29.57	1774	2.555
0.14	0.4312	3.226	193.5	0.2787	0.64	4.044	30.25	1815	2.614
0.15	0.4778	3.575	214.5	0.3088	0.65	4.136	30.94	1856	2.673
0.16	0.5260	3.935	236.1	0.3399	0.66	4.228	31.63	1898	2.733
0.17	0.5756	4.306	258.3	0.3720	0.67	4.321	32.32	1939	2.793
0.18	0.6266	4.688	281.2	0.4050	0.68	4.414	33.02	1981	2.853
0.19	0.6790	5.080	304.7	0.4388	0.69	4.508	33.73	2023	2.914
0.20	0.7327	5.481	328.8	0.4735	0.70	4.603	34.43	2066	2.975
0.21	0.7877	5.893	353.5	0.5091	0.71	4.698	35.14	2108	3.036
0.22	0.8439	6.313	378.8	0.5454	0.72	4.793	35.86	2151	3.098
0.23	0.9014	6.743	404.5	0.5826	0.73	4.889	36.58	2194	3.160
0.24	0.9600	7.182	430.9	0.6205	0.74	4.986	37.30	2238	3.222
0.25	1.020	7.629	457.7	0.6591	0.75	5.083	38.02	2281	3.285
0.26	1.081	8.085	485.0	0.6985	0.76	5.180	38.75	2325	3.348
0.27	1.143	8.549	512.9	0.7386	0.77	5.278	39.49	2369	3.411
0.28	1.206	9.021	541.2	0.7793	0.78	5.377	40.23	2413	3.475
0.29	1.270	9.501	570.0	0.8208	0.79	5.476	40.97	2458	3.539
0.30	1.335	9.988	599.2	0.8629	0.80	5.576	41.71	2502	3.604
0.31	1.401	10.48	628.9	0.9056	0.81	5.676	42.46	2547	3.668
0.32	1.468	10.99	659.0	0.9490	0.82	5.776	43.21	2592	3.733
0.33	1.537	11.49	689.6	0.9930	0.83	5.877	43.97	2638	3.798
0.34	1.606	12.01	720.6	1.038	0.84	5.978	44.73	2683	3.864
0.35	1.676	12.53	752.0	1.083	0.85	6.080	45.49	2729	3.930
0.36	1.746	13.06	783.8	1.129	0.86	6.183	46.25	2775	3.996
0.37	1.818	13.60	816.0	1.175	0.87	6.285	47.02	2821	4.062
0.38	1.891	14.15	848.6	1.222	0.88	6.389	47.79	2867	4.129
0.39	1.964	14.70	881.6	1.270	0.89	6.492	48.57	2914	4.196
0.40	2.039	15.25	915.0	1.318	0.90	6.596	49.35	2960	4.263
0.41	2.114	15.81	948.7	1.366	0.91	6.701	50.13	3007	4.331
0.42	2.190	16.38	982.8	1.415	0.92	6.806	50.91	3054	4.398
0.43	2.267	16.96	1017	1.465	0.93	6.911	51.70	3102	4.466
0.44	2.344	17.54	1052	1.515	0.94	7.017	52.49	3149	4.535
0.45	2.423	18.12	1087	1.566	0.95	7.123	53.28	3197	4.603
0.46	2.502	18.72	1123	1.617	0.96	7.229	54.08	3244	4.672
0.47	2.582	19.31	1159	1.668	0.97	7.336	54.88	3292	4.741
0.48	2.662	19.92	1195	1.721	0.98	7.443	55.68	3341	4.811
0.49	2.744	20.52	1231	1.773	0.99	7.551	56.49	3389	4.880
0.50	2.826	21.14	1268	1.826	1.00	7.659	57.30	3437	4.950

9

Formulas: $CFS = 3.330(2.5-0.2H)H^{1.5}$ $GPS = CFS \times 7.481$
$GPM = CFS \times 448.8$ $MGD = CFS \times 0.6463$

Head Feet	CFS	GPS	GPM	MGD	Head Feet	CFS	GPS	GPM	MGD
1.01	7.767	58.11	3486	5.020	1.51	13.58	101.6	6095	8.778
1.02	7.876	58.92	3535	5.090	1.52	13.70	102.5	6150	8.857
1.03	7.985	59.74	3584	5.161	1.53	13.83	103.4	6205	8.936
1.04	8.095	60.56	3633	5.232	1.54	13.95	104.4	6261	9.016
1.05	8.205	61.38	3682	5.303	1.55	14.07	105.3	6316	9.095
1.06	8.315	62.20	3732	5.374	1.56	14.20	106.2	6371	9.175
1.07	8.426	63.03	3781	5.445	1.57	14.32	107.1	6427	9.255
1.08	8.536	63.86	3831	5.517	1.58	14.44	108.1	6482	9.335
1.09	8.648	64.69	3881	5.589	1.59	14.57	109.0	6538	9.415
1.10	8.759	65.53	3931	5.661	1.60	14.69	109.9	6594	9.495
1.11	8.871	66.37	3981	5.733	1.61	14.82	110.8	6650	9.576
1.12	8.983	67.21	4032	5.806	1.62	14.94	111.8	6705	9.656
1.13	9.096	68.05	4082	5.879	1.63	15.07	112.7	6761	9.737
1.14	9.209	68.89	4133	5.952	1.64	15.19	113.6	6817	9.818
1.15	9.322	69.74	4184	6.025	1.65	15.32	114.6	6874	9.898
1.16	9.436	70.59	4235	6.098	1.66	15.44	115.5	6930	9.979
1.17	9.550	71.44	4286	6.172	1.67	15.57	116.4	6986	10.06
1.18	9.664	72.29	4337	6.246	1.68	15.69	117.4	7042	10.14
1.19	9.778	73.15	4388	6.320	1.69	15.82	118.3	7099	10.22
1.20	9.893	74.01	4440	6.394	1.70	15.94	119.3	7155	10.30
1.21	10.01	74.87	4492	6.468	1.71	16.07	120.2	7212	10.39
1.22	10.12	75.73	4543	6.543	1.72	16.20	121.2	7268	10.47
1.23	10.24	76.60	4595	6.617	1.73	16.32	122.1	7325	10.55
1.24	10.35	77.46	4647	6.692	1.74	16.45	123.0	7382	10.63
1.25	10.47	78.33	4699	6.767	1.75	16.57	124.0	7439	10.71
1.26	10.59	79.21	4752	6.843	1.76	16.70	124.9	7495	10.79
1.27	10.70	80.08	4804	6.918	1.77	16.83	125.9	7552	10.88
1.28	10.82	80.95	4857	6.994	1.78	16.96	126.8	7609	10.96
1.29	10.94	81.83	4909	7.070	1.79	17.08	127.8	7666	11.04
1.30	11.06	82.71	4962	7.146	1.80	17.21	128.7	7724	11.12
1.31	11.17	83.59	5015	7.222	1.81	17.34	129.7	7781	11.20
1.32	11.29	84.48	5068	7.298	1.82	17.46	130.7	7838	11.29
1.33	11.41	85.36	5121	7.375	1.83	17.59	131.6	7895	11.37
1.34	11.53	86.25	5174	7.451	1.84	17.72	132.6	7953	11.45
1.35	11.65	87.14	5228	7.528	1.85	17.85	133.5	8010	11.53
1.36	11.77	88.03	5281	7.605	1.86	17.98	134.5	8067	11.62
1.37	11.89	88.92	5335	7.682	1.87	18.10	135.4	8125	11.70
1.38	12.01	89.82	5388	7.759	1.88	18.23	136.4	8183	11.78
1.39	12.13	90.71	5442	7.837	1.89	18.36	137.4	8240	11.87
1.40	12.25	91.61	5496	7.914	1.90	18.49	138.3	8298	11.95
1.41	12.37	92.51	5550	7.992	1.91	18.62	139.3	8356	12.03
1.42	12.49	93.41	5604	8.070	1.92	18.75	140.2	8413	12.12
1.43	12.61	94.32	5658	8.148	1.93	18.87	141.2	8471	12.20
1.44	12.73	95.22	5712	8.226	1.94	19.00	142.2	8529	12.28
1.45	12.85	96.13	5767	8.305	1.95	19.13	143.1	8587	12.37
1.46	12.97	97.04	5821	8.383	1.96	19.26	144.1	8645	12.45
1.47	13.09	97.95	5876	8.462	1.97	19.39	145.1	8703	12.53
1.48	13.21	98.86	5931	8.540	1.98	19.52	146.0	8761	12.62
1.49	13.34	99.77	5985	8.619	1.99	19.65	147.0	8819	12.70
1.50	13.46	100.7	6040	8.698	2.00	19.78	148.0	8877	12.78

Formulas: CFS $=3.330(2.5-0.2H)H^{1.5}$ GPS = CFS x 7.481
          GPM = CFS x 448.8   MGD = CFS x 0.6463

Head Feet	CFS	GPS	GPM	MGD	Head Feet	CFS	GPS	GPM	MGD
2.01	19.91	148.9	8935	12.87	2.51	26.46	197.9	11870	17.10
2.02	20.04	149.9	8993	12.95	2.52	26.59	198.9	11930	17.18
2.03	20.17	150.9	9051	13.03	2.53	26.72	199.9	11990	17.27
2.04	20.30	151.8	9110	13.12	2.54	26.85	200.9	12050	17.35
2.05	20.43	152.8	9168	13.20	2.55	26.98	201.9	12110	17.44
2.06	20.56	153.8	9226	13.29	2.56	27.12	202.9	12170	17.52
2.07	20.69	154.8	9285	13.37	2.57	27.25	203.8	12230	17.61
2.08	20.82	155.7	9343	13.45	2.58	27.38	204.8	12290	17.69
2.09	20.95	156.7	9402	13.54	2.59	27.51	205.8	12350	17.78
2.10	21.08	157.7	9460	13.62	2.60	27.64	206.8	12410	17.87
2.11	21.21	158.7	9518	13.71	2.61	27.77	207.8	12460	17.95
2.12	21.34	159.6	9577	13.79	2.62	27.91	208.8	12520	18.04
2.13	21.47	160.6	9636	13.88	2.63	28.04	209.7	12580	18.12
2.14	21.60	161.6	9694	13.96	2.64	28.17	210.7	12640	18.21
2.15	21.73	162.6	9753	14.04	2.65	28.30	211.7	12700	18.29
2.16	21.86	163.5	9811	14.13	2.66	28.43	212.7	12760	18.37
2.17	21.99	164.5	9870	14.21	2.67	28.56	213.7	12820	18.46
2.18	22.12	165.5	9929	14.30	2.68	28.69	214.7	12880	18.54
2.19	22.25	166.5	9987	14.38	2.69	28.83	215.6	12940	18.63
2.20	22.38	167.5	10050	14.47	2.70	28.96	216.6	13000	18.71
2.21	22.52	168.4	10100	14.55	2.71	29.09	217.6	13050	18.80
2.22	22.65	169.4	10160	14.64	2.72	29.22	218.6	13110	18.88
2.23	22.78	170.4	10220	14.72	2.73	29.35	219.6	13170	18.97
2.24	22.91	171.4	10280	14.81	2.74	29.48	220.6	13230	19.05
2.25	23.04	172.4	10340	14.89	2.75	29.61	221.5	13290	19.14
2.26	23.17	173.3	10400	14.98	2.76	29.74	222.5	13350	19.22
2.27	23.30	174.3	10460	15.06	2.77	29.87	223.5	13410	19.31
2.28	23.43	175.3	10520	15.14	2.78	30.01	224.5	13470	19.39
2.29	23.56	176.3	10580	15.23	2.79	30.14	225.5	13530	19.48
2.30	23.70	177.3	10630	15.31	2.80	30.27	226.4	13580	19.56
2.31	23.83	178.2	10690	15.40	2.81	30.40	227.4	13640	19.65
2.32	23.96	179.2	10750	15.48	2.82	30.53	228.4	13700	19.73
2.33	24.09	180.2	10810	15.57	2.83	30.66	229.4	13760	19.82
2.34	24.22	181.2	10870	15.65	2.84	30.79	230.4	13820	19.90
2.35	24.35	182.2	10930	15.74	2.85	30.92	231.3	13880	19.98
2.36	24.48	183.2	10990	15.82	2.86	31.05	232.3	13940	20.07
2.37	24.62	184.1	11050	15.91	2.87	31.18	233.3	14000	20.15
2.38	24.75	185.1	11110	15.99	2.88	31.31	234.3	14050	20.24
2.39	24.88	186.1	11170	16.08	2.89	31.44	235.2	14110	20.32
2.40	25.01	187.1	11220	16.16	2.90	31.57	236.2	14170	20.41
2.41	25.14	188.1	11280	16.25	2.91	31.71	237.2	14230	20.49
2.42	25.27	189.1	11340	16.33	2.92	31.84	238.2	14290	20.58
2.43	25.40	190.1	11400	16.42	2.93	31.97	239.1	14350	20.66
2.44	25.54	191.0	11460	16.50	2.94	32.10	240.1	14400	20.74
2.45	25.67	192.0	11520	16.59	2.95	32.23	241.1	14460	20.83
2.46	25.80	193.0	11580	16.67	2.96	32.36	242.1	14520	20.91
2.47	25.93	194.0	11640	16.76	2.97	32.49	243.0	14580	21.00
2.48	26.06	195.0	11700	16.84	2.98	32.62	244.0	14640	21.08
2.49	26.19	196.0	11760	16.93	2.99	32.75	245.0	14700	21.16
2.50	26.33	196.9	11820	17.01	3.00	32.88	245.9	14750	21.25

9

9-5: 3 ft. Rectangular Weir with End Contractions Discharge Table

Formulas: CFS = 3.330(3.0-0.2H)H$^{1.5}$ GPS = CFS x 7.481
         GPM = CFS x 448.8   MGD = CFS x 0.6463

Head Feet	CFS	GPS	GPM	MGD	Head Feet	CFS	GPS	GPM	MGD
0.01	0.0100	0.0747	4.481	0.0065	0.51	3.515	26.29	1577	2.272
0.02	0.0282	0.2111	12.66	0.0182	0.52	3.616	27.05	1623	2.337
0.03	0.0518	0.3876	23.25	0.0335	0.53	3.718	27.82	1669	2.403
0.04	0.0797	0.5963	35.77	0.0515	0.54	3.821	28.59	1715	2.470
0.05	0.1113	0.8328	49.96	0.0719	0.55	3.925	29.37	1762	2.537
0.06	0.1462	1.094	65.63	0.0945	0.56	4.030	30.15	1809	2.605
0.07	0.1842	1.378	82.65	0.1190	0.57	4.136	30.94	1856	2.673
0.08	0.2248	1.682	100.9	0.1453	0.58	4.242	31.74	1904	2.742
0.09	0.2681	2.006	120.3	0.1733	0.59	4.349	32.54	1952	2.811
0.10	0.3138	2.348	140.8	0.2028	0.60	4.457	33.34	2000	2.881
0.11	0.3618	2.707	162.4	0.2338	0.61	4.566	34.16	2049	2.951
0.12	0.4120	3.082	184.9	0.2662	0.62	4.675	34.98	2098	3.022
0.13	0.4642	3.473	208.3	0.3000	0.63	4.786	35.80	2148	3.093
0.14	0.5184	3.878	232.7	0.3351	0.64	4.897	36.63	2198	3.165
0.15	0.5746	4.298	257.9	0.3713	0.65	5.008	37.47	2248	3.237
0.16	0.6325	4.732	283.9	0.4088	0.66	5.121	38.31	2298	3.310
0.17	0.6923	5.179	310.7	0.4474	0.67	5.234	39.16	2349	3.383
0.18	0.7538	5.639	338.3	0.4872	0.68	5.348	40.01	2400	3.456
0.19	0.8169	6.111	366.6	0.5280	0.69	5.462	40.86	2452	3.530
0.20	0.8816	6.595	395.7	0.5698	0.70	5.578	41.73	2503	3.605
0.21	0.9479	7.091	425.4	0.6126	0.71	5.694	42.59	2555	3.680
0.22	1.016	7.599	455.9	0.6565	0.72	5.810	43.47	2608	3.755
0.23	1.085	8.117	487.0	0.7013	0.73	5.928	44.34	2660	3.831
0.24	1.156	8.646	518.7	0.7470	0.74	6.046	45.23	2713	3.907
0.25	1.228	9.186	551.1	0.7936	0.75	6.164	46.11	2767	3.984
0.26	1.301	9.736	584.1	0.8411	0.76	6.284	47.01	2820	4.061
0.27	1.376	10.30	617.7	0.8895	0.77	6.403	47.90	2874	4.139
0.28	1.453	10.87	651.9	0.9388	0.78	6.524	48.81	2928	4.216
0.29	1.530	11.45	686.7	0.9888	0.79	6.645	49.71	2982	4.295
0.30	1.609	12.03	722.0	1.040	0.80	6.767	50.62	3037	4.374
0.31	1.689	12.63	757.9	1.091	0.81	6.889	51.54	3092	4.453
0.32	1.770	13.24	794.3	1.144	0.82	7.012	52.46	3147	4.532
0.33	1.852	13.86	831.2	1.197	0.83	7.136	53.39	3203	4.612
0.34	1.936	14.48	868.7	1.251	0.84	7.260	54.31	3258	4.692
0.35	2.020	15.11	906.7	1.306	0.85	7.385	55.25	3314	4.773
0.36	2.106	15.76	945.2	1.361	0.86	7.511	56.19	3371	4.854
0.37	2.193	16.41	984.2	1.417	0.87	7.637	57.13	3427	4.935
0.38	2.281	17.06	1024	1.474	0.88	7.763	58.08	3484	5.017
0.39	2.370	17.73	1064	1.532	0.89	7.890	59.03	3541	5.099
0.40	2.460	18.40	1104	1.590	0.90	8.018	59.98	3598	5.182
0.41	2.551	19.08	1145	1.649	0.91	8.146	60.94	3656	5.265
0.42	2.643	19.77	1186	1.708	0.92	8.275	61.90	3714	5.348
0.43	2.736	20.47	1228	1.768	0.93	8.404	62.87	3772	5.432
0.44	2.830	21.17	1270	1.829	0.94	8.534	63.84	3830	5.516
0.45	2.925	21.88	1313	1.891	0.95	8.664	64.82	3889	5.600
0.46	3.021	22.60	1356	1.953	0.96	8.795	65.80	3947	5.684
0.47	3.118	23.33	1399	2.015	0.97	8.927	66.78	4006	5.769
0.48	3.216	24.06	1443	2.078	0.98	9.059	67.77	4066	5.855
0.49	3.315	24.80	1488	2.142	0.99	9.191	68.76	4125	5.940
0.50	3.414	25.54	1532	2.207	1.00	9.324	69.75	4185	6.026

9

9-5: 3 ft. Rectangular Weir with End Contractions Discharge Table *(Continued)*

Formulas: $CFS = 3.330(3.0-0.2H)H^{1.5}$ $GPS = CFS \times 7.481$
$GPM = CFS \times 448.8$ $MGD = CFS \times 0.6463$

Head Feet	CFS	GPS	GPM	MGD	Head Feet	CFS	GPS	GPM	MGD
1.01	9.457	70.75	4245	6.112	1.51	16.67	124.7	7482	10.77
1.02	9.591	71.75	4305	6.199	1.52	16.82	125.9	7551	10.87
1.03	9.726	72.76	4365	6.286	1.53	16.98	127.0	7620	10.97
1.04	9.861	73.77	4426	6.373	1.54	17.13	128.2	7689	11.07
1.05	9.996	74.78	4486	6.461	1.55	17.29	129.3	7758	11.17
1.06	10.13	75.80	4547	6.548	1.56	17.44	130.5	7827	11.27
1.07	10.27	76.82	4608	6.636	1.57	17.60	131.6	7897	11.37
1.08	10.41	77.84	4670	6.725	1.58	17.75	132.8	7966	11.47
1.09	10.54	78.87	4731	6.814	1.59	17.91	134.0	8036	11.57
1.10	10.68	79.90	4793	6.903	1.60	18.06	135.1	8106	11.67
1.11	10.82	80.93	4855	6.992	1.61	18.22	136.3	8176	11.77
1.12	10.96	81.97	4917	7.081	1.62	18.37	137.5	8246	11.88
1.13	11.10	83.01	4980	7.171	1.63	18.53	138.6	8316	11.98
1.14	11.24	84.05	5043	7.262	1.64	18.69	139.8	8387	12.08
1.15	11.38	85.10	5105	7.352	1.65	18.84	141.0	8457	12.18
1.16	11.52	86.15	5168	7.443	1.66	19.00	142.2	8528	12.28
1.17	11.66	87.20	5232	7.534	1.67	19.16	143.3	8599	12.38
1.18	11.80	88.26	5295	7.625	1.68	19.32	144.5	8670	12.48
1.19	11.94	89.32	5358	7.717	1.69	19.48	145.7	8740	12.59
1.20	12.08	90.38	5422	7.808	1.70	19.63	146.9	8812	12.69
1.21	12.22	91.45	5486	7.900	1.71	19.79	148.1	8883	12.79
1.22	12.37	92.52	5550	7.993	1.72	19.95	149.3	8954	12.89
1.23	12.51	93.59	5615	8.085	1.73	20.11	150.4	9025	13.00
1.24	12.65	94.66	5679	8.178	1.74	20.27	151.6	9097	13.10
1.25	12.80	95.74	5744	8.271	1.75	20.43	152.8	9169	13.20
1.26	12.94	96.82	5809	8.365	1.76	20.59	154.0	9240	13.31
1.27	13.09	97.91	5874	8.458	1.77	20.75	155.2	9312	13.41
1.28	13.23	98.99	5939	8.552	1.78	20.91	156.4	9384	13.51
1.29	13.38	100.1	6004	8.646	1.79	21.07	157.6	9456	13.62
1.30	13.52	101.2	6070	8.741	1.80	21.23	158.8	9528	13.72
1.31	13.67	102.3	6135	8.835	1.81	21.39	160.0	9600	13.83
1.32	13.82	103.4	6201	8.930	1.82	21.55	161.2	9673	13.93
1.33	13.96	104.5	6267	9.025	1.83	21.71	162.4	9745	14.03
1.34	14.11	105.6	6333	9.120	1.84	21.88	163.7	9818	14.14
1.35	14.26	106.7	6400	9.216	1.85	22.04	164.9	9890	14.24
1.36	14.41	107.8	6466	9.312	1.86	22.20	166.1	9963	14.35
1.37	14.56	108.9	6533	9.408	1.87	22.36	167.3	10040	14.45
1.38	14.71	110.0	6600	9.504	1.88	22.52	168.5	10110	14.56
1.39	14.85	111.1	6667	9.600	1.89	22.69	169.7	10180	14.66
1.40	15.00	112.2	6734	9.697	1.90	22.85	170.9	10250	14.77
1.41	15.15	113.4	6801	9.794	1.91	23.01	172.2	10330	14.87
1.42	15.30	114.5	6868	9.891	1.92	23.18	173.4	10400	14.98
1.43	15.45	115.6	6936	9.988	1.93	23.34	174.6	10470	15.08
1.44	15.61	116.7	7004	10.09	1.94	23.50	175.8	10550	15.19
1.45	15.76	117.9	7072	10.18	1.95	23.67	177.1	10620	15.30
1.46	15.91	119.0	7140	10.28	1.96	23.83	178.3	10700	15.40
1.47	16.06	120.1	7208	10.38	1.97	23.99	179.5	10770	15.51
1.48	16.21	121.3	7276	10.48	1.98	24.16	180.7	10840	15.61
1.49	16.36	122.4	7344	10.58	1.99	24.32	182.0	10920	15.72
1.50	16.52	123.6	7413	10.68	2.00	24.49	183.2	10990	15.83

9

Formulas: CFS $=3.330(3.0-0.2H)H^{1.5}$ GPS = CFS x 7.481
$\quad\quad\quad$ GPM = CFS x 448.8 $\quad\quad$ MGD = CFS x 0.6463

Head Feet	CFS	GPS	GPM	MGD	Head Feet	CFS	GPS	GPM	MGD
2.01	24.65	184.4	11060	15.93	2.51	33.08	247.5	14850	21.38
2.02	24.82	185.7	11140	16.04	2.52	33.25	248.7	14920	21.49
2.03	24.98	186.9	11210	16.15	2.53	33.42	250.0	15000	21.60
2.04	25.15	188.1	11290	16.25	2.54	33.59	251.3	15080	21.71
2.05	25.31	189.4	11360	16.36	2.55	33.76	252.6	15150	21.82
2.06	25.48	190.6	11440	16.47	2.56	33.94	253.9	15230	21.93
2.07	25.65	191.9	11510	16.58	2.57	34.11	255.2	15310	22.04
2.08	25.81	193.1	11580	16.68	2.58	34.28	256.4	15380	22.15
2.09	25.98	194.3	11660	16.79	2.59	34.45	257.7	15460	22.27
2.10	26.15	195.6	11730	16.90	2.60	34.62	259.0	15540	22.38
2.11	26.31	196.8	11810	17.01	2.61	34.79	260.3	15620	22.49
2.12	26.48	198.1	11880	17.11	2.62	34.97	261.6	15690	22.60
2.13	26.65	199.3	11960	17.22	2.63	35.14	262.9	15770	22.71
2.14	26.81	200.6	12030	17.33	2.64	35.31	264.2	15850	22.82
2.15	26.98	201.8	12110	17.44	2.65	35.48	265.4	15920	22.93
2.16	27.15	203.1	12180	17.55	2.66	35.65	266.7	16000	23.04
2.17	27.31	204.3	12260	17.65	2.67	35.83	268.0	16080	23.15
2.18	27.48	205.6	12330	17.76	2.68	36.00	269.3	16160	23.27
2.19	27.65	206.8	12410	17.87	2.69	36.17	270.6	16230	23.38
2.20	27.82	208.1	12480	17.98	2.70	36.34	271.9	16310	23.49
2.21	27.99	209.4	12560	18.09	2.71	36.52	273.2	16390	23.60
2.22	28.15	210.6	12640	18.20	2.72	36.69	274.5	16470	23.71
2.23	28.32	211.9	12710	18.30	2.73	36.86	275.8	16540	23.82
2.24	28.49	213.1	12790	18.41	2.74	37.03	277.0	16620	23.93
2.25	28.66	214.4	12860	18.52	2.75	37.21	278.3	16700	24.05
2.26	28.83	215.7	12940	18.63	2.76	37.38	279.6	16780	24.16
2.27	29.00	216.9	13010	18.74	2.77	37.55	280.9	16850	24.27
2.28	29.17	218.2	13090	18.85	2.78	37.72	282.2	16930	24.38
2.29	29.33	219.4	13170	18.96	2.79	37.90	283.5	17010	24.49
2.30	29.50	220.7	13240	19.07	2.80	38.07	284.8	17090	24.60
2.31	29.67	222.0	13320	19.18	2.81	38.24	286.1	17160	24.72
2.32	29.84	223.2	13390	19.29	2.82	38.41	287.4	17240	24.83
2.33	30.01	224.5	13470	19.40	2.83	38.59	288.7	17320	24.94
2.34	30.18	225.8	13550	19.51	2.84	38.76	290.0	17400	25.05
2.35	30.35	227.1	13620	19.62	2.85	38.93	291.3	17470	25.16
2.36	30.52	228.3	13700	19.73	2.86	39.11	292.6	17550	25.27
2.37	30.69	229.6	13770	19.84	2.87	39.28	293.8	17630	25.39
2.38	30.86	230.9	13850	19.94	2.88	39.45	295.1	17710	25.50
2.39	31.03	232.1	13930	20.05	2.89	39.62	296.4	17780	25.61
2.40	31.20	233.4	14000	20.16	2.90	39.80	297.7	17860	25.72
2.41	31.37	234.7	14080	20.27	2.91	39.97	299.0	17940	25.83
2.42	31.54	236.0	14160	20.39	2.92	40.14	300.3	18020	25.94
2.43	31.71	237.2	14230	20.50	2.93	40.32	301.6	18090	26.06
2.44	31.88	238.5	14310	20.61	2.94	40.49	302.9	18170	26.17
2.45	32.05	239.8	14390	20.72	2.95	40.66	304.2	18250	26.28
2.46	32.22	241.1	14460	20.83	2.96	40.84	305.5	18330	26.39
2.47	32.39	242.3	14540	20.94	2.97	41.01	306.8	18400	26.50
2.48	32.57	243.6	14620	21.05	2.98	41.18	308.1	18480	26.62
2.49	32.74	244.9	14690	21.16	2.99	41.35	309.4	18560	26.73
2.50	32.91	246.2	14770	21.27	3.00	41.53	310.7	18640	26.84

9

9-6: 4 ft. Rectangular Weir with End Contractions Discharge Table

Formulas: CFS $= 3.330(3.0-0.2H)H^{1.5}$ GPS $=$ CFS x 7.481
GPM $=$ CFS x 448.8 MGD $=$ CFS x 0.6463

Head Feet	CFS	GPS	GPM	MGD	Head Feet	CFS	GPS	GPM	MGD
0.01	0.0133	0.0996	5.975	0.0086	0.51	4.728	35.37	2122	3.055
0.02	0.0376	0.2816	16.89	0.0243	0.52	4.865	36.39	2183	3.144
0.03	0.0691	0.5170	31.02	0.0447	0.53	5.003	37.43	2245	3.234
0.04	0.1063	0.7956	47.73	0.0687	0.54	5.143	38.47	2308	3.324
0.05	0.1485	1.111	66.67	0.0960	0.55	5.284	39.53	2371	3.415
0.06	0.1952	1.460	87.59	0.1261	0.56	5.426	40.59	2435	3.507
0.07	0.2458	1.839	110.3	0.1589	0.57	5.569	41.66	2499	3.599
0.08	0.3002	2.246	134.7	0.1940	0.58	5.713	42.74	2564	3.692
0.09	0.3580	2.678	160.7	0.2314	0.59	5.858	43.83	2629	3.786
0.10	0.4191	3.135	188.1	0.2709	0.60	6.005	44.92	2695	3.881
0.11	0.4833	3.615	216.9	0.3123	0.61	6.152	46.03	2761	3.976
0.12	0.5504	4.117	247.0	0.3557	0.62	6.301	47.14	2828	4.072
0.13	0.6203	4.640	278.4	0.4009	0.63	6.451	48.26	2895	4.169
0.14	0.6929	5.183	311.0	0.4478	0.64	6.602	49.39	2963	4.267
0.15	0.7680	5.746	344.7	0.4964	0.65	6.753	50.52	3031	4.365
0.16	0.8457	6.326	379.5	0.5466	0.66	6.906	51.67	3100	4.464
0.17	0.9257	6.925	415.5	0.5983	0.67	7.060	52.82	3169	4.563
0.18	1.008	7.541	452.4	0.6515	0.68	7.215	53.98	3238	4.663
0.19	1.093	8.174	490.4	0.7062	0.69	7.371	55.14	3308	4.764
0.20	1.179	8.824	529.3	0.7623	0.70	7.528	56.32	3379	4.865
0.21	1.268	9.489	569.2	0.8198	0.71	7.686	57.50	3449	4.967
0.22	1.359	10.17	610.1	0.8786	0.72	7.845	58.69	3521	5.070
0.23	1.452	10.87	651.8	0.9387	0.73	8.005	59.88	3592	5.173
0.24	1.547	11.58	694.4	1.000	0.74	8.165	61.09	3665	5.277
0.25	1.644	12.30	737.9	1.063	0.75	8.327	62.30	3737	5.382
0.26	1.743	13.04	782.2	1.126	0.76	8.490	63.51	3810	5.487
0.27	1.844	13.79	827.4	1.191	0.77	8.653	64.74	3884	5.593
0.28	1.946	14.56	873.3	1.258	0.78	8.818	65.97	3958	5.699
0.29	2.050	15.34	920.0	1.325	0.79	8.983	67.21	4032	5.806
0.30	2.156	16.13	967.6	1.393	0.80	9.150	68.45	4106	5.913
0.31	2.263	16.93	1016	1.463	0.81	9.317	69.70	4181	6.022
0.32	2.373	17.75	1065	1.533	0.82	9.485	70.96	4257	6.130
0.33	2.483	18.58	1115	1.605	0.83	9.654	72.22	4333	6.239
0.34	2.596	19.42	1165	1.678	0.84	9.824	73.49	4409	6.349
0.35	2.710	20.27	1216	1.751	0.85	9.995	74.77	4486	6.460
0.36	2.825	21.14	1268	1.826	0.86	10.17	76.05	4563	6.570
0.37	2.942	22.01	1321	1.902	0.87	10.34	77.34	4640	6.682
0.38	3.061	22.90	1374	1.978	0.88	10.51	78.64	4718	6.794
0.39	3.181	23.80	1428	2.056	0.89	10.69	79.94	4796	6.906
0.40	3.302	24.70	1482	2.134	0.90	10.86	81.25	4874	7.019
0.41	3.425	25.62	1537	2.214	0.91	11.04	82.57	4953	7.133
0.42	3.549	26.55	1593	2.294	0.92	11.21	83.89	5033	7.247
0.43	3.675	27.49	1649	2.375	0.93	11.39	85.21	5112	7.362
0.44	3.802	28.44	1706	2.457	0.94	11.57	86.55	5192	7.477
0.45	3.930	29.40	1764	2.540	0.95	11.75	87.88	5272	7.593
0.46	4.060	30.37	1822	2.624	0.96	11.93	89.23	5353	7.709
0.47	4.191	31.35	1881	2.709	0.97	12.11	90.58	5434	7.825
0.48	4.323	32.34	1940	2.794	0.98	12.29	91.94	5515	7.943
0.49	4.457	33.34	2000	2.880	0.99	12.47	93.30	5597	8.060
0.50	4.592	34.35	2061	2.968	1.00	12.65	94.66	5679	8.178

9

Formulas: CFS = $3.330(4.0-0.2H)H^{1.5}$ GPS = CFS x 7.481
GPM = CFS x 448.8   MGD = CFS x 0.6463

Head Feet	CFS	GPS	GPM	MGD	Head Feet	CFS	GPS	GPM	MGD
1.01	12.84	96.04	5761	8.297	1.51	22.85	170.9	10250	14.77
1.02	13.02	97.42	5844	8.416	1.52	23.06	172.5	10350	14.91
1.03	13.21	98.80	5927	8.536	1.53	23.28	174.2	10450	15.05
1.04	13.39	100.2	6011	8.656	1.54	23.50	175.8	10540	15.19
1.05	13.58	101.6	6094	8.776	1.55	23.71	177.4	10640	15.33
1.06	13.77	103.0	6178	8.897	1.56	23.93	179.0	10740	15.47
1.07	13.95	104.4	6263	9.019	1.57	24.15	180.6	10840	15.61
1.08	14.14	105.8	6347	9.140	1.58	24.36	182.3	10930	15.75
1.09	14.33	107.2	6432	9.263	1.59	24.58	183.9	11030	15.89
1.10	14.52	108.6	6517	9.386	1.60	24.80	185.5	11130	16.03
1.11	14.71	110.1	6603	9.509	1.61	25.02	187.2	11230	16.17
1.12	14.90	111.5	6689	9.632	1.62	25.24	188.8	11330	16.31
1.13	15.10	112.9	6775	9.757	1.63	25.46	190.5	11430	16.46
1.14	15.29	114.4	6862	9.881	1.64	25.68	192.1	11530	16.60
1.15	15.48	115.8	6948	10.01	1.65	25.90	193.8	11620	16.74
1.16	15.68	117.3	7035	10.13	1.66	26.12	195.4	11720	16.88
1.17	15.87	118.7	7123	10.26	1.67	26.35	197.1	11820	17.03
1.18	16.07	120.2	7211	10.38	1.68	26.57	198.8	11920	17.17
1.19	16.26	121.7	7299	10.51	1.69	26.79	200.4	12020	17.32
1.20	16.46	123.1	7387	10.64	1.70	27.01	202.1	12120	17.46
1.21	16.66	124.6	7475	10.76	1.71	27.24	203.8	12220	17.60
1.22	16.85	126.1	7564	10.89	1.72	27.46	205.4	12330	17.75
1.23	17.05	127.6	7653	11.02	1.73	27.69	207.1	12430	17.89
1.24	17.25	129.1	7743	11.15	1.74	27.91	208.8	12530	18.04
1.25	17.45	130.6	7832	11.28	1.75	28.14	210.5	12630	18.19
1.26	17.65	132.1	7922	11.41	1.76	28.36	212.2	12730	18.33
1.27	17.85	133.6	8013	11.54	1.77	28.59	213.9	12830	18.48
1.28	18.05	135.1	8103	11.67	1.78	28.82	215.6	12930	18.62
1.29	18.26	136.6	8194	11.80	1.79	29.04	217.3	13040	18.77
1.30	18.46	138.1	8285	11.93	1.80	29.27	219.0	13140	18.92
1.31	18.66	139.6	8376	12.06	1.81	29.50	220.7	13240	19.07
1.32	18.87	141.1	8468	12.19	1.82	29.73	222.4	13340	19.21
1.33	19.07	142.7	8560	12.33	1.83	29.96	224.1	13440	19.36
1.34	19.28	144.2	8652	12.46	1.84	30.19	225.8	13550	19.51
1.35	19.48	145.8	8744	12.59	1.85	30.42	227.5	13650	19.66
1.36	19.69	147.3	8837	12.73	1.86	30.65	229.3	13750	19.81
1.37	19.90	148.8	8929	12.86	1.87	30.88	231.0	13860	19.96
1.38	20.10	150.4	9022	12.99	1.88	31.11	232.7	13960	20.10
1.39	20.31	152.0	9116	13.13	1.89	31.34	234.4	14060	20.25
1.40	20.52	153.5	9209	13.26	1.90	31.57	236.2	14170	20.40
1.41	20.73	155.1	9303	13.40	1.91	31.80	237.9	14270	20.55
1.42	20.94	156.6	9397	13.53	1.92	32.03	239.7	14380	20.70
1.43	21.15	158.2	9492	13.67	1.93	32.27	241.4	14480	20.85
1.44	21.36	159.8	9586	13.80	1.94	32.50	243.1	14590	21.01
1.45	21.57	161.4	9681	13.94	1.95	32.73	244.9	14690	21.16
1.46	21.78	163.0	9776	14.08	1.96	32.97	246.6	14800	21.31
1.47	22.00	164.5	9871	14.22	1.97	33.20	248.4	14900	21.46
1.48	22.21	166.1	9967	14.35	1.98	33.44	250.1	15010	21.61
1.49	22.42	167.7	10060	14.49	1.99	33.67	251.9	15110	21.76
1.50	22.64	169.3	10160	14.63	2.00	33.91	253.7	15220	21.91

9

9-6: 4 ft. Rectangular Weir with End Contractions
Discharge Table *(Continued)*

Formulas: $CFS = 3.330(4.0-0.2H)H^{1.5}$

$GPM = CFS \times 448.8$

$GPS = CFS \times 7.481$

$MGD = CFS \times 0.6463$

Head Feet	CFS	GPS	GPM	MGD	Head Feet	CFS	GPS	GPM	MGD
2.01	34.14	255.4	15320	22.07	2.51	46.32	346.5	20790	29.94
2.02	34.38	257.2	15430	22.22	2.52	46.57	348.4	20900	30.10
2.03	34.62	259.0	15540	22.37	2.53	46.82	350.3	21010	30.26
2.04	34.85	260.7	15640	22.52	2.54	47.07	352.2	21130	30.42
2.05	35.09	262.5	15750	22.68	2.55	47.32	354.0	21240	30.59
2.06	35.33	264.3	15850	22.83	2.56	47.58	355.9	21350	30.75
2.07	35.56	266.1	15960	22.98	2.57	47.83	357.8	21460	30.91
2.08	35.80	267.8	16070	23.14	2.58	48.08	359.7	21580	31.07
2.09	36.04	269.6	16170	23.29	2.59	48.33	361.6	21690	31.24
2.10	36.28	271.4	16280	23.45	2.60	48.58	363.4	21800	31.40
2.11	36.52	273.2	16390	23.60	2.61	48.84	365.3	21920	31.56
2.12	36.76	275.0	16500	23.76	2.62	49.09	367.2	22030	31.73
2.13	37.00	276.8	16600	23.91	2.63	49.34	369.1	22140	31.89
2.14	37.24	278.6	16710	24.07	2.64	49.59	371.0	22260	32.05
2.15	37.48	280.4	16820	24.22	2.65	49.85	372.9	22370	32.22
2.16	37.72	282.2	16930	24.38	2.66	50.10	374.8	22490	32.38
2.17	37.96	284.0	17040	24.53	2.67	50.35	376.7	22600	32.54
2.18	38.20	285.8	17140	24.69	2.68	50.61	378.6	22710	32.71
2.19	38.44	287.6	17250	24.84	2.69	50.86	380.5	22830	32.87
2.20	38.68	289.4	17360	25.00	2.70	51.12	382.4	22940	33.04
2.21	38.93	291.2	17470	25.16	2.71	51.37	384.3	23060	33.20
2.22	39.17	293.0	17580	25.31	2.72	51.63	386.2	23170	33.37
2.23	39.41	294.8	17690	25.47	2.73	51.88	388.1	23280	33.53
2.24	39.65	296.7	17800	25.63	2.74	52.14	390.0	23400	33.70
2.25	39.90	298.5	17910	25.79	2.75	52.39	391.9	23510	33.86
2.26	40.14	300.3	18020	25.94	2.76	52.65	393.9	23630	34.03
2.27	40.39	302.1	18120	26.10	2.77	52.90	395.8	23740	34.19
2.28	40.63	303.9	18230	26.26	2.78	53.16	397.7	23860	34.36
2.29	40.87	305.8	18340	26.42	2.79	53.41	399.6	23970	34.52
2.30	41.12	307.6	18450	26.58	2.80	53.67	401.5	24090	34.69
2.31	41.36	309.4	18560	26.73	2.81	53.93	403.4	24200	34.85
2.32	41.61	311.3	18670	26.89	2.82	54.18	405.4	24320	35.02
2.33	41.85	313.1	18780	27.05	2.83	54.44	407.3	24430	35.19
2.34	42.10	315.0	18890	27.21	2.84	54.70	409.2	24550	35.35
2.35	42.35	316.8	19010	27.37	2.85	54.95	411.1	24660	35.52
2.36	42.59	318.6	19120	27.53	2.86	55.21	413.0	24780	35.68
2.37	42.84	320.5	19230	27.69	2.87	55.47	415.0	24890	35.85
2.38	43.09	322.3	19340	27.85	2.88	55.73	416.9	25010	36.02
2.39	43.33	324.2	19450	28.01	2.89	55.98	418.8	25130	36.18
2.40	43.58	326.0	19560	28.17	2.90	56.24	420.8	25240	36.35
2.41	43.83	327.9	19670	28.33	2.91	56.50	422.7	25360	36.52
2.42	44.08	329.7	19780	28.49	2.92	56.76	424.6	25470	36.68
2.43	44.33	331.6	19890	28.65	2.93	57.02	426.5	25590	36.85
2.44	44.57	333.5	20000	28.81	2.94	57.28	428.5	25710	37.02
2.45	44.82	335.3	20120	28.97	2.95	57.53	430.4	25820	37.18
2.46	45.07	337.2	20230	29.13	2.96	57.79	432.4	25940	37.35
2.47	45.32	339.0	20340	29.29	2.97	58.05	434.3	26050	37.52
2.48	45.57	340.9	20450	29.45	2.98	58.31	436.2	26170	37.69
2.49	45.82	342.8	20560	29.61	2.99	58.57	438.2	26290	37.85
2.50	46.07	344.7	20680	29.78	3.00	58.83	440.1	26400	38.02

9

9-7: 5 ft. Rectangular Weir with End Contractions Discharge Table

Formulas: $CFS = 3.330(4.0\text{-}0.2H)H^{1.5}$ $GPS = CFS \times 7.481$
$GPM = CFS \times 448.8$ $MGD = CFS \times 0.6463$

Head Feet	CFS	GPS	GPM	MGD	Head Feet	CFS	GPS	GPM	MGD
0.01	0.0166	0.1245	7.470	0.0108	0.51	5.940	44.44	2666	3.839
0.02	0.0471	0.3520	21.12	0.0304	0.52	6.114	45.74	2744	3.951
0.03	0.0864	0.6464	38.78	0.0558	0.53	6.288	47.04	2822	4.064
0.04	0.1330	0.9949	59.68	0.0859	0.54	6.464	48.36	2901	4.178
0.05	0.1858	1.390	83.38	0.1201	0.55	6.642	49.69	2981	4.293
0.06	0.2441	1.826	109.6	0.1578	0.56	6.821	51.03	3061	4.409
0.07	0.3075	2.300	138.0	0.1987	0.57	7.002	52.38	3142	4.525
0.08	0.3755	2.809	168.5	0.2427	0.58	7.184	53.74	3224	4.643
0.09	0.4479	3.351	201.0	0.2895	0.59	7.367	55.12	3307	4.762
0.10	0.5244	3.923	235.4	0.3389	0.60	7.553	56.50	3390	4.881
0.11	0.6048	4.524	271.4	0.3909	0.61	7.739	57.89	3473	5.002
0.12	0.6888	5.153	309.1	0.4452	0.62	7.927	59.30	3558	5.123
0.13	0.7764	5.808	348.4	0.5018	0.63	8.116	60.72	3642	5.245
0.14	0.8673	6.488	389.2	0.5605	0.64	8.307	62.14	3728	5.369
0.15	0.9615	7.193	431.5	0.6214	0.65	8.499	63.58	3814	5.493
0.16	1.059	7.921	475.2	0.6843	0.66	8.692	65.02	3901	5.618
0.17	1.159	8.671	520.2	0.7491	0.67	8.886	66.48	3988	5.743
0.18	1.262	9.444	566.5	0.8159	0.68	9.082	67.95	4076	5.870
0.19	1.368	10.24	614.2	0.8844	0.69	9.280	69.42	4165	5.997
0.20	1.477	11.05	663.0	0.9548	0.70	9.478	70.91	4254	6.126
0.21	1.589	11.89	713.1	1.027	0.71	9.678	72.40	4344	6.255
0.22	1.703	12.74	764.3	1.101	0.72	9.879	73.91	4434	6.385
0.23	1.820	13.61	816.7	1.176	0.73	10.08	75.42	4525	6.516
0.24	1.939	14.50	870.2	1.253	0.74	10.29	76.94	4616	6.647
0.25	2.060	15.41	924.7	1.332	0.75	10.49	78.48	4708	6.780
0.26	2.184	16.34	980.4	1.412	0.76	10.70	80.02	4800	6.913
0.27	2.311	17.29	1037	1.493	0.77	10.90	81.57	4893	7.047
0.28	2.439	18.25	1095	1.576	0.78	11.11	83.13	4987	7.182
0.29	2.570	19.23	1153	1.661	0.79	11.32	84.70	5081	7.317
0.30	2.703	20.22	1213	1.747	0.80	11.53	86.27	5176	7.453
0.31	2.838	21.23	1274	1.834	0.81	11.74	87.86	5271	7.591
0.32	2.975	22.26	1335	1.923	0.82	11.96	89.46	5367	7.728
0.33	3.115	23.30	1398	2.013	0.83	12.17	91.06	5463	7.867
0.34	3.256	24.36	1461	2.104	0.84	12.39	92.67	5560	8.006
0.35	3.399	25.43	1526	2.197	0.85	12.60	94.29	5657	8.146
0.36	3.545	26.52	1591	2.291	0.86	12.82	95.92	5755	8.287
0.37	3.692	27.62	1657	2.386	0.87	13.04	97.56	5853	8.428
0.38	3.841	28.73	1724	2.482	0.88	13.26	99.21	5952	8.571
0.39	3.992	29.86	1792	2.580	0.89	13.48	100.9	6051	8.713
0.40	4.145	31.01	1860	2.679	0.90	13.70	102.5	6150	8.857
0.41	4.299	32.16	1930	2.779	0.91	13.93	104.2	6251	9.001
0.42	4.456	33.33	2000	2.880	0.92	14.15	105.9	6351	9.146
0.43	4.614	34.52	2071	2.982	0.93	14.38	107.6	6452	9.292
0.44	4.774	35.71	2143	3.085	0.94	14.60	109.2	6554	9.438
0.45	4.936	36.92	2215	3.190	0.95	14.83	111.0	6656	9.585
0.46	5.099	38.15	2288	3.295	0.96	15.06	112.7	6759	9.733
0.47	5.264	39.38	2362	3.402	0.97	15.29	114.4	6862	9.881
0.48	5.431	40.63	2437	3.510	0.98	15.52	116.1	6965	10.03
0.49	5.599	41.89	2513	3.619	0.99	15.75	117.8	7069	10.18
0.50	5.769	43.16	2589	3.728	1.00	15.98	119.6	7174	10.33

9

Formulas: $CFS = 3.330(4.0-0.2H)H^{1.5}$

$GPM = CFS \times 448.8$

$GPS = CFS \times 7.481$

$MGD = CFS \times 0.6463$

Head Feet	CFS	GPS	GPM	MGD	Head Feet	CFS	GPS	GPM	MGD
1.01	16.22	121.3	7278	10.48	1.51	29.03	217.2	13030	18.76
1.02	16.45	123.1	7384	10.63	1.52	29.30	219.2	13150	18.94
1.03	16.69	124.8	7489	10.79	1.53	29.58	221.3	13280	19.12
1.04	16.92	126.6	7596	10.94	1.54	29.86	223.4	13400	19.30
1.05	17.16	128.4	7702	11.09	1.55	30.14	225.5	13530	19.48
1.06	17.40	130.2	7809	11.25	1.56	30.42	227.6	13650	19.66
1.07	17.64	132.0	7917	11.40	1.57	30.70	229.6	13780	19.84
1.08	17.88	133.8	8025	11.56	1.58	30.98	231.7	13900	20.02
1.09	18.12	135.6	8133	11.71	1.59	31.26	233.8	14030	20.20
1.10	18.36	137.4	8242	11.87	1.60	31.54	236.0	14160	20.38
1.11	18.61	139.2	8351	12.03	1.61	31.82	238.1	14280	20.57
1.12	18.85	141.0	8460	12.18	1.62	32.11	240.2	14410	20.75
1.13	19.10	142.9	8570	12.34	1.63	32.39	242.3	14540	20.93
1.14	19.34	144.7	8681	12.50	1.64	32.67	244.4	14660	21.12
1.15	19.59	146.5	8791	12.66	1.65	32.96	246.6	14790	21.30
1.16	19.84	148.4	8903	12.82	1.66	33.25	248.7	14920	21.49
1.17	20.09	150.3	9014	12.98	1.67	33.53	250.9	15050	21.67
1.18	20.33	152.1	9126	13.14	1.68	33.82	253.0	15180	21.86
1.19	20.59	154.0	9239	13.30	1.69	34.11	255.2	15310	22.04
1.20	20.84	155.9	9351	13.47	1.70	34.40	257.3	15440	22.23
1.21	21.09	157.8	9465	13.63	1.71	34.68	259.5	15570	22.42
1.22	21.34	159.7	9578	13.79	1.72	34.97	261.6	15700	22.60
1.23	21.60	161.6	9692	13.96	1.73	35.26	263.8	15830	22.79
1.24	21.85	163.5	9806	14.12	1.74	35.56	266.0	15960	22.98
1.25	22.11	165.4	9921	14.29	1.75	35.85	268.2	16090	23.17
1.26	22.36	167.3	10040	14.45	1.76	36.14	270.4	16220	23.36
1.27	22.62	169.2	10150	14.62	1.77	36.43	272.5	16350	23.55
1.28	22.88	171.1	10270	14.79	1.78	36.73	274.7	16480	23.74
1.29	23.14	173.1	10380	14.95	1.79	37.02	276.9	16610	23.93
1.30	23.40	175.0	10500	15.12	1.80	37.31	279.1	16750	24.12
1.31	23.66	177.0	10620	15.29	1.81	37.61	281.4	16880	24.31
1.32	23.92	178.9	10730	15.46	1.82	37.90	283.6	17010	24.50
1.33	24.18	180.9	10850	15.63	1.83	38.20	285.8	17140	24.69
1.34	24.44	182.9	10970	15.80	1.84	38.50	288.0	17280	24.88
1.35	24.71	184.8	11090	15.97	1.85	38.80	290.2	17410	25.07
1.36	24.97	186.8	11210	16.14	1.86	39.09	292.5	17550	25.27
1.37	25.24	188.8	11330	16.31	1.87	39.39	294.7	17680	25.46
1.38	25.50	190.8	11450	16.48	1.88	39.69	296.9	17810	25.65
1.39	25.77	192.8	11560	16.65	1.89	39.99	299.2	17950	25.85
1.40	26.04	194.8	11690	16.83	1.90	40.29	301.4	18080	26.04
1.41	26.30	196.8	11810	17.00	1.91	40.59	303.7	18220	26.24
1.42	26.57	198.8	11930	17.17	1.92	40.89	305.9	18350	26.43
1.43	26.84	200.8	12050	17.35	1.93	41.20	308.2	18490	26.63
1.44	27.11	202.8	12170	17.52	1.94	41.50	310.5	18620	26.82
1.45	27.39	204.9	12290	17.70	1.95	41.80	312.7	18760	27.02
1.46	27.66	206.9	12410	17.87	1.96	42.11	315.0	18900	27.21
1.47	27.93	208.9	12540	18.05	1.97	42.41	317.3	19030	27.41
1.48	28.20	211.0	12660	18.23	1.98	42.71	319.5	19170	27.61
1.49	28.48	213.0	12780	18.41	1.99	43.02	321.8	19310	27.80
1.50	28.75	215.1	12900	18.58	2.00	43.33	324.1	19440	28.00

9

Formulas: $CFS = 3.330(4.0-0.2H)H^{1.5}$ $GPS = CFS \times 7.481$
$GPM = CFS \times 448.8$ $MGD = CFS \times 0.6463$

Head Feet	CFS	GPS	GPM	MGD	Head Feet	CFS	GPS	GPM	MGD
2.01	43.63	326.4	19580	28.20	2.51	59.56	445.6	26730	38.50
2.02	43.94	328.7	19720	28.40	2.52	59.89	448.1	26880	38.71
2.03	44.25	331.0	19860	28.60	2.53	60.22	450.5	27030	38.92
2.04	44.55	333.3	20000	28.80	2.54	60.55	453.0	27180	39.14
2.05	44.86	335.6	20130	28.99	2.55	60.88	455.5	27320	39.35
2.06	45.17	337.9	20270	29.19	2.56	61.21	457.9	27470	39.56
2.07	45.48	340.2	20410	29.39	2.57	61.55	460.4	27620	39.78
2.08	45.79	342.6	20550	29.59	2.58	61.88	462.9	27770	39.99
2.09	46.10	344.9	20690	29.80	2.59	62.21	465.4	27920	40.21
2.10	46.41	347.2	20830	30.00	2.60	62.54	467.9	28070	40.42
2.11	46.72	349.5	20970	30.20	2.61	62.88	470.4	28220	40.64
2.12	47.04	351.9	21110	30.40	2.62	63.21	472.9	28370	40.85
2.13	47.35	354.2	21250	30.60	2.63	63.54	475.4	28520	41.07
2.14	47.66	356.6	21390	30.80	2.64	63.88	477.9	28670	41.28
2.15	47.98	358.9	21530	31.01	2.65	64.21	480.4	28820	41.50
2.16	48.29	361.3	21670	31.21	2.66	64.55	482.9	28970	41.72
2.17	48.60	363.6	21810	31.41	2.67	64.88	485.4	29120	41.93
2.18	48.92	366.0	21950	31.62	2.68	65.22	487.9	29270	42.15
2.19	49.23	368.3	22100	31.82	2.69	65.55	490.4	29420	42.37
2.20	49.55	370.7	22240	32.02	2.70	65.89	492.9	29570	42.59
2.21	49.87	373.0	22380	32.23	2.71	66.23	495.4	29720	42.80
2.22	50.18	375.4	22520	32.43	2.72	66.56	498.0	29870	43.02
2.23	50.50	377.8	22660	32.64	2.73	66.90	500.5	30030	43.24
2.24	50.82	380.2	22810	32.84	2.74	67.24	503.0	30180	43.46
2.25	51.14	382.6	22950	33.05	2.75	67.58	505.5	30330	43.68
2.26	51.45	384.9	23090	33.26	2.76	67.92	508.1	30480	43.89
2.27	51.77	387.3	23240	33.46	2.77	68.25	510.6	30630	44.11
2.28	52.09	389.7	23380	33.67	2.78	68.59	513.2	30780	44.33
2.29	52.41	392.1	23520	33.87	2.79	68.93	515.7	30940	44.55
2.30	52.73	394.5	23670	34.08	2.80	69.27	518.2	31090	44.77
2.31	53.06	396.9	23810	34.29	2.81	69.61	520.8	31240	44.99
2.32	53.38	399.3	23960	34.50	2.82	69.95	523.3	31400	45.21
2.33	53.70	401.7	24100	34.71	2.83	70.29	525.9	31550	45.43
2.34	54.02	404.1	24240	34.91	2.84	70.64	528.4	31700	45.65
2.35	54.34	406.5	24390	35.12	2.85	70.98	531.0	31850	45.87
2.36	54.67	409.0	24530	35.33	2.86	71.32	533.5	32010	46.09
2.37	54.99	411.4	24680	35.54	2.87	71.66	536.1	32160	46.31
2.38	55.31	413.8	24820	35.75	2.88	72.00	538.7	32310	46.54
2.39	55.64	416.2	24970	35.96	2.89	72.35	541.2	32470	46.76
2.40	55.96	418.7	25120	36.17	2.90	72.69	543.8	32620	46.98
2.41	56.29	421.1	25260	36.38	2.91	73.03	546.3	32780	47.20
2.42	56.61	423.5	25410	36.59	2.92	73.37	548.9	32930	47.42
2.43	56.94	426.0	25550	36.80	2.93	73.72	551.5	33080	47.64
2.44	57.27	428.4	25700	37.01	2.94	74.06	554.1	33240	47.87
2.45	57.59	430.9	25850	37.22	2.95	74.41	556.6	33390	48.09
2.46	57.92	433.3	25990	37.43	2.96	74.75	559.2	33550	48.31
2.47	58.25	435.8	26140	37.65	2.97	75.10	561.8	33700	48.54
2.48	58.58	438.2	26290	37.86	2.98	75.44	564.4	33860	48.76
2.49	58.90	440.7	26440	38.07	2.99	75.79	567.0	34010	48.98
2.50	59.23	443.1	26580	38.28	3.00	76.13	569.6	34170	49.21

9-8: 6 ft. Rectangular Weir with End Contractions Discharge Table

Formulas: CFS $= 3.330(4.0-0.2H)H^{1.5}$ GPS = CFS x 7.481
GPM = CFS x 448.8   MGD = CFS x 0.6463

Head Feet	CFS	GPS	GPM	MGD	Head Feet	CFS	GPS	GPM	MGD
0.01	0.0200	0.1494	8.964	0.0129	0.51	7.153	53.51	3210	4.623
0.02	0.0565	0.4225	25.35	0.0365	0.52	7.362	55.08	3304	4.758
0.03	0.1037	0.7759	46.55	0.0670	0.53	7.573	56.65	3399	4.894
0.04	0.1596	1.194	71.64	0.1032	0.54	7.786	58.24	3494	5.032
0.05	0.2230	1.668	100.1	0.1441	0.55	8.000	59.85	3591	5.171
0.06	0.2931	2.192	131.5	0.1894	0.56	8.217	61.47	3688	5.310
0.07	0.3692	2.762	165.7	0.2386	0.57	8.435	63.10	3786	5.451
0.08	0.4509	3.373	202.4	0.2914	0.58	8.655	64.75	3884	5.594
0.09	0.5378	4.024	241.4	0.3476	0.59	8.877	66.41	3984	5.737
0.10	0.6297	4.711	282.6	0.4070	0.60	9.100	68.08	4084	5.881
0.11	0.7263	5.433	325.9	0.4694	0.61	9.325	69.76	4185	6.027
0.12	0.8272	6.189	371.3	0.5346	0.62	9.552	71.46	4287	6.174
0.13	0.9324	6.976	418.5	0.6026	0.63	9.781	73.17	4390	6.322
0.14	1.042	7.793	467.5	0.6733	0.64	10.01	74.90	4493	6.470
0.15	1.155	8.640	518.3	0.7464	0.65	10.24	76.63	4597	6.620
0.16	1.272	9.515	570.8	0.8220	0.66	10.48	78.38	4702	6.771
0.17	1.393	10.42	625.0	0.9000	0.67	10.71	80.14	4808	6.924
0.18	1.517	11.35	680.7	0.9802	0.68	10.95	81.91	4914	7.077
0.19	1.644	12.30	737.9	1.063	0.69	11.19	83.70	5021	7.231
0.20	1.775	13.28	796.7	1.147	0.70	11.43	85.50	5129	7.386
0.21	1.909	14.28	856.9	1.234	0.71	11.67	87.31	5238	7.542
0.22	2.047	15.31	918.5	1.323	0.72	11.91	89.13	5347	7.700
0.23	2.187	16.36	981.5	1.413	0.73	12.16	90.96	5457	7.858
0.24	2.330	17.43	1046	1.506	0.74	12.40	92.80	5567	8.017
0.25	2.477	18.53	1112	1.601	0.75	12.65	94.66	5679	8.178
0.26	2.626	19.64	1178	1.697	0.76	12.90	96.52	5791	8.339
0.27	2.778	20.78	1247	1.795	0.77	13.15	98.40	5903	8.501
0.28	2.933	21.94	1316	1.895	0.78	13.41	100.3	6017	8.664
0.29	3.090	23.12	1387	1.997	0.79	13.66	102.2	6131	8.828
0.30	3.250	24.31	1459	2.101	0.80	13.92	104.1	6245	8.993
0.31	3.413	25.53	1532	2.206	0.81	14.17	106.0	6360	9.159
0.32	3.578	26.77	1606	2.313	0.82	14.43	108.0	6476	9.326
0.33	3.746	28.02	1681	2.421	0.83	14.69	109.9	6593	9.494
0.34	3.916	29.30	1758	2.531	0.84	14.95	111.9	6710	9.663
0.35	4.089	30.59	1835	2.643	0.85	15.21	113.8	6828	9.833
0.36	4.264	31.90	1914	2.756	0.86	15.48	115.8	6946	10.00
0.37	4.441	33.23	1993	2.870	0.87	15.74	117.8	7066	10.17
0.38	4.621	34.57	2074	2.987	0.88	16.01	119.8	7185	10.35
0.39	4.803	35.93	2156	3.104	0.89	16.28	121.8	7306	10.52
0.40	4.987	37.31	2238	3.223	0.90	16.55	123.8	7426	10.69
0.41	5.174	38.70	2322	3.344	0.91	16.82	125.8	7548	10.87
0.42	5.362	40.11	2407	3.466	0.92	17.09	127.9	7670	11.05
0.43	5.553	41.54	2492	3.589	0.93	17.36	129.9	7793	11.22
0.44	5.746	42.99	2579	3.714	0.94	17.64	132.0	7916	11.40
0.45	5.941	44.44	2666	3.840	0.95	17.91	134.0	8040	11.58
0.46	6.138	45.92	2755	3.967	0.96	18.19	136.1	8165	11.76
0.47	6.337	47.41	2844	4.096	0.97	18.47	138.2	8290	11.94
0.48	6.538	48.91	2934	4.226	0.98	18.75	140.3	8415	12.12
0.49	6.741	50.43	3025	4.357	0.99	19.03	142.4	8541	12.30
0.50	6.946	51.96	3117	4.489	1.00	19.31	144.5	8668	12.48

9

9-8: 6 ft. Rectangular Weir with End Contractions Discharge Table (Continued)

Formulas: CFS $= 3.330(4.0-0.2H)H^{1.5}$ GPS = CFS x 7.481
GPM = CFS x 448.8   MGD = CFS x 0.6463

Head Feet	CFS	GPS	GPM	MGD	Head Feet	CFS	GPS	GPM	MGD
1.01	19.60	146.6	8795	12.67	1.51	35.21	263.4	15800	22.75
1.02	19.88	148.7	8923	12.85	1.52	35.55	265.9	15950	22.97
1.03	20.17	150.9	9052	13.04	1.53	35.88	268.4	16100	23.19
1.04	20.46	153.0	9181	13.22	1.54	36.22	271.0	16260	23.41
1.05	20.74	155.2	9310	13.41	1.55	36.56	273.5	16410	23.63
1.06	21.03	157.4	9440	13.59	1.56	36.91	276.1	16560	23.85
1.07	21.33	159.5	9571	13.78	1.57	37.25	278.7	16720	24.07
1.08	21.62	161.7	9702	13.97	1.58	37.59	281.2	16870	24.30
1.09	21.91	163.9	9834	14.16	1.59	37.94	283.8	17030	24.52
1.10	22.21	166.1	9966	14.35	1.60	38.28	286.4	17180	24.74
1.11	22.50	168.3	10100	14.54	1.61	38.63	289.0	17340	24.96
1.12	22.80	170.6	10230	14.73	1.62	38.97	291.6	17490	25.19
1.13	23.10	172.8	10370	14.93	1.63	39.32	294.2	17650	25.41
1.14	23.40	175.0	10500	15.12	1.64	39.67	296.8	17800	25.64
1.15	23.70	177.3	10630	15.31	1.65	40.02	299.4	17960	25.86
1.16	24.00	179.5	10770	15.51	1.66	40.37	302.0	18120	26.09
1.17	24.30	181.8	10910	15.70	1.67	40.72	304.6	18270	26.32
1.18	24.60	184.1	11040	15.90	1.68	41.07	307.2	18430	26.54
1.19	24.91	186.3	11180	16.10	1.69	41.42	309.9	18590	26.77
1.20	25.21	188.6	11320	16.30	1.70	41.78	312.5	18750	27.00
1.21	25.52	190.9	11450	16.49	1.71	42.13	315.2	18910	27.23
1.22	25.83	193.2	11590	16.69	1.72	42.49	317.8	19070	27.46
1.23	26.14	195.5	11730	16.89	1.73	42.84	320.5	19230	27.69
1.24	26.45	197.9	11870	17.09	1.74	43.20	323.2	19390	27.92
1.25	26.76	200.2	12010	17.29	1.75	43.56	325.8	19550	28.15
1.26	27.07	202.5	12150	17.50	1.76	43.91	328.5	19710	28.38
1.27	27.39	204.9	12290	17.70	1.77	44.27	331.2	19870	28.61
1.28	27.70	207.2	12430	17.90	1.78	44.63	333.9	20030	28.85
1.29	28.02	209.6	12570	18.11	1.79	44.99	336.6	20190	29.08
1.30	28.33	211.9	12720	18.31	1.80	45.36	339.3	20360	29.31
1.31	28.65	214.3	12860	18.52	1.81	45.72	342.0	20520	29.55
1.32	28.97	216.7	13000	18.72	1.82	46.08	344.7	20680	29.78
1.33	29.29	219.1	13140	18.93	1.83	46.44	347.5	20840	30.02
1.34	29.61	221.5	13290	19.14	1.84	46.81	350.2	21010	30.25
1.35	29.93	223.9	13430	19.34	1.85	47.17	352.9	21170	30.49
1.36	30.25	226.3	13580	19.55	1.86	47.54	355.7	21340	30.73
1.37	30.58	228.7	13720	19.76	1.87	47.91	358.4	21500	30.96
1.38	30.90	231.2	13870	19.97	1.88	48.28	361.1	21670	31.20
1.39	31.23	233.6	14010	20.18	1.89	48.64	363.9	21830	31.44
1.40	31.55	236.0	14160	20.39	1.90	49.01	366.7	22000	31.68
1.41	31.88	238.5	14310	20.60	1.91	49.38	369.4	22160	31.92
1.42	32.21	241.0	14460	20.82	1.92	49.75	372.2	22330	32.16
1.43	32.54	243.4	14600	21.03	1.93	50.12	375.0	22500	32.40
1.44	32.87	245.9	14750	21.24	1.94	50.50	377.8	22660	32.64
1.45	33.20	248.4	14900	21.46	1.95	50.87	380.6	22830	32.88
1.46	33.53	250.9	15050	21.67	1.96	51.24	383.4	23000	33.12
1.47	33.87	253.3	15200	21.89	1.97	51.62	386.2	23170	33.36
1.48	34.20	255.8	15350	22.10	1.98	51.99	389.0	23330	33.60
1.49	34.53	258.4	15500	22.32	1.99	52.37	391.8	23500	33.85
1.50	34.87	260.9	15650	22.54	2.00	52.74	394.6	23670	34.09

9-8: 6 ft. Rectangular Weir with End Contractions
Discharge Table *(Continued)*

Formulas: CFS $=3.330(4.0-0.2H)H^{1.5}$ GPS = CFS x 7.481
  GPM = CFS x 448.8   MGD = CFS x 0.6463

Head Feet	CFS	GPS	GPM	MGD	Head Feet	CFS	GPS	GPM	MGD
2.01	53.12	397.4	23840	34.33	2.51	72.80	544.7	32670	47.05
2.02	53.50	400.2	24010	34.58	2.52	73.21	547.7	32860	47.32
2.03	53.88	403.1	24180	34.82	2.53	73.62	550.8	33040	47.58
2.04	54.26	405.9	24350	35.07	2.54	74.03	553.8	33230	47.85
2.05	54.64	408.7	24520	35.31	2.55	74.44	556.9	33410	48.11
2.06	55.02	411.6	24690	35.56	2.56	74.85	560.0	33590	48.38
2.07	55.40	414.4	24860	35.80	2.57	75.27	563.1	33780	48.64
2.08	55.78	417.3	25030	36.05	2.58	75.68	566.1	33960	48.91
2.09	56.16	420.2	25210	36.30	2.59	76.09	569.2	34150	49.18
2.10	56.55	423.0	25380	36.55	2.60	76.50	572.3	34340	49.44
2.11	56.93	425.9	25550	36.79	2.61	76.92	575.4	34520	49.71
2.12	57.32	428.8	25720	37.04	2.62	77.33	578.5	34710	49.98
2.13	57.70	431.7	25900	37.29	2.63	77.75	581.6	34890	50.25
2.14	58.09	434.5	26070	37.54	2.64	78.16	584.7	35080	50.52
2.15	58.47	437.4	26240	37.79	2.65	78.58	587.8	35270	50.78
2.16	58.86	440.3	26420	38.04	2.66	78.99	591.0	35450	51.05
2.17	59.25	443.2	26590	38.29	2.67	79.41	594.1	35640	51.32
2.18	59.64	446.1	26770	38.54	2.68	79.83	597.2	35830	51.59
2.19	60.03	449.1	26940	38.79	2.69	80.25	600.3	36010	51.86
2.20	60.42	452.0	27110	39.05	2.70	80.66	603.5	36200	52.13
2.21	60.81	454.9	27290	39.30	2.71	81.08	606.6	36390	52.40
2.22	61.20	457.8	27470	39.55	2.72	81.50	609.7	36580	52.68
2.23	61.59	460.8	27640	39.81	2.73	81.92	612.9	36770	52.95
2.24	61.98	463.7	27820	40.06	2.74	82.34	616.0	36960	53.22
2.25	62.38	466.6	27990	40.31	2.75	82.76	619.2	37140	53.49
2.26	62.77	469.6	28170	40.57	2.76	83.18	622.3	37330	53.76
2.27	63.16	472.5	28350	40.82	2.77	83.61	625.5	37520	54.04
2.28	63.56	475.5	28520	41.08	2.78	84.03	628.6	37710	54.31
2.29	63.95	478.4	28700	41.33	2.79	84.45	631.8	37900	54.58
2.30	64.35	481.4	28880	41.59	2.80	84.88	635.0	38090	54.85
2.31	64.75	484.4	29060	41.85	2.81	85.30	638.1	38280	55.13
2.32	65.14	487.3	29240	42.10	2.82	85.72	641.3	38470	55.40
2.33	65.54	490.3	29420	42.36	2.83	86.15	644.5	38660	55.68
2.34	65.94	493.3	29590	42.62	2.84	86.57	647.7	38850	55.95
2.35	66.34	496.3	29770	42.88	2.85	87.00	650.8	39040	56.23
2.36	66.74	499.3	29950	43.13	2.86	87.42	654.0	39240	56.50
2.37	67.14	502.3	30130	43.39	2.87	87.85	657.2	39430	56.78
2.38	67.54	505.3	30310	43.65	2.88	88.28	660.4	39620	57.05
2.39	67.94	508.3	30490	43.91	2.89	88.71	663.6	39810	57.33
2.40	68.34	511.3	30670	44.17	2.90	89.13	666.8	40000	57.61
2.41	68.75	514.3	30850	44.43	2.91	89.56	670.0	40200	57.88
2.42	69.15	517.3	31030	44.69	2.92	89.99	673.2	40390	58.16
2.43	69.55	520.3	31220	44.95	2.93	90.42	676.4	40580	58.44
2.44	69.96	523.4	31400	45.21	2.94	90.85	679.6	40770	58.72
2.45	70.36	526.4	31580	45.48	2.95	91.28	682.9	40970	58.99
2.46	70.77	529.4	31760	45.74	2.96	91.71	686.1	41160	59.27
2.47	71.17	532.5	31940	46.00	2.97	92.14	689.3	41350	59.55
2.48	71.58	535.5	32130	46.26	2.98	92.57	692.5	41550	59.83
2.49	71.99	538.5	32310	46.53	2.99	93.00	695.8	41740	60.11
2.50	72.40	541.6	32490	46.79	3.00	93.44	699.0	41930	60.39

9

9-9: 8 ft. Rectangular Weir with End Contractions Discharge Table

Formulas: CFS $= 3.330(4.0-0.2H)H^{1.5}$ GPS = CFS x 7.481

GPM = CFS x 448.8   MGD = CFS x 0.6463

Head Feet	CFS	GPS	GPM	MGD	Head Feet	CFS	GPS	GPM	MGD
0.01	0.0266	0.1992	11.95	0.0172	0.51	9.579	71.66	4299	6.191
0.02	0.0753	0.5634	33.80	0.0487	0.52	9.860	73.76	4425	6.372
0.03	0.1383	1.035	62.08	0.0894	0.53	10.14	75.88	4552	6.555
0.04	0.2129	1.593	95.55	0.1376	0.54	10.43	78.02	4680	6.740
0.05	0.2975	2.225	133.5	0.1923	0.55	10.72	80.17	4810	6.926
0.06	0.3909	2.925	175.5	0.2527	0.56	11.01	82.35	4940	7.114
0.07	0.4925	3.685	221.0	0.3183	0.57	11.30	84.54	5072	7.304
0.08	0.6016	4.500	270.0	0.3888	0.58	11.60	86.75	5205	7.495
0.09	0.7177	5.369	322.1	0.4638	0.59	11.89	88.99	5338	7.688
0.10	0.8403	6.286	377.1	0.5431	0.60	12.20	91.23	5473	7.882
0.11	0.9692	7.251	435.0	0.6264	0.61	12.50	93.50	5609	8.078
0.12	1.104	8.260	495.5	0.7136	0.62	12.80	95.78	5746	8.275
0.13	1.245	9.311	558.6	0.8044	0.63	13.11	98.09	5884	8.474
0.14	1.391	10.40	624.1	0.8987	0.64	13.42	100.4	6024	8.674
0.15	1.542	11.53	692.0	0.9965	0.65	13.73	102.7	6164	8.876
0.16	1.698	12.70	762.1	1.098	0.66	14.05	105.1	6305	9.079
0.17	1.859	13.91	834.5	1.202	0.67	14.37	107.5	6447	9.284
0.18	2.025	15.15	908.9	1.309	0.68	14.68	109.9	6590	9.490
0.19	2.196	16.43	985.5	1.419	0.69	15.01	112.3	6734	9.698
0.20	2.371	17.74	1064	1.532	0.70	15.33	114.7	6880	9.907
0.21	2.550	19.08	1145	1.648	0.71	15.65	117.1	7026	10.12
0.22	2.734	20.45	1227	1.767	0.72	15.98	119.6	7173	10.33
0.23	2.922	21.86	1311	1.888	0.73	16.31	122.0	7321	10.54
0.24	3.113	23.29	1397	2.012	0.74	16.64	124.5	7470	10.76
0.25	3.309	24.76	1485	2.139	0.75	16.98	127.0	7620	10.97
0.26	3.509	26.25	1575	2.268	0.76	17.32	129.5	7771	11.19
0.27	3.712	27.77	1666	2.399	0.77	17.65	132.1	7923	11.41
0.28	3.919	29.32	1759	2.533	0.78	17.99	134.6	8076	11.63
0.29	4.130	30.90	1854	2.669	0.79	18.34	137.2	8229	11.85
0.30	4.345	32.50	1950	2.808	0.80	18.68	139.8	8384	12.07
0.31	4.562	34.13	2048	2.949	0.81	19.03	142.3	8539	12.30
0.32	4.784	35.79	2147	3.092	0.82	19.38	145.0	8696	12.52
0.33	5.008	37.47	2248	3.237	0.83	19.73	147.6	8853	12.75
0.34	5.237	39.17	2350	3.384	0.84	20.08	150.2	9011	12.98
0.35	5.468	40.91	2454	3.534	0.85	20.43	152.9	9170	13.21
0.36	5.702	42.66	2559	3.685	0.86	20.79	155.5	9330	13.44
0.37	5.940	44.44	2666	3.839	0.87	21.15	158.2	9491	13.67
0.38	6.181	46.24	2774	3.995	0.88	21.51	160.9	9653	13.90
0.39	6.425	48.07	2884	4.153	0.89	21.87	163.6	9815	14.13
0.40	6.672	49.91	2994	4.312	0.90	22.23	166.3	9979	14.37
0.41	6.922	51.78	3107	4.474	0.91	22.60	169.1	10140	14.61
0.42	7.175	53.68	3220	4.637	0.92	22.97	171.8	10310	14.84
0.43	7.431	55.59	3335	4.803	0.93	23.34	174.6	10470	15.08
0.44	7.690	57.53	3451	4.970	0.94	23.71	177.4	10640	15.32
0.45	7.951	59.48	3569	5.139	0.95	24.08	180.2	10810	15.56
0.46	8.216	61.46	3687	5.310	0.96	24.46	183.0	10980	15.81
0.47	8.483	63.46	3807	5.483	0.97	24.83	185.8	11150	16.05
0.48	8.753	65.48	3928	5.657	0.98	25.21	188.6	11310	16.29
0.49	9.026	67.52	4051	5.833	0.99	25.59	191.5	11490	16.54
0.50	9.301	69.58	4174	6.011	1.00	25.97	194.3	11660	16.79

9

9-9: 8 ft. Rectangular Weir with End Contractions Discharge Table *(Continued)*

Formulas: CFS $=3.330(4.0-0.2H)H^{1.5}$ GPS = CFS x 7.481

   GPM = CFS x 448.8   MGD = CFS x 0.6463

Head Feet	CFS	GPS	GPM	MGD	Head Feet	CFS	GPS	GPM	MGD
1.01	26.36	197.2	11830	17.04	1.51	47.57	355.8	21350	30.74
1.02	26.74	200.1	12000	17.28	1.52	48.03	359.3	21550	31.04
1.03	27.13	203.0	12180	17.53	1.53	48.49	362.7	21760	31.34
1.04	27.52	205.9	12350	17.79	1.54	48.95	366.2	21970	31.64
1.05	27.91	208.8	12530	18.04	1.55	49.42	369.7	22180	31.94
1.06	28.30	211.7	12700	18.29	1.56	49.88	373.2	22390	32.24
1.07	28.70	214.7	12880	18.55	1.57	50.35	376.7	22600	32.54
1.08	29.09	217.6	13060	18.80	1.58	50.82	380.2	22810	32.84
1.09	29.49	220.6	13240	19.06	1.59	51.29	383.7	23020	33.15
1.10	29.89	223.6	13410	19.32	1.60	51.76	387.2	23230	33.45
1.11	30.29	226.6	13590	19.58	1.61	52.23	390.7	23440	33.76
1.12	30.69	229.6	13770	19.84	1.62	52.70	394.3	23650	34.06
1.13	31.10	232.6	13960	20.10	1.63	53.18	397.8	23870	34.37
1.14	31.50	235.7	14140	20.36	1.64	53.66	401.4	24080	34.68
1.15	31.91	238.7	14320	20.62	1.65	54.13	405.0	24300	34.99
1.16	32.32	241.8	14500	20.89	1.66	54.61	408.6	24510	35.30
1.17	32.73	244.8	14690	21.15	1.67	55.09	412.1	24730	35.61
1.18	33.14	247.9	14870	21.42	1.68	55.57	415.7	24940	35.92
1.19	33.55	251.0	15060	21.69	1.69	56.06	419.3	25160	36.23
1.20	33.97	254.1	15250	21.95	1.70	56.54	423.0	25370	36.54
1.21	34.39	257.2	15430	22.22	1.71	57.02	426.6	25590	36.85
1.22	34.80	260.4	15620	22.49	1.72	57.51	430.2	25810	37.17
1.23	35.22	263.5	15810	22.76	1.73	58.00	433.9	26030	37.48
1.24	35.64	266.7	16000	23.04	1.74	58.48	437.5	26250	37.80
1.25	36.07	269.8	16190	23.31	1.75	58.97	441.2	26470	38.12
1.26	36.49	273.0	16380	23.58	1.76	59.46	444.9	26690	38.43
1.27	36.92	276.2	16570	23.86	1.77	59.96	448.5	26910	38.75
1.28	37.34	279.4	16760	24.14	1.78	60.45	452.2	27130	39.07
1.29	37.77	282.6	16950	24.41	1.79	60.94	455.9	27350	39.39
1.30	38.20	285.8	17150	24.69	1.80	61.44	459.6	27570	39.71
1.31	38.63	289.0	17340	24.97	1.81	61.94	463.3	27800	40.03
1.32	39.07	292.3	17530	25.25	1.82	62.43	467.1	28020	40.35
1.33	39.50	295.5	17730	25.53	1.83	62.93	470.8	28240	40.67
1.34	39.94	298.8	17920	25.81	1.84	63.43	474.5	28470	41.00
1.35	40.38	302.1	18120	26.10	1.85	63.93	478.3	28690	41.32
1.36	40.81	305.3	18320	26.38	1.86	64.44	482.0	28920	41.64
1.37	41.26	308.6	18520	26.66	1.87	64.94	485.8	29140	41.97
1.38	41.70	311.9	18710	26.95	1.88	65.44	489.6	29370	42.30
1.39	42.14	315.3	18910	27.24	1.89	65.95	493.4	29600	42.62
1.40	42.58	318.6	19110	27.52	1.90	66.46	497.2	29830	42.95
1.41	43.03	321.9	19310	27.81	1.91	66.96	501.0	30050	43.28
1.42	43.48	325.3	19510	28.10	1.92	67.47	504.8	30280	43.61
1.43	43.93	328.6	19710	28.39	1.93	67.98	508.6	30510	43.94
1.44	44.38	332.0	19920	28.68	1.94	68.49	512.4	30740	44.27
1.45	44.83	335.4	20120	28.97	1.95	69.01	516.2	30970	44.60
1.46	45.28	338.7	20320	29.27	1.96	69.52	520.1	31200	44.93
1.47	45.74	342.1	20530	29.56	1.97	70.03	523.9	31430	45.26
1.48	46.19	345.6	20730	29.85	1.98	70.55	527.8	31660	45.60
1.49	46.65	349.0	20940	30.15	1.99	71.06	531.6	31890	45.93
1.50	47.11	352.4	21140	30.44	2.00	71.58	535.5	32130	46.26

9

Formulas: CFS = $3.330(4.0-0.2H)H^{1.5}$ GPS = CFS x 7.481
GPM = CFS x 448.8   MGD = CFS x 0.6463

Head Feet	CFS	GPS	GPM	MGD	Head Feet	CFS	GPS	GPM	MGD
2.01	72.10	539.4	32360	46.60	2.51	99.29	742.8	44560	64.17
2.02	72.62	543.3	32590	46.93	2.52	99.86	747.0	44820	64.54
2.03	73.14	547.2	32830	47.27	2.53	100.4	751.3	45070	64.90
2.04	73.66	551.1	33060	47.61	2.54	101.0	755.5	45330	65.27
2.05	74.19	555.0	33290	47.95	2.55	101.6	759.8	45580	65.64
2.06	74.71	558.9	33530	48.28	2.56	102.1	764.1	45840	66.01
2.07	75.23	562.8	33760	48.62	2.57	102.7	768.3	46090	66.38
2.08	75.76	566.8	34000	48.96	2.58	103.3	772.6	46350	66.75
2.09	76.29	570.7	34240	49.30	2.59	103.9	776.9	46610	67.12
2.10	76.81	574.6	34470	49.65	2.60	104.4	781.2	46870	67.49
2.11	77.34	578.6	34710	49.99	2.61	105.0	785.5	47120	67.86
2.12	77.87	582.6	34950	50.33	2.62	105.6	789.8	47380	68.23
2.13	78.40	586.5	35190	50.67	2.63	106.2	794.1	47640	68.61
2.14	78.94	590.5	35430	51.02	2.64	106.7	798.4	47900	68.98
2.15	79.47	594.5	35670	51.36	2.65	107.3	802.8	48160	69.35
2.16	80.00	598.5	35910	51.71	2.66	107.9	807.1	48420	69.73
2.17	80.54	602.5	36150	52.05	2.67	108.5	811.4	48680	70.10
2.18	81.07	606.5	36390	52.40	2.68	109.0	815.8	48940	70.48
2.19	81.61	610.5	36630	52.74	2.69	109.6	820.1	49200	70.85
2.20	82.15	614.6	36870	53.09	2.70	110.2	824.5	49460	71.23
2.21	82.69	618.6	37110	53.44	2.71	110.8	828.9	49720	71.61
2.22	83.23	622.6	37350	53.79	2.72	111.4	833.2	49990	71.98
2.23	83.77	626.7	37600	54.14	2.73	112.0	837.6	50250	72.36
2.24	84.31	630.7	37840	54.49	2.74	112.5	842.0	50510	72.74
2.25	84.85	634.8	38080	54.84	2.75	113.1	846.4	50780	73.12
2.26	85.40	638.8	38330	55.19	2.76	113.7	850.8	51040	73.50
2.27	85.94	642.9	38570	55.54	2.77	114.3	855.2	51300	73.88
2.28	86.49	647.0	38820	55.90	2.78	114.9	859.6	51570	74.26
2.29	87.03	651.1	39060	56.25	2.79	115.5	864.0	51830	74.64
2.30	87.58	655.2	39310	56.60	2.80	116.1	868.4	52100	75.02
2.31	88.13	659.3	39550	56.96	2.81	116.7	872.8	52360	75.40
2.32	88.68	663.4	39800	57.31	2.82	117.3	877.2	52630	75.79
2.33	89.23	667.5	40050	57.67	2.83	117.9	881.7	52890	76.17
2.34	89.78	671.6	40290	58.02	2.84	118.4	886.1	53160	76.55
2.35	90.33	675.8	40540	58.38	2.85	119.0	890.6	53430	76.94
2.36	90.88	679.9	40790	58.74	2.86	119.6	895.0	53690	77.32
2.37	91.44	684.1	41040	59.10	2.87	120.2	899.5	53960	77.71
2.38	91.99	688.2	41290	59.46	2.88	120.8	903.9	54230	78.09
2.39	92.55	692.4	41540	59.81	2.89	121.4	908.4	54500	78.48
2.40	93.11	696.5	41790	60.17	2.90	122.0	912.9	54760	78.86
2.41	93.66	700.7	42040	60.53	2.91	122.6	917.3	55030	79.25
2.42	94.22	704.9	42290	60.90	2.92	123.2	921.8	55300	79.64
2.43	94.78	709.1	42540	61.26	2.93	123.8	926.3	55570	80.03
2.44	95.34	713.3	42790	61.62	2.94	124.4	930.8	55840	80.41
2.45	95.90	717.5	43040	61.98	2.95	125.0	935.3	56110	80.80
2.46	96.47	721.7	43290	62.35	2.96	125.6	939.8	56380	81.19
2.47	97.03	725.9	43550	62.71	2.97	126.2	944.3	56650	81.58
2.48	97.59	730.1	43800	63.07	2.98	126.8	948.8	56920	81.97
2.49	98.16	734.3	44050	63.44	2.99	127.4	953.4	57190	82.36
2.50	98.72	738.5	44310	63.80	3.00	128.0	957.9	57470	82.75

9-10: 10 ft. Rectangular Weir with End Contractions Discharge Table

Formulas: CFS $=3.330(4.0-0.2H)H^{1.5}$ GPS = CFS x 7.481

GPM = CFS x 448.8   MGD = CFS x 0.6463

Head Feet	CFS	GPS	GPM	MGD	Head Feet	CFS	GPS	GPM	MGD
0.01	0.0333	0.2491	14.94	0.0215	0.51	12.00	89.81	5388	7.759
0.02	0.0941	0.7043	42.25	0.0608	0.52	12.36	92.44	5546	7.986
0.03	0.1729	1.294	77.61	0.1118	0.53	12.71	95.10	5705	8.216
0.04	0.2662	1.991	119.5	0.1720	0.54	13.07	97.79	5866	8.448
0.05	0.3719	2.782	166.9	0.2404	0.55	13.43	100.5	6029	8.682
0.06	0.4888	3.657	219.4	0.3159	0.56	13.80	103.2	6193	8.918
0.07	0.6159	4.607	276.4	0.3980	0.57	14.17	106.0	6358	9.156
0.08	0.7523	5.628	337.6	0.4862	0.58	14.54	108.8	6525	9.396
0.09	0.8975	6.714	402.8	0.5800	0.59	14.91	111.6	6693	9.638
0.10	1.051	7.862	471.7	0.6792	0.60	15.29	114.4	6862	9.882
0.11	1.212	9.069	544.0	0.7834	0.61	15.67	117.2	7033	10.128
0.12	1.381	10.33	619.8	0.8925	0.62	16.06	120.1	7206	10.38
0.13	1.557	11.65	698.7	1.006	0.63	16.44	123.0	7379	10.63
0.14	1.739	13.01	780.7	1.124	0.64	16.83	125.9	7554	10.88
0.15	1.929	14.43	865.6	1.247	0.65	17.22	128.9	7730	11.13
0.16	2.124	15.89	953.4	1.373	0.66	17.62	131.8	7908	11.39
0.17	2.326	17.40	1044	1.503	0.67	18.02	134.8	8086	11.64
0.18	2.534	18.96	1137	1.638	0.68	18.42	137.8	8266	11.90
0.19	2.747	20.55	1233	1.776	0.69	18.82	140.8	8448	12.17
0.20	2.967	22.19	1331	1.917	0.70	19.23	143.9	8630	12.43
0.21	3.191	23.87	1432	2.062	0.71	19.64	146.9	8814	12.69
0.22	3.421	25.59	1535	2.211	0.72	20.05	150.0	8999	12.96
0.23	3.656	27.35	1641	2.363	0.73	20.47	153.1	9185	13.23
0.24	3.896	29.15	1749	2.518	0.74	20.88	156.2	9373	13.50
0.25	4.142	30.98	1859	2.677	0.75	21.30	159.4	9561	13.77
0.26	4.392	32.85	1971	2.838	0.76	21.73	162.5	9751	14.04
0.27	4.647	34.76	2085	3.003	0.77	22.15	165.7	9942	14.32
0.28	4.906	36.70	2202	3.171	0.78	22.58	168.9	10140	14.59
0.29	5.170	38.68	2320	3.342	0.79	23.01	172.2	10330	14.87
0.30	5.439	40.69	2441	3.515	0.80	23.45	175.4	10520	15.15
0.31	5.712	42.73	2564	3.692	0.81	23.88	178.7	10720	15.44
0.32	5.989	44.81	2688	3.871	0.82	24.32	181.9	10920	15.72
0.33	6.271	46.91	2814	4.053	0.83	24.76	185.2	11110	16.00
0.34	6.557	49.05	2943	4.238	0.84	25.21	188.6	11310	16.29
0.35	6.847	51.22	3073	4.425	0.85	25.65	191.9	11510	16.58
0.36	7.141	53.42	3205	4.615	0.86	26.10	195.3	11710	16.87
0.37	7.439	55.65	3339	4.808	0.87	26.55	198.6	11920	17.16
0.38	7.741	57.91	3474	5.003	0.88	27.01	202.0	12120	17.45
0.39	8.047	60.20	3612	5.201	0.89	27.46	205.4	12320	17.75
0.40	8.357	62.52	3751	5.401	0.90	27.92	208.9	12530	18.04
0.41	8.670	64.86	3891	5.604	0.91	28.38	212.3	12740	18.34
0.42	8.988	67.24	4034	5.809	0.92	28.84	215.8	12950	18.64
0.43	9.309	69.64	4178	6.016	0.93	29.31	219.3	13150	18.94
0.44	9.634	72.07	4324	6.226	0.94	29.78	222.8	13360	19.25
0.45	9.962	74.52	4471	6.438	0.95	30.25	226.3	13580	19.55
0.46	10.29	77.01	4620	6.653	0.96	30.72	229.8	13790	19.85
0.47	10.63	79.51	4770	6.869	0.97	31.20	233.4	14000	20.16
0.48	10.97	82.05	4922	7.088	0.98	31.67	236.9	14210	20.47
0.49	11.31	84.61	5076	7.310	0.99	32.15	240.5	14430	20.78
0.50	11.66	87.20	5231	7.533	1.00	32.63	244.1	14650	21.09

9

9-10: 10 ft. Rectangular Weir with End Contractions Discharge Table (Continued)

Formulas: CFS = $3.330(4.0-0.2H)H^{1.5}$ GPS = CFS x 7.481

          GPM = CFS x 448.8   MGD = CFS x 0.6463

Head Feet	CFS	GPS	GPM	MGD	Head Feet	CFS	GPS	GPM	MGD
1.01	33.12	247.8	14860	21.40	1.51	59.92	448.3	26890	38.73
1.02	33.60	251.4	15080	21.72	1.52	60.51	452.6	27160	39.11
1.03	34.09	255.0	15300	22.03	1.53	61.09	457.0	27420	39.48
1.04	34.58	258.7	15520	22.35	1.54	61.68	461.4	27680	39.86
1.05	35.08	262.4	15740	22.67	1.55	62.27	465.8	27950	40.24
1.06	35.57	266.1	15960	22.99	1.56	62.86	470.2	28210	40.63
1.07	36.07	269.8	16190	23.31	1.57	63.45	474.7	28480	41.01
1.08	36.57	273.6	16410	23.63	1.58	64.04	479.1	28740	41.39
1.09	37.07	277.3	16640	23.96	1.59	64.64	483.6	29010	41.78
1.10	37.57	281.1	16860	24.28	1.60	65.24	488.0	29280	42.16
1.11	38.08	284.9	17090	24.61	1.61	65.84	492.5	29550	42.55
1.12	38.59	288.7	17320	24.94	1.62	66.44	497.0	29820	42.94
1.13	39.10	292.5	17550	25.27	1.63	67.04	501.5	30090	43.33
1.14	39.61	296.3	17780	25.60	1.64	67.64	506.0	30360	43.72
1.15	40.12	300.2	18010	25.93	1.65	68.25	510.6	30630	44.11
1.16	40.64	304.0	18240	26.26	1.66	68.86	515.1	30900	44.50
1.17	41.16	307.9	18470	26.60	1.67	69.46	519.7	31180	44.90
1.18	41.68	311.8	18700	26.94	1.68	70.08	524.2	31450	45.29
1.19	42.20	315.7	18940	27.27	1.69	70.69	528.8	31720	45.69
1.20	42.72	319.6	19170	27.61	1.70	71.30	533.4	32000	46.08
1.21	43.25	323.6	19410	27.95	1.71	71.92	538.0	32280	46.48
1.22	43.78	327.5	19650	28.29	1.72	72.53	542.6	32550	46.88
1.23	44.31	331.5	19890	28.64	1.73	73.15	547.2	32830	47.28
1.24	44.84	335.5	20120	28.98	1.74	73.77	551.9	33110	47.68
1.25	45.37	339.4	20360	29.33	1.75	74.39	556.5	33390	48.08
1.26	45.91	343.5	20600	29.67	1.76	75.02	561.1	33670	48.48
1.27	46.45	347.5	20850	30.02	1.77	75.64	565.9	33950	48.89
1.28	46.99	351.5	21090	30.37	1.78	76.27	570.5	34230	49.29
1.29	47.53	355.6	21330	30.72	1.79	76.89	575.2	34510	49.70
1.30	48.07	359.6	21580	31.07	1.80	77.52	579.9	34790	50.10
1.31	48.62	363.7	21820	31.42	1.81	78.15	584.7	35080	50.51
1.32	49.17	367.8	22070	31.78	1.82	78.79	589.4	35360	50.92
1.33	49.72	371.9	22310	32.13	1.83	79.42	594.1	35640	51.33
1.34	50.27	376.1	22560	32.49	1.84	80.05	598.9	35930	51.74
1.35	50.82	380.2	22810	32.85	1.85	80.69	603.7	36210	52.15
1.36	51.38	384.4	23060	33.21	1.86	81.33	608.4	36500	52.56
1.37	51.93	388.5	23310	33.57	1.87	81.97	613.2	36790	52.98
1.38	52.49	392.7	23560	33.93	1.88	82.61	618.0	37080	53.39
1.39	53.05	396.9	23810	34.29	1.89	83.25	622.8	37360	53.81
1.40	53.62	401.1	24060	34.65	1.90	83.90	627.6	37650	54.22
1.41	54.18	405.3	24320	35.02	1.91	84.54	632.5	37940	54.64
1.42	54.75	409.6	24570	35.38	1.92	85.19	637.3	38230	55.06
1.43	55.32	413.8	24830	35.75	1.93	85.84	642.2	38520	55.48
1.44	55.89	418.1	25080	36.12	1.94	86.49	647.0	38820	55.90
1.45	56.46	422.4	25340	36.49	1.95	87.14	651.9	39110	56.32
1.46	57.03	426.6	25600	36.86	1.96	87.79	656.8	39400	56.74
1.47	57.61	430.9	25850	37.23	1.97	88.45	661.7	39700	57.16
1.48	58.18	435.3	26110	37.60	1.98	89.10	666.6	39990	57.59
1.49	58.76	439.6	26370	37.98	1.99	89.76	671.5	40280	58.01
1.50	59.34	443.9	26630	38.35	2.00	90.42	676.4	40580	58.44

9

9-10: 10 ft. Rectangular Weir with End Contractions Discharge Table (Continued)

Formulas: CFS =3.330(4.0-0.2H)H$^{1.5}$ GPS = CFS x 7.481
GPM = CFS x 448.8   MGD = CFS x 0.6463

Head Feet	CFS	GPS	GPM	MGD	Head Feet	CFS	GPS	GPM	MGD
2.01	91.08	681.4	40880	58.86	2.51	125.8	940.9	56450	81.29
2.02	91.74	686.3	41170	59.29	2.52	126.5	946.3	56770	81.76
2.03	92.40	691.3	41470	59.72	2.53	127.2	951.8	57100	82.23
2.04	93.07	696.2	41770	60.15	2.54	128.0	957.2	57430	82.70
2.05	93.73	701.2	42070	60.58	2.55	128.7	962.7	57750	83.17
2.06	94.40	706.2	42370	61.01	2.56	129.4	968.1	58080	83.64
2.07	95.07	711.2	42670	61.44	2.57	130.1	973.6	58410	84.11
2.08	95.74	716.2	42970	61.88	2.58	130.9	979.1	58740	84.59
2.09	96.41	721.2	43270	62.31	2.59	131.6	984.6	59070	85.06
2.10	97.08	726.3	43570	62.74	2.60	132.3	990.1	59400	85.54
2.11	97.76	731.3	43870	63.18	2.61	133.1	995.6	59730	86.01
2.12	98.43	736.4	44180	63.62	2.62	133.8	1001	60060	86.49
2.13	99.11	741.4	44480	64.05	2.63	134.6	1007	60390	86.97
2.14	99.79	746.5	44780	64.49	2.64	135.3	1012	60720	87.44
2.15	100.5	751.6	45090	64.93	2.65	136.0	1018	61050	87.92
2.16	101.1	756.7	45390	65.37	2.66	136.8	1023	61390	88.40
2.17	101.8	761.8	45700	65.81	2.67	137.5	1029	61720	88.88
2.18	102.5	766.9	46010	66.25	2.68	138.3	1034	62050	89.36
2.19	103.2	772.0	46310	66.70	2.69	139.0	1040	62390	89.84
2.20	103.9	777.1	46620	67.14	2.70	139.8	1046	62720	90.33
2.21	104.6	782.3	46930	67.58	2.71	140.5	1051	63060	90.81
2.22	105.3	787.4	47240	68.03	2.72	141.3	1057	63400	91.29
2.23	105.9	792.6	47550	68.47	2.73	142.0	1062	63730	91.78
2.24	106.6	797.8	47860	68.92	2.74	142.8	1068	64070	92.26
2.25	107.3	802.9	48170	69.37	2.75	143.5	1074	64410	92.75
2.26	108.0	808.1	48480	69.82	2.76	144.3	1079	64740	93.24
2.27	108.7	813.3	48790	70.26	2.77	145.0	1085	65080	93.72
2.28	109.4	818.5	49110	70.71	2.78	145.8	1091	65420	94.21
2.29	110.1	823.8	49420	71.17	2.79	146.5	1096	65760	94.70
2.30	110.8	829.0	49730	71.62	2.80	147.3	1102	66100	95.19
2.31	111.5	834.2	50050	72.07	2.81	148.0	1107	66440	95.68
2.32	112.2	839.5	50360	72.52	2.82	148.8	1113	66780	96.17
2.33	112.9	844.7	50680	72.98	2.83	149.6	1119	67120	96.66
2.34	113.6	850.0	50990	73.43	2.84	150.3	1125	67460	97.15
2.35	114.3	855.3	51310	73.89	2.85	151.1	1130	67810	97.65
2.36	115.0	860.5	51630	74.34	2.86	151.8	1136	68150	98.14
2.37	115.7	865.8	51940	74.80	2.87	152.6	1142	68490	98.63
2.38	116.4	871.1	52260	75.26	2.88	153.4	1147	68840	99.13
2.39	117.2	876.5	52580	75.72	2.89	154.1	1153	69180	99.62
2.40	117.9	881.8	52900	76.18	2.90	154.9	1159	69530	100.1
2.41	118.6	887.1	53220	76.64	2.91	155.7	1165	69870	100.6
2.42	119.3	892.4	53540	77.10	2.92	156.5	1170	70220	101.1
2.43	120.0	897.8	53860	77.56	2.93	157.2	1176	70560	101.6
2.44	120.7	903.2	54180	78.03	2.94	158.0	1182	70910	102.1
2.45	121.4	908.5	54500	78.49	2.95	158.8	1188	71260	102.6
2.46	122.2	913.9	54830	78.95	2.96	159.5	1194	71600	103.1
2.47	122.9	919.3	55150	79.42	2.97	160.3	1199	71950	103.6
2.48	123.6	924.7	55470	79.88	2.98	161.1	1205	72300	104.1
2.49	124.3	930.1	55800	80.35	2.99	161.9	1211	72650	104.6
2.50	125.0	935.5	56120	80.82	3.00	162.6	1217	73000	105.1

9

Chapter 10

This chapter contains discharge (flow rate vs head) tables for rectangular weirs without end contractions. Note that all of the tabular data is for free flow. If the flow is submerged, corrections will have to be made to determine the discharge, as discussed in Chapter 3.

Rectangular weir without end contractions discharge tables

Note also that in many cases, discharges are listed for heads which are above the maximum recommended operating head or below the minimum recommended operating head of the weir in question. Discharge for these heads outside the normal operating range are listed for reference only; it should not be implied that the primary device is intended to be used in these regions. Refer to Chapter 3 for minimum and maximum recommended heads.

Rectangular weirs
without end contractions

Note: The discharges of the weirs are listed in four different units:

CFS—cubic feet per second   GPS—gallons per second

GPM—gallons per minute   MGD—million gallons per day.

The equation used to develop each table is listed on the table.

10-1: 1 ft. Rectangular Weir without End Contractions Discharge Table

Formulas: $CFS = 3.330H^{1.5}$ $GPS = CFS \times 7.481$
$GPM = CFS \times 448.8$ $MGD = CFS \times 0.6463$

Head Feet	CFS	GPS	GPM	MGD	Head Feet	CFS	GPS	GPM	MGD
0.01	0.0033	0.0249	1.495	0.0022	0.51	1.213	9.073	544.3	0.7839
0.02	0.0094	0.0705	4.227	0.0061	0.52	1.249	9.341	560.4	0.8070
0.03	0.0173	0.1294	7.766	0.0112	0.53	1.285	9.612	576.6	0.8304
0.04	0.0266	0.1993	11.96	0.0172	0.54	1.321	9.885	593.0	0.8540
0.05	0.0372	0.2785	16.71	0.0241	0.55	1.358	10.16	609.6	0.8779
0.06	0.0489	0.3661	21.96	0.0316	0.56	1.395	10.44	626.3	0.9019
0.07	0.0617	0.4614	27.68	0.0399	0.57	1.433	10.72	643.1	0.9262
0.08	0.0753	0.5637	33.82	0.0487	0.58	1.471	11.00	660.1	0.9506
0.09	0.0899	0.6726	40.35	0.0581	0.59	1.509	11.29	677.3	0.9753
0.10	0.1053	0.7878	47.26	0.0681	0.60	1.548	11.58	694.6	1.000
0.11	0.1215	0.9089	54.52	0.0785	0.61	1.586	11.87	712.0	1.025
0.12	0.1384	1.036	62.13	0.0895	0.62	1.626	12.16	729.6	1.051
0.13	0.1561	1.168	70.05	0.1009	0.63	1.665	12.46	747.3	1.076
0.14	0.1744	1.305	78.29	0.1127	0.64	1.705	12.75	765.2	1.102
0.15	0.1935	1.447	86.82	0.1250	0.65	1.745	13.05	783.2	1.128
0.16	0.2131	1.594	95.65	0.1377	0.66	1.786	13.36	801.3	1.154
0.17	0.2334	1.746	104.8	0.1509	0.67	1.826	13.66	819.6	1.180
0.18	0.2543	1.902	114.1	0.1644	0.68	1.867	13.97	838.0	1.207
0.19	0.2758	2.063	123.8	0.1782	0.69	1.909	14.28	856.6	1.234
0.20	0.2978	2.228	133.7	0.1925	0.70	1.950	14.59	875.3	1.260
0.21	0.3205	2.397	143.8	0.2071	0.71	1.992	14.90	894.1	1.288
0.22	0.3436	2.571	154.2	0.2221	0.72	2.034	15.22	913.1	1.315
0.23	0.3673	2.748	164.8	0.2374	0.73	2.077	15.54	932.1	1.342
0.24	0.3915	2.929	175.7	0.2530	0.74	2.120	15.86	951.4	1.370
0.25	0.4163	3.114	186.8	0.2690	0.75	2.163	16.18	970.7	1.398
0.26	0.4415	3.303	198.1	0.2853	0.76	2.206	16.51	990.2	1.426
0.27	0.4672	3.495	209.7	0.3019	0.77	2.250	16.83	1010	1.454
0.28	0.4934	3.691	221.4	0.3189	0.78	2.294	17.16	1030	1.483
0.29	0.5200	3.890	233.4	0.3361	0.79	2.338	17.49	1049	1.511
0.30	0.5472	4.093	245.6	0.3536	0.80	2.383	17.83	1069	1.540
0.31	0.5748	4.300	258.0	0.3715	0.81	2.428	18.16	1089	1.569
0.32	0.6028	4.510	270.5	0.3896	0.82	2.473	18.50	1110	1.598
0.33	0.6313	4.723	283.3	0.4080	0.83	2.518	18.84	1130	1.627
0.34	0.6602	4.939	296.3	0.4267	0.84	2.564	19.18	1151	1.657
0.35	0.6895	5.158	309.5	0.4456	0.85	2.610	19.52	1171	1.687
0.36	0.7193	5.381	322.8	0.4649	0.86	2.656	19.87	1192	1.716
0.37	0.7495	5.607	336.4	0.4844	0.87	2.702	20.22	1213	1.746
0.38	0.7800	5.836	350.1	0.5041	0.88	2.749	20.56	1234	1.777
0.39	0.8110	6.067	364.0	0.5242	0.89	2.796	20.92	1255	1.807
0.40	0.8424	6.302	378.1	0.5445	0.90	2.843	21.27	1276	1.838
0.41	0.8742	6.540	392.3	0.5650	0.91	2.891	21.63	1297	1.868
0.42	0.9064	6.781	406.8	0.5858	0.92	2.939	21.98	1319	1.899
0.43	0.9390	7.024	421.4	0.6068	0.93	2.987	22.34	1340	1.930
0.44	0.9719	7.271	436.2	0.6281	0.94	3.035	22.70	1362	1.961
0.45	1.005	7.520	451.1	0.6497	0.95	3.083	23.07	1384	1.993
0.46	1.039	7.772	466.3	0.6715	0.96	3.132	23.43	1406	2.024
0.47	1.073	8.027	481.6	0.6935	0.97	3.181	23.80	1428	2.056
0.48	1.107	8.284	497.0	0.7157	0.98	3.231	24.17	1450	2.088
0.49	1.142	8.545	512.6	0.7382	0.99	3.280	24.54	1472	2.120
0.50	1.177	8.808	528.4	0.7609	1.00	3.330	24.91	1495	2.152

10

10-1: 1 ft. Rectangular Weir without End Contractions Discharge Table (Continued)

Formulas: $CFS = 3.330H^{1.5}$ $GPS = CFS \times 7.481$
$GPM = CFS \times 448.8$ $MGD = CFS \times 0.6463$

Head Feet	CFS	GPS	GPM	MGD	Head Feet	CFS	GPS	GPM	MGD
1.01	3.380	25.29	1517	2.185	1.51	6.179	46.22	2773	3.993
1.02	3.430	25.66	1540	2.217	1.52	6.240	46.68	2801	4.033
1.03	3.481	26.04	1562	2.250	1.53	6.302	47.15	2828	4.073
1.04	3.532	26.42	1585	2.283	1.54	6.364	47.61	2856	4.113
1.05	3.583	26.80	1608	2.316	1.55	6.426	48.07	2884	4.153
1.06	3.634	27.19	1631	2.349	1.56	6.488	48.54	2912	4.193
1.07	3.686	27.57	1654	2.382	1.57	6.551	49.01	2940	4.234
1.08	3.737	27.96	1677	2.416	1.58	6.613	49.48	2968	4.274
1.09	3.790	28.35	1701	2.449	1.59	6.676	49.95	2996	4.315
1.10	3.842	28.74	1724	2.483	1.60	6.739	50.42	3025	4.356
1.11	3.894	29.13	1748	2.517	1.61	6.803	50.89	3053	4.397
1.12	3.947	29.53	1771	2.551	1.62	6.866	51.37	3082	4.438
1.13	4.000	29.92	1795	2.585	1.63	6.930	51.84	3110	4.479
1.14	4.053	30.32	1819	2.620	1.64	6.994	52.32	3139	4.520
1.15	4.107	30.72	1843	2.654	1.65	7.058	52.80	3168	4.561
1.16	4.160	31.12	1867	2.689	1.66	7.122	53.28	3196	4.603
1.17	4.214	31.53	1891	2.724	1.67	7.187	53.76	3225	4.645
1.18	4.268	31.93	1916	2.759	1.68	7.251	54.25	3254	4.686
1.19	4.323	32.34	1940	2.794	1.69	7.316	54.73	3283	4.728
1.20	4.377	32.75	1965	2.829	1.70	7.381	55.22	3313	4.770
1.21	4.432	33.16	1989	2.865	1.71	7.446	55.71	3342	4.813
1.22	4.487	33.57	2014	2.900	1.72	7.512	56.19	3371	4.855
1.23	4.543	33.98	2039	2.936	1.73	7.577	56.69	3401	4.897
1.24	4.598	34.40	2064	2.972	1.74	7.643	57.18	3430	4.940
1.25	4.654	34.82	2089	3.008	1.75	7.709	57.67	3460	4.982
1.26	4.710	35.23	2114	3.044	1.76	7.775	58.17	3490	5.025
1.27	4.766	35.65	2139	3.080	1.77	7.842	58.66	3519	5.068
1.28	4.822	36.08	2164	3.117	1.78	7.908	59.16	3549	5.111
1.29	4.879	36.50	2190	3.153	1.79	7.975	59.66	3579	5.154
1.30	4.936	36.92	2215	3.190	1.80	8.042	60.16	3609	5.197
1.31	4.993	37.35	2241	3.227	1.81	8.109	60.66	3639	5.241
1.32	5.050	37.78	2267	3.264	1.82	8.176	61.17	3669	5.284
1.33	5.108	38.21	2292	3.301	1.83	8.244	61.67	3700	5.328
1.34	5.165	38.64	2318	3.338	1.84	8.311	62.18	3730	5.372
1.35	5.223	39.08	2344	3.376	1.85	8.379	62.68	3761	5.415
1.36	5.281	39.51	2370	3.413	1.86	8.447	63.19	3791	5.459
1.37	5.340	39.95	2397	3.451	1.87	8.515	63.70	3822	5.504
1.38	5.398	40.39	2423	3.489	1.88	8.584	64.22	3852	5.548
1.39	5.457	40.82	2449	3.527	1.89	8.652	64.73	3883	5.592
1.40	5.516	41.27	2476	3.565	1.90	8.721	65.24	3914	5.636
1.41	5.575	41.71	2502	3.603	1.91	8.790	65.76	3945	5.681
1.42	5.635	42.15	2529	3.642	1.92	8.859	66.28	3976	5.726
1.43	5.694	42.60	2556	3.680	1.93	8.929	66.79	4007	5.771
1.44	5.754	43.05	2583	3.719	1.94	8.998	67.31	4038	5.815
1.45	5.814	43.50	2609	3.758	1.95	9.068	67.84	4070	5.860
1.46	5.875	43.95	2636	3.797	1.96	9.138	68.36	4101	5.906
1.47	5.935	44.40	2664	3.836	1.97	9.208	68.88	4132	5.951
1.48	5.996	44.85	2691	3.875	1.98	9.278	69.41	4164	5.996
1.49	6.057	45.31	2718	3.914	1.99	9.348	69.93	4195	6.042
1.50	6.118	45.77	2746	3.954	2.00	9.419	70.46	4227	6.087

Formulas: $CFS = 3.330H^{1.5}$ $GPS = CFS \times 7.481$
$GPM = CFS \times 448.8$ $MGD = CFS \times 0.6463$

Head Feet	CFS	GPS	GPM	MGD	Head Feet	CFS	GPS	GPM	MGD
2.01	9.489	70.99	4259	6.133	2.51	13.24	99.06	5943	8.558
2.02	9.560	71.52	4291	6.179	2.52	13.32	99.66	5979	8.610
2.03	9.631	72.05	4323	6.225	2.53	13.40	100.3	6014	8.661
2.04	9.703	72.59	4355	6.271	2.54	13.48	100.8	6050	8.712
2.05	9.774	73.12	4387	6.317	2.55	13.56	101.4	6086	8.764
2.06	9.846	73.66	4419	6.363	2.56	13.64	102.0	6121	8.815
2.07	9.917	74.19	4451	6.410	2.57	13.72	102.6	6157	8.867
2.08	9.989	74.73	4483	6.456	2.58	13.80	103.2	6193	8.919
2.09	10.06	75.27	4516	6.503	2.59	13.88	103.8	6229	8.971
2.10	10.13	75.81	4548	6.549	2.60	13.96	104.4	6266	9.023
2.11	10.21	76.35	4581	6.596	2.61	14.04	105.0	6302	9.075
2.12	10.28	76.90	4613	6.643	2.62	14.12	105.6	6338	9.127
2.13	10.35	77.44	4646	6.690	2.63	14.20	106.3	6374	9.179
2.14	10.42	77.99	4679	6.738	2.64	14.28	106.9	6411	9.232
2.15	10.50	78.53	4711	6.785	2.65	14.37	107.5	6447	9.284
2.16	10.57	79.08	4744	6.832	2.66	14.45	108.1	6484	9.337
2.17	10.64	79.63	4777	6.880	2.67	14.53	108.7	6520	9.390
2.18	10.72	80.18	4810	6.927	2.68	14.61	109.3	6557	9.442
2.19	10.79	80.74	4844	6.975	2.69	14.69	109.9	6594	9.495
2.20	10.87	81.29	4877	7.023	2.70	14.77	110.5	6630	9.548
2.21	10.94	81.85	4910	7.071	2.71	14.86	111.1	6667	9.601
2.22	11.01	82.40	4943	7.119	2.72	14.94	111.8	6704	9.655
2.23	11.09	82.96	4977	7.167	2.73	15.02	112.4	6741	9.708
2.24	11.16	83.52	5010	7.215	2.74	15.10	113.0	6778	9.761
2.25	11.24	84.08	5044	7.264	2.75	15.19	113.6	6815	9.815
2.26	11.31	84.64	5078	7.312	2.76	15.27	114.2	6853	9.868
2.27	11.39	85.20	5111	7.361	2.77	15.35	114.8	6890	9.922
2.28	11.46	85.76	5145	7.409	2.78	15.44	115.5	6927	9.976
2.29	11.54	86.33	5179	7.458	2.79	15.52	116.1	6965	10.03
2.30	11.62	86.90	5213	7.507	2.80	15.60	116.7	7002	10.08
2.31	11.69	87.46	5247	7.556	2.81	15.69	117.3	7040	10.14
2.32	11.77	88.03	5281	7.605	2.82	15.77	118.0	7077	10.19
2.33	11.84	88.60	5315	7.654	2.83	15.85	118.6	7115	10.25
2.34	11.92	89.17	5350	7.704	2.84	15.94	119.2	7153	10.30
2.35	12.00	89.74	5384	7.753	2.85	16.02	119.9	7191	10.35
2.36	12.07	90.32	5418	7.803	2.86	16.11	120.5	7228	10.41
2.37	12.15	90.89	5453	7.852	2.87	16.19	121.1	7266	10.46
2.38	12.23	91.47	5487	7.902	2.88	16.28	121.8	7304	10.52
2.39	12.30	92.05	5522	7.952	2.89	16.36	122.4	7342	10.57
2.40	12.38	92.62	5557	8.002	2.90	16.45	123.0	7381	10.63
2.41	12.46	93.20	5591	8.052	2.91	16.53	123.7	7419	10.68
2.42	12.54	93.78	5626	8.102	2.92	16.62	124.3	7457	10.74
2.43	12.61	94.37	5661	8.152	2.93	16.70	124.9	7495	10.79
2.44	12.69	94.95	5696	8.203	2.94	16.79	125.6	7534	10.85
2.45	12.77	95.53	5731	8.253	2.95	16.87	126.2	7572	10.90
2.46	12.85	96.12	5766	8.304	2.96	16.96	126.9	7611	10.96
2.47	12.93	96.71	5802	8.355	2.97	17.04	127.5	7649	11.02
2.48	13.01	97.29	5837	8.405	2.98	17.13	128.2	7688	11.07
2.49	13.08	97.88	5872	8.456	2.99	17.22	128.8	7727	11.13
2.50	13.16	98.47	5908	8.507	3.00	17.30	129.4	7766	11.18

10

10-2: 1 ½ ft. Rectangular Weir without End Contractions Discharge Table

Formulas: $CFS = 4.995H^{1.5}$ $GPS = CFS \times 7.481$
$GPM = CFS \times 448.8$ $MGD = CFS \times 0.6463$

Head Feet	CFS	GPS	GPM	MGD	Head Feet	CFS	GPS	GPM	MGD
0.01	0.0050	0.0374	2.242	0.0032	0.51	1.819	13.61	816.5	1.176
0.02	0.0141	0.1057	6.341	0.0091	0.52	1.873	14.01	840.6	1.211
0.03	0.0260	0.1942	11.65	0.0168	0.53	1.927	14.42	865.0	1.246
0.04	0.0400	0.2989	17.93	0.0258	0.54	1.982	14.83	889.6	1.281
0.05	0.0558	0.4178	25.06	0.0361	0.55	2.037	15.24	914.4	1.317
0.06	0.0734	0.5492	32.95	0.0474	0.56	2.093	15.66	939.4	1.353
0.07	0.0925	0.6921	41.52	0.0598	0.57	2.150	16.08	964.7	1.389
0.08	0.1130	0.8455	50.73	0.0730	0.58	2.206	16.51	990.2	1.426
0.09	0.1349	1.009	60.53	0.0872	0.59	2.264	16.93	1016	1.463
0.10	0.1580	1.182	70.89	0.1021	0.60	2.321	17.37	1042	1.500
0.11	0.1822	1.363	81.79	0.1178	0.61	2.380	17.80	1068	1.538
0.12	0.2076	1.553	93.19	0.1342	0.62	2.439	18.24	1094	1.576
0.13	0.2341	1.752	105.1	0.1513	0.63	2.498	18.69	1121	1.614
0.14	0.2617	1.957	117.4	0.1691	0.64	2.557	19.13	1148	1.653
0.15	0.2902	2.171	130.2	0.1875	0.65	2.618	19.58	1175	1.692
0.16	0.3197	2.392	143.5	0.2066	0.66	2.678	20.04	1202	1.731
0.17	0.3501	2.619	157.1	0.2263	0.67	2.739	20.49	1229	1.770
0.18	0.3815	2.854	171.2	0.2465	0.68	2.801	20.95	1257	1.810
0.19	0.4137	3.095	185.7	0.2674	0.69	2.863	21.42	1285	1.850
0.20	0.4468	3.342	200.5	0.2887	0.70	2.925	21.88	1313	1.891
0.21	0.4807	3.596	215.7	0.3107	0.71	2.988	22.36	1341	1.931
0.22	0.5154	3.856	231.3	0.3331	0.72	3.052	22.83	1370	1.972
0.23	0.5510	4.122	247.3	0.3561	0.73	3.115	23.31	1398	2.014
0.24	0.5873	4.394	263.6	0.3796	0.74	3.180	23.79	1427	2.055
0.25	0.6244	4.671	280.2	0.4035	0.75	3.244	24.27	1456	2.097
0.26	0.6622	4.954	297.2	0.4280	0.76	3.309	24.76	1485	2.139
0.27	0.7008	5.243	314.5	0.4529	0.77	3.375	25.25	1515	2.181
0.28	0.7401	5.536	332.1	0.4783	0.78	3.441	25.74	1544	2.224
0.29	0.7801	5.836	350.1	0.5042	0.79	3.507	26.24	1574	2.267
0.30	0.8208	6.140	368.4	0.5305	0.80	3.574	26.74	1604	2.310
0.31	0.8621	6.450	386.9	0.5572	0.81	3.641	27.24	1634	2.353
0.32	0.9042	6.764	405.8	0.5844	0.82	3.709	27.75	1665	2.397
0.33	0.9469	7.084	425.0	0.6120	0.83	3.777	28.26	1695	2.441
0.34	0.9903	7.408	444.4	0.6400	0.84	3.846	28.77	1726	2.485
0.35	1.034	7.737	464.2	0.6685	0.85	3.914	29.28	1757	2.530
0.36	1.079	8.071	484.2	0.6973	0.86	3.984	29.80	1788	2.575
0.37	1.124	8.410	504.5	0.7266	0.87	4.053	30.32	1819	2.620
0.38	1.170	8.753	525.1	0.7562	0.88	4.123	30.85	1851	2.665
0.39	1.217	9.101	546.0	0.7863	0.89	4.194	31.37	1882	2.711
0.40	1.264	9.453	567.1	0.8167	0.90	4.265	31.91	1914	2.756
0.41	1.311	9.810	588.5	0.8475	0.91	4.336	32.44	1946	2.802
0.42	1.360	10.17	610.2	0.8787	0.92	4.408	32.97	1978	2.849
0.43	1.408	10.54	632.1	0.9103	0.93	4.480	33.51	2011	2.895
0.44	1.458	10.91	654.3	0.9422	0.94	4.552	34.06	2043	2.942
0.45	1.508	11.28	676.7	0.9745	0.95	4.625	34.60	2076	2.989
0.46	1.558	11.66	699.4	1.0072	0.96	4.698	35.15	2109	3.037
0.47	1.609	12.04	722.3	1.040	0.97	4.772	35.70	2142	3.084
0.48	1.661	12.43	745.5	1.074	0.98	4.846	36.25	2175	3.132
0.49	1.713	12.82	768.9	1.107	0.99	4.920	36.81	2208	3.180
0.50	1.766	13.21	792.6	1.141	1.00	4.995	37.37	2242	3.228

10

10-2: 1 ¹/₂ ft. Rectangular Weir without End Contractions Discharge Table *(Continued)*

Formulas: $CFS = 4.995H^{1.5}$ $GPS = CFS \times 7.481$
$GPM = CFS \times 448.8$ $MGD = CFS \times 0.6463$

Head Feet	CFS	GPS	GPM	MGD	Head Feet	CFS	GPS	GPM	MGD
1.01	5.070	37.93	2275	3.277	1.51	9.268	69.34	4160	5.990
1.02	5.146	38.49	2309	3.326	1.52	9.361	70.03	4201	6.050
1.03	5.221	39.06	2343	3.375	1.53	9.453	70.72	4243	6.110
1.04	5.298	39.63	2378	3.424	1.54	9.546	71.41	4284	6.170
1.05	5.374	40.20	2412	3.473	1.55	9.639	72.11	4326	6.230
1.06	5.451	40.78	2447	3.523	1.56	9.732	72.81	4368	6.290
1.07	5.529	41.36	2481	3.573	1.57	9.826	73.51	4410	6.351
1.08	5.606	41.94	2516	3.623	1.58	9.920	74.21	4452	6.411
1.09	5.684	42.52	2551	3.674	1.59	10.02	74.92	4495	6.472
1.10	5.763	43.11	2586	3.724	1.60	10.11	75.63	4537	6.534
1.11	5.841	43.70	2622	3.775	1.61	10.20	76.34	4580	6.595
1.12	5.921	44.29	2657	3.826	1.62	10.30	77.05	4622	6.656
1.13	6.000	44.89	2693	3.878	1.63	10.39	77.76	4665	6.718
1.14	6.080	45.48	2729	3.929	1.64	10.49	78.48	4708	6.780
1.15	6.160	46.08	2765	3.981	1.65	10.59	79.20	4751	6.842
1.16	6.241	46.69	2801	4.033	1.66	10.68	79.92	4795	6.904
1.17	6.321	47.29	2837	4.086	1.67	10.78	80.64	4838	6.967
1.18	6.403	47.90	2874	4.138	1.68	10.88	81.37	4881	7.030
1.19	6.484	48.51	2910	4.191	1.69	10.97	82.10	4925	7.093
1.20	6.566	49.12	2947	4.244	1.70	11.07	82.83	4969	7.156
1.21	6.648	49.74	2984	4.297	1.71	11.17	83.56	5013	7.219
1.22	6.731	50.35	3021	4.350	1.72	11.27	84.29	5057	7.282
1.23	6.814	50.97	3058	4.404	1.73	11.37	85.03	5101	7.346
1.24	6.897	51.60	3095	4.458	1.74	11.46	85.77	5145	7.410
1.25	6.981	52.22	3133	4.512	1.75	11.56	86.51	5190	7.474
1.26	7.065	52.85	3171	4.566	1.76	11.66	87.25	5234	7.538
1.27	7.149	53.48	3208	4.620	1.77	11.76	87.99	5279	7.602
1.28	7.234	54.11	3246	4.675	1.78	11.86	88.74	5324	7.667
1.29	7.318	54.75	3285	4.730	1.79	11.96	89.49	5369	7.731
1.30	7.404	55.39	3323	4.785	1.80	12.06	90.24	5414	7.796
1.31	7.489	56.03	3361	4.840	1.81	12.16	90.99	5459	7.861
1.32	7.575	56.67	3400	4.896	1.82	12.26	91.75	5504	7.926
1.33	7.661	57.32	3438	4.952	1.83	12.37	92.51	5550	7.992
1.34	7.748	57.96	3477	5.008	1.84	12.47	93.27	5595	8.057
1.35	7.835	58.61	3516	5.064	1.85	12.57	94.03	5641	8.123
1.36	7.922	59.27	3555	5.120	1.86	12.67	94.79	5687	8.189
1.37	8.010	59.92	3595	5.177	1.87	12.77	95.56	5733	8.255
1.38	8.098	60.58	3634	5.233	1.88	12.88	96.32	5779	8.322
1.39	8.186	61.24	3674	5.290	1.89	12.98	97.09	5825	8.388
1.40	8.274	61.90	3713	5.348	1.90	13.08	97.86	5871	8.455
1.41	8.363	62.56	3753	5.405	1.91	13.19	98.64	5918	8.522
1.42	8.452	63.23	3793	5.463	1.92	13.29	99.41	5964	8.589
1.43	8.542	63.90	3833	5.520	1.93	13.39	100.2	6011	8.656
1.44	8.631	64.57	3874	5.578	1.94	13.50	101.0	6057	8.723
1.45	8.721	65.24	3914	5.637	1.95	13.60	101.8	6104	8.791
1.46	8.812	65.92	3955	5.695	1.96	13.71	102.5	6151	8.858
1.47	8.902	66.60	3995	5.754	1.97	13.81	103.3	6199	8.926
1.48	8.993	67.28	4036	5.812	1.98	13.92	104.1	6246	8.994
1.49	9.085	67.96	4077	5.871	1.99	14.02	104.9	6293	9.063
1.50	9.176	68.65	4118	5.931	2.00	14.13	105.7	6341	9.131

10

10-2: 1 1/2 ft. Rectangular Weir without End Contractions Discharge Table *(Continued)*

Formulas: CFS = 4.995H$^{1.5}$ GPS = CFS x 7.481
GPM = CFS x 448.8 MGD = CFS x 0.6463

Head Feet	CFS	GPS	GPM	MGD	Head Feet	CFS	GPS	GPM	MGD
2.01	14.23	106.5	6388	9.199	2.51	19.86	148.6	8915	12.84
2.02	14.34	107.3	6436	9.268	2.52	19.98	149.5	8968	12.91
2.03	14.45	108.1	6484	9.337	2.53	20.10	150.4	9021	12.99
2.04	14.55	108.9	6532	9.406	2.54	20.22	151.3	9075	13.07
2.05	14.66	109.7	6580	9.475	2.55	20.34	152.2	9128	13.15
2.06	14.77	110.5	6628	9.545	2.56	20.46	153.1	9182	13.22
2.07	14.88	111.3	6676	9.614	2.57	20.58	154.0	9236	13.30
2.08	14.98	112.1	6725	9.684	2.58	20.70	154.9	9290	13.38
2.09	15.09	112.9	6773	9.754	2.59	20.82	155.8	9344	13.46
2.10	15.20	113.7	6822	9.824	2.60	20.94	156.7	9398	13.53
2.11	15.31	114.5	6871	9.894	2.61	21.06	157.6	9453	13.61
2.12	15.42	115.3	6920	9.965	2.62	21.18	158.5	9507	13.69
2.13	15.53	116.2	6969	10.04	2.63	21.30	159.4	9561	13.77
2.14	15.64	117.0	7018	10.11	2.64	21.43	160.3	9616	13.85
2.15	15.75	117.8	7067	10.18	2.65	21.55	161.2	9671	13.93
2.16	15.86	118.6	7117	10.25	2.66	21.67	162.1	9725	14.01
2.17	15.97	119.4	7166	10.32	2.67	21.79	163.0	9780	14.08
2.18	16.08	120.3	7216	10.39	2.68	21.91	163.9	9835	14.16
2.19	16.19	121.1	7265	10.46	2.69	22.04	164.9	9890	14.24
2.20	16.30	121.9	7315	10.53	2.70	22.16	165.8	9946	14.32
2.21	16.41	122.8	7365	10.61	2.71	22.28	166.7	10000	14.40
2.22	16.52	123.6	7415	10.68	2.72	22.41	167.6	10060	14.48
2.23	16.63	124.4	7465	10.75	2.73	22.53	168.6	10110	14.56
2.24	16.75	125.3	7516	10.82	2.74	22.65	169.5	10170	14.64
2.25	16.86	126.1	7566	10.90	2.75	22.78	170.4	10220	14.72
2.26	16.97	127.0	7616	10.97	2.76	22.90	171.3	10280	14.80
2.27	17.08	127.8	7667	11.04	2.77	23.03	172.3	10330	14.88
2.28	17.20	128.6	7718	11.11	2.78	23.15	173.2	10390	14.96
2.29	17.31	129.5	7769	11.19	2.79	23.28	174.1	10450	15.04
2.30	17.42	130.3	7820	11.26	2.80	23.40	175.1	10500	15.13
2.31	17.54	131.2	7871	11.33	2.81	23.53	176.0	10560	15.21
2.32	17.65	132.0	7922	11.41	2.82	23.65	177.0	10620	15.29
2.33	17.77	132.9	7973	11.48	2.83	23.78	177.9	10670	15.37
2.34	17.88	133.8	8024	11.56	2.84	23.91	178.8	10730	15.45
2.35	17.99	134.6	8076	11.63	2.85	24.03	179.8	10790	15.53
2.36	18.11	135.5	8127	11.70	2.86	24.16	180.7	10840	15.61
2.37	18.22	136.3	8179	11.78	2.87	24.29	181.7	10900	15.70
2.38	18.34	137.2	8231	11.85	2.88	24.41	182.6	10960	15.78
2.39	18.46	138.1	8283	11.93	2.89	24.54	183.6	11010	15.86
2.40	18.57	138.9	8335	12.00	2.90	24.67	184.5	11070	15.94
2.41	18.69	139.8	8387	12.08	2.91	24.80	185.5	11130	16.03
2.42	18.80	140.7	8439	12.15	2.92	24.92	186.5	11190	16.11
2.43	18.92	141.5	8492	12.23	2.93	25.05	187.4	11240	16.19
2.44	19.04	142.4	8544	12.30	2.94	25.18	188.4	11300	16.27
2.45	19.16	143.3	8597	12.38	2.95	25.31	189.3	11360	16.36
2.46	19.27	144.2	8649	12.46	2.96	25.44	190.3	11420	16.44
2.47	19.39	145.1	8702	12.53	2.97	25.57	191.3	11470	16.52
2.48	19.51	145.9	8755	12.61	2.98	25.70	192.2	11530	16.61
2.49	19.63	146.8	8808	12.68	2.99	25.83	193.2	11590	16.69
2.50	19.74	147.7	8861	12.76	3.00	25.95	194.2	11650	16.77

10

10-3: 2 ft. Rectangular Weir without End Contractions Discharge Table

Formulas: $CFS = 6.660H^{1.5}$ $GPS = CFS \times 7.481$

$GPM = CFS \times 448.8$ $MGD = CFS \times 0.6463$

Head Feet	CFS	GPS	GPM	MGD	Head Feet	CFS	GPS	GPM	MGD
0.01	0.0067	0.0498	2.989	0.0043	0.51	2.426	18.15	1089	1.568
0.02	0.0188	0.1409	8.454	0.0122	0.52	2.497	18.68	1121	1.614
0.03	0.0346	0.2589	15.53	0.0224	0.53	2.570	19.22	1153	1.661
0.04	0.0533	0.3986	23.91	0.0344	0.54	2.643	19.77	1186	1.708
0.05	0.0745	0.5570	33.42	0.0481	0.55	2.717	20.32	1219	1.756
0.06	0.0979	0.7323	43.93	0.0633	0.56	2.791	20.88	1253	1.804
0.07	0.1233	0.9227	55.36	0.0797	0.57	2.866	21.44	1286	1.852
0.08	0.1507	1.127	67.63	0.0974	0.58	2.942	22.01	1320	1.901
0.09	0.1798	1.345	80.70	0.1162	0.59	3.018	22.58	1355	1.951
0.10	0.2106	1.576	94.52	0.1361	0.60	3.095	23.16	1389	2.000
0.11	0.2430	1.818	109.0	0.1570	0.61	3.173	23.74	1424	2.051
0.12	0.2769	2.071	124.3	0.1789	0.62	3.251	24.32	1459	2.101
0.13	0.3122	2.335	140.1	0.2018	0.63	3.330	24.91	1495	2.152
0.14	0.3489	2.610	156.6	0.2255	0.64	3.410	25.51	1530	2.204
0.15	0.3869	2.894	173.6	0.2501	0.65	3.490	26.11	1566	2.256
0.16	0.4262	3.189	191.3	0.2755	0.66	3.571	26.71	1603	2.308
0.17	0.4668	3.492	209.5	0.3017	0.67	3.652	27.32	1639	2.361
0.18	0.5086	3.805	228.3	0.3287	0.68	3.735	27.94	1676	2.414
0.19	0.5516	4.126	247.5	0.3565	0.69	3.817	28.56	1713	2.467
0.20	0.5957	4.456	267.3	0.3850	0.70	3.901	29.18	1751	2.521
0.21	0.6409	4.795	287.6	0.4142	0.71	3.984	29.81	1788	2.575
0.22	0.6872	5.141	308.4	0.4442	0.72	4.069	30.44	1826	2.630
0.23	0.7346	5.496	329.7	0.4748	0.73	4.154	31.08	1864	2.685
0.24	0.7831	5.858	351.4	0.5061	0.74	4.240	31.72	1903	2.740
0.25	0.8325	6.228	373.6	0.5380	0.75	4.326	32.36	1941	2.796
0.26	0.8829	6.605	396.3	0.5706	0.76	4.413	33.01	1980	2.852
0.27	0.9344	6.990	419.3	0.6039	0.77	4.500	33.66	2020	2.908
0.28	0.9868	7.382	442.9	0.6377	0.78	4.588	34.32	2059	2.965
0.29	1.040	7.781	466.8	0.6722	0.79	4.676	34.98	2099	3.022
0.30	1.094	8.187	491.1	0.7073	0.80	4.766	35.65	2139	3.080
0.31	1.150	8.600	515.9	0.7429	0.81	4.855	36.32	2179	3.138
0.32	1.206	9.019	541.1	0.7792	0.82	4.945	37.00	2219	3.196
0.33	1.263	9.445	566.6	0.8160	0.83	5.036	37.67	2260	3.255
0.34	1.320	9.878	592.6	0.8533	0.84	5.127	38.36	2301	3.314
0.35	1.379	10.32	618.9	0.8913	0.85	5.219	39.04	2342	3.373
0.36	1.439	10.76	645.6	0.9297	0.86	5.312	39.74	2384	3.433
0.37	1.499	11.21	672.7	0.9687	0.87	5.404	40.43	2426	3.493
0.38	1.560	11.67	700.2	1.008	0.88	5.498	41.13	2467	3.553
0.39	1.622	12.13	728.0	1.048	0.89	5.592	41.83	2510	3.614
0.40	1.685	12.60	756.2	1.089	0.90	5.686	42.54	2552	3.675
0.41	1.748	13.08	784.7	1.130	0.91	5.781	43.25	2595	3.737
0.42	1.813	13.56	813.6	1.172	0.92	5.877	43.97	2638	3.798
0.43	1.878	14.05	842.8	1.214	0.93	5.973	44.68	2681	3.860
0.44	1.944	14.54	872.4	1.256	0.94	6.070	45.41	2724	3.923
0.45	2.010	15.04	902.3	1.299	0.95	6.167	46.13	2768	3.986
0.46	2.078	15.54	932.5	1.343	0.96	6.264	46.86	2811	4.049
0.47	2.146	16.05	963.1	1.387	0.97	6.363	47.60	2856	4.112
0.48	2.215	16.57	994.0	1.431	0.98	6.461	48.34	2900	4.176
0.49	2.284	17.09	1025	1.476	0.99	6.560	49.08	2944	4.240
0.50	2.355	17.62	1057	1.522	1.00	6.660	49.82	2989	4.304

10

10-3: 2 ft. Rectangular Weir without End Contractions Discharge Table *(Continued)*

Formulas: CFS = 6.660H$^{1.5}$ GPS = CFS x 7.481
GPM = CFS x 448.8   MGD = CFS x 0.6463

Head Feet	CFS	GPS	GPM	MGD	Head Feet	CFS	GPS	GPM	MGD
1.01	6.760	50.57	3034	4.369	1.51	12.36	92.45	5546	7.987
1.02	6.861	51.33	3079	4.434	1.52	12.48	93.37	5601	8.066
1.03	6.962	52.08	3125	4.499	1.53	12.60	94.29	5657	8.146
1.04	7.064	52.84	3170	4.565	1.54	12.73	95.22	5712	8.226
1.05	7.166	53.61	3216	4.631	1.55	12.85	96.15	5768	8.306
1.06	7.268	54.37	3262	4.698	1.56	12.98	97.08	5824	8.387
1.07	7.371	55.15	3308	4.764	1.57	13.10	98.01	5880	8.468
1.08	7.475	55.92	3355	4.831	1.58	13.23	98.95	5936	8.549
1.09	7.579	56.70	3401	4.898	1.59	13.35	99.89	5993	8.630
1.10	7.684	57.48	3448	4.966	1.60	13.48	100.8	6049	8.711
1.11	7.789	58.27	3496	5.034	1.61	13.61	101.8	6106	8.793
1.12	7.894	59.06	3543	5.102	1.62	13.73	102.7	6163	8.875
1.13	8.000	59.85	3590	5.170	1.63	13.86	103.7	6220	8.958
1.14	8.106	60.64	3638	5.239	1.64	13.99	104.6	6278	9.040
1.15	8.213	61.44	3686	5.308	1.65	14.12	105.6	6335	9.123
1.16	8.321	62.25	3734	5.378	1.66	14.24	106.6	6393	9.206
1.17	8.429	63.05	3783	5.447	1.67	14.37	107.5	6451	9.289
1.18	8.537	63.86	3831	5.517	1.68	14.50	108.5	6509	9.373
1.19	8.646	64.68	3880	5.588	1.69	14.63	109.5	6567	9.457
1.20	8.755	65.49	3929	5.658	1.70	14.76	110.4	6625	9.541
1.21	8.864	66.32	3978	5.729	1.71	14.89	111.4	6684	9.625
1.22	8.975	67.14	4028	5.800	1.72	15.02	112.4	6742	9.710
1.23	9.085	67.97	4077	5.872	1.73	15.15	113.4	6801	9.794
1.24	9.196	68.80	4127	5.943	1.74	15.29	114.4	6860	9.879
1.25	9.308	69.63	4177	6.016	1.75	15.42	115.3	6920	9.965
1.26	9.420	70.47	4227	6.088	1.76	15.55	116.3	6979	10.05
1.27	9.532	71.31	4278	6.160	1.77	15.68	117.3	7039	10.14
1.28	9.645	72.15	4329	6.233	1.78	15.82	118.3	7098	10.22
1.29	9.758	73.00	4379	6.307	1.79	15.95	119.3	7158	10.31
1.30	9.872	73.85	4430	6.380	1.80	16.08	120.3	7218	10.39
1.31	9.986	74.70	4482	6.454	1.81	16.22	121.3	7279	10.48
1.32	10.10	75.56	4533	6.528	1.82	16.35	122.3	7339	10.57
1.33	10.22	76.42	4585	6.602	1.83	16.49	123.3	7400	10.66
1.34	10.33	77.28	4636	6.677	1.84	16.62	124.4	7460	10.74
1.35	10.45	78.15	4688	6.752	1.85	16.76	125.4	7521	10.83
1.36	10.56	79.02	4741	6.827	1.86	16.89	126.4	7582	10.92
1.37	10.68	79.89	4793	6.902	1.87	17.03	127.4	7643	11.01
1.38	10.80	80.77	4846	6.978	1.88	17.17	128.4	7705	11.10
1.39	10.91	81.65	4898	7.054	1.89	17.30	129.5	7766	11.18
1.40	11.03	82.53	4951	7.130	1.90	17.44	130.5	7828	11.27
1.41	11.15	83.42	5004	7.207	1.91	17.58	131.5	7890	11.36
1.42	11.27	84.31	5058	7.284	1.92	17.72	132.6	7952	11.45
1.43	11.39	85.20	5111	7.361	1.93	17.86	133.6	8014	11.54
1.44	11.51	86.09	5165	7.438	1.94	18.00	134.6	8077	11.63
1.45	11.63	86.99	5219	7.516	1.95	18.14	135.7	8139	11.72
1.46	11.75	87.89	5273	7.593	1.96	18.28	136.7	8202	11.81
1.47	11.87	88.80	5327	7.672	1.97	18.42	137.8	8265	11.90
1.48	11.99	89.71	5382	7.750	1.98	18.56	138.8	8328	11.99
1.49	12.11	90.62	5436	7.829	1.99	18.70	139.9	8391	12.08
1.50	12.24	91.53	5491	7.908	2.00	18.84	140.9	8454	12.17

10

10-3: 2 ft. Rectangular Weir without End Contractions Discharge Table *(Continued)*

Formulas: CFS = 6.660H$^{1.5}$ GPS = CFS x 7.481
GPM = CFS x 448.8   MGD = CFS x 0.6463

Head Feet	CFS	GPS	GPM	MGD	Head Feet	CFS	GPS	GPM	MGD
2.01	18.98	142.0	8518	12.27	2.51	26.48	198.1	11890	17.12
2.02	19.12	143.0	8581	12.36	2.52	26.64	199.3	11960	17.22
2.03	19.26	144.1	8645	12.45	2.53	26.80	200.5	12030	17.32
2.04	19.41	145.2	8709	12.54	2.54	26.96	201.7	12100	17.42
2.05	19.55	146.2	8773	12.63	2.55	27.12	202.9	12170	17.53
2.06	19.69	147.3	8837	12.73	2.56	27.28	204.1	12240	17.63
2.07	19.83	148.4	8902	12.82	2.57	27.44	205.3	12310	17.73
2.08	19.98	149.5	8966	12.91	2.58	27.60	206.5	12390	17.84
2.09	20.12	150.5	9031	13.01	2.59	27.76	207.7	12460	17.94
2.10	20.27	151.6	9096	13.10	2.60	27.92	208.9	12530	18.05
2.11	20.41	152.7	9161	13.19	2.61	28.08	210.1	12600	18.15
2.12	20.56	153.8	9226	13.29	2.62	28.24	211.3	12680	18.25
2.13	20.70	154.9	9292	13.38	2.63	28.41	212.5	12750	18.36
2.14	20.85	156.0	9357	13.48	2.64	28.57	213.7	12820	18.46
2.15	21.00	157.1	9423	13.57	2.65	28.73	214.9	12890	18.57
2.16	21.14	158.2	9489	13.66	2.66	28.89	216.2	12970	18.67
2.17	21.29	159.3	9555	13.76	2.67	29.06	217.4	13040	18.78
2.18	21.44	160.4	9621	13.85	2.68	29.22	218.6	13110	18.88
2.19	21.58	161.5	9687	13.95	2.69	29.38	219.8	13190	18.99
2.20	21.73	162.6	9754	14.05	2.70	29.55	221.0	13260	19.10
2.21	21.88	163.7	9820	14.14	2.71	29.71	222.3	13330	19.20
2.22	22.03	164.8	9887	14.24	2.72	29.88	223.5	13410	19.31
2.23	22.18	165.9	9954	14.33	2.73	30.04	224.7	13480	19.42
2.24	22.33	167.0	10020	14.43	2.74	30.21	226.0	13560	19.52
2.25	22.48	168.2	10090	14.53	2.75	30.37	227.2	13630	19.63
2.26	22.63	169.3	10160	14.62	2.76	30.54	228.5	13710	19.74
2.27	22.78	170.4	10220	14.72	2.77	30.70	229.7	13780	19.84
2.28	22.93	171.5	10290	14.82	2.78	30.87	230.9	13850	19.95
2.29	23.08	172.7	10360	14.92	2.79	31.04	232.2	13930	20.06
2.30	23.23	173.8	10430	15.01	2.80	31.20	233.4	14000	20.17
2.31	23.38	174.9	10490	15.11	2.81	31.37	234.7	14080	20.28
2.32	23.53	176.1	10560	15.21	2.82	31.54	235.9	14150	20.38
2.33	23.69	177.2	10630	15.31	2.83	31.71	237.2	14230	20.49
2.34	23.84	178.3	10700	15.41	2.84	31.88	238.5	14310	20.60
2.35	23.99	179.5	10770	15.51	2.85	32.04	239.7	14380	20.71
2.36	24.15	180.6	10840	15.61	2.86	32.21	241.0	14460	20.82
2.37	24.30	181.8	10910	15.70	2.87	32.38	242.2	14530	20.93
2.38	24.45	182.9	10970	15.80	2.88	32.55	243.5	14610	21.04
2.39	24.61	184.1	11040	15.90	2.89	32.72	244.8	14680	21.15
2.40	24.76	185.2	11110	16.00	2.90	32.89	246.1	14760	21.26
2.41	24.92	186.4	11180	16.10	2.91	33.06	247.3	14840	21.37
2.42	25.07	187.6	11250	16.20	2.92	33.23	248.6	14910	21.48
2.43	25.23	188.7	11320	16.30	2.93	33.40	249.9	14990	21.59
2.44	25.38	189.9	11390	16.41	2.94	33.57	251.2	15070	21.70
2.45	25.54	191.1	11460	16.51	2.95	33.74	252.4	15140	21.81
2.46	25.70	192.2	11530	16.61	2.96	33.92	253.7	15220	21.92
2.47	25.85	193.4	11600	16.71	2.97	34.09	255.0	15300	22.03
2.48	26.01	194.6	11670	16.81	2.98	34.26	256.3	15380	22.14
2.49	26.17	195.8	11740	16.91	2.99	34.43	257.6	15450	22.25
2.50	26.33	196.9	11820	17.01	3.00	34.61	258.9	15530	22.37

10

10-4: 2 1/2 ft. Rectangular Weir without End Contractions Discharge Table

Formulas: CFS = 8.325H$^{1.5}$ GPS = CFS x 7.481
          GPM = CFS x 448.8   MGD = CFS x 0.6463

Head Feet	CFS	GPS	GPM	MGD	Head Feet	CFS	GPS	GPM	MGD
0.01	0.0083	0.0623	3.736	0.0054	0.51	3.032	22.68	1361	1.960
0.02	0.0235	0.1762	10.57	0.0152	0.52	3.122	23.35	1401	2.018
0.03	0.0433	0.3236	19.41	0.0280	0.53	3.212	24.03	1442	2.076
0.04	0.0666	0.4982	29.89	0.0430	0.54	3.304	24.71	1483	2.135
0.05	0.0931	0.6963	41.77	0.0602	0.55	3.396	25.40	1524	2.195
0.06	0.1224	0.9153	54.91	0.0791	0.56	3.489	26.10	1566	2.255
0.07	0.1542	1.153	69.20	0.0996	0.57	3.583	26.80	1608	2.315
0.08	0.1884	1.409	84.54	0.1217	0.58	3.677	27.51	1650	2.377
0.09	0.2248	1.682	100.9	0.1453	0.59	3.773	28.22	1693	2.438
0.10	0.2633	1.969	118.2	0.1701	0.60	3.869	28.94	1736	2.501
0.11	0.3037	2.272	136.3	0.1963	0.61	3.966	29.67	1780	2.563
0.12	0.3461	2.589	155.3	0.2237	0.62	4.064	30.40	1824	2.627
0.13	0.3902	2.919	175.1	0.2522	0.63	4.163	31.14	1868	2.690
0.14	0.4361	3.262	195.7	0.2818	0.64	4.262	31.89	1913	2.755
0.15	0.4836	3.618	217.1	0.3126	0.65	4.363	32.64	1958	2.820
0.16	0.5328	3.986	239.1	0.3443	0.66	4.464	33.39	2003	2.885
0.17	0.5835	4.365	261.9	0.3771	0.67	4.566	34.16	2049	2.951
0.18	0.6358	4.756	285.3	0.4109	0.68	4.668	34.92	2095	3.017
0.19	0.6895	5.158	309.4	0.4456	0.69	4.772	35.70	2141	3.084
0.20	0.7446	5.570	334.2	0.4812	0.70	4.876	36.47	2188	3.151
0.21	0.8011	5.993	359.6	0.5178	0.71	4.980	37.26	2235	3.219
0.22	0.8590	6.427	385.5	0.5552	0.72	5.086	38.05	2283	3.287
0.23	0.9183	6.870	412.1	0.5935	0.73	5.192	38.84	2330	3.356
0.24	0.9788	7.323	439.3	0.6326	0.74	5.299	39.65	2378	3.425
0.25	1.041	7.785	467.0	0.6726	0.75	5.407	40.45	2427	3.495
0.26	1.104	8.257	495.3	0.7133	0.76	5.516	41.26	2475	3.565
0.27	1.168	8.738	524.2	0.7549	0.77	5.625	42.08	2524	3.635
0.28	1.233	9.227	553.6	0.7972	0.78	5.735	42.90	2574	3.706
0.29	1.300	9.726	583.5	0.8403	0.79	5.846	43.73	2623	3.778
0.30	1.368	10.23	613.9	0.8841	0.80	5.957	44.56	2673	3.850
0.31	1.437	10.75	644.9	0.9287	0.81	6.069	45.40	2724	3.922
0.32	1.507	11.27	676.3	0.9740	0.82	6.182	46.24	2774	3.995
0.33	1.578	11.81	708.3	1.020	0.83	6.295	47.09	2825	4.069
0.34	1.650	12.35	740.7	1.067	0.84	6.409	47.95	2876	4.142
0.35	1.724	12.90	773.6	1.114	0.85	6.524	48.81	2928	4.216
0.36	1.798	13.45	807.0	1.162	0.86	6.639	49.67	2980	4.291
0.37	1.874	14.02	840.9	1.211	0.87	6.756	50.54	3032	4.366
0.38	1.950	14.59	875.2	1.260	0.88	6.872	51.41	3084	4.442
0.39	2.028	15.17	910.0	1.310	0.89	6.990	52.29	3137	4.518
0.40	2.106	15.76	945.2	1.361	0.90	7.108	53.18	3190	4.594
0.41	2.186	16.35	980.9	1.413	0.91	7.227	54.06	3243	4.671
0.42	2.266	16.95	1017	1.465	0.92	7.346	54.96	3297	4.748
0.43	2.347	17.56	1054	1.517	0.93	7.466	55.86	3351	4.826
0.44	2.430	18.18	1090	1.570	0.94	7.587	56.76	3405	4.904
0.45	2.513	18.80	1128	1.624	0.95	7.708	57.67	3460	4.982
0.46	2.597	19.43	1166	1.679	0.96	7.831	58.58	3514	5.061
0.47	2.682	20.07	1204	1.734	0.97	7.953	59.50	3569	5.140
0.48	2.769	20.71	1243	1.789	0.98	8.077	60.42	3625	5.220
0.49	2.855	21.36	1282	1.845	0.99	8.200	61.35	3680	5.300
0.50	2.943	22.02	1321	1.902	1.00	8.325	62.28	3736	5.380

10

10-4: 2 ¹/₂ ft. Rectangular Weir without End Contractions Discharge Table (Continued)

Formulas: CFS = 8.325H$^{1.5}$ GPS = CFS x 7.481
           GPM = CFS x 448.8   MGD = CFS x 0.6463

Head Feet	CFS	GPS	GPM	MGD	Head Feet	CFS	GPS	GPM	MGD
1.01	8.450	63.22	3792	5.461	1.51	15.45	115.6	6933	9.984
1.02	8.576	64.16	3849	5.543	1.52	15.60	116.7	7002	10.08
1.03	8.702	65.10	3906	5.624	1.53	15.76	117.9	7071	10.18
1.04	8.829	66.05	3963	5.706	1.54	15.91	119.0	7140	10.28
1.05	8.957	67.01	4020	5.789	1.55	16.07	120.2	7210	10.38
1.06	9.085	67.97	4078	5.872	1.56	16.22	121.3	7280	10.48
1.07	9.214	68.93	4135	5.955	1.57	16.38	122.5	7350	10.58
1.08	9.344	69.90	4193	6.039	1.58	16.53	123.7	7420	10.69
1.09	9.474	70.87	4252	6.123	1.59	16.69	124.9	7491	10.79
1.10	9.604	71.85	4310	6.207	1.60	16.85	126.0	7562	10.89
1.11	9.736	72.83	4369	6.292	1.61	17.01	127.2	7633	10.99
1.12	9.868	73.82	4429	6.377	1.62	17.17	128.4	7704	11.09
1.13	10.00	74.81	4488	6.463	1.63	17.32	129.6	7775	11.20
1.14	10.13	75.81	4548	6.549	1.64	17.48	130.8	7847	11.30
1.15	10.27	76.81	4608	6.635	1.65	17.64	132.0	7919	11.40
1.16	10.40	77.81	4668	6.722	1.66	17.81	133.2	7991	11.51
1.17	10.54	78.82	4728	6.809	1.67	17.97	134.4	8063	11.61
1.18	10.67	79.83	4789	6.897	1.68	18.13	135.6	8136	11.72
1.19	10.81	80.85	4850	6.985	1.69	18.29	136.8	8209	11.82
1.20	10.94	81.87	4911	7.073	1.70	18.45	138.0	8282	11.93
1.21	11.08	82.89	4973	7.161	1.71	18.62	139.3	8355	12.03
1.22	11.22	83.92	5035	7.250	1.72	18.78	140.5	8428	12.14
1.23	11.36	84.96	5097	7.340	1.73	18.94	141.7	8502	12.24
1.24	11.50	86.00	5159	7.429	1.74	19.11	142.9	8576	12.35
1.25	11.63	87.04	5222	7.519	1.75	19.27	144.2	8650	12.46
1.26	11.77	88.08	5284	7.610	1.76	19.44	145.4	8724	12.56
1.27	11.91	89.14	5347	7.701	1.77	19.60	146.7	8798	12.67
1.28	12.06	90.19	5411	7.792	1.78	19.77	147.9	8873	12.78
1.29	12.20	91.25	5474	7.883	1.79	19.94	149.2	8948	12.89
1.30	12.34	92.31	5538	7.975	1.80	20.10	150.4	9023	12.99
1.31	12.48	93.38	5602	8.067	1.81	20.27	151.7	9098	13.10
1.32	12.63	94.45	5666	8.160	1.82	20.44	152.9	9174	13.21
1.33	12.77	95.53	5731	8.253	1.83	20.61	154.2	9249	13.32
1.34	12.91	96.61	5796	8.346	1.84	20.78	155.4	9325	13.43
1.35	13.06	97.69	5861	8.440	1.85	20.95	156.7	9401	13.54
1.36	13.20	98.78	5926	8.533	1.86	21.12	158.0	9478	13.65
1.37	13.35	99.87	5991	8.628	1.87	21.29	159.3	9554	13.76
1.38	13.50	101.0	6057	8.722	1.88	21.46	160.5	9631	13.87
1.39	13.64	102.1	6123	8.817	1.89	21.63	161.8	9708	13.98
1.40	13.79	103.2	6189	8.913	1.90	21.80	163.1	9785	14.09
1.41	13.94	104.3	6256	9.008	1.91	21.98	164.4	9863	14.20
1.42	14.09	105.4	6322	9.104	1.92	22.15	165.7	9940	14.31
1.43	14.24	106.5	6389	9.201	1.93	22.32	167.0	10020	14.43
1.44	14.39	107.6	6456	9.297	1.94	22.50	168.3	10100	14.54
1.45	14.54	108.7	6524	9.394	1.95	22.67	169.6	10170	14.65
1.46	14.69	109.9	6591	9.492	1.96	22.84	170.9	10250	14.76
1.47	14.84	111.0	6659	9.589	1.97	23.02	172.2	10330	14.88
1.48	14.99	112.1	6727	9.687	1.98	23.19	173.5	10410	14.99
1.49	15.14	113.3	6795	9.786	1.99	23.37	174.8	10490	15.10
1.50	15.29	114.4	6864	9.885	2.00	23.55	176.2	10570	15.22

10

10-4: 2 $^1/_2$ ft. Rectangular Weir without End Contractions Discharge Table *(Continued)*

Formulas: CFS = $8.325H^{1.5}$ GPS = CFS x 7.481
GPM = CFS x 448.8   MGD = CFS x 0.6463

Head Feet	CFS	GPS	GPM	MGD	Head Feet	CFS	GPS	GPM	MGD
2.01	23.72	177.5	10650	15.33	2.51	33.11	247.7	14860	21.40
2.02	23.90	178.8	10730	15.45	2.52	33.30	249.1	14950	21.52
2.03	24.08	180.1	10810	15.56	2.53	33.50	250.6	15040	21.65
2.04	24.26	181.5	10890	15.68	2.54	33.70	252.1	15120	21.78
2.05	24.44	182.8	10970	15.79	2.55	33.90	253.6	15210	21.91
2.06	24.61	184.1	11050	15.91	2.56	34.10	255.1	15300	22.04
2.07	24.79	185.5	11130	16.02	2.57	34.30	256.6	15390	22.17
2.08	24.97	186.8	11210	16.14	2.58	34.50	258.1	15480	22.30
2.09	25.15	188.2	11290	16.26	2.59	34.70	259.6	15570	22.43
2.10	25.33	189.5	11370	16.37	2.60	34.90	261.1	15660	22.56
2.11	25.52	190.9	11450	16.49	2.61	35.10	262.6	15750	22.69
2.12	25.70	192.2	11530	16.61	2.62	35.30	264.1	15840	22.82
2.13	25.88	193.6	11610	16.73	2.63	35.51	265.6	15940	22.95
2.14	26.06	195.0	11700	16.84	2.64	35.71	267.1	16030	23.08
2.15	26.24	196.3	11780	16.96	2.65	35.91	268.7	16120	23.21
2.16	26.43	197.7	11860	17.08	2.66	36.12	270.2	16210	23.34
2.17	26.61	199.1	11940	17.20	2.67	36.32	271.7	16300	23.47
2.18	26.80	200.5	12030	17.32	2.68	36.52	273.2	16390	23.61
2.19	26.98	201.8	12110	17.44	2.69	36.73	274.8	16480	23.74
2.20	27.17	203.2	12190	17.56	2.70	36.93	276.3	16580	23.87
2.21	27.35	204.6	12280	17.68	2.71	37.14	277.8	16670	24.00
2.22	27.54	206.0	12360	17.80	2.72	37.35	279.4	16760	24.14
2.23	27.72	207.4	12440	17.92	2.73	37.55	280.9	16850	24.27
2.24	27.91	208.8	12530	18.04	2.74	37.76	282.5	16950	24.40
2.25	28.10	210.2	12610	18.16	2.75	37.96	284.0	17040	24.54
2.26	28.28	211.6	12690	18.28	2.76	38.17	285.6	17130	24.67
2.27	28.47	213.0	12780	18.40	2.77	38.38	287.1	17220	24.80
2.28	28.66	214.4	12860	18.52	2.78	38.59	288.7	17320	24.94
2.29	28.85	215.8	12950	18.65	2.79	38.80	290.2	17410	25.07
2.30	29.04	217.2	13030	18.77	2.80	39.01	291.8	17510	25.21
2.31	29.23	218.7	13120	18.89	2.81	39.21	293.4	17600	25.34
2.32	29.42	220.1	13200	19.01	2.82	39.45	295.1	17700	25.49
2.33	29.61	221.5	13290	19.14	2.83	39.63	296.5	17790	25.62
2.34	29.80	222.9	13370	19.26	2.84	39.84	298.1	17880	25.75
2.35	29.99	224.4	13460	19.38	2.85	40.05	299.6	17980	25.89
2.36	30.18	225.8	13550	19.51	2.86	40.27	301.2	18070	26.02
2.37	30.37	227.2	13630	19.63	2.87	40.48	302.8	18170	26.16
2.38	30.57	228.7	13720	19.76	2.88	40.69	304.4	18260	26.30
2.39	30.76	230.1	13800	19.88	2.89	40.90	306.0	18360	26.43
2.40	30.95	231.6	13890	20.00	2.90	41.11	307.6	18450	26.57
2.41	31.15	233.0	13980	20.13	2.91	41.33	309.2	18550	26.71
2.42	31.34	234.5	14070	20.26	2.92	41.54	310.8	18640	26.85
2.43	31.54	235.9	14150	20.38	2.93	41.75	312.4	18740	26.98
2.44	31.73	237.4	14240	20.51	2.94	41.97	314.0	18830	27.12
2.45	31.93	238.8	14330	20.63	2.95	42.18	315.6	18930	27.26
2.46	32.12	240.3	14420	20.76	2.96	42.40	317.2	19030	27.40
2.47	32.32	241.8	14500	20.89	2.97	42.61	318.8	19120	27.54
2.48	32.51	243.2	14590	21.01	2.98	42.83	320.4	19220	27.68
2.49	32.71	244.7	14680	21.14	2.99	43.04	322.0	19320	27.82
2.50	32.91	246.2	14770	21.27	3.00	43.26	323.6	19410	27.96

10-5: 3 ft. Rectangular Weir without End Contractions Discharge Table

Formulas: $CFS = 9.990H^{1.5}$ $GPS = CFS \times 7.481$
$GPM = CFS \times 448.8$ $MGD = CFS \times 0.6463$

Head Feet	CFS	GPS	GPM	MGD	Head Feet	CFS	GPS	GPM	MGD
0.01	0.0100	0.0747	4.484	0.0065	0.51	3.638	27.22	1633	2.352
0.02	0.0283	0.2114	12.68	0.0183	0.52	3.746	28.02	1681	2.421
0.03	0.0519	0.3883	23.30	0.0335	0.53	3.855	28.84	1730	2.491
0.04	0.0799	0.5979	35.87	0.0517	0.54	3.964	29.66	1779	2.562
0.05	0.1117	0.8356	50.13	0.0722	0.55	4.075	30.48	1829	2.634
0.06	0.1468	1.098	65.89	0.0949	0.56	4.186	31.32	1879	2.706
0.07	0.1850	1.384	83.04	0.1196	0.57	4.299	32.16	1929	2.779
0.08	0.2260	1.691	101.5	0.1461	0.58	4.413	33.01	1980	2.852
0.09	0.2697	2.018	121.1	0.1743	0.59	4.527	33.87	2032	2.926
0.10	0.3159	2.363	141.8	0.2042	0.60	4.643	34.73	2084	3.001
0.11	0.3645	2.727	163.6	0.2356	0.61	4.759	35.61	2136	3.076
0.12	0.4153	3.107	186.4	0.2684	0.62	4.877	36.48	2189	3.152
0.13	0.4683	3.503	210.2	0.3026	0.63	4.995	37.37	2242	3.229
0.14	0.5233	3.915	234.9	0.3382	0.64	5.115	38.26	2296	3.306
0.15	0.5804	4.342	260.5	0.3751	0.65	5.235	39.16	2350	3.384
0.16	0.6394	4.783	286.9	0.4132	0.66	5.357	40.07	2404	3.462
0.17	0.7002	5.238	314.3	0.4526	0.67	5.479	40.99	2459	3.541
0.18	0.7629	5.707	342.4	0.4931	0.68	5.602	41.91	2514	3.620
0.19	0.8274	6.189	371.3	0.5347	0.69	5.726	42.84	2570	3.701
0.20	0.8935	6.685	401.0	0.5775	0.70	5.851	43.77	2626	3.781
0.21	0.9614	7.192	431.5	0.6213	0.71	5.977	44.71	2682	3.863
0.22	1.031	7.712	462.6	0.6662	0.72	6.103	45.66	2739	3.945
0.23	1.102	8.244	494.5	0.7122	0.73	6.231	46.61	2796	4.027
0.24	1.175	8.787	527.2	0.7591	0.74	6.359	47.57	2854	4.110
0.25	1.249	9.342	560.4	0.8071	0.75	6.489	48.54	2912	4.194
0.26	1.324	9.908	594.4	0.8560	0.76	6.619	49.52	2971	4.278
0.27	1.402	10.49	629.0	0.9058	0.77	6.750	50.50	3029	4.363
0.28	1.480	11.07	664.3	0.9566	0.78	6.882	51.48	3089	4.448
0.29	1.560	11.67	700.2	1.008	0.79	7.015	52.48	3148	4.534
0.30	1.642	12.28	736.7	1.061	0.80	7.148	53.48	3208	4.620
0.31	1.724	12.90	773.9	1.114	0.81	7.283	54.48	3268	4.707
0.32	1.808	13.53	811.6	1.169	0.82	7.418	55.49	3329	4.794
0.33	1.894	14.17	849.9	1.224	0.83	7.554	56.51	3390	4.882
0.34	1.981	14.82	888.9	1.280	0.84	7.691	57.54	3452	4.971
0.35	2.069	15.47	928.4	1.337	0.85	7.829	58.57	3514	5.060
0.36	2.158	16.14	968.4	1.395	0.86	7.967	59.60	3576	5.149
0.37	2.248	16.82	1009	1.453	0.87	8.107	60.65	3638	5.239
0.38	2.340	17.51	1050	1.512	0.88	8.247	61.69	3701	5.330
0.39	2.433	18.20	1092	1.573	0.89	8.388	62.75	3764	5.421
0.40	2.527	18.91	1134	1.633	0.90	8.530	63.81	3828	5.513
0.41	2.623	19.62	1177	1.695	0.91	8.672	64.88	3892	5.605
0.42	2.719	20.34	1220	1.757	0.92	8.816	65.95	3956	5.697
0.43	2.817	21.07	1264	1.821	0.93	8.960	67.03	4021	5.791
0.44	2.916	21.81	1309	1.884	0.94	9.105	68.11	4086	5.884
0.45	3.016	22.56	1353	1.949	0.95	9.250	69.20	4151	5.978
0.46	3.117	23.32	1399	2.014	0.96	9.397	70.30	4217	6.073
0.47	3.219	24.08	1445	2.080	0.97	9.544	71.40	4283	6.168
0.48	3.322	24.85	1491	2.147	0.98	9.692	72.50	4350	6.264
0.49	3.427	25.63	1538	2.215	0.99	9.841	73.62	4416	6.360
0.50	3.532	26.42	1585	2.283	1.00	9.990	74.74	4484	6.457

10

10-5: 3 ft. Rectangular Weir without End Contractions Discharge Table (Continued)

Formulas: CFS = $9.990H^{1.5}$ GPS = CFS x 7.481
GPM = CFS x 448.8   MGD = CFS x 0.6463

Head Feet	CFS	GPS	GPM	MGD	Head Feet	CFS	GPS	GPM	MGD
1.01	10.14	75.86	4551	6.554	1.51	18.54	138.7	8319	11.98
1.02	10.29	76.99	4619	6.651	1.52	18.72	140.1	8402	12.10
1.03	10.44	78.12	4687	6.749	1.53	18.91	141.4	8485	12.22
1.04	10.60	79.26	4755	6.848	1.54	19.09	142.8	8568	12.34
1.05	10.75	80.41	4824	6.947	1.55	19.28	144.2	8652	12.46
1.06	10.90	81.56	4893	7.046	1.56	19.46	145.6	8736	12.58
1.07	11.06	82.72	4962	7.146	1.57	19.65	147.0	8820	12.70
1.08	11.21	83.88	5032	7.247	1.58	19.84	148.4	8904	12.82
1.09	11.37	85.05	5102	7.347	1.59	20.03	149.8	8989	12.94
1.10	11.53	86.22	5173	7.449	1.60	20.22	151.3	9074	13.07
1.11	11.68	87.40	5243	7.551	1.61	20.41	152.7	9159	13.19
1.12	11.84	88.58	5314	7.653	1.62	20.60	154.1	9245	13.31
1.13	12.00	89.77	5386	7.756	1.63	20.79	155.5	9330	13.44
1.14	12.16	90.97	5457	7.859	1.64	20.98	157.0	9416	13.56
1.15	12.32	92.17	5529	7.962	1.65	21.17	158.4	9503	13.68
1.16	12.48	93.37	5602	8.067	1.66	21.37	159.8	9589	13.81
1.17	12.64	94.58	5674	8.171	1.67	21.56	161.3	9676	13.93
1.18	12.81	95.80	5747	8.276	1.68	21.75	162.7	9763	14.06
1.19	12.97	97.02	5820	8.381	1.69	21.95	164.2	9850	14.19
1.20	13.13	98.24	5894	8.487	1.70	22.14	165.7	9938	14.31
1.21	13.30	99.47	5968	8.594	1.71	22.34	167.1	10030	14.44
1.22	13.46	100.7	6042	8.700	1.72	22.54	168.6	10110	14.56
1.23	13.63	101.9	6116	8.808	1.73	22.73	170.1	10200	14.69
1.24	13.79	103.2	6191	8.915	1.74	22.93	171.5	10290	14.82
1.25	13.96	104.4	6266	9.023	1.75	23.13	173.0	10380	14.95
1.26	14.13	105.7	6341	9.132	1.76	23.33	174.5	10470	15.08
1.27	14.30	107.0	6417	9.241	1.77	23.52	176.0	10560	15.20
1.28	14.47	108.2	6493	9.350	1.78	23.72	177.5	10650	15.33
1.29	14.64	109.5	6569	9.460	1.79	23.92	179.0	10740	15.46
1.30	14.81	110.8	6646	9.570	1.80	24.13	180.5	10830	15.59
1.31	14.98	112.1	6722	9.681	1.81	24.33	182.0	10920	15.72
1.32	15.15	113.3	6800	9.792	1.82	24.53	183.5	11010	15.85
1.33	15.32	114.6	6877	9.903	1.83	24.73	185.0	11100	15.98
1.34	15.50	115.9	6955	10.02	1.84	24.93	186.5	11190	16.11
1.35	15.67	117.2	7033	10.13	1.85	25.14	188.1	11280	16.25
1.36	15.84	118.5	7111	10.24	1.86	25.34	189.6	11370	16.38
1.37	16.02	119.8	7190	10.35	1.87	25.55	191.1	11470	16.51
1.38	16.20	121.2	7268	10.47	1.88	25.75	192.6	11560	16.64
1.39	16.37	122.5	7348	10.58	1.89	25.96	194.2	11650	16.78
1.40	16.55	123.8	7427	10.70	1.90	26.16	195.7	11740	16.91
1.41	16.73	125.1	7507	10.81	1.91	26.37	197.3	11840	17.04
1.42	16.90	126.5	7587	10.93	1.92	26.58	198.8	11930	17.18
1.43	17.08	127.8	7667	11.04	1.93	26.79	200.4	12020	17.31
1.44	17.26	129.1	7748	11.16	1.94	26.99	201.9	12110	17.45
1.45	17.44	130.5	7828	11.27	1.95	27.20	203.5	12210	17.58
1.46	17.62	131.8	7909	11.39	1.96	27.41	205.1	12300	17.72
1.47	17.80	133.2	7991	11.51	1.97	27.62	206.6	12400	17.85
1.48	17.99	134.6	8073	11.62	1.98	27.83	208.2	12490	17.99
1.49	18.17	135.9	8155	11.74	1.99	28.04	209.8	12590	18.13
1.50	18.35	137.3	8237	11.86	2.00	28.26	211.4	12680	18.26

10

Formulas: CFS $=9.990H^{1.5}$ GPS = CFS x 7.481
GPM = CFS x 448.8 MGD = CFS x 0.6463

Head Feet	CFS	GPS	GPM	MGD	Head Feet	CFS	GPS	GPM	MGD
2.01	28.47	213.0	12780	18.40	2.51	39.73	297.2	17830	25.67
2.02	28.68	214.6	12870	18.54	2.52	39.96	299.0	17940	25.83
2.03	28.89	216.2	12970	18.67	2.53	40.20	300.8	18040	25.98
2.04	29.11	217.8	13060	18.81	2.54	40.44	302.5	18150	26.14
2.05	29.32	219.4	13160	18.95	2.55	40.68	304.3	18260	26.29
2.06	29.54	221.0	13260	19.09	2.56	40.92	306.1	18360	26.45
2.07	29.75	222.6	13350	19.23	2.57	41.16	307.9	18470	26.60
2.08	29.97	224.2	13450	19.37	2.58	41.40	309.7	18580	26.76
2.09	30.18	225.8	13550	19.51	2.59	41.64	311.5	18690	26.91
2.10	30.40	227.4	13640	19.65	2.60	41.88	313.3	18800	27.07
2.11	30.62	229.1	13740	19.79	2.61	42.12	315.1	18910	27.22
2.12	30.84	230.7	13840	19.93	2.62	42.37	316.9	19010	27.38
2.13	31.06	232.3	13940	20.07	2.63	42.61	318.8	19120	27.54
2.14	31.27	234.0	14040	20.21	2.64	42.85	320.6	19230	27.70
2.15	31.49	235.6	14130	20.35	2.65	43.10	322.4	19340	27.85
2.16	31.71	237.2	14230	20.50	2.66	43.34	324.2	19450	28.01
2.17	31.93	238.9	14330	20.64	2.67	43.58	326.1	19560	28.17
2.18	32.16	240.6	14430	20.78	2.68	43.83	327.9	19670	28.33
2.19	32.38	242.2	14530	20.93	2.69	44.08	329.7	19780	28.49
2.20	32.60	243.9	14630	21.07	2.70	44.32	331.6	19890	28.64
2.21	32.82	245.5	14730	21.21	2.71	44.57	333.4	20000	28.80
2.22	33.04	247.2	14830	21.36	2.72	44.81	335.3	20110	28.96
2.23	33.27	248.9	14930	21.50	2.73	45.06	337.1	20220	29.12
2.24	33.49	250.6	15030	21.65	2.74	45.31	339.0	20340	29.28
2.25	33.72	252.2	15130	21.79	2.75	45.56	340.8	20450	29.44
2.26	33.94	253.9	15230	21.94	2.76	45.81	342.7	20560	29.60
2.27	34.17	255.6	15330	22.08	2.77	46.06	344.5	20670	29.77
2.28	34.39	257.3	15440	22.23	2.78	46.31	346.4	20780	29.93
2.29	34.62	259.0	15540	22.37	2.79	46.56	348.3	20890	30.09
2.30	34.85	260.7	15640	22.52	2.80	46.81	350.2	21010	30.25
2.31	35.07	262.4	15740	22.67	2.81	47.06	352.0	21120	30.41
2.32	35.30	264.1	15840	22.82	2.82	47.31	353.9	21230	30.58
2.33	35.53	265.8	15950	22.96	2.83	47.56	355.8	21350	30.74
2.34	35.76	267.5	16050	23.11	2.84	47.81	357.7	21460	30.90
2.35	35.99	269.2	16150	23.26	2.85	48.07	359.6	21570	31.06
2.36	36.22	271.0	16250	23.41	2.86	48.32	361.5	21690	31.23
2.37	36.45	272.7	16360	23.56	2.87	48.57	363.4	21800	31.39
2.38	36.68	274.4	16460	23.71	2.88	48.83	365.3	21910	31.56
2.39	36.91	276.1	16570	23.86	2.89	49.08	367.2	22030	31.72
2.40	37.14	277.9	16670	24.01	2.90	49.34	369.1	22140	31.89
2.41	37.38	279.6	16770	24.16	2.91	49.59	371.0	22260	32.05
2.42	37.61	281.4	16880	24.31	2.92	49.85	372.9	22370	32.22
2.43	37.84	283.1	16980	24.46	2.93	50.10	374.8	22490	32.38
2.44	38.08	284.8	17090	24.61	2.94	50.36	376.7	22600	32.55
2.45	38.31	286.6	17190	24.76	2.95	50.62	378.7	22720	32.71
2.46	38.55	288.4	17300	24.91	2.96	50.87	380.6	22830	32.88
2.47	38.78	290.1	17400	25.06	2.97	51.13	382.5	22950	33.05
2.48	39.02	291.9	17510	25.22	2.98	51.39	384.5	23060	33.21
2.49	39.25	293.6	17620	25.37	2.99	51.65	386.4	23180	33.38
2.50	39.49	295.4	17720	25.52	3.00	51.91	388.3	23300	33.55

10

10-6: 4 ft. Rectangular Weir without End Contractions Discharge Table

Formulas: $CFS = 13.32H^{1.5}$ $GPS = CFS \times 7.481$
$GPM = CFS \times 448.8$ $MGD = CFS \times 0.6463$

Head Feet	CFS	GPS	GPM	MGD	Head Feet	CFS	GPS	GPM	MGD
0.01	0.0133	0.0996	5.978	0.0086	0.51	4.851	36.29	2177	3.135
0.02	0.0377	0.2818	16.91	0.0243	0.52	4.995	37.37	2242	3.228
0.03	0.0692	0.5178	31.06	0.0447	0.53	5.139	38.45	2307	3.322
0.04	0.1066	0.7972	47.82	0.0689	0.54	5.286	39.54	2372	3.416
0.05	0.1489	1.114	66.84	0.0962	0.55	5.433	40.65	2438	3.511
0.06	0.1958	1.465	87.86	0.1265	0.56	5.582	41.76	2505	3.608
0.07	0.2467	1.845	110.7	0.1594	0.57	5.732	42.88	2573	3.705
0.08	0.3014	2.255	135.3	0.1948	0.58	5.884	44.02	2641	3.803
0.09	0.3596	2.690	161.4	0.2324	0.59	6.036	45.16	2709	3.901
0.10	0.4212	3.151	189.0	0.2722	0.60	6.191	46.31	2778	4.001
0.11	0.4860	3.635	218.1	0.3141	0.61	6.346	47.47	2848	4.101
0.12	0.5537	4.142	248.5	0.3579	0.62	6.503	48.65	2918	4.203
0.13	0.6243	4.671	280.2	0.4035	0.63	6.661	49.83	2989	4.305
0.14	0.6977	5.220	313.1	0.4510	0.64	6.820	51.02	3061	4.408
0.15	0.7738	5.789	347.3	0.5001	0.65	6.980	52.22	3133	4.511
0.16	0.8525	6.377	382.6	0.5510	0.66	7.142	53.43	3205	4.616
0.17	0.9336	6.985	419.0	0.6034	0.67	7.305	54.65	3278	4.721
0.18	1.017	7.610	456.5	0.6574	0.68	7.469	55.88	3352	4.827
0.19	1.103	8.253	495.1	0.7130	0.69	7.634	57.11	3426	4.934
0.20	1.191	8.913	534.7	0.7700	0.70	7.801	58.36	3501	5.042
0.21	1.282	9.589	575.3	0.8285	0.71	7.969	59.61	3576	5.150
0.22	1.374	10.28	616.9	0.8883	0.72	8.138	60.88	3652	5.259
0.23	1.469	10.99	659.4	0.9496	0.73	8.308	62.15	3729	5.369
0.24	1.566	11.72	702.9	1.012	0.74	8.479	63.43	3805	5.480
0.25	1.665	12.46	747.3	1.076	0.75	8.652	64.72	3883	5.592
0.26	1.766	13.21	792.5	1.141	0.76	8.825	66.02	3961	5.704
0.27	1.869	13.98	838.7	1.208	0.77	9.000	67.33	4039	5.817
0.28	1.974	14.76	885.7	1.275	0.78	9.176	68.64	4118	5.930
0.29	2.080	15.56	933.6	1.344	0.79	9.353	69.97	4198	6.045
0.30	2.189	16.37	982.3	1.415	0.80	9.531	71.30	4278	6.160
0.31	2.299	17.20	1032	1.486	0.81	9.710	72.64	4358	6.276
0.32	2.411	18.04	1082	1.558	0.82	9.891	73.99	4439	6.392
0.33	2.525	18.89	1133	1.632	0.83	10.07	75.35	4520	6.510
0.34	2.641	19.76	1185	1.707	0.84	10.25	76.72	4602	6.628
0.35	2.758	20.63	1238	1.783	0.85	10.44	78.09	4685	6.746
0.36	2.877	21.52	1291	1.859	0.86	10.62	79.47	4768	6.866
0.37	2.998	22.43	1345	1.937	0.87	10.81	80.86	4851	6.986
0.38	3.120	23.34	1400	2.017	0.88	11.00	82.26	4935	7.107
0.39	3.244	24.27	1456	2.097	0.89	11.18	83.67	5019	7.228
0.40	3.370	25.21	1512	2.178	0.90	11.37	85.08	5104	7.350
0.41	3.497	26.16	1569	2.260	0.91	11.56	86.50	5189	7.473
0.42	3.626	27.12	1627	2.343	0.92	11.75	87.93	5275	7.597
0.43	3.756	28.10	1686	2.427	0.93	11.95	89.37	5361	7.721
0.44	3.888	29.08	1745	2.513	0.94	12.14	90.81	5448	7.846
0.45	4.021	30.08	1805	2.599	0.95	12.33	92.27	5535	7.971
0.46	4.156	31.09	1865	2.686	0.96	12.53	93.73	5623	8.097
0.47	4.292	32.11	1926	2.774	0.97	12.73	95.20	5711	8.224
0.48	4.430	33.14	1988	2.863	0.98	12.92	96.67	5800	8.352
0.49	4.569	34.18	2050	2.953	0.99	13.12	98.16	5889	8.480
0.50	4.709	35.23	2114	3.044	1.00	13.32	99.65	5978	8.609

10.

Formulas: CFS = 13.32H$^{1.5}$ GPS = CFS x 7.481
GPM = CFS x 448.8 MGD = CFS x 0.6463

Head Feet	CFS	GPS	GPM	MGD	Head Feet	CFS	GPS	GPM	MGD
1.01	13.52	101.1	6068	8.738	1.51	24.72	184.9	11090	15.97
1.02	13.72	102.7	6158	8.868	1.52	24.96	186.7	11200	16.13
1.03	13.92	104.2	6249	8.999	1.53	25.21	188.6	11310	16.29
1.04	14.13	105.7	6340	9.130	1.54	25.46	190.4	11430	16.45
1.05	14.33	107.2	6432	9.262	1.55	25.70	192.3	11540	16.61
1.06	14.54	108.7	6524	9.395	1.56	25.95	194.2	11650	16.77
1.07	14.74	110.3	6617	9.528	1.57	26.20	196.0	11760	16.94
1.08	14.95	111.8	6710	9.662	1.58	26.45	197.9	11870	17.10
1.09	15.16	113.4	6803	9.797	1.59	26.71	199.8	11990	17.26
1.10	15.37	115.0	6897	9.932	1.60	26.96	201.7	12100	17.42
1.11	15.58	116.5	6991	10.07	1.61	27.21	203.6	12210	17.59
1.12	15.79	118.1	7086	10.20	1.62	27.46	205.5	12330	17.75
1.13	16.00	119.7	7181	10.34	1.63	27.72	207.4	12440	17.92
1.14	16.21	121.3	7276	10.48	1.64	27.97	209.3	12560	18.08
1.15	16.43	122.9	7372	10.62	1.65	28.23	211.2	12670	18.25
1.16	16.64	124.5	7469	10.76	1.66	28.49	213.1	12790	18.41
1.17	16.86	126.1	7565	10.89	1.67	28.75	215.0	12900	18.58
1.18	17.07	127.7	7663	11.03	1.68	29.00	217.0	13020	18.75
1.19	17.29	129.4	7760	11.18	1.69	29.26	218.9	13130	18.91
1.20	17.51	131.0	7858	11.32	1.70	29.52	220.9	13250	19.08
1.21	17.73	132.6	7957	11.46	1.71	29.79	222.8	13370	19.25
1.22	17.95	134.3	8056	11.60	1.72	30.05	224.8	13490	19.42
1.23	18.17	135.9	8155	11.74	1.73	30.31	226.7	13600	19.59
1.24	18.39	137.6	8254	11.89	1.74	30.57	228.7	13720	19.76
1.25	18.62	139.3	8355	12.03	1.75	30.84	230.7	13840	19.93
1.26	18.84	140.9	8455	12.18	1.76	31.10	232.7	13960	20.10
1.27	19.06	142.6	8556	12.32	1.77	31.37	234.7	14080	20.27
1.28	19.29	144.3	8657	12.47	1.78	31.63	236.6	14200	20.44
1.29	19.52	146.0	8759	12.61	1.79	31.90	238.6	14320	20.62
1.30	19.74	147.7	8861	12.76	1.80	32.17	240.6	14440	20.79
1.31	19.97	149.4	8963	12.91	1.81	32.44	242.7	14560	20.96
1.32	20.20	151.1	9066	13.06	1.82	32.70	244.7	14680	21.14
1.33	20.43	152.8	9169	13.20	1.83	32.97	246.7	14800	21.31
1.34	20.66	154.6	9273	13.35	1.84	33.25	248.7	14920	21.49
1.35	20.89	156.3	9377	13.50	1.85	33.52	250.7	15040	21.66
1.36	21.13	158.0	9481	13.65	1.86	33.79	252.8	15170	21.84
1.37	21.36	159.8	9586	13.80	1.87	34.06	254.8	15290	22.01
1.38	21.59	161.5	9691	13.96	1.88	34.34	256.9	15410	22.19
1.39	21.83	163.3	9797	14.11	1.89	34.61	258.9	15530	22.37
1.40	22.06	165.1	9903	14.26	1.90	34.88	261.0	15660	22.55
1.41	22.30	166.8	10010	14.41	1.91	35.16	263.0	15780	22.72
1.42	22.54	168.6	10120	14.57	1.92	35.44	265.1	15904	22.90
1.43	22.78	170.4	10220	14.72	1.93	35.71	267.2	16029	23.08
1.44	23.02	172.2	10330	14.88	1.94	35.99	269.3	16150	23.26
1.45	23.26	174.0	10440	15.03	1.95	36.27	271.3	16280	23.44
1.46	23.50	175.8	10550	15.19	1.96	36.55	273.4	16400	23.62
1.47	23.74	177.6	10660	15.34	1.97	36.83	275.5	16530	23.80
1.48	23.98	179.4	10760	15.50	1.98	37.11	277.6	16660	23.98
1.49	24.23	181.2	10870	15.66	1.99	37.39	279.7	16780	24.17
1.50	24.47	183.1	10980	15.82	2.00	37.67	281.8	16910	24.35

10

Formulas: CFS $=13.32H^{1.5}$ GPS = CFS x 7.481
           GPM = CFS x 448.8   MGD = CFS x 0.6463

Head Feet	CFS	GPS	GPM	MGD	Head Feet	CFS	GPS	GPM	MGD
2.01	37.96	284.0	17040	24.53	2.51	52.97	396.3	23770	34.23
2.02	38.24	286.1	17160	24.72	2.52	53.29	398.6	23910	34.44
2.03	38.53	288.2	17290	24.90	2.53	53.60	401.0	24060	34.64
2.04	38.81	290.3	17420	25.08	2.54	53.92	403.4	24200	34.85
2.05	39.10	292.5	17550	25.27	2.55	54.24	405.8	24340	35.05
2.06	39.38	294.6	17670	25.45	2.56	54.56	408.2	24490	35.26
2.07	39.67	296.8	17800	25.64	2.57	54.88	410.5	24630	35.47
2.08	39.96	298.9	17930	25.82	2.58	55.20	412.9	24770	35.68
2.09	40.25	301.1	18060	26.01	2.59	55.52	415.3	24920	35.88
2.10	40.54	303.2	18190	26.20	2.60	55.84	417.8	25060	36.09
2.11	40.83	305.4	18320	26.39	2.61	56.16	420.2	25210	36.30
2.12	41.12	307.6	18450	26.57	2.62	56.49	422.6	25350	36.51
2.13	41.41	309.8	18580	26.76	2.63	56.81	425.0	25500	36.72
2.14	41.70	311.9	18710	26.95	2.64	57.14	427.4	25640	36.93
2.15	41.99	314.1	18850	27.14	2.65	57.46	429.9	25790	37.14
2.16	42.28	316.3	18980	27.33	2.66	57.79	432.3	25930	37.35
2.17	42.58	318.5	19110	27.52	2.67	58.11	434.7	26080	37.56
2.18	42.87	320.7	19240	27.71	2.68	58.44	437.2	26230	37.77
2.19	43.17	322.9	19370	27.90	2.69	58.77	439.6	26370	37.98
2.20	43.46	325.2	19510	28.09	2.70	59.09	442.1	26520	38.19
2.21	43.76	327.4	19640	28.28	2.71	59.42	444.5	26670	38.41
2.22	44.06	329.6	19770	28.48	2.72	59.75	447.0	26820	38.62
2.23	44.36	331.8	19910	28.67	2.73	60.08	449.5	26970	38.83
2.24	44.66	334.1	20040	28.86	2.74	60.41	451.9	27110	39.04
2.25	44.95	336.3	20180	29.05	2.75	60.74	454.4	27260	39.26
2.26	45.26	338.6	20310	29.25	2.76	61.08	456.9	27410	39.47
2.27	45.56	340.8	20450	29.44	2.77	61.41	459.4	27560	39.69
2.28	45.86	343.1	20580	29.64	2.78	61.74	461.9	27710	39.90
2.29	46.16	345.3	20720	29.83	2.79	62.07	464.4	27860	40.12
2.30	46.46	347.6	20850	30.03	2.80	62.41	466.9	28010	40.33
2.31	46.77	349.8	20990	30.22	2.81	62.74	469.4	28160	40.55
2.32	47.07	352.1	21120	30.42	2.82	63.08	471.9	28310	40.77
2.33	47.37	354.4	21260	30.62	2.83	63.41	474.4	28460	40.98
2.34	47.68	356.7	21400	30.81	2.84	63.75	476.9	28610	41.20
2.35	47.99	359.0	21540	31.01	2.85	64.09	479.4	28760	41.42
2.36	48.29	361.3	21670	31.21	2.86	64.42	482.0	28910	41.64
2.37	48.60	363.6	21810	31.41	2.87	64.76	484.5	29070	41.86
2.38	48.91	365.9	21950	31.61	2.88	65.10	487.0	29220	42.08
2.39	49.22	368.2	22090	31.81	2.89	65.44	489.6	29370	42.29
2.40	49.52	370.5	22230	32.01	2.90	65.78	492.1	29520	42.51
2.41	49.83	372.8	22370	32.21	2.91	66.12	494.7	29680	42.73
2.42	50.14	375.1	22510	32.41	2.92	66.46	497.2	29830	42.95
2.43	50.46	377.5	22640	32.61	2.93	66.80	499.8	29980	43.18
2.44	50.77	379.8	22780	32.81	2.94	67.15	502.3	30140	43.40
2.45	51.08	382.1	22920	33.01	2.95	67.49	504.9	30290	43.62
2.46	51.39	384.5	23070	33.22	2.96	67.83	507.5	30440	43.84
2.47	51.71	386.8	23210	33.42	2.97	68.18	510.0	30600	44.06
2.48	52.02	389.2	23350	33.62	2.98	68.52	512.6	30750	44.29
2.49	52.34	391.5	23490	33.82	2.99	68.87	515.2	30910	44.51
2.50	52.65	393.9	23630	34.03	3.00	69.21	517.8	31060	44.73

10

10-7: 5 ft. Rectangular Weir without End Contractions Discharge Table

Formulas: CFS = 16.65H$^{1.5}$ GPS = CFS x 7.481
GPM = CFS x 448.8   MGD = CFS x 0.6463

Head Feet	CFS	GPS	GPM	MGD	Head Feet	CFS	GPS	GPM	MGD
0.01	0.0166	0.1246	7.473	0.0108	0.51	6.064	45.37	2722	3.919
0.02	0.0471	0.3523	21.14	0.0304	0.52	6.243	46.71	2802	4.035
0.03	0.0865	0.6472	38.83	0.0559	0.53	6.424	48.06	2883	4.152
0.04	0.1332	0.9965	59.78	0.0861	0.54	6.607	49.43	2965	4.270
0.05	0.1862	1.393	83.55	0.1203	0.55	6.791	50.81	3048	4.389
0.06	0.2447	1.831	109.8	0.1582	0.56	6.977	52.20	3131	4.510
0.07	0.3084	2.307	138.4	0.1993	0.57	7.165	53.60	3216	4.631
0.08	0.3767	2.818	169.1	0.2435	0.58	7.355	55.02	3301	4.753
0.09	0.4495	3.363	201.8	0.2905	0.59	7.546	56.45	3386	4.877
0.10	0.5265	3.939	236.3	0.3403	0.60	7.738	57.89	3473	5.001
0.11	0.6074	4.544	272.6	0.3926	0.61	7.932	59.34	3560	5.127
0.12	0.6921	5.178	310.6	0.4473	0.62	8.128	60.81	3648	5.253
0.13	0.7804	5.838	350.3	0.5044	0.63	8.326	62.29	3737	5.381
0.14	0.8722	6.525	391.4	0.5637	0.64	8.525	63.77	3826	5.510
0.15	0.9673	7.236	434.1	0.6252	0.65	8.725	65.27	3916	5.639
0.16	1.066	7.972	478.2	0.6887	0.66	8.928	66.79	4007	5.770
0.17	1.167	8.731	523.8	0.7543	0.67	9.131	68.31	4098	5.901
0.18	1.272	9.512	570.7	0.8218	0.68	9.336	69.85	4190	6.034
0.19	1.379	10.32	618.9	0.8912	0.69	9.543	71.39	4283	6.168
0.20	1.489	11.14	668.4	0.9625	0.70	9.751	72.95	4376	6.302
0.21	1.602	11.99	719.1	1.036	0.71	9.961	74.52	4470	6.438
0.22	1.718	12.85	771.1	1.110	0.72	10.17	76.10	4565	6.574
0.23	1.837	13.74	824.2	1.187	0.73	10.38	77.69	4661	6.712
0.24	1.958	14.65	878.6	1.265	0.74	10.60	79.29	4757	6.850
0.25	2.081	15.57	934.1	1.345	0.75	10.81	80.90	4854	6.989
0.26	2.207	16.51	990.7	1.427	0.76	11.03	82.53	4951	7.130
0.27	2.336	17.48	1048	1.510	0.77	11.25	84.16	5049	7.271
0.28	2.467	18.45	1107	1.594	0.78	11.47	85.81	5148	7.413
0.29	2.600	19.45	1167	1.681	0.79	11.69	87.46	5247	7.556
0.30	2.736	20.47	1228	1.768	0.80	11.91	89.13	5347	7.700
0.31	2.874	21.50	1290	1.857	0.81	12.14	90.80	5447	7.845
0.32	3.014	22.55	1353	1.948	0.82	12.36	92.49	5549	7.990
0.33	3.156	23.61	1417	2.040	0.83	12.59	94.19	5650	8.137
0.34	3.301	24.69	1481	2.133	0.84	12.82	95.89	5753	8.285
0.35	3.448	25.79	1547	2.228	0.85	13.05	97.61	5856	8.433
0.36	3.596	26.90	1614	2.324	0.86	13.28	99.34	5960	8.582
0.37	3.747	28.03	1682	2.422	0.87	13.51	101.1	6064	8.732
0.38	3.900	29.18	1750	2.521	0.88	13.74	102.8	6169	8.883
0.39	4.055	30.34	1820	2.621	0.89	13.98	104.6	6274	9.035
0.40	4.212	31.51	1890	2.722	0.90	14.22	106.4	6380	9.188
0.41	4.371	32.70	1962	2.825	0.91	14.45	108.1	6487	9.341
0.42	4.532	33.90	2034	2.929	0.92	14.69	109.9	6594	9.496
0.43	4.695	35.12	2107	3.034	0.93	14.93	111.7	6702	9.651
0.44	4.860	36.35	2181	3.141	0.94	15.17	113.5	6810	9.807
0.45	5.026	37.60	2256	3.248	0.95	15.42	115.3	6919	9.964
0.46	5.195	38.86	2331	3.357	0.96	15.66	117.2	7029	10.12
0.47	5.365	40.13	2408	3.467	0.97	15.91	119.0	7139	10.28
0.48	5.537	41.42	2485	3.579	0.98	16.15	120.8	7249	10.44
0.49	5.711	42.72	2563	3.691	0.99	16.40	122.7	7361	10.60
0.50	5.887	44.04	2642	3.805	1.00	16.65	124.6	7473	10.76

10

10-7: 5 ft. Rectangular Weir without End Contractions Discharge Table (Continued)

Formulas: CFS = 16.65H$^{1.5}$ GPS = CFS x 7.481
GPM = CFS x 448.8   MGD = CFS x 0.6463

Head Feet	CFS	GPS	GPM	MGD	Head Feet	CFS	GPS	GPM	MGD
1.01	16.90	126.4	7585	10.92	1.51	30.89	231.1	13870	19.97
1.02	17.15	128.3	7698	11.09	1.52	31.20	233.4	14000	20.17
1.03	17.40	130.2	7811	11.25	1.53	31.51	235.7	14140	20.37
1.04	17.66	132.1	7925	11.41	1.54	31.82	238.0	14280	20.57
1.05	17.91	134.0	8040	11.58	1.55	32.13	240.4	14420	20.77
1.06	18.17	135.9	8155	11.74	1.56	32.44	242.7	14560	20.97
1.07	18.43	137.9	8271	11.91	1.57	32.75	245.0	14700	21.17
1.08	18.69	139.8	8387	12.08	1.58	33.07	247.4	14840	21.37
1.09	18.95	141.7	8504	12.25	1.59	33.38	249.7	14980	21.57
1.10	19.21	143.7	8621	12.41	1.60	33.70	252.1	15120	21.78
1.11	19.47	145.7	8739	12.58	1.61	34.01	254.5	15270	21.98
1.12	19.74	147.6	8857	12.75	1.62	34.33	256.8	15410	22.19
1.13	20.00	149.6	8976	12.93	1.63	34.65	259.2	15550	22.39
1.14	20.27	151.6	9095	13.10	1.64	34.97	261.6	15690	22.60
1.15	20.53	153.6	9215	13.27	1.65	35.29	264.0	15840	22.81
1.16	20.80	155.6	9336	13.44	1.66	35.61	266.4	15980	23.01
1.17	21.07	157.6	9457	13.62	1.67	35.93	268.8	16130	23.22
1.18	21.34	159.7	9578	13.79	1.68	36.26	271.2	16270	23.43
1.19	21.61	161.7	9700	13.97	1.69	36.58	273.7	16420	23.64
1.20	21.89	163.7	9823	14.15	1.70	36.91	276.1	16560	23.85
1.21	22.16	165.8	9946	14.32	1.71	37.23	278.5	16710	24.06
1.22	22.44	167.8	10070	14.50	1.72	37.56	281.0	16860	24.27
1.23	22.71	169.9	10200	14.68	1.73	37.89	283.4	17000	24.49
1.24	22.99	172.0	10320	14.86	1.74	38.22	285.9	17150	24.70
1.25	23.27	174.1	10440	15.04	1.75	38.55	288.4	17300	24.91
1.26	23.55	176.2	10570	15.22	1.76	38.88	290.8	17450	25.13
1.27	23.83	178.3	10700	15.40	1.77	39.21	293.3	17600	25.34
1.28	24.11	180.4	10820	15.58	1.78	39.54	295.8	17750	25.56
1.29	24.39	182.5	10950	15.77	1.79	39.87	298.3	17900	25.77
1.30	24.68	184.6	11080	15.95	1.80	40.21	300.8	18050	25.99
1.31	24.96	186.8	11200	16.13	1.81	40.54	303.3	18200	26.20
1.32	25.25	188.9	11330	16.32	1.82	40.88	305.8	18350	26.42
1.33	25.54	191.1	11460	16.51	1.83	41.22	308.4	18500	26.64
1.34	25.83	193.2	11590	16.69	1.84	41.56	310.9	18650	26.86
1.35	26.12	195.4	11720	16.88	1.85	41.90	313.4	18800	27.08
1.36	26.41	197.6	11850	17.07	1.86	42.24	316.0	18960	27.30
1.37	26.70	199.7	11980	17.26	1.87	42.58	318.5	19110	27.52
1.38	26.99	201.9	12110	17.44	1.88	42.92	321.1	19260	27.74
1.39	27.29	204.1	12250	17.63	1.89	43.26	323.6	19420	27.96
1.40	27.58	206.3	12380	17.83	1.90	43.61	326.2	19570	28.18
1.41	27.88	208.5	12510	18.02	1.91	43.95	328.8	19730	28.41
1.42	28.17	210.8	12640	18.21	1.92	44.30	331.4	19880	28.63
1.43	28.47	213.0	12780	18.40	1.93	44.64	334.0	20040	28.85
1.44	28.77	215.2	12910	18.59	1.94	44.99	336.6	20190	29.08
1.45	29.07	217.5	13050	18.79	1.95	45.34	339.2	20350	29.30
1.46	29.37	219.7	13180	18.98	1.96	45.69	341.8	20500	29.53
1.47	29.67	222.0	13320	19.18	1.97	46.04	344.4	20660	29.75
1.48	29.98	224.3	13450	19.37	1.98	46.39	347.0	20820	29.98
1.49	30.28	226.5	13590	19.57	1.99	46.74	349.7	20980	30.21
1.50	30.59	228.8	13730	19.77	2.00	47.09	352.3	21140	30.44

10-7: 5 ft. Rectangular Weir without End Contractions Discharge Table *(Continued)*

Formulas: CFS $=16.65H^{1.5}$ GPS = CFS x 7.481
GPM = CFS x 448.8 MGD = CFS x 0.6463

Head Feet	CFS	GPS	GPM	MGD	Head Feet	CFS	GPS	GPM	MGD
2.01	47.45	355.0	21290	30.66	2.51	66.21	495.3	29720	42.79
2.02	47.80	357.6	21450	30.89	2.52	66.61	498.3	29890	43.05
2.03	48.16	360.3	21610	31.12	2.53	67.00	501.3	30070	43.30
2.04	48.51	362.9	21770	31.35	2.54	67.40	504.2	30250	43.56
2.05	48.87	365.6	21930	31.58	2.55	67.80	507.2	30430	43.82
2.06	49.23	368.3	22090	31.82	2.56	68.20	510.2	30610	44.08
2.07	49.59	371.0	22250	32.05	2.57	68.60	513.2	30790	44.34
2.08	49.95	373.7	22420	32.28	2.58	69.00	516.2	30970	44.59
2.09	50.31	376.4	22580	32.51	2.59	69.40	519.2	31150	44.85
2.10	50.67	379.1	22740	32.75	2.60	69.80	522.2	31330	45.11
2.11	51.03	381.8	22900	32.98	2.61	70.21	525.2	31510	45.37
2.12	51.39	384.5	23070	33.22	2.62	70.61	528.2	31690	45.64
2.13	51.76	387.2	23230	33.45	2.63	71.01	531.3	31870	45.90
2.14	52.12	389.9	23390	33.69	2.64	71.42	534.3	32050	46.16
2.15	52.49	392.7	23560	33.92	2.65	71.83	537.3	32240	46.42
2.16	52.86	395.4	23720	34.16	2.66	72.23	540.4	32420	46.68
2.17	53.22	398.2	23890	34.40	2.67	72.64	543.4	32600	46.95
2.18	53.59	400.9	24050	34.64	2.68	73.05	546.5	32780	47.21
2.19	53.96	403.7	24220	34.88	2.69	73.46	549.5	32970	47.48
2.20	54.33	406.5	24380	35.11	2.70	73.87	552.6	33150	47.74
2.21	54.70	409.2	24550	35.35	2.71	74.28	555.7	33340	48.01
2.22	55.07	412.0	24720	35.59	2.72	74.69	558.8	33520	48.27
2.23	55.45	414.8	24880	35.83	2.73	75.10	561.8	33710	48.54
2.24	55.82	417.6	25050	36.08	2.74	75.52	564.9	33890	48.81
2.25	56.19	420.4	25220	36.32	2.75	75.93	568.0	34080	49.07
2.26	56.57	423.2	25390	36.56	2.76	76.34	571.1	34260	49.34
2.27	56.94	426.0	25560	36.80	2.77	76.76	574.2	34450	49.61
2.28	57.32	428.8	25730	37.05	2.78	77.18	577.4	34640	49.88
2.29	57.70	431.6	25900	37.29	2.79	77.59	580.5	34820	50.15
2.30	58.08	434.5	26070	37.54	2.80	78.01	583.6	35010	50.42
2.31	58.46	437.3	26240	37.78	2.81	78.43	586.7	35200	50.69
2.32	58.84	440.2	26410	38.03	2.82	78.85	589.9	35390	50.96
2.33	59.22	443.0	26580	38.27	2.83	79.27	593.0	35580	51.23
2.34	59.60	445.9	26750	38.52	2.84	79.69	596.1	35760	51.50
2.35	59.98	448.7	26920	38.77	2.85	80.11	599.3	35950	51.77
2.36	60.36	451.6	27090	39.01	2.86	80.53	602.5	36140	52.05
2.37	60.75	454.5	27260	39.26	2.87	80.95	605.6	36330	52.32
2.38	61.13	457.3	27440	39.51	2.88	81.38	608.8	36520	52.59
2.39	61.52	460.2	27610	39.76	2.89	81.80	612.0	36710	52.87
2.40	61.91	463.1	27780	40.01	2.90	82.23	615.1	36900	53.14
2.41	62.29	466.0	27960	40.26	2.91	82.65	618.3	37090	53.42
2.42	62.68	468.9	28130	40.51	2.92	83.08	621.5	37290	53.69
2.43	63.07	471.8	28310	40.76	2.93	83.51	624.7	37480	53.97
2.44	63.46	474.7	28480	41.01	2.94	83.93	627.9	37670	54.25
2.45	63.85	477.7	28660	41.27	2.95	84.36	631.1	37860	54.52
2.46	64.24	480.6	28830	41.52	2.96	84.79	634.3	38050	54.80
2.47	64.63	483.5	29010	41.77	2.97	85.22	637.5	38250	55.08
2.48	65.03	486.5	29180	42.03	2.98	85.65	640.8	38440	55.36
2.49	65.42	489.4	29360	42.28	2.99	86.08	644.0	38630	55.64
2.50	65.81	492.4	29540	42.54	3.00	86.52	647.2	38830	55.92

10

10-8: 6 ft. Rectangular Weir without End Contractions Discharge Table

Formulas: CFS = 19.98H$^{1.5}$ GPS = CFS x 7.481
GPM = CFS x 448.8   MGD = CFS x 0.6463

Head Feet	CFS	GPS	GPM	MGD	Head Feet	CFS	GPS	GPM	MGD
0.01	0.0200	0.1495	8.967	0.0129	0.51	7.277	54.44	3266	4.703
0.02	0.0565	0.4228	25.36	0.0365	0.52	7.492	56.05	3362	4.842
0.03	0.1038	0.7767	46.59	0.0671	0.53	7.709	57.67	3460	4.982
0.04	0.1598	1.196	71.74	0.1033	0.54	7.928	59.31	3558	5.124
0.05	0.2234	1.671	100.3	0.1444	0.55	8.150	60.97	3658	5.267
0.06	0.2936	2.197	131.8	0.1898	0.56	8.373	62.64	3758	5.411
0.07	0.3700	2.768	166.1	0.2392	0.57	8.598	64.32	3859	5.557
0.08	0.4521	3.382	202.9	0.2922	0.58	8.825	66.02	3961	5.704
0.09	0.5395	4.036	242.1	0.3487	0.59	9.055	67.74	4064	5.852
0.10	0.6318	4.727	283.6	0.4083	0.60	9.286	69.47	4167	6.001
0.11	0.7289	5.453	327.1	0.4711	0.61	9.519	71.21	4272	6.152
0.12	0.8306	6.213	372.8	0.5368	0.62	9.754	72.97	4378	6.304
0.13	0.9365	7.006	420.3	0.6053	0.63	9.991	74.74	4484	6.457
0.14	1.047	7.830	469.7	0.6764	0.64	10.23	76.53	4591	6.611
0.15	1.161	8.683	520.9	0.7502	0.65	10.47	78.33	4699	6.767
0.16	1.279	9.566	573.9	0.8264	0.66	10.71	80.14	4808	6.924
0.17	1.400	10.48	628.5	0.9051	0.67	10.96	81.97	4918	7.082
0.18	1.526	11.41	684.8	0.9861	0.68	11.20	83.81	5028	7.241
0.19	1.655	12.38	742.6	1.069	0.69	11.45	85.67	5140	7.401
0.20	1.787	13.37	802.0	1.155	0.70	11.70	87.54	5252	7.563
0.21	1.923	14.38	862.9	1.243	0.71	11.95	89.42	5365	7.725
0.22	2.062	15.42	925.3	1.332	0.72	12.21	91.32	5478	7.889
0.23	2.204	16.49	989.1	1.424	0.73	12.46	93.23	5593	8.054
0.24	2.349	17.57	1054	1.518	0.74	12.72	95.15	5708	8.220
0.25	2.498	18.68	1121	1.614	0.75	12.98	97.08	5824	8.387
0.26	2.649	19.82	1189	1.712	0.76	13.24	99.03	5941	8.556
0.27	2.803	20.97	1258	1.812	0.77	13.50	101.0	6059	8.725
0.28	2.960	22.15	1329	1.913	0.78	13.76	103.0	6177	8.896
0.29	3.120	23.34	1400	2.017	0.79	14.03	105.0	6296	9.067
0.30	3.283	24.56	1473	2.122	0.80	14.30	107.0	6416	9.240
0.31	3.449	25.80	1548	2.229	0.81	14.57	109.0	6537	9.414
0.32	3.617	27.06	1623	2.338	0.82	14.84	111.0	6658	9.588
0.33	3.788	28.34	1700	2.448	0.83	15.11	113.0	6781	9.764
0.34	3.961	29.63	1778	2.560	0.84	15.38	115.1	6903	9.941
0.35	4.137	30.95	1857	2.674	0.85	15.66	117.1	7027	10.12
0.36	4.316	32.29	1937	2.789	0.86	15.93	119.2	7151	10.30
0.37	4.497	33.64	2018	2.906	0.87	16.21	121.3	7277	10.48
0.38	4.680	35.01	2101	3.025	0.88	16.49	123.4	7402	10.66
0.39	4.866	36.40	2184	3.145	0.89	16.78	125.5	7529	10.84
0.40	5.055	37.81	2268	3.267	0.90	17.06	127.6	7656	11.03
0.41	5.245	39.24	2354	3.390	0.91	17.34	129.8	7784	11.21
0.42	5.438	40.68	2441	3.515	0.92	17.63	131.9	7913	11.39
0.43	5.634	42.15	2528	3.641	0.93	17.92	134.1	8042	11.58
0.44	5.831	43.62	2617	3.769	0.94	18.21	136.2	8172	11.77
0.45	6.031	45.12	2707	3.898	0.95	18.50	138.4	8303	11.96
0.46	6.234	46.63	2798	4.029	0.96	18.79	140.6	8434	12.15
0.47	6.438	48.16	2889	4.161	0.97	19.09	142.8	8567	12.34
0.48	6.644	49.71	2982	4.294	0.98	19.38	145.0	8699	12.53
0.49	6.853	51.27	3076	4.429	0.99	19.68	147.2	8833	12.72
0.50	7.064	52.85	3170	4.565	1.00	19.98	149.5	8967	12.91

Formulas: $CFS = 19.98H^{1.5}$ $GPS = CFS \times 7.481$
$GPM = CFS \times 448.8$ $MGD = CFS \times 0.6463$

Head Feet	CFS	GPS	GPM	MGD	Head Feet	CFS	GPS	GPM	MGD
1.01	20.28	151.7	9102	13.11	1.51	37.07	277.3	16640	23.96
1.02	20.58	154.0	9237	13.30	1.52	37.44	280.1	16800	24.20
1.03	20.89	156.2	9374	13.50	1.53	37.81	282.9	16970	24.44
1.04	21.19	158.5	9510	13.70	1.54	38.18	285.7	17140	24.68
1.05	21.50	160.8	9648	13.89	1.55	38.56	288.4	17300	24.92
1.06	21.80	163.1	9786	14.09	1.56	38.93	291.2	17470	25.16
1.07	22.11	165.4	9925	14.29	1.57	39.30	294.0	17640	25.40
1.08	22.42	167.8	10060	14.49	1.58	39.68	296.9	17810	25.65
1.09	22.74	170.1	10200	14.69	1.59	40.06	299.7	17980	25.89
1.10	23.05	172.4	10350	14.90	1.60	40.44	302.5	18150	26.13
1.11	23.37	174.8	10490	15.10	1.61	40.82	305.3	18320	26.38
1.12	23.68	177.2	10630	15.31	1.62	41.20	308.2	18490	26.63
1.13	24.00	179.5	10770	15.51	1.63	41.58	311.1	18660	26.87
1.14	24.32	181.9	10920	15.72	1.64	41.96	313.9	18830	27.12
1.15	24.64	184.3	11060	15.92	1.65	42.35	316.8	19010	27.37
1.16	24.96	186.7	11200	16.13	1.66	42.73	319.7	19180	27.62
1.17	25.29	189.2	11350	16.34	1.67	43.12	322.6	19350	27.87
1.18	25.61	191.6	11490	16.55	1.68	43.51	325.5	19530	28.12
1.19	25.94	194.0	11640	16.76	1.69	43.90	328.4	19700	28.37
1.20	26.26	196.5	11790	16.97	1.70	44.29	331.3	19880	28.62
1.21	26.59	198.9	11940	17.19	1.71	44.68	334.2	20050	28.88
1.22	26.92	201.4	12080	17.40	1.72	45.07	337.2	20230	29.13
1.23	27.26	203.9	12230	17.62	1.73	45.46	340.1	20400	29.38
1.24	27.59	206.4	12380	17.83	1.74	45.86	343.1	20580	29.64
1.25	27.92	208.9	12530	18.05	1.75	46.25	346.0	20760	29.89
1.26	28.26	211.4	12680	18.26	1.76	46.65	349.0	20940	30.15
1.27	28.60	213.9	12830	18.48	1.77	47.05	352.0	21120	30.41
1.28	28.93	216.5	12990	18.70	1.78	47.45	355.0	21395	30.67
1.29	29.27	219.0	13140	18.92	1.79	47.85	358.0	21480	30.92
1.30	29.61	221.5	13290	19.14	1.80	48.25	361.0	21660	31.18
1.31	29.96	224.1	13450	19.36	1.81	48.65	364.0	21840	31.44
1.32	30.30	226.7	13600	19.58	1.82	49.06	367.0	22020	31.71
1.33	30.65	229.3	13750	19.81	1.83	49.46	370.0	22200	31.97
1.34	30.99	231.9	13910	20.03	1.84	49.87	373.1	22380	32.23
1.35	31.34	234.5	14070	20.25	1.85	50.28	376.1	22560	32.49
1.36	31.69	237.1	14220	20.48	1.86	50.68	379.2	22750	32.76
1.37	32.04	239.7	14380	20.71	1.87	51.09	382.2	22930	33.02
1.38	32.39	242.3	14540	20.93	1.88	51.50	385.3	23120	33.29
1.39	32.74	244.9	14700	21.16	1.89	51.91	388.4	23300	33.55
1.40	33.10	247.6	14850	21.39	1.90	52.33	391.5	23480	33.82
1.41	33.45	250.3	15010	21.62	1.91	52.74	394.6	23670	34.09
1.42	33.81	252.9	15170	21.85	1.92	53.16	397.7	23860	34.35
1.43	34.17	255.6	15330	22.08	1.93	53.57	400.8	24040	34.62
1.44	34.53	258.3	15500	22.31	1.94	53.99	403.9	24230	34.89
1.45	34.89	261.0	15660	22.55	1.95	54.41	407.0	24420	35.16
1.46	35.25	263.7	15820	22.78	1.96	54.83	410.1	24610	35.43
1.47	35.61	266.4	15980	23.01	1.97	55.25	413.3	24790	35.70
1.48	35.97	269.1	16150	23.25	1.98	55.67	416.4	24980	35.98
1.49	36.34	271.9	16310	23.49	1.99	56.09	419.6	25170	36.25
1.50	36.71	274.6	16470	23.72	2.00	56.51	422.8	25360	36.52

10

10-8: 6 ft. Rectangular Weir without End Contractions Discharge Table *(Continued)*

Formulas: $CFS = 19.98H^{1.5}$ $GPS = CFS \times 7.481$
$GPM = CFS \times 448.8$ $MGD = CFS \times 0.6463$

Head Feet	CFS	GPS	GPM	MGD	Head Feet	CFS	GPS	GPM	MGD
2.01	56.94	425.9	25550	36.80	2.51	79.45	594.4	35660	51.35
2.02	57.36	429.1	25740	37.07	2.52	79.93	597.9	35870	51.66
2.03	57.79	432.3	25940	37.35	2.53	80.40	601.5	36090	51.96
2.04	58.22	435.5	26130	37.62	2.54	80.88	605.1	36300	52.27
2.05	58.64	438.7	26320	37.90	2.55	81.36	608.6	36510	52.58
2.06	59.07	441.9	26510	38.18	2.56	81.84	612.2	36730	52.89
2.07	59.50	445.2	26710	38.46	2.57	82.32	615.8	36940	53.20
2.08	59.94	448.4	26900	38.74	2.58	82.80	619.4	37160	53.51
2.09	60.37	451.6	27090	39.02	2.59	83.28	623.0	37380	53.82
2.10	60.80	454.9	27290	39.30	2.60	83.76	626.6	37590	54.14
2.11	61.24	458.1	27480	39.58	2.61	84.25	630.3	37810	54.45
2.12	61.67	461.4	27680	39.86	2.62	84.73	633.9	38030	54.76
2.13	62.11	464.6	27880	40.14	2.63	85.22	637.5	38250	55.08
2.14	62.55	467.9	28070	40.43	2.64	85.70	641.2	38460	55.39
2.15	62.99	471.2	28270	40.71	2.65	86.19	644.8	38680	55.71
2.16	63.43	474.5	28470	40.99	2.66	86.68	648.5	38900	56.02
2.17	63.87	477.8	28660	41.28	2.67	87.17	652.1	39120	56.34
2.18	64.31	481.1	28860	41.56	2.68	87.66	655.8	39340	56.65
2.19	64.75	484.4	29060	41.85	2.69	88.15	659.5	39560	56.97
2.20	65.20	487.7	29260	42.14	2.70	88.64	663.1	39780	57.29
2.21	65.64	491.1	29460	42.42	2.71	89.14	666.8	40000	57.61
2.22	66.09	494.4	29660	42.71	2.72	89.63	670.5	40230	57.93
2.23	66.54	497.8	29860	43.00	2.73	90.12	674.2	40450	58.25
2.24	66.98	501.1	30060	43.29	2.74	90.62	677.9	40670	58.57
2.25	67.43	504.5	30260	43.58	2.75	91.12	681.6	40890	58.89
2.26	67.88	507.8	30470	43.87	2.76	91.61	685.4	41120	59.21
2.27	68.33	511.2	30670	44.16	2.77	92.11	689.1	41340	59.53
2.28	68.79	514.6	30870	44.46	2.78	92.61	692.8	41560	59.85
2.29	69.24	518.0	31070	44.75	2.79	93.11	696.6	41790	60.18
2.30	69.69	521.4	31280	45.04	2.80	93.61	700.3	42010	60.50
2.31	70.15	524.8	31480	45.34	2.81	94.11	704.1	42240	60.83
2.32	70.60	528.2	31690	45.63	2.82	94.62	707.8	42460	61.15
2.33	71.06	531.6	31890	45.93	2.83	95.12	711.6	42690	61.48
2.34	71.52	535.0	32100	46.22	2.84	95.63	715.4	42920	61.80
2.35	71.98	538.5	32300	46.52	2.85	96.13	719.2	43140	62.13
2.36	72.44	541.9	32510	46.82	2.86	96.64	722.9	43370	62.46
2.37	72.90	545.4	32720	47.11	2.87	97.14	726.7	43600	62.78
2.38	73.36	548.8	32920	47.41	2.88	97.65	730.5	43830	63.11
2.39	73.82	552.3	33130	47.71	2.89	98.16	734.3	44050	63.44
2.40	74.29	555.7	33340	48.01	2.90	98.67	738.2	44280	63.77
2.41	74.75	559.2	33550	48.31	2.91	99.18	742.0	44510	64.10
2.42	75.22	562.7	33760	48.61	2.92	99.69	745.8	44740	64.43
2.43	75.68	566.2	33970	48.91	2.93	100.2	749.6	44970	64.76
2.44	76.15	569.7	34180	49.22	2.94	100.7	753.5	45200	65.10
2.45	76.62	573.2	34390	49.52	2.95	101.2	757.3	45430	65.43
2.46	77.09	576.7	34600	49.82	2.96	101.7	761.2	45670	65.76
2.47	77.56	580.2	34810	50.13	2.97	102.3	765.0	45900	66.09
2.48	78.03	583.8	35020	50.43	2.98	102.8	768.9	46130	66.43
2.49	78.50	587.3	35230	50.74	2.99	103.3	772.8	46360	66.76
2.50	78.98	590.8	35450	51.04	3.00	103.8	776.7	46590	67.10

10

10-9: 8 ft. Rectangular Weir without End Contractions Discharge Table

Formulas: $CFS = 26.64H^{1.5}$ $GPS = CFS \times 7.481$
$GPM = CFS \times 448.8$ $MGD = CFS \times 0.6463$

Head Feet	CFS	GPS	GPM	MGD	Head Feet	CFS	GPS	GPM	MGD
0.01	0.0266	0.1993	11.96	0.0172	0.51	9.703	72.59	4355	6.271
0.02	0.0753	0.5637	33.82	0.0487	0.52	9.989	74.73	4483	6.456
0.03	0.1384	1.036	62.13	0.0895	0.53	10.28	76.90	4613	6.643
0.04	0.2131	1.594	95.65	0.1377	0.54	10.57	79.08	4744	6.832
0.05	0.2978	2.228	133.7	0.1925	0.55	10.87	81.29	4877	7.023
0.06	0.3915	2.929	175.7	0.2530	0.56	11.16	83.52	5010	7.215
0.07	0.4934	3.691	221.4	0.3189	0.57	11.46	85.76	5145	7.409
0.08	0.6028	4.510	270.5	0.3896	0.58	11.77	88.03	5281	7.605
0.09	0.7193	5.381	322.8	0.4649	0.59	12.07	90.32	5418	7.803
0.10	0.8424	6.302	378.1	0.5445	0.60	12.38	92.62	5557	8.002
0.11	0.9719	7.271	436.2	0.6281	0.61	12.69	94.95	5696	8.203
0.12	1.107	8.284	497.0	0.7157	0.62	13.01	97.29	5837	8.405
0.13	1.249	9.341	560.4	0.8070	0.63	13.32	99.66	5979	8.610
0.14	1.395	10.44	626.3	0.9019	0.64	13.64	102.0	6121	8.815
0.15	1.548	11.58	694.6	1.000	0.65	13.96	104.4	6266	9.023
0.16	1.705	12.75	765.2	1.102	0.66	14.28	106.9	6411	9.232
0.17	1.867	13.97	838.0	1.207	0.67	14.61	109.3	6557	9.442
0.18	2.034	15.22	913.1	1.315	0.68	14.94	111.8	6704	9.655
0.19	2.206	16.51	990.2	1.426	0.69	15.27	114.2	6853	9.868
0.20	2.383	17.83	1069	1.540	0.70	15.60	116.7	7002	10.08
0.21	2.564	19.18	1151	1.657	0.71	15.94	119.2	7153	10.30
0.22	2.749	20.56	1234	1.777	0.72	16.28	121.8	7304	10.52
0.23	2.939	21.98	1319	1.899	0.73	16.62	124.3	7457	10.74
0.24	3.132	23.43	1406	2.024	0.74	16.96	126.9	7611	10.96
0.25	3.330	24.91	1495	2.152	0.75	17.30	129.4	7766	11.18
0.26	3.532	26.42	1585	2.283	0.76	17.65	132.0	7922	11.41
0.27	3.737	27.96	1677	2.416	0.77	18.00	134.7	8078	11.63
0.28	3.947	29.53	1771	2.551	0.78	18.35	137.3	8236	11.86
0.29	4.160	31.12	1867	2.689	0.79	18.71	139.9	8395	12.09
0.30	4.377	32.75	1965	2.829	0.80	19.06	142.6	8555	12.32
0.31	4.598	34.40	2064	2.972	0.81	19.42	145.3	8716	12.55
0.32	4.822	36.08	2164	3.117	0.82	19.78	148.0	8878	12.78
0.33	5.050	37.78	2267	3.264	0.83	20.14	150.7	9041	13.02
0.34	5.281	39.51	2370	3.413	0.84	20.51	153.4	9205	13.26
0.35	5.516	41.27	2476	3.565	0.85	20.88	156.2	9369	13.49
0.36	5.754	43.05	2583	3.719	0.86	21.25	158.9	9535	13.73
0.37	5.996	44.85	2691	3.875	0.87	21.62	161.7	9702	13.97
0.38	6.240	46.68	2801	4.033	0.88	21.99	164.5	9870	14.21
0.39	6.488	48.54	2912	4.193	0.89	22.37	167.3	10040	14.46
0.40	6.739	50.42	3025	4.356	0.90	22.75	170.2	10210	14.70
0.41	6.994	52.32	3139	4.520	0.91	23.13	173.0	10380	14.95
0.42	7.251	54.25	3254	4.686	0.92	23.51	175.9	10550	15.19
0.43	7.512	56.19	3371	4.855	0.93	23.89	178.7	10720	15.44
0.44	7.775	58.17	3490	5.025	0.94	24.28	181.6	10900	15.69
0.45	8.042	60.16	3609	5.197	0.95	24.67	184.5	11070	15.94
0.46	8.311	62.18	3730	5.372	0.96	25.06	187.5	11250	16.19
0.47	8.584	64.22	3852	5.548	0.97	25.45	190.4	11420	16.45
0.48	8.859	66.28	3976	5.726	0.98	25.84	193.3	11600	16.70
0.49	9.138	68.36	4101	5.906	0.99	26.24	196.3	11780	16.96
0.50	9.419	70.46	4227	6.087	1.00	26.64	199.3	11960	17.22

10

10-9: 8 ft. Rectangular Weir without End Contractions Discharge Table (Continued)

Formulas: $CFS = 26.64H^{1.5}$ $GPS = CFS \times 7.481$
$GPM = CFS \times 448.8$ $MGD = CFS \times 0.6463$

Head Feet	CFS	GPS	GPM	MGD	Head Feet	CFS	GPS	GPM	MGD
1.01	27.04	202.3	12140	17.48	1.51	49.43	369.8	22190	31.95
1.02	27.44	205.3	12320	17.74	1.52	49.92	373.5	22410	32.27
1.03	27.85	208.3	12500	18.00	1.53	50.42	377.2	22630	32.58
1.04	28.25	211.4	12680	18.26	1.54	50.91	380.9	22850	32.90
1.05	28.66	214.4	12860	18.52	1.55	51.41	384.6	23070	33.23
1.06	29.07	217.5	13050	18.79	1.56	51.91	388.3	23300	33.55
1.07	29.49	220.6	13230	19.06	1.57	52.41	392.1	23520	33.87
1.08	29.90	223.7	13420	19.32	1.58	52.91	395.8	23750	34.19
1.09	30.32	226.8	13610	19.59	1.59	53.41	399.6	23970	34.52
1.10	30.73	229.9	13790	19.86	1.60	53.92	403.3	24200	34.85
1.11	31.15	233.1	13980	20.14	1.61	54.42	407.1	24430	35.17
1.12	31.58	236.2	14170	20.41	1.62	54.93	410.9	24650	35.50
1.13	32.00	239.4	14360	20.68	1.63	55.44	414.7	24880	35.83
1.14	32.43	242.6	14550	20.96	1.64	55.95	418.6	25110	36.16
1.15	32.85	245.8	14750	21.23	1.65	56.46	422.4	25340	36.49
1.16	33.28	249.0	14940	21.51	1.66	56.98	426.2	25570	36.82
1.17	33.71	252.2	15130	21.79	1.67	57.49	430.1	25800	37.16
1.18	34.15	255.5	15330	22.07	1.68	58.01	434.0	26040	37.49
1.19	34.58	258.7	15520	22.35	1.69	58.53	437.8	26270	37.83
1.20	35.02	262.0	15720	22.63	1.70	59.05	441.7	26500	38.16
1.21	35.46	265.3	15910	22.92	1.71	59.57	445.6	26740	38.50
1.22	35.90	268.6	16110	23.20	1.72	60.09	449.6	26970	38.84
1.23	36.34	271.9	16310	23.49	1.73	60.62	453.5	27210	39.18
1.24	36.78	275.2	16510	23.77	1.74	61.14	457.4	27440	39.52
1.25	37.23	278.5	16710	24.06	1.75	61.67	461.4	27680	39.86
1.26	37.68	281.9	16910	24.35	1.76	62.20	465.3	27920	40.20
1.27	38.13	285.2	17110	24.64	1.77	62.73	469.3	28150	40.54
1.28	38.58	288.6	17310	24.93	1.78	63.27	473.3	28390	40.89
1.29	39.03	292.0	17520	25.23	1.79	63.80	477.3	28630	41.23
1.30	39.49	295.4	17720	25.52	1.80	64.33	481.3	28870	41.58
1.31	39.94	298.8	17930	25.82	1.81	64.87	485.3	29110	41.93
1.32	40.40	302.2	18130	26.11	1.82	65.41	489.3	29360	42.27
1.33	40.86	305.7	18340	26.41	1.83	65.95	493.4	29600	42.62
1.34	41.32	309.1	18550	26.71	1.84	66.49	497.4	29840	42.97
1.35	41.79	312.6	18750	27.01	1.85	67.03	501.5	30090	43.32
1.36	42.25	316.1	18960	27.31	1.86	67.58	505.5	30330	43.68
1.37	42.72	319.6	19170	27.61	1.87	68.12	509.6	30570	44.03
1.38	43.19	323.1	19380	27.91	1.88	68.67	513.7	30820	44.38
1.39	43.66	326.6	19590	28.22	1.89	69.22	517.8	31070	44.74
1.40	44.13	330.1	19810	28.52	1.90	69.77	521.9	31310	45.09
1.41	44.60	333.7	20020	28.83	1.91	70.32	526.1	31560	45.45
1.42	45.08	337.2	20230	29.13	1.92	70.87	530.2	31810	45.81
1.43	45.56	340.8	20450	29.44	1.93	71.43	534.4	32060	46.16
1.44	46.03	344.4	20660	29.75	1.94	71.98	538.5	32310	46.52
1.45	46.51	348.0	20880	30.06	1.95	72.54	542.7	32560	46.88
1.46	47.00	351.6	21090	30.37	1.96	73.10	546.9	32810	47.24
1.47	47.48	355.2	21310	30.69	1.97	73.66	551.1	33060	47.61
1.48	47.97	358.8	21530	31.00	1.98	74.22	555.3	33310	47.97
1.49	48.45	362.5	21750	31.31	1.99	74.78	559.5	33560	48.33
1.50	48.94	366.1	21970	31.63	2.00	75.35	563.7	33820	48.70

10

Formulas: CFS = $26.64H^{1.5}$ GPS = CFS x 7.481
GPM = CFS x 448.8 MGD = CFS x 0.6463

Head Feet	CFS	GPS	GPM	MGD	Head Feet	CFS	GPS	GPM	MGD
2.01	75.92	567.9	34070	49.06	2.51	105.9	792.5	47540	68.47
2.02	76.48	572.2	34330	49.43	2.52	106.6	797.3	47830	68.88
2.03	77.05	576.4	34580	49.80	2.53	107.2	802.0	48110	69.29
2.04	77.62	580.7	34840	50.17	2.54	107.8	806.8	48400	69.70
2.05	78.19	585.0	35090	50.54	2.55	108.5	811.5	48690	70.11
2.06	78.77	589.2	35350	50.91	2.56	109.1	816.3	48970	70.52
2.07	79.34	593.5	35610	51.28	2.57	109.8	821.1	49260	70.94
2.08	79.92	597.8	35870	51.65	2.58	110.4	825.9	49550	71.35
2.09	80.49	602.2	36120	52.02	2.59	111.0	830.7	49840	71.77
2.10	81.07	606.5	36380	52.40	2.60	111.7	835.5	50120	72.18
2.11	81.65	610.8	36640	52.77	2.61	112.3	840.3	50410	72.60
2.12	82.23	615.2	36910	53.15	2.62	113.0	845.2	50700	73.02
2.13	82.81	619.5	37170	53.52	2.63	113.6	850.0	50990	73.43
2.14	83.40	623.9	37430	53.90	2.64	114.3	854.9	51290	73.85
2.15	83.98	628.3	37690	54.28	2.65	114.9	859.7	51580	74.27
2.16	84.57	632.7	37950	54.66	2.66	115.6	864.6	51870	74.69
2.17	85.16	637.1	38220	55.04	2.67	116.2	869.5	52160	75.12
2.18	85.75	641.5	38480	55.42	2.68	116.9	874.4	52460	75.54
2.19	86.34	645.9	38750	55.80	2.69	117.5	879.3	52750	75.96
2.20	86.93	650.3	39010	56.18	2.70	118.2	884.2	53040	76.39
2.21	87.52	654.8	39280	56.57	2.71	118.8	889.1	53340	76.81
2.22	88.12	659.2	39550	56.95	2.72	119.5	894.0	53630	77.24
2.23	88.71	663.7	39810	57.34	2.73	120.2	899.0	53930	77.66
2.24	89.31	668.1	40080	57.72	2.74	120.8	903.9	54230	78.09
2.25	89.91	672.6	40350	58.11	2.75	121.5	908.9	54520	78.52
2.26	90.51	677.1	40620	58.50	2.76	122.2	913.8	54820	78.95
2.27	91.11	681.6	40890	58.89	2.77	122.8	918.8	55120	79.38
2.28	91.71	686.1	41160	59.27	2.78	123.5	923.8	55420	79.81
2.29	92.32	690.6	41430	59.67	2.79	124.1	928.8	55720	80.24
2.30	92.92	695.2	41700	60.06	2.80	124.8	933.8	56020	80.67
2.31	93.53	699.7	41980	60.45	2.81	125.5	938.8	56320	81.10
2.32	94.14	704.2	42250	60.84	2.82	126.2	943.8	56620	81.53
2.33	94.75	708.8	42520	61.24	2.83	126.8	948.8	56920	81.97
2.34	95.36	713.4	42800	61.63	2.84	127.5	953.8	57220	82.40
2.35	95.97	718.0	43070	62.03	2.85	128.2	958.9	57520	82.84
2.36	96.58	722.5	43350	62.42	2.86	128.8	963.9	57830	83.28
2.37	97.20	727.1	43620	62.82	2.87	129.5	969.0	58130	83.71
2.38	97.81	731.7	43900	63.22	2.88	130.2	974.1	58440	84.15
2.39	98.43	736.4	44180	63.62	2.89	130.9	979.1	58740	84.59
2.40	99.05	741.0	44450	64.02	2.90	131.6	984.2	59050	85.03
2.41	99.67	745.6	44730	64.42	2.91	132.2	989.3	59350	85.47
2.42	100.3	750.3	45010	64.82	2.92	132.9	994.4	59660	85.91
2.43	100.9	754.9	45290	65.22	2.93	133.6	999.5	59960	86.35
2.44	101.5	759.6	45570	65.62	2.94	134.3	1005	60270	86.79
2.45	102.2	764.3	45850	66.03	2.95	135.0	1010	60580	87.24
2.46	102.8	768.9	46130	66.43	2.96	135.7	1015	60890	87.68
2.47	103.4	773.6	46410	66.84	2.97	136.4	1020	61200	88.13
2.48	104.0	778.3	46690	67.24	2.98	137.0	1025	61510	88.57
2.49	104.7	783.1	46980	67.65	2.99	137.7	1030	61810	89.02
2.50	105.3	787.8	47260	68.06	3.00	138.4	1036	62130	89.46

8

10-10: 10 ft. Rectangular Weir without End Contractions Discharge Table

Formulas: $CFS = 33.30H^{1.5}$ $GPS = CFS \times 7.481$
$GPM = CFS \times 448.8$ $MGD = CFS \times 0.6463$

Head Feet	CFS	GPS	GPM	MGD	Head Feet	CFS	GPS	GPM	MGD
0.01	0.0333	0.2491	14.95	0.0215	0.51	12.13	90.73	5443	7.839
0.02	0.0942	0.7046	42.27	0.0609	0.52	12.49	93.41	5604	8.070
0.03	0.1730	1.294	77.66	0.1118	0.53	12.85	96.12	5766	8.304
0.04	0.2664	1.993	119.6	0.1722	0.54	13.21	98.85	5930	8.540
0.05	0.3723	2.785	167.1	0.2406	0.55	13.58	101.6	6096	8.779
0.06	0.4894	3.661	219.6	0.3163	0.56	13.95	104.4	6263	9.019
0.07	0.6167	4.614	276.8	0.3986	0.57	14.33	107.2	6431	9.262
0.08	0.7535	5.637	338.2	0.4870	0.58	14.71	110.0	6601	9.506
0.09	0.8991	6.726	403.5	0.5811	0.59	15.09	112.9	6773	9.753
0.10	1.053	7.878	472.6	0.6806	0.60	15.48	115.8	6946	10.00
0.11	1.215	9.089	545.2	0.7852	0.61	15.86	118.7	7120	10.25
0.12	1.384	10.36	621.3	0.8946	0.62	16.26	121.6	7296	10.51
0.13	1.561	11.68	700.5	1.009	0.63	16.65	124.6	7473	10.76
0.14	1.744	13.05	782.9	1.127	0.64	17.05	127.5	7652	11.02
0.15	1.935	14.47	868.2	1.250	0.65	17.45	130.5	7832	11.28
0.16	2.131	15.94	956.5	1.377	0.66	17.86	133.6	8013	11.54
0.17	2.334	17.46	1048	1.509	0.67	18.26	136.6	8196	11.80
0.18	2.543	19.02	1141	1.644	0.68	18.67	139.7	8380	12.07
0.19	2.758	20.63	1238	1.782	0.69	19.09	142.8	8566	12.34
0.20	2.978	22.28	1337	1.925	0.70	19.50	145.9	8753	12.60
0.21	3.205	23.97	1438	2.071	0.71	19.92	149.0	8941	12.88
0.22	3.436	25.71	1542	2.221	0.72	20.34	152.2	9131	13.15
0.23	3.673	27.48	1648	2.374	0.73	20.77	155.4	9321	13.42
0.24	3.915	29.29	1757	2.530	0.74	21.20	158.6	9514	13.70
0.25	4.162	31.14	1868	2.690	0.75	21.63	161.8	9707	13.98
0.26	4.415	33.03	1981	2.853	0.76	22.06	165.1	9902	14.26
0.27	4.672	34.95	2097	3.019	0.77	22.50	168.3	10100	14.54
0.28	4.934	36.91	2214	3.189	0.78	22.94	171.6	10300	14.83
0.29	5.200	38.90	2334	3.361	0.79	23.38	174.9	10500	15.11
0.30	5.472	40.93	2456	3.536	0.80	23.83	178.3	10700	15.40
0.31	5.748	43.00	2580	3.715	0.81	24.28	181.6	10900	15.69
0.32	6.028	45.10	2705	3.896	0.82	24.73	185.0	11100	15.98
0.33	6.313	47.23	2833	4.080	0.83	25.18	188.4	11300	16.27
0.34	6.602	49.39	2963	4.267	0.84	25.64	191.8	11510	16.57
0.35	6.895	51.58	3095	4.456	0.85	26.10	195.2	11710	16.87
0.36	7.193	53.81	3228	4.649	0.86	26.56	198.7	11920	17.16
0.37	7.495	56.07	3364	4.844	0.87	27.02	202.2	12130	17.46
0.38	7.800	58.36	3501	5.041	0.88	27.49	205.6	12340	17.77
0.39	8.110	60.67	3640	5.242	0.89	27.96	209.2	12550	18.07
0.40	8.424	63.02	3781	5.445	0.90	28.43	212.7	12760	18.38
0.41	8.742	65.40	3923	5.650	0.91	28.91	216.3	12970	18.68
0.42	9.064	67.81	4068	5.858	0.92	29.39	219.8	13190	18.99
0.43	9.390	70.24	4214	6.068	0.93	29.87	223.4	13400	19.30
0.44	9.719	72.71	4362	6.281	0.94	30.35	227.0	13620	19.61
0.45	10.05	75.20	4511	6.497	0.95	30.83	230.7	13840	19.93
0.46	10.39	77.72	4663	6.715	0.96	31.32	234.3	14060	20.24
0.47	10.73	80.27	4816	6.935	0.97	31.81	238.0	14280	20.56
0.48	11.07	82.84	4970	7.157	0.98	32.31	241.7	14500	20.88
0.49	11.42	85.45	5126	7.382	0.99	32.80	245.4	14720	21.20
0.50	11.77	88.08	5284	7.609	1.00	33.30	249.1	14950	21.52

8

Formulas: $CFS = 33.30H^{1.5}$ $GPS = CFS \times 7.481$
$GPM = CFS \times 448.8$ $MGD = CFS \times 0.6463$

Head Feet	CFS	GPS	GPM	MGD	Head Feet	CFS	GPS	GPM	MGD
1.01	33.80	252.9	15170	21.85	1.51	61.79	462.2	27730	39.93
1.02	34.30	256.6	15400	22.17	1.52	62.40	466.8	28010	40.33
1.03	34.81	260.4	15600	22.50	1.53	63.02	471.5	28280	40.73
1.04	35.32	264.2	15850	22.83	1.54	63.64	476.1	28560	41.13
1.05	35.83	268.0	16080	23.16	1.55	64.26	480.7	28840	41.53
1.06	36.34	271.9	16310	23.49	1.56	64.88	485.4	29120	41.93
1.07	36.86	275.7	16540	23.82	1.57	65.51	490.1	29400	42.34
1.08	37.37	279.6	16770	24.16	1.58	66.13	494.8	29680	42.74
1.09	37.90	283.5	17010	24.49	1.59	66.76	499.5	29960	43.15
1.10	38.42	287.4	17240	24.83	1.60	67.39	504.2	30250	43.56
1.11	38.94	291.3	17480	25.17	1.61	68.03	508.9	30530	43.97
1.12	39.47	295.3	17710	25.51	1.62	68.66	513.7	30820	44.38
1.13	40.00	299.2	17950	25.85	1.63	69.30	518.4	31100	44.79
1.14	40.53	303.2	18190	26.20	1.64	69.94	523.2	31390	45.20
1.15	41.07	307.2	18430	26.54	1.65	70.58	528.0	31680	45.61
1.16	41.60	311.2	18670	26.89	1.66	71.22	532.8	31960	46.03
1.17	42.14	315.3	18910	27.24	1.67	71.87	537.6	32250	46.45
1.18	42.68	319.3	19160	27.59	1.68	72.51	542.5	32540	46.86
1.19	43.23	323.4	19400	27.94	1.69	73.16	547.3	32830	47.28
1.20	43.77	327.5	19650	28.29	1.70	73.81	552.2	33130	47.70
1.21	44.32	331.6	19890	28.65	1.71	74.46	557.1	33420	48.13
1.22	44.87	335.7	20140	29.00	1.72	75.12	561.9	33710	48.55
1.23	45.43	339.8	20390	29.36	1.73	75.77	566.9	34010	48.97
1.24	45.98	344.0	20640	29.72	1.74	76.43	571.8	34300	49.40
1.25	46.54	348.2	20890	30.08	1.75	77.09	576.7	34600	49.82
1.26	47.10	352.3	21140	30.44	1.76	77.75	581.7	34900	50.25
1.27	47.66	356.5	21390	30.80	1.77	78.42	586.6	35190	50.68
1.28	48.22	360.8	21640	31.17	1.78	79.08	591.6	35490	51.11
1.29	48.79	365.0	21900	31.53	1.79	79.75	596.6	35790	51.54
1.30	49.36	369.2	22150	31.90	1.80	80.42	601.6	36090	51.97
1.31	49.93	373.5	22410	32.27	1.81	81.09	606.6	36390	52.41
1.32	50.50	377.8	22670	32.64	1.82	81.76	611.7	36700	52.84
1.33	51.08	382.1	22920	33.01	1.83	82.44	616.7	37000	53.28
1.34	51.65	386.4	23180	33.38	1.84	83.11	621.8	37300	53.72
1.35	52.23	390.8	23440	33.76	1.85	83.79	626.8	37610	54.15
1.36	52.81	395.1	23700	34.13	1.86	84.47	631.9	37910	54.59
1.37	53.40	399.5	23970	34.51	1.87	85.15	637.0	38220	55.04
1.38	53.98	403.9	24230	34.89	1.88	85.84	642.2	38520	55.48
1.39	54.57	408.2	24490	35.27	1.89	86.52	647.3	38830	55.92
1.40	55.16	412.7	24760	35.65	1.90	87.21	652.4	39140	56.36
1.41	55.75	417.1	25020	36.03	1.91	87.90	657.6	39450	56.81
1.42	56.35	421.5	25290	36.42	1.92	88.59	662.8	39760	57.26
1.43	56.94	426.0	25560	36.80	1.93	89.29	667.9	40070	57.71
1.44	57.54	430.5	25830	37.19	1.94	89.98	673.1	40380	58.15
1.45	58.14	435.0	26100	37.58	1.95	90.68	678.4	40700	58.60
1.46	58.75	439.5	26370	37.97	1.96	91.38	683.6	41010	59.06
1.47	59.35	444.0	26640	38.36	1.97	92.08	688.8	41320	59.51
1.48	59.96	448.5	26910	38.75	1.98	92.78	694.1	41640	59.96
1.49	60.57	453.1	27180	39.14	1.99	93.48	699.3	41950	60.42
1.50	61.18	457.7	27460	39.54	2.00	94.19	704.6	42270	60.87

Formulas: CFS $=33.30H^{1.5}$ GPS = CFS x 7.481
            GPM = CFS x 448.8   MGD = CFS x 0.6463

Head Feet	CFS	GPS	GPM	MGD	Head Feet	CFS	GPS	GPM	MGD
2.01	94.89	709.9	42590	61.33	2.51	132.4	990.6	59430	85.58
2.02	95.60	715.2	42910	61.79	2.52	133.2	996.6	59790	86.10
2.03	96.31	720.5	43230	62.25	2.53	134.0	1003	60140	86.61
2.04	97.03	725.9	43550	62.71	2.54	134.8	1008	60500	87.12
2.05	97.74	731.2	43870	63.17	2.55	135.6	1014	60860	87.64
2.06	98.46	736.6	44190	63.63	2.56	136.4	1020	61210	88.15
2.07	99.17	741.9	44510	64.10	2.57	137.2	1026	61570	88.67
2.08	99.89	747.3	44830	64.56	2.58	138.0	1032	61930	89.19
2.09	100.6	752.7	45160	65.03	2.59	138.8	1038	62290	89.71
2.10	101.3	758.1	45480	65.49	2.60	139.6	1044	62660	90.23
2.11	102.1	763.5	45810	65.96	2.61	140.4	1050	63020	90.75
2.12	102.8	769.0	46130	66.43	2.62	141.2	1056	63380	91.27
2.13	103.5	774.4	46460	66.90	2.63	142.0	1063	63740	91.79
2.14	104.2	779.9	46790	67.38	2.64	142.8	1069	64110	92.32
2.15	105.0	785.3	47110	67.85	2.65	143.7	1075	64470	92.84
2.16	105.7	790.8	47440	68.32	2.66	144.5	1081	64840	93.37
2.17	106.4	796.3	47770	68.80	2.67	145.3	1087	65200	93.90
2.18	107.2	801.8	48100	69.27	2.68	146.1	1093	65570	94.42
2.19	107.9	807.4	48440	69.75	2.69	146.9	1099	65940	94.95
2.20	108.7	812.9	48770	70.23	2.70	147.7	1105	66300	95.48
2.21	109.4	818.5	49100	70.71	2.71	148.6	1111	66670	96.01
2.22	110.1	824.0	49430	71.19	2.72	149.4	1118	67040	96.55
2.23	110.9	829.6	49770	71.67	2.73	150.2	1124	67410	97.08
2.24	111.6	835.2	50100	72.15	2.74	151.0	1130	67780	97.61
2.25	112.4	840.8	50440	72.64	2.75	151.9	1136	68150	98.15
2.26	113.1	846.4	50780	73.12	2.76	152.7	1142	68530	98.68
2.27	113.9	852.0	51110	73.61	2.77	153.5	1148	68900	99.22
2.28	114.6	857.6	51450	74.09	2.78	154.4	1155	69270	99.76
2.29	115.4	863.3	51790	74.58	2.79	155.2	1161	69650	100.3
2.30	116.2	869.0	52130	75.07	2.80	156.0	1167	70020	100.8
2.31	116.9	874.6	52470	75.56	2.81	156.9	1173	70400	101.4
2.32	117.7	880.3	52810	76.05	2.82	157.7	1180	70770	101.9
2.33	118.4	886.0	53150	76.54	2.83	158.5	1186	71150	102.5
2.34	119.2	891.7	53500	77.04	2.84	159.4	1192	71530	103.0
2.35	120.0	897.4	53840	77.53	2.85	160.2	1199	71910	103.5
2.36	120.7	903.2	54180	78.03	2.86	161.1	1205	72280	104.1
2.37	121.5	908.9	54530	78.52	2.87	161.9	1211	72660	104.6
2.38	122.3	914.7	54870	79.02	2.88	162.8	1218	73040	105.2
2.39	123.0	920.5	55220	79.52	2.89	163.6	1224	73420	105.7
2.40	123.8	926.2	55570	80.02	2.90	164.5	1230	73810	106.3
2.41	124.6	932.0	55910	80.52	2.91	165.3	1237	74190	106.8
2.42	125.4	937.8	56260	81.02	2.92	166.2	1243	74570	107.4
2.43	126.1	943.7	56610	81.52	2.93	167.0	1249	74950	107.9
2.44	126.9	949.5	56960	82.03	2.94	167.9	1256	75340	108.5
2.45	127.7	955.3	57310	82.53	2.95	168.7	1262	75720	109.0
2.46	128.5	961.2	57660	83.04	2.96	169.6	1269	76110	109.6
2.47	129.3	967.1	58020	83.55	2.97	170.4	1275	76490	110.2
2.48	130.1	972.9	58370	84.05	2.98	171.3	1282	76880	110.7
2.49	130.8	978.8	58720	84.56	2.99	172.2	1288	77270	111.3
2.50	131.6	984.7	59080	85.07	3.00	173.0	1294	77660	111.8

10

Chapter 11

Cipolletti weir discharge tables

This chapter contains discharge (flow rate vs head) tables for Cipolletti weirs. Note that all of the tabular data is for free flow. If the flow is submerged, corrections will have to be made to determine the discharge, as discussed in Chapter 3. Note also that in many cases, discharges are listed for heads which are above the maximum recommended operating head or below the minimum recommended operating head of the weir in question. Discharge for these heads outside the normal operating range are listed for reference only; it should not be implied that the primary device is intended to be used in these regions. Refer to Chapter 3 for minimum and maximum recommended heads.

Cipolletti weirs

11-1: 1 ft. Crest Length Cipolletti Weir

11-2: 1½ ft. Crest Length Cipolletti Weir

11-3: 2 ft. Crest Length Cipolletti Weir

11-4: 2½ ft. Crest Length Cipolletti Weir

11-5: 3 ft. Crest Length Cipolletti Weir

11-6: 4 ft. Crest Length Cipolletti Weir

11-7: 5 ft. Crest Length Cipolletti Weir

11-8: 6 ft. Crest Length Cipolletti Weir

11-9: 8 ft. Crest Length Cipolletti Weir

11-10: 10 ft. Crest Length Cipolletti Weir

Note: The discharges of the weirs are listed in four different units:

CFS—cubic feet per second   GPS—gallons per second

GPM—gallons per minute   MGD—million gallons per day.

The equation used to develop each table is listed on the table.

11-1: 1 ft. Cipolletti Weir Discharge Table

Formulas: $CFS = 3.367 \, H^{1.5}$ $GPS = CFS \times 7.481$
$GPM = CFS \times 448.8$ $MGD = CFS \times 0.6463$

Head Feet	CFS	GPS	GPM	MGD	Head Feet	CFS	GPS	GPM	MGD
0.01	0.0034	0.0252	1.511	0.0022	0.51	1.226	9.174	550.4	0.7926
0.02	0.0095	0.0712	4.274	0.0062	0.52	1.263	9.445	566.6	0.8160
0.03	0.0175	0.1309	7.852	0.0113	0.53	1.299	9.719	583.1	0.8396
0.04	0.0269	0.2015	12.09	0.0174	0.54	1.336	9.995	599.6	0.8635
0.05	0.0376	0.2816	16.89	0.0243	0.55	1.373	10.27	616.4	0.8876
0.06	0.0495	0.3702	22.21	0.0320	0.56	1.411	10.56	633.3	0.9119
0.07	0.0624	0.4665	27.99	0.0403	0.57	1.449	10.84	650.3	0.9365
0.08	0.0762	0.5700	34.19	0.0492	0.58	1.487	11.13	667.5	0.9612
0.09	0.0909	0.6801	40.80	0.0588	0.59	1.526	11.42	684.8	0.9862
0.10	0.1065	0.7965	47.79	0.0688	0.60	1.565	11.71	702.3	1.011
0.11	0.1228	0.9189	55.13	0.0794	0.61	1.604	12.00	719.9	1.037
0.12	0.1400	1.047	62.82	0.0905	0.62	1.644	12.30	737.7	1.062
0.13	0.1578	1.181	70.83	0.1020	0.63	1.684	12.60	755.6	1.088
0.14	0.1764	1.319	79.16	0.1140	0.64	1.724	12.90	773.7	1.114
0.15	0.1956	1.463	87.79	0.1264	0.65	1.764	13.20	791.9	1.140
0.16	0.2155	1.612	96.71	0.1393	0.66	1.805	13.51	810.2	1.167
0.17	0.2360	1.766	105.9	0.1525	0.67	1.847	13.81	828.7	1.193
0.18	0.2571	1.924	115.4	0.1662	0.68	1.888	14.12	847.3	1.220
0.19	0.2789	2.086	125.1	0.1802	0.69	1.930	14.44	866.1	1.247
0.20	0.3012	2.253	135.2	0.1946	0.70	1.972	14.75	885.0	1.274
0.21	0.3240	2.424	145.4	0.2094	0.71	2.014	15.07	904.0	1.302
0.22	0.3474	2.599	155.9	0.2245	0.72	2.057	15.39	923.2	1.329
0.23	0.3714	2.778	166.7	0.2400	0.73	2.100	15.71	942.5	1.357
0.24	0.3959	2.962	177.7	0.2559	0.74	2.143	16.03	961.9	1.385
0.25	0.4209	3.149	188.9	0.2720	0.75	2.187	16.36	981.5	1.413
0.26	0.4464	3.339	200.3	0.2885	0.76	2.231	16.69	1001	1.442
0.27	0.4724	3.534	212.0	0.3053	0.77	2.275	17.02	1021	1.470
0.28	0.4989	3.732	223.9	0.3224	0.78	2.319	17.35	1041	1.499
0.29	0.5258	3.934	236.0	0.3398	0.79	2.364	17.69	1061	1.528
0.30	0.5533	4.139	248.3	0.3576	0.80	2.409	18.02	1081	1.557
0.31	0.5811	4.348	260.8	0.3756	0.81	2.455	18.36	1102	1.586
0.32	0.6095	4.560	273.5	0.3939	0.82	2.500	18.70	1122	1.616
0.33	0.6383	4.775	286.5	0.4125	0.83	2.546	19.05	1143	1.645
0.34	0.6675	4.994	299.6	0.4314	0.84	2.592	19.39	1163	1.675
0.35	0.6972	5.216	312.9	0.4506	0.85	2.639	19.74	1184	1.705
0.36	0.7273	5.441	326.4	0.4700	0.86	2.685	20.09	1205	1.736
0.37	0.7578	5.669	340.1	0.4898	0.87	2.732	20.44	1226	1.766
0.38	0.7887	5.900	354.0	0.5097	0.88	2.780	20.79	1247	1.796
0.39	0.8200	6.135	368.0	0.5300	0.89	2.827	21.15	1269	1.827
0.40	0.8518	6.372	382.3	0.5505	0.90	2.875	21.51	1290	1.858
0.41	0.8839	6.613	396.7	0.5713	0.91	2.923	21.87	1312	1.889
0.42	0.9165	6.856	411.3	0.5923	0.92	2.971	22.23	1333	1.920
0.43	0.9494	7.102	426.1	0.6136	0.93	3.020	22.59	1355	1.952
0.44	0.9827	7.352	441.0	0.6351	0.94	3.069	22.96	1377	1.983
0.45	1.016	7.604	456.2	0.6569	0.95	3.118	23.32	1399	2.015
0.46	1.050	7.858	471.4	0.6789	0.96	3.167	23.69	1421	2.047
0.47	1.085	8.116	486.9	0.7012	0.97	3.217	24.06	1444	2.079
0.48	1.120	8.377	502.5	0.7237	0.98	3.266	24.44	1466	2.111
0.49	1.155	8.640	518.3	0.7464	0.99	3.317	24.81	1488	2.144
0.50	1.190	8.905	534.3	0.7694	1.00	3.367	25.19	1511	2.176

11

11-1: 1 ft. Cipolletti Weir Discharge Table *(Continued)*

Formulas: $CFS = 3.367\ H^{1.5}$ $GPS = CFS \times 7.481$
$GPM = CFS \times 448.8$ $MGD = CFS \times 0.6463$

Head Feet	CFS	GPS	GPM	MGD	Head Feet	CFS	GPS	GPM	MGD
1.01	3.418	25.57	1534	2.209	1.51	6.248	46.74	2804	4.038
1.02	3.469	25.95	1557	2.242	1.52	6.310	47.20	2832	4.078
1.03	3.520	26.33	1580	2.275	1.53	6.372	47.67	2860	4.118
1.04	3.571	26.71	1603	2.308	1.54	6.435	48.14	2888	4.159
1.05	3.623	27.10	1626	2.341	1.55	6.497	48.61	2916	4.199
1.06	3.675	27.49	1649	2.375	1.56	6.560	49.08	2944	4.240
1.07	3.727	27.88	1673	2.409	1.57	6.624	49.55	2973	4.281
1.08	3.779	28.27	1696	2.442	1.58	6.687	50.03	3001	4.322
1.09	3.832	28.66	1720	2.476	1.59	6.751	50.50	3030	4.363
1.10	3.884	29.06	1743	2.511	1.60	6.814	50.98	3058	4.404
1.11	3.938	29.46	1767	2.545	1.61	6.878	51.46	3087	4.445
1.12	3.991	29.86	1791	2.579	1.62	6.942	51.94	3116	4.487
1.13	4.044	30.26	1815	2.614	1.63	7.007	52.42	3145	4.529
1.14	4.098	30.66	1839	2.649	1.64	7.071	52.90	3174	4.570
1.15	4.152	31.06	1864	2.684	1.65	7.136	53.39	3203	4.612
1.16	4.207	31.47	1888	2.719	1.66	7.201	53.87	3232	4.654
1.17	4.261	31.88	1912	2.754	1.67	7.266	54.36	3261	4.696
1.18	4.316	32.29	1937	2.789	1.68	7.332	54.85	3290	4.739
1.19	4.371	32.70	1962	2.825	1.69	7.397	55.34	3320	4.781
1.20	4.426	33.11	1986	2.861	1.70	7.463	55.83	3349	4.823
1.21	4.481	33.53	2011	2.896	1.71	7.529	56.32	3379	4.866
1.22	4.537	33.94	2036	2.932	1.72	7.595	56.82	3409	4.909
1.23	4.593	34.36	2061	2.968	1.73	7.661	57.32	3438	4.952
1.24	4.649	34.78	2087	3.005	1.74	7.728	57.81	3468	4.995
1.25	4.706	35.20	2112	3.041	1.75	7.795	58.31	3498	5.038
1.26	4.762	35.63	2137	3.078	1.76	7.862	58.81	3528	5.081
1.27	4.819	36.05	2163	3.114	1.77	7.929	59.31	3558	5.124
1.28	4.876	36.48	2188	3.151	1.78	7.996	59.82	3589	5.168
1.29	4.933	36.91	2214	3.188	1.79	8.063	60.32	3619	5.211
1.30	4.991	37.34	2240	3.225	1.80	8.131	60.83	3649	5.255
1.31	5.048	37.77	2266	3.263	1.81	8.199	61.34	3680	5.299
1.32	5.106	38.20	2292	3.300	1.82	8.267	61.85	3710	5.343
1.33	5.164	38.63	2318	3.338	1.83	8.335	62.36	3741	5.387
1.34	5.223	39.07	2344	3.375	1.84	8.404	62.87	3772	5.431
1.35	5.281	39.51	2370	3.413	1.85	8.472	63.38	3802	5.476
1.36	5.340	39.95	2397	3.451	1.86	8.541	63.90	3833	5.520
1.37	5.399	40.39	2423	3.489	1.87	8.610	64.41	3864	5.565
1.38	5.458	40.83	2450	3.528	1.88	8.679	64.93	3895	5.609
1.39	5.518	41.28	2476	3.566	1.89	8.749	65.45	3926	5.654
1.40	5.577	41.72	2503	3.605	1.90	8.818	65.97	3958	5.699
1.41	5.637	42.17	2530	3.643	1.91	8.888	66.49	3989	5.744
1.42	5.697	42.62	2557	3.682	1.92	8.958	67.01	4020	5.789
1.43	5.758	43.07	2584	3.721	1.93	9.028	67.54	4052	5.835
1.44	5.818	43.53	2611	3.760	1.94	9.098	68.06	4083	5.880
1.45	5.879	43.98	2638	3.800	1.95	9.168	68.59	4115	5.926
1.46	5.940	44.44	2666	3.839	1.96	9.239	69.12	4146	5.971
1.47	6.001	44.89	2693	3.878	1.97	9.310	69.65	4178	6.017
1.48	6.062	45.35	2721	3.918	1.98	9.381	70.18	4210	6.063
1.49	6.124	45.81	2748	3.958	1.99	9.452	70.71	4242	6.109
1.50	6.186	46.27	2776	3.998	2.00	9.523	71.24	4274	6.155

11

11-1: 1 ft. Cipolletti Weir Discharge Table *(Continued)*

Formulas: $CFS = 3.367\ H^{1.5}$ $GPS = CFS \times 7.481$
$GPM = CFS \times 448.8$ $MGD = CFS \times 0.6463$

Head Feet	CFS	GPS	GPM	MGD	Head Feet	CFS	GPS	GPM	MGD
2.01	9.595	71.78	4306	6.201	2.51	13.39	100.2	6009	8.653
2.02	9.667	72.32	4338	6.247	2.52	13.47	100.8	6045	8.705
2.03	9.738	72.85	4371	6.294	2.53	13.55	101.4	6081	8.757
2.04	9.810	73.39	4403	6.340	2.54	13.63	102.0	6117	8.809
2.05	9.883	73.93	4435	6.387	2.55	13.71	102.6	6153	8.861
2.06	9.955	74.47	4468	6.434	2.56	13.79	103.2	6190	8.913
2.07	10.03	75.02	4500	6.481	2.57	13.87	103.8	6226	8.966
2.08	10.10	75.56	4533	6.528	2.58	13.95	104.4	6262	9.018
2.09	10.17	76.11	4566	6.575	2.59	14.03	105.0	6299	9.070
2.10	10.25	76.65	4599	6.622	2.60	14.12	105.6	6335	9.123
2.11	10.32	77.20	4631	6.670	2.61	14.20	106.2	6372	9.176
2.12	10.39	77.75	4664	6.717	2.62	14.28	106.8	6408	9.228
2.13	10.47	78.30	4697	6.765	2.63	14.36	107.4	6445	9.281
2.14	10.54	78.85	4731	6.812	2.64	14.44	108.0	6482	9.334
2.15	10.61	79.41	4764	6.860	2.65	14.52	108.7	6519	9.387
2.16	10.69	79.96	4797	6.908	2.66	14.61	109.3	6556	9.441
2.17	10.76	80.52	4830	6.956	2.67	14.69	109.9	6593	9.494
2.18	10.84	81.08	4864	7.004	2.68	14.77	110.5	6630	9.547
2.19	10.91	81.63	4897	7.053	2.69	14.85	111.1	6667	9.601
2.20	10.99	82.19	4931	7.101	2.70	14.94	111.8	6704	9.654
2.21	11.06	82.75	4965	7.149	2.71	15.02	112.4	6741	9.708
2.22	11.14	83.32	4998	7.198	2.72	15.10	113.0	6779	9.762
2.23	11.21	83.88	5032	7.247	2.73	15.19	113.6	6816	9.816
2.24	11.29	84.45	5066	7.295	2.74	15.27	114.2	6854	9.870
2.25	11.36	85.01	5100	7.344	2.75	15.35	114.9	6891	9.924
2.26	11.44	85.58	5134	7.393	2.76	15.44	115.5	6929	9.978
2.27	11.52	86.15	5168	7.442	2.77	15.52	116.1	6967	10.03
2.28	11.59	86.72	5202	7.492	2.78	15.61	116.8	7004	10.09
2.29	11.67	87.29	5237	7.541	2.79	15.69	117.4	7042	10.14
2.30	11.74	87.86	5271	7.590	2.80	15.78	118.0	7080	10.20
2.31	11.82	88.43	5305	7.640	2.81	15.86	118.6	7118	10.25
2.32	11.90	89.01	5340	7.690	2.82	15.94	119.3	7156	10.31
2.33	11.98	89.59	5374	7.739	2.83	16.03	119.9	7194	10.36
2.34	12.05	90.16	5409	7.789	2.84	16.11	120.6	7232	10.41
2.35	12.13	90.74	5444	7.839	2.85	16.20	121.2	7270	10.47
2.36	12.21	91.32	5479	7.889	2.86	16.29	121.8	7309	10.53
2.37	12.28	91.90	5513	7.940	2.87	16.37	122.5	7347	10.58
2.38	12.36	92.48	5548	7.990	2.88	16.46	123.1	7386	10.64
2.39	12.44	93.07	5583	8.040	2.89	16.54	123.8	7424	10.69
2.40	12.52	93.65	5618	8.091	2.90	16.63	124.4	7463	10.75
2.41	12.60	94.24	5654	8.141	2.91	16.71	125.0	7501	10.80
2.42	12.68	94.83	5689	8.192	2.92	16.80	125.7	7540	10.86
2.43	12.75	95.41	5724	8.243	2.93	16.89	126.3	7579	10.91
2.44	12.83	96.00	5759	8.294	2.94	16.97	127.0	7618	10.97
2.45	12.91	96.59	5795	8.345	2.95	17.06	127.6	7656	11.03
2.46	12.99	97.19	5830	8.396	2.96	17.15	128.3	7695	11.08
2.47	13.07	97.78	5866	8.447	2.97	17.23	128.9	7734	11.14
2.48	13.15	98.37	5902	8.499	2.98	17.32	129.6	7774	11.19
2.49	13.23	98.97	5937	8.550	2.99	17.41	130.2	7813	11.25
2.50	13.31	99.57	5973	8.602	3.00	17.50	130.9	7852	11.31

11

11-2: 1 ½ ft. Cipolletti Weir Discharge Table

Formulas: CFS = 5.051 $H^{1.5}$ GPS = CFS x 7.481
           GPM = CFS x 448.8   MGD = CFS x 0.6463

Head Feet	CFS	GPS	GPM	MGD	Head Feet	CFS	GPS	GPM	MGD
0.01	0.0051	0.0378	2.267	0.0033	0.51	1.840	13.76	825.6	1.189
0.02	0.0143	0.1069	6.412	0.0092	0.52	1.894	14.17	850.0	1.224
0.03	0.0262	0.1963	11.78	0.0170	0.53	1.949	14.58	874.7	1.260
0.04	0.0404	0.3023	18.14	0.0261	0.54	2.004	14.99	899.5	1.295
0.05	0.0565	0.4225	25.34	0.0365	0.55	2.060	15.41	924.6	1.332
0.06	0.0742	0.5553	33.32	0.0480	0.56	2.117	15.84	950.0	1.368
0.07	0.0935	0.6998	41.98	0.0605	0.57	2.174	16.26	975.5	1.405
0.08	0.1143	0.8550	51.29	0.0739	0.58	2.231	16.69	1001	1.442
0.09	0.1364	1.020	61.21	0.0881	0.59	2.289	17.12	1027	1.479
0.10	0.1597	1.195	71.69	0.1032	0.60	2.347	17.56	1054	1.517
0.11	0.1843	1.379	82.70	0.1191	0.61	2.406	18.00	1080	1.555
0.12	0.2100	1.571	94.23	0.1357	0.62	2.466	18.45	1107	1.594
0.13	0.2368	1.771	106.3	0.1530	0.63	2.526	18.90	1134	1.632
0.14	0.2646	1.979	118.7	0.1710	0.64	2.586	19.35	1161	1.671
0.15	0.2934	2.195	131.7	0.1896	0.65	2.647	19.80	1188	1.711
0.16	0.3233	2.418	145.1	0.2089	0.66	2.708	20.26	1215	1.750
0.17	0.3540	2.649	158.9	0.2288	0.67	2.770	20.72	1243	1.790
0.18	0.3857	2.886	173.1	0.2493	0.68	2.832	21.19	1271	1.831
0.19	0.4183	3.129	187.7	0.2704	0.69	2.895	21.66	1299	1.871
0.20	0.4518	3.380	202.8	0.2920	0.70	2.958	22.13	1328	1.912
0.21	0.4861	3.636	218.2	0.3142	0.71	3.022	22.61	1356	1.953
0.22	0.5212	3.899	233.9	0.3369	0.72	3.086	23.09	1385	1.994
0.23	0.5571	4.168	250.0	0.3601	0.73	3.150	23.57	1414	2.036
0.24	0.5939	4.443	266.5	0.3838	0.74	3.215	24.05	1443	2.078
0.25	0.6314	4.723	283.4	0.4081	0.75	3.281	24.54	1472	2.120
0.26	0.6696	5.010	300.5	0.4328	0.76	3.347	25.04	1502	2.163
0.27	0.7086	5.301	318.0	0.4580	0.77	3.413	25.53	1532	2.206
0.28	0.7484	5.599	335.9	0.4837	0.78	3.480	26.03	1562	2.249
0.29	0.7888	5.901	354.0	0.5098	0.79	3.547	26.53	1592	2.292
0.30	0.8300	6.209	372.5	0.5364	0.80	3.614	27.04	1622	2.336
0.31	0.8718	6.522	391.3	0.5634	0.81	3.682	27.55	1653	2.380
0.32	0.9143	6.840	410.4	0.5909	0.82	3.751	28.06	1683	2.424
0.33	0.9575	7.163	429.7	0.6188	0.83	3.819	28.57	1714	2.468
0.34	1.001	7.491	449.4	0.6472	0.84	3.889	29.09	1745	2.513
0.35	1.046	7.824	469.4	0.6759	0.85	3.958	29.61	1776	2.558
0.36	1.091	8.162	489.6	0.7051	0.86	4.028	30.14	1808	2.604
0.37	1.137	8.504	510.2	0.7347	0.87	4.099	30.66	1840	2.649
0.38	1.183	8.851	531.0	0.7647	0.88	4.170	31.19	1871	2.695
0.39	1.230	9.203	552.1	0.7951	0.89	4.241	31.73	1903	2.741
0.40	1.278	9.559	573.5	0.8259	0.90	4.313	32.26	1936	2.787
0.41	1.326	9.920	595.1	0.8570	0.91	4.385	32.80	1968	2.834
0.42	1.375	10.29	617.0	0.8886	0.92	4.457	33.34	2000	2.881
0.43	1.424	10.65	639.2	0.9205	0.93	4.530	33.89	2033	2.928
0.44	1.474	11.03	661.6	0.9528	0.94	4.603	34.44	2066	2.975
0.45	1.525	11.41	684.3	0.9854	0.95	4.677	34.99	2099	3.023
0.46	1.576	11.79	707.2	1.018	0.96	4.751	35.54	2132	3.071
0.47	1.628	12.18	730.4	1.052	0.97	4.825	36.10	2166	3.119
0.48	1.680	12.57	753.9	1.086	0.98	4.900	36.66	2199	3.167
0.49	1.732	12.96	777.5	1.120	0.99	4.975	37.22	2233	3.216
0.50	1.786	13.36	801.5	1.154	1.00	5.051	37.79	2267	3.264

11

11-2: 1 ¹/₂ ft. Cipolletti Weir Discharge Table
(Continued)

Formulas: $CFS = 5.051\ H^{1.5}$ $GPS = CFS \times 7.481$
$GPM = CFS \times 448.8$ $MGD = CFS \times 0.6463$

Head Feet	CFS	GPS	GPM	MGD	Head Feet	CFS	GPS	GPM	MGD
1.01	5.127	38.35	2301	3.314	1.51	9.372	70.11	4206	6.057
1.02	5.203	38.93	2335	3.363	1.52	9.465	70.81	4248	6.118
1.03	5.280	39.50	2370	3.412	1.53	9.559	71.51	4290	6.178
1.04	5.357	40.08	2404	3.462	1.54	9.653	72.21	4332	6.239
1.05	5.435	40.66	2439	3.512	1.55	9.747	72.92	4374	6.300
1.06	5.512	41.24	2474	3.563	1.56	9.842	73.62	4417	6.361
1.07	5.591	41.82	2509	3.613	1.57	9.936	74.33	4459	6.422
1.08	5.669	42.41	2544	3.664	1.58	10.03	75.05	4502	6.483
1.09	5.748	43.00	2580	3.715	1.59	10.13	75.76	4545	6.545
1.10	5.827	43.59	2615	3.766	1.60	10.22	76.47	4588	6.607
1.11	5.907	44.19	2651	3.818	1.61	10.32	77.19	4631	6.669
1.12	5.987	44.79	2687	3.869	1.62	10.41	77.91	4674	6.731
1.13	6.067	45.39	2723	3.921	1.63	10.51	78.64	4717	6.793
1.14	6.148	45.99	2759	3.973	1.64	10.61	79.36	4761	6.856
1.15	6.229	46.60	2796	4.026	1.65	10.71	80.09	4805	6.919
1.16	6.311	47.21	2832	4.078	1.66	10.80	80.82	4848	6.982
1.17	6.392	47.82	2869	4.131	1.67	10.90	81.55	4892	7.045
1.18	6.474	48.44	2906	4.184	1.68	11.00	82.28	4936	7.108
1.19	6.557	49.05	2943	4.238	1.69	11.10	83.02	4980	7.172
1.20	6.640	49.67	2980	4.291	1.70	11.20	83.75	5025	7.236
1.21	6.723	50.29	3017	4.345	1.71	11.29	84.50	5069	7.300
1.22	6.806	50.92	3055	4.399	1.72	11.39	85.24	5114	7.364
1.23	6.890	51.55	3092	4.453	1.73	11.49	85.98	5158	7.428
1.24	6.974	52.18	3130	4.508	1.74	11.59	86.73	5203	7.493
1.25	7.059	52.81	3168	4.562	1.75	11.69	87.48	5248	7.557
1.26	7.144	53.44	3206	4.617	1.76	11.79	88.23	5293	7.622
1.27	7.229	54.08	3244	4.672	1.77	11.89	88.98	5338	7.687
1.28	7.315	54.72	3283	4.727	1.78	12.00	89.74	5383	7.752
1.29	7.401	55.36	3321	4.783	1.79	12.10	90.49	5429	7.818
1.30	7.487	56.01	3360	4.839	1.80	12.20	91.25	5474	7.884
1.31	7.573	56.66	3399	4.895	1.81	12.30	92.01	5520	7.949
1.32	7.660	57.31	3438	4.951	1.82	12.40	92.78	5566	8.015
1.33	7.747	57.96	3477	5.007	1.83	12.50	93.54	5612	8.081
1.34	7.835	58.61	3516	5.064	1.84	12.61	94.31	5658	8.148
1.35	7.923	59.27	3556	5.120	1.85	12.71	95.08	5704	8.214
1.36	8.011	59.93	3595	5.177	1.86	12.81	95.85	5750	8.281
1.37	8.100	60.59	3635	5.235	1.87	12.92	96.63	5797	8.348
1.38	8.188	61.26	3675	5.292	1.88	13.02	97.40	5843	8.415
1.39	8.278	61.92	3715	5.350	1.89	13.12	98.18	5890	8.482
1.40	8.367	62.59	3755	5.408	1.90	13.23	98.96	5937	8.550
1.41	8.457	63.27	3795	5.466	1.91	13.33	99.74	5984	8.617
1.42	8.547	63.94	3836	5.524	1.92	13.44	100.5	6031	8.685
1.43	8.637	64.62	3876	5.582	1.93	13.54	101.3	6078	8.753
1.44	8.728	65.30	3917	5.641	1.94	13.65	102.1	6125	8.821
1.45	8.819	65.98	3958	5.700	1.95	13.75	102.9	6173	8.889
1.46	8.911	66.66	3999	5.759	1.96	13.86	103.7	6220	8.958
1.47	9.002	67.35	4040	5.818	1.97	13.97	104.5	6268	9.026
1.48	9.094	68.03	4082	5.878	1.98	14.07	105.3	6316	9.095
1.49	9.187	68.73	4123	5.937	1.99	14.18	106.1	6364	9.164
1.50	9.279	69.42	4165	5.997	2.00	14.29	106.9	6412	9.233

11

11-2: 1 $\frac{1}{2}$ ft. Cipolletti Weir Discharge Table
(Continued)

Formulas: CFS $= 5.051$ H$^{1.5}$ GPS $=$ CFS x 7.481
              GPM $=$ CFS x 448.8   MGD $=$ CFS x 0.6463

Head Feet	CFS	GPS	GPM	MGD	Head Feet	CFS	GPS	GPM	MGD
2.01	14.39	107.7	6460	9.303	2.51	20.09	150.3	9014	12.98
2.02	14.50	108.5	6508	9.372	2.52	20.21	151.2	9068	13.06
2.03	14.61	109.3	6557	9.442	2.53	20.33	152.1	9122	13.14
2.04	14.72	110.1	6605	9.512	2.54	20.45	153.0	9177	13.21
2.05	14.83	110.9	6654	9.582	2.55	20.57	153.9	9231	13.29
2.06	14.93	111.7	6702	9.652	2.56	20.69	154.8	9285	13.37
2.07	15.04	112.5	6751	9.722	2.57	20.81	155.7	9340	13.45
2.08	15.15	113.4	6800	9.793	2.58	20.93	156.6	9394	13.53
2.09	15.26	114.2	6849	9.863	2.59	21.05	157.5	9449	13.61
2.10	15.37	115.0	6899	9.934	2.60	21.18	158.4	9504	13.69
2.11	15.48	115.8	6948	10.01	2.61	21.30	159.3	9559	13.76
2.12	15.59	116.6	6997	10.08	2.62	21.42	160.2	9614	13.84
2.13	15.70	117.5	7047	10.15	2.63	21.54	161.2	9669	13.92
2.14	15.81	118.3	7097	10.22	2.64	21.67	162.1	9724	14.00
2.15	15.92	119.1	7146	10.29	2.65	21.79	163.0	9779	14.08
2.16	16.03	120.0	7196	10.36	2.66	21.91	163.9	9835	14.16
2.17	16.15	120.8	7246	10.44	2.67	22.04	164.9	9890	14.24
2.18	16.26	121.6	7297	10.51	2.68	22.16	165.8	9946	14.32
2.19	16.37	122.5	7347	10.58	2.69	22.28	166.7	10000	14.40
2.20	16.48	123.3	7397	10.65	2.70	22.41	167.6	10060	14.48
2.21	16.59	124.1	7448	10.73	2.71	22.53	168.6	10110	14.56
2.22	16.71	125.0	7498	10.80	2.72	22.66	169.5	10170	14.64
2.23	16.82	125.8	7549	10.87	2.73	22.78	170.4	10230	14.73
2.24	16.93	126.7	7600	10.94	2.74	22.91	171.4	10280	14.81
2.25	17.05	127.5	7651	11.02	2.75	23.03	172.3	10340	14.89
2.26	17.16	128.4	7702	11.09	2.76	23.16	173.3	10390	14.97
2.27	17.27	129.2	7753	11.16	2.77	23.29	174.2	10450	15.05
2.28	17.39	130.1	7804	11.24	2.78	23.41	175.1	10510	15.13
2.29	17.50	130.9	7856	11.31	2.79	23.54	176.1	10560	15.21
2.30	17.62	131.8	7907	11.39	2.80	23.67	177.0	10620	15.29
2.31	17.73	132.7	7959	11.46	2.81	23.79	178.0	10680	15.38
2.32	17.85	133.5	8011	11.54	2.82	23.92	178.9	10740	15.46
2.33	17.96	134.4	8062	11.61	2.83	24.05	179.9	10790	15.54
2.34	18.08	135.3	8114	11.69	2.84	24.17	180.8	10850	15.62
2.35	18.20	136.1	8166	11.76	2.85	24.30	181.8	10910	15.71
2.36	18.31	137.0	8219	11.84	2.86	24.43	182.8	10960	15.79
2.37	18.43	137.9	8271	11.91	2.87	24.56	183.7	11020	15.87
2.38	18.55	138.7	8323	11.99	2.88	24.69	184.7	11080	15.96
2.39	18.66	139.6	8376	12.06	2.89	24.82	185.6	11140	16.04
2.40	18.78	140.5	8428	12.14	2.90	24.94	186.6	11200	16.12
2.41	18.90	141.4	8481	12.21	2.91	25.07	187.6	11250	16.21
2.42	19.02	142.3	8534	12.29	2.92	25.20	188.5	11310	16.29
2.43	19.13	143.1	8587	12.37	2.93	25.33	189.5	11370	16.37
2.44	19.25	144.0	8640	12.44	2.94	25.46	190.5	11430	16.46
2.45	19.37	144.9	8693	12.52	2.95	25.59	191.5	11490	16.54
2.46	19.49	145.8	8746	12.60	2.96	25.72	192.4	11540	16.62
2.47	19.61	146.7	8800	12.67	2.97	25.85	193.4	11600	16.71
2.48	19.73	147.6	8853	12.75	2.98	25.98	194.4	11660	16.79
2.49	19.85	148.5	8907	12.83	2.99	26.11	195.4	11720	16.88
2.50	19.97	149.4	8961	12.90	3.00	26.25	196.3	11780	16.96

11

11-3: 2 ft. Cipolletti Weir Discharge Table

Formulas: CFS $= 6.734 \, H^{1.5}$ GPS = CFS x 7.481
$\quad\quad\quad$ GPM = CFS x 448.8   MGD = CFS x 0.6463

Head Feet	CFS	GPS	GPM	MGD	Head Feet	CFS	GPS	GPM	MGD
0.01	0.0067	0.0504	3.022	0.0044	0.51	2.453	18.35	1101	1.585
0.02	0.0190	0.1425	8.548	0.0123	0.52	2.525	18.89	1133	1.632
0.03	0.0350	0.2618	15.70	0.0226	0.53	2.598	19.44	1166	1.679
0.04	0.0539	0.4030	24.18	0.0348	0.54	2.672	19.99	1199	1.727
0.05	0.0753	0.5632	33.79	0.0487	0.55	2.747	20.55	1233	1.775
0.06	0.0990	0.7404	44.42	0.0640	0.56	2.822	21.11	1267	1.824
0.07	0.1247	0.9330	55.97	0.0806	0.57	2.898	21.68	1301	1.873
0.08	0.1524	1.140	68.39	0.0985	0.58	2.975	22.25	1335	1.922
0.09	0.1818	1.360	81.60	0.1175	0.59	3.052	22.83	1370	1.972
0.10	0.2129	1.593	95.57	0.1376	0.60	3.130	23.41	1405	2.023
0.11	0.2457	1.838	110.3	0.1588	0.61	3.208	24.00	1440	2.073
0.12	0.2799	2.094	125.6	0.1809	0.62	3.287	24.59	1475	2.125
0.13	0.3156	2.361	141.7	0.2040	0.63	3.367	25.19	1511	2.176
0.14	0.3527	2.639	158.3	0.2280	0.64	3.448	25.79	1547	2.228
0.15	0.3912	2.927	175.6	0.2528	0.65	3.529	26.40	1584	2.281
0.16	0.4310	3.224	193.4	0.2785	0.66	3.611	27.01	1620	2.334
0.17	0.4720	3.531	211.8	0.3051	0.67	3.693	27.63	1657	2.387
0.18	0.5143	3.847	230.8	0.3324	0.68	3.776	28.25	1695	2.440
0.19	0.5577	4.172	250.3	0.3604	0.69	3.860	28.87	1732	2.494
0.20	0.6023	4.506	270.3	0.3893	0.70	3.944	29.50	1770	2.549
0.21	0.6480	4.848	290.8	0.4188	0.71	4.029	30.14	1808	2.604
0.22	0.6949	5.198	311.9	0.4491	0.72	4.114	30.78	1846	2.659
0.23	0.7428	5.557	333.4	0.4801	0.73	4.200	31.42	1885	2.715
0.24	0.7918	5.923	355.3	0.5117	0.74	4.287	32.07	1924	2.770
0.25	0.8417	6.297	377.8	0.5440	0.75	4.374	32.72	1963	2.827
0.26	0.8928	6.679	400.7	0.5770	0.76	4.462	33.38	2002	2.884
0.27	0.9448	7.068	424.0	0.6106	0.77	4.550	34.04	2042	2.941
0.28	0.9977	7.464	447.8	0.6448	0.78	4.639	34.70	2082	2.998
0.29	1.052	7.867	472.0	0.6797	0.79	4.728	35.37	2122	3.056
0.30	1.107	8.278	496.6	0.7151	0.80	4.818	36.05	2163	3.114
0.31	1.162	8.695	521.6	0.7512	0.81	4.909	36.72	2203	3.173
0.32	1.219	9.119	547.1	0.7878	0.82	5.000	37.41	2244	3.232
0.33	1.277	9.550	572.9	0.8250	0.83	5.092	38.09	2285	3.291
0.34	1.335	9.987	599.2	0.8628	0.84	5.184	38.78	2327	3.351
0.35	1.394	10.43	625.8	0.9012	0.85	5.277	39.48	2368	3.411
0.36	1.455	10.88	652.8	0.9401	0.86	5.371	40.18	2410	3.471
0.37	1.516	11.34	680.2	0.9795	0.87	5.465	40.88	2452	3.532
0.38	1.577	11.80	707.9	1.019	0.88	5.559	41.59	2495	3.593
0.39	1.640	12.27	736.1	1.060	0.89	5.654	42.30	2538	3.654
0.40	1.704	12.74	764.6	1.101	0.90	5.750	43.01	2580	3.716
0.41	1.768	13.23	793.4	1.143	0.91	5.846	43.73	2624	3.778
0.42	1.833	13.71	822.6	1.185	0.92	5.942	44.45	2667	3.841
0.43	1.899	14.20	852.2	1.227	0.93	6.039	45.18	2711	3.903
0.44	1.965	14.70	882.1	1.270	0.94	6.137	45.91	2754	3.966
0.45	2.033	15.21	912.3	1.314	0.95	6.235	46.65	2798	4.030
0.46	2.101	15.72	942.9	1.358	0.96	6.334	47.38	2843	4.094
0.47	2.170	16.23	973.8	1.402	0.97	6.433	48.13	2887	4.158
0.48	2.239	16.75	1005	1.447	0.98	6.533	48.87	2932	4.222
0.49	2.310	17.28	1037	1.493	0.99	6.633	49.62	2977	4.287
0.50	2.381	17.81	1069	1.539	1.00	6.734	50.38	3022	4.352

11

11-3: 2 ft. Cipolletti Weir Discharge Table *(Continued)*

Formulas: CFS = 6.734 H$^{1.5}$ GPS = CFS x 7.481
GPM = CFS x 448.8   MGD = CFS x 0.6463

Head Feet	CFS	GPS	GPM	MGD	Head Feet	CFS	GPS	GPM	MGD
1.01	6.835	51.13	3068	4.418	1.51	12.50	93.48	5608	8.076
1.02	6.937	51.90	3113	4.483	1.52	12.62	94.41	5664	8.156
1.03	7.039	52.66	3159	4.549	1.53	12.74	95.34	5720	8.237
1.04	7.142	53.43	3205	4.616	1.54	12.87	96.28	5776	8.317
1.05	7.245	54.20	3252	4.683	1.55	12.99	97.21	5832	8.399
1.06	7.349	54.98	3298	4.750	1.56	13.12	98.16	5889	8.480
1.07	7.453	55.76	3345	4.817	1.57	13.25	99.10	5945	8.562
1.08	7.558	56.54	3392	4.885	1.58	13.37	100.1	6002	8.644
1.09	7.663	57.33	3439	4.953	1.59	13.50	101.0	6059	8.726
1.10	7.769	58.12	3487	5.021	1.60	13.63	102.0	6117	8.808
1.11	7.875	58.91	3534	5.090	1.61	13.76	102.9	6174	8.891
1.12	7.982	59.71	3582	5.159	1.62	13.88	103.9	6232	8.974
1.13	8.089	60.51	3630	5.228	1.63	14.01	104.8	6289	9.057
1.14	8.197	61.32	3679	5.297	1.64	14.14	105.8	6347	9.141
1.15	8.305	62.13	3727	5.367	1.65	14.27	106.8	6405	9.224
1.16	8.413	62.94	3776	5.437	1.66	14.40	107.7	6464	9.308
1.17	8.522	63.75	3825	5.508	1.67	14.53	108.7	6522	9.393
1.18	8.632	64.57	3874	5.579	1.68	14.66	109.7	6581	9.477
1.19	8.742	65.40	3923	5.650	1.69	14.79	110.7	6640	9.562
1.20	8.852	66.22	3973	5.721	1.70	14.93	111.7	6699	9.647
1.21	8.963	67.05	4023	5.793	1.71	15.06	112.6	6758	9.732
1.22	9.074	67.88	4073	5.865	1.72	15.19	113.6	6817	9.817
1.23	9.186	68.72	4123	5.937	1.73	15.32	114.6	6877	9.903
1.24	9.298	69.56	4173	6.010	1.74	15.46	115.6	6937	9.989
1.25	9.411	70.40	4224	6.082	1.75	15.59	116.6	6997	10.08
1.26	9.524	71.25	4274	6.155	1.76	15.72	117.6	7057	10.16
1.27	9.638	72.10	4325	6.229	1.77	15.86	118.6	7117	10.25
1.28	9.752	72.95	4377	6.303	1.78	15.99	119.6	7177	10.34
1.29	9.866	73.81	4428	6.377	1.79	16.13	120.6	7238	10.42
1.30	9.981	74.67	4480	6.451	1.80	16.26	121.7	7299	10.51
1.31	10.10	75.53	4531	6.526	1.81	16.40	122.7	7359	10.60
1.32	10.21	76.40	4583	6.600	1.82	16.53	123.7	7420	10.69
1.33	10.33	77.27	4636	6.676	1.83	16.67	124.7	7482	10.77
1.34	10.45	78.14	4688	6.751	1.84	16.81	125.7	7543	10.86
1.35	10.56	79.02	4741	6.827	1.85	16.94	126.8	7605	10.95
1.36	10.68	79.90	4793	6.903	1.86	17.08	127.8	7666	11.04
1.37	10.80	80.78	4846	6.979	1.87	17.22	128.8	7728	11.13
1.38	10.92	81.67	4899	7.055	1.88	17.36	129.9	7790	11.22
1.39	11.04	82.56	4953	7.132	1.89	17.50	130.9	7853	11.31
1.40	11.15	83.45	5006	7.209	1.90	17.64	131.9	7915	11.40
1.41	11.27	84.35	5060	7.287	1.91	17.78	133.0	7978	11.49
1.42	11.39	85.24	5114	7.364	1.92	17.92	134.0	8040	11.58
1.43	11.52	86.15	5168	7.442	1.93	18.06	135.1	8103	11.67
1.44	11.64	87.05	5222	7.521	1.94	18.20	136.1	8166	11.76
1.45	11.76	87.96	5277	7.599	1.95	18.34	137.2	8230	11.85
1.46	11.88	88.87	5332	7.678	1.96	18.48	138.2	8293	11.94
1.47	12.00	89.79	5386	7.757	1.97	18.62	139.3	8357	12.03
1.48	12.12	90.70	5441	7.836	1.98	18.76	140.4	8420	12.13
1.49	12.25	91.62	5497	7.916	1.99	18.90	141.4	8484	12.22
1.50	12.37	92.55	5552	7.995	2.00	19.05	142.5	8548	12.31

11

Formulas: CFS =6.734 H$^{1.5}$ GPS = CFS x 7.481
GPM = CFS x 448.8   MGD = CFS x 0.6463

Head Feet	CFS	GPS	GPM	MGD	Head Feet	CFS	GPS	GPM	MGD
2.01	19.19	143.6	8612	12.40	2.51	26.78	200.3	12020	17.31
2.02	19.33	144.6	8677	12.49	2.52	26.94	201.5	12090	17.41
2.03	19.48	145.7	8741	12.59	2.53	27.10	202.7	12160	17.51
2.04	19.62	146.8	8806	12.68	2.54	27.26	203.9	12230	17.62
2.05	19.77	147.9	8871	12.77	2.55	27.42	205.1	12310	17.72
2.06	19.91	148.9	8936	12.87	2.56	27.58	206.3	12380	17.83
2.07	20.06	150.0	9001	12.96	2.57	27.74	207.6	12450	17.93
2.08	20.20	151.1	9066	13.06	2.58	27.91	208.8	12520	18.04
2.09	20.35	152.2	9132	13.15	2.59	28.07	210.0	12600	18.14
2.10	20.49	153.3	9197	13.24	2.60	28.23	211.2	12670	18.25
2.11	20.64	154.4	9263	13.34	2.61	28.39	212.4	12740	18.35
2.12	20.79	155.5	9329	13.43	2.62	28.56	213.6	12820	18.46
2.13	20.93	156.6	9395	13.53	2.63	28.72	214.9	12890	18.56
2.14	21.08	157.7	9461	13.62	2.64	28.89	216.1	12960	18.67
2.15	21.23	158.8	9528	13.72	2.65	29.05	217.3	13040	18.77
2.16	21.38	159.9	9594	13.82	2.66	29.21	218.6	13110	18.88
2.17	21.53	161.0	9661	13.91	2.67	29.38	219.8	13190	18.99
2.18	21.67	162.2	9728	14.01	2.68	29.54	221.0	13260	19.09
2.19	21.82	163.3	9795	14.11	2.69	29.71	222.3	13330	19.20
2.20	21.97	164.4	9862	14.20	2.70	29.88	223.5	13410	19.31
2.21	22.12	165.5	9929	14.30	2.71	30.04	224.7	13480	19.42
2.22	22.27	166.6	10000	14.40	2.72	30.21	226.0	13560	19.52
2.23	22.42	167.8	10060	14.49	2.73	30.38	227.2	13630	19.63
2.24	22.58	168.9	10130	14.59	2.74	30.54	228.5	13710	19.74
2.25	22.73	170.0	10200	14.69	2.75	30.71	229.7	13780	19.85
2.26	22.88	171.2	10270	14.79	2.76	30.88	231.0	13860	19.96
2.27	23.03	172.3	10340	14.88	2.77	31.05	232.2	13930	20.06
2.28	23.18	173.4	10400	14.98	2.78	31.21	233.5	14010	20.17
2.29	23.34	174.6	10470	15.08	2.79	31.38	234.8	14080	20.28
2.30	23.49	175.7	10540	15.18	2.80	31.55	236.0	14160	20.39
2.31	23.64	176.9	10610	15.28	2.81	31.72	237.3	14240	20.50
2.32	23.80	178.0	10680	15.38	2.82	31.89	238.6	14310	20.61
2.33	23.95	179.2	10750	15.48	2.83	32.06	239.8	14390	20.72
2.34	24.10	180.3	10820	15.58	2.84	32.23	241.1	14460	20.83
2.35	24.26	181.5	10890	15.68	2.85	32.40	242.4	14540	20.94
2.36	24.41	182.6	10960	15.78	2.86	32.57	243.7	14620	21.05
2.37	24.57	183.8	11030	15.88	2.87	32.74	244.9	14690	21.16
2.38	24.73	185.0	11100	15.98	2.88	32.91	246.2	14770	21.27
2.39	24.88	186.1	11170	16.08	2.89	33.08	247.5	14850	21.38
2.40	25.04	187.3	11240	16.18	2.90	33.26	248.8	14930	21.49
2.41	25.19	188.5	11310	16.28	2.91	33.43	250.1	15000	21.60
2.42	25.35	189.7	11380	16.38	2.92	33.60	251.4	15080	21.72
2.43	25.51	190.8	11450	16.49	2.93	33.77	252.7	15160	21.83
2.44	25.67	192.0	11520	16.59	2.94	33.95	254.0	15240	21.94
2.45	25.82	193.2	11590	16.69	2.95	34.12	255.3	15310	22.05
2.46	25.98	194.4	11660	16.79	2.96	34.29	256.5	15390	22.16
2.47	26.14	195.6	11730	16.89	2.97	34.47	257.9	15470	22.28
2.48	26.30	196.7	11800	17.00	2.98	34.64	259.2	15550	22.39
2.49	26.46	197.9	11870	17.10	2.99	34.82	260.5	15630	22.50
2.50	26.62	199.1	11950	17.20	3.00	34.99	261.8	15700	22.61

11

11-4: 2 $^1/_2$ ft. Cipolletti Weir Discharge Table

Formulas: CFS = 8.418 H$^{1.5}$ GPS = CFS x 7.481
  GPM = CFS x 448.8   MGD = CFS x 0.6463

Head Feet	CFS	GPS	GPM	MGD	Head Feet	CFS	GPS	GPM	MGD
0.01	0.0084	0.0630	3.778	0.0054	0.51	3.066	22.94	1376	1.982
0.02	0.0238	0.1781	10.69	0.0154	0.52	3.157	23.61	1417	2.040
0.03	0.0437	0.3272	19.63	0.0283	0.53	3.248	24.30	1458	2.099
0.04	0.0673	0.5038	30.22	0.0435	0.54	3.340	24.99	1499	2.159
0.05	0.0941	0.7041	42.24	0.0608	0.55	3.434	25.69	1541	2.219
0.06	0.1237	0.9255	55.53	0.0800	0.56	3.528	26.39	1583	2.280
0.07	0.1559	1.166	69.97	0.1008	0.57	3.623	27.10	1626	2.341
0.08	0.1905	1.425	85.49	0.1231	0.58	3.718	27.82	1669	2.403
0.09	0.2273	1.700	102.0	0.1469	0.59	3.815	28.54	1712	2.466
0.10	0.2662	1.991	119.5	0.1720	0.60	3.912	29.27	1756	2.529
0.11	0.3071	2.298	137.8	0.1985	0.61	4.011	30.00	1800	2.592
0.12	0.3499	2.618	157.0	0.2262	0.62	4.110	30.74	1844	2.656
0.13	0.3946	2.952	177.1	0.2550	0.63	4.209	31.49	1889	2.721
0.14	0.4410	3.299	197.9	0.2850	0.64	4.310	32.24	1934	2.786
0.15	0.4890	3.659	219.5	0.3161	0.65	4.411	33.00	1980	2.851
0.16	0.5388	4.030	241.8	0.3482	0.66	4.514	33.77	2026	2.917
0.17	0.5900	4.414	264.8	0.3813	0.67	4.617	34.54	2072	2.984
0.18	0.6429	4.809	288.5	0.4155	0.68	4.720	35.31	2118	3.051
0.19	0.6972	5.216	312.9	0.4506	0.69	4.825	36.09	2165	3.118
0.20	0.7529	5.633	337.9	0.4866	0.70	4.930	36.88	2213	3.186
0.21	0.8101	6.060	363.6	0.5236	0.71	5.036	37.68	2260	3.255
0.22	0.8686	6.498	389.8	0.5614	0.72	5.143	38.47	2308	3.324
0.23	0.9285	6.946	416.7	0.6001	0.73	5.250	39.28	2356	3.393
0.24	0.9898	7.404	444.2	0.6397	0.74	5.359	40.09	2405	3.463
0.25	1.052	7.872	472.2	0.6801	0.75	5.468	40.90	2454	3.534
0.26	1.116	8.349	500.9	0.7213	0.76	5.577	41.72	2503	3.605
0.27	1.181	8.835	530.0	0.7633	0.77	5.688	42.55	2553	3.676
0.28	1.247	9.331	559.8	0.8061	0.78	5.799	43.38	2603	3.748
0.29	1.315	9.835	590.0	0.8497	0.79	5.911	44.22	2653	3.820
0.30	1.383	10.35	620.8	0.8940	0.80	6.023	45.06	2703	3.893
0.31	1.453	10.87	652.1	0.9390	0.81	6.137	45.91	2754	3.966
0.32	1.524	11.40	683.9	0.9848	0.82	6.251	46.76	2805	4.040
0.33	1.596	11.94	716.2	1.031	0.83	6.365	47.62	2857	4.114
0.34	1.669	12.48	749.0	1.079	0.84	6.481	48.48	2909	4.189
0.35	1.743	13.04	782.3	1.127	0.85	6.597	49.35	2961	4.264
0.36	1.818	13.60	816.0	1.175	0.86	6.714	50.22	3013	4.339
0.37	1.895	14.17	850.3	1.224	0.87	6.831	51.10	3066	4.415
0.38	1.972	14.75	885.0	1.274	0.88	6.949	51.99	3119	4.491
0.39	2.050	15.34	920.2	1.325	0.89	7.068	52.88	3172	4.568
0.40	2.130	15.93	955.8	1.376	0.90	7.187	53.77	3226	4.645
0.41	2.210	16.53	991.8	1.428	0.91	7.308	54.67	3280	4.723
0.42	2.291	17.14	1028	1.481	0.92	7.428	55.57	3334	4.801
0.43	2.374	17.76	1065	1.534	0.93	7.550	56.48	3388	4.879
0.44	2.457	18.38	1103	1.588	0.94	7.672	57.39	3443	4.958
0.45	2.541	19.01	1140	1.642	0.95	7.795	58.31	3498	5.038
0.46	2.626	19.65	1179	1.697	0.96	7.918	59.23	3554	5.117
0.47	2.712	20.29	1217	1.753	0.97	8.042	60.16	3609	5.198
0.48	2.799	20.94	1256	1.809	0.98	8.167	61.10	3665	5.278
0.49	2.887	21.60	1296	1.866	0.99	8.292	62.03	3721	5.359
0.50	2.976	22.27	1336	1.924	1.00	8.418	62.98	3780	5.441

11

11-4: 2 $^{1}/_{2}$ ft. Cipolletti Weir Discharge Table (Continued)

Formulas: CFS = 8.418 H$^{1.5}$ GPS = CFS x 7.481
GPM = CFS x 448.8   MGD = CFS x 0.6463

Head Feet	CFS	GPS	GPM	MGD	Head Feet	CFS	GPS	GPM	MGD
1.01	8.545	63.92	3835	5.522	1.51	15.62	116.9	7010	10.10
1.02	8.672	64.87	3892	5.605	1.52	15.78	118.0	7080	10.20
1.03	8.800	65.83	3949	5.687	1.53	15.93	119.2	7150	10.30
1.04	8.928	66.79	4007	5.770	1.54	16.09	120.4	7220	10.40
1.05	9.057	67.76	4065	5.854	1.55	16.24	121.5	7291	10.50
1.06	9.187	68.73	4123	5.937	1.56	16.40	122.7	7361	10.60
1.07	9.317	69.70	4182	6.022	1.57	16.56	123.9	7432	10.70
1.08	9.448	70.68	4240	6.106	1.58	16.72	125.1	7503	10.81
1.09	9.580	71.67	4299	6.191	1.59	16.88	126.3	7575	10.91
1.10	9.712	72.65	4359	6.277	1.60	17.04	127.5	7646	11.01
1.11	9.844	73.65	4418	6.362	1.61	17.20	128.6	7718	11.11
1.12	9.978	74.64	4478	6.449	1.62	17.36	129.8	7790	11.22
1.13	10.11	75.65	4538	6.535	1.63	17.52	131.1	7862	11.32
1.14	10.25	76.65	4599	6.622	1.64	17.68	132.3	7935	11.43
1.15	10.38	77.66	4659	6.709	1.65	17.84	133.5	8007	11.53
1.16	10.52	78.68	4720	6.797	1.66	18.00	134.7	8080	11.64
1.17	10.65	79.70	4781	6.885	1.67	18.17	135.9	8153	11.74
1.18	10.79	80.72	4843	6.974	1.68	18.33	137.1	8227	11.85
1.19	10.93	81.75	4904	7.063	1.69	18.49	138.4	8300	11.95
1.20	11.07	82.78	4966	7.152	1.70	18.66	139.6	8374	12.06
1.21	11.20	83.82	5029	7.241	1.71	18.82	140.8	8448	12.17
1.22	11.34	84.86	5091	7.331	1.72	18.99	142.1	8522	12.27
1.23	11.48	85.91	5154	7.422	1.73	19.15	143.3	8597	12.38
1.24	11.62	86.96	5217	7.512	1.74	19.32	144.5	8671	12.49
1.25	11.76	88.01	5280	7.603	1.75	19.49	145.8	8746	12.60
1.26	11.91	89.07	5343	7.695	1.76	19.66	147.0	8821	12.70
1.27	12.05	90.13	5407	7.787	1.77	19.82	148.3	8897	12.81
1.28	12.19	91.20	5471	7.879	1.78	19.99	149.6	8972	12.92
1.29	12.33	92.27	5535	7.971	1.79	20.16	150.8	9048	13.03
1.30	12.48	93.34	5600	8.064	1.80	20.33	152.1	9124	13.14
1.31	12.62	94.42	5665	8.157	1.81	20.50	153.4	9200	13.25
1.32	12.77	95.51	5730	8.251	1.82	20.67	154.6	9276	13.36
1.33	12.91	96.59	5795	8.345	1.83	20.84	155.9	9353	13.47
1.34	13.06	97.68	5860	8.439	1.84	21.01	157.2	9429	13.58
1.35	13.20	98.78	5926	8.534	1.85	21.18	158.5	9506	13.69
1.36	13.35	99.88	5992	8.629	1.86	21.35	159.7	9584	13.80
1.37	13.50	101.0	6058	8.724	1.87	21.53	161.0	9661	13.91
1.38	13.65	102.1	6125	8.820	1.88	21.70	162.3	9739	14.02
1.39	13.80	103.2	6191	8.916	1.89	21.87	163.6	9816	14.14
1.40	13.94	104.3	6258	9.012	1.90	22.05	164.9	9894	14.25
1.41	14.09	105.4	6325	9.109	1.91	22.22	166.2	9973	14.36
1.42	14.24	106.6	6393	9.206	1.92	22.40	167.5	10050	14.47
1.43	14.40	107.7	6460	9.304	1.93	22.57	168.9	10130	14.59
1.44	14.55	108.8	6528	9.401	1.94	22.75	170.2	10210	14.70
1.45	14.70	110.0	6597	9.499	1.95	22.92	171.5	10290	14.81
1.46	14.85	111.1	6665	9.598	1.96	23.10	172.8	10370	14.93
1.47	15.00	112.2	6733	9.697	1.97	23.28	174.1	10450	15.04
1.48	15.16	113.4	6802	9.796	1.98	23.45	175.5	10530	15.16
1.49	15.31	114.5	6871	9.895	1.99	23.63	176.8	10610	15.27
1.50	15.46	115.7	6941	9.995	2.00	23.81	178.1	10690	15.39

11

11-4: 2 ^{1}/2 ft. Cipolletti Weir Discharge Table (Continued)

Formulas: CFS = 8.418 H$^{1.5}$ GPS = CFS x 7.481
GPM = CFS x 448.8 MGD = CFS x 0.6463

Head Feet	CFS	GPS	GPM	MGD	Head Feet	CFS	GPS	GPM	MGD
2.01	23.99	179.5	10770	15.50	2.51	33.47	250.4	15020	21.63
2.02	24.17	180.8	10850	15.62	2.52	33.68	251.9	15110	21.76
2.03	24.35	182.1	10930	15.74	2.53	33.88	253.4	15200	21.89
2.04	24.53	183.5	11010	15.85	2.54	34.08	254.9	15290	22.02
2.05	24.71	184.8	11090	15.97	2.55	34.28	256.4	15380	22.15
2.06	24.89	186.2	11170	16.09	2.56	34.48	257.9	15470	22.28
2.07	25.07	187.6	11250	16.20	2.57	34.68	259.5	15570	22.42
2.08	25.25	188.9	11330	16.32	2.58	34.88	261.0	15660	22.55
2.09	25.43	190.3	11420	16.44	2.59	35.09	262.5	15750	22.68
2.10	25.62	191.6	11500	16.56	2.60	35.29	264.0	15840	22.81
2.11	25.80	193.0	11580	16.68	2.61	35.50	265.5	15930	22.94
2.12	25.98	194.4	11660	16.79	2.62	35.70	267.1	16020	23.07
2.13	26.17	195.8	11740	16.91	2.63	35.90	268.6	16110	23.20
2.14	26.35	197.1	11830	17.03	2.64	36.11	270.1	16210	23.34
2.15	26.54	198.5	11910	17.15	2.65	36.31	271.7	16300	23.47
2.16	26.72	199.9	11990	17.27	2.66	36.52	273.2	16390	23.60
2.17	26.91	201.3	12080	17.39	2.67	36.73	274.7	16480	23.74
2.18	27.10	202.7	12160	17.51	2.68	36.93	276.3	16580	23.87
2.19	27.28	204.1	12240	17.63	2.69	37.14	277.8	16670	24.00
2.20	27.47	205.5	12330	17.75	2.70	37.35	279.4	16760	24.14
2.21	27.66	206.9	12410	17.87	2.71	37.55	280.9	16850	24.27
2.22	27.84	208.3	12500	18.00	2.72	37.76	282.5	16950	24.41
2.23	28.03	209.7	12580	18.12	2.73	37.97	284.1	17040	24.54
2.24	28.22	211.1	12670	18.24	2.74	38.18	285.6	17140	24.68
2.25	28.41	212.5	12750	18.36	2.75	38.39	287.2	17230	24.81
2.26	28.60	214.0	12840	18.48	2.76	38.60	288.8	17320	24.95
2.27	28.79	215.4	12920	18.61	2.77	38.81	290.3	17420	25.08
2.28	28.98	216.8	13010	18.73	2.78	39.02	291.9	17510	25.22
2.29	29.17	218.2	13090	18.85	2.79	39.23	293.5	17610	25.35
2.30	29.36	219.7	13180	18.98	2.80	39.44	295.1	17700	25.49
2.31	29.55	221.1	13260	19.10	2.81	39.65	296.6	17800	25.63
2.32	29.75	222.5	13350	19.23	2.82	39.86	298.2	17890	25.76
2.33	29.94	224.0	13440	19.35	2.83	40.08	299.8	17990	25.90
2.34	30.13	225.4	13520	19.47	2.84	40.29	301.4	18080	26.04
2.35	30.33	226.9	13610	19.60	2.85	40.50	303.0	18180	26.18
2.36	30.52	228.3	13700	19.72	2.86	40.72	304.6	18270	26.31
2.37	30.71	229.8	13780	19.85	2.87	40.93	306.2	18370	26.45
2.38	30.91	231.2	13870	19.98	2.88	41.14	307.8	18470	26.59
2.39	31.10	232.7	13960	20.10	2.89	41.36	309.4	18560	26.73
2.40	31.30	234.1	14050	20.23	2.90	41.57	311.0	18660	26.87
2.41	31.49	235.6	14130	20.35	2.91	41.79	312.6	18750	27.01
2.42	31.69	237.1	14220	20.48	2.92	42.00	314.2	18850	27.15
2.43	31.89	238.5	14310	20.61	2.93	42.22	315.8	18950	27.29
2.44	32.08	240.0	14400	20.74	2.94	42.44	317.5	19050	27.43
2.45	32.28	241.5	14490	20.86	2.95	42.65	319.1	19140	27.57
2.46	32.48	243.0	14580	20.99	2.96	42.87	320.7	19240	27.71
2.47	32.68	244.5	14670	21.12	2.97	43.09	322.3	19340	27.85
2.48	32.88	245.9	14760	21.25	2.98	43.30	324.0	19440	27.99
2.49	33.08	247.4	14840	21.38	2.99	43.52	325.6	19530	28.13
2.50	33.28	248.9	14930	21.51	3.00	43.74	327.2	19630	28.27

11

11-5: 3 ft. Cipolletti Weir Discharge Table

Formulas: CFS = 10.10 $H^{1.5}$ GPS = CFS x 7.481
GPM = CFS x 448.8   MGD = CFS x 0.6463

Head Feet	CFS	GPS	GPM	MGD	Head Feet	CFS	GPS	GPM	MGD
0.01	0.0101	0.0756	4.533	0.0065	0.51	3.679	27.52	1651	2.377
0.02	0.0286	0.2137	12.82	0.0185	0.52	3.787	28.33	1700	2.448
0.03	0.0525	0.3926	23.55	0.0339	0.53	3.897	29.15	1749	2.519
0.04	0.0808	0.6045	36.26	0.0522	0.54	4.008	29.98	1799	2.590
0.05	0.1129	0.8448	50.68	0.0730	0.55	4.120	30.82	1849	2.663
0.06	0.1484	1.110	66.62	0.0959	0.56	4.233	31.66	1900	2.736
0.07	0.1871	1.399	83.95	0.1209	0.57	4.346	32.52	1951	2.809
0.08	0.2285	1.710	102.6	0.1477	0.58	4.461	33.38	2002	2.883
0.09	0.2727	2.040	122.4	0.1762	0.59	4.577	34.24	2054	2.958
0.10	0.3194	2.389	143.3	0.2064	0.60	4.694	35.12	2107	3.034
0.11	0.3685	2.757	165.4	0.2381	0.61	4.812	36.00	2160	3.110
0.12	0.4198	3.141	188.4	0.2713	0.62	4.931	36.89	2213	3.187
0.13	0.4734	3.542	212.5	0.3060	0.63	5.050	37.78	2267	3.264
0.14	0.5291	3.958	237.4	0.3419	0.64	5.171	38.69	2321	3.342
0.15	0.5868	4.390	263.3	0.3792	0.65	5.293	39.60	2375	3.421
0.16	0.6464	4.836	290.1	0.4178	0.66	5.415	40.51	2430	3.500
0.17	0.7079	5.296	317.7	0.4575	0.67	5.539	41.44	2486	3.580
0.18	0.7713	5.770	346.2	0.4985	0.68	5.663	42.37	2542	3.660
0.19	0.8365	6.258	375.4	0.5406	0.69	5.789	43.31	2598	3.741
0.20	0.9034	6.758	405.4	0.5838	0.70	5.915	44.25	2655	3.823
0.21	0.9720	7.271	436.2	0.6282	0.71	6.042	45.20	2712	3.905
0.22	1.042	7.797	467.7	0.6736	0.72	6.170	46.16	2769	3.988
0.23	1.114	8.334	500.0	0.7200	0.73	6.299	47.13	2827	4.071
0.24	1.188	8.884	533.0	0.7675	0.74	6.429	48.10	2886	4.155
0.25	1.262	9.445	566.6	0.8160	0.75	6.560	49.08	2944	4.240
0.26	1.339	10.02	600.9	0.8654	0.76	6.692	50.06	3003	4.325
0.27	1.417	10.60	635.9	0.9158	0.77	6.824	51.05	3063	4.411
0.28	1.496	11.19	671.6	0.9671	0.78	6.958	52.05	3123	4.497
0.29	1.577	11.80	707.9	1.019	0.79	7.092	53.05	3183	4.583
0.30	1.660	12.42	744.8	1.073	0.80	7.227	54.06	3243	4.671
0.31	1.743	13.04	782.4	1.127	0.81	7.363	55.08	3304	4.759
0.32	1.828	13.68	820.5	1.182	0.82	7.500	56.11	3366	4.847
0.33	1.915	14.32	859.3	1.237	0.83	7.637	57.13	3428	4.936
0.34	2.002	14.98	898.7	1.294	0.84	7.776	58.17	3490	5.025
0.35	2.091	15.65	938.6	1.352	0.85	7.915	59.21	3552	5.115
0.36	2.182	16.32	979.1	1.410	0.86	8.055	60.26	3615	5.206
0.37	2.273	17.01	1020	1.469	0.87	8.196	61.31	3678	5.297
0.38	2.366	17.70	1062	1.529	0.88	8.338	62.37	3742	5.389
0.39	2.460	18.40	1104	1.590	0.89	8.480	63.44	3806	5.481
0.40	2.555	19.11	1147	1.651	0.90	8.624	64.51	3870	5.573
0.41	2.652	19.84	1190	1.714	0.91	8.768	65.59	3935	5.667
0.42	2.749	20.57	1234	1.777	0.92	8.913	66.67	4000	5.760
0.43	2.848	21.31	1278	1.841	0.93	9.058	67.77	4065	5.854
0.44	2.948	22.05	1323	1.905	0.94	9.205	68.86	4131	5.949
0.45	3.049	22.81	1368	1.970	0.95	9.352	69.96	4197	6.044
0.46	3.151	23.57	1414	2.037	0.96	9.500	71.07	4264	6.140
0.47	3.254	24.35	1461	2.103	0.97	9.649	72.18	4330	6.236
0.48	3.359	25.13	1507	2.171	0.98	9.799	73.30	4398	6.333
0.49	3.464	25.92	1555	2.239	0.99	9.949	74.43	4465	6.430
0.50	3.571	26.71	1603	2.308	1.00	10.10	75.56	4533	6.528

11

11-5: 3 ft. Cipolletti Weir Discharge Table *(Continued)*

Formulas: $CFS = 10.10 \; H^{1.5}$ $GPS = CFS \times 7.481$
$GPM = CFS \times 448.8$ $MGD = CFS \times 0.6463$

Head Feet	CFS	GPS	GPM	MGD	Head Feet	CFS	GPS	GPM	MGD
1.01	10.25	76.69	4601	6.626	1.51	18.74	140.2	8411	12.11
1.02	10.40	77.84	4670	6.724	1.52	18.93	141.6	8495	12.23
1.03	10.56	78.98	4738	6.824	1.53	19.11	143.0	8579	12.35
1.04	10.71	80.14	4808	6.923	1.54	19.30	144.4	8663	12.47
1.05	10.87	81.30	4877	7.023	1.55	19.49	145.8	8747	12.60
1.06	11.02	82.46	4947	7.124	1.56	19.68	147.2	8832	12.72
1.07	11.18	83.63	5017	7.225	1.57	19.87	148.6	8917	12.84
1.08	11.34	84.80	5088	7.326	1.58	20.06	150.1	9002	12.96
1.09	11.49	85.98	5158	7.428	1.59	20.25	151.5	9088	13.09
1.10	11.65	87.17	5230	7.531	1.60	20.44	152.9	9174	13.21
1.11	11.81	88.36	5301	7.634	1.61	20.63	154.4	9260	13.34
1.12	11.97	89.56	5373	7.737	1.62	20.83	155.8	9346	13.46
1.13	12.13	90.76	5445	7.841	1.63	21.02	157.2	9433	13.58
1.14	12.29	91.97	5517	7.945	1.64	21.21	158.7	9520	13.71
1.15	12.46	93.18	5590	8.050	1.65	21.41	160.1	9607	13.84
1.16	12.62	94.40	5663	8.155	1.66	21.60	161.6	9695	13.96
1.17	12.78	95.62	5737	8.261	1.67	21.80	163.1	9782	14.09
1.18	12.95	96.85	5810	8.367	1.68	21.99	164.5	9870	14.21
1.19	13.11	98.08	5884	8.474	1.69	22.19	166.0	9959	14.34
1.20	13.28	99.32	5959	8.581	1.70	22.39	167.5	10050	14.47
1.21	13.44	100.6	6033	8.688	1.71	22.58	169.0	10140	14.60
1.22	13.61	101.8	6108	8.796	1.72	22.78	170.4	10230	14.72
1.23	13.78	103.1	6183	8.905	1.73	22.98	171.9	10310	14.85
1.24	13.95	104.3	6259	9.013	1.74	23.18	173.4	10400	14.98
1.25	14.12	105.6	6335	9.123	1.75	23.38	174.9	10490	15.11
1.26	14.28	106.9	6411	9.232	1.76	23.58	176.4	10580	15.24
1.27	14.46	108.1	6488	9.342	1.77	23.78	177.9	10670	15.37
1.28	14.63	109.4	6564	9.453	1.78	23.99	179.4	10760	15.50
1.29	14.80	110.7	6641	9.564	1.79	24.19	181.0	10860	15.63
1.30	14.97	112.0	6719	9.675	1.80	24.39	182.5	10950	15.76
1.31	15.14	113.3	6796	9.787	1.81	24.59	184.0	11040	15.90
1.32	15.32	114.6	6874	9.900	1.82	24.80	185.5	11130	16.03
1.33	15.49	115.9	6953	10.01	1.83	25.00	187.0	11220	16.16
1.34	15.67	117.2	7031	10.13	1.84	25.21	188.6	11310	16.29
1.35	15.84	118.5	7110	10.24	1.85	25.41	190.1	11410	16.43
1.36	16.02	119.8	7189	10.35	1.86	25.62	191.7	11500	16.56
1.37	16.20	121.2	7269	10.47	1.87	25.83	193.2	11590	16.69
1.38	16.37	122.5	7348	10.58	1.88	26.04	194.8	11680	16.83
1.39	16.55	123.8	7428	10.70	1.89	26.24	196.3	11780	16.96
1.40	16.73	125.2	7509	10.81	1.90	26.45	197.9	11870	17.10
1.41	16.91	126.5	7589	10.93	1.91	26.66	199.4	11970	17.23
1.42	17.09	127.9	7670	11.05	1.92	26.87	201.0	12060	17.37
1.43	17.27	129.2	7751	11.16	1.93	27.08	202.6	12150	17.50
1.44	17.45	130.6	7833	11.28	1.94	27.29	204.2	12250	17.64
1.45	17.63	131.9	7915	11.40	1.95	27.50	205.7	12340	17.77
1.46	17.82	133.3	7997	11.52	1.96	27.71	207.3	12440	17.91
1.47	18.00	134.7	8079	11.63	1.97	27.93	208.9	12530	18.05
1.48	18.19	136.0	8161	11.75	1.98	28.14	210.5	12630	18.19
1.49	18.37	137.4	8244	11.87	1.99	28.35	212.1	12720	18.32
1.50	18.55	138.8	8327	11.99	2.00	28.57	213.7	12820	18.46

11

Formulas: CFS = 10.10 H$^{1.5}$ GPS = CFS x 7.481
GPM = CFS x 448.8   MGD = CFS x 0.6463

Head Feet	CFS	GPS	GPM	MGD	Head Feet	CFS	GPS	GPM	MGD
2.01	28.78	215.3	12920	18.60	2.51	40.16	300.5	18030	25.96
2.02	29.00	216.9	13010	18.74	2.52	40.40	302.3	18130	26.11
2.03	29.21	218.5	13110	18.88	2.53	40.64	304.1	18240	26.27
2.04	29.43	220.2	13210	19.02	2.54	40.89	305.9	18350	26.42
2.05	29.65	221.8	13300	19.16	2.55	41.13	307.7	18460	26.58
2.06	29.86	223.4	13400	19.30	2.56	41.37	309.5	18570	26.74
2.07	30.08	225.0	13500	19.44	2.57	41.61	311.3	18680	26.89
2.08	30.30	226.7	13600	19.58	2.58	41.86	313.1	18780	27.05
2.09	30.52	228.3	13700	19.72	2.59	42.10	314.9	18890	27.21
2.10	30.74	229.9	13790	19.86	2.60	42.34	316.8	19000	27.37
2.11	30.96	231.6	13890	20.01	2.61	42.59	318.6	19110	27.52
2.12	31.18	233.2	13990	20.15	2.62	42.83	320.4	19220	27.68
2.13	31.40	234.9	14090	20.29	2.63	43.08	322.3	19330	27.84
2.14	31.62	236.5	14190	20.44	2.64	43.32	324.1	19440	28.00
2.15	31.84	238.2	14290	20.58	2.65	43.57	325.9	19550	28.16
2.16	32.06	239.9	14390	20.72	2.66	43.82	327.8	19670	28.32
2.17	32.29	241.5	14490	20.87	2.67	44.06	329.6	19780	28.48
2.18	32.51	243.2	14590	21.01	2.68	44.31	331.5	19890	28.64
2.19	32.73	244.9	14690	21.16	2.69	44.56	333.4	20000	28.80
2.20	32.96	246.6	14790	21.30	2.70	44.81	335.2	20110	28.96
2.21	33.18	248.2	14890	21.45	2.71	45.06	337.1	20220	29.12
2.22	33.41	249.9	14990	21.59	2.72	45.31	338.9	20330	29.28
2.23	33.63	251.6	15090	21.74	2.73	45.56	340.8	20450	29.44
2.24	33.86	253.3	15200	21.88	2.74	45.81	342.7	20560	29.61
2.25	34.09	255.0	15300	22.03	2.75	46.06	344.6	20670	29.77
2.26	34.32	256.7	15400	22.18	2.76	46.31	346.5	20780	29.93
2.27	34.54	258.4	15500	22.33	2.77	46.56	348.3	20900	30.09
2.28	34.77	260.1	15610	22.47	2.78	46.82	350.2	21010	30.26
2.29	35.00	261.8	15710	22.62	2.79	47.07	352.1	21120	30.42
2.30	35.23	263.6	15810	22.77	2.80	47.32	354.0	21240	30.58
2.31	35.46	265.3	15910	22.92	2.81	47.58	355.9	21350	30.75
2.32	35.69	267.0	16020	23.07	2.82	47.83	357.8	21470	30.91
2.33	35.92	268.7	16120	23.22	2.83	48.08	359.7	21580	31.08
2.34	36.15	270.5	16230	23.37	2.84	48.34	361.6	21690	31.24
2.35	36.39	272.2	16330	23.52	2.85	48.59	363.5	21810	31.41
2.36	36.62	273.9	16430	23.67	2.86	48.85	365.5	21920	31.57
2.37	36.85	275.7	16540	23.82	2.87	49.11	367.4	22040	31.74
2.38	37.08	277.4	16640	23.97	2.88	49.36	369.3	22150	31.90
2.39	37.32	279.2	16750	24.12	2.89	49.62	371.2	22270	32.07
2.40	37.55	280.9	16850	24.27	2.90	49.88	373.1	22390	32.24
2.41	37.79	282.7	16960	24.42	2.91	50.14	375.1	22500	32.40
2.42	38.02	284.4	17060	24.57	2.92	50.40	377.0	22620	32.57
2.43	38.26	286.2	17170	24.73	2.93	50.66	379.0	22730	32.74
2.44	38.50	288.0	17280	24.88	2.94	50.91	380.9	22850	32.91
2.45	38.73	289.8	17380	25.03	2.95	51.17	382.8	22970	33.07
2.46	38.97	291.5	17490	25.19	2.96	51.44	384.8	23080	33.24
2.47	39.21	293.3	17600	25.34	2.97	51.70	386.7	23200	33.41
2.48	39.45	295.1	17700	25.49	2.98	51.96	388.7	23320	33.58
2.49	39.68	296.9	17810	25.65	2.99	52.22	390.6	23440	33.75
2.50	39.92	298.7	17920	25.80	3.00	52.48	392.6	23550	33.92

11-6: 4 ft. Cipolletti Weir Discharge Table

Formulas: CFS = 13.47 H$^{1.5}$ GPS = CFS x 7.481
          GPM = CFS x 448.8   MGD = CFS x 0.6463

Head Feet	CFS	GPS	GPM	MGD	Head Feet	CFS	GPS	GPM	MGD
0.01	0.0135	0.1008	6.044	0.0087	0.51	4.905	36.70	2201	3.170
0.02	0.0381	0.2850	17.10	0.0246	0.52	5.050	37.78	2267	3.264
0.03	0.0700	0.5235	31.41	0.0452	0.53	5.197	38.88	2332	3.359
0.04	0.1077	0.8060	48.36	0.0696	0.54	5.344	39.98	2399	3.454
0.05	0.1506	1.126	67.58	0.0973	0.55	5.493	41.10	2465	3.550
0.06	0.1979	1.481	88.83	0.1279	0.56	5.644	42.22	2533	3.648
0.07	0.2494	1.866	111.9	0.1612	0.57	5.796	43.36	2601	3.746
0.08	0.3047	2.280	136.8	0.1970	0.58	5.949	44.50	2670	3.845
0.09	0.3636	2.720	163.2	0.2350	0.59	6.104	45.66	2739	3.945
0.10	0.4259	3.186	191.1	0.2753	0.60	6.259	46.83	2809	4.045
0.11	0.4914	3.676	220.5	0.3176	0.61	6.416	48.00	2880	4.147
0.12	0.5599	4.188	251.3	0.3618	0.62	6.575	49.19	2951	4.249
0.13	0.6313	4.723	283.3	0.4080	0.63	6.735	50.38	3023	4.353
0.14	0.7055	5.278	316.6	0.4560	0.64	6.896	51.59	3095	4.457
0.15	0.7824	5.853	351.2	0.5057	0.65	7.058	52.80	3168	4.561
0.16	0.8620	6.448	386.8	0.5571	0.66	7.221	54.02	3241	4.667
0.17	0.9440	7.062	423.7	0.6101	0.67	7.386	55.26	3315	4.774
0.18	1.029	7.694	461.6	0.6647	0.68	7.552	56.50	3389	4.881
0.19	1.115	8.344	500.6	0.7209	0.69	7.719	57.75	3464	4.989
0.20	1.205	9.012	540.6	0.7785	0.70	7.888	59.01	3540	5.098
0.21	1.296	9.696	581.7	0.8377	0.71	8.057	60.28	3616	5.207
0.22	1.390	10.40	623.7	0.8982	0.72	8.228	61.55	3693	5.318
0.23	1.486	11.11	666.7	0.9601	0.73	8.400	62.84	3770	5.429
0.24	1.584	11.85	710.7	1.023	0.74	8.573	64.14	3848	5.541
0.25	1.683	12.59	755.6	1.088	0.75	8.748	65.44	3926	5.654
0.26	1.786	13.36	801.3	1.154	0.76	8.923	66.75	4005	5.767
0.27	1.890	14.14	848.0	1.221	0.77	9.100	68.08	4084	5.881
0.28	1.995	14.93	895.6	1.290	0.78	9.278	69.41	4164	5.996
0.29	2.103	15.73	944.0	1.359	0.79	9.457	70.75	4240	6.112
0.30	2.213	16.56	993.2	1.430	0.80	9.637	72.09	4330	6.228
0.31	2.325	17.39	1043	1.502	0.81	9.818	73.45	4410	6.345
0.32	2.438	18.24	1094	1.576	0.82	10.00	74.81	4490	6.463
0.33	2.553	19.10	1146	1.650	0.83	10.18	76.19	4570	6.582
0.34	2.670	19.97	1198	1.726	0.84	10.37	77.57	4650	6.701
0.35	2.789	20.86	1252	1.802	0.85	10.55	78.96	4740	6.821
0.36	2.909	21.76	1306	1.880	0.86	10.74	80.35	4820	6.942
0.37	3.031	22.68	1360	1.959	0.87	10.93	81.76	4900	7.063
0.38	3.155	23.60	1416	2.039	0.88	11.12	83.17	4990	7.186
0.39	3.280	24.54	1472	2.120	0.89	11.31	84.60	5080	7.308
0.40	3.407	25.49	1529	2.202	0.90	11.50	86.03	5160	7.432
0.41	3.536	26.45	1587	2.285	0.91	11.69	87.46	5250	7.556
0.42	3.666	27.42	1645	2.369	0.92	11.88	88.91	5330	7.681
0.43	3.798	28.41	1704	2.454	0.93	12.08	90.36	5420	7.807
0.44	3.931	29.41	1764	2.540	0.94	12.27	91.82	5510	7.933
0.45	4.066	30.41	1825	2.628	0.95	12.47	93.29	5600	8.060
0.46	4.202	31.43	1886	2.716	0.96	12.67	94.77	5690	8.187
0.47	4.340	32.46	1948	2.805	0.97	12.87	96.25	5770	8.316
0.48	4.479	33.51	2010	2.895	0.98	13.07	97.75	5860	8.445
0.49	4.620	34.56	2073	2.986	0.99	13.27	99.25	5950	8.574
0.50	4.762	35.62	2137	3.077	1.00	13.47	100.8	6040	8.704

11

Formulas: $CFS = 13.47\ H^{1.5}$ $GPS = CFS \times 7.481$
$GPM = CFS \times 448.8$ $MGD = CFS \times 0.6463$

Head Feet	CFS	GPS	GPM	MGD	Head Feet	CFS	GPS	GPM	MGD
1.01	13.67	102.3	6140	8.835	1.51	24.99	187.0	11220	16.15
1.02	13.87	103.8	6230	8.967	1.52	25.24	188.8	11330	16.31
1.03	14.08	105.3	6320	9.099	1.53	25.49	190.7	11440	16.47
1.04	14.28	106.9	6410	9.232	1.54	25.74	192.6	11550	16.63
1.05	14.49	108.4	6500	9.365	1.55	25.99	194.4	11660	16.80
1.06	14.70	110.0	6600	9.499	1.56	26.24	196.3	11780	16.96
1.07	14.91	111.5	6690	9.634	1.57	26.49	198.2	11890	17.12
1.08	15.12	113.1	6780	9.770	1.58	26.75	200.1	12000	17.29
1.09	15.33	114.7	6880	9.906	1.59	27.00	202.0	12120	17.45
1.10	15.54	116.2	6970	10.04	1.60	27.26	203.9	12230	17.62
1.11	15.75	117.8	7070	10.18	1.61	27.51	205.8	12350	17.78
1.12	15.96	119.4	7160	10.32	1.62	27.77	207.7	12460	17.95
1.13	16.18	121.0	7260	10.46	1.63	28.03	209.7	12580	18.11
1.14	16.39	122.6	7360	10.59	1.64	28.29	211.6	12690	18.28
1.15	16.61	124.3	7450	10.73	1.65	28.54	213.5	12810	18.45
1.16	16.83	125.9	7550	10.87	1.66	28.80	215.5	12930	18.62
1.17	17.04	127.5	7650	11.02	1.67	29.07	217.4	13040	18.79
1.18	17.26	129.1	7750	11.16	1.68	29.33	219.4	13160	18.95
1.19	17.48	130.8	7850	11.30	1.69	29.59	221.4	13280	19.12
1.20	17.70	132.4	7950	11.44	1.70	29.85	223.3	13400	19.29
1.21	17.93	134.1	8050	11.59	1.71	30.12	225.3	13520	19.46
1.22	18.15	135.8	8150	11.73	1.72	30.38	227.3	13630	19.63
1.23	18.37	137.4	8250	11.87	1.73	30.65	229.3	13750	19.81
1.24	18.60	139.1	8350	12.02	1.74	30.91	231.3	13870	19.98
1.25	18.82	140.8	8450	12.16	1.75	31.18	233.2	13990	20.15
1.26	19.05	142.5	8550	12.31	1.76	31.45	235.3	14110	20.32
1.27	19.28	144.2	8650	12.46	1.77	31.71	237.3	14230	20.50
1.28	19.50	145.9	8750	12.61	1.78	31.98	239.3	14350	20.67
1.29	19.73	147.6	8860	12.75	1.79	32.25	241.3	14480	20.85
1.30	19.96	149.3	8960	12.90	1.80	32.52	243.3	14600	21.02
1.31	20.19	151.1	9060	13.05	1.81	32.80	245.3	14720	21.20
1.32	20.43	152.8	9170	13.20	1.82	33.07	247.4	14840	21.37
1.33	20.66	154.5	9270	13.35	1.83	33.34	249.4	14960	21.55
1.34	20.89	156.3	9380	13.50	1.84	33.61	251.5	15090	21.73
1.35	21.13	158.0	9480	13.65	1.85	33.89	253.5	15210	21.90
1.36	21.36	159.8	9590	13.81	1.86	34.16	255.6	15330	22.08
1.37	21.60	161.6	9690	13.96	1.87	34.44	257.6	15460	22.26
1.38	21.83	163.3	9800	14.11	1.88	34.72	259.7	15580	22.44
1.39	22.07	165.1	9910	14.26	1.89	34.99	261.8	15710	22.62
1.40	22.31	166.9	10010	14.42	1.90	35.27	263.9	15830	22.80
1.41	22.55	168.7	10120	14.57	1.91	35.55	266.0	15960	22.98
1.42	22.79	170.5	10230	14.73	1.92	35.83	268.0	16080	23.16
1.43	23.03	172.3	10340	14.88	1.93	36.11	270.1	16210	23.34
1.44	23.27	174.1	10440	15.04	1.94	36.39	272.2	16330	23.52
1.45	23.52	175.9	10550	15.20	1.95	36.67	274.4	16460	23.70
1.46	23.76	177.7	10660	15.36	1.96	36.96	276.5	16590	23.88
1.47	24.00	179.6	10770	15.51	1.97	37.24	278.6	16710	24.07
1.48	24.25	181.4	10880	15.67	1.98	37.52	280.7	16840	24.25
1.49	24.50	183.2	10990	15.83	1.99	37.81	282.8	16970	24.44
1.50	24.74	185.1	11100	15.99	2.00	38.09	285.0	17100	24.62

11-6: 4 ft. Cipolletti Weir Discharge Table *(Continued)*

Formulas: $CFS = 13.47 \; H^{1.5}$ $GPS = CFS \times 7.481$
          $GPM = CFS \times 448.8$ $MGD = CFS \times 0.6463$

Head Feet	CFS	GPS	GPM	MGD	Head Feet	CFS	GPS	GPM	MGD
2.01	38.38	287.1	17220	24.80	2.51	53.56	400.7	24040	34.61
2.02	38.67	289.3	17350	24.99	2.52	53.88	403.1	24180	34.82
2.03	38.95	291.4	17480	25.18	2.53	54.20	405.5	24320	35.03
2.04	39.24	293.6	17610	25.36	2.54	54.52	407.9	24470	35.24
2.05	39.53	295.7	17740	25.55	2.55	54.84	410.3	24610	35.44
2.06	39.82	297.9	17870	25.74	2.56	55.16	412.7	24760	35.65
2.07	40.11	300.1	18000	25.92	2.57	55.49	415.1	24900	35.86
2.08	40.40	302.2	18130	26.11	2.58	55.81	417.5	25050	36.07
2.09	40.69	304.4	18260	26.30	2.59	56.14	420.0	25190	36.28
2.10	40.99	306.6	18390	26.49	2.60	56.46	422.4	25340	36.49
2.11	41.28	308.8	18530	26.68	2.61	56.79	424.8	25490	36.70
2.12	41.57	311.0	18660	26.87	2.62	57.12	427.3	25630	36.91
2.13	41.87	313.2	18790	27.06	2.63	57.44	429.7	25780	37.13
2.14	42.16	315.4	18920	27.25	2.64	57.77	432.2	25930	37.34
2.15	42.46	317.6	19060	27.44	2.65	58.10	434.6	26080	37.55
2.16	42.75	319.8	19190	27.63	2.66	58.43	437.1	26220	37.76
2.17	43.05	322.1	19320	27.82	2.67	58.76	439.6	26370	37.98
2.18	43.35	324.3	19460	28.02	2.68	59.09	442.0	26520	38.19
2.19	43.65	326.5	19590	28.21	2.69	59.42	444.5	26670	38.40
2.20	43.95	328.8	19720	28.40	2.70	59.75	447.0	26820	38.62
2.21	44.25	331.0	19860	28.60	2.71	60.08	449.5	26970	38.83
2.22	44.55	333.3	19990	28.79	2.72	60.42	452.0	27110	39.05
2.23	44.85	335.5	20130	28.99	2.73	60.75	454.5	27260	39.26
2.24	45.15	337.8	20260	29.18	2.74	61.08	457.0	27410	39.48
2.25	45.45	340.0	20400	29.38	2.75	61.42	459.5	27560	39.70
2.26	45.76	342.3	20540	29.57	2.76	61.75	462.0	27720	39.91
2.27	46.06	344.6	20670	29.77	2.77	62.09	464.5	27870	40.13
2.28	46.37	346.9	20810	29.97	2.78	62.43	467.0	28020	40.35
2.29	46.67	349.2	20950	30.16	2.79	62.76	469.5	28170	40.56
2.30	46.98	351.4	21080	30.36	2.80	63.10	472.1	28320	40.78
2.31	47.28	353.7	21220	30.56	2.81	63.44	474.6	28470	41.00
2.32	47.59	356.0	21360	30.76	2.82	63.78	477.1	28620	41.22
2.33	47.90	358.3	21500	30.96	2.83	64.12	479.7	28780	41.44
2.34	48.21	360.7	21640	31.16	2.84	64.46	482.2	28930	41.66
2.35	48.52	363.0	21770	31.36	2.85	64.80	484.8	29080	41.88
2.36	48.83	365.3	21910	31.56	2.86	65.14	487.3	29240	42.10
2.37	49.14	367.6	22050	31.76	2.87	65.48	489.9	29390	42.32
2.38	49.45	369.9	22190	31.96	2.88	65.83	492.4	29540	42.54
2.39	49.76	372.3	22330	32.16	2.89	66.17	495.0	29700	42.76
2.40	50.07	374.6	22470	32.36	2.90	66.51	497.6	29850	42.99
2.41	50.39	377.0	22610	32.57	2.91	66.86	500.2	30010	43.21
2.42	50.70	379.3	22760	32.77	2.92	67.20	502.7	30160	43.43
2.43	51.02	381.7	22900	32.97	2.93	67.55	505.3	30310	43.66
2.44	51.33	384.0	23040	33.18	2.94	67.89	507.9	30470	43.88
2.45	51.65	386.4	23180	33.38	2.95	68.24	510.5	30630	44.10
2.46	51.96	388.7	23320	33.58	2.96	68.59	513.1	30780	44.33
2.47	52.28	391.1	23460	33.79	2.97	68.93	515.7	30940	44.55
2.48	52.60	393.5	23610	33.99	2.98	69.28	518.3	31090	44.78
2.49	52.92	395.9	23750	34.20	2.99	69.63	520.9	31250	45.00
2.50	53.24	398.3	23890	34.41	3.00	69.98	523.5	31410	45.23

11

11-7: 5 ft. Cipolletti Weir Discharge Table

Formulas: $CFS = 16.84\ H^{1.5}$ $GPS = CFS \times 7.481$

$GPM = CFS \times 448.8$ $MGD = CFS \times 0.6463$

Head Feet	CFS	GPS	GPM	MGD	Head Feet	CFS	GPS	GPM	MGD
0.01	0.0168	0.1260	7.558	0.0109	0.51	6.133	45.88	2753	3.964
0.02	0.0476	0.3563	21.38	0.0308	0.52	6.315	47.24	2834	4.081
0.03	0.0875	0.6546	39.27	0.0566	0.53	6.498	48.61	2916	4.199
0.04	0.1347	1.008	60.46	0.0871	0.54	6.682	49.99	2999	4.319
0.05	0.1883	1.408	84.50	0.1217	0.55	6.869	51.39	3083	4.439
0.06	0.2475	1.852	111.1	0.1600	0.56	7.057	52.79	3167	4.561
0.07	0.3119	2.333	140.0	0.2016	0.57	7.247	54.21	3252	4.684
0.08	0.3810	2.851	171.0	0.2463	0.58	7.438	55.65	3338	4.807
0.09	0.4547	3.401	204.1	0.2939	0.59	7.632	57.09	3425	4.932
0.10	0.5325	3.984	239.0	0.3442	0.60	7.827	58.55	3513	5.058
0.11	0.6144	4.596	275.7	0.3971	0.61	8.023	60.02	3601	5.185
0.12	0.7000	5.237	314.2	0.4524	0.62	8.221	61.50	3690	5.313
0.13	0.7893	5.905	354.3	0.5101	0.63	8.421	63.00	3779	5.442
0.14	0.8821	6.599	395.9	0.5701	0.64	8.622	64.50	3870	5.572
0.15	0.9783	7.319	439.1	0.6323	0.65	8.825	66.02	3961	5.704
0.16	1.078	8.063	483.7	0.6966	0.66	9.029	67.55	4052	5.836
0.17	1.180	8.830	529.7	0.7629	0.67	9.235	69.09	4145	5.969
0.18	1.286	9.621	577.2	0.8312	0.68	9.443	70.64	4238	6.103
0.19	1.395	10.43	625.9	0.9014	0.69	9.652	72.21	4332	6.238
0.20	1.506	11.27	676.0	0.9735	0.70	9.863	73.78	4426	6.374
0.21	1.621	12.12	727.3	1.047	0.71	10.07	75.37	4521	6.511
0.22	1.738	13.00	779.9	1.123	0.72	10.29	76.97	4617	6.649
0.23	1.858	13.90	833.7	1.201	0.73	10.50	78.58	4714	6.788
0.24	1.980	14.81	888.6	1.280	0.74	10.72	80.20	4811	6.928
0.25	2.105	15.75	944.7	1.360	0.75	10.94	81.83	4909	7.069
0.26	2.233	16.70	1002	1.443	0.76	11.16	83.47	5007	7.211
0.27	2.363	17.67	1060	1.527	0.77	11.38	85.12	5107	7.354
0.28	2.495	18.67	1120	1.613	0.78	11.60	86.78	5206	7.498
0.29	2.630	19.67	1180	1.700	0.79	11.82	88.46	5307	7.642
0.30	2.767	20.70	1242	1.788	0.80	12.05	90.14	5408	7.788
0.31	2.907	21.74	1304	1.879	0.81	12.28	91.84	5510	7.934
0.32	3.048	22.80	1368	1.970	0.82	12.50	93.55	5612	8.082
0.33	3.192	23.88	1433	2.063	0.83	12.73	95.26	5715	8.230
0.34	3.339	24.98	1498	2.158	0.84	12.96	96.99	5819	8.379
0.35	3.487	26.09	1565	2.254	0.85	13.20	98.73	5923	8.529
0.36	3.637	27.21	1632	2.351	0.86	13.43	100.5	6028	8.680
0.37	3.790	28.35	1701	2.450	0.87	13.67	102.2	6133	8.832
0.38	3.945	29.51	1770	2.549	0.88	13.90	104.0	6239	8.985
0.39	4.101	30.68	1841	2.651	0.89	14.14	105.8	6346	9.138
0.40	4.260	31.87	1912	2.753	0.90	14.38	107.6	6453	9.293
0.41	4.421	33.07	1984	2.857	0.91	14.62	109.4	6561	9.448
0.42	4.584	34.29	2057	2.962	0.92	14.86	111.2	6669	9.604
0.43	4.748	35.52	2131	3.069	0.93	15.10	113.0	6778	9.761
0.44	4.915	36.77	2206	3.177	0.94	15.35	114.8	6888	9.919
0.45	5.083	38.03	2281	3.285	0.95	15.59	116.7	6998	10.08
0.46	5.254	39.30	2358	3.396	0.96	15.84	118.5	7109	10.24
0.47	5.426	40.59	2435	3.507	0.97	16.09	120.4	7220	10.40
0.48	5.600	41.90	2513	3.619	0.98	16.34	122.2	7332	10.56
0.49	5.776	43.21	2592	3.733	0.99	16.59	124.1	7445	10.72
0.50	5.954	44.54	2672	3.848	1.00	16.84	126.0	7558	10.88

11

Formulas: CFS = 16.84 H$^{1.5}$ GPS = CFS x 7.481
GPM = CFS x 448.8   MGD = CFS x 0.6463

Head Feet	CFS	GPS	GPM	MGD	Head Feet	CFS	GPS	GPM	MGD
1.01	17.09	127.9	7671	11.05	1.51	31.25	233.8	14020	20.19
1.02	17.35	129.8	7786	11.21	1.52	31.56	236.1	14160	20.40
1.03	17.60	131.7	7900	11.38	1.53	31.87	238.4	14300	20.60
1.04	17.86	133.6	8016	11.54	1.54	32.18	240.8	14440	20.80
1.05	18.12	135.5	8132	11.71	1.55	32.50	243.1	14580	21.00
1.06	18.38	137.5	8248	11.88	1.56	32.81	245.5	14730	21.21
1.07	18.64	139.4	8365	12.05	1.57	33.13	247.8	14870	21.41
1.08	18.90	141.4	8483	12.22	1.58	33.44	250.2	15010	21.62
1.09	19.16	143.4	8601	12.39	1.59	33.76	252.6	15150	21.82
1.10	19.43	145.3	8719	12.56	1.60	34.08	255.0	15300	22.03
1.11	19.69	147.3	8839	12.73	1.61	34.40	257.4	15440	22.23
1.12	19.96	149.3	8958	12.90	1.62	34.72	259.8	15580	22.44
1.13	20.23	151.3	9078	13.07	1.63	35.04	262.2	15730	22.65
1.14	20.50	153.3	9199	13.25	1.64	35.37	264.6	15870	22.86
1.15	20.77	155.4	9321	13.42	1.65	35.69	267.0	16020	23.07
1.16	21.04	157.4	9442	13.60	1.66	36.02	269.4	16160	23.28
1.17	21.31	159.4	9565	13.77	1.67	36.34	271.9	16310	23.49
1.18	21.59	161.5	9688	13.95	1.68	36.67	274.3	16460	23.70
1.19	21.86	163.5	9811	14.13	1.69	37.00	276.8	16600	23.91
1.20	22.14	165.6	9935	14.31	1.70	37.33	279.2	16750	24.12
1.21	22.41	167.7	10060	14.49	1.71	37.66	281.7	16900	24.34
1.22	22.69	169.8	10180	14.67	1.72	37.99	284.2	17050	24.55
1.23	22.97	171.9	10310	14.85	1.73	38.32	286.7	17200	24.77
1.24	23.25	174.0	10440	15.03	1.74	38.65	289.2	17350	24.98
1.25	23.53	176.1	10560	15.21	1.75	38.99	291.6	17500	25.20
1.26	23.82	178.2	10690	15.39	1.76	39.32	294.2	17650	25.41
1.27	24.10	180.3	10820	15.58	1.77	39.66	296.7	17800	25.63
1.28	24.39	182.4	10940	15.76	1.78	39.99	299.2	17950	25.85
1.29	24.67	184.6	11070	15.95	1.79	40.33	301.7	18100	26.06
1.30	24.96	186.7	11200	16.13	1.80	40.67	304.2	18250	26.28
1.31	25.25	188.9	11330	16.32	1.81	41.01	306.8	18400	26.50
1.32	25.54	191.1	11460	16.51	1.82	41.35	309.3	18560	26.72
1.33	25.83	193.2	11590	16.69	1.83	41.69	311.9	18710	26.94
1.34	26.12	195.4	11720	16.88	1.84	42.03	314.4	18860	27.16
1.35	26.41	197.6	11850	17.07	1.85	42.37	317.0	19020	27.39
1.36	26.71	199.8	11990	17.26	1.86	42.72	319.6	19170	27.61
1.37	27.00	202.0	12120	17.45	1.87	43.06	322.2	19330	27.83
1.38	27.30	204.2	12250	17.64	1.88	43.41	324.7	19480	28.06
1.39	27.60	206.5	12390	17.84	1.89	43.76	327.3	19640	28.28
1.40	27.90	208.7	12520	18.03	1.90	44.10	329.9	19790	28.50
1.41	28.19	210.9	12650	18.22	1.91	44.45	332.5	19950	28.73
1.42	28.50	213.2	12790	18.42	1.92	44.80	335.2	20110	28.96
1.43	28.80	215.4	12920	18.61	1.93	45.15	337.8	20260	29.18
1.44	29.10	217.7	13060	18.81	1.94	45.50	340.4	20420	29.41
1.45	29.40	220.0	13200	19.00	1.95	45.86	343.0	20580	29.64
1.46	29.71	222.2	13330	19.20	1.96	46.21	345.7	20740	29.86
1.47	30.01	224.5	13470	19.40	1.97	46.56	348.3	20900	30.09
1.48	30.32	226.8	13610	19.60	1.98	46.92	351.0	21060	30.32
1.49	30.63	229.1	13750	19.80	1.99	47.27	353.7	21220	30.55
1.50	30.94	231.4	13880	19.99	2.00	47.63	356.3	21380	30.78

11

Formulas: $CFS = 16.84\ H^{1.5}$ $GPS = CFS \times 7.481$

$GPM = CFS \times 448.8$ $MGD = CFS \times 0.6463$

Head Feet	CFS	GPS	GPM	MGD	Head Feet	CFS	GPS	GPM	MGD
2.01	47.99	359.0	21540	31.01	2.51	66.97	501.0	30050	43.28
2.02	48.35	361.7	21700	31.25	2.52	67.37	504.0	30230	43.54
2.03	48.71	364.4	21860	31.48	2.53	67.77	507.0	30410	43.80
2.04	49.07	367.1	22020	31.71	2.54	68.17	510.0	30590	44.06
2.05	49.43	369.8	22180	31.95	2.55	68.57	513.0	30780	44.32
2.06	49.79	372.5	22350	32.18	2.56	68.98	516.0	30960	44.58
2.07	50.15	375.2	22510	32.41	2.57	69.38	519.0	31140	44.84
2.08	50.52	377.9	22670	32.65	2.58	69.79	522.1	31320	45.10
2.09	50.88	380.6	22840	32.88	2.59	70.19	525.1	31500	45.37
2.10	51.25	383.4	23000	33.12	2.60	70.60	528.2	31690	45.63
2.11	51.61	386.1	23160	33.36	2.61	71.01	531.2	31870	45.89
2.12	51.98	388.9	23330	33.60	2.62	71.42	534.3	32050	46.16
2.13	52.35	391.6	23490	33.83	2.63	71.83	537.3	32240	46.42
2.14	52.72	394.4	23660	34.07	2.64	72.24	540.4	32420	46.69
2.15	53.09	397.2	23830	34.31	2.65	72.65	543.5	32600	46.95
2.16	53.46	399.9	23990	34.55	2.66	73.06	546.5	32790	47.22
2.17	53.83	402.7	24160	34.79	2.67	73.47	549.6	32970	47.48
2.18	54.20	405.5	24330	35.03	2.68	73.88	552.7	33160	47.75
2.19	54.58	408.3	24490	35.27	2.69	74.30	555.8	33340	48.02
2.20	54.95	411.1	24660	35.51	2.70	74.71	558.9	33530	48.29
2.21	55.33	413.9	24830	35.76	2.71	75.13	562.0	33720	48.55
2.22	55.70	416.7	25000	36.00	2.72	75.54	565.1	33900	48.82
2.23	56.08	419.5	25170	36.24	2.73	75.96	568.3	34090	49.09
2.24	56.46	422.4	25340	36.49	2.74	76.38	571.4	34280	49.36
2.25	56.84	425.2	25510	36.73	2.75	76.80	574.5	34470	49.63
2.26	57.21	428.0	25680	36.98	2.76	77.22	577.7	34650	49.90
2.27	57.59	430.9	25850	37.22	2.77	77.64	580.8	34840	50.18
2.28	57.98	433.7	26020	37.47	2.78	78.06	583.9	35030	50.45
2.29	58.36	436.6	26190	37.72	2.79	78.48	587.1	35220	50.72
2.30	58.74	439.4	26360	37.96	2.80	78.90	590.3	35410	50.99
2.31	59.12	442.3	26530	38.21	2.81	79.32	593.4	35600	51.27
2.32	59.51	445.2	26710	38.46	2.82	79.75	596.6	35790	51.54
2.33	59.89	448.1	26880	38.71	2.83	80.17	599.8	35980	51.82
2.34	60.28	450.9	27050	38.96	2.84	80.60	602.9	36170	52.09
2.35	60.67	453.8	27230	39.21	2.85	81.02	606.1	36360	52.37
2.36	61.05	456.7	27400	39.46	2.86	81.45	609.3	36550	52.64
2.37	61.44	459.6	27580	39.71	2.87	81.88	612.5	36750	52.92
2.38	61.83	462.6	27750	39.96	2.88	82.31	615.7	36940	53.19
2.39	62.22	465.5	27920	40.21	2.89	82.73	618.9	37130	53.47
2.40	62.61	468.4	28100	40.47	2.90	83.16	622.2	37320	53.75
2.41	63.00	471.3	28280	40.72	2.91	83.60	625.4	37520	54.03
2.42	63.40	474.3	28450	40.97	2.92	84.03	628.6	37710	54.31
2.43	63.79	477.2	28630	41.23	2.93	84.46	631.8	37900	54.59
2.44	64.18	480.2	28810	41.48	2.94	84.89	635.1	38100	54.87
2.45	64.58	483.1	28980	41.74	2.95	85.32	638.3	38290	55.15
2.46	64.97	486.1	29160	41.99	2.96	85.76	641.6	38490	55.43
2.47	65.37	489.0	29340	42.25	2.97	86.19	644.8	38680	55.71
2.48	65.77	492.0	29520	42.51	2.98	86.63	648.1	38880	55.99
2.49	66.17	495.0	29700	42.76	2.99	87.07	651.3	39080	56.27
2.50	66.57	498.0	29870	43.02	3.00	87.50	654.6	39270	56.55

11

11-8: 6 ft. Cipolletti Weir Discharge Table

Formulas: CFS = 20.20 H$^{1.5}$ GPS = CFS x 7.481
          GPM = CFS x 448.8   MGD = CFS x 0.6463

Head Feet	CFS	GPS	GPM	MGD	Head Feet	CFS	GPS	GPM	MGD
0.01	0.0202	0.1511	9.066	0.0131	0.51	7.357	55.04	3302	4.755
0.02	0.0571	0.4274	25.64	0.0369	0.52	7.575	56.67	3399	4.895
0.03	0.1050	0.7852	47.11	0.0678	0.53	7.794	58.31	3498	5.037
0.04	0.1616	1.209	72.53	0.1044	0.54	8.016	59.97	3597	5.181
0.05	0.2258	1.690	101.4	0.1460	0.55	8.239	61.64	3698	5.325
0.06	0.2969	2.221	133.2	0.1919	0.56	8.465	63.33	3799	5.471
0.07	0.3741	2.799	167.9	0.2418	0.57	8.693	65.03	3901	5.618
0.08	0.4571	3.419	205.1	0.2954	0.58	8.923	66.75	4004	5.767
0.09	0.5454	4.080	244.8	0.3525	0.59	9.154	68.48	4108	5.916
0.10	0.6388	4.779	286.7	0.4128	0.60	9.388	70.23	4213	6.068
0.11	0.7370	5.513	330.7	0.4763	0.61	9.624	72.00	4319	6.220
0.12	0.8397	6.282	376.9	0.5427	0.62	9.861	73.77	4426	6.373
0.13	0.9468	7.083	424.9	0.6119	0.63	10.10	75.57	4533	6.528
0.14	1.058	7.916	474.9	0.6839	0.64	10.34	77.37	4642	6.684
0.15	1.174	8.779	526.7	0.7584	0.65	10.59	79.19	4751	6.842
0.16	1.293	9.671	580.2	0.8355	0.66	10.83	81.03	4861	7.000
0.17	1.416	10.59	635.4	0.9151	0.67	11.08	82.87	4972	7.160
0.18	1.543	11.54	692.3	0.9970	0.68	11.33	84.74	5084	7.321
0.19	1.673	12.52	750.8	1.081	0.69	11.58	86.61	5196	7.483
0.20	1.807	13.52	810.9	1.168	0.70	11.83	88.50	5309	7.646
0.21	1.944	14.54	872.4	1.256	0.71	12.08	90.41	5424	7.810
0.22	2.084	15.59	935.5	1.347	0.72	12.34	92.32	5539	7.976
0.23	2.228	16.67	1000	1.440	0.73	12.60	94.25	5654	8.143
0.24	2.375	17.77	1066	1.535	0.74	12.86	96.20	5771	8.311
0.25	2.525	18.89	1133	1.632	0.75	13.12	98.15	5888	8.480
0.26	2.678	20.03	1202	1.731	0.76	13.38	100.1	6007	8.650
0.27	2.834	21.20	1272	1.832	0.77	13.65	102.1	6125	8.821
0.28	2.993	22.39	1343	1.934	0.78	13.92	104.1	6245	8.993
0.29	3.155	23.60	1416	2.039	0.79	14.18	106.1	6366	9.167
0.30	3.319	24.83	1490	2.145	0.80	14.45	108.1	6487	9.342
0.31	3.487	26.08	1565	2.253	0.81	14.73	110.2	6609	9.517
0.32	3.657	27.35	1641	2.363	0.82	15.00	112.2	6732	9.694
0.33	3.829	28.65	1719	2.475	0.83	15.27	114.3	6855	9.872
0.34	4.005	29.96	1797	2.588	0.84	15.55	116.3	6979	10.05
0.35	4.183	31.29	1877	2.703	0.85	15.83	118.4	7104	10.23
0.36	4.363	32.64	1958	2.820	0.86	16.11	120.5	7230	10.41
0.37	4.546	34.01	2040	2.938	0.87	16.39	122.6	7357	10.59
0.38	4.732	35.40	2124	3.058	0.88	16.68	124.7	7484	10.78
0.39	4.920	36.81	2208	3.180	0.89	16.96	126.9	7612	10.96
0.40	5.110	38.23	2293	3.303	0.90	17.25	129.0	7740	11.15
0.41	5.303	39.67	2380	3.427	0.91	17.54	131.2	7870	11.33
0.42	5.498	41.13	2468	3.554	0.92	17.83	133.3	8000	11.52
0.43	5.696	42.61	2556	3.681	0.93	18.12	135.5	8131	11.71
0.44	5.896	44.11	2646	3.810	0.94	18.41	137.7	8262	11.90
0.45	6.098	45.62	2737	3.941	0.95	18.70	139.9	8394	12.09
0.46	6.302	47.15	2828	4.073	0.96	19.00	142.1	8527	12.28
0.47	6.509	48.69	2921	4.207	0.97	19.30	144.4	8661	12.47
0.48	6.718	50.25	3015	4.342	0.98	19.60	146.6	8795	12.67
0.49	6.929	51.83	3110	4.478	0.99	19.90	148.9	8930	12.86
0.50	7.142	53.43	3205	4.616	1.00	20.20	151.1	9066	13.06

11

Formulas: CFS = 20.20 H$^{1.5}$ GPS = CFS x 7.481
GPM = CFS x 448.8   MGD = CFS x 0.6463

Head Feet	CFS	GPS	GPM	MGD	Head Feet	CFS	GPS	GPM	MGD
1.01	20.50	153.4	9202	13.25	1.51	37.48	280.4	16820	24.22
1.02	20.81	155.7	9339	13.45	1.52	37.85	283.2	16990	24.47
1.03	21.12	158.0	9477	13.65	1.53	38.23	286.0	17160	24.71
1.04	21.42	160.3	9615	13.85	1.54	38.60	288.8	17330	24.95
1.05	21.73	162.6	9754	14.05	1.55	38.98	291.6	17490	25.19
1.06	22.05	164.9	9894	14.25	1.56	39.36	294.4	17660	25.44
1.07	22.36	167.3	10030	14.45	1.57	39.74	297.3	17830	25.68
1.08	22.67	169.6	10180	14.65	1.58	40.12	300.1	18000	25.93
1.09	22.99	172.0	10320	14.86	1.59	40.50	303.0	18180	26.17
1.10	23.30	174.3	10460	15.06	1.60	40.88	305.8	18350	26.42
1.11	23.62	176.7	10600	15.27	1.61	41.27	308.7	18520	26.67
1.12	23.94	179.1	10750	15.47	1.62	41.65	311.6	18690	26.92
1.13	24.26	181.5	10890	15.68	1.63	42.04	314.5	18870	27.17
1.14	24.59	183.9	11030	15.89	1.64	42.42	317.4	19040	27.42
1.15	24.91	186.4	11180	16.10	1.65	42.81	320.3	19210	27.67
1.16	25.24	188.8	11330	16.31	1.66	43.20	323.2	19390	27.92
1.17	25.56	191.2	11470	16.52	1.67	43.59	326.1	19560	28.17
1.18	25.89	193.7	11620	16.73	1.68	43.99	329.1	19740	28.43
1.19	26.22	196.2	11770	16.95	1.69	44.38	332.0	19920	28.68
1.20	26.55	198.6	11920	17.16	1.70	44.77	335.0	20090	28.94
1.21	26.89	201.1	12070	17.38	1.71	45.17	337.9	20270	29.19
1.22	27.22	203.6	12220	17.59	1.72	45.57	340.9	20450	29.45
1.23	27.56	206.1	12370	17.81	1.73	45.96	343.9	20630	29.71
1.24	27.89	208.7	12520	18.03	1.74	46.36	346.8	20810	29.96
1.25	28.23	211.2	12670	18.25	1.75	46.76	349.8	20990	30.22
1.26	28.57	213.7	12820	18.46	1.76	47.17	352.8	21170	30.48
1.27	28.91	216.3	12980	18.68	1.77	47.57	355.9	21350	30.74
1.28	29.25	218.8	13130	18.91	1.78	47.97	358.9	21530	31.00
1.29	29.60	221.4	13280	19.13	1.79	48.38	361.9	21710	31.27
1.30	29.94	224.0	13440	19.35	1.80	48.78	364.9	21890	31.53
1.31	30.29	226.6	13590	19.57	1.81	49.19	368.0	22080	31.79
1.32	30.63	229.2	13750	19.80	1.82	49.60	371.0	22260	32.05
1.33	30.98	231.8	13910	20.02	1.83	50.01	374.1	22440	32.32
1.34	31.33	234.4	14060	20.25	1.84	50.42	377.2	22630	32.58
1.35	31.68	237.0	14220	20.48	1.85	50.83	380.2	22810	32.85
1.36	32.04	239.7	14380	20.71	1.86	51.24	383.3	23000	33.12
1.37	32.39	242.3	14540	20.93	1.87	51.66	386.4	23180	33.38
1.38	32.75	245.0	14700	21.16	1.88	52.07	389.5	23370	33.65
1.39	33.10	247.6	14860	21.39	1.89	52.49	392.6	23560	33.92
1.40	33.46	250.3	15020	21.63	1.90	52.90	395.8	23740	34.19
1.41	33.82	253.0	15180	21.86	1.91	53.32	398.9	23930	34.46
1.42	34.18	255.7	15340	22.09	1.92	53.74	402.0	24120	34.73
1.43	34.54	258.4	15500	22.32	1.93	54.16	405.2	24310	35.00
1.44	34.91	261.1	15670	22.56	1.94	54.58	408.3	24500	35.28
1.45	35.27	263.9	15830	22.79	1.95	55.01	411.5	24690	35.55
1.46	35.64	266.6	15990	23.03	1.96	55.43	414.7	24880	35.82
1.47	36.00	269.3	16160	23.27	1.97	55.85	417.8	25070	36.10
1.48	36.37	272.1	16320	23.51	1.98	56.28	421.0	25260	36.37
1.49	36.74	274.8	16490	23.74	1.99	56.71	424.2	25450	36.65
1.50	37.11	277.6	16650	23.98	2.00	57.13	427.4	25640	36.93

Formulas: CFS = 20.20 H$^{1.5}$ GPS = CFS x 7.481
            GPM = CFS x 448.8   MGD = CFS x 0.6463

Head Feet	CFS	GPS	GPM	MGD	Head Feet	CFS	GPS	GPM	MGD
2.01	57.56	430.6	25830	37.20	2.51	80.33	600.9	36050	51.92
2.02	57.99	433.8	26030	37.48	2.52	80.81	604.5	36270	52.23
2.03	58.42	437.1	26220	37.76	2.53	81.29	608.1	36480	52.54
2.04	58.86	440.3	26410	38.04	2.54	81.77	611.7	36700	52.85
2.05	59.29	443.5	26610	38.32	2.55	82.25	615.3	36920	53.16
2.06	59.72	446.8	26800	38.60	2.56	82.74	619.0	37130	53.47
2.07	60.16	450.1	27000	38.88	2.57	83.22	622.6	37350	53.79
2.08	60.60	453.3	27200	39.16	2.58	83.71	626.2	37570	54.10
2.09	61.03	456.6	27390	39.45	2.59	84.20	629.9	37790	54.42
2.10	61.47	459.9	27590	39.73	2.60	84.69	633.5	38010	54.73
2.11	61.91	463.2	27790	40.01	2.61	85.17	637.2	38230	55.05
2.12	62.35	466.5	27980	40.30	2.62	85.66	640.9	38450	55.37
2.13	62.79	469.8	28180	40.58	2.63	86.16	644.5	38670	55.68
2.14	63.24	473.1	28380	40.87	2.64	86.65	648.2	38890	56.00
2.15	63.68	476.4	28580	41.16	2.65	87.14	651.9	39110	56.32
2.16	64.13	479.7	28780	41.44	2.66	87.63	655.6	39330	56.64
2.17	64.57	483.1	28980	41.73	2.67	88.13	659.3	39550	56.96
2.18	65.02	486.4	29180	42.02	2.68	88.62	663.0	39770	57.28
2.19	65.47	489.8	29380	42.31	2.69	89.12	666.7	40000	57.60
2.20	65.92	493.1	29580	42.60	2.70	89.62	670.4	40220	57.92
2.21	66.37	496.5	29780	42.89	2.71	90.12	674.2	40440	58.24
2.22	66.82	499.9	29990	43.18	2.72	90.62	677.9	40670	58.57
2.23	67.27	503.2	30190	43.48	2.73	91.12	681.6	40890	58.89
2.24	67.72	506.6	30390	43.77	2.74	91.62	685.4	41120	59.21
2.25	68.17	510.0	30600	44.06	2.75	92.12	689.1	41340	59.54
2.26	68.63	513.4	30800	44.36	2.76	92.62	692.9	41570	59.86
2.27	69.09	516.8	31010	44.65	2.77	93.13	696.7	41790	60.19
2.28	69.54	520.3	31210	44.95	2.78	93.63	700.5	42020	60.51
2.29	70.00	523.7	31420	45.24	2.79	94.14	704.2	42250	60.84
2.30	70.46	527.1	31620	45.54	2.80	94.64	708.0	42480	61.17
2.31	70.92	530.6	31830	45.84	2.81	95.15	711.8	42700	61.50
2.32	71.38	534.0	32040	46.13	2.82	95.66	715.6	42930	61.82
2.33	71.84	537.5	32240	46.43	2.83	96.17	719.4	43160	62.15
2.34	72.31	540.9	32450	46.73	2.84	96.68	723.3	43390	62.48
2.35	72.77	544.4	32660	47.03	2.85	97.19	727.1	43620	62.81
2.36	73.24	547.9	32870	47.33	2.86	97.70	730.9	43850	63.14
2.37	73.70	551.4	33080	47.63	2.87	98.21	734.7	44080	63.48
2.38	74.17	554.9	33290	47.93	2.88	98.73	738.6	44310	63.81
2.39	74.64	558.4	33500	48.24	2.89	99.24	742.4	44540	64.14
2.40	75.10	561.9	33710	48.54	2.90	99.76	746.3	44770	64.47
2.41	75.57	565.4	33920	48.84	2.91	100.3	750.2	45000	64.81
2.42	76.05	568.9	34130	49.15	2.92	100.8	754.0	45240	65.14
2.43	76.52	572.4	34340	49.45	2.93	101.3	757.9	45470	65.48
2.44	76.99	576.0	34550	49.76	2.94	101.8	761.8	45700	65.81
2.45	77.46	579.5	34770	50.07	2.95	102.3	765.7	45930	66.15
2.46	77.94	583.1	34980	50.37	2.96	102.9	769.6	46170	66.48
2.47	78.41	586.6	35190	50.68	2.97	103.4	773.5	46400	66.82
2.48	78.89	590.2	35410	50.99	2.98	103.9	777.4	46640	67.16
2.49	79.37	593.8	35620	51.30	2.99	104.4	781.3	46870	67.50
2.50	79.85	597.3	35840	51.61	3.00	105.0	785.2	47110	67.84

11

11-9: 8 ft. Cipolletti Weir Discharge Table

Formulas: CFS = 26.94 H$^{1.5}$ GPS = CFS x 7.481
           GPM = CFS x 448.8   MGD = CFS x 0.6463

Head Feet	CFS	GPS	GPM	MGD	Head Feet	CFS	GPS	GPM	MGD
0.01	0.0269	0.2015	12.09	0.0174	0.51	9.812	73.40	4404	6.341
0.02	0.0762	0.5700	34.20	0.0492	0.52	10.10	75.57	4534	6.529
0.03	0.1400	1.047	62.82	0.0905	0.53	10.39	77.76	4665	6.718
0.04	0.2155	1.612	96.73	0.1393	0.54	10.69	79.97	4798	6.909
0.05	0.3012	2.253	135.2	0.1947	0.55	10.99	82.21	4932	7.102
0.06	0.3959	2.962	177.7	0.2559	0.56	11.29	84.46	5067	7.296
0.07	0.4989	3.733	223.9	0.3225	0.57	11.59	86.73	5203	7.493
0.08	0.6096	4.560	273.6	0.3940	0.58	11.90	89.02	5341	7.691
0.09	0.7274	5.442	326.4	0.4701	0.59	12.21	91.33	5479	7.891
0.10	0.8519	6.373	382.3	0.5506	0.60	12.52	93.67	5619	8.092
0.11	0.9828	7.353	441.1	0.6352	0.61	12.83	96.02	5760	8.295
0.12	1.120	8.378	502.6	0.7238	0.62	13.15	98.39	5903	8.500
0.13	1.263	9.447	566.7	0.8161	0.63	13.47	100.8	6046	8.706
0.14	1.411	10.56	633.3	0.9121	0.64	13.79	103.2	6190	8.915
0.15	1.565	11.71	702.4	1.012	0.65	14.12	105.6	6336	9.124
0.16	1.724	12.90	773.8	1.114	0.66	14.44	108.1	6483	9.336
0.17	1.888	14.13	847.5	1.220	0.67	14.77	110.5	6631	9.549
0.18	2.057	15.39	923.3	1.330	0.68	15.11	113.0	6780	9.763
0.19	2.231	16.69	1001	1.442	0.69	15.44	115.5	6930	9.979
0.20	2.410	18.03	1081	1.557	0.70	15.78	118.0	7081	10.20
0.21	2.593	19.39	1164	1.676	0.71	16.12	120.6	7233	10.42
0.22	2.780	20.80	1248	1.797	0.72	16.46	123.1	7387	10.64
0.23	2.972	22.23	1334	1.921	0.73	16.80	125.7	7541	10.86
0.24	3.167	23.70	1422	2.047	0.74	17.15	128.3	7697	11.08
0.25	3.368	25.19	1511	2.176	0.75	17.50	130.9	7853	11.31
0.26	3.572	26.72	1603	2.308	0.76	17.85	133.5	8011	11.54
0.27	3.780	28.28	1696	2.443	0.77	18.20	136.2	8169	11.76
0.28	3.991	29.86	1791	2.580	0.78	18.56	138.8	8329	11.99
0.29	4.207	31.47	1888	2.719	0.79	18.92	141.5	8490	12.23
0.30	4.427	33.12	1987	2.861	0.80	19.28	144.2	8651	12.46
0.31	4.650	34.79	2087	3.005	0.81	19.64	146.9	8814	12.69
0.32	4.877	36.48	2189	3.152	0.82	20.00	149.7	8978	12.93
0.33	5.107	38.21	2292	3.301	0.83	20.37	152.4	9143	13.17
0.34	5.341	39.96	2397	3.452	0.84	20.74	155.2	9308	13.40
0.35	5.578	41.73	2504	3.605	0.85	21.11	157.9	9475	13.64
0.36	5.819	43.53	2612	3.761	0.86	21.49	160.7	9643	13.89
0.37	6.063	45.36	2721	3.919	0.87	21.86	163.5	9811	14.13
0.38	6.311	47.21	2832	4.079	0.88	22.24	166.4	9981	14.37
0.39	6.561	49.09	2945	4.241	0.89	22.62	169.2	10150	14.62
0.40	6.815	50.99	3059	4.405	0.90	23.00	172.1	10320	14.87
0.41	7.073	52.91	3174	4.571	0.91	23.39	175.0	10500	15.11
0.42	7.333	54.86	3291	4.739	0.92	23.77	177.8	10670	15.36
0.43	7.596	56.83	3409	4.909	0.93	24.16	180.8	10840	15.62
0.44	7.863	58.82	3529	5.082	0.94	24.55	183.7	11020	15.87
0.45	8.132	60.84	3650	5.256	0.95	24.94	186.6	11200	16.12
0.46	8.405	62.88	3772	5.432	0.96	25.34	189.6	11370	16.38
0.47	8.680	64.94	3896	5.610	0.97	25.74	192.5	11550	16.63
0.48	8.959	67.02	4021	5.790	0.98	26.14	195.5	11730	16.89
0.49	9.240	69.13	4147	5.972	0.99	26.54	198.5	11910	17.15
0.50	9.525	71.25	4275	6.156	1.00	26.94	201.5	12090	17.41

11

Formulas: $CFS = 26.94\ H^{1.5}$ $GPS = CFS \times 7.481$

$GPM = CFS \times 448.8$ $MGD = CFS \times 0.6463$

Head Feet	CFS	GPS	GPM	MGD	Head Feet	CFS	GPS	GPM	MGD
1.01	27.35	204.6	12270	17.67	1.51	49.99	374.0	22430	32.31
1.02	27.75	207.6	12460	17.94	1.52	50.49	377.7	22660	32.63
1.03	28.16	210.7	12640	18.20	1.53	50.98	381.4	22880	32.95
1.04	28.57	213.8	12820	18.47	1.54	51.48	385.2	23110	33.27
1.05	28.99	216.8	13010	18.73	1.55	51.99	388.9	23330	33.60
1.06	29.40	219.9	13190	19.00	1.56	52.49	392.7	23560	33.92
1.07	29.82	223.1	13380	19.27	1.57	53.00	396.5	23780	34.25
1.08	30.24	226.2	13570	19.54	1.58	53.50	400.3	24010	34.58
1.09	30.66	229.3	13760	19.81	1.59	54.01	404.1	24240	34.91
1.10	31.08	232.5	13950	20.09	1.60	54.52	407.9	24470	35.24
1.11	31.51	235.7	14140	20.36	1.61	55.03	411.7	24700	35.57
1.12	31.93	238.9	14330	20.64	1.62	55.55	415.6	24930	35.90
1.13	32.36	242.1	14520	20.91	1.63	56.06	419.4	25160	36.23
1.14	32.79	245.3	14720	21.19	1.64	56.58	423.3	25390	36.57
1.15	33.22	248.5	14910	21.47	1.65	57.10	427.2	25630	36.90
1.16	33.66	251.8	15110	21.75	1.66	57.62	431.0	25860	37.24
1.17	34.09	255.1	15300	22.03	1.67	58.14	434.9	26090	37.58
1.18	34.53	258.3	15500	22.32	1.68	58.66	438.9	26330	37.91
1.19	34.97	261.6	15700	22.60	1.69	59.19	442.8	26560	38.25
1.20	35.41	264.9	15890	22.89	1.70	59.71	446.7	26800	38.59
1.21	35.86	268.2	16090	23.17	1.71	60.24	450.7	27040	38.93
1.22	36.30	271.6	16290	23.46	1.72	60.77	454.6	27270	39.28
1.23	36.75	274.9	16490	23.75	1.73	61.30	458.6	27510	39.62
1.24	37.20	278.3	16690	24.04	1.74	61.83	462.6	27750	39.96
1.25	37.65	281.7	16900	24.33	1.75	62.37	466.6	27990	40.31
1.26	38.10	285.0	17100	24.63	1.76	62.90	470.6	28230	40.65
1.27	38.56	288.4	17300	24.92	1.77	63.44	474.6	28470	41.00
1.28	39.01	291.9	17510	25.21	1.78	63.98	478.6	28710	41.35
1.29	39.47	295.3	17710	25.51	1.79	64.52	482.7	28960	41.70
1.30	39.93	298.7	17920	25.81	1.80	65.06	486.7	29200	42.05
1.31	40.39	302.2	18130	26.11	1.81	65.60	490.8	29440	42.40
1.32	40.86	305.6	18340	26.41	1.82	66.15	494.8	29690	42.75
1.33	41.32	309.1	18550	26.71	1.83	66.69	498.9	29930	43.10
1.34	41.79	312.6	18750	27.01	1.84	67.24	503.0	30180	43.46
1.35	42.26	316.1	18960	27.31	1.85	67.79	507.1	30420	43.81
1.36	42.73	319.6	19180	27.61	1.86	68.34	511.2	30670	44.17
1.37	43.20	323.2	19390	27.92	1.87	68.89	515.4	30920	44.52
1.38	43.67	326.7	19600	28.23	1.88	69.44	519.5	31170	44.88
1.39	44.15	330.3	19810	28.53	1.89	70.00	523.7	31420	45.24
1.40	44.63	333.8	20030	28.84	1.90	70.56	527.8	31670	45.60
1.41	45.11	337.4	20240	29.15	1.91	71.11	532.0	31920	45.96
1.42	45.59	341.0	20460	29.46	1.92	71.67	536.2	32170	46.32
1.43	46.07	344.6	20680	29.77	1.93	72.23	540.4	32420	46.68
1.44	46.55	348.3	20890	30.09	1.94	72.79	544.6	32670	47.05
1.45	47.04	351.9	21110	30.40	1.95	73.36	548.8	32920	47.41
1.46	47.53	355.5	21330	30.72	1.96	73.92	553.0	33180	47.78
1.47	48.01	359.2	21550	31.03	1.97	74.49	557.3	33430	48.14
1.48	48.51	362.9	21770	31.35	1.98	75.06	561.5	33690	48.51
1.49	49.00	366.6	21990	31.67	1.99	75.63	565.8	33940	48.88
1.50	49.49	370.2	22210	31.99	2.00	76.20	570.0	34200	49.25

11

11-9: 8 ft. Cipolletti Weir Discharge Table *(Continued)*

Formulas: CFS = 26.94 H$^{1.5}$ GPS = CFS x 7.481
GPM = CFS x 448.8   MGD = CFS x 0.6463

Head Feet	CFS	GPS	GPM	MGD	Head Feet	CFS	GPS	GPM	MGD
2.01	76.77	574.3	34450	49.62	2.51	107.1	801.4	48080	69.24
2.02	77.34	578.6	34710	49.99	2.52	107.8	806.2	48370	69.65
2.03	77.92	582.9	34970	50.36	2.53	108.4	811.0	48660	70.07
2.04	78.50	587.2	35230	50.73	2.54	109.1	815.8	48940	70.48
2.05	79.07	591.5	35490	51.10	2.55	109.7	820.7	49230	70.90
2.06	79.65	595.9	35750	51.48	2.56	110.3	825.5	49520	71.32
2.07	80.23	600.2	36010	51.85	2.57	111.0	830.3	49810	71.74
2.08	80.82	604.6	36270	52.23	2.58	111.6	835.2	50100	72.15
2.09	81.40	608.9	36530	52.61	2.59	112.3	840.1	50400	72.57
2.10	81.98	613.3	36790	52.99	2.60	112.9	844.9	50690	72.99
2.11	82.57	617.7	37060	53.36	2.61	113.6	849.8	50980	73.42
2.12	83.16	622.1	37320	53.74	2.62	114.2	854.7	51270	73.84
2.13	83.75	626.5	37590	54.13	2.63	114.9	859.6	51570	74.26
2.14	84.34	630.9	37850	54.51	2.64	115.6	864.5	51860	74.69
2.15	84.93	635.4	38120	54.89	2.65	116.2	869.4	52160	75.11
2.16	85.52	639.8	38380	55.27	2.66	116.9	874.3	52450	75.54
2.17	86.12	644.2	38650	55.66	2.67	117.5	879.3	52750	75.96
2.18	86.71	648.7	38920	56.04	2.68	118.2	884.2	53050	76.39
2.19	87.31	653.2	39180	56.43	2.69	118.9	889.2	53340	76.82
2.20	87.91	657.6	39450	56.82	2.70	119.5	894.1	53640	77.25
2.21	88.51	662.1	39720	57.20	2.71	120.2	899.1	53940	77.68
2.22	89.11	666.6	39990	57.59	2.72	120.9	904.1	54240	78.11
2.23	89.71	671.1	40260	57.98	2.73	121.5	909.1	54540	78.54
2.24	90.32	675.7	40530	58.37	2.74	122.2	914.1	54840	78.97
2.25	90.92	680.2	40810	58.76	2.75	122.9	919.1	55140	79.40
2.26	91.53	684.7	41080	59.16	2.76	123.5	924.1	55440	79.84
2.27	92.14	689.3	41350	59.55	2.77	124.2	929.1	55740	80.27
2.28	92.75	693.8	41620	59.94	2.78	124.9	934.2	56040	80.70
2.29	93.36	698.4	41900	60.34	2.79	125.5	939.2	56350	81.14
2.30	93.97	703.0	42170	60.73	2.80	126.2	944.3	56650	81.58
2.31	94.58	707.6	42450	61.13	2.81	126.9	949.3	56950	82.01
2.32	95.20	712.2	42730	61.53	2.82	127.6	954.4	57260	82.45
2.33	95.81	716.8	43000	61.92	2.83	128.3	959.5	57560	82.89
2.34	96.43	721.4	43280	62.32	2.84	128.9	964.6	57870	83.33
2.35	97.05	726.0	43560	62.72	2.85	129.6	969.7	58170	83.77
2.36	97.67	730.7	43830	63.12	2.86	130.3	974.8	58480	84.21
2.37	98.29	735.3	44110	63.53	2.87	131.0	979.9	58790	84.66
2.38	98.92	740.0	44390	63.93	2.88	131.7	985.0	59090	85.10
2.39	99.54	744.7	44670	64.33	2.89	132.4	990.2	59400	85.54
2.40	100.2	749.3	44950	64.74	2.90	133.0	995.3	59710	85.99
2.41	100.8	754.0	45240	65.14	2.91	133.7	1000	60020	86.43
2.42	101.4	758.7	45520	65.55	2.92	134.4	1006	60330	86.88
2.43	102.0	763.4	45800	65.95	2.93	135.1	1011	60640	87.32
2.44	102.7	768.1	46080	66.36	2.94	135.8	1016	60950	87.77
2.45	103.3	772.9	46370	66.77	2.95	136.5	1021	61260	88.22
2.46	103.9	777.6	46650	67.18	2.96	137.2	1026	61570	88.67
2.47	104.6	782.4	46930	67.59	2.97	137.9	1032	61880	89.12
2.48	105.2	787.1	47220	68.00	2.98	138.6	1037	62200	89.57
2.49	105.9	791.9	47510	68.41	2.99	139.3	1042	62510	90.02
2.50	106.5	796.6	47790	68.82	3.00	140.0	1047	62820	90.47

11-10: 10 ft. Cipolletti Weir Discharge Table

Formulas: CFS = $33.67\ H^{1.5}$ GPS = CFS x 7.481

GPM = CFS x 448.8 MGD = CFS x 0.6463

Head Feet	CFS	GPS	GPM	MGD	Head Feet	CFS	GPS	GPM	MGD
0.01	0.0337	0.2519	15.11	0.0218	0.51	12.26	91.74	5504	7.926
0.02	0.0952	0.7124	42.74	0.0615	0.52	12.63	94.45	5666	8.160
0.03	0.1750	1.309	78.52	0.1131	0.53	12.99	97.19	5831	8.396
0.04	0.2694	2.015	120.9	0.1741	0.54	13.36	99.95	5996	8.635
0.05	0.3764	2.816	168.9	0.2433	0.55	13.73	102.7	6164	8.876
0.06	0.4948	3.702	222.1	0.3198	0.56	14.11	105.6	6333	9.119
0.07	0.6236	4.665	279.9	0.4030	0.57	14.49	108.4	6503	9.365
0.08	0.7619	5.700	341.9	0.4924	0.58	14.87	111.3	6675	9.612
0.09	0.9091	6.801	408.0	0.5875	0.59	15.26	114.2	6848	9.862
0.10	1.065	7.965	477.9	0.6881	0.60	15.65	117.1	7023	10.11
0.11	1.228	9.189	551.3	0.7939	0.61	16.04	120.0	7199	10.37
0.12	1.400	10.47	628.2	0.9046	0.62	16.44	123.0	7377	10.62
0.13	1.578	11.81	708.3	1.020	0.63	16.84	126.0	7556	10.88
0.14	1.764	13.19	791.6	1.140	0.64	17.24	129.0	7737	11.14
0.15	1.956	14.63	877.9	1.264	0.65	17.64	132.0	7919	11.40
0.16	2.155	16.12	967.1	1.393	0.66	18.05	135.1	8102	11.67
0.17	2.360	17.66	1059	1.525	0.67	18.47	138.1	8287	11.93
0.18	2.571	19.24	1154	1.662	0.68	18.88	141.2	8473	12.20
0.19	2.789	20.86	1251	1.802	0.69	19.30	144.4	8661	12.47
0.20	3.012	22.53	1352	1.946	0.70	19.72	147.5	8850	12.74
0.21	3.240	24.24	1454	2.094	0.71	20.14	150.7	9040	13.02
0.22	3.474	25.99	1559	2.245	0.72	20.57	153.9	9232	13.29
0.23	3.714	27.78	1667	2.400	0.73	21.00	157.1	9425	13.57
0.24	3.959	29.62	1777	2.559	0.74	21.43	160.3	9619	13.85
0.25	4.209	31.49	1889	2.720	0.75	21.87	163.6	9815	14.13
0.26	4.464	33.39	2003	2.885	0.76	22.31	166.9	10010	14.42
0.27	4.724	35.34	2120	3.053	0.77	22.75	170.2	10210	14.70
0.28	4.989	37.32	2239	3.224	0.78	23.19	173.5	10410	14.99
0.29	5.258	39.34	2360	3.398	0.79	23.64	176.9	10610	15.28
0.30	5.533	41.39	2483	3.576	0.80	24.09	180.2	10810	15.57
0.31	5.811	43.48	2608	3.756	0.81	24.55	183.6	11020	15.86
0.32	6.095	45.60	2735	3.939	0.82	25.00	187.0	11220	16.16
0.33	6.383	47.75	2865	4.125	0.83	25.46	190.5	11430	16.45
0.34	6.675	49.94	2996	4.314	0.84	25.92	193.9	11630	16.75
0.35	6.972	52.16	3129	4.506	0.85	26.39	197.4	11840	17.05
0.36	7.273	54.41	3264	4.700	0.86	26.85	200.9	12050	17.36
0.37	7.578	56.69	3401	4.898	0.87	27.32	204.4	12260	17.66
0.38	7.887	59.00	3540	5.097	0.88	27.80	207.9	12470	17.96
0.39	8.200	61.35	3680	5.300	0.89	28.27	211.5	12690	18.27
0.40	8.518	63.72	3823	5.505	0.90	28.75	215.1	12900	18.58
0.41	8.839	66.13	3967	5.713	0.91	29.23	218.7	13120	18.89
0.42	9.165	68.56	4113	5.923	0.92	29.71	222.3	13330	19.20
0.43	9.494	71.02	4261	6.136	0.93	30.20	225.9	13550	19.52
0.44	9.827	73.52	4410	6.351	0.94	30.69	229.6	13770	19.83
0.45	10.16	76.04	4562	6.569	0.95	31.18	233.2	13990	20.15
0.46	10.50	78.58	4714	6.789	0.96	31.67	236.9	14210	20.47
0.47	10.85	81.16	4869	7.012	0.97	32.17	240.6	14440	20.79
0.48	11.20	83.77	5025	7.237	0.98	32.66	244.4	14660	21.11
0.49	11.55	86.40	5183	7.464	0.99	33.17	248.1	14880	21.44
0.50	11.90	89.05	5343	7.694	1.00	33.67	251.9	15110	21.76

11

Formulas: $CFS = 33.67 \, H^{1.5}$ $GPS = CFS \times 7.481$
$GPM = CFS \times 448.8$ $MGD = CFS \times 0.6463$

Head Feet	CFS	GPS	GPM	MGD	Head Feet	CFS	GPS	GPM	MGD
1.01	34.18	255.7	15340	22.09	1.51	62.48	467.4	28040	40.38
1.02	34.69	259.5	15570	22.42	1.52	63.10	472.0	28320	40.78
1.03	35.20	263.3	15800	22.75	1.53	63.72	476.7	28600	41.18
1.04	35.71	267.1	16030	23.08	1.54	64.35	481.4	28880	41.59
1.05	36.23	271.0	16260	23.41	1.55	64.97	486.1	29160	41.99
1.06	36.75	274.9	16490	23.75	1.56	65.60	490.8	29440	42.40
1.07	37.27	278.8	16730	24.09	1.57	66.24	495.5	29730	42.81
1.08	37.79	282.7	16960	24.42	1.58	66.87	500.3	30010	43.22
1.09	38.32	286.6	17200	24.76	1.59	67.51	505.0	30300	43.63
1.10	38.84	290.6	17430	25.11	1.60	68.14	509.8	30580	44.04
1.11	39.38	294.6	17670	25.45	1.61	68.78	514.6	30870	44.45
1.12	39.91	298.6	17910	25.79	1.62	69.42	519.4	31160	44.87
1.13	40.44	302.6	18150	26.14	1.63	70.07	524.2	31450	45.29
1.14	40.98	306.6	18390	26.49	1.64	70.71	529.0	31740	45.70
1.15	41.52	310.6	18640	26.84	1.65	71.36	533.9	32030	46.12
1.16	42.07	314.7	18880	27.19	1.66	72.01	538.7	32320	46.54
1.17	42.61	318.8	19120	27.54	1.67	72.66	543.6	32610	46.96
1.18	43.16	322.9	19370	27.89	1.68	73.32	548.5	32900	47.39
1.19	43.71	327.0	19620	28.25	1.69	73.97	553.4	33200	47.81
1.20	44.26	331.1	19860	28.61	1.70	74.63	558.3	33490	48.23
1.21	44.81	335.3	20110	28.96	1.71	75.29	563.2	33790	48.66
1.22	45.37	339.4	20360	29.32	1.72	75.95	568.2	34090	49.09
1.23	45.93	343.6	20610	29.68	1.73	76.61	573.2	34380	49.52
1.24	46.49	347.8	20870	30.05	1.74	77.28	578.1	34680	49.95
1.25	47.06	352.0	21120	30.41	1.75	77.95	583.1	34980	50.38
1.26	47.62	356.3	21370	30.78	1.76	78.62	588.1	35280	50.81
1.27	48.19	360.5	21630	31.14	1.77	79.29	593.1	35580	51.24
1.28	48.76	364.8	21880	31.51	1.78	79.96	598.2	35890	51.68
1.29	49.33	369.1	22140	31.88	1.79	80.63	603.2	36190	52.11
1.30	49.91	373.4	22400	32.25	1.80	81.31	608.3	36490	52.55
1.31	50.48	377.7	22660	32.63	1.81	81.99	613.4	36800	52.99
1.32	51.06	382.0	22920	33.00	1.82	82.67	618.5	37100	53.43
1.33	51.64	386.3	23180	33.38	1.83	83.35	623.6	37410	53.87
1.34	52.23	390.7	23440	33.75	1.84	84.04	628.7	37720	54.31
1.35	52.81	395.1	23700	34.13	1.85	84.72	633.8	38020	54.76
1.36	53.40	399.5	23970	34.51	1.86	85.41	639.0	38330	55.20
1.37	53.99	403.9	24230	34.89	1.87	86.10	644.1	38640	55.65
1.38	54.58	408.3	24500	35.28	1.88	86.79	649.3	38950	56.09
1.39	55.18	412.8	24760	35.66	1.89	87.49	654.5	39260	56.54
1.40	55.77	417.2	25030	36.05	1.90	88.18	659.7	39580	56.99
1.41	56.37	421.7	25300	36.43	1.91	88.88	664.9	39890	57.44
1.42	56.97	426.2	25570	36.82	1.92	89.58	670.1	40200	57.89
1.43	57.58	430.7	25840	37.21	1.93	90.28	675.4	40520	58.35
1.44	58.18	435.3	26110	37.60	1.94	90.98	680.6	40830	58.80
1.45	58.79	439.8	26380	38.00	1.95	91.68	685.9	41150	59.26
1.46	59.40	444.4	26660	38.39	1.96	92.39	691.2	41460	59.71
1.47	60.01	448.9	26930	38.78	1.97	93.10	696.5	41780	60.17
1.48	60.62	453.5	27210	39.18	1.98	93.81	701.8	42100	60.63
1.49	61.24	458.1	27480	39.58	1.99	94.52	707.1	42420	61.09
1.50	61.86	462.7	27760	39.98	2.00	95.23	712.4	42740	61.55

11-10: 10 ft. Cipolletti Weir Discharge Table (Continued)

Formulas: $CFS = 33.67\ H^{1.5}$ $GPS = CFS \times 7.481$
$GPM = CFS \times 448.8$ $MGD = CFS \times 0.6463$

Head Feet	CFS	GPS	GPM	MGD	Head Feet	CFS	GPS	GPM	MGD
2.01	95.95	717.8	43060	62.01	2.51	133.9	1002	60090	86.53
2.02	96.67	723.2	43380	62.47	2.52	134.7	1008	60450	87.05
2.03	97.38	728.5	43710	62.94	2.53	135.5	1014	60810	87.57
2.04	98.10	733.9	44030	63.40	2.54	136.3	1020	61170	88.09
2.05	98.83	739.3	44350	63.87	2.55	137.1	1026	61530	88.61
2.06	99.55	744.7	44680	64.34	2.56	137.9	1032	61900	89.13
2.07	100.3	750.2	45000	64.81	2.57	138.7	1038	62260	89.66
2.08	101.0	755.6	45330	65.28	2.58	139.5	1044	62620	90.18
2.09	101.7	761.1	45660	65.75	2.59	140.3	1050	62990	90.70
2.10	102.5	766.5	45990	66.22	2.60	141.2	1056	63350	91.23
2.11	103.2	772.0	46310	66.70	2.61	142.0	1062	63720	91.76
2.12	103.9	777.5	46640	67.17	2.62	142.8	1068	64080	92.28
2.13	104.7	783.0	46970	67.65	2.63	143.6	1074	64450	92.81
2.14	105.4	788.5	47310	68.12	2.64	144.4	1080	64820	93.34
2.15	106.1	794.1	47640	68.60	2.65	145.2	1087	65190	93.87
2.16	106.9	799.6	47970	69.08	2.66	146.1	1093	65560	94.41
2.17	107.6	805.2	48300	69.56	2.67	146.9	1099	65930	94.94
2.18	108.4	810.8	48640	70.04	2.68	147.7	1105	66300	95.47
2.19	109.1	816.3	48970	70.53	2.69	148.5	1111	66670	96.01
2.20	109.9	821.9	49310	71.01	2.70	149.4	1118	67040	96.54
2.21	110.6	827.5	49650	71.49	2.71	150.2	1124	67410	97.08
2.22	111.4	833.2	49980	71.98	2.72	151.0	1130	67790	97.62
2.23	112.1	838.8	50320	72.47	2.73	151.9	1136	68160	98.16
2.24	112.9	844.5	50660	72.95	2.74	152.7	1142	68540	98.70
2.25	113.6	850.1	51000	73.44	2.75	153.5	1149	68910	99.24
2.26	114.4	855.8	51340	73.93	2.76	154.4	1155	69290	99.78
2.27	115.2	861.5	51680	74.42	2.77	155.2	1161	69670	100.3
2.28	115.9	867.2	52020	74.92	2.78	156.1	1168	70040	100.9
2.29	116.7	872.9	52370	75.41	2.79	156.9	1174	70420	101.4
2.30	117.4	878.6	52710	75.90	2.80	157.8	1180	70800	102.0
2.31	118.2	884.3	53050	76.40	2.81	158.6	1186	71180	102.5
2.32	119.0	890.1	53400	76.90	2.82	159.4	1193	71560	103.1
2.33	119.8	895.9	53740	77.39	2.83	160.3	1199	71940	103.6
2.34	120.5	901.6	54090	77.89	2.84	161.1	1206	72320	104.1
2.35	121.3	907.4	54440	78.39	2.85	162.0	1212	72700	104.7
2.36	122.1	913.2	54790	78.89	2.86	162.9	1218	73090	105.3
2.37	122.8	919.0	55130	79.40	2.87	163.7	1225	73470	105.8
2.38	123.6	924.8	55480	79.90	2.88	164.6	1231	73860	106.4
2.39	124.4	930.7	55830	80.40	2.89	165.4	1238	74240	106.9
2.40	125.2	936.5	56180	80.91	2.90	166.3	1244	74630	107.5
2.41	126.0	942.4	56540	81.41	2.91	167.1	1250	75010	108.0
2.42	126.8	948.3	56890	81.92	2.92	168.0	1257	75400	108.6
2.43	127.5	954.1	57240	82.43	2.93	168.9	1263	75790	109.1
2.44	128.3	960.0	57590	82.94	2.94	169.7	1270	76180	109.7
2.45	129.1	965.9	57950	83.45	2.95	170.6	1276	76560	110.3
2.46	129.9	971.9	58300	83.96	2.96	171.5	1283	76950	110.8
2.47	130.7	977.8	58660	84.47	2.97	172.3	1289	77340	111.4
2.48	131.5	983.7	59020	84.99	2.98	173.2	1296	77740	111.9
2.49	132.3	989.7	59370	85.50	2.99	174.1	1302	78130	112.5
2.50	133.1	995.7	59730	86.02	3.00	175.0	1309	78520	113.1

11

Chapter

12

Parshall flume
discharge
tables

· *This chapter contains discharge (flow rate*
· *vs head) tables for Parshall flumes. Note*
· *that all of the tabular data is for free flow.*
· *If the flow is submerged, corrections will*
· *have to be made to determine the dis-*
· *charge, as discussed in Chapter 4.*
· *Note also that in many cases, discharges*
· *are listed for heads which are above the*
· *maximum recommended operating head*
· *or below the minimum recommended*
· *operating head of the flume in question.*
· *Discharge for these heads outside the nor-*
· *mal operating range are listed for refer-*
· *ence only; it should not be implied that the*
· *primary device is intended to be used in*
· *these regions. Refer to Chapter 4 for mini-*
· *mum and maximum recommended heads.*
·

Parshall flumes

12-1: 1 in. Throat Width Parshall Flume
12-2: 2 in. Throat Width Parshall Flume
12-3: 3 in. Throat Width Parshall Flume
12-4: 6 in. Throat Width Parshall Flume
12-5: 9 in. Throat Width Parshall Flume
12-6: 1 ft. Throat Width Parshall Flume
12-7: 1 1/2 ft. Throat Width Parshall Flume
12-8: 2 ft. Throat Width Parshall Flume
12-9: 3 ft. Throat Width Parshall Flume
12-10: 4 ft. Throat Width Parshall Flume
12-11: 5 ft. Throat Width Parshall Flume
12-12: 6 ft. Throat Width Parshall Flume
12-13: 8 ft. Throat Width Parshall Flume
12-14: 10 ft. Throat Width Parshall Flume
12-15: 12 ft. Throat Width Parshall Flume

Note: The discharges of the flumes are listed in four different units:

CFS—cubic feet per second   GPS—gallons per second
GPM—gallons per minute   MGD—million gallons per day

The equation used to develop each table is listed on the table.

12-1: 1 in. Parshall Flume Discharge Table

Formulas: $CFS = 0.3380H^{1.550}$ $GPS = CFS \times 7.481$
$GPM = CFS \times 448.8$ $MGD = CFS \times 0.6463$

Head Feet	CFS	GPS	GPM	MGD	Head Feet	CFS	GPS	GPM	MGD
0.01	0.0003	0.0020	0.1205	0.0002	0.51	0.1190	0.8905	53.42	0.0769
0.02	0.0008	0.0059	0.3528	0.0005	0.52	0.1227	0.9177	55.05	0.0793
0.03	0.0015	0.0110	0.6615	0.0010	0.53	0.1263	0.9452	56.70	0.0817
0.04	0.0023	0.0172	1.033	0.0015	0.54	0.1301	0.9729	58.37	0.0841
0.05	0.0033	0.0243	1.460	0.0021	0.55	0.1338	1.001	60.05	0.0865
0.06	0.0043	0.0323	1.937	0.0028	0.56	0.1376	1.029	61.75	0.0889
0.07	0.0055	0.0410	2.460	0.0035	0.57	0.1414	1.058	63.47	0.0914
0.08	0.0067	0.0504	3.025	0.0044	0.58	0.1453	1.087	65.21	0.0939
0.09	0.0081	0.0605	3.631	0.0052	0.59	0.1492	1.116	66.96	0.0964
0.10	0.0095	0.0713	4.275	0.0062	0.60	0.1531	1.146	68.72	0.0990
0.11	0.0110	0.0826	4.956	0.0071	0.61	0.1571	1.175	70.51	0.1015
0.12	0.0126	0.0945	5.672	0.0082	0.62	0.1611	1.205	72.31	0.1041
0.13	0.0143	0.1070	6.421	0.0092	0.63	0.1652	1.236	74.12	0.1067
0.14	0.0160	0.1201	7.202	0.0104	0.64	0.1692	1.266	75.95	0.1094
0.15	0.0179	0.1336	8.015	0.0115	0.65	0.1734	1.297	77.80	0.1120
0.16	0.0197	0.1477	8.858	0.0128	0.66	0.1775	1.328	79.66	0.1147
0.17	0.0217	0.1622	9.731	0.0140	0.67	0.1817	1.359	81.54	0.1174
0.18	0.0237	0.1772	10.63	0.0153	0.68	0.1859	1.391	83.44	0.1202
0.19	0.0258	0.1927	11.56	0.0167	0.69	0.1902	1.423	85.35	0.1229
0.20	0.0279	0.2087	12.52	0.0180	0.70	0.1945	1.455	87.27	0.1257
0.21	0.0301	0.2251	13.50	0.0194	0.71	0.1988	1.487	89.21	0.1285
0.22	0.0323	0.2419	14.51	0.0209	0.72	0.2031	1.520	91.17	0.1313
0.23	0.0346	0.2592	15.55	0.0224	0.73	0.2075	1.552	93.14	0.1341
0.24	0.0370	0.2768	16.61	0.0239	0.74	0.2119	1.586	95.12	0.1370
0.25	0.0394	0.2949	17.69	0.0255	0.75	0.2164	1.619	97.12	0.1399
0.26	0.0419	0.3134	18.80	0.0271	0.76	0.2209	1.652	99.14	0.1428
0.27	0.0444	0.3323	19.93	0.0287	0.77	0.2254	1.686	101.2	0.1457
0.28	0.0470	0.3515	21.09	0.0304	0.78	0.2300	1.720	103.2	0.1486
0.29	0.0496	0.3712	22.27	0.0321	0.79	0.2346	1.755	105.3	0.1516
0.30	0.0523	0.3912	23.47	0.0338	0.80	0.2392	1.789	107.3	0.1546
0.31	0.0550	0.4116	24.69	0.0356	0.81	0.2438	1.824	109.4	0.1576
0.32	0.0578	0.4324	25.94	0.0374	0.82	0.2485	1.859	111.5	0.1606
0.33	0.0606	0.4535	27.21	0.0392	0.83	0.2532	1.894	113.6	0.1637
0.34	0.0635	0.4750	28.49	0.0410	0.84	0.2580	1.930	115.8	0.1667
0.35	0.0664	0.4968	29.80	0.0429	0.85	0.2627	1.966	117.9	0.1698
0.36	0.0694	0.5190	31.13	0.0448	0.86	0.2675	2.001	120.1	0.1729
0.37	0.0724	0.5415	32.48	0.0468	0.87	0.2724	2.038	122.2	0.1760
0.38	0.0754	0.5643	33.86	0.0488	0.88	0.2772	2.074	124.4	0.1792
0.39	0.0785	0.5875	35.25	0.0508	0.89	0.2821	2.111	126.6	0.1823
0.40	0.0817	0.6110	36.66	0.0528	0.90	0.2871	2.148	128.8	0.1855
0.41	0.0849	0.6349	38.09	0.0548	0.91	0.2920	2.185	131.1	0.1887
0.42	0.0881	0.6590	39.54	0.0569	0.92	0.2970	2.222	133.3	0.1920
0.43	0.0914	0.6835	41.01	0.0591	0.93	0.3020	2.260	135.6	0.1952
0.44	0.0947	0.7083	42.49	0.0612	0.94	0.3071	2.297	137.8	0.1985
0.45	0.0980	0.7334	44.00	0.0634	0.95	0.3122	2.335	140.1	0.2018
0.46	0.1014	0.7588	45.52	0.0656	0.96	0.3173	2.374	142.4	0.2051
0.47	0.1049	0.7846	47.07	0.0678	0.97	0.3224	2.412	144.7	0.2084
0.48	0.1084	0.8106	48.63	0.0700	0.98	0.3276	2.451	147.0	0.2117
0.49	0.1119	0.8369	50.21	0.0723	0.99	0.3328	2.489	149.3	0.2151
0.50	0.1154	0.8635	51.81	0.0746	1.00	0.3380	2.529	151.7	0.2184

12

12-1: 1 in. Parshall Flume Discharge Table *(Continued)*

Formulas: CFS = $0.3380H^{1.550}$ GPS = CFS x 7.481
 GPM = CFS x 448.8   MGD = CFS x 0.6463

Head Feet	CFS	GPS	GPM	MGD	Head Feet	CFS	GPS	GPM	MGD
1.01	0.3433	2.568	154.1	0.2218	1.51	0.6402	4.790	287.3	0.4138
1.02	0.3485	2.607	156.4	0.2253	1.52	0.6468	4.839	290.3	0.4180
1.03	0.3538	2.647	158.8	0.2287	1.53	0.6534	4.888	293.3	0.4223
1.04	0.3592	2.687	161.2	0.2321	1.54	0.6600	4.938	296.2	0.4266
1.05	0.3646	2.727	163.6	0.2356	1.55	0.6667	4.988	299.2	0.4309
1.06	0.3699	2.768	166.0	0.2391	1.56	0.6734	5.038	302.2	0.4352
1.07	0.3754	2.808	168.5	0.2426	1.57	0.6801	5.088	305.2	0.4395
1.08	0.3808	2.849	170.9	0.2461	1.58	0.6868	5.138	308.2	0.4439
1.09	0.3863	2.890	173.4	0.2497	1.59	0.6936	5.189	311.3	0.4482
1.10	0.3918	2.931	175.8	0.2532	1.60	0.7003	5.239	314.3	0.4526
1.11	0.3973	2.973	178.3	0.2568	1.61	0.7071	5.290	317.4	0.4570
1.12	0.4029	3.014	180.8	0.2604	1.62	0.7139	5.341	320.4	0.4614
1.13	0.4085	3.056	183.3	0.2640	1.63	0.7208	5.392	323.5	0.4658
1.14	0.4141	3.098	185.9	0.2676	1.64	0.7277	5.444	326.6	0.4703
1.15	0.4198	3.140	188.4	0.2713	1.65	0.7345	5.495	329.7	0.4747
1.16	0.4254	3.183	190.9	0.2750	1.66	0.7415	5.547	332.8	0.4792
1.17	0.4311	3.225	193.5	0.2786	1.67	0.7484	5.599	335.9	0.4837
1.18	0.4369	3.268	196.1	0.2823	1.68	0.7553	5.651	339.0	0.4882
1.19	0.4426	3.311	198.6	0.2861	1.69	0.7623	5.703	342.1	0.4927
1.20	0.4484	3.354	201.2	0.2898	1.70	0.7693	5.755	345.3	0.4972
1.21	0.4542	3.398	203.8	0.2935	1.71	0.7764	5.808	348.4	0.5018
1.22	0.4600	3.441	206.5	0.2973	1.72	0.7834	5.861	351.6	0.5063
1.23	0.4659	3.485	209.1	0.3011	1.73	0.7905	5.914	354.8	0.5109
1.24	0.4718	3.529	211.7	0.3049	1.74	0.7976	5.967	357.9	0.5155
1.25	0.4777	3.573	214.4	0.3087	1.75	0.8047	6.020	361.1	0.5201
1.26	0.4836	3.618	217.0	0.3126	1.76	0.8118	6.073	364.3	0.5247
1.27	0.4896	3.662	219.7	0.3164	1.77	0.8190	6.127	367.6	0.5293
1.28	0.4956	3.707	222.4	0.3203	1.78	0.8262	6.181	370.8	0.5340
1.29	0.5016	3.752	225.1	0.3242	1.79	0.8334	6.234	374.0	0.5386
1.30	0.5076	3.797	227.8	0.3281	1.80	0.8406	6.289	377.3	0.5433
1.31	0.5137	3.843	230.5	0.3320	1.81	0.8478	6.343	380.5	0.5480
1.32	0.5198	3.888	233.3	0.3359	1.82	0.8551	6.397	383.8	0.5527
1.33	0.5259	3.934	236.0	0.3399	1.83	0.8624	6.452	387.1	0.5574
1.34	0.5320	3.980	238.8	0.3438	1.84	0.8697	6.506	390.3	0.5621
1.35	0.5382	4.026	241.5	0.3478	1.85	0.8771	6.561	393.6	0.5668
1.36	0.5444	4.073	244.3	0.3518	1.86	0.8844	6.616	396.9	0.5716
1.37	0.5506	4.119	247.1	0.3559	1.87	0.8918	6.672	400.2	0.5764
1.38	0.5568	4.166	249.9	0.3599	1.88	0.8992	6.727	403.6	0.5812
1.39	0.5631	4.213	252.7	0.3639	1.89	0.9066	6.783	406.9	0.5860
1.40	0.5694	4.260	255.5	0.3680	1.90	0.9141	6.838	410.2	0.5908
1.41	0.5757	4.307	258.4	0.3721	1.91	0.9215	6.894	413.6	0.5956
1.42	0.5821	4.354	261.2	0.3762	1.92	0.9290	6.950	417.0	0.6004
1.43	0.5884	4.402	264.1	0.3803	1.93	0.9365	7.006	420.3	0.6053
1.44	0.5948	4.450	267.0	0.3844	1.94	0.9441	7.063	423.7	0.6102
1.45	0.6012	4.498	269.8	0.3886	1.95	0.9516	7.119	427.1	0.6150
1.46	0.6077	4.546	272.7	0.3927	1.96	0.9592	7.176	430.5	0.6199
1.47	0.6141	4.594	275.6	0.3969	1.97	0.9668	7.233	433.9	0.6248
1.48	0.6206	4.643	278.5	0.4011	1.98	0.9744	7.290	437.3	0.6298
1.49	0.6271	4.692	281.5	0.4053	1.99	0.9821	7.347	440.7	0.6347
1.50	0.6337	4.740	284.4	0.4095	2.00	0.9897	7.404	444.2	0.6397

12

Formulas: $CFS = 0.3380H^{1.550}$ $GPS = CFS \times 7.481$
$GPM = CFS \times 448.8$ $MGD = CFS \times 0.6463$

Head Feet	CFS	GPS	GPM	MGD	Head Feet	CFS	GPS	GPM	MGD
2.01	0.997	7.462	447.6	0.6446	2.51	1.407	10.53	631.6	0.9096
2.02	1.005	7.519	451.1	0.6496	2.52	1.416	10.59	635.5	0.9152
2.03	1.013	7.577	454.6	0.6546	2.53	1.425	10.66	639.4	0.9208
2.04	1.021	7.635	458.0	0.6596	2.54	1.434	10.72	643.4	0.9265
2.05	1.028	7.693	461.5	0.6646	2.55	1.442	10.79	647.3	0.9322
2.06	1.036	7.751	465.0	0.6696	2.56	1.451	10.86	651.2	0.9378
2.07	1.044	7.810	468.5	0.6747	2.57	1.460	10.92	655.2	0.9435
2.08	1.052	7.868	472.0	0.6797	2.58	1.469	10.99	659.1	0.9492
2.09	1.060	7.927	475.6	0.6848	2.59	1.478	11.05	663.1	0.9549
2.10	1.067	7.986	479.1	0.6899	2.60	1.486	11.12	667.1	0.9606
2.11	1.075	8.045	482.6	0.6950	2.61	1.495	11.19	671.1	0.9664
2.12	1.083	8.104	486.2	0.7001	2.62	1.504	11.25	675.1	0.9721
2.13	1.091	8.163	489.7	0.7052	2.63	1.513	11.32	679.0	0.9779
2.14	1.099	8.223	493.3	0.7104	2.64	1.522	11.39	683.1	0.9836
2.15	1.107	8.282	496.9	0.7155	2.65	1.531	11.45	687.1	0.9894
2.16	1.115	8.342	500.5	0.7207	2.66	1.540	11.52	691.1	0.9952
2.17	1.123	8.402	504.1	0.7259	2.67	1.549	11.59	695.1	1.001
2.18	1.131	8.462	507.7	0.7311	2.68	1.558	11.65	699.2	1.007
2.19	1.139	8.522	511.3	0.7363	2.69	1.567	11.72	703.2	1.013
2.20	1.147	8.583	514.9	0.7415	2.70	1.576	11.79	707.3	1.019
2.21	1.155	8.643	518.5	0.7467	2.71	1.585	11.86	711.3	1.024
2.22	1.163	8.704	522.2	0.7520	2.72	1.594	11.92	715.4	1.030
2.23	1.172	8.765	525.8	0.7572	2.73	1.603	11.99	719.5	1.036
2.24	1.180	8.826	529.5	0.7625	2.74	1.612	12.06	723.6	1.042
2.25	1.188	8.887	533.2	0.7678	2.75	1.621	12.13	727.7	1.048
2.26	1.196	8.948	536.8	0.7731	2.76	1.631	12.20	731.8	1.054
2.27	1.204	9.010	540.5	0.7784	2.77	1.640	12.27	735.9	1.060
2.28	1.213	9.071	544.2	0.7837	2.78	1.649	12.34	740.0	1.066
2.29	1.221	9.133	547.9	0.7890	2.79	1.658	12.40	744.1	1.072
2.30	1.229	9.195	551.6	0.7944	2.80	1.667	12.47	748.3	1.078
2.31	1.237	9.257	555.4	0.7997	2.81	1.677	12.54	752.4	1.084
2.32	1.246	9.319	559.1	0.8051	2.82	1.686	12.61	756.6	1.090
2.33	1.254	9.382	562.8	0.8105	2.83	1.695	12.68	760.7	1.096
2.34	1.262	9.444	566.6	0.8159	2.84	1.704	12.75	764.9	1.102
2.35	1.271	9.507	570.3	0.8213	2.85	1.714	12.82	769.1	1.108
2.36	1.279	9.570	574.1	0.8267	2.86	1.723	12.89	773.3	1.114
2.37	1.288	9.632	577.9	0.8322	2.87	1.732	12.96	777.5	1.120
2.38	1.296	9.696	581.7	0.8376	2.88	1.742	13.03	781.7	1.126
2.39	1.304	9.759	585.4	0.8431	2.89	1.751	13.10	785.9	1.132
2.40	1.313	9.822	589.2	0.8486	2.90	1.760	13.17	790.1	1.138
2.41	1.321	9.886	593.1	0.8540	2.91	1.770	13.24	794.3	1.144
2.42	1.330	9.949	596.9	0.8595	2.92	1.779	13.31	798.6	1.150
2.43	1.338	10.01	600.7	0.8650	2.93	1.789	13.38	802.8	1.156
2.44	1.347	10.08	604.5	0.8706	2.94	1.798	13.45	807.1	1.162
2.45	1.356	10.14	608.4	0.8761	2.95	1.808	13.52	811.3	1.168
2.46	1.364	10.21	612.2	0.8817	2.96	1.817	13.59	815.6	1.174
2.47	1.373	10.27	616.1	0.8872	2.97	1.827	13.67	819.9	1.181
2.48	1.381	10.33	620.0	0.8928	2.98	1.836	13.74	824.1	1.187
2.49	1.390	10.40	623.8	0.8984	2.99	1.846	13.81	828.4	1.193
2.50	1.399	10.46	627.7	0.9040	3.00	1.855	13.88	832.7	1.199

12

12-2: 2 in. Parshall Flume Discharge Table

Formulas: $CFS = 0.6760H^{1.550}$ $GPS = CFS \times 7.481$
$GPM = CFS \times 448.8$ $MGD = CFS \times 0.6463$

Head Feet	CFS	GPS	GPM	MGD	Head Feet	CFS	GPS	GPM	MGD
0.01	0.0005	0.0040	0.2410	0.0003	0.51	0.2381	1.781	106.8	0.1539
0.02	0.0016	0.0118	0.7057	0.0010	0.52	0.2453	1.835	110.1	0.1586
0.03	0.0029	0.0221	1.323	0.0019	0.53	0.2527	1.890	113.4	0.1633
0.04	0.0046	0.0344	2.066	0.0030	0.54	0.2601	1.946	116.7	0.1681
0.05	0.0065	0.0487	2.920	0.0042	0.55	0.2676	2.002	120.1	0.1730
0.06	0.0086	0.0646	3.874	0.0056	0.56	0.2752	2.059	123.5	0.1779
0.07	0.0110	0.0820	4.919	0.0071	0.57	0.2828	2.116	126.9	0.1828
0.08	0.0135	0.1009	6.050	0.0087	0.58	0.2906	2.174	130.4	0.1878
0.09	0.0162	0.1211	7.262	0.0105	0.59	0.2984	2.232	133.9	0.1928
0.10	0.0191	0.1425	8.551	0.0123	0.60	0.3063	2.291	137.4	0.1979
0.11	0.0221	0.1652	9.912	0.0143	0.61	0.3142	2.351	141.0	0.2031
0.12	0.0253	0.1891	11.34	0.0163	0.62	0.3222	2.411	144.6	0.2083
0.13	0.0286	0.2141	12.84	0.0185	0.63	0.3303	2.471	148.2	0.2135
0.14	0.0321	0.2401	14.40	0.0207	0.64	0.3385	2.532	151.9	0.2188
0.15	0.0357	0.2672	16.03	0.0231	0.65	0.3467	2.594	155.6	0.2241
0.16	0.0395	0.2953	17.72	0.0255	0.66	0.3550	2.656	159.3	0.2294
0.17	0.0434	0.3244	19.46	0.0280	0.67	0.3634	2.718	163.1	0.2349
0.18	0.0474	0.3545	21.27	0.0306	0.68	0.3718	2.782	166.9	0.2403
0.19	0.0515	0.3855	23.12	0.0333	0.69	0.3803	2.845	170.7	0.2458
0.20	0.0558	0.4174	25.04	0.0361	0.70	0.3889	2.909	174.5	0.2514
0.21	0.0602	0.4501	27.00	0.0389	0.71	0.3976	2.974	178.4	0.2569
0.22	0.0647	0.4838	29.02	0.0418	0.72	0.4063	3.039	182.3	0.2626
0.23	0.0693	0.5183	31.09	0.0448	0.73	0.4150	3.105	186.3	0.2682
0.24	0.0740	0.5536	33.21	0.0478	0.74	0.4239	3.171	190.2	0.2740
0.25	0.0788	0.5898	35.38	0.0510	0.75	0.4328	3.238	194.2	0.2797
0.26	0.0838	0.6268	37.60	0.0541	0.76	0.4418	3.305	198.3	0.2855
0.27	0.0888	0.6645	39.87	0.0574	0.77	0.4508	3.373	202.3	0.2914
0.28	0.0940	0.7031	42.18	0.0607	0.78	0.4599	3.441	206.4	0.2973
0.29	0.0992	0.7424	44.54	0.0641	0.79	0.4691	3.509	210.5	0.3032
0.30	0.1046	0.7824	46.94	0.0676	0.80	0.4783	3.578	214.7	0.3092
0.31	0.1100	0.8232	49.39	0.0711	0.81	0.4876	3.648	218.9	0.3152
0.32	0.1156	0.8647	51.88	0.0747	0.82	0.4970	3.718	223.1	0.3212
0.33	0.1212	0.9070	54.41	0.0784	0.83	0.5064	3.789	227.3	0.3273
0.34	0.1270	0.9499	56.99	0.0821	0.84	0.5159	3.860	231.5	0.3334
0.35	0.1328	0.9936	59.61	0.0858	0.85	0.5255	3.931	235.8	0.3396
0.36	0.1387	1.038	62.27	0.0897	0.86	0.5351	4.003	240.1	0.3458
0.37	0.1448	1.083	64.97	0.0936	0.87	0.5448	4.075	244.5	0.3521
0.38	0.1509	1.129	67.71	0.0975	0.88	0.5545	4.148	248.9	0.3584
0.39	0.1571	1.175	70.49	0.1015	0.89	0.5643	4.221	253.3	0.3647
0.40	0.1634	1.222	73.31	0.1056	0.90	0.5741	4.295	257.7	0.3711
0.41	0.1697	1.270	76.18	0.1097	0.91	0.5841	4.369	262.1	0.3775
0.42	0.1762	1.318	79.07	0.1139	0.92	0.5940	4.444	266.6	0.3839
0.43	0.1827	1.367	82.01	0.1181	0.93	0.6041	4.519	271.1	0.3904
0.44	0.1894	1.417	84.99	0.1224	0.94	0.6142	4.595	275.6	0.3969
0.45	0.1961	1.467	88.00	0.1267	0.95	0.6243	4.671	280.2	0.4035
0.46	0.2029	1.518	91.05	0.1311	0.96	0.6346	4.747	284.8	0.4101
0.47	0.2097	1.569	94.14	0.1356	0.97	0.6448	4.824	289.4	0.4168
0.48	0.2167	1.621	97.26	0.1401	0.98	0.6552	4.901	294.0	0.4234
0.49	0.2237	1.674	100.4	0.1446	0.99	0.6656	4.979	298.7	0.4301
0.50	0.2309	1.727	103.6	0.1492	1.00	0.6760	5.057	303.4	0.4369

12

Formulas: $CFS = 0.6760H^{1.550}$ $GPS = CFS \times 7.481$
$GPM = CFS \times 448.8$ $MGD = CFS \times 0.6463$

Head Feet	CFS	GPS	GPM	MGD	Head Feet	CFS	GPS	GPM	MGD
1.01	0.6865	5.136	308.1	0.4437	1.51	1.280	9.579	574.7	0.8276
1.02	0.6971	5.215	312.8	0.4505	1.52	1.294	9.678	580.6	0.8361
1.03	0.7077	5.294	317.6	0.4574	1.53	1.307	9.776	586.5	0.8446
1.04	0.7184	5.374	322.4	0.4643	1.54	1.320	9.876	592.5	0.8532
1.05	0.7291	5.454	327.2	0.4712	1.55	1.333	9.975	598.4	0.8618
1.06	0.7399	5.535	332.1	0.4782	1.56	1.347	10.08	604.4	0.8704
1.07	0.7507	5.616	336.9	0.4852	1.57	1.360	10.18	610.4	0.8791
1.08	0.7616	5.698	341.8	0.4923	1.58	1.374	10.28	616.5	0.8878
1.09	0.7726	5.780	346.7	0.4993	1.59	1.387	10.38	622.5	0.8965
1.10	0.7836	5.862	351.7	0.5065	1.60	1.401	10.48	628.6	0.9052
1.11	0.7947	5.945	356.7	0.5136	1.61	1.414	10.58	634.7	0.9140
1.12	0.8058	6.028	361.6	0.5208	1.62	1.428	10.68	640.8	0.9228
1.13	0.8170	6.112	366.7	0.5280	1.63	1.442	10.78	647.0	0.9317
1.14	0.8282	6.196	371.7	0.5353	1.64	1.455	10.89	653.1	0.9406
1.15	0.8395	6.280	376.8	0.5426	1.65	1.469	10.99	659.3	0.9495
1.16	0.8509	6.365	381.9	0.5499	1.66	1.483	11.09	665.5	0.9584
1.17	0.8623	6.451	387.0	0.5573	1.67	1.497	11.20	671.8	0.9674
1.18	0.8737	6.536	392.1	0.5647	1.68	1.511	11.30	678.0	0.9764
1.19	0.8852	6.622	397.3	0.5721	1.69	1.525	11.41	684.3	0.9854
1.20	0.8968	6.709	402.5	0.5796	1.70	1.539	11.51	690.6	0.9944
1.21	0.9084	6.796	407.7	0.5871	1.71	1.553	11.62	696.9	1.004
1.22	0.9200	6.883	412.9	0.5946	1.72	1.567	11.72	703.2	1.013
1.23	0.9318	6.970	418.2	0.6022	1.73	1.581	11.83	709.5	1.022
1.24	0.9435	7.058	423.5	0.6098	1.74	1.595	11.93	715.9	1.031
1.25	0.9553	7.147	428.8	0.6174	1.75	1.609	12.04	722.3	1.040
1.26	0.9672	7.236	434.1	0.6251	1.76	1.624	12.15	728.7	1.049
1.27	0.9791	7.325	439.4	0.6328	1.77	1.638	12.25	735.1	1.059
1.28	0.9911	7.414	444.8	0.6406	1.78	1.652	12.36	741.6	1.068
1.29	1.003	7.504	450.2	0.6483	1.79	1.667	12.47	748.0	1.077
1.30	1.015	7.595	455.6	0.6561	1.80	1.681	12.58	754.5	1.087
1.31	1.027	7.686	461.1	0.6640	1.81	1.696	12.69	761.0	1.096
1.32	1.040	7.777	466.5	0.6718	1.82	1.710	12.79	767.6	1.105
1.33	1.052	7.868	472.0	0.6798	1.83	1.725	12.90	774.1	1.115
1.34	1.064	7.960	477.5	0.6877	1.84	1.739	13.01	780.7	1.124
1.35	1.076	8.052	483.1	0.6957	1.85	1.754	13.12	787.3	1.134
1.36	1.089	8.145	488.6	0.7037	1.86	1.769	13.23	793.9	1.143
1.37	1.101	8.238	494.2	0.7117	1.87	1.784	13.34	800.5	1.153
1.38	1.114	8.331	499.8	0.7198	1.88	1.798	13.45	807.1	1.162
1.39	1.126	8.425	505.4	0.7279	1.89	1.813	13.57	813.8	1.172
1.40	1.139	8.519	511.1	0.7360	1.90	1.828	13.68	820.5	1.182
1.41	1.151	8.614	516.8	0.7442	1.91	1.843	13.79	827.2	1.191
1.42	1.164	8.709	522.5	0.7524	1.92	1.858	13.90	833.9	1.201
1.43	1.177	8.804	528.2	0.7606	1.93	1.873	14.01	840.6	1.211
1.44	1.190	8.900	533.9	0.7689	1.94	1.888	14.13	847.4	1.220
1.45	1.202	8.996	539.7	0.7771	1.95	1.903	14.24	854.2	1.230
1.46	1.215	9.092	545.4	0.7855	1.96	1.918	14.35	861.0	1.240
1.47	1.228	9.189	551.2	0.7938	1.97	1.934	14.47	867.8	1.250
1.48	1.241	9.286	557.1	0.8022	1.98	1.949	14.58	874.6	1.260
1.49	1.254	9.383	562.9	0.8106	1.99	1.964	14.69	881.5	1.269
1.50	1.267	9.481	568.8	0.8191	2.00	1.979	14.81	888.4	1.279

12

Formulas: $CFS = 0.6760H^{1.550}$ $GPS = CFS \times 7.481$
$GPM = CFS \times 448.8$ $MGD = CFS \times 0.6463$

Head Feet	CFS	GPS	GPM	MGD	Head Feet	CFS	GPS	GPM	MGD
2.01	1.995	14.92	895.3	1.289	2.51	2.815	21.06	1263	1.819
2.02	2.010	15.04	902.2	1.299	2.52	2.832	21.19	1271	1.830
2.03	2.026	15.15	909.1	1.309	2.53	2.850	21.32	1279	1.842
2.04	2.041	15.27	916.1	1.319	2.54	2.867	21.45	1287	1.853
2.05	2.057	15.39	923.0	1.329	2.55	2.885	21.58	1295	1.864
2.06	2.072	15.50	930.0	1.339	2.56	2.902	21.71	1302	1.876
2.07	2.088	15.62	937.0	1.349	2.57	2.920	21.84	1310	1.887
2.08	2.104	15.74	944.1	1.359	2.58	2.937	21.97	1318	1.898
2.09	2.119	15.85	951.1	1.370	2.59	2.955	22.11	1326	1.910
2.10	2.135	15.97	958.2	1.380	2.60	2.973	22.24	1334	1.921
2.11	2.151	16.09	965.2	1.390	2.61	2.990	22.37	1342	1.933
2.12	2.167	16.21	972.3	1.400	2.62	3.008	22.50	1350	1.944
2.13	2.182	16.33	979.5	1.410	2.63	3.026	22.64	1358	1.956
2.14	2.198	16.45	986.6	1.421	2.64	3.044	22.77	1366	1.967
2.15	2.214	16.56	993.8	1.431	2.65	3.062	22.91	1374	1.979
2.16	2.230	16.68	1001	1.441	2.66	3.080	23.04	1382	1.990
2.17	2.246	16.80	1008	1.452	2.67	3.098	23.17	1390	2.002
2.18	2.262	16.92	1015	1.462	2.68	3.116	23.31	1398	2.014
2.19	2.278	17.04	1023	1.473	2.69	3.134	23.44	1406	2.025
2.20	2.295	17.17	1030	1.483	2.70	3.152	23.58	1415	2.037
2.21	2.311	17.29	1037	1.493	2.71	3.170	23.71	1423	2.049
2.22	2.327	17.41	1044	1.504	2.72	3.188	23.85	1431	2.060
2.23	2.343	17.53	1052	1.514	2.73	3.206	23.99	1439	2.072
2.24	2.360	17.65	1059	1.525	2.74	3.224	24.12	1447	2.084
2.25	2.376	17.77	1066	1.536	2.75	3.243	24.26	1455	2.096
2.26	2.392	17.90	1074	1.546	2.76	3.261	24.40	1464	2.108
2.27	2.409	18.02	1081	1.557	2.77	3.279	24.53	1472	2.119
2.28	2.425	18.14	1088	1.567	2.78	3.298	24.67	1480	2.131
2.29	2.442	18.27	1096	1.578	2.79	3.316	24.81	1488	2.143
2.30	2.458	18.39	1103	1.589	2.80	3.335	24.95	1497	2.155
2.31	2.475	18.51	1111	1.599	2.81	3.353	25.08	1505	2.167
2.32	2.491	18.64	1118	1.610	2.82	3.372	25.22	1513	2.179
2.33	2.508	18.76	1126	1.621	2.83	3.390	25.36	1521	2.191
2.34	2.525	18.89	1133	1.632	2.84	3.409	25.50	1530	2.203
2.35	2.542	19.01	1141	1.643	2.85	3.427	25.64	1538	2.215
2.36	2.558	19.14	1148	1.653	2.86	3.446	25.78	1547	2.227
2.37	2.575	19.26	1156	1.664	2.87	3.465	25.92	1555	2.239
2.38	2.592	19.39	1163	1.675	2.88	3.483	26.06	1563	2.251
2.39	2.609	19.52	1171	1.686	2.89	3.502	26.20	1572	2.263
2.40	2.626	19.64	1178	1.697	2.90	3.521	26.34	1580	2.276
2.41	2.643	19.77	1186	1.708	2.91	3.540	26.48	1589	2.288
2.42	2.660	19.90	1194	1.719	2.92	3.559	26.62	1597	2.300
2.43	2.677	20.03	1201	1.730	2.93	3.578	26.76	1606	2.312
2.44	2.694	20.15	1209	1.741	2.94	3.597	26.91	1614	2.324
2.45	2.711	20.28	1217	1.752	2.95	3.616	27.05	1623	2.337
2.46	2.728	20.41	1224	1.763	2.96	3.635	27.19	1631	2.349
2.47	2.746	20.54	1232	1.774	2.97	3.654	27.33	1640	2.361
2.48	2.763	20.67	1240	1.786	2.98	3.673	27.48	1648	2.374
2.49	2.780	20.80	1248	1.797	2.99	3.692	27.62	1657	2.386
2.50	2.797	20.93	1255	1.808	3.00	3.711	27.76	1665	2.398

12-3: 3 in. Parshall Flume Discharge Table

Formulas: CFS = 0.9920H$^{1.547}$ GPS = CFS x 7.481
          GPM = CFS x 448.8   MGD = CFS x 0.6463

Head Feet	CFS	GPS	GPM	MGD	Head Feet	CFS	GPS	GPM	MGD
0.01	0.0008	0.0060	0.3586	0.0005	0.51	0.3500	2.619	157.1	0.2262
0.02	0.0023	0.0175	1.048	0.0015	0.52	0.3607	2.699	161.9	0.2331
0.03	0.0044	0.0327	1.962	0.0028	0.53	0.3715	2.779	166.7	0.2401
0.04	0.0068	0.0510	3.062	0.0044	0.54	0.3824	2.861	171.6	0.2471
0.05	0.0096	0.0721	4.324	0.0062	0.55	0.3934	2.943	176.6	0.2543
0.06	0.0128	0.0956	5.733	0.0083	0.56	0.4045	3.026	181.6	0.2615
0.07	0.0162	0.1213	7.277	0.0105	0.57	0.4158	3.110	186.6	0.2687
0.08	0.0199	0.1491	8.946	0.0129	0.58	0.4271	3.195	191.7	0.2760
0.09	0.0239	0.1789	10.73	0.0155	0.59	0.4386	3.281	196.8	0.2834
0.10	0.0282	0.2106	12.63	0.0182	0.60	0.4501	3.367	202.0	0.2909
0.11	0.0326	0.2441	14.64	0.0211	0.61	0.4618	3.454	207.2	0.2984
0.12	0.0373	0.2792	16.75	0.0241	0.62	0.4735	3.542	212.5	0.3060
0.13	0.0422	0.3160	18.96	0.0273	0.63	0.4854	3.631	217.8	0.3137
0.14	0.0474	0.3544	21.26	0.0306	0.64	0.4974	3.721	223.2	0.3214
0.15	0.0527	0.3944	23.66	0.0341	0.65	0.5094	3.811	228.6	0.3292
0.16	0.0582	0.4358	26.14	0.0376	0.66	0.5216	3.902	234.1	0.3371
0.17	0.0640	0.4786	28.71	0.0413	0.67	0.5339	3.994	239.6	0.3451
0.18	0.0699	0.5229	31.37	0.0452	0.68	0.5463	4.087	245.2	0.3531
0.19	0.0760	0.5685	34.10	0.0491	0.69	0.5587	4.180	250.8	0.3611
0.20	0.0823	0.6154	36.92	0.0532	0.70	0.5713	4.274	256.4	0.3692
0.21	0.0887	0.6637	39.81	0.0573	0.71	0.5840	4.369	262.1	0.3774
0.22	0.0953	0.7132	42.79	0.0616	0.72	0.5968	4.464	267.8	0.3857
0.23	0.1021	0.7639	45.83	0.0660	0.73	0.6096	4.561	273.6	0.3940
0.24	0.1091	0.8159	48.95	0.0705	0.74	0.6226	4.658	279.4	0.4024
0.25	0.1162	0.8691	52.14	0.0751	0.75	0.6357	4.755	285.3	0.4108
0.26	0.1234	0.9235	55.40	0.0798	0.76	0.6488	4.854	291.2	0.4193
0.27	0.1309	0.9790	58.73	0.0846	0.77	0.6621	4.953	297.1	0.4279
0.28	0.1384	1.036	62.13	0.0895	0.78	0.6754	5.053	303.1	0.4365
0.29	0.1462	1.093	65.60	0.0945	0.79	0.6889	5.153	309.2	0.4452
0.30	0.1540	1.152	69.13	0.0996	0.80	0.7024	5.255	315.2	0.4540
0.31	0.1620	1.212	72.73	0.1047	0.81	0.7160	5.357	321.4	0.4628
0.32	0.1702	1.273	76.39	0.1100	0.82	0.7298	5.459	327.5	0.4716
0.33	0.1785	1.335	80.11	0.1154	0.83	0.7436	5.563	333.7	0.4806
0.34	0.1869	1.399	83.90	0.1208	0.84	0.7575	5.667	340.0	0.4896
0.35	0.1955	1.463	87.75	0.1264	0.85	0.7715	5.771	346.2	0.4986
0.36	0.2042	1.528	91.66	0.1320	0.86	0.7856	5.877	352.6	0.5077
0.37	0.2131	1.594	95.63	0.1377	0.87	0.7997	5.983	358.9	0.5169
0.38	0.2220	1.661	99.65	0.1435	0.88	0.8140	6.090	365.3	0.5261
0.39	0.2311	1.729	103.7	0.1494	0.89	0.8284	6.197	371.8	0.5354
0.40	0.2404	1.798	107.9	0.1554	0.90	0.8428	6.305	378.2	0.5447
0.41	0.2497	1.868	112.1	0.1614	0.91	0.8573	6.414	384.8	0.5541
0.42	0.2592	1.939	116.3	0.1675	0.92	0.8719	6.523	391.3	0.5635
0.43	0.2688	2.011	120.7	0.1737	0.93	0.8867	6.633	397.9	0.5730
0.44	0.2786	2.084	125.0	0.1800	0.94	0.9014	6.744	404.6	0.5826
0.45	0.2884	2.158	129.4	0.1864	0.95	0.9163	6.855	411.2	0.5922
0.46	0.2984	2.232	133.9	0.1929	0.96	0.9313	6.967	418.0	0.6019
0.47	0.3085	2.308	138.5	0.1994	0.97	0.9463	7.080	424.7	0.6116
0.48	0.3187	2.384	143.0	0.2060	0.98	0.9615	7.193	431.5	0.6214
0.49	0.3290	2.462	147.7	0.2127	0.99	0.9767	7.307	438.3	0.6312
0.50	0.3395	2.540	152.4	0.2194	1.00	0.9920	7.421	445.2	0.6411

12

12-3: 3 in. Parshall Flume Discharge Table *(Continued)*

Formulas: $CFS = 0.9920H^{1.547}$ $GPS = CFS \times 7.481$
$GPM = CFS \times 448.8$ $MGD = CFS \times 0.6463$

Head Feet	CFS	GPS	GPM	MGD	Head Feet	CFS	GPS	GPM	MGD
1.01	1.007	7.536	452.1	0.6511	1.51	1.877	14.04	842.3	1.213
1.02	1.023	7.652	459.1	0.6611	1.52	1.896	14.18	850.9	1.225
1.03	1.038	7.768	466.0	0.6711	1.53	1.915	14.33	859.6	1.238
1.04	1.054	7.885	473.1	0.6812	1.54	1.935	14.47	868.3	1.250
1.05	1.070	8.003	480.1	0.6914	1.55	1.954	14.62	877.0	1.263
1.06	1.086	8.121	487.2	0.7016	1.56	1.974	14.77	885.8	1.276
1.07	1.101	8.240	494.3	0.7119	1.57	1.993	14.91	894.6	1.288
1.08	1.117	8.359	501.5	0.7222	1.58	2.013	15.06	903.4	1.301
1.09	1.133	8.479	508.7	0.7326	1.59	2.033	15.21	912.3	1.314
1.10	1.150	8.600	515.9	0.7430	1.60	2.053	15.35	921.2	1.327
1.11	1.166	8.721	523.2	0.7535	1.61	2.072	15.50	930.1	1.339
1.12	1.182	8.843	530.5	0.7640	1.62	2.092	15.65	939.0	1.352
1.13	1.198	8.966	537.9	0.7746	1.63	2.112	15.80	948.0	1.365
1.14	1.215	9.089	545.3	0.7852	1.64	2.132	15.95	957.0	1.378
1.15	1.231	9.212	552.7	0.7959	1.65	2.153	16.10	966.1	1.391
1.16	1.248	9.337	560.1	0.8066	1.66	2.173	16.25	975.2	1.404
1.17	1.265	9.461	567.6	0.8174	1.67	2.193	16.41	984.3	1.417
1.18	1.281	9.587	575.1	0.8282	1.68	2.213	16.56	993.4	1.431
1.19	1.298	9.713	582.7	0.8391	1.69	2.234	16.71	1003	1.444
1.20	1.315	9.839	590.3	0.8500	1.70	2.254	16.86	1012	1.457
1.21	1.332	9.966	597.9	0.8610	1.71	2.275	17.02	1021	1.470
1.22	1.349	10.09	605.6	0.8721	1.72	2.295	17.17	1030	1.484
1.23	1.366	10.22	613.3	0.8831	1.73	2.316	17.33	1039	1.497
1.24	1.384	10.35	621.0	0.8943	1.74	2.337	17.48	1049	1.510
1.25	1.401	10.48	628.8	0.9055	1.75	2.358	17.64	1058	1.524
1.26	1.418	10.61	636.6	0.9167	1.76	2.379	17.79	1068	1.537
1.27	1.436	10.74	644.4	0.9280	1.77	2.400	17.95	1077	1.551
1.28	1.453	10.87	652.3	0.9393	1.78	2.421	18.11	1086	1.564
1.29	1.471	11.00	660.2	0.9507	1.79	2.442	18.27	1096	1.578
1.30	1.489	11.14	668.1	0.9621	1.80	2.463	18.42	1105	1.592
1.31	1.506	11.27	676.1	0.9736	1.81	2.484	18.58	1115	1.605
1.32	1.524	11.40	684.1	0.9851	1.82	2.505	18.74	1124	1.619
1.33	1.542	11.54	692.1	0.9967	1.83	2.527	18.90	1134	1.633
1.34	1.560	11.67	700.2	1.008	1.84	2.548	19.06	1144	1.647
1.35	1.578	11.81	708.3	1.020	1.85	2.569	19.22	1153	1.661
1.36	1.596	11.94	716.4	1.032	1.86	2.591	19.38	1163	1.674
1.37	1.614	12.08	724.6	1.043	1.87	2.612	19.54	1172	1.688
1.38	1.633	12.21	732.8	1.055	1.88	2.634	19.71	1182	1.702
1.39	1.651	12.35	741.0	1.067	1.89	2.656	19.87	1192	1.716
1.40	1.669	12.49	749.2	1.079	1.90	2.678	20.03	1202	1.731
1.41	1.688	12.63	757.5	1.091	1.91	2.699	20.19	1211	1.745
1.42	1.706	12.77	765.9	1.103	1.92	2.721	20.36	1221	1.759
1.43	1.725	12.91	774.2	1.115	1.93	2.743	20.52	1231	1.773
1.44	1.744	13.05	782.6	1.127	1.94	2.765	20.69	1241	1.787
1.45	1.763	13.19	791.0	1.139	1.95	2.787	20.85	1251	1.801
1.46	1.781	13.33	799.5	1.151	1.96	2.810	21.02	1261	1.816
1.47	1.800	13.47	808.0	1.164	1.97	2.832	21.18	1271	1.830
1.48	1.819	13.61	816.5	1.176	1.98	2.854	21.35	1281	1.845
1.49	1.838	13.75	825.1	1.188	1.99	2.876	21.52	1291	1.859
1.50	1.857	13.90	833.6	1.200	2.00	2.899	21.69	1301	1.873

12

12-3: 3 in. Parshall Flume Discharge Table *(Continued)*

Formulas: $CFS = 0.9920H^{1.547}$ $GPS = CFS \times 7.481$
$GPM = CFS \times 448.8$ $MGD = CFS \times 0.6463$

Head Feet	CFS	GPS	GPM	MGD	Head Feet	CFS	GPS	GPM	MGD
2.01	2.921	21.85	1311	1.888	2.51	4.119	30.82	1849	2.662
2.02	2.944	22.02	1321	1.902	2.52	4.145	31.01	1860	2.679
2.03	2.966	22.19	1331	1.917	2.53	4.170	31.20	1872	2.695
2.04	2.989	22.36	1341	1.932	2.54	4.196	31.39	1883	2.712
2.05	3.012	22.53	1352	1.946	2.55	4.221	31.58	1894	2.728
2.06	3.034	22.70	1362	1.961	2.56	4.247	31.77	1906	2.745
2.07	3.057	22.87	1372	1.976	2.57	4.272	31.96	1917	2.761
2.08	3.080	23.04	1382	1.991	2.58	4.298	32.15	1929	2.778
2.09	3.103	23.21	1393	2.005	2.59	4.324	32.35	1941	2.795
2.10	3.126	23.39	1403	2.020	2.60	4.350	32.54	1952	2.811
2.11	3.149	23.56	1413	2.035	2.61	4.376	32.74	1964	2.828
2.12	3.172	23.73	1424	2.050	2.62	4.402	32.93	1975	2.845
2.13	3.195	23.90	1434	2.065	2.63	4.428	33.12	1987	2.862
2.14	3.219	24.08	1444	2.080	2.64	4.454	33.32	1999	2.879
2.15	3.242	24.25	1455	2.095	2.65	4.480	33.51	2011	2.895
2.16	3.265	24.43	1465	2.110	2.66	4.506	33.71	2022	2.912
2.17	3.289	24.60	1476	2.125	2.67	4.532	33.91	2034	2.929
2.18	3.312	24.78	1486	2.141	2.68	4.559	34.10	2046	2.946
2.19	3.336	24.95	1497	2.156	2.69	4.585	34.30	2058	2.963
2.20	3.359	25.13	1508	2.171	2.70	4.611	34.50	2070	2.980
2.21	3.383	25.31	1518	2.186	2.71	4.638	34.70	2081	2.997
2.22	3.407	25.48	1529	2.202	2.72	4.664	34.89	2093	3.015
2.23	3.430	25.66	1540	2.217	2.73	4.691	35.09	2105	3.032
2.24	3.454	25.84	1550	2.232	2.74	4.717	35.29	2117	3.049
2.25	3.478	26.02	1561	2.248	2.75	4.744	35.49	2129	3.066
2.26	3.502	26.20	1572	2.263	2.76	4.771	35.69	2141	3.083
2.27	3.526	26.38	1582	2.279	2.77	4.798	35.89	2153	3.101
2.28	3.550	26.56	1593	2.294	2.78	4.824	36.09	2165	3.118
2.29	3.574	26.74	1604	2.310	2.79	4.851	36.29	2177	3.135
2.30	3.598	26.92	1615	2.326	2.80	4.878	36.49	2189	3.153
2.31	3.623	27.10	1626	2.341	2.81	4.905	36.70	2201	3.170
2.32	3.647	27.28	1637	2.357	2.82	4.932	36.90	2214	3.188
2.33	3.671	27.46	1648	2.373	2.83	4.959	37.10	2226	3.205
2.34	3.696	27.65	1659	2.388	2.84	4.986	37.30	2238	3.223
2.35	3.720	27.83	1670	2.404	2.85	5.014	37.51	2250	3.240
2.36	3.745	28.01	1681	2.420	2.86	5.041	37.71	2262	3.258
2.37	3.769	28.20	1692	2.436	2.87	5.068	37.92	2275	3.276
2.38	3.794	28.38	1703	2.452	2.88	5.096	38.12	2287	3.293
2.39	3.819	28.57	1714	2.468	2.89	5.123	38.32	2299	3.311
2.40	3.843	28.75	1725	2.484	2.90	5.150	38.53	2312	3.329
2.41	3.868	28.94	1736	2.500	2.91	5.178	38.74	2324	3.346
2.42	3.893	29.12	1747	2.516	2.92	5.205	38.94	2336	3.364
2.43	3.918	29.31	1758	2.532	2.93	5.233	39.15	2349	3.382
2.44	3.943	29.50	1770	2.548	2.94	5.261	39.36	2361	3.400
2.45	3.968	29.68	1781	2.564	2.95	5.288	39.56	2373	3.418
2.46	3.993	29.87	1792	2.581	2.96	5.316	39.77	2386	3.436
2.47	4.018	30.06	1803	2.597	2.97	5.344	39.98	2398	3.454
2.48	4.043	30.25	1815	2.613	2.98	5.372	40.19	2411	3.472
2.49	4.068	30.44	1826	2.629	2.99	5.400	40.40	2423	3.490
2.50	4.094	30.63	1837	2.646	3.00	5.428	40.60	2436	3.508

12-4: 6 in. Parshall Flume Discharge Table

Formulas: CFS = $2.060H^{1.580}$ GPS = CFS x 7.481
GPM = CFS x 448.8   MGD = CFS x 0.6463

Head Feet	CFS	GPS	GPM	MGD	Head Feet	CFS	GPS	GPM	MGD
0.01	0.0014	0.0107	0.6396	0.0009	0.51	0.7109	5.318	319.1	0.4595
0.02	0.0043	0.0319	1.912	0.0028	0.52	0.7331	5.484	329.0	0.4738
0.03	0.0081	0.0605	3.629	0.0052	0.53	0.7555	5.652	339.1	0.4883
0.04	0.0127	0.0953	5.717	0.0082	0.54	0.7781	5.821	349.2	0.5029
0.05	0.0181	0.1356	8.134	0.0117	0.55	0.8010	5.992	359.5	0.5177
0.06	0.0242	0.1808	10.85	0.0156	0.56	0.8241	6.165	369.9	0.5326
0.07	0.0308	0.2307	13.84	0.0199	0.57	0.8475	6.340	380.4	0.5478
0.08	0.0381	0.2849	17.09	0.0246	0.58	0.8711	6.517	391.0	0.5630
0.09	0.0459	0.3432	20.59	0.0296	0.59	0.8950	6.695	401.7	0.5784
0.10	0.0542	0.4053	24.32	0.0350	0.60	0.9191	6.876	412.5	0.5940
0.11	0.0630	0.4712	28.27	0.0407	0.61	0.9434	7.057	423.4	0.6097
0.12	0.0723	0.5407	32.44	0.0467	0.62	0.9679	7.241	434.4	0.6256
0.13	0.0820	0.6136	36.81	0.0530	0.63	0.9927	7.427	445.5	0.6416
0.14	0.0922	0.6898	41.38	0.0596	0.64	1.018	7.614	456.8	0.6578
0.15	0.1028	0.7692	46.15	0.0665	0.65	1.043	7.802	468.1	0.6741
0.16	0.1139	0.8518	51.10	0.0736	0.66	1.068	7.993	479.5	0.6905
0.17	0.1253	0.9374	56.24	0.0810	0.67	1.094	8.185	491.0	0.7071
0.18	0.1372	1.026	61.55	0.0886	0.68	1.120	8.379	502.7	0.7239
0.19	0.1494	1.118	67.04	0.0965	0.69	1.146	8.574	514.4	0.7408
0.20	0.1620	1.212	72.70	0.1047	0.70	1.173	8.772	526.2	0.7578
0.21	0.1750	1.309	78.53	0.1131	0.71	1.199	8.970	538.2	0.7750
0.22	0.1883	1.409	84.52	0.1217	0.72	1.226	9.171	550.2	0.7923
0.23	0.2020	1.511	90.67	0.1306	0.73	1.253	9.373	562.3	0.8098
0.24	0.2161	1.616	96.97	0.1396	0.74	1.280	9.577	574.5	0.8273
0.25	0.2305	1.724	103.4	0.1490	0.75	1.308	9.782	586.8	0.8451
0.26	0.2452	1.834	110.0	0.1585	0.76	1.335	9.989	599.2	0.8630
0.27	0.2603	1.947	116.8	0.1682	0.77	1.363	10.20	611.8	0.8810
0.28	0.2757	2.062	123.7	0.1782	0.78	1.391	10.41	624.4	0.8991
0.29	0.2914	2.180	130.8	0.1883	0.79	1.419	10.62	637.0	0.9174
0.30	0.3074	2.300	138.0	0.1987	0.80	1.448	10.83	649.8	0.9358
0.31	0.3238	2.422	145.3	0.2092	0.81	1.477	11.05	662.7	0.9544
0.32	0.3404	2.547	152.8	0.2200	0.82	1.506	11.26	675.7	0.9730
0.33	0.3574	2.673	160.4	0.2310	0.83	1.535	11.48	688.8	0.9918
0.34	0.3746	2.803	168.1	0.2421	0.84	1.564	11.70	701.9	1.011
0.35	0.3922	2.934	176.0	0.2535	0.85	1.593	11.92	715.2	1.030
0.36	0.4100	3.068	184.0	0.2650	0.86	1.623	12.14	728.5	1.049
0.37	0.4282	3.203	192.2	0.2767	0.87	1.653	12.37	741.9	1.068
0.38	0.4466	3.341	200.4	0.2886	0.88	1.683	12.59	755.4	1.088
0.39	0.4653	3.481	208.8	0.3007	0.89	1.714	12.82	769.1	1.107
0.40	0.4843	3.623	217.4	0.3130	0.90	1.744	13.05	782.8	1.127
0.41	0.5036	3.767	226.0	0.3255	0.91	1.775	13.28	796.5	1.147
0.42	0.5231	3.913	234.8	0.3381	0.92	1.806	13.51	810.4	1.167
0.43	0.5429	4.062	243.7	0.3509	0.93	1.837	13.74	824.4	1.187
0.44	0.5630	4.212	252.7	0.3639	0.94	1.868	13.98	838.4	1.207
0.45	0.5834	4.364	261.8	0.3770	0.95	1.900	14.21	852.6	1.228
0.46	0.6040	4.518	271.1	0.3904	0.96	1.931	14.45	866.8	1.248
0.47	0.6249	4.675	280.4	0.4038	0.97	1.963	14.69	881.1	1.269
0.48	0.6460	4.833	289.9	0.4175	0.98	1.995	14.93	895.5	1.290
0.49	0.6674	4.993	299.5	0.4313	0.99	2.028	15.17	910.0	1.310
0.50	0.6890	5.155	309.2	0.4453	1.00	2.060	15.41	924.5	1.331

12

Formulas: CFS = $2.060H^{1.580}$ GPS = CFS x 7.481
GPM = CFS x 448.8   MGD = CFS x 0.6463

Head Feet	CFS	GPS	GPM	MGD	Head Feet	CFS	GPS	GPM	MGD
1.01	2.093	15.66	939.2	1.352	1.51	3.950	29.55	1773	2.553
1.02	2.125	15.90	953.9	1.374	1.52	3.992	29.86	1792	2.580
1.03	2.158	16.15	968.7	1.395	1.53	4.033	30.17	1810	2.607
1.04	2.192	16.40	983.6	1.416	1.54	4.075	30.49	1829	2.634
1.05	2.225	16.65	998.6	1.438	1.55	4.117	30.80	1848	2.661
1.06	2.259	16.90	1014	1.460	1.56	4.159	31.11	1867	2.688
1.07	2.292	17.15	1029	1.482	1.57	4.201	31.43	1886	2.715
1.08	2.326	17.40	1044	1.504	1.58	4.244	31.75	1905	2.743
1.09	2.360	17.66	1059	1.526	1.59	4.286	32.07	1924	2.770
1.10	2.395	17.92	1075	1.548	1.60	4.329	32.38	1943	2.798
1.11	2.429	18.17	1090	1.570	1.61	4.372	32.70	1962	2.825
1.12	2.464	18.43	1106	1.592	1.62	4.415	33.03	1981	2.853
1.13	2.499	18.69	1121	1.615	1.63	4.458	33.35	2001	2.881
1.14	2.534	18.96	1137	1.638	1.64	4.501	33.67	2020	2.909
1.15	2.569	19.22	1153	1.660	1.65	4.545	34.00	2040	2.937
1.16	2.604	19.48	1169	1.683	1.66	4.588	34.32	2059	2.965
1.17	2.640	19.75	1185	1.706	1.67	4.632	34.65	2079	2.994
1.18	2.676	20.02	1201	1.729	1.68	4.676	34.98	2098	3.022
1.19	2.712	20.29	1217	1.753	1.69	4.720	35.31	2118	3.050
1.20	2.748	20.56	1233	1.776	1.70	4.764	35.64	2138	3.079
1.21	2.784	20.83	1249	1.799	1.71	4.808	35.97	2158	3.108
1.22	2.820	21.10	1266	1.823	1.72	4.853	36.30	2178	3.136
1.23	2.857	21.37	1282	1.847	1.73	4.898	36.64	2198	3.165
1.24	2.894	21.65	1299	1.870	1.74	4.942	36.97	2218	3.194
1.25	2.931	21.93	1315	1.894	1.75	4.987	37.31	2238	3.223
1.26	2.968	22.20	1332	1.918	1.76	5.032	37.65	2259	3.252
1.27	3.005	22.48	1349	1.942	1.77	5.078	37.99	2279	3.282
1.28	3.043	22.76	1366	1.966	1.78	5.123	38.33	2299	3.311
1.29	3.080	23.04	1382	1.991	1.79	5.169	38.67	2320	3.340
1.30	3.118	23.33	1399	2.015	1.80	5.214	39.01	2340	3.370
1.31	3.156	23.61	1416	2.040	1.81	5.260	39.35	2361	3.400
1.32	3.194	23.90	1434	2.064	1.82	5.306	39.70	2381	3.429
1.33	3.233	24.18	1451	2.089	1.83	5.352	40.04	2402	3.459
1.34	3.271	24.47	1468	2.114	1.84	5.399	40.39	2423	3.489
1.35	3.310	24.76	1485	2.139	1.85	5.445	40.73	2444	3.519
1.36	3.349	25.05	1503	2.164	1.86	5.492	41.08	2465	3.549
1.37	3.388	25.34	1520	2.189	1.87	5.538	41.43	2486	3.579
1.38	3.427	25.64	1538	2.215	1.88	5.585	41.78	2507	3.610
1.39	3.466	25.93	1556	2.240	1.89	5.632	42.13	2528	3.640
1.40	3.505	26.22	1573	2.266	1.90	5.679	42.49	2549	3.671
1.41	3.545	26.52	1591	2.291	1.91	5.727	42.84	2570	3.701
1.42	3.585	26.82	1609	2.317	1.92	5.774	43.20	2591	3.732
1.43	3.625	27.12	1627	2.343	1.93	5.822	43.55	2613	3.763
1.44	3.665	27.42	1645	2.369	1.94	5.869	43.91	2634	3.793
1.45	3.705	27.72	1663	2.395	1.95	5.917	44.27	2656	3.824
1.46	3.746	28.02	1681	2.421	1.96	5.965	44.63	2677	3.855
1.47	3.786	28.33	1699	2.447	1.97	6.013	44.99	2699	3.886
1.48	3.827	28.63	1718	2.474	1.98	6.062	45.35	2721	3.918
1.49	3.868	28.94	1736	2.500	1.99	6.110	45.71	2742	3.949
1.50	3.909	29.24	1754	2.527	2.00	6.159	46.07	2764	3.980

12

Formulas: CFS = $2.060H^{1.580}$ GPS = CFS x 7.481
GPM = CFS x 448.8   MGD = CFS x 0.6463

Head Feet	CFS	GPS	GPM	MGD	Head Feet	CFS	GPS	GPM	MGD
2.01	6.208	46.44	2786	4.012	2.51	8.818	65.96	3957	5.699
2.02	6.256	46.80	2808	4.043	2.52	8.873	66.38	3982	5.735
2.03	6.305	47.17	2830	4.075	2.53	8.929	66.80	4007	5.771
2.04	6.355	47.54	2852	4.107	2.54	8.985	67.21	4032	5.807
2.05	6.404	47.91	2874	4.139	2.55	9.041	67.63	4057	5.843
2.06	6.453	48.28	2896	4.171	2.56	9.097	68.05	4083	5.879
2.07	6.503	48.65	2918	4.203	2.57	9.153	68.47	4108	5.916
2.08	6.553	49.02	2941	4.235	2.58	9.209	68.89	4133	5.952
2.09	6.602	49.39	2963	4.267	2.59	9.266	69.32	4158	5.988
2.10	6.652	49.77	2986	4.299	2.60	9.322	69.74	4184	6.025
2.11	6.702	50.14	3008	4.332	2.61	9.379	70.16	4209	6.062
2.12	6.753	50.52	3031	4.364	2.62	9.436	70.59	4235	6.098
2.13	6.803	50.89	3053	4.397	2.63	9.493	71.02	4260	6.135
2.14	6.854	51.27	3076	4.430	2.64	9.550	71.44	4286	6.172
2.15	6.904	51.65	3099	4.462	2.65	9.607	71.87	4312	6.209
2.16	6.955	52.03	3121	4.495	2.66	9.665	72.30	4337	6.246
2.17	7.006	52.41	3144	4.528	2.67	9.722	72.73	4363	6.283
2.18	7.057	52.79	3167	4.561	2.68	9.780	73.16	4389	6.321
2.19	7.108	53.18	3190	4.594	2.69	9.837	73.59	4415	6.358
2.20	7.160	53.56	3213	4.627	2.70	9.895	74.03	4441	6.395
2.21	7.211	53.95	3236	4.661	2.71	9.953	74.46	4467	6.433
2.22	7.263	54.33	3260	4.694	2.72	10.01	74.89	4493	6.470
2.23	7.315	54.72	3283	4.727	2.73	10.07	75.33	4519	6.508
2.24	7.366	55.11	3306	4.761	2.74	10.13	75.77	4545	6.546
2.25	7.418	55.50	3329	4.795	2.75	10.19	76.20	4572	6.583
2.26	7.471	55.89	3353	4.828	2.76	10.24	76.64	4598	6.621
2.27	7.523	56.28	3376	4.862	2.77	10.30	77.08	4624	6.659
2.28	7.575	56.67	3400	4.896	2.78	10.36	77.52	4651	6.697
2.29	7.628	57.06	3423	4.930	2.79	10.42	77.96	4677	6.735
2.30	7.681	57.46	3447	4.964	2.80	10.48	78.40	4704	6.773
2.31	7.733	57.85	3471	4.998	2.81	10.54	78.85	4730	6.812
2.32	7.786	58.25	3495	5.032	2.82	10.60	79.29	4757	6.850
2.33	7.840	58.65	3518	5.067	2.83	10.66	79.74	4783	6.888
2.34	7.893	59.05	3542	5.101	2.84	10.72	80.18	4810	6.927
2.35	7.946	59.44	3566	5.136	2.85	10.78	80.63	4837	6.966
2.36	8.000	59.84	3590	5.170	2.86	10.84	81.07	4864	7.004
2.37	8.053	60.25	3614	5.205	2.87	10.90	81.52	4891	7.043
2.38	8.107	60.65	3638	5.240	2.88	10.96	81.97	4918	7.082
2.39	8.161	61.05	3663	5.274	2.89	11.02	82.42	4945	7.121
2.40	8.215	61.46	3687	5.309	2.90	11.08	82.87	4972	7.160
2.41	8.269	61.86	3711	5.344	2.91	11.14	83.33	4999	7.199
2.42	8.323	62.27	3735	5.379	2.92	11.20	83.78	5026	7.238
2.43	8.378	62.67	3760	5.415	2.93	11.26	84.23	5053	7.277
2.44	8.432	63.08	3784	5.450	2.94	11.32	84.69	5081	7.316
2.45	8.487	63.49	3809	5.485	2.95	11.38	85.14	5108	7.356
2.46	8.542	63.90	3834	5.521	2.96	11.44	85.60	5135	7.395
2.47	8.597	64.31	3858	5.556	2.97	11.50	86.06	5163	7.435
2.48	8.652	64.72	3883	5.592	2.98	11.56	86.51	5190	7.474
2.49	8.707	65.14	3908	5.627	2.99	11.63	86.97	5218	7.514
2.50	8.762	65.55	3932	5.663	3.00	11.69	87.43	5245	7.554

12

12-5: 9 in. Parshall Flume Discharge Table

Formulas: $CFS = 3.070H^{1.530}$ $GPS = CFS \times 7.481$
$GPM = CFS \times 448.8$ $MGD = CFS \times 0.6463$

Head Feet	CFS	GPS	GPM	MGD	Head Feet	CFS	GPS	GPM	MGD
0.01	0.0027	0.0200	1.200	0.0017	0.51	1.096	8.197	491.8	0.7082
0.02	0.0077	0.0578	3.466	0.0050	0.52	1.129	8.445	506.6	0.7296
0.03	0.0144	0.1074	6.444	0.0093	0.53	1.162	8.694	521.6	0.7511
0.04	0.0223	0.1668	10.01	0.0144	0.54	1.196	8.947	536.7	0.7729
0.05	0.0314	0.2347	14.08	0.0203	0.55	1.230	9.201	552.0	0.7949
0.06	0.0415	0.3102	18.61	0.0268	0.56	1.264	9.459	567.4	0.8171
0.07	0.0525	0.3927	23.56	0.0339	0.57	1.299	9.718	583.0	0.8396
0.08	0.0644	0.4818	28.90	0.0416	0.58	1.334	9.980	598.7	0.8622
0.09	0.0771	0.5769	34.61	0.0498	0.59	1.369	10.24	614.6	0.8851
0.10	0.0906	0.6778	40.66	0.0586	0.60	1.405	10.51	630.6	0.9081
0.11	0.1048	0.7842	47.05	0.0677	0.61	1.441	10.78	646.8	0.9314
0.12	0.1198	0.8959	53.75	0.0774	0.62	1.477	11.05	663.1	0.9548
0.13	0.1354	1.013	60.75	0.0875	0.63	1.514	11.33	679.5	0.9785
0.14	0.1516	1.134	68.04	0.0980	0.64	1.551	11.60	696.1	1.002
0.15	0.1685	1.260	75.62	0.1089	0.65	1.588	11.88	712.8	1.026
0.16	0.1860	1.391	83.46	0.1202	0.66	1.626	12.16	729.6	1.051
0.17	0.2040	1.526	91.58	0.1319	0.67	1.664	12.44	746.6	1.075
0.18	0.2227	1.666	99.94	0.1439	0.68	1.702	12.73	763.7	1.100
0.19	0.2419	1.810	108.6	0.1563	0.69	1.740	13.02	781.0	1.125
0.20	0.2616	1.957	117.4	0.1691	0.70	1.779	13.31	798.3	1.150
0.21	0.2819	2.109	126.5	0.1822	0.71	1.818	13.60	815.9	1.175
0.22	0.3027	2.265	135.9	0.1956	0.72	1.857	13.89	833.5	1.200
0.23	0.3240	2.424	145.4	0.2094	0.73	1.897	14.19	851.3	1.226
0.24	0.3458	2.587	155.2	0.2235	0.74	1.937	14.49	869.2	1.252
0.25	0.3681	2.754	165.2	0.2379	0.75	1.977	14.79	887.2	1.278
0.26	0.3909	2.924	175.4	0.2526	0.76	2.017	15.09	905.4	1.304
0.27	0.4141	3.098	185.9	0.2676	0.77	2.058	15.40	923.7	1.330
0.28	0.4378	3.275	196.5	0.2830	0.78	2.099	15.70	942.1	1.357
0.29	0.4620	3.456	207.3	0.2986	0.79	2.140	16.01	960.6	1.383
0.30	0.4866	3.640	218.4	0.3145	0.80	2.182	16.32	979.3	1.410
0.31	0.5116	3.827	229.6	0.3306	0.81	2.224	16.64	998.1	1.437
0.32	0.5371	4.018	241.0	0.3471	0.82	2.266	16.95	1017	1.465
0.33	0.5629	4.211	252.6	0.3638	0.83	2.308	17.27	1036	1.492
0.34	0.5893	4.408	264.5	0.3808	0.84	2.351	17.59	1055	1.520
0.35	0.6160	4.608	276.4	0.3981	0.85	2.394	17.91	1074	1.547
0.36	0.6431	4.811	288.6	0.4156	0.86	2.437	18.23	1094	1.575
0.37	0.6706	5.017	301.0	0.4334	0.87	2.481	18.56	1113	1.603
0.38	0.6986	5.226	313.5	0.4515	0.88	2.525	18.89	1133	1.632
0.39	0.7269	5.438	326.2	0.4698	0.89	2.569	19.22	1153	1.660
0.40	0.7556	5.653	339.1	0.4883	0.90	2.613	19.55	1173	1.689
0.41	0.7847	5.870	352.2	0.5071	0.91	2.657	19.88	1193	1.718
0.42	0.8142	6.091	365.4	0.5262	0.92	2.702	20.22	1213	1.746
0.43	0.8440	6.314	378.8	0.5455	0.93	2.747	20.55	1233	1.775
0.44	0.8742	6.540	392.4	0.5650	0.94	2.793	20.89	1253	1.805
0.45	0.9048	6.769	406.1	0.5848	0.95	2.838	21.23	1274	1.834
0.46	0.9357	7.000	420.0	0.6048	0.96	2.884	21.58	1294	1.864
0.47	0.9670	7.234	434.0	0.6250	0.97	2.930	21.92	1315	1.894
0.48	0.9987	7.471	448.2	0.6455	0.98	2.977	22.27	1336	1.924
0.49	1.031	7.711	462.6	0.6662	0.99	3.023	22.62	1357	1.954
0.50	1.063	7.953	477.1	0.6871	1.00	3.070	22.97	1378	1.984

12

Formulas: CFS = $3.070H^{1.530}$ GPS = CFS x 7.481
GPM = CFS x 448.8   MGD = CFS x 0.6463

Head Feet	CFS	GPS	GPM	MGD	Head Feet	CFS	GPS	GPM	MGD
1.01	3.117	23.32	1399	2.015	1.51	5.767	43.15	2588	3.727
1.02	3.164	23.67	1420	2.045	1.52	5.826	43.58	2615	3.765
1.03	3.212	24.03	1442	2.076	1.53	5.885	44.02	2641	3.803
1.04	3.260	24.39	1463	2.107	1.54	5.944	44.46	2667	3.841
1.05	3.308	24.75	1485	2.138	1.55	6.003	44.91	2694	3.880
1.06	3.356	25.11	1506	2.169	1.56	6.062	45.35	2721	3.918
1.07	3.405	25.47	1528	2.201	1.57	6.122	45.80	2747	3.956
1.08	3.454	25.84	1550	2.232	1.58	6.181	46.24	2774	3.995
1.09	3.503	26.20	1572	2.264	1.59	6.241	46.69	2801	4.034
1.10	3.552	26.57	1594	2.296	1.60	6.301	47.14	2828	4.073
1.11	3.601	26.94	1616	2.328	1.61	6.362	47.59	2855	4.112
1.12	3.651	27.32	1639	2.360	1.62	6.422	48.05	2882	4.151
1.13	3.701	27.69	1661	2.392	1.63	6.483	48.50	2910	4.190
1.14	3.751	28.06	1684	2.425	1.64	6.544	48.96	2937	4.229
1.15	3.802	28.44	1706	2.457	1.65	6.605	49.41	2964	4.269
1.16	3.853	28.82	1729	2.490	1.66	6.667	49.87	2992	4.309
1.17	3.904	29.20	1752	2.523	1.67	6.728	50.33	3020	4.348
1.18	3.955	29.59	1775	2.556	1.68	6.790	50.80	3047	4.388
1.19	4.006	29.97	1798	2.589	1.69	6.852	51.26	3075	4.428
1.20	4.058	30.36	1821	2.623	1.70	6.914	51.72	3103	4.468
1.21	4.110	30.74	1844	2.656	1.71	6.976	52.19	3131	4.509
1.22	4.162	31.13	1868	2.690	1.72	7.039	52.66	3159	4.549
1.23	4.214	31.52	1891	2.723	1.73	7.101	53.13	3187	4.590
1.24	4.267	31.92	1915	2.757	1.74	7.164	53.60	3215	4.630
1.25	4.319	32.31	1938	2.792	1.75	7.227	54.07	3244	4.671
1.26	4.372	32.71	1962	2.826	1.76	7.291	54.54	3272	4.712
1.27	4.425	33.11	1986	2.860	1.77	7.354	55.02	3301	4.753
1.28	4.479	33.51	2010	2.895	1.78	7.418	55.49	3329	4.794
1.29	4.533	33.91	2034	2.929	1.79	7.482	55.97	3358	4.835
1.30	4.586	34.31	2058	2.964	1.80	7.546	56.45	3387	4.877
1.31	4.640	34.72	2083	2.999	1.81	7.610	56.93	3415	4.918
1.32	4.695	35.12	2107	3.034	1.82	7.674	57.41	3444	4.960
1.33	4.749	35.53	2131	3.069	1.83	7.739	57.90	3473	5.002
1.34	4.804	35.94	2156	3.105	1.84	7.804	58.38	3502	5.044
1.35	4.859	36.35	2181	3.140	1.85	7.869	58.87	3532	5.086
1.36	4.914	36.76	2205	3.176	1.86	7.934	59.35	3561	5.128
1.37	4.970	37.18	2230	3.212	1.87	7.999	59.84	3590	5.170
1.38	5.025	37.59	2255	3.248	1.88	8.065	60.33	3620	5.212
1.39	5.081	38.01	2280	3.284	1.89	8.131	60.83	3649	5.255
1.40	5.137	38.43	2306	3.320	1.90	8.197	61.32	3679	5.297
1.41	5.193	38.85	2331	3.356	1.91	8.263	61.81	3708	5.340
1.42	5.250	39.27	2356	3.393	1.92	8.329	62.31	3738	5.383
1.43	5.306	39.70	2382	3.430	1.93	8.395	62.81	3768	5.426
1.44	5.363	40.12	2407	3.466	1.94	8.462	63.30	3798	5.469
1.45	5.420	40.55	2433	3.503	1.95	8.529	63.80	3828	5.512
1.46	5.478	40.98	2458	3.540	1.96	8.596	64.31	3858	5.556
1.47	5.535	41.41	2484	3.577	1.97	8.663	64.81	3888	5.599
1.48	5.593	41.84	2510	3.615	1.98	8.730	65.31	3918	5.642
1.49	5.651	42.27	2536	3.652	1.99	8.798	65.82	3949	5.686
1.50	5.709	42.71	2562	3.690	2.00	8.866	66.32	3979	5.730

12

Formulas: $CFS = 3.070H^{1.530}$ $GPS = CFS \times 7.481$
$GPM = CFS \times 448.8$ $MGD = CFS \times 0.6463$

Head Feet	CFS	GPS	GPM	MGD	Head Feet	CFS	GPS	GPM	MGD
2.01	8.934	66.83	4009	5.774	2.51	12.55	93.89	5632	8.111
2.02	9.002	67.34	4040	5.818	2.52	12.63	94.46	5667	8.160
2.03	9.070	67.85	4071	5.862	2.53	12.70	95.03	5701	8.210
2.04	9.138	68.36	4101	5.906	2.54	12.78	95.61	5736	8.260
2.05	9.207	68.88	4132	5.951	2.55	12.86	96.18	5770	8.310
2.06	9.276	69.39	4163	5.995	2.56	12.93	96.76	5805	8.359
2.07	9.345	69.91	4194	6.040	2.57	13.01	97.34	5840	8.410
2.08	9.414	70.43	4225	6.084	2.58	13.09	97.92	5874	8.460
2.09	9.483	70.95	4256	6.129	2.59	13.17	98.50	5909	8.510
2.10	9.553	71.47	4287	6.174	2.60	13.24	99.08	5944	8.560
2.11	9.623	71.99	4319	6.219	2.61	13.32	99.67	5979	8.611
2.12	9.692	72.51	4350	6.264	2.62	13.40	100.3	6014	8.661
2.13	9.762	73.03	4381	6.309	2.63	13.48	100.8	6050	8.712
2.14	9.833	73.56	4413	6.355	2.64	13.56	101.4	6085	8.762
2.15	9.903	74.08	4444	6.400	2.65	13.64	102.0	6120	8.813
2.16	9.974	74.61	4476	6.446	2.66	13.72	102.6	6155	8.864
2.17	10.04	75.14	4508	6.492	2.67	13.79	103.2	6191	8.915
2.18	10.12	75.67	4540	6.537	2.68	13.87	103.8	6226	8.966
2.19	10.19	76.20	4572	6.583	2.69	13.95	104.4	6262	9.018
2.20	10.26	76.74	4604	6.629	2.70	14.03	105.0	6298	9.069
2.21	10.33	77.27	4636	6.676	2.71	14.11	105.6	6333	9.120
2.22	10.40	77.81	4668	6.722	2.72	14.19	106.2	6369	9.172
2.23	10.47	78.34	4700	6.768	2.73	14.27	106.8	6405	9.224
2.24	10.54	78.88	4732	6.815	2.74	14.35	107.4	6441	9.275
2.25	10.62	79.42	4765	6.861	2.75	14.43	108.0	6477	9.327
2.26	10.69	79.96	4797	6.908	2.76	14.51	108.6	6513	9.379
2.27	10.76	80.50	4830	6.955	2.77	14.59	109.2	6549	9.431
2.28	10.83	81.05	4862	7.002	2.78	14.67	109.8	6585	9.483
2.29	10.91	81.59	4895	7.049	2.79	14.75	110.4	6622	9.536
2.30	10.98	82.14	4928	7.096	2.80	14.84	111.0	6658	9.588
2.31	11.05	82.68	4960	7.143	2.81	14.92	111.6	6694	9.640
2.32	11.13	83.23	4993	7.191	2.82	15.00	112.2	6731	9.693
2.33	11.20	83.78	5026	7.238	2.83	15.08	112.8	6767	9.746
2.34	11.27	84.33	5059	7.286	2.84	15.16	113.4	6804	9.798
2.35	11.35	84.89	5092	7.333	2.85	15.24	114.0	6841	9.851
2.36	11.42	85.44	5126	7.381	2.86	15.32	114.6	6878	9.904
2.37	11.49	85.99	5159	7.429	2.87	15.41	115.3	6914	9.957
2.38	11.57	86.55	5192	7.477	2.88	15.49	115.9	6951	10.01
2.39	11.64	87.11	5226	7.525	2.89	15.57	116.5	6988	10.06
2.40	11.72	87.66	5259	7.573	2.90	15.65	117.1	7025	10.12
2.41	11.79	88.22	5293	7.622	2.91	15.74	117.7	7062	10.17
2.42	11.87	88.78	5326	7.670	2.92	15.82	118.3	7099	10.22
2.43	11.94	89.35	5360	7.719	2.93	15.90	119.0	7137	10.28
2.44	12.02	89.91	5394	7.767	2.94	15.98	119.6	7174	10.33
2.45	12.09	90.47	5428	7.816	2.95	16.07	120.2	7211	10.38
2.46	12.17	91.04	5462	7.865	2.96	16.15	120.8	7249	10.44
2.47	12.25	91.61	5496	7.914	2.97	16.24	121.5	7286	10.49
2.48	12.32	92.17	5530	7.963	2.98	16.32	122.1	7324	10.55
2.49	12.40	92.74	5564	8.012	2.99	16.40	122.7	7362	10.60
2.50	12.47	93.31	5598	8.062	3.00	16.49	123.3	7399	10.66

12

12-6: 1 ft. Parshall Flume Discharge Table

Formulas: CFS = $4.000H^{1.522}$ GPS = CFS x 7.481
$\qquad$ GPM = CFS x 448.8   MGD = CFS x 0.6463

Head Feet	CFS	GPS	GPM	MGD	Head Feet	CFS	GPS	GPM	MGD
0.01	0.0036	0.0270	1.622	0.0023	0.51	1.435	10.74	644.2	0.9277
0.02	0.0104	0.0777	4.659	0.0067	0.52	1.478	11.06	663.5	0.9555
0.03	0.0192	0.1439	8.636	0.0124	0.53	1.522	11.39	683.1	0.9837
0.04	0.0298	0.2230	13.38	0.0193	0.54	1.566	11.71	702.8	1.012
0.05	0.0419	0.3132	18.79	0.0271	0.55	1.610	12.05	722.7	1.041
0.06	0.0553	0.4134	24.80	0.0357	0.56	1.655	12.38	742.8	1.070
0.07	0.0699	0.5227	31.36	0.0452	0.57	1.700	12.72	763.1	1.099
0.08	0.0856	0.6405	38.43	0.0553	0.58	1.746	13.06	783.5	1.128
0.09	0.1024	0.7663	45.97	0.0662	0.59	1.792	13.40	804.2	1.158
0.10	0.1202	0.8995	53.97	0.0777	0.60	1.838	13.75	825.0	1.188
0.11	0.1390	1.040	62.39	0.0898	0.61	1.885	14.10	846.0	1.218
0.12	0.1587	1.187	71.22	0.1026	0.62	1.932	14.46	867.2	1.249
0.13	0.1793	1.341	80.45	0.1159	0.63	1.980	14.81	888.6	1.280
0.14	0.2007	1.501	90.06	0.1297	0.64	2.028	15.17	910.2	1.311
0.15	0.2229	1.667	100.0	0.1440	0.65	2.076	15.53	931.9	1.342
0.16	0.2459	1.839	110.4	0.1589	0.66	2.125	15.90	953.8	1.374
0.17	0.2697	2.017	121.0	0.1743	0.67	2.174	16.27	975.9	1.405
0.18	0.2942	2.201	132.0	0.1901	0.68	2.224	16.64	998.1	1.437
0.19	0.3194	2.389	143.3	0.2064	0.69	2.274	17.01	1021	1.470
0.20	0.3453	2.583	155.0	0.2232	0.70	2.324	17.39	1043	1.502
0.21	0.3719	2.783	166.9	0.2404	0.71	2.375	17.77	1066	1.535
0.22	0.3992	2.987	179.2	0.2580	0.72	2.426	18.15	1089	1.568
0.23	0.4272	3.196	191.7	0.2761	0.73	2.478	18.54	1112	1.601
0.24	0.4558	3.410	204.5	0.2946	0.74	2.529	18.92	1135	1.635
0.25	0.4850	3.628	217.7	0.3134	0.75	2.582	19.31	1159	1.669
0.26	0.5148	3.851	231.0	0.3327	0.76	2.634	19.71	1182	1.703
0.27	0.5452	4.079	244.7	0.3524	0.77	2.687	20.10	1206	1.737
0.28	0.5763	4.311	258.6	0.3725	0.78	2.740	20.50	1230	1.771
0.29	0.6079	4.548	272.8	0.3929	0.79	2.794	20.90	1254	1.806
0.30	0.6401	4.788	287.3	0.4137	0.80	2.848	21.31	1278	1.841
0.31	0.6728	5.034	302.0	0.4349	0.81	2.903	21.71	1303	1.876
0.32	0.7062	5.283	316.9	0.4564	0.82	2.957	22.12	1327	1.911
0.33	0.7400	5.536	332.1	0.4783	0.83	3.012	22.53	1352	1.947
0.34	0.7744	5.793	347.6	0.5005	0.84	3.068	22.95	1377	1.983
0.35	0.8093	6.055	363.2	0.5231	0.85	3.123	23.37	1402	2.019
0.36	0.8448	6.320	379.1	0.5460	0.86	3.180	23.79	1427	2.055
0.37	0.8808	6.589	395.3	0.5692	0.87	3.236	24.21	1452	2.091
0.38	0.9173	6.862	411.7	0.5928	0.88	3.293	24.63	1478	2.128
0.39	0.9542	7.139	428.3	0.6167	0.89	3.350	25.06	1503	2.165
0.40	0.9917	7.419	445.1	0.6410	0.90	3.407	25.49	1529	2.202
0.41	1.030	7.703	462.1	0.6655	0.91	3.465	25.92	1555	2.240
0.42	1.068	7.991	479.4	0.6904	0.92	3.523	26.36	1581	2.277
0.43	1.107	8.282	496.9	0.7155	0.93	3.582	26.79	1607	2.315
0.44	1.147	8.577	514.6	0.7410	0.94	3.640	27.23	1634	2.353
0.45	1.186	8.876	532.5	0.7668	0.95	3.700	27.68	1660	2.391
0.46	1.227	9.178	550.6	0.7929	0.96	3.759	28.12	1687	2.429
0.47	1.268	9.483	568.9	0.8193	0.97	3.819	28.57	1714	2.468
0.48	1.309	9.792	587.4	0.8459	0.98	3.879	29.02	1741	2.507
0.49	1.351	10.10	606.2	0.8729	0.99	3.939	29.47	1768	2.546
0.50	1.393	10.42	625.1	0.9002	1.00	4.000	29.92	1795	2.585

12

12-6: 1 ft. Parshall Flume Discharge Table *(Continued)*

Formulas: $CFS = 4.000H^{1.520}$ $GPS = CFS \times 7.481$
$GPM = CFS \times 448.8$ $MGD = CFS \times 0.6463$

Head Feet	CFS	GPS	GPM	MGD	Head Feet	CFS	GPS	GPM	MGD
1.01	4.061	30.38	1823	2.625	1.51	7.490	56.03	3361	4.841
1.02	4.122	30.84	1850	2.664	1.52	7.565	56.60	3395	4.889
1.03	4.184	31.30	1878	2.704	1.53	7.641	57.16	3429	4.938
1.04	4.246	31.76	1906	2.744	1.54	7.717	57.73	3464	4.988
1.05	4.308	32.23	1934	2.784	1.55	7.794	58.30	3498	5.037
1.06	4.371	32.70	1962	2.825	1.56	7.870	58.88	3532	5.087
1.07	4.434	33.17	1990	2.866	1.57	7.947	59.45	3567	5.136
1.08	4.497	33.64	2018	2.906	1.58	8.024	60.03	3601	5.186
1.09	4.561	34.12	2047	2.948	1.59	8.102	60.61	3636	5.236
1.10	4.624	34.60	2075	2.989	1.60	8.180	61.19	3671	5.286
1.11	4.689	35.08	2104	3.030	1.61	8.258	61.77	3706	5.337
1.12	4.753	35.56	2133	3.072	1.62	8.336	62.36	3741	5.387
1.13	4.818	36.04	2162	3.114	1.63	8.414	62.95	3776	5.438
1.14	4.883	36.53	2191	3.156	1.64	8.493	63.53	3812	5.489
1.15	4.948	37.02	2221	3.198	1.65	8.572	64.13	3847	5.540
1.16	5.014	37.51	2250	3.240	1.66	8.651	64.72	3883	5.591
1.17	5.080	38.00	2280	3.283	1.67	8.730	65.31	3918	5.642
1.18	5.146	38.50	2309	3.326	1.68	8.810	65.91	3954	5.694
1.19	5.212	38.99	2339	3.369	1.69	8.890	66.51	3990	5.746
1.20	5.279	39.49	2369	3.412	1.70	8.970	67.11	4026	5.797
1.21	5.346	40.00	2399	3.455	1.71	9.051	67.71	4062	5.849
1.22	5.414	40.50	2430	3.499	1.72	9.131	68.31	4098	5.902
1.23	5.481	41.01	2460	3.543	1.73	9.212	68.92	4134	5.954
1.24	5.549	41.52	2491	3.587	1.74	9.293	69.52	4171	6.006
1.25	5.618	42.03	2521	3.631	1.75	9.375	70.13	4207	6.059
1.26	5.686	42.54	2552	3.675	1.76	9.456	70.74	4244	6.112
1.27	5.755	43.05	2583	3.719	1.77	9.538	71.36	4281	6.165
1.28	5.824	43.57	2614	3.764	1.78	9.621	71.97	4318	6.218
1.29	5.894	44.09	2645	3.809	1.79	9.703	72.59	4355	6.271
1.30	5.963	44.61	2676	3.854	1.80	9.786	73.21	4392	6.324
1.31	6.033	45.13	2708	3.899	1.81	9.868	73.83	4429	6.378
1.32	6.103	45.66	2739	3.945	1.82	9.952	74.45	4466	6.432
1.33	6.174	46.19	2771	3.990	1.83	10.03	75.07	4504	6.486
1.34	6.245	46.72	2803	4.036	1.84	10.12	75.70	4541	6.540
1.35	6.316	47.25	2835	4.082	1.85	10.20	76.32	4579	6.594
1.36	6.387	47.78	2867	4.128	1.86	10.29	76.95	4616	6.648
1.37	6.459	48.32	2899	4.174	1.87	10.37	77.58	4654	6.703
1.38	6.531	48.86	2931	4.221	1.88	10.46	78.21	4692	6.757
1.39	6.603	49.40	2963	4.267	1.89	10.54	78.85	4730	6.812
1.40	6.675	49.94	2996	4.314	1.90	10.62	79.48	4768	6.867
1.41	6.748	50.48	3028	4.361	1.91	10.71	80.12	4807	6.922
1.42	6.821	51.03	3061	4.408	1.92	10.80	80.76	4845	6.977
1.43	6.894	51.58	3094	4.456	1.93	10.88	81.40	4883	7.033
1.44	6.968	52.13	3127	4.503	1.94	10.97	82.05	4922	7.088
1.45	7.041	52.68	3160	4.551	1.95	11.05	82.69	4961	7.144
1.46	7.115	53.23	3193	4.599	1.96	11.14	83.34	5000	7.200
1.47	7.190	53.79	3227	4.647	1.97	11.23	83.98	5038	7.256
1.48	7.264	54.34	3260	4.695	1.98	11.31	84.63	5077	7.312
1.49	7.339	54.90	3294	4.743	1.99	11.40	85.29	5116	7.368
1.50	7.414	55.47	3328	4.792	2.00	11.49	85.94	5156	7.424

12

12-6: 1 ft. Parshall Flume Discharge Table (Continued)

Formulas: $CFS = 4.000H^{1.522}$ $GPS = CFS \times 7.481$
$GPM = CFS \times 448.8$ $MGD = CFS \times 0.6463$

Head Feet	CFS	GPS	GPM	MGD	Head Feet	CFS	GPS	GPM	MGD
2.01	11.58	86.59	5195	7.481	2.51	16.23	121.4	7285	10.49
2.02	11.66	87.25	5234	7.538	2.52	16.33	122.2	7329	10.55
2.03	11.75	87.91	5274	7.595	2.53	16.43	122.9	7373	10.62
2.04	11.84	88.57	5313	7.652	2.54	16.53	123.6	7418	10.68
2.05	11.93	89.23	5353	7.709	2.55	16.63	124.4	7462	10.75
2.06	12.02	89.89	5393	7.766	2.56	16.73	125.1	7507	10.81
2.07	12.11	90.56	5433	7.823	2.57	16.83	125.9	7551	10.87
2.08	12.19	91.22	5473	7.881	2.58	16.93	126.6	7596	10.94
2.09	12.28	91.89	5513	7.939	2.59	17.03	127.4	7641	11.00
2.10	12.37	92.56	5553	7.997	2.60	17.13	128.1	7686	11.07
2.11	12.46	93.23	5593	8.055	2.61	17.23	128.9	7731	11.13
2.12	12.55	93.91	5634	8.113	2.62	17.33	129.6	7776	11.20
2.13	12.64	94.58	5674	8.171	2.63	17.43	130.4	7821	11.26
2.14	12.73	95.26	5715	8.230	2.64	17.53	131.1	7867	11.33
2.15	12.82	95.94	5756	8.288	2.65	17.63	131.9	7912	11.39
2.16	12.92	96.62	5796	8.347	2.66	17.73	132.6	7958	11.46
2.17	13.01	97.30	5837	8.406	2.67	17.83	133.4	8003	11.53
2.18	13.10	97.98	5878	8.465	2.68	17.93	134.2	8049	11.59
2.19	13.19	98.67	5919	8.524	2.69	18.04	134.9	8095	11.66
2.20	13.28	99.35	5960	8.583	2.70	18.14	135.7	8140	11.72
2.21	13.37	100.0	6002	8.643	2.71	18.24	136.5	8186	11.79
2.22	13.47	100.7	6043	8.702	2.72	18.34	137.2	8232	11.86
2.23	13.56	101.4	6085	8.762	2.73	18.45	138.0	8279	11.92
2.24	13.65	102.1	6126	8.822	2.74	18.55	138.8	8325	11.99
2.25	13.74	102.8	6168	8.882	2.75	18.65	139.5	8371	12.05
2.26	13.84	103.5	6210	8.942	2.76	18.76	140.3	8417	12.12
2.27	13.93	104.2	6251	9.003	2.77	18.86	141.1	8464	12.19
2.28	14.02	104.9	6293	9.063	2.78	18.96	141.9	8510	12.26
2.29	14.12	105.6	6336	9.124	2.79	19.07	142.6	8557	12.32
2.30	14.21	106.3	6378	9.184	2.80	19.17	143.4	8604	12.39
2.31	14.30	107.0	6420	9.245	2.81	19.27	144.2	8651	12.46
2.32	14.40	107.7	6462	9.306	2.82	19.38	145.0	8697	12.52
2.33	14.49	108.4	6505	9.367	2.83	19.48	145.8	8744	12.59
2.34	14.59	109.1	6547	9.428	2.84	19.59	146.5	8792	12.66
2.35	14.68	109.8	6590	9.490	2.85	19.69	147.3	8839	12.73
2.36	14.78	110.6	6633	9.551	2.86	19.80	148.1	8886	12.80
2.37	14.87	111.3	6675	9.613	2.87	19.90	148.9	8933	12.86
2.38	14.97	112.0	6718	9.675	2.88	20.01	149.7	8981	12.93
2.39	15.07	112.7	6761	9.737	2.89	20.12	150.5	9028	13.00
2.40	15.16	113.4	6804	9.799	2.90	20.22	151.3	9076	13.07
2.41	15.26	114.1	6848	9.861	2.91	20.33	152.1	9123	13.14
2.42	15.35	114.9	6891	9.923	2.92	20.43	152.9	9171	13.21
2.43	15.45	115.6	6934	9.986	2.93	20.54	153.7	9219	13.28
2.44	15.55	116.3	6978	10.05	2.94	20.65	154.5	9267	13.35
2.45	15.64	117.0	7021	10.11	2.95	20.76	155.3	9315	13.41
2.46	15.74	117.8	7065	10.17	2.96	20.86	156.1	9363	13.48
2.47	15.84	118.5	7109	10.24	2.97	20.97	156.9	9411	13.55
2.48	15.94	119.2	7153	10.30	2.98	21.08	157.7	9460	13.62
2.49	16.04	120.0	7197	10.36	2.99	21.19	158.5	9508	13.69
2.50	16.13	120.7	7241	10.43	3.00	21.29	159.3	9556	13.76

12

Formulas:
$$CFS = 6.000H^{1.538} \qquad GPS = CFS \times 7.481$$
$$GPM = CFS \times 448.8 \qquad MGD = CFS \times 0.6463$$

Head Feet	CFS	GPS	GPM	MGD	Head Feet	CFS	GPS	GPM	MGD
0.01	0.0050	0.0377	2.260	0.0033	0.51	2.130	15.94	956.0	1.377
0.02	0.0146	0.1094	6.564	0.0095	0.52	2.195	16.42	985.0	1.418
0.03	0.0273	0.2041	12.25	0.0176	0.53	2.260	16.91	1014	1.461
0.04	0.0425	0.3177	19.06	0.0275	0.54	2.326	17.40	1044	1.503
0.05	0.0599	0.4478	26.87	0.0387	0.55	2.392	17.90	1074	1.546
0.06	0.0792	0.5928	35.56	0.0512	0.56	2.460	18.40	1104	1.590
0.07	0.1004	0.7514	45.08	0.0649	0.57	2.527	18.91	1134	1.634
0.08	0.1233	0.9227	55.35	0.0797	0.58	2.596	19.42	1165	1.678
0.09	0.1478	1.106	66.35	0.0955	0.59	2.665	19.94	1196	1.722
0.10	0.1738	1.301	78.02	0.1124	0.60	2.735	20.46	1227	1.768
0.11	0.2013	1.506	90.34	0.1301	0.61	2.805	20.99	1259	1.813
0.12	0.2301	1.721	103.3	0.1487	0.62	2.876	21.52	1291	1.859
0.13	0.2603	1.947	116.8	0.1682	0.63	2.948	22.05	1323	1.905
0.14	0.2917	2.182	130.9	0.1885	0.64	3.020	22.60	1356	1.952
0.15	0.3243	2.426	145.6	0.2096	0.65	3.093	23.14	1388	1.999
0.16	0.3582	2.679	160.7	0.2315	0.66	3.167	23.69	1421	2.047
0.17	0.3932	2.941	176.5	0.2541	0.67	3.241	24.24	1454	2.095
0.18	0.4293	3.212	192.7	0.2775	0.68	3.316	24.80	1488	2.143
0.19	0.4665	3.490	209.4	0.3015	0.69	3.391	25.37	1522	2.191
0.20	0.5048	3.777	226.6	0.3263	0.70	3.467	25.93	1556	2.241
0.21	0.5442	4.071	244.2	0.3517	0.71	3.543	26.51	1590	2.290
0.22	0.5845	4.373	262.3	0.3778	0.72	3.620	27.08	1625	2.340
0.23	0.6259	4.682	280.9	0.4045	0.73	3.698	27.66	1660	2.390
0.24	0.6682	4.999	299.9	0.4319	0.74	3.776	28.25	1695	2.440
0.25	0.7115	5.323	319.3	0.4599	0.75	3.855	28.84	1730	2.491
0.26	0.7558	5.654	339.2	0.4884	0.76	3.934	29.43	1766	2.543
0.27	0.8009	5.992	359.5	0.5176	0.77	4.014	30.03	1801	2.594
0.28	0.8470	6.336	380.1	0.5474	0.78	4.094	30.63	1838	2.646
0.29	0.8940	6.688	401.2	0.5778	0.79	4.175	31.24	1874	2.699
0.30	0.9418	7.046	422.7	0.6087	0.80	4.257	31.85	1911	2.751
0.31	0.9905	7.410	444.5	0.6402	0.81	4.339	32.46	1947	2.804
0.32	1.040	7.781	466.8	0.6722	0.82	4.422	33.08	1984	2.858
0.33	1.091	8.158	489.4	0.7048	0.83	4.505	33.70	2022	2.912
0.34	1.142	8.541	512.4	0.7379	0.84	4.589	34.33	2059	2.966
0.35	1.194	8.931	535.8	0.7715	0.85	4.673	34.96	2097	3.020
0.36	1.247	9.326	559.5	0.8057	0.86	4.758	35.59	2135	3.075
0.37	1.300	9.728	583.6	0.8404	0.87	4.843	36.23	2174	3.130
0.38	1.355	10.13	608.0	0.8756	0.88	4.929	36.87	2212	3.186
0.39	1.410	10.55	632.8	0.9113	0.89	5.015	37.52	2251	3.242
0.40	1.466	10.97	657.9	0.9474	0.90	5.102	38.17	2290	3.298
0.41	1.523	11.39	683.4	0.9841	0.91	5.190	38.83	2329	3.354
0.42	1.580	11.82	709.2	1.021	0.92	5.278	39.48	2369	3.411
0.43	1.638	12.26	735.3	1.059	0.93	5.366	40.15	2408	3.468
0.44	1.697	12.70	761.8	1.097	0.94	5.455	40.81	2448	3.526
0.45	1.757	13.14	788.6	1.136	0.95	5.545	41.48	2489	3.584
0.46	1.817	13.60	815.7	1.175	0.96	5.635	42.15	2529	3.642
0.47	1.879	14.05	843.1	1.214	0.97	5.725	42.83	2570	3.700
0.48	1.940	14.52	870.9	1.254	0.98	5.816	43.51	2610	3.759
0.49	2.003	14.98	898.9	1.295	0.99	5.908	44.20	2651	3.818
0.50	2.066	15.46	927.3	1.335	1.00	6.000	44.89	2693	3.878

12

12-7: 1½ ft. Parshall Flume Discharge Table (Continued)

Formulas: $CFS = 6.000H^{1.538}$ $GPS = CFS \times 7.481$
$GPM = CFS \times 448.8$ $MGD = CFS \times 0.6463$

Head Feet	CFS	GPS	GPM	MGD	Head Feet	CFS	GPS	GPM	MGD
1.01	6.093	45.58	2734	3.938	1.51	11.31	84.60	5075	7.309
1.02	6.186	46.27	2776	3.998	1.52	11.42	85.46	5127	7.383
1.03	6.279	46.97	2818	4.058	1.53	11.54	86.33	5179	7.458
1.04	6.373	47.68	2860	4.119	1.54	11.66	87.20	5231	7.533
1.05	6.468	48.38	2903	4.180	1.55	11.77	88.07	5284	7.609
1.06	6.563	49.09	2945	4.241	1.56	11.89	88.95	5336	7.684
1.07	6.658	49.81	2988	4.303	1.57	12.01	89.83	5389	7.760
1.08	6.754	50.53	3031	4.365	1.58	12.13	90.71	5442	7.836
1.09	6.850	51.25	3074	4.427	1.59	12.24	91.59	5495	7.913
1.10	6.947	51.97	3118	4.490	1.60	12.36	92.48	5548	7.990
1.11	7.045	52.70	3162	4.553	1.61	12.48	93.37	5601	8.066
1.12	7.142	53.43	3206	4.616	1.62	12.60	94.26	5655	8.144
1.13	7.241	54.17	3250	4.680	1.63	12.72	95.16	5709	8.221
1.14	7.340	54.91	3294	4.744	1.64	12.84	96.06	5763	8.299
1.15	7.439	55.65	3339	4.808	1.65	12.96	96.96	5817	8.377
1.16	7.539	56.40	3383	4.872	1.66	13.08	97.87	5871	8.455
1.17	7.639	57.15	3428	4.937	1.67	13.20	98.78	5926	8.533
1.18	7.739	57.90	3473	5.002	1.68	13.33	99.69	5980	8.612
1.19	7.840	58.65	3519	5.067	1.69	13.45	100.6	6035	8.691
1.20	7.942	59.41	3564	5.133	1.70	13.57	101.5	6090	8.770
1.21	8.044	60.18	3610	5.199	1.71	13.69	102.4	6145	8.850
1.22	8.147	60.94	3656	5.265	1.72	13.82	103.4	6201	8.930
1.23	8.249	61.71	3702	5.332	1.73	13.94	104.3	6256	9.009
1.24	8.353	62.49	3749	5.398	1.74	14.06	105.2	6312	9.090
1.25	8.457	63.26	3795	5.466	1.75	14.19	106.1	6368	9.170
1.26	8.561	64.04	3842	5.533	1.76	14.31	107.1	6424	9.251
1.27	8.666	64.83	3889	5.601	1.77	14.44	108.0	6480	9.332
1.28	8.771	65.61	3936	5.669	1.78	14.56	109.0	6537	9.413
1.29	8.876	66.40	3984	5.737	1.79	14.69	109.9	6593	9.495
1.30	8.982	67.20	4031	5.805	1.80	14.82	110.8	6650	9.576
1.31	9.089	67.99	4079	5.874	1.81	14.94	111.8	6707	9.658
1.32	9.196	68.79	4127	5.943	1.82	15.07	112.7	6764	9.740
1.33	9.303	69.60	4175	6.013	1.83	15.20	113.7	6821	9.823
1.34	9.411	70.40	4224	6.082	1.84	15.33	114.7	6879	9.905
1.35	9.519	71.21	4272	6.152	1.85	15.45	115.6	6936	9.988
1.36	9.628	72.03	4321	6.223	1.86	15.58	116.6	6994	10.07
1.37	9.737	72.84	4370	6.293	1.87	15.71	117.5	7052	10.15
1.38	9.847	73.66	4419	6.364	1.88	15.84	118.5	7110	10.24
1.39	9.957	74.48	4468	6.435	1.89	15.97	119.5	7168	10.32
1.40	10.07	75.31	4518	6.506	1.90	16.10	120.5	7226	10.41
1.41	10.18	76.14	4568	6.578	1.91	16.23	121.4	7285	10.49
1.42	10.29	76.97	4618	6.650	1.92	16.36	122.4	7344	10.58
1.43	10.40	77.81	4668	6.722	1.93	16.49	123.4	7403	10.66
1.44	10.51	78.65	4718	6.794	1.94	16.63	124.4	7462	10.75
1.45	10.63	79.49	4769	6.867	1.95	16.76	125.4	7521	10.83
1.46	10.74	80.33	4819	6.940	1.96	16.89	126.4	7580	10.92
1.47	10.85	81.18	4870	7.013	1.97	17.02	127.4	7640	11.00
1.48	10.97	82.03	4921	7.087	1.98	17.16	128.3	7700	11.09
1.49	11.08	82.88	4972	7.161	1.99	17.29	129.3	7760	11.17
1.50	11.19	83.74	5024	7.235	2.00	17.42	130.3	7820	11.26

12

12-7: 1¹/₂ ft. Parshall Flume Discharge Table (Continued)

Formulas: CFS = $6.000H^{1.538}$ GPS = CFS x 7.481
GPM = CFS x 448.8 MGD = CFS x 0.6463

Head Feet	CFS	GPS	GPM	MGD	Head Feet	CFS	GPS	GPM	MGD
2.01	17.56	131.3	7880	11.35	2.51	24.71	184.8	11090	15.97
2.02	17.69	132.4	7940	11.43	2.52	24.86	186.0	11160	16.07
2.03	17.83	133.4	8001	11.52	2.53	25.01	187.1	11230	16.17
2.04	17.96	134.4	8061	11.61	2.54	25.16	188.3	11290	16.26
2.05	18.10	135.4	8122	11.70	2.55	25.32	189.4	11360	16.36
2.06	18.23	136.4	8183	11.78	2.56	25.47	190.5	11430	16.46
2.07	18.37	137.4	8245	11.87	2.57	25.62	191.7	11500	16.56
2.08	18.51	138.4	8306	11.96	2.58	25.78	192.8	11570	16.66
2.09	18.64	139.5	8367	12.05	2.59	25.93	194.0	11640	16.76
2.10	18.78	140.5	8429	12.14	2.60	26.08	195.1	11710	16.86
2.11	18.92	141.5	8491	12.23	2.61	26.24	196.3	11780	16.96
2.12	19.06	142.6	8553	12.32	2.62	26.39	197.5	11850	17.06
2.13	19.20	143.6	8615	12.41	2.63	26.55	198.6	11920	17.16
2.14	19.33	144.6	8677	12.50	2.64	26.70	199.8	11980	17.26
2.15	19.47	145.7	8740	12.59	2.65	26.86	200.9	12050	17.36
2.16	19.61	146.7	8802	12.68	2.66	27.02	202.1	12120	17.46
2.17	19.75	147.8	8865	12.77	2.67	27.17	203.3	12190	17.56
2.18	19.89	148.8	8928	12.86	2.68	27.33	204.4	12270	17.66
2.19	20.03	149.9	8991	12.95	2.69	27.49	205.6	12340	17.76
2.20	20.17	150.9	9054	13.04	2.70	27.64	206.8	12410	17.87
2.21	20.32	152.0	9118	13.13	2.71	27.80	208.0	12480	17.97
2.22	20.46	153.0	9181	13.22	2.72	27.96	209.2	12550	18.07
2.23	20.60	154.1	9245	13.31	2.73	28.12	210.3	12620	18.17
2.24	20.74	155.2	9309	13.41	2.74	28.28	211.5	12690	18.27
2.25	20.88	156.2	9373	13.50	2.75	28.43	212.7	12760	18.38
2.26	21.03	157.3	9437	13.59	2.76	28.59	213.9	12830	18.48
2.27	21.17	158.4	9501	13.68	2.77	28.75	215.1	12900	18.58
2.28	21.31	159.4	9566	13.77	2.78	28.91	216.3	12980	18.69
2.29	21.46	160.5	9630	13.87	2.79	29.07	217.5	13050	18.79
2.30	21.60	161.6	9695	13.96	2.80	29.23	218.7	13120	18.89
2.31	21.75	162.7	9760	14.05	2.81	29.39	219.9	13190	19.00
2.32	21.89	163.8	9825	14.15	2.82	29.56	221.1	13260	19.10
2.33	22.04	164.9	9890	14.24	2.83	29.72	222.3	13340	19.21
2.34	22.18	165.9	9955	14.34	2.84	29.88	223.5	13410	19.31
2.35	22.33	167.0	10020	14.43	2.85	30.04	224.7	13480	19.41
2.36	22.47	168.1	10090	14.53	2.86	30.20	225.9	13550	19.52
2.37	22.62	169.2	10150	14.62	2.87	30.37	227.2	13630	19.62
2.38	22.77	170.3	10220	14.72	2.88	30.53	228.4	13700	19.73
2.39	22.92	171.4	10280	14.81	2.89	30.69	229.6	13770	19.84
2.40	23.06	172.5	10350	14.91	2.90	30.85	230.8	13850	19.94
2.41	23.21	173.6	10420	15.00	2.91	31.02	232.0	13920	20.05
2.42	23.36	174.8	10480	15.10	2.92	31.18	233.3	13990	20.15
2.43	23.51	175.9	10550	15.19	2.93	31.35	234.5	14070	20.26
2.44	23.66	177.0	10620	15.29	2.94	31.51	235.7	14140	20.37
2.45	23.81	178.1	10680	15.39	2.95	31.68	237.0	14220	20.47
2.46	23.96	179.2	10750	15.48	2.96	31.84	238.2	14290	20.58
2.47	24.11	180.3	10820	15.58	2.97	32.01	239.4	14360	20.69
2.48	24.26	181.5	10890	15.68	2.98	32.17	240.7	14440	20.79
2.49	24.41	182.6	10950	15.77	2.99	32.34	241.9	14510	20.90
2.50	24.56	183.7	11020	15.87	3.00	32.51	243.2	14590	21.01

12

12-8: 2 ft. Parshall Flume Discharge Table

Formulas: $CFS = 8.000H^{1.550}$ $GPS = CFS \times 7.481$
$GPM = CFS \times 448.8$ $MGD = CFS \times 0.6463$

Head Feet	CFS	GPS	GPM	MGD	Head Feet	CFS	GPS	GPM	MGD
0.01	0.0064	0.0475	2.852	0.0041	0.51	2.817	21.08	1264	1.821
0.02	0.0186	0.1392	8.351	0.0120	0.52	2.903	21.72	1303	1.876
0.03	0.0349	0.2610	15.66	0.0225	0.53	2.990	22.37	1342	1.933
0.04	0.0545	0.4076	24.45	0.0352	0.54	3.078	23.03	1382	1.989
0.05	0.0770	0.5760	34.56	0.0498	0.55	3.167	23.69	1421	2.047
0.06	0.1021	0.7642	45.84	0.0660	0.56	3.257	24.36	1462	2.105
0.07	0.1297	0.9704	58.22	0.0838	0.57	3.347	25.04	1502	2.163
0.08	0.1595	1.194	71.60	0.1031	0.58	3.439	25.73	1543	2.222
0.09	0.1915	1.433	85.94	0.1238	0.59	3.531	26.42	1585	2.282
0.10	0.2255	1.687	101.2	0.1457	0.60	3.624	27.11	1627	2.342
0.11	0.2614	1.955	117.3	0.1689	0.61	3.718	27.82	1669	2.403
0.12	0.2991	2.238	134.2	0.1933	0.62	3.813	28.53	1711	2.465
0.13	0.3386	2.533	152.0	0.2188	0.63	3.909	29.24	1754	2.526
0.14	0.3798	2.842	170.5	0.2455	0.64	4.006	29.97	1798	2.589
0.15	0.4227	3.162	189.7	0.2732	0.65	4.103	30.69	1841	2.652
0.16	0.4672	3.495	209.7	0.3019	0.66	4.201	31.43	1886	2.715
0.17	0.5132	3.839	230.3	0.3317	0.67	4.300	32.17	1930	2.779
0.18	0.5607	4.195	251.7	0.3624	0.68	4.400	32.92	1975	2.844
0.19	0.6098	4.562	273.7	0.3941	0.69	4.501	33.67	2020	2.909
0.20	0.6602	4.939	296.3	0.4267	0.70	4.602	34.43	2066	2.975
0.21	0.7121	5.327	319.6	0.4602	0.71	4.705	35.20	2112	3.041
0.22	0.7653	5.725	343.5	0.4946	0.72	4.808	35.97	2158	3.107
0.23	0.8199	6.134	368.0	0.5299	0.73	4.912	36.75	2204	3.174
0.24	0.8758	6.552	393.1	0.5660	0.74	5.016	37.53	2251	3.242
0.25	0.9330	6.980	418.7	0.6030	0.75	5.122	38.32	2299	3.310
0.26	0.9915	7.418	445.0	0.6408	0.76	5.228	39.11	2346	3.379
0.27	1.051	7.864	471.8	0.6794	0.77	5.335	39.91	2394	3.448
0.28	1.112	8.320	499.2	0.7188	0.78	5.443	40.72	2443	3.518
0.29	1.174	8.786	527.1	0.7590	0.79	5.552	41:53	2492	3.588
0.30	1.238	9.260	555.5	0.7999	0.80	5.661	42.35	2541	3.659
0.31	1.302	9.742	584.5	0.8417	0.81	5.771	43.17	2590	3.730
0.32	1.368	10.23	613.9	0.8841	0.82	5.882	44.00	2640	3.801
0.33	1.435	10.73	643.9	0.9273	0.83	5.993	44.84	2690	3.873
0.34	1.503	11.24	674.4	0.9712	0.84	6.106	45.68	2740	3.946
0.35	1.572	11.76	705.4	1.016	0.85	6.219	46.52	2791	4.019
0.36	1.642	12.28	736.9	1.061	0.86	6.332	47.37	2842	4.093
0.37	1.713	12.82	768.9	1.107	0.87	6.447	48.23	2893	4.167
0.38	1.785	13.36	801.3	1.154	0.88	6.562	49.09	2945	4.241
0.39	1.859	13.91	834.2	1.201	0.89	6.678	49.96	2997	4.316
0.40	1.933	14.46	867.6	1.249	0.90	6.795	50.83	3049	4.391
0.41	2.009	15.03	901.5	1.298	0.91	6.912	51.71	3102	4.467
0.42	2.085	15.60	935.8	1.348	0.92	7.030	52.59	3155	4.544
0.43	2.163	16.18	970.6	1.398	0.93	7.149	53.48	3208	4.620
0.44	2.241	16.76	1006	1.448	0.94	7.268	54.37	3262	4.698
0.45	2.320	17.36	1041	1.500	0.95	7.389	55.27	3316	4.775
0.46	2.401	17.96	1078	1.552	0.96	7.509	56.18	3370	4.853
0.47	2.482	18.57	1114	1.604	0.97	7.631	57.09	3425	4.932
0.48	2.565	19.19	1151	1.657	0.98	7.753	58.00	3480	5.011
0.49	2.648	19.81	1188	1.711	0.99	7.876	58.92	3535	5.090
0.50	2.732	20.44	1226	1.766	1.00	8.000	59.85	3590	5.170

12

Formulas: CFS $=8.000H^{1.550}$ GPS = CFS x 7.481
GPM = CFS x 448.8   MGD = CFS x 0.6463

Head Feet	CFS	GPS	GPM	MGD	Head Feet	CFS	GPS	GPM	MGD
1.01	8.124	60.78	3646	5.251	1.51	15.15	113.4	6801	9.794
1.02	8.249	61.71	3702	5.332	1.52	15.31	114.5	6871	9.894
1.03	8.375	62.65	3759	5.413	1.53	15.47	115.7	6941	9.995
1.04	8.501	63.60	3815	5.494	1.54	15.62	116.9	7011	10.10
1.05	8.628	64.55	3872	5.577	1.55	15.78	118.0	7082	10.20
1.06	8.756	65.50	3930	5.659	1.56	15.94	119.2	7153	10.30
1.07	8.885	66.47	3987	5.742	1.57	16.10	120.4	7224	10.40
1.08	9.014	67.43	4045	5.825	1.58	16.26	121.6	7296	10.51
1.09	9.143	68.40	4103	5.909	1.59	16.42	122.8	7367	10.61
1.10	9.274	69.38	4162	5.994	1.60	16.58	124.0	7439	10.71
1.11	9.405	70.36	4221	6.078	1.61	16.74	125.2	7511	10.82
1.12	9.536	71.34	4280	6.163	1.62	16.90	126.4	7584	10.92
1.13	9.669	72.33	4339	6.249	1.63	17.06	127.6	7657	11.03
1.14	9.801	73.33	4399	6.335	1.64	17.22	128.8	7729	11.13
1.15	9.935	74.32	4459	6.421	1.65	17.39	130.1	7803	11.24
1.16	10.07	75.33	4519	6.508	1.66	17.55	131.3	7876	11.34
1.17	10.20	76.34	4580	6.595	1.67	17.71	132.5	7950	11.45
1.18	10.34	77.35	4640	6.683	1.68	17.88	133.7	8024	11.55
1.19	10.48	78.37	4702	6.771	1.69	18.04	135.0	8098	11.66
1.20	10.61	79.39	4763	6.859	1.70	18.21	136.2	8172	11.77
1.21	10.75	80.42	4825	6.948	1.71	18.38	137.5	8247	11.88
1.22	10.89	81.45	4887	7.037	1.72	18.54	138.7	8322	11.98
1.23	11.03	82.49	4949	7.127	1.73	18.71	140.0	8397	12.09
1.24	11.17	83.53	5011	7.217	1.74	18.88	141.2	8472	12.20
1.25	11.31	84.58	5074	7.307	1.75	19.05	142.5	8548	12.31
1.26	11.45	85.63	5137	7.398	1.76	19.21	143.7	8624	12.42
1.27	11.59	86.69	5200	7.489	1.77	19.38	145.0	8700	12.53
1.28	11.73	87.75	5264	7.581	1.78	19.55	146.3	8776	12.64
1.29	11.87	88.81	5328	7.673	1.79	19.72	147.6	8852	12.75
1.30	12.01	89.88	5392	7.765	1.80	19.90	148.8	8929	12.86
1.31	12.16	90.95	5456	7.858	1.81	20.07	150.1	9006	12.97
1.32	12.30	92.03	5521	7.951	1.82	20.24	151.4	9084	13.08
1.33	12.45	93.12	5586	8.044	1.83	20.41	152.7	9161	13.19
1.34	12.59	94.20	5651	8.138	1.84	20.59	154.0	9239	13.30
1.35	12.74	95.29	5717	8.233	1.85	20.76	155.3	9317	13.42
1.36	12.88	96.39	5783	8.327	1.86	20.93	156.6	9395	13.53
1.37	13.03	97.49	5849	8.423	1.87	21.11	157.9	9473	13.64
1.38	13.18	98.60	5915	8.518	1.88	21.28	159.2	9552	13.76
1.39	13.33	99.71	5982	8.614	1.89	21.46	160.5	9631	13.87
1.40	13.48	100.8	6048	8.710	1.90	21.64	161.9	9710	13.98
1.41	13.63	101.9	6116	8.807	1.91	21.81	163.2	9789	14.10
1.42	13.78	103.1	6183	8.904	1.92	21.99	164.5	9869	14.21
1.43	13.93	104.2	6250	9.001	1.93	22.17	165.8	9948	14.33
1.44	14.08	105.3	6318	9.099	1.94	22.35	167.2	10030	14.44
1.45	14.23	106.5	6387	9.197	1.95	22.52	168.5	10110	14.56
1.46	14.38	107.6	6455	9.295	1.96	22.70	169.8	10190	14.67
1.47	14.54	108.7	6524	9.394	1.97	22.88	171.2	10270	14.79
1.48	14.69	109.9	6592	9.494	1.98	23.06	172.5	10350	14.91
1.49	14.84	111.0	6662	9.593	1.99	23.24	173.9	10430	15.02
1.50	15.00	112.2	6731	9.693	2.00	23.43	175.2	10510	15.14

12

12-8: 2 ft. Parshall Flume Discharge Table (Continued)

Formulas: CFS $=8.000H^{1.550}$ GPS = CFS x 7.481
GPM = CFS x 448.8 MGD = CFS x 0.6463

Head Feet	CFS	GPS	GPM	MGD	Head Feet	CFS	GPS	GPM	MGD
2.01	23.61	176.6	10590	15.26	2.51	33.31	249.2	14950	21.53
2.02	23.79	178.0	10680	15.38	2.52	33.52	250.7	15040	21.66
2.03	23.97	179.3	10760	15.49	2.53	33.72	252.3	15130	21.80
2.04	24.16	180.7	10840	15.61	2.54	33.93	253.8	15230	21.93
2.05	24.34	182.1	10920	15.73	2.55	34.14	255.4	15320	22.06
2.06	24.52	183.5	11010	15.85	2.56	34.34	256.9	15410	22.20
2.07	24.71	184.8	11090	15.97	2.57	34.55	258.5	15510	22.33
2.08	24.89	186.2	11170	16.09	2.58	34.76	260.1	15600	22.47
2.09	25.08	187.6	11260	16.21	2.59	34.97	261.6	15690	22.60
2.10	25.27	189.0	11340	16.33	2.60	35.18	263.2	15790	22.74
2.11	25.45	190.4	11420	16.45	2.61	35.39	264.8	15880	22.87
2.12	25.64	191.8	11510	16.57	2.62	35.60	266.3	15980	23.01
2.13	25.83	193.2	11590	16.69	2.63	35.81	267.9	16070	23.14
2.14	26.02	194.6	11680	16.81	2.64	36.02	269.5	16170	23.28
2.15	26.20	196.0	11760	16.94	2.65	36.23	271.1	16260	23.42
2.16	26.39	197.4	11850	17.06	2.66	36.45	272.7	16360	23.56
2.17	26.58	198.9	11930	17.18	2.67	36.66	274.2	16450	23.69
2.18	26.77	200.3	12020	17.30	2.68	36.87	275.8	16550	23.83
2.19	26.96	201.7	12100	17.43	2.69	37.09	277.4	16640	23.97
2.20	27.15	203.1	12190	17.55	2.70	37.30	279.0	16740	24.11
2.21	27.35	204.6	12270	17.67	2.71	37.51	280.6	16840	24.25
2.22	27.54	206.0	12360	17.80	2.72	37.73	282.2	16930	24.38
2.23	27.73	207.5	12450	17.92	2.73	37.94	283.9	17030	24.52
2.24	27.92	208.9	12530	18.05	2.74	38.16	285.5	17130	24.66
2.25	28.12	210.3	12620	18.17	2.75	38.38	287.1	17220	24.80
2.26	28.31	211.8	12710	18.30	2.76	38.59	288.7	17320	24.94
2.27	28.51	213.3	12790	18.42	2.77	38.81	290.3	17420	25.08
2.28	28.70	214.7	12880	18.55	2.78	39.03	292.0	17520	25.22
2.29	28.90	216.2	12970	18.68	2.79	39.24	293.6	17610	25.36
2.30	29.09	217.6	13060	18.80	2.80	39.46	295.2	17710	25.50
2.31	29.29	219.1	13140	18.93	2.81	39.68	296.9	17810	25.65
2.32	29.48	220.6	13230	19.06	2.82	39.90	298.5	17910	25.79
2.33	29.68	222.1	13320	19.18	2.83	40.12	300.1	18010	25.93
2.34	29.88	223.5	13410	19.31	2.84	40.34	301.8	18100	26.07
2.35	30.08	225.0	13500	19.44	2.85	40.56	303.4	18200	26.21
2.36	30.28	226.5	13590	19.57	2.86	40.78	305.1	18300	26.36
2.37	30.48	228.0	13680	19.70	2.87	41.00	306.7	18400	26.50
2.38	30.67	229.5	13770	19.83	2.88	41.22	308.4	18500	26.64
2.39	30.87	231.0	13860	19.95	2.89	41.45	310.1	18600	26.79
2.40	31.08	232.5	13950	20.08	2.90	41.67	311.7	18700	26.93
2.41	31.28	234.0	14040	20.21	2.91	41.89	313.4	18800	27.07
2.42	31.48	235.5	14130	20.34	2.92	42.11	315.1	18900	27.22
2.43	31.68	237.0	14220	20.47	2.93	42.34	316.7	19000	27.36
2.44	31.88	238.5	14310	20.61	2.94	42.56	318.4	19100	27.51
2.45	32.08	240.0	14400	20.74	2.95	42.79	320.1	19200	27.65
2.46	32.29	241.5	14490	20.87	2.96	43.01	321.8	19300	27.80
2.47	32.49	243.1	14580	21.00	2.97	43.24	323.5	19410	27.94
2.48	32.70	244.6	14670	21.13	2.98	43.46	325.2	19510	28.09
2.49	32.90	246.1	14770	21.26	2.99	43.69	326.8	19610	28.24
2.50	33.11	247.7	14860	21.40	3.00	43.92	328.5	19710	28.38

12

12-9: 3 ft. Parshall Flume Discharge Table

Formulas: CFS $= 12.00H^{1.566}$ GPS = CFS x 7.481
GPM = CFS x 448.8   MGD = CFS x 0.6463

Head Feet	CFS	GPS	GPM	MGD	Head Feet	CFS	GPS	GPM	MGD
0.01	0.0089	0.0662	3.974	0.0057	0.51	4.181	31.27	1876	2.702
0.02	0.0262	0.1961	11.77	0.0169	0.52	4.310	32.24	1934	2.785
0.03	0.0495	0.3701	22.20	0.0320	0.53	4.440	33.22	1993	2.870
0.04	0.0776	0.5807	34.84	0.0502	0.54	4.572	34.20	2052	2.955
0.05	0.1101	0.8236	49.41	0.0712	0.55	4.705	35.20	2112	3.041
0.06	0.1465	1.096	65.74	0.0947	0.56	4.840	36.21	2172	3.128
0.07	0.1865	1.395	83.69	0.1205	0.57	4.976	37.23	2233	3.216
0.08	0.2298	1.719	103.2	0.1485	0.58	5.113	38.25	2295	3.305
0.09	0.2764	2.068	124.0	0.1786	0.59	5.252	39.29	2357	3.394
0.10	0.3260	2.439	146.3	0.2107	0.60	5.392	40.34	2420	3.485
0.11	0.3784	2.831	169.8	0.2446	0.61	5.534	41.40	2483	3.576
0.12	0.4337	3.244	194.6	0.2803	0.62	5.676	42.46	2548	3.669
0.13	0.4916	3.678	220.6	0.3177	0.63	5.820	43.54	2612	3.762
0.14	0.5521	4.130	247.8	0.3568	0.64	5.966	44.63	2677	3.856
0.15	0.6151	4.602	276.1	0.3975	0.65	6.112	45.73	2743	3.950
0.16	0.6805	5.091	305.4	0.4398	0.66	6.260	46.83	2810	4.046
0.17	0.7483	5.598	335.8	0.4836	0.67	6.409	47.95	2877	4.142
0.18	0.8183	6.122	367.3	0.5289	0.68	6.560	49.07	2944	4.240
0.19	0.8907	6.663	399.7	0.5756	0.69	6.711	50.21	3012	4.338
0.20	0.9651	7.220	433.2	0.6238	0.70	6.864	51.35	3081	4.436
0.21	1.042	7.794	467.6	0.6733	0.71	7.019	52.51	3150	4.536
0.22	1.121	8.383	502.9	0.7242	0.72	7.174	53.67	3220	4.637
0.23	1.201	8.987	539.1	0.7764	0.73	7.331	54.84	3290	4.738
0.24	1.284	9.606	576.3	0.8299	0.74	7.489	56.02	3361	4.840
0.25	1.369	10.24	614.3	0.8847	0.75	7.648	57.21	3432	4.943
0.26	1.456	10.89	653.3	0.9407	0.76	7.808	58.41	3504	5.046
0.27	1.544	11.55	693.0	0.9980	0.77	7.969	59.62	3577	5.151
0.28	1.635	12.23	733.6	1.056	0.78	8.132	60.84	3650	5.256
0.29	1.727	12.92	775.1	1.116	0.79	8.296	62.06	3723	5.362
0.30	1.821	13.62	817.3	1.177	0.80	8.461	63.30	3797	5.468
0.31	1.917	14.34	860.4	1.239	0.81	8.627	64.54	3872	5.576
0.32	2.015	15.07	904.3	1.302	0.82	8.795	65.79	3947	5.684
0.33	2.114	15.82	948.9	1.366	0.83	8.963	67.05	4023	5.793
0.34	2.216	16.57	994.3	1.432	0.84	9.133	68.32	4099	5.903
0.35	2.318	17.34	1041	1.498	0.85	9.304	69.60	4175	6.013
0.36	2.423	18.13	1087	1.566	0.86	9.476	70.89	4253	6.124
0.37	2.529	18.92	1135	1.635	0.87	9.649	72.18	4330	6.236
0.38	2.637	19.73	1184	1.704	0.88	9.823	73.49	4409	6.349
0.39	2.747	20.55	1233	1.775	0.89	9.998	74.80	4487	6.462
0.40	2.858	21.38	1283	1.847	0.90	10.17	76.12	4566	6.576
0.41	2.970	22.22	1333	1.920	0.91	10.35	77.45	4646	6.691
0.42	3.085	23.08	1384	1.994	0.92	10.53	78.78	4726	6.806
0.43	3.200	23.94	1436	2.068	0.93	10.71	80.13	4807	6.922
0.44	3.318	24.82	1489	2.144	0.94	10.89	81.48	4888	7.039
0.45	3.436	25.71	1542	2.221	0.95	11.07	82.84	4970	7.157
0.46	3.557	26.61	1596	2.299	0.96	11.26	84.21	5052	7.275
0.47	3.679	27.52	1651	2.378	0.97	11.44	85.59	5135	7.394
0.48	3.802	28.44	1706	2.457	0.98	11.63	86.98	5218	7.514
0.49	3.927	29.38	1762	2.538	0.99	11.81	88.37	5302	7.634
0.50	4.053	30.32	1819	2.619	1.00	12.00	89.77	5386	7.756

12

12-9: 3 ft. Parshall Flume Discharge Table *(Continued)*

Formulas: $CFS = 12.00H^{1.566}$ $GPS = CFS \times 7.481$
$GPM = CFS \times 448.8$ $MGD = CFS \times 0.6463$

Head Feet	CFS	GPS	GPM	MGD	Head Feet	CFS	GPS	GPM	MGD
1.01	12.19	91.18	5470	7.877	1.51	22.88	171.2	10270	14.79
1.02	12.38	92.60	5555	8.000	1.52	23.12	172.9	10380	14.94
1.03	12.57	94.03	5641	8.123	1.53	23.36	174.7	10480	15.10
1.04	12.76	95.46	5727	8.247	1.54	23.60	176.5	10590	15.25
1.05	12.95	96.90	5813	8.371	1.55	23.84	178.3	10700	15.41
1.06	13.15	98.35	5900	8.497	1.56	24.08	180.1	10810	15.56
1.07	13.34	99.81	5988	8.622	1.57	24.32	181.9	10910	15.72
1.08	13.54	101.3	6075	8.749	1.58	24.56	183.8	11020	15.87
1.09	13.73	102.7	6164	8.876	1.59	24.81	185.6	11130	16.03
1.10	13.93	104.2	6253	9.004	1.60	25.05	187.4	11240	16.19
1.11	14.13	105.7	6342	9.133	1.61	25.30	189.2	11350	16.35
1.12	14.33	107.2	6431	9.262	1.62	25.54	191.1	11460	16.51
1.13	14.53	108.7	6522	9.392	1.63	25.79	192.9	11570	16.67
1.14	14.73	110.2	6612	9.522	1.64	26.04	194.8	11690	16.83
1.15	14.94	111.7	6703	9.653	1.65	26.29	196.7	11800	16.99
1.16	15.14	113.3	6795	9.785	1.66	26.54	198.5	11910	17.15
1.17	15.34	114.8	6887	9.917	1.67	26.79	200.4	12020	17.31
1.18	15.55	116.3	6979	10.05	1.68	27.04	202.3	12140	17.48
1.19	15.76	117.9	7072	10.18	1.69	27.29	204.2	12250	17.64
1.20	15.97	119.4	7165	10.32	1.70	27.55	206.1	12360	17.80
1.21	16.17	121.0	7259	10.45	1.71	27.80	208.0	12480	17.97
1.22	16.38	122.6	7353	10.59	1.72	28.06	209.9	12590	18.13
1.23	16.59	124.1	7448	10.73	1.73	28.31	211.8	12710	18.30
1.24	16.81	125.7	7543	10.86	1.74	28.57	213.7	12820	18.46
1.25	17.02	127.3	7638	11.00	1.75	28.83	215.6	12940	18.63
1.26	17.23	128.9	7734	11.14	1.76	29.08	217.6	13050	18.80
1.27	17.45	130.5	7831	11.28	1.77	29.34	219.5	13170	18.96
1.28	17.66	132.1	7927	11.42	1.78	29.60	221.5	13290	19.13
1.29	17.88	133.8	8024	11.56	1.79	29.86	223.4	13400	19.30
1.30	18.10	135.4	8122	11.70	1.80	30.13	225.4	13520	19.47
1.31	18.32	137.0	8220	11.84	1.81	30.39	227.3	13640	19.64
1.32	18.54	138.7	8319	11.98	1.82	30.65	229.3	13760	19.81
1.33	18.76	140.3	8418	12.12	1.83	30.92	231.3	13870	19.98
1.34	18.98	142.0	8517	12.26	1.84	31.18	233.3	13990	20.15
1.35	19.20	143.6	8617	12.41	1.85	31.45	235.3	14110	20.32
1.36	19.42	145.3	8717	12.55	1.86	31.71	237.2	14230	20.50
1.37	19.65	147.0	8817	12.70	1.87	31.98	239.2	14350	20.67
1.38	19.87	148.7	8918	12.84	1.88	32.25	241.3	14470	20.84
1.39	20.10	150.3	9020	12.99	1.89	32.52	243.3	14590	21.02
1.40	20.32	152.0	9122	13.14	1.90	32.79	245.3	14720	21.19
1.41	20.55	153.8	9224	13.28	1.91	33.06	247.3	14840	21.37
1.42	20.78	155.5	9326	13.43	1.92	33.33	249.3	14960	21.54
1.43	21.01	157.2	9430	13.58	1.93	33.60	251.4	15080	21.72
1.44	21.24	158.9	9533	13.73	1.94	33.87	253.4	15200	21.89
1.45	21.47	160.6	9637	13.88	1.95	34.15	255.5	15330	22.07
1.46	21.70	162.4	9741	14.03	1.96	34.42	257.5	15450	22.25
1.47	21.94	164.1	9846	14.18	1.97	34.70	259.6	15570	22.43
1.48	22.17	165.9	9951	14.33	1.98	34.98	261.6	15700	22.60
1.49	22.41	167.6	10060	14.48	1.99	35.25	263.7	15820	22.78
1.50	22.64	169.4	10160	14.63	2.00	35.53	265.8	15950	22.96

12

12-9: 3 ft. Parshall Flume Discharge Table *(Continued)*

Formulas: CFS $=12.00H^{1.566}$ GPS = CFS x 7.481
GPM = CFS x 448.8   MGD = CFS x 0.6463

Head Feet	CFS	GPS	GPM	MGD	Head Feet	CFS	GPS	GPM	MGD
2.01	35.81	267.9	16070	23.14	2.51	50.71	379.3	22760	32.77
2.02	36.09	270.0	16200	23.32	2.52	51.02	381.7	22900	32.98
2.03	36.37	272.1	16320	23.50	2.53	51.34	384.1	23040	33.18
2.04	36.65	274.2	16450	23.69	2.54	51.66	386.5	23180	33.39
2.05	36.93	276.3	16570	23.87	2.55	51.98	388.9	23330	33.59
2.06	37.21	278.4	16700	24.05	2.56	52.30	391.2	23470	33.80
2.07	37.50	280.5	16830	24.23	2.57	52.62	393.6	23620	34.01
2.08	37.78	282.6	16960	24.42	2.58	52.94	396.0	23760	34.21
2.09	38.07	284.8	17080	24.60	2.59	53.26	398.4	23900	34.42
2.10	38.35	286.9	17210	24.79	2.60	53.58	400.9	24050	34.63
2.11	38.64	289.0	17340	24.97	2.61	53.91	403.3	24190	34.84
2.12	38.92	291.2	17470	25.16	2.62	54.23	405.7	24340	35.05
2.13	39.21	293.3	17600	25.34	2.63	54.55	408.1	24480	35.26
2.14	39.50	295.5	17730	25.53	2.64	54.88	410.6	24630	35.47
2.15	39.79	297.7	17860	25.72	2.65	55.21	413.0	24780	35.68
2.16	40.08	299.8	17990	25.90	2.66	55.53	415.4	24920	35.89
2.17	40.37	302.0	18120	26.09	2.67	55.86	417.9	25070	36.10
2.18	40.66	304.2	18250	26.28	2.68	56.19	420.3	25220	36.31
2.19	40.96	306.4	18380	26.47	2.69	56.52	422.8	25360	36.53
2.20	41.25	308.6	18510	26.66	2.70	56.85	425.3	25510	36.74
2.21	41.54	310.8	18640	26.85	2.71	57.18	427.7	25660	36.95
2.22	41.84	313.0	18780	27.04	2.72	57.51	430.2	25810	37.17
2.23	42.13	315.2	18910	27.23	2.73	57.84	432.7	25960	37.38
2.24	42.43	317.4	19040	27.42	2.74	58.17	435.2	26110	37.60
2.25	42.73	319.6	19180	27.61	2.75	58.50	437.7	26260	37.81
2.26	43.02	321.9	19310	27.81	2.76	58.84	440.2	26410	38.03
2.27	43.32	324.1	19440	28.00	2.77	59.17	442.7	26560	38.24
2.28	43.62	326.3	19580	28.19	2.78	59.51	445.2	26710	38.46
2.29	43.92	328.6	19710	28.39	2.79	59.84	447.7	26860	38.68
2.30	44.22	330.8	19850	28.58	2.80	60.18	450.2	27010	38.89
2.31	44.52	333.1	19980	28.78	2.81	60.51	452.7	27160	39.11
2.32	44.83	335.3	20120	28.97	2.82	60.85	455.2	27310	39.33
2.33	45.13	337.6	20250	29.17	2.83	61.19	457.8	27460	39.55
2.34	45.43	339.9	20390	29.36	2.84	61.53	460.3	27610	39.77
2.35	45.74	342.2	20530	29.56	2.85	61.87	462.8	27770	39.99
2.36	46.04	344.4	20660	29.76	2.86	62.21	465.4	27920	40.21
2.37	46.35	346.7	20800	29.96	2.87	62.55	467.9	28070	40.43
2.38	46.66	349.0	20940	30.15	2.88	62.89	470.5	28230	40.65
2.39	46.96	351.3	21080	30.35	2.89	63.23	473.0	28380	40.87
2.40	47.27	353.6	21220	30.55	2.90	63.58	475.6	28530	41.09
2.41	47.58	355.9	21350	30.75	2.91	63.92	478.2	28690	41.31
2.42	47.89	358.3	21490	30.95	2.92	64.26	480.8	28840	41.53
2.43	48.20	360.6	21630	31.15	2.93	64.61	483.3	29000	41.76
2.44	48.51	362.9	21770	31.35	2.94	64.96	485.9	29150	41.98
2.45	48.82	365.2	21910	31.55	2.95	65.30	488.5	29310	42.20
2.46	49.13	367.6	22050	31.76	2.96	65.65	491.1	29460	42.43
2.47	49.45	369.9	22190	31.96	2.97	66.00	493.7	29620	42.65
2.48	49.76	372.3	22330	32.16	2.98	66.34	496.3	29780	42.88
2.49	50.08	374.6	22470	32.36	2.99	66.69	498.9	29930	43.10
2.50	50.39	377.0	22620	32.57	3.00	67.04	501.5	30090	43.33

12

12-10: 4 ft. Parshall Flume Discharge Table

Formulas: CFS $= 16.00H^{1.578}$ GPS = CFS x 7.481
           GPM = CFS x 448.8   MGD = CFS x 0.6463

Head Feet	CFS	GPS	GPM	MGD	Head Feet	CFS	GPS	GPM	MGD
0.01	0.0112	0.0836	5.014	0.0072	0.51	5.529	41.36	2482	3.574
0.02	0.0334	0.2495	14.97	0.0216	0.52	5.701	42.65	2559	3.685
0.03	0.0632	0.4731	28.38	0.0409	0.53	5.875	43.95	2637	3.797
0.04	0.0996	0.7450	44.69	0.0644	0.54	6.051	45.27	2716	3.911
0.05	0.1416	1.059	63.55	0.0915	0.55	6.229	46.60	2796	4.026
0.06	0.1888	1.413	84.74	0.1220	0.56	6.409	47.94	2876	4.142
0.07	0.2408	1.802	108.1	0.1556	0.57	6.590	49.30	2958	4.259
0.08	0.2973	2.224	133.4	0.1921	0.58	6.773	50.67	3040	4.378
0.09	0.3580	2.678	160.7	0.2314	0.59	6.959	52.06	3123	4.497
0.10	0.4228	3.163	189.7	0.2732	0.60	7.146	53.46	3207	4.618
0.11	0.4914	3.676	220.5	0.3176	0.61	7.334	54.87	3292	4.740
0.12	0.5637	4.217	253.0	0.3643	0.62	7.525	56.30	3377	4.863
0.13	0.6396	4.785	287.1	0.4134	0.63	7.718	57.73	3464	4.988
0.14	0.7190	5.379	322.7	0.4647	0.64	7.912	59.19	3551	5.113
0.15	0.8017	5.997	359.8	0.5181	0.65	8.108	60.65	3639	5.240
0.16	0.8876	6.640	398.4	0.5737	0.66	8.305	62.13	3727	5.368
0.17	0.9767	7.307	438.4	0.6313	0.67	8.505	63.62	3817	5.497
0.18	1.069	7.996	479.7	0.6908	0.68	8.706	65.13	3907	5.627
0.19	1.164	8.709	522.5	0.7524	0.69	8.909	66.65	3998	5.758
0.20	1.262	9.443	566.5	0.8158	0.70	9.113	68.18	4090	5.890
0.21	1.363	10.20	611.8	0.8811	0.71	9.320	69.72	4183	6.023
0.22	1.467	10.98	658.4	0.9482	0.72	9.528	71.28	4276	6.158
0.23	1.574	11.77	706.3	1.017	0.73	9.737	72.85	4370	6.293
0.24	1.683	12.59	755.3	1.088	0.74	9.949	74.43	4465	6.430
0.25	1.795	13.43	805.6	1.160	0.75	10.16	76.02	4561	6.568
0.26	1.910	14.29	857.0	1.234	0.76	10.38	77.63	4657	6.706
0.27	2.027	15.16	909.6	1.310	0.77	10.59	79.24	4754	6.846
0.28	2.147	16.06	963.4	1.387	0.78	10.81	80.87	4852	6.987
0.29	2.269	16.97	1018	1.466	0.79	11.03	82.52	4950	7.129
0.30	2.393	17.91	1074	1.547	0.80	11.25	84.17	5050	7.272
0.31	2.521	18.86	1131	1.629	0.81	11.47	85.84	5149	7.416
0.32	2.650	19.82	1189	1.713	0.82	11.70	87.51	5250	7.561
0.33	2.782	20.81	1248	1.798	0.83	11.92	89.20	5352	7.707
0.34	2.916	21.81	1309	1.885	0.84	12.15	90.91	5454	7.854
0.35	3.053	22.84	1370	1.973	0.85	12.38	92.62	5556	8.002
0.36	3.191	23.87	1432	2.063	0.86	12.61	94.34	5660	8.151
0.37	3.332	24.93	1496	2.154	0.87	12.84	96.08	5764	8.301
0.38	3.476	26.00	1560	2.246	0.88	13.08	97.83	5869	8.452
0.39	3.621	27.09	1625	2.340	0.89	13.31	99.59	5975	8.604
0.40	3.769	28.19	1691	2.436	0.90	13.55	101.4	6081	8.757
0.41	3.918	29.31	1759	2.532	0.91	13.79	103.1	6188	8.911
0.42	4.070	30.45	1827	2.631	0.92	14.03	104.9	6295	9.066
0.43	4.224	31.60	1896	2.730	0.93	14.27	106.7	6404	9.222
0.44	4.380	32.77	1966	2.831	0.94	14.51	108.6	6513	9.379
0.45	4.538	33.95	2037	2.933	0.95	14.76	110.4	6622	9.537
0.46	4.698	35.15	2109	3.037	0.96	15.00	112.2	6733	9.696
0.47	4.861	36.36	2181	3.141	0.97	15.25	114.1	6844	9.856
0.48	5.025	37.59	2255	3.248	0.98	15.50	115.9	6955	10.02
0.49	5.191	38.83	2330	3.355	0.99	15.75	117.8	7068	10.18
0.50	5.359	40.09	2405	3.464	1.00	16.00	119.7	7181	10.34

12

12-10: 4 ft. Parshall Flume Discharge Table (Continued)

Formulas: CFS = 16.00H$^{1.578}$ GPS = CFS x 7.481
GPM = CFS x 448.8 MGD = CFS x 0.6463

Head Feet	CFS	GPS	GPM	MGD	Head Feet	CFS	GPS	GPM	MGD
1.01	16.25	121.6	7294	10.50	1.51	30.66	229.4	13760	19.81
1.02	16.51	123.5	7409	10.67	1.52	30.98	231.8	13900	20.02
1.03	16.76	125.4	7524	10.83	1.53	31.30	234.2	14050	20.23
1.04	17.02	127.3	7639	11.00	1.54	31.62	236.6	14190	20.44
1.05	17.28	129.3	7755	11.17	1.55	31.95	239.0	14340	20.65
1.06	17.54	131.2	7872	11.34	1.56	32.28	241.5	14490	20.86
1.07	17.80	133.2	7990	11.51	1.57	32.60	243.9	14630	21.07
1.08	18.07	135.2	8108	11.68	1.58	32.93	246.4	14780	21.28
1.09	18.33	137.1	8227	11.85	1.59	33.26	248.8	14930	21.50
1.10	18.60	139.1	8346	12.02	1.60	33.59	251.3	15080	21.71
1.11	18.86	141.1	8466	12.19	1.61	33.92	253.8	15220	21.92
1.12	19.13	143.1	8587	12.37	1.62	34.26	256.3	15370	22.14
1.13	19.40	145.2	8708	12.54	1.63	34.59	258.8	15520	22.36
1.14	19.68	147.2	8830	12.72	1.64	34.93	261.3	15670	22.57
1.15	19.95	149.2	8953	12.89	1.65	35.26	263.8	15830	22.79
1.16	20.22	151.3	9076	13.07	1.66	35.60	266.3	15980	23.01
1.17	20.50	153.3	9200	13.25	1.67	35.94	268.9	16130	23.23
1.18	20.78	155.4	9324	13.43	1.68	36.28	271.4	16280	23.45
1.19	21.05	157.5	9449	13.61	1.69	36.62	274.0	16440	23.67
1.20	21.33	159.6	9575	13.79	1.70	36.96	276.5	16590	23.89
1.21	21.62	161.7	9701	13.97	1.71	37.31	279.1	16740	24.11
1.22	21.90	163.8	9828	14.15	1.72	37.65	281.7	16900	24.33
1.23	22.18	165.9	9955	14.34	1.73	38.00	284.3	17050	24.56
1.24	22.47	168.1	10080	14.52	1.74	38.34	286.9	17210	24.78
1.25	22.75	170.2	10210	14.71	1.75	38.69	289.5	17370	25.01
1.26	23.04	172.4	10340	14.89	1.76	39.04	292.1	17520	25.23
1.27	23.33	174.5	10470	15.08	1.77	39.39	294.7	17680	25.46
1.28	23.62	176.7	10600	15.27	1.78	39.75	297.3	17840	25.69
1.29	23.91	178.9	10730	15.45	1.79	40.10	300.0	18000	25.92
1.30	24.21	181.1	10860	15.64	1.80	40.45	302.6	18150	26.14
1.31	24.50	183.3	11000	15.83	1.81	40.81	305.3	18310	26.37
1.32	24.80	185.5	11130	16.03	1.82	41.16	307.9	18470	26.60
1.33	25.09	187.7	11260	16.22	1.83	41.52	310.6	18630	26.84
1.34	25.39	190.0	11400	16.41	1.84	41.88	313.3	18800	27.07
1.35	25.69	192.2	11530	16.60	1.85	42.24	316.0	18960	27.30
1.36	25.99	194.4	11670	16.80	1.86	42.60	318.7	19120	27.53
1.37	26.29	196.7	11800	16.99	1.87	42.96	321.4	19280	27.77
1.38	26.60	199.0	11940	17.19	1.88	43.33	324.1	19440	28.00
1.39	26.90	201.3	12070	17.39	1.89	43.69	326.8	19610	28.24
1.40	27.21	203.5	12210	17.59	1.90	44.05	329.6	19770	28.47
1.41	27.52	205.8	12350	17.78	1.91	44.42	332.3	19940	28.71
1.42	27.82	208.2	12490	17.98	1.92	44.79	335.1	20100	28.95
1.43	28.13	210.5	12630	18.18	1.93	45.16	337.8	20270	29.19
1.44	28.45	212.8	12770	18.38	1.94	45.53	340.6	20430	29.42
1.45	28.76	215.1	12910	18.59	1.95	45.90	343.4	20600	29.66
1.46	29.07	217.5	13050	18.79	1.96	46.27	346.1	20770	29.90
1.47	29.39	219.8	13190	18.99	1.97	46.64	348.9	20930	30.15
1.48	29.70	222.2	13330	19.20	1.98	47.02	351.7	21100	30.39
1.49	30.02	224.6	13470	19.40	1.99	47.39	354.5	21270	30.63
1.50	30.34	227.0	13620	19.61	2.00	47.77	357.4	21440	30.87

12

12-10: 4 ft. Parshall Flume Discharge Table (Continued)

Formulas: $CFS = 16.00H^{1.578}$ $GPS = CFS \times 7.481$
$GPM = CFS \times 448.8$ $MGD = CFS \times 0.6463$

Head Feet	CFS	GPS	GPM	MGD	Head Feet	CFS	GPS	GPM	MGD
2.01	48.15	360.2	21610	31.12	2.51	68.36	511.4	30680	44.18
2.02	48.52	363.0	21780	31.36	2.52	68.79	514.6	30870	44.46
2.03	48.90	365.9	21950	31.61	2.53	69.22	517.8	31070	44.74
2.04	49.29	368.7	22120	31.85	2.54	69.65	521.1	31260	45.02
2.05	49.67	371.6	22290	32.10	2.55	70.09	524.3	31460	45.30
2.06	50.05	374.4	22460	32.35	2.56	70.52	527.6	31650	45.58
2.07	50.43	377.3	22630	32.60	2.57	70.96	530.8	31850	45.86
2.08	50.82	380.2	22810	32.84	2.58	71.39	534.1	32040	46.14
2.09	51.20	383.1	22980	33.09	2.59	71.83	537.4	32240	46.42
2.10	51.59	386.0	23150	33.34	2.60	72.27	540.6	32430	46.71
2.11	51.98	388.9	23330	33.59	2.61	72.71	543.9	32630	46.99
2.12	52.37	391.8	23500	33.85	2.62	73.15	547.2	32830	47.28
2.13	52.76	394.7	23680	34.10	2.63	73.59	550.5	33030	47.56
2.14	53.15	397.6	23850	34.35	2.64	74.03	553.8	33220	47.85
2.15	53.54	400.6	24030	34.61	2.65	74.47	557.1	33420	48.13
2.16	53.94	403.5	24210	34.86	2.66	74.92	560.5	33620	48.42
2.17	54.33	406.5	24380	35.11	2.67	75.36	563.8	33820	48.71
2.18	54.73	409.4	24560	35.37	2.68	75.81	567.1	34020	48.99
2.19	55.12	412.4	24740	35.63	2.69	76.26	570.5	34220	49.28
2.20	55.52	415.4	24920	35.88	2.70	76.70	573.8	34420	49.57
2.21	55.92	418.3	25100	36.14	2.71	77.15	577.2	34630	49.86
2.22	56.32	421.3	25280	36.40	2.72	77.60	580.5	34830	50.15
2.23	56.72	424.3	25460	36.66	2.73	78.05	583.9	35030	50.45
2.24	57.12	427.3	25640	36.92	2.74	78.50	587.3	35230	50.74
2.25	57.53	430.4	25820	37.18	2.75	78.96	590.7	35440	51.03
2.26	57.93	433.4	26000	37.44	2.76	79.41	594.1	35640	51.32
2.27	58.33	436.4	26180	37.70	2.77	79.86	597.5	35840	51.62
2.28	58.74	439.4	26360	37.96	2.78	80.32	600.9	36050	51.91
2.29	59.15	442.5	26550	38.23	2.79	80.78	604.3	36250	52.21
2.30	59.56	445.5	26730	38.49	2.80	81.23	607.7	36460	52.50
2.31	59.97	448.6	26910	38.76	2.81	81.69	611.1	36660	52.80
2.32	60.38	451.7	27100	39.02	2.82	82.15	614.6	36870	53.09
2.33	60.79	454.7	27280	39.29	2.83	82.61	618.0	37080	53.39
2.34	61.20	457.8	27470	39.55	2.84	83.07	621.5	37280	53.69
2.35	61.61	460.9	27650	39.82	2.85	83.53	624.9	37490	53.99
2.36	62.03	464.0	27840	40.09	2.86	84.00	628.4	37700	54.29
2.37	62.44	467.1	28020	40.36	2.87	84.46	631.9	37910	54.59
2.38	62.86	470.2	28210	40.62	2.88	84.93	635.3	38110	54.89
2.39	63.27	473.4	28400	40.89	2.89	85.39	638.8	38320	55.19
2.40	63.69	476.5	28590	41.16	2.90	85.86	642.3	38530	55.49
2.41	64.11	479.6	28770	41.44	2.91	86.33	645.8	38740	55.79
2.42	64.53	482.8	28960	41.71	2.92	86.79	649.3	38950	56.10
2.43	64.95	485.9	29150	41.98	2.93	87.26	652.8	39160	56.40
2.44	65.38	489.1	29340	42.25	2.94	87.73	656.3	39380	56.70
2.45	65.80	492.2	29530	42.53	2.95	88.21	659.9	39590	57.01
2.46	66.22	495.4	29720	42.80	2.96	88.68	663.4	39800	57.31
2.47	66.65	498.6	29910	43.08	2.97	89.15	666.9	40010	57.62
2.48	67.08	501.8	30100	43.35	2.98	89.63	670.5	40220	57.93
2.49	67.50	505.0	30300	43.63	2.99	90.10	674.0	40440	58.23
2.50	67.93	508.2	30490	43.90	3.00	90.58	677.6	40650	58.54

12

12-11: 5 ft. Parshall Flume Discharge Table

Formulas: $CFS = 20.00H^{1.587}$ $GPS = CFS \times 7.481$
$GPM = CFS \times 448.8$ $MGD = CFS \times 0.6463$

Head Feet	CFS	GPS	GPM	MGD	Head Feet	CFS	GPS	GPM	MGD
0.01	0.0134	0.1002	6.013	0.0087	0.51	6.870	51.39	3083	4.440
0.02	0.0402	0.3011	18.06	0.0260	0.52	7.085	53.00	3180	4.579
0.03	0.0766	0.5730	34.38	0.0495	0.53	7.302	54.63	3277	4.719
0.04	0.1209	0.9046	54.27	0.0782	0.54	7.522	56.27	3376	4.862
0.05	0.1723	1.289	77.33	0.1114	0.55	7.744	57.94	3476	5.005
0.06	0.2301	1.722	103.3	0.1487	0.56	7.969	59.62	3576	5.150
0.07	0.2939	2.199	131.9	0.1899	0.57	8.196	61.31	3678	5.297
0.08	0.3633	2.718	163.0	0.2348	0.58	8.425	63.03	3781	5.445
0.09	0.4379	3.276	196.5	0.2830	0.59	8.657	64.76	3885	5.595
0.10	0.5176	3.872	232.3	0.3346	0.60	8.891	66.51	3990	5.746
0.11	0.6022	4.505	270.3	0.3892	0.61	9.127	68.28	4096	5.899
0.12	0.6913	5.172	310.3	0.4468	0.62	9.366	70.07	4203	6.053
0.13	0.7850	5.872	352.3	0.5073	0.63	9.607	71.87	4312	6.209
0.14	0.8829	6.605	396.3	0.5706	0.64	9.850	73.69	4421	6.366
0.15	0.9851	7.370	442.1	0.6367	0.65	10.10	75.52	4531	6.525
0.16	1.091	8.164	489.8	0.7053	0.66	10.34	77.38	4642	6.685
0.17	1.202	8.989	539.3	0.7766	0.67	10.59	79.24	4754	6.846
0.18	1.316	9.843	590.5	0.8503	0.68	10.84	81.13	4867	7.009
0.19	1.434	10.72	643.4	0.9265	0.69	11.10	83.03	4981	7.173
0.20	1.555	11.63	697.9	1.005	0.70	11.36	84.95	5096	7.339
0.21	1.680	12.57	754.1	1.086	0.71	11.61	86.88	5212	7.506
0.22	1.809	13.53	811.9	1.169	0.72	11.87	88.83	5329	7.675
0.23	1.941	14.52	871.3	1.255	0.73	12.14	90.80	5447	7.844
0.24	2.077	15.54	932.1	1.342	0.74	12.40	92.78	5566	8.016
0.25	2.216	16.58	994.5	1.432	0.75	12.67	94.78	5686	8.188
0.26	2.358	17.64	1058	1.524	0.76	12.94	96.79	5807	8.362
0.27	2.504	18.73	1124	1.618	0.77	13.21	98.82	5928	8.537
0.28	2.653	19.84	1190	1.714	0.78	13.48	100.9	6051	8.714
0.29	2.805	20.98	1259	1.813	0.79	13.76	102.9	6175	8.892
0.30	2.960	22.14	1328	1.913	0.80	14.04	105.0	6299	9.071
0.31	3.118	23.32	1399	2.015	0.81	14.32	107.1	6425	9.252
0.32	3.279	24.53	1471	2.119	0.82	14.60	109.2	6551	9.434
0.33	3.443	25.76	1545	2.225	0.83	14.88	111.3	6678	9.617
0.34	3.610	27.01	1620	2.333	0.84	15.17	113.5	6806	9.802
0.35	3.780	28.28	1696	2.443	0.85	15.45	115.6	6935	9.987
0.36	3.953	29.57	1774	2.555	0.86	15.74	117.8	7065	10.17
0.37	4.128	30.88	1853	2.668	0.87	16.03	120.0	7196	10.36
0.38	4.307	32.22	1933	2.783	0.88	16.33	122.1	7328	10.55
0.39	4.488	33.57	2014	2.901	0.89	16.62	124.4	7460	10.74
0.40	4.672	34.95	2097	3.019	0.90	16.92	126.6	7594	10.94
0.41	4.859	36.35	2181	3.140	0.91	17.22	128.8	7728	11.13
0.42	5.048	37.76	2266	3.263	0.92	17.52	131.1	7863	11.32
0.43	5.240	39.20	2352	3.387	0.93	17.82	133.3	8000	11.52
0.44	5.435	40.66	2439	3.513	0.94	18.13	135.6	8136	11.72
0.45	5.632	42.13	2528	3.640	0.95	18.44	137.9	8274	11.92
0.46	5.832	43.63	2617	3.769	0.96	18.75	140.2	8413	12.12
0.47	6.035	45.14	2708	3.900	0.97	19.06	142.6	8552	12.32
0.48	6.240	46.68	2800	4.033	0.98	19.37	144.9	8693	12.52
0.49	6.447	48.23	2894	4.167	0.99	19.68	147.3	8834	12.72
0.50	6.657	49.80	2988	4.303	1.00	20.00	149.6	8976	12.93

12

12-11: 5 ft. Parshall Flume Discharge Table (*Continued*)

Formulas: CFS = $20.00H^{1.587}$ GPS = CFS x 7.481
GPM = CFS x 448.8   MGD = CFS x 0.6463

Head Feet	CFS	GPS	GPM	MGD	Head Feet	CFS	GPS	GPM	MGD
1.01	20.32	152.0	9119	13.13	1.51	38.47	287.8	17260	24.86
1.02	20.64	154.4	9263	13.34	1.52	38.87	290.8	17440	25.12
1.03	20.96	156.8	9407	13.55	1.53	39.28	293.8	17630	25.38
1.04	21.28	159.2	9552	13.76	1.54	39.68	296.9	17810	25.65
1.05	21.61	161.7	9699	13.97	1.55	40.09	299.9	17990	25.91
1.06	21.94	164.1	9846	14.18	1.56	40.51	303.0	18180	26.18
1.07	22.27	166.6	9993	14.39	1.57	40.92	306.1	18360	26.45
1.08	22.60	169.1	10140	14.61	1.58	41.33	309.2	18550	26.71
1.09	22.93	171.5	10290	14.82	1.59	41.75	312.3	18740	26.98
1.10	23.27	174.1	10440	15.04	1.60	42.17	315.4	18920	27.25
1.11	23.60	176.6	10590	15.25	1.61	42.59	318.6	19110	27.52
1.12	23.94	179.1	10740	15.47	1.62	43.01	321.7	19300	27.79
1.13	24.28	181.6	10900	15.69	1.63	43.43	324.9	19490	28.07
1.14	24.62	184.2	11050	15.91	1.64	43.85	328.1	19680	28.34
1.15	24.97	186.8	11200	16.14	1.65	44.28	331.2	19870	28.62
1.16	25.31	189.4	11360	16.36	1.66	44.70	334.4	20060	28.89
1.17	25.66	192.0	11520	16.58	1.67	45.13	337.6	20260	29.17
1.18	26.01	194.6	11670	16.81	1.68	45.56	340.8	20450	29.45
1.19	26.36	197.2	11830	17.04	1.69	45.99	344.1	20640	29.72
1.20	26.71	199.8	11990	17.26	1.70	46.43	347.3	20840	30.00
1.21	27.07	202.5	12150	17.49	1.71	46.86	350.6	21030	30.29
1.22	27.42	205.1	12310	17.72	1.72	47.29	353.8	21230	30.57
1.23	27.78	207.8	12470	17.95	1.73	47.73	357.1	21420	30.85
1.24	28.14	210.5	12630	18.19	1.74	48.17	360.4	21620	31.13
1.25	28.50	213.2	12790	18.42	1.75	48.61	363.7	21820	31.42
1.26	28.86	215.9	12950	18.65	1.76	49.05	367.0	22010	31.70
1.27	29.23	218.6	13120	18.89	1.77	49.50	370.3	22210	31.99
1.28	29.59	221.4	13280	19.13	1.78	49.94	373.6	22410	32.28
1.29	29.96	224.1	13450	19.36	1.79	50.39	376.9	22610	32.56
1.30	30.33	226.9	13610	19.60	1.80	50.83	380.3	22810	32.85
1.31	30.70	229.7	13780	19.84	1.81	51.28	383.6	23020	33.14
1.32	31.07	232.5	13950	20.08	1.82	51.73	387.0	23220	33.43
1.33	31.45	235.3	14110	20.32	1.83	52.18	390.4	23420	33.73
1.34	31.82	238.1	14280	20.57	1.84	52.64	393.8	23620	34.02
1.35	32.20	240.9	14450	20.81	1.85	53.09	397.2	23830	34.31
1.36	32.58	243.7	14620	21.06	1.86	53.55	400.6	24030	34.61
1.37	32.96	246.6	14790	21.30	1.87	54.01	404.0	24240	34.90
1.38	33.34	249.4	14960	21.55	1.88	54.47	407.5	24440	35.20
1.39	33.73	252.3	15140	21.80	1.89	54.93	410.9	24650	35.50
1.40	34.11	255.2	15310	22.05	1.90	55.39	414.4	24860	35.80
1.41	34.50	258.1	15480	22.30	1.91	55.85	417.8	25070	36.10
1.42	34.89	261.0	15660	22.55	1.92	56.32	421.3	25270	36.40
1.43	35.28	263.9	15830	22.80	1.93	56.78	424.8	25480	36.70
1.44	35.67	266.9	16010	23.06	1.94	57.25	428.3	25690	37.00
1.45	36.07	269.8	16190	23.31	1.95	57.72	431.8	25900	37.30
1.46	36.46	272.8	16360	23.57	1.96	58.19	435.3	26120	37.61
1.47	36.86	275.8	16540	23.82	1.97	58.66	438.8	26330	37.91
1.48	37.26	278.7	16720	24.08	1.98	59.13	442.4	26540	38.22
1.49	37.66	281.7	16900	24.34	1.99	59.61	445.9	26750	38.53
1.50	38.06	284.7	17080	24.60	2.00	60.08	449.5	26970	38.83

12

12-11: 5 ft. Parshall Flume Discharge Table (Continued)

Formulas: $CFS = 20.00H^{1.587}$ $GPS = CFS \times 7.481$
$GPM = CFS \times 448.8$ $MGD = CFS \times 0.6463$

Head Feet	CFS	GPS	GPM	MGD	Head Feet	CFS	GPS	GPM	MGD
2.01	60.56	453.1	27180	39.14	2.51	86.16	644.6	38670	55.69
2.02	61.04	456.6	27400	39.45	2.52	86.71	648.7	38910	56.04
2.03	61.52	460.2	27610	39.76	2.53	87.25	652.7	39160	56.39
2.04	62.00	463.8	27830	40.07	2.54	87.80	656.8	39410	56.75
2.05	62.49	467.5	28040	40.38	2.55	88.35	661.0	39650	57.10
2.06	62.97	471.1	28260	40.70	2.56	88.90	665.1	39900	57.46
2.07	63.46	474.7	28480	41.01	2.57	89.45	669.2	40150	57.81
2.08	63.94	478.4	28700	41.33	2.58	90.01	673.3	40390	58.17
2.09	64.43	482.0	28920	41.64	2.59	90.56	677.5	40640	58.53
2.10	64.92	485.7	29140	41.96	2.60	91.12	681.6	40890	58.89
2.11	65.41	489.4	29360	42.28	2.61	91.67	685.8	41140	59.25
2.12	65.91	493.0	29580	42.60	2.62	92.23	690.0	41390	59.61
2.13	66.40	496.7	29800	42.91	2.63	92.79	694.2	41640	59.97
2.14	66.90	500.4	30020	43.23	2.64	93.35	698.4	41900	60.33
2.15	67.39	504.2	30250	43.56	2.65	93.91	702.6	42150	60.70
2.16	67.89	507.9	30470	43.88	2.66	94.48	706.8	42400	61.06
2.17	68.39	511.6	30690	44.20	2.67	95.04	711.0	42650	61.42
2.18	68.89	515.4	30920	44.52	2.68	95.60	715.2	42910	61.79
2.19	69.39	519.1	31140	44.85	2.69	96.17	719.5	43160	62.16
2.20	69.90	522.9	31370	45.17	2.70	96.74	723.7	43420	62.52
2.21	70.40	526.7	31600	45.50	2.71	97.31	728.0	43670	62.89
2.22	70.91	530.5	31820	45.83	2.72	97.88	732.2	43930	63.26
2.23	71.42	534.3	32050	46.16	2.73	98.45	736.5	44180	63.63
2.24	71.92	538.1	32280	46.48	2.74	99.02	740.8	44440	64.00
2.25	72.43	541.9	32510	46.81	2.75	99.60	745.1	44700	64.37
2.26	72.95	545.7	32740	47.14	2.76	100.2	749.4	44960	64.74
2.27	73.46	549.5	32970	47.48	2.77	100.8	753.7	45220	65.11
2.28	73.97	553.4	33200	47.81	2.78	101.3	758.0	45480	65.49
2.29	74.49	557.2	33430	48.14	2.79	101.9	762.4	45740	65.86
2.30	75.01	561.1	33660	48.48	2.80	102.5	766.7	46000	66.24
2.31	75.52	565.0	33890	48.81	2.81	103.1	771.1	46260	66.61
2.32	76.04	568.9	34130	49.15	2.82	103.7	775.4	46520	66.99
2.33	76.56	572.8	34360	49.48	2.83	104.2	779.8	46780	67.37
2.34	77.09	576.7	34600	49.82	2.84	104.8	784.2	47040	67.75
2.35	77.61	580.6	34830	50.16	2.85	105.4	788.5	47310	68.12
2.36	78.13	584.5	35070	50.50	2.86	106.0	792.9	47570	68.50
2.37	78.66	588.5	35300	50.84	2.87	106.6	797.3	47830	68.88
2.38	79.19	592.4	35540	51.18	2.88	107.2	801.8	48100	69.27
2.39	79.72	596.4	35780	51.52	2.89	107.8	806.2	48360	69.65
2.40	80.25	600.3	36010	51.86	2.90	108.4	810.6	48630	70.03
2.41	80.78	604.3	36250	52.21	2.91	109.0	815.1	48900	70.41
2.42	81.31	608.3	36490	52.55	2.92	109.5	819.5	49160	70.80
2.43	81.84	612.3	36730	52.90	2.93	110.1	824.0	49430	71.18
2.44	82.38	616.3	36970	53.24	2.94	110.7	828.4	49700	71.57
2.45	82.92	620.3	37210	53.59	2.95	111.3	832.9	49970	71.96
2.46	83.45	624.3	37450	53.94	2.96	111.9	837.4	50240	72.34
2.47	83.99	628.3	37700	54.28	2.97	112.5	841.9	50510	72.73
2.48	84.53	632.4	37940	54.63	2.98	113.1	846.4	50780	73.12
2.49	85.07	636.4	38180	54.98	2.99	113.7	850.9	51050	73.51
2.50	85.62	640.5	38420	55.33	3.00	114.3	855.4	51320	73.90

12

12-12: 6 ft. Parshall Flume Discharge Table

Formulas: $CFS = 24.00H^{1.595}$ $GPS = CFS \times 7.481$
$GPM = CFS \times 448.8$ $MGD = CFS \times 0.6463$

Head Feet	CFS	GPS	GPM	MGD	Head Feet	CFS	GPS	GPM	MGD
0.01	0.0155	0.1159	6.954	0.0100	0.51	8.199	61.34	3680	5.299
0.02	0.0468	0.3502	21.01	0.0303	0.52	8.457	63.27	3796	5.466
0.03	0.0894	0.6686	40.11	0.0578	0.53	8.718	65.22	3913	5.635
0.04	0.1414	1.058	63.47	0.0914	0.54	8.982	67.20	4031	5.805
0.05	0.2019	1.510	90.60	0.1305	0.55	9.249	69.19	4151	5.978
0.06	0.2700	2.020	121.2	0.1745	0.56	9.519	71.21	4272	6.152
0.07	0.3453	2.583	155.0	0.2231	0.57	9.791	73.25	4394	6.328
0.08	0.4272	3.196	191.7	0.2761	0.58	10.07	75.31	4518	6.506
0.09	0.5155	3.856	231.4	0.3332	0.59	10.34	77.39	4643	6.686
0.10	0.6098	4.562	273.7	0.3941	0.60	10.63	79.49	4769	6.867
0.11	0.7100	5.311	318.6	0.4588	0.61	10.91	81.62	4896	7.051
0.12	0.8157	6.102	366.1	0.5272	0.62	11.20	83.76	5025	7.236
0.13	0.9267	6.933	415.9	0.5989	0.63	11.49	85.92	5155	7.423
0.14	1.043	7.803	468.1	0.6741	0.64	11.78	88.11	5286	7.612
0.15	1.164	8.710	522.6	0.7525	0.65	12.07	90.32	5418	7.803
0.16	1.291	9.655	579.2	0.8341	0.66	12.37	92.54	5552	7.995
0.17	1.422	10.63	638.0	0.9188	0.67	12.67	94.79	5687	8.189
0.18	1.557	11.65	698.9	1.006	0.68	12.97	97.06	5823	8.385
0.19	1.698	12.70	761.9	1.097	0.69	13.28	99.34	5960	8.582
0.20	1.842	13.78	826.8	1.191	0.70	13.59	101.6	6098	8.782
0.21	1.991	14.90	893.7	1.287	0.71	13.90	104.0	6238	8.983
0.22	2.145	16.04	962.6	1.386	0.72	14.21	106.3	6378	9.185
0.23	2.302	17.22	1033	1.488	0.73	14.53	108.7	6520	9.390
0.24	2.464	18.43	1106	1.593	0.74	14.85	111.1	6663	9.596
0.25	2.630	19.67	1180	1.700	0.75	15.17	113.5	6807	9.803
0.26	2.800	20.94	1256	1.809	0.76	15.49	115.9	6953	10.01
0.27	2.973	22.24	1334	1.922	0.77	15.82	118.3	7099	10.22
0.28	3.151	23.57	1414	2.036	0.78	16.15	120.8	7247	10.44
0.29	3.332	24.93	1496	2.154	0.79	16.48	123.3	7396	10.65
0.30	3.517	26.31	1579	2.273	0.80	16.81	125.8	7546	10.87
0.31	3.706	27.73	1663	2.395	0.81	17.15	128.3	7697	11.08
0.32	3.899	29.17	1750	2.520	0.82	17.49	130.8	7849	11.30
0.33	4.095	30.63	1838	2.647	0.83	17.83	133.4	8002	11.52
0.34	4.295	32.13	1927	2.776	0.84	18.17	136.0	8156	11.75
0.35	4.498	33.65	2019	2.907	0.85	18.52	138.5	8312	11.97
0.36	4.705	35.19	2111	3.041	0.86	18.87	141.2	8468	12.19
0.37	4.915	36.77	2206	3.176	0.87	19.22	143.8	8626	12.42
0.38	5.128	38.36	2302	3.314	0.88	19.57	146.4	8784	12.65
0.39	5.345	39.99	2399	3.455	0.89	19.93	149.1	8944	12.88
0.40	5.565	41.63	2498	3.597	0.90	20.29	151.8	9105	13.11
0.41	5.789	43.31	2598	3.741	0.91	20.65	154.5	9267	13.34
0.42	6.016	45.00	2700	3.888	0.92	21.01	157.2	9430	13.58
0.43	6.246	46.73	2803	4.037	0.93	21.38	159.9	9594	13.82
0.44	6.479	48.47	2908	4.187	0.94	21.74	162.7	9759	14.05
0.45	6.716	50.24	3014	4.340	0.95	22.11	165.4	9925	14.29
0.46	6.955	52.03	3121	4.495	0.96	22.49	168.2	10090	14.53
0.47	7.198	53.85	3230	4.652	0.97	22.86	171.0	10260	14.78
0.48	7.444	55.69	3341	4.811	0.98	23.24	173.9	10430	15.02
0.49	7.693	57.55	3452	4.972	0.99	23.62	176.7	10600	15.26
0.50	7.945	59.43	3566	5.135	1.00	24.00	179.5	10770	15.51

12

12-12: 6 ft. Parshall Flume Discharge Table (Continued)

Formulas: CFS = $24.00H^{1.595}$ GPS = CFS x 7.481
           GPM = CFS x 448.8   MGD = CFS x 0.6463

Head Feet	CFS	GPS	GPM	MGD	Head Feet	CFS	GPS	GPM	MGD
1.01	24.38	182.4	10940	15.76	1.51	46.31	346.4	20780	29.93
1.02	24.77	185.3	11120	16.01	1.52	46.80	350.1	21000	30.25
1.03	25.16	188.2	11290	16.26	1.53	47.29	353.8	21220	30.57
1.04	25.55	191.1	11470	16.51	1.54	47.79	357.5	21450	30.88
1.05	25.94	194.1	11640	16.77	1.55	48.28	361.2	21670	31.21
1.06	26.34	197.0	11820	17.02	1.56	48.78	364.9	21890	31.53
1.07	26.73	200.0	12000	17.28	1.57	49.28	368.7	22120	31.85
1.08	27.13	203.0	12180	17.54	1.58	49.78	372.4	22340	32.17
1.09	27.54	206.0	12360	17.80	1.59	50.29	376.2	22570	32.50
1.10	27.94	209.0	12540	18.06	1.60	50.79	380.0	22790	32.83
1.11	28.35	212.1	12720	18.32	1.61	51.30	383.8	23020	33.15
1.12	28.76	215.1	12910	18.58	1.62	51.81	387.6	23250	33.48
1.13	29.17	218.2	13090	18.85	1.63	52.32	391.4	23480	33.81
1.14	29.58	221.3	13270	19.12	1.64	52.83	395.2	23710	34.14
1.15	29.99	224.4	13460	19.38	1.65	53.35	399.1	23940	34.48
1.16	30.41	227.5	13650	19.65	1.66	53.86	402.9	24170	34.81
1.17	30.83	230.6	13840	19.93	1.67	54.38	406.8	24410	35.15
1.18	31.25	233.8	14030	20.20	1.68	54.90	410.7	24640	35.48
1.19	31.67	237.0	14220	20.47	1.69	55.42	414.6	24870	35.82
1.20	32.10	240.1	14410	20.75	1.70	55.95	418.5	25110	36.16
1.21	32.53	243.3	14600	21.02	1.71	56.47	422.5	25350	36.50
1.22	32.96	246.6	14790	21.30	1.72	57.00	426.4	25580	36.84
1.23	33.39	249.8	14990	21.58	1.73	57.53	430.4	25820	37.18
1.24	33.82	253.0	15180	21.86	1.74	58.06	434.4	26060	37.53
1.25	34.26	256.3	15380	22.14	1.75	58.59	438.3	26300	37.87
1.26	34.70	259.6	15570	22.43	1.76	59.13	442.3	26540	38.22
1.27	35.14	262.9	15770	22.71	1.77	59.67	446.4	26780	38.56
1.28	35.58	266.2	15970	23.00	1.78	60.20	450.4	27020	38.91
1.29	36.02	269.5	16170	23.28	1.79	60.75	454.4	27260	39.26
1.30	36.47	272.8	16370	23.57	1.80	61.29	458.5	27510	39.61
1.31	36.92	276.2	16570	23.86	1.81	61.83	462.6	27750	39.96
1.32	37.37	279.6	16770	24.15	1.82	62.38	466.6	27990	40.31
1.33	37.82	283.0	16970	24.44	1.83	62.92	470.7	28240	40.67
1.34	38.28	286.4	17180	24.74	1.84	63.47	474.8	28490	41.02
1.35	38.73	289.8	17380	25.03	1.85	64.03	479.0	28730	41.38
1.36	39.19	293.2	17590	25.33	1.86	64.58	483.1	28980	41.74
1.37	39.65	296.6	17800	25.63	1.87	65.13	487.3	29230	42.10
1.38	40.12	300.1	18000	25.93	1.88	65.69	491.4	29480	42.45
1.39	40.58	303.6	18210	26.23	1.89	66.25	495.6	29730	42.82
1.40	41.05	307.1	18420	26.53	1.90	66.81	499.8	29980	43.18
1.41	41.52	310.6	18630	26.83	1.91	67.37	504.0	30240	43.54
1.42	41.99	314.1	18840	27.14	1.92	67.93	508.2	30490	43.90
1.43	42.46	317.6	19060	27.44	1.93	68.50	512.4	30740	44.27
1.44	42.93	321.2	19270	27.75	1.94	69.06	516.7	31000	44.64
1.45	43.41	324.8	19480	28.06	1.95	69.63	520.9	31250	45.00
1.46	43.89	328.3	19700	28.37	1.96	70.20	525.2	31510	45.37
1.47	44.37	331.9	19910	28.68	1.97	70.78	529.5	31760	45.74
1.48	44.85	335.5	20130	28.99	1.98	71.35	533.8	32020	46.11
1.49	45.34	339.2	20350	29.30	1.99	71.93	538.1	32280	46.49
1.50	45.82	342.8	20570	29.61	2.00	72.50	542.4	32540	46.86

12

12-12: 6 ft. Parshall Flume Discharge Table (Continued)

Formulas: $CFS = 24.00H^{1.595}$ $GPS = CFS \times 7.481$
$GPM = CFS \times 448.8$ $MGD = CFS \times 0.6463$

Head Feet	CFS	GPS	GPM	MGD	Head Feet	CFS	GPS	GPM	MGD
2.01	73.08	546.7	32800	47.23	2.51	104.2	779.2	46750	67.32
2.02	73.66	551.1	33060	47.61	2.52	104.8	784.2	47040	67.75
2.03	74.25	555.4	33320	47.98	2.53	105.5	789.1	47340	68.17
2.04	74.83	559.8	33580	48.36	2.54	106.2	794.1	47640	68.60
2.05	75.42	564.2	33850	48.74	2.55	106.8	799.1	47940	69.04
2.06	76.00	568.6	34110	49.12	2.56	107.5	804.1	48240	69.47
2.07	76.59	573.0	34370	49.50	2.57	108.2	809.1	48540	69.90
2.08	77.18	577.4	34640	49.88	2.58	108.8	814.1	48840	70.34
2.09	77.78	581.8	34910	50.27	2.59	109.5	819.2	49140	70.77
2.10	78.37	586.3	35170	50.65	2.60	110.2	824.2	49450	71.21
2.11	78.97	590.7	35440	51.04	2.61	110.9	829.3	49750	71.65
2.12	79.56	595.2	35710	51.42	2.62	111.5	834.4	50060	72.08
2.13	80.16	599.7	35980	51.81	2.63	112.2	839.5	50360	72.52
2.14	80.76	604.2	36250	52.20	2.64	112.9	844.6	50670	72.96
2.15	81.37	608.7	36520	52.59	2.65	113.6	849.7	50970	73.40
2.16	81.97	613.2	36790	52.98	2.66	114.3	854.8	51280	73.85
2.17	82.58	617.8	37060	53.37	2.67	114.9	859.9	51590	74.29
2.18	83.19	622.3	37330	53.76	2.68	115.6	865.1	51900	74.73
2.19	83.80	626.9	37610	54.16	2.69	116.3	870.2	52210	75.18
2.20	84.41	631.4	37880	54.55	2.70	117.0	875.4	52520	75.63
2.21	85.02	636.0	38160	54.95	2.71	117.7	880.6	52830	76.07
2.22	85.63	640.6	38430	55.35	2.72	118.4	885.7	53140	76.52
2.23	86.25	645.2	38710	55.74	2.73	119.1	890.9	53450	76.97
2.24	86.87	649.9	38990	56.14	2.74	119.8	896.2	53760	77.42
2.25	87.49	654.5	39260	56.54	2.75	120.5	901.4	54080	77.87
2.26	88.11	659.1	39540	56.94	2.76	121.2	906.6	54390	78.32
2.27	88.73	663.8	39820	57.35	2.77	121.9	911.9	54700	78.78
2.28	89.35	668.5	40100	57.75	2.78	122.6	917.1	55020	79.23
2.29	89.98	673.1	40380	58.15	2.79	123.3	922.4	55340	79.69
2.30	90.61	677.8	40660	58.56	2.80	124.0	927.7	55650	80.14
2.31	91.24	682.5	40950	58.97	2.81	124.7	932.9	55970	80.60
2.32	91.87	687.3	41230	59.37	2.82	125.4	938.2	56290	81.06
2.33	92.50	692.0	41510	59.78	2.83	126.1	943.6	56610	81.52
2.34	93.13	696.7	41800	60.19	2.84	126.8	948.9	56930	81.98
2.35	93.77	701.5	42080	60.60	2.85	127.6	954.2	57250	82.44
2.36	94.41	706.3	42370	61.02	2.86	128.3	959.6	57570	82.90
2.37	95.05	711.0	42660	61.43	2.87	129.0	964.9	57890	83.36
2.38	95.69	715.8	42940	61.84	2.88	129.7	970.3	58210	83.83
2.39	96.33	720.6	43230	62.26	2.89	130.4	975.7	58530	84.29
2.40	96.97	725.5	43520	62.67	2.90	131.1	981.1	58860	84.76
2.41	97.62	730.3	43810	63.09	2.91	131.9	986.5	59180	85.22
2.42	98.26	735.1	44100	63.51	2.92	132.6	991.9	59500	85.69
2.43	98.91	740.0	44390	63.93	2.93	133.3	997.3	59830	86.16
2.44	99.56	744.8	44680	64.35	2.94	134.0	1003	60160	86.63
2.45	100.2	749.7	44980	64.77	2.95	134.8	1008	60480	87.10
2.46	100.9	754.6	45270	65.19	2.96	135.5	1014	60810	87.57
2.47	101.5	759.5	45560	65.61	2.97	136.2	1019	61140	88.04
2.48	102.2	764.4	45860	66.04	2.98	137.0	1025	61470	88.52
2.49	102.8	769.3	46150	66.46	2.99	137.7	1030	61800	88.99
2.50	103.5	774.3	46450	66.89	3.00	138.4	1036	62130	89.47

12

12-13: 8 ft. Parshall Flume Discharge Table

Formulas: $CFS = 32.00H^{1.607}$ $GPS = CFS \times 7.481$

$GPM = CFS \times 448.8$ $MGD = CFS \times 0.6463$

Head Feet	CFS	GPS	GPM	MGD	Head Feet	CFS	GPS	GPM	MGD
0.01	0.0196	0.1463	8.774	0.0126	0.51	10.84	81.13	4867	7.009
0.02	0.0596	0.4455	26.73	0.0385	0.52	11.19	83.70	5021	7.231
0.03	0.1143	0.8548	51.28	0.0738	0.53	11.54	86.30	5177	7.456
0.04	0.1814	1.357	81.42	0.1172	0.54	11.89	88.93	5335	7.683
0.05	0.2597	1.942	116.5	0.1678	0.55	12.24	91.60	5495	7.913
0.06	0.3480	2.604	156.2	0.2249	0.56	12.60	94.29	5656	8.146
0.07	0.4459	3.336	200.1	0.2882	0.57	12.97	97.01	5820	8.381
0.08	0.5526	4.134	248.0	0.3571	0.58	13.33	99.76	5985	8.618
0.09	0.6678	4.995	299.7	0.4316	0.59	13.71	102.5	6151	8.858
0.10	0.7910	5.917	355.0	0.5112	0.60	14.08	105.3	6320	9.101
0.11	0.9219	6.896	413.7	0.5958	0.61	14.46	108.2	6490	9.346
0.12	1.060	7.931	475.8	0.6852	0.62	14.84	111.0	6662	9.593
0.13	1.206	9.020	541.1	0.7793	0.63	15.23	113.9	6835	9.843
0.14	1.358	10.16	609.6	0.8778	0.64	15.62	116.9	7010	10.10
0.15	1.517	11.35	681.1	0.9808	0.65	16.01	119.8	7187	10.35
0.16	1.683	12.59	755.5	1.088	0.66	16.41	122.8	7366	10.61
0.17	1.856	13.88	832.8	1.199	0.67	16.81	125.8	7546	10.87
0.18	2.034	15.22	912.9	1.315	0.68	17.22	128.8	7728	11.13
0.19	2.219	16.60	995.8	1.434	0.69	17.63	131.9	7911	11.39
0.20	2.409	18.02	1081	1.557	0.70	18.04	135.0	8096	11.66
0.21	2.606	19.49	1170	1.684	0.71	18.46	138.1	8283	11.93
0.22	2.808	21.01	1260	1.815	0.72	18.87	141.2	8471	12.20
0.23	3.016	22.56	1354	1.949	0.73	19.30	144.4	8661	12.47
0.24	3.230	24.16	1449	2.087	0.74	19.72	147.6	8852	12.75
0.25	3.449	25.80	1548	2.229	0.75	20.15	150.8	9045	13.03
0.26	3.673	27.48	1648	2.374	0.76	20.59	154.0	9240	13.31
0.27	3.903	29.20	1751	2.522	0.77	21.03	157.3	9436	13.59
0.28	4.137	30.95	1857	2.674	0.78	21.47	160.6	9634	13.87
0.29	4.377	32.75	1965	2.829	0.79	21.91	163.9	9833	14.16
0.30	4.623	34.58	2075	2.988	0.80	22.36	167.3	10030	14.45
0.31	4.873	36.45	2187	3.149	0.81	22.81	170.6	10240	14.74
0.32	5.128	38.36	2301	3.314	0.82	23.26	174.0	10440	15.03
0.33	5.388	40.31	2418	3.482	0.83	23.72	177.4	10650	15.33
0.34	5.652	42.29	2537	3.653	0.84	24.18	180.9	10850	15.63
0.35	5.922	44.30	2658	3.827	0.85	24.64	184.4	11060	15.93
0.36	6.196	46.35	2781	4.005	0.86	25.11	187.9	11270	16.23
0.37	6.475	48.44	2906	4.185	0.87	25.58	191.4	11480	16.53
0.38	6.759	50.56	3033	4.368	0.88	26.06	194.9	11690	16.84
0.39	7.047	52.72	3163	4.554	0.89	26.54	198.5	11910	17.15
0.40	7.339	54.91	3294	4.743	0.90	27.02	202.1	12120	17.46
0.41	7.636	57.13	3427	4.935	0.91	27.50	205.7	12340	17.77
0.42	7.938	59.38	3563	5.130	0.92	27.99	209.4	12560	18.09
0.43	8.244	61.67	3700	5.328	0.93	28.48	213.0	12780	18.41
0.44	8.554	63.99	3839	5.529	0.94	28.97	216.7	13000	18.72
0.45	8.869	66.35	3980	5.732	0.95	29.47	220.5	13230	19.05
0.46	9.188	68.73	4123	5.938	0.96	29.97	224.2	13450	19.37
0.47	9.511	71.15	4268	6.147	0.97	30.47	228.0	13680	19.69
0.48	9.838	73.60	4415	6.358	0.98	30.98	231.7	13900	20.02
0.49	10.17	76.08	4564	6.572	0.99	31.49	235.6	14130	20.35
0.50	10.50	78.59	4715	6.789	1.00	32.00	239.4	14360	20.68

12

12-13: 8 ft. Parshall Flume Discharge Table (Continued)

Formulas: CFS = $32.00H^{1.607}$ GPS = CFS x 7.481
GPM = CFS x 448.8   MGD = CFS x 0.6463

Head Feet	CFS	GPS	GPM	MGD	Head Feet	CFS	GPS	GPM	MGD
1.01	32.52	243.3	14590	21.01	1.51	62.05	464.2	27850	40.11
1.02	33.03	247.1	14830	21.35	1.52	62.72	469.2	28150	40.53
1.03	33.56	251.0	15060	21.69	1.53	63.38	474.1	28440	40.96
1.04	34.08	255.0	15300	22.03	1.54	64.05	479.1	28740	41.39
1.05	34.61	258.9	15530	22.37	1.55	64.72	484.1	29040	41.83
1.06	35.14	262.9	15770	22.71	1.56	65.39	489.2	29350	42.26
1.07	35.68	266.9	16010	23.06	1.57	66.06	494.2	29650	42.70
1.08	36.21	270.9	16250	23.40	1.58	66.74	499.3	29950	43.13
1.09	36.75	275.0	16490	23.75	1.59	67.42	504.4	30260	43.57
1.10	37.30	279.0	16740	24.10	1.60	68.10	509.5	30560	44.02
1.11	37.84	283.1	16980	24.46	1.61	68.79	514.6	30870	44.46
1.12	38.39	287.2	17230	24.81	1.62	69.48	519.8	31180	44.90
1.13	38.94	291.3	17480	25.17	1.63	70.17	524.9	31490	45.35
1.14	39.50	295.5	17730	25.53	1.64	70.86	530.1	31800	45.80
1.15	40.06	299.7	17980	25.89	1.65	71.56	535.3	32110	46.25
1.16	40.62	303.9	18230	26.25	1.66	72.25	540.5	32430	46.70
1.17	41.18	308.1	18480	26.62	1.67	72.96	545.8	32740	47.15
1.18	41.75	312.3	18740	26.98	1.68	73.66	551.0	33060	47.61
1.19	42.32	316.6	18990	27.35	1.69	74.36	556.3	33370	48.06
1.20	42.89	320.9	19250	27.72	1.70	75.07	561.6	33690	48.52
1.21	43.47	325.2	19510	28.09	1.71	75.78	566.9	34010	48.98
1.22	44.05	329.5	19770	28.47	1.72	76.50	572.3	34330	49.44
1.23	44.63	333.9	20030	28.84	1.73	77.21	577.6	34650	49.90
1.24	45.21	338.3	20290	29.22	1.74	77.93	583.0	34980	50.37
1.25	45.80	342.6	20560	29.60	1.75	78.65	588.4	35300	50.83
1.26	46.39	347.1	20820	29.98	1.76	79.38	593.8	35620	51.30
1.27	46.99	351.5	21090	30.37	1.77	80.10	599.2	35950	51.77
1.28	47.58	356.0	21350	30.75	1.78	80.83	604.7	36280	52.24
1.29	48.18	360.4	21620	31.14	1.79	81.56	610.2	36600	52.71
1.30	48.78	364.9	21890	31.53	1.80	82.29	615.6	36930	53.19
1.31	49.39	369.5	22160	31.92	1.81	83.03	621.2	37260	53.66
1.32	49.99	374.0	22440	32.31	1.82	83.77	626.7	37600	54.14
1.33	50.60	378.6	22710	32.70	1.83	84.51	632.2	37930	54.62
1.34	51.22	383.1	22990	33.10	1.84	85.25	637.8	38260	55.10
1.35	51.83	387.8	23260	33.50	1.85	86.00	643.4	38600	55.58
1.36	52.45	392.4	23540	33.90	1.86	86.75	649.0	38930	56.06
1.37	53.07	397.0	23820	34.30	1.87	87.50	654.6	39270	56.55
1.38	53.70	401.7	24100	34.70	1.88	88.25	660.2	39610	57.04
1.39	54.32	406.4	24380	35.11	1.89	89.01	665.9	39950	57.53
1.40	54.95	411.1	24660	35.52	1.90	89.76	671.5	40290	58.02
1.41	55.58	415.8	24950	35.92	1.91	90.53	677.2	40630	58.51
1.42	56.22	420.6	25230	36.33	1.92	91.29	682.9	40970	59.00
1.43	56.86	425.3	25520	36.75	1.93	92.05	688.7	41310	59.49
1.44	57.50	430.1	25800	37.16	1.94	92.82	694.4	41660	59.99
1.45	58.14	434.9	26090	37.58	1.95	93.59	700.2	42000	60.49
1.46	58.78	439.8	26380	37.99	1.96	94.36	705.9	42350	60.99
1.47	59.43	444.6	26670	38.41	1.97	95.14	711.7	42700	61.49
1.48	60.08	449.5	26970	38.83	1.98	95.92	717.5	43050	61.99
1.49	60.74	454.4	27260	39.25	1.99	96.70	723.4	43400	62.49
1.50	61.39	459.3	27550	39.68	2.00	97.48	729.2	43750	63.00

12

12-13: 8 ft. Parshall Flume Discharge Table (Continued)

Formulas: CFS = $32.00H^{1.607}$ GPS = CFS x 7.481
GPM = CFS x 448.8   MGD = CFS x 0.6463

Head Feet	CFS	GPS	GPM	MGD	Head Feet	CFS	GPS	GPM	MGD
2.01	98.26	735.1	44100	63.51	2.51	140.4	1050	63020	90.75
2.02	99.05	741.0	44450	64.02	2.52	141.3	1057	63420	91.33
2.03	99.84	746.9	44810	64.53	2.53	142.2	1064	63830	91.92
2.04	100.6	752.8	45160	65.04	2.54	143.1	1071	64230	92.50
2.05	101.4	758.7	45520	65.55	2.55	144.0	1078	64640	93.09
2.06	102.2	764.7	45880	66.06	2.56	144.9	1084	65050	93.68
2.07	103.0	770.7	46230	66.58	2.57	145.9	1091	65460	94.26
2.08	103.8	776.7	46590	67.10	2.58	146.8	1098	65870	94.85
2.09	104.6	782.7	46950	67.62	2.59	147.7	1105	66280	95.45
2.10	105.4	788.7	47320	68.14	2.60	148.6	1112	66690	96.04
2.11	106.2	794.8	47680	68.66	2.61	149.5	1119	67100	96.63
2.12	107.0	800.8	48040	69.18	2.62	150.4	1125	67520	97.23
2.13	107.9	806.9	48410	69.71	2.63	151.4	1132	67930	97.83
2.14	108.7	813.0	48770	70.24	2.64	152.3	1139	68350	98.42
2.15	109.5	819.1	49140	70.76	2.65	153.2	1146	68760	99.02
2.16	110.3	825.2	49510	71.29	2.66	154.1	1153	69180	99.63
2.17	111.1	831.4	49880	71.82	2.67	155.1	1160	69600	100.2
2.18	112.0	837.5	50250	72.36	2.68	156.0	1167	70020	100.8
2.19	112.8	843.7	50620	72.89	2.69	157.0	1174	70440	101.4
2.20	113.6	849.9	50990	73.43	2.70	157.9	1181	70860	102.0
2.21	114.4	856.1	51360	73.96	2.71	158.8	1188	71280	102.7
2.22	115.3	862.4	51740	74.50	2.72	159.8	1195	71710	103.3
2.23	116.1	868.6	52110	75.04	2.73	160.7	1202	72130	103.9
2.24	116.9	874.9	52490	75.58	2.74	161.7	1209	72560	104.5
2.25	117.8	881.2	52860	76.13	2.75	162.6	1217	72980	105.1
2.26	118.6	887.5	53240	76.67	2.76	163.6	1224	73410	105.7
2.27	119.5	893.8	53620	77.22	2.77	164.5	1231	73840	106.3
2.28	120.3	900.1	54000	77.77	2.78	165.5	1238	74260	106.9
2.29	121.2	906.5	54380	78.31	2.79	166.4	1245	74690	107.6
2.30	122.0	912.9	54760	78.86	2.80	167.4	1252	75130	108.2
2.31	122.9	919.3	55150	79.42	2.81	168.4	1259	75560	108.8
2.32	123.7	925.7	55530	79.97	2.82	169.3	1267	75990	109.4
2.33	124.6	932.1	55920	80.52	2.83	170.3	1274	76420	110.1
2.34	125.5	938.5	56300	81.08	2.84	171.3	1281	76860	110.7
2.35	126.3	945.0	56690	81.64	2.85	172.2	1288	77290	111.3
2.36	127.2	951.4	57080	82.20	2.86	173.2	1296	77730	111.9
2.37	128.0	957.9	57470	82.76	2.87	174.2	1303	78170	112.6
2.38	128.9	964.4	57860	83.32	2.88	175.1	1310	78600	113.2
2.39	129.8	970.9	58250	83.88	2.89	176.1	1318	79040	113.8
2.40	130.7	977.5	58640	84.45	2.90	177.1	1325	79480	114.5
2.41	131.5	984.0	59030	85.01	2.91	178.1	1332	79920	115.1
2.42	132.4	990.6	59430	85.58	2.92	179.1	1340	80370	115.7
2.43	133.3	997.2	59820	86.15	2.93	180.1	1347	80810	116.4
2.44	134.2	1004	60220	86.72	2.94	181.0	1354	81250	117.0
2.45	135.1	1010	60620	87.29	2.95	182.0	1362	81700	117.6
2.46	136.0	1017	61010	87.87	2.96	183.0	1369	82140	118.3
2.47	136.8	1024	61410	88.44	2.97	184.0	1377	82590	118.9
2.48	137.7	1030	61810	89.02	2.98	185.0	1384	83040	119.6
2.49	138.6	1037	62220	89.59	2.99	186.0	1392	83480	120.2
2.50	139.5	1044	62620	90.17	3.00	187.0	1399	83930	120.9

12-14: 10 ft. Parshall Flume Discharge Table

Formulas: $CFS = 39.38H^{1.6}$ $GPS = CFS \times 7.481$

          $GPM = CFS \times 448.8$ $MGD = CFS \times 0.6463$

Head Feet	CFS	GPS	GPM	MGD	Head Feet	CFS	GPS	GPM	MGD
0.01	0.0248	0.1859	11.15	0.0161	0.51	13.41	100.3	6018	8.666
0.02	0.0753	0.5635	33.80	0.0487	0.52	13.83	103.5	6208	8.940
0.03	0.1441	1.078	64.67	0.0931	0.53	14.26	106.7	6400	9.216
0.04	0.2283	1.708	102.5	0.1476	0.54	14.69	109.9	6594	9.496
0.05	0.3263	2.441	146.4	0.2109	0.55	15.13	113.2	6791	9.779
0.06	0.4368	3.268	196.1	0.2823	0.56	15.57	116.5	6989	10.06
0.07	0.5590	4.182	250.9	0.3613	0.57	16.02	119.8	7190	10.35
0.08	0.6922	5.178	310.7	0.4474	0.58	16.47	123.2	7393	10.65
0.09	0.8357	6.252	375.1	0.5401	0.59	16.93	126.6	7598	10.94
0.10	0.9892	7.400	443.9	0.6393	0.60	17.39	130.1	7805	11.24
0.11	1.152	8.619	517.1	0.7446	0.61	17.86	133.6	8014	11.54
0.12	1.324	9.907	594.3	0.8559	0.62	18.33	137.1	8225	11.85
0.13	1.505	11.26	675.5	0.9728	0.63	18.80	140.7	8439	12.15
0.14	1.695	12.68	760.6	1.095	0.64	19.28	144.3	8654	12.46
0.15	1.892	14.16	849.3	1.223	0.65	19.77	147.9	8871	12.78
0.16	2.098	15.70	941.7	1.356	0.66	20.26	151.5	9091	13.09
0.17	2.312	17.30	1038	1.494	0.67	20.75	155.2	9312	13.41
0.18	2.533	18.95	1137	1.637	0.68	21.25	158.9	9535	13.73
0.19	2.762	20.67	1240	1.785	0.69	21.75	162.7	9761	14.06
0.20	2.999	22.43	1346	1.938	0.70	22.26	166.5	9988	14.38
0.21	3.242	24.25	1455	2.095	0.71	22.77	170.3	10220	14.71
0.22	3.493	26.13	1567	2.257	0.72	23.28	174.2	10450	15.05
0.23	3.750	28.05	1683	2.424	0.73	23.80	178.1	10680	15.38
0.24	4.014	30.03	1802	2.594	0.74	24.32	182.0	10920	15.72
0.25	4.285	32.06	1923	2.770	0.75	24.85	185.9	11150	16.06
0.26	4.563	34.13	2048	2.949	0.76	25.39	189.9	11390	16.41
0.27	4.847	36.26	2175	3.133	0.77	25.92	193.9	11630	16.75
0.28	5.137	38.43	2306	3.320	0.78	26.46	198.0	11880	17.10
0.29	5.434	40.65	2439	3.512	0.79	27.01	202.0	12120	17.45
0.30	5.737	42.92	2575	3.708	0.80	27.56	206.1	12370	17.81
0.31	6.046	45.23	2713	3.907	0.81	28.11	210.3	12620	18.17
0.32	6.361	47.59	2855	4.111	0.82	28.67	214.5	12870	18.53
0.33	6.682	49.99	2999	4.318	0.83	29.23	218.7	13120	18.89
0.34	7.009	52.43	3146	4.530	0.84	29.79	222.9	13370	19.26
0.35	7.341	54.92	3295	4.745	0.85	30.36	227.1	13630	19.62
0.36	7.680	57.45	3447	4.964	0.86	30.94	231.4	13880	19.99
0.37	8.024	60.03	3601	5.186	0.87	31.51	235.8	14140	20.37
0.38	8.374	62.65	3758	5.412	0.88	32.10	240.1	14400	20.74
0.39	8.729	65.30	3918	5.642	0.89	32.68	244.5	14670	21.12
0.40	9.090	68.00	4080	5.875	0.90	33.27	248.9	14930	21.50
0.41	9.456	70.74	4244	6.112	0.91	33.86	253.3	15200	21.89
0.42	9.828	73.52	4411	6.352	0.92	34.46	257.8	15470	22.27
0.43	10.21	76.35	4580	6.596	0.93	35.06	262.3	15740	22.66
0.44	10.59	79.21	4752	6.843	0.94	35.67	266.8	16010	23.05
0.45	10.98	82.11	4926	7.093	0.95	36.28	271.4	16280	23.45
0.46	11.37	85.04	5102	7.347	0.96	36.89	276.0	16560	23.84
0.47	11.77	88.02	5281	7.604	0.97	37.51	280.6	16830	24.24
0.48	12.17	91.04	5462	7.865	0.98	38.13	285.2	17110	24.64
0.49	12.58	94.09	5645	8.129	0.99	38.75	289.9	17390	25.05
0.50	12.99	97.18	5830	8.396	1.00	39.38	294.6	17670	25.45

12

12-14: 10 ft. Parshall Flume Discharge Table (Continued)

Formulas: CFS $=39.38H^{1.6}$ GPS = CFS x 7.481
$\quad\quad\quad$ GPM = CFS x 448.8   MGD = CFS x 0.6463

Head Feet	CFS	GPS	GPM	MGD	Head Feet	CFS	GPS	GPM	MGD
1.01	40.01	299.3	17960	25.86	1.51	76.14	569.6	34170	49.21
1.02	40.65	304.1	18240	26.27	1.52	76.95	575.7	34540	49.73
1.03	41.29	308.9	18530	26.68	1.53	77.76	581.8	34900	50.26
1.04	41.93	313.7	18820	27.10	1.54	78.58	587.9	35270	50.79
1.05	42.58	318.5	19110	27.52	1.55	79.40	594.0	35630	51.31
1.06	43.23	323.4	19400	27.94	1.56	80.22	600.1	36000	51.85
1.07	43.88	328.3	19690	28.36	1.57	81.04	606.3	36370	52.38
1.08	44.54	333.2	19990	28.79	1.58	81.87	612.5	36740	52.91
1.09	45.20	338.2	20290	29.21	1.59	82.70	618.7	37120	53.45
1.10	45.87	343.1	20590	29.64	1.60	83.53	624.9	37490	53.99
1.11	46.54	348.1	20890	30.08	1.61	84.37	631.2	37870	54.53
1.12	47.21	353.2	21190	30.51	1.62	85.21	637.5	38240	55.07
1.13	47.89	358.2	21490	30.95	1.63	86.05	643.8	38620	55.62
1.14	48.57	363.3	21800	31.39	1.64	86.90	650.1	39000	56.16
1.15	49.25	368.4	22100	31.83	1.65	87.75	656.5	39380	56.71
1.16	49.94	373.6	22410	32.27	1.66	88.60	662.8	39770	57.26
1.17	50.63	378.7	22720	32.72	1.67	89.46	669.2	40150	57.82
1.18	51.32	383.9	23030	33.17	1.68	90.32	675.7	40530	58.37
1.19	52.02	389.1	23350	33.62	1.69	91.18	682.1	40920	58.93
1.20	52.72	394.4	23660	34.07	1.70	92.04	688.6	41310	59.49
1.21	53.42	399.7	23980	34.53	1.71	92.91	695.1	41700	60.05
1.22	54.13	405.0	24290	34.99	1.72	93.78	701.6	42090	60.61
1.23	54.84	410.3	24610	35.45	1.73	94.66	708.1	42480	61.18
1.24	55.56	415.6	24930	35.91	1.74	95.53	714.7	42880	61.74
1.25	56.28	421.0	25260	36.37	1.75	96.41	721.3	43270	62.31
1.26	57.00	426.4	25580	36.84	1.76	97.30	727.9	43670	62.88
1.27	57.72	431.8	25910	37.31	1.77	98.18	734.5	44060	63.46
1.28	58.45	437.3	26230	37.78	1.78	99.07	741.2	44460	64.03
1.29	59.19	442.8	26560	38.25	1.79	99.96	747.8	44860	64.61
1.30	59.92	448.3	26890	38.73	1.80	100.9	754.5	45270	65.18
1.31	60.66	453.8	27220	39.21	1.81	101.8	761.2	45670	65.77
1.32	61.40	459.4	27560	39.69	1.82	102.7	768.0	46070	66.35
1.33	62.15	464.9	27890	40.17	1.83	103.6	774.7	46480	66.93
1.34	62.90	470.5	28230	40.65	1.84	104.5	781.5	46890	67.52
1.35	63.65	476.2	28570	41.14	1.85	105.4	788.3	47290	68.11
1.36	64.41	481.8	28910	41.63	1.86	106.3	795.2	47700	68.70
1.37	65.17	487.5	29250	42.12	1.87	107.2	802.0	48110	69.29
1.38	65.93	493.2	29590	42.61	1.88	108.1	808.9	48530	69.88
1.39	66.70	499.0	29930	43.11	1.89	109.0	815.8	48940	70.48
1.40	67.47	504.7	30280	43.60	1.90	110.0	822.7	49360	71.07
1.41	68.24	510.5	30630	44.10	1.91	110.9	829.6	49770	71.67
1.42	69.01	516.3	30970	44.60	1.92	111.8	836.6	50190	72.28
1.43	69.79	522.1	31320	45.11	1.93	112.8	843.6	50610	72.88
1.44	70.58	528.0	31670	45.61	1.94	113.7	850.6	51030	73.48
1.45	71.36	533.9	32030	46.12	1.95	114.6	857.6	51450	74.09
1.46	72.15	539.8	32380	46.63	1.96	115.6	864.7	51870	74.70
1.47	72.94	545.7	32740	47.14	1.97	116.5	871.7	52300	75.31
1.48	73.74	551.6	33090	47.66	1.98	117.5	878.8	52720	75.92
1.49	74.54	557.6	33450	48.17	1.99	118.4	885.9	53150	76.54
1.50	75.34	563.6	33810	48.69	2.00	119.4	893.1	53580	77.15

12

12-14: 10 ft. Parshall Flume Discharge Table (Continued)

Formulas: CFS = $39.38H^{1.6}$ GPS = CFS x 7.481

GPM = CFS x 448.8 MGD = CFS x 0.6463

Head Feet	CFS	GPS	GPM	MGD	Head Feet	CFS	GPS	GPM	MGD
2.01	120.3	900.2	54010	77.77	2.51	171.7	1284	77060	111.0
2.02	121.3	907.4	54440	78.39	2.52	172.8	1293	77550	111.7
2.03	122.3	914.6	54870	79.01	2.53	173.9	1301	78040	112.4
2.04	123.2	921.8	55300	79.64	2.54	175.0	1309	78530	113.1
2.05	124.2	929.1	55740	80.26	2.55	176.1	1317	79030	113.8
2.06	125.2	936.3	56170	80.89	2.56	177.2	1326	79530	114.5
2.07	126.1	943.6	56610	81.52	2.57	178.3	1334	80020	115.2
2.08	127.1	950.9	57050	82.15	2.58	179.4	1342	80520	116.0
2.09	128.1	958.2	57490	82.78	2.59	180.5	1351	81020	116.7
2.10	129.1	965.6	57930	83.42	2.60	181.6	1359	81520	117.4
2.11	130.1	972.9	58370	84.05	2.61	182.8	1367	82030	118.1
2.12	131.0	980.3	58810	84.69	2.62	183.9	1376	82530	118.8
2.13	132.0	987.7	59260	85.33	2.63	185.0	1384	83030	119.6
2.14	133.0	995.2	59700	85.97	2.64	186.1	1393	83540	120.3
2.15	134.0	1003	60150	86.62	2.65	187.3	1401	84050	121.0
2.16	135.0	1010	60600	87.26	2.66	188.4	1409	84550	121.8
2.17	136.0	1018	61050	87.91	2.67	189.5	1418	85060	122.5
2.18	137.0	1025	61500	88.56	2.68	190.7	1426	85570	123.2
2.19	138.0	1033	61950	89.21	2.69	191.8	1435	86090	124.0
2.20	139.0	1040	62400	89.86	2.70	193.0	1444	86600	124.7
2.21	140.1	1048	62860	90.52	2.71	194.1	1452	87110	125.4
2.22	141.1	1055	63310	91.17	2.72	195.2	1461	87630	126.2
2.23	142.1	1063	63770	91.83	2.73	196.4	1469	88140	126.9
2.24	143.1	1071	64230	92.49	2.74	197.5	1478	88660	127.7
2.25	144.1	1078	64690	93.15	2.75	198.7	1487	89180	128.4
2.26	145.2	1086	65150	93.82	2.76	199.9	1495	89700	129.2
2.27	146.2	1094	65610	94.48	2.77	201.0	1504	90220	129.9
2.28	147.2	1101	66070	95.15	2.78	202.2	1513	90740	130.7
2.29	148.3	1109	66540	95.82	2.79	203.3	1521	91260	131.4
2.30	149.3	1117	67000	96.49	2.80	204.5	1530	91790	132.2
2.31	150.3	1125	67470	97.16	2.81	205.7	1539	92310	132.9
2.32	151.4	1132	67940	97.83	2.82	206.9	1548	92840	133.7
2.33	152.4	1140	68410	98.51	2.83	208.0	1556	93370	134.5
2.34	153.5	1148	68880	99.19	2.84	209.2	1565	93890	135.2
2.35	154.5	1156	69350	99.87	2.85	210.4	1574	94420	136.0
2.36	155.6	1164	69820	100.5	2.86	211.6	1583	94950	136.7
2.37	156.6	1172	70300	101.2	2.87	212.8	1592	95490	137.5
2.38	157.7	1180	70770	101.9	2.88	213.9	1601	96020	138.3
2.39	158.7	1188	71250	102.6	2.89	215.1	1609	96550	139.0
2.40	159.8	1196	71720	103.3	2.90	216.3	1618	97090	139.8
2.41	160.9	1204	72200	104.0	2.91	217.5	1627	97620	140.6
2.42	161.9	1212	72680	104.7	2.92	218.7	1636	98160	141.4
2.43	163.0	1220	73160	105.4	2.93	219.9	1645	98700	142.1
2.44	164.1	1228	73650	106.1	2.94	221.1	1654	99240	142.9
2.45	165.2	1236	74130	106.8	2.95	222.3	1663	99780	143.7
2.46	166.3	1244	74610	107.4	2.96	223.5	1672	100320	144.5
2.47	167.3	1252	75100	108.1	2.97	224.7	1681	100860	145.3
2.48	168.4	1260	75590	108.9	2.98	226.0	1690	101410	146.0
2.49	169.5	1268	76080	109.6	2.99	227.2	1699	101950	146.8
2.50	170.6	1276	76570	110.3	3.00	228.4	1709	102500	147.6

12

12-15: 12 ft. Parshall Flume Discharge Table

Formulas: CFS $= 46.75H^{1.6}$ GPS = CFS x 7.481
GPM = CFS x 448.8   MGD = CFS x 0.6463

Head Feet	CFS	GPS	GPM	MGD	Head Feet	CFS	GPS	GPM	MGD
0.01	0.0295	0.2207	13.24	0.0191	0.51	15.92	119.1	7144	10.29
0.02	0.0894	0.6689	40.13	0.0578	0.52	16.42	122.8	7370	10.61
0.03	0.1711	1.280	76.78	0.1106	0.53	16.93	126.6	7598	10.94
0.04	0.2711	2.028	121.7	0.1752	0.54	17.44	130.5	7828	11.27
0.05	0.3874	2.898	173.9	0.2504	0.55	17.96	134.4	8061	11.61
0.06	0.5186	3.880	232.7	0.3352	0.56	18.49	138.3	8297	11.95
0.07	0.6636	4.965	297.8	0.4289	0.57	19.02	142.3	8536	12.29
0.08	0.8217	6.147	368.8	0.5311	0.58	19.56	146.3	8776	12.64
0.09	0.9921	7.422	445.3	0.6412	0.59	20.10	150.4	9020	12.99
0.10	1.174	8.785	527.0	0.7590	0.60	20.65	154.4	9266	13.34
0.11	1.368	10.23	613.9	0.8840	0.61	21.20	158.6	9514	13.70
0.12	1.572	11.76	705.5	1.016	0.62	21.76	162.8	9765	14.06
0.13	1.787	13.37	801.9	1.155	0.63	22.32	167.0	10020	14.43
0.14	2.012	15.05	902.9	1.300	0.64	22.89	171.2	10270	14.79
0.15	2.247	16.81	1008	1.452	0.65	23.47	175.6	10530	15.17
0.16	2.491	18.64	1118	1.610	0.66	24.05	179.9	10790	15.54
0.17	2.745	20.53	1232	1.774	0.67	24.63	184.3	11050	15.92
0.18	3.008	22.50	1350	1.944	0.68	25.22	188.7	11320	16.30
0.19	3.279	24.53	1472	2.119	0.69	25.82	193.2	11590	16.69
0.20	3.560	26.63	1598	2.301	0.70	26.42	197.7	11860	17.08
0.21	3.849	28.79	1727	2.488	0.71	27.03	202.2	12130	17.47
0.22	4.146	31.02	1861	2.680	0.72	27.64	206.8	12400	17.86
0.23	4.452	33.30	1998	2.877	0.73	28.26	211.4	12680	18.26
0.24	4.766	35.65	2139	3.080	0.74	28.88	216.0	12960	18.66
0.25	5.087	38.06	2283	3.288	0.75	29.50	220.7	13240	19.07
0.26	5.417	40.52	2431	3.501	0.76	30.14	225.4	13520	19.48
0.27	5.754	43.05	2582	3.719	0.77	30.77	230.2	13810	19.89
0.28	6.099	45.62	2737	3.942	0.78	31.41	235.0	14100	20.30
0.29	6.451	48.26	2895	4.169	0.79	32.06	239.9	14390	20.72
0.30	6.810	50.95	3057	4.402	0.80	32.71	244.7	14680	21.14
0.31	7.177	53.69	3221	4.639	0.81	33.37	249.6	14980	21.57
0.32	7.551	56.49	3389	4.880	0.82	34.03	254.6	15270	21.99
0.33	7.932	59.34	3560	5.127	0.83	34.70	259.6	15570	22.43
0.34	8.320	62.25	3734	5.378	0.84	35.37	264.6	15870	22.86
0.35	8.715	65.20	3911	5.633	0.85	36.05	269.7	16180	23.30
0.36	9.117	68.21	4092	5.893	0.86	36.73	274.8	16480	23.74
0.37	9.526	71.26	4275	6.157	0.87	37.41	279.9	16790	24.18
0.38	9.941	74.37	4462	6.425	0.88	38.10	285.0	17100	24.63
0.39	10.36	77.53	4651	6.698	0.89	38.80	290.2	17410	25.07
0.40	10.79	80.73	4843	6.974	0.90	39.50	295.5	17730	25.53
0.41	11.23	83.98	5038	7.256	0.91	40.20	300.8	18040	25.98
0.42	11.67	87.29	5236	7.541	0.92	40.91	306.1	18360	26.44
0.43	12.12	90.63	5437	7.830	0.93	41.63	311.4	18680	26.90
0.44	12.57	94.03	5641	8.123	0.94	42.34	316.8	19000	27.37
0.45	13.03	97.47	5848	8.421	0.95	43.07	322.2	19330	27.83
0.46	13.50	101.0	6057	8.722	0.96	43.79	327.6	19650	28.30
0.47	13.97	104.5	6269	9.028	0.97	44.53	333.1	19980	28.78
0.48	14.45	108.1	6484	9.337	0.98	45.26	338.6	20310	29.25
0.49	14.93	111.7	6701	9.650	0.99	46.00	344.2	20650	29.73
0.50	15.42	115.4	6921	9.967	1.00	46.75	349.7	20980	30.21

12

12-15: 12 ft. Parshall Flume Discharge Table
(Continued)

Formulas: $CFS = 46.75H^{1.6}$ $GPS = CFS \times 7.481$
$GPM = CFS \times 448.8$ $MGD = CFS \times 0.6463$

Head Feet	CFS	GPS	GPM	MGD	Head Feet	CFS	GPS	GPM	MGD
1.01	47.50	355.3	21320	30.70	1.51	90.40	676.2	40570	58.42
1.02	48.25	361.0	21660	31.19	1.52	91.35	683.4	41000	59.04
1.03	49.01	366.7	22000	31.68	1.53	92.32	690.6	41430	59.67
1.04	49.78	372.4	22340	32.17	1.54	93.29	697.9	41870	60.29
1.05	50.55	378.1	22680	32.67	1.55	94.26	705.1	42300	60.92
1.06	51.32	383.9	23030	33.17	1.56	95.23	712.4	42740	61.55
1.07	52.09	389.7	23380	33.67	1.57	96.21	719.7	43180	62.18
1.08	52.88	395.6	23730	34.17	1.58	97.19	727.1	43620	62.82
1.09	53.66	401.4	24080	34.68	1.59	98.18	734.5	44060	63.45
1.10	54.45	407.4	24440	35.19	1.60	99.17	741.9	44510	64.09
1.11	55.25	413.3	24790	35.71	1.61	100.2	749.3	44950	64.73
1.12	56.04	419.3	25150	36.22	1.62	101.2	756.8	45400	65.38
1.13	56.85	425.3	25510	36.74	1.63	102.2	764.3	45850	66.03
1.14	57.65	431.3	25880	37.26	1.64	103.2	771.8	46300	66.68
1.15	58.47	437.4	26240	37.79	1.65	104.2	779.3	46750	67.33
1.16	59.28	443.5	26610	38.31	1.66	105.2	786.9	47210	67.98
1.17	60.10	449.6	26970	38.84	1.67	106.2	794.5	47660	68.64
1.18	60.92	455.8	27340	39.38	1.68	107.2	802.1	48120	69.30
1.19	61.75	462.0	27710	39.91	1.69	108.2	809.8	48580	69.96
1.20	62.59	468.2	28090	40.45	1.70	109.3	817.4	49040	70.62
1.21	63.42	474.5	28460	40.99	1.71	110.3	825.2	49500	71.29
1.22	64.26	480.7	28840	41.53	1.72	111.3	832.9	49970	71.96
1.23	65.11	487.1	29220	42.08	1.73	112.4	840.6	50430	72.63
1.24	65.96	493.4	29600	42.63	1.74	113.4	848.4	50900	73.30
1.25	66.81	499.8	29980	43.18	1.75	114.5	856.3	51370	73.97
1.26	67.67	506.2	30370	43.73	1.76	115.5	864.1	51840	74.65
1.27	68.53	512.7	30760	44.29	1.77	116.6	872.0	52310	75.33
1.28	69.39	519.1	31140	44.85	1.78	117.6	879.9	52780	76.01
1.29	70.26	525.6	31530	45.41	1.79	118.7	887.8	53260	76.70
1.30	71.14	532.2	31930	45.98	1.80	119.7	895.7	53740	77.38
1.31	72.01	538.7	32320	46.54	1.81	120.8	903.7	54220	78.07
1.32	72.90	545.3	32720	47.11	1.82	121.9	911.7	54700	78.76
1.33	73.78	552.0	33110	47.68	1.83	122.9	919.7	55180	79.46
1.34	74.67	558.6	33510	48.26	1.84	124.0	927.8	55660	80.15
1.35	75.56	565.3	33910	48.84	1.85	125.1	935.9	56140	80.85
1.36	76.46	572.0	34320	49.42	1.86	126.2	944.0	56630	81.55
1.37	77.36	578.8	34720	50.00	1.87	127.3	952.1	57120	82.26
1.38	78.27	585.5	35130	50.59	1.88	128.4	960.3	57610	82.96
1.39	79.18	592.3	35540	51.17	1.89	129.5	968.5	58100	83.67
1.40	80.09	599.2	35950	51.76	1.90	130.6	976.7	58590	84.38
1.41	81.01	606.0	36360	52.36	1.91	131.7	984.9	59090	85.09
1.42	81.93	612.9	36770	52.95	1.92	132.8	993.2	59580	85.80
1.43	82.86	619.8	37190	53.55	1.93	133.9	1001	60080	86.52
1.44	83.78	626.8	37600	54.15	1.94	135.0	1010	60580	87.24
1.45	84.72	633.8	38020	54.75	1.95	136.1	1018	61080	87.96
1.46	85.65	640.8	38440	55.36	1.96	137.2	1026	61580	88.68
1.47	86.59	647.8	38860	55.97	1.97	138.3	1035	62080	89.40
1.48	87.54	654.9	39290	56.58	1.98	139.5	1043	62590	90.13
1.49	88.49	662.0	39710	57.19	1.99	140.6	1052	63100	90.86
1.50	89.44	669.1	40140	57.80	2.00	141.7	1060	63600	91.59

12

12-15: 12 ft. Parshall Flume Discharge Table (Continued)

Formulas: $CFS = 46.75H^{1.6}$ $GPS = CFS \times 7.481$
$GPM = CFS \times 448.8$ $MGD = CFS \times 0.6463$

Head Feet	CFS	GPS	GPM	MGD	Head Feet	CFS	GPS	GPM	MGD
2.01	142.9	1069	64110	92.33	2.51	203.8	1525	91480	131.7
2.02	144.0	1077	64620	93.06	2.52	205.1	1535	92060	132.6
2.03	145.1	1086	65140	93.80	2.53	206.4	1544	92650	133.4
2.04	146.3	1094	65650	94.54	2.54	207.7	1554	93230	134.3
2.05	147.4	1103	66170	95.28	2.55	209.0	1564	93820	135.1
2.06	148.6	1112	66680	96.03	2.56	210.4	1574	94410	136.0
2.07	149.7	1120	67200	96.78	2.57	211.7	1584	95000	136.8
2.08	150.9	1129	67720	97.53	2.58	213.0	1593	95590	137.7
2.09	152.1	1138	68240	98.28	2.59	214.3	1603	96190	138.5
2.10	153.2	1146	68770	99.03	2.60	215.6	1613	96780	139.4
2.11	154.4	1155	69290	99.79	2.61	217.0	1623	97380	140.2
2.12	155.6	1164	69820	100.5	2.62	218.3	1633	97980	141.1
2.13	156.7	1173	70350	101.3	2.63	219.6	1643	98570	142.0
2.14	157.9	1181	70880	102.1	2.64	221.0	1653	99170	142.8
2.15	159.1	1190	71410	102.8	2.65	222.3	1663	99780	143.7
2.16	160.3	1199	71940	103.6	2.66	223.7	1673	100380	144.6
2.17	161.5	1208	72470	104.4	2.67	225.0	1683	100980	145.4
2.18	162.7	1217	73010	105.1	2.68	226.4	1693	101590	146.3
2.19	163.9	1226	73540	105.9	2.69	227.7	1704	102200	147.2
2.20	165.1	1235	74080	106.7	2.70	229.1	1714	102810	148.0
2.21	166.3	1244	74620	107.5	2.71	230.4	1724	103420	148.9
2.22	167.5	1253	75160	108.2	2.72	231.8	1734	104030	149.8
2.23	168.7	1262	75700	109.0	2.73	233.2	1744	104640	150.7
2.24	169.9	1271	76250	109.8	2.74	234.5	1754	105250	151.6
2.25	171.1	1280	76790	110.6	2.75	235.9	1765	105870	152.5
2.26	172.3	1289	77340	111.4	2.76	237.3	1775	106490	153.3
2.27	173.5	1298	77890	112.2	2.77	238.6	1785	107100	154.2
2.28	174.8	1307	78440	113.0	2.78	240.0	1796	107720	155.1
2.29	176.0	1317	78990	113.8	2.79	241.4	1806	108340	156.0
2.30	177.2	1326	79540	114.5	2.80	242.8	1816	108970	156.9
2.31	178.5	1335	80100	115.3	2.81	244.2	1827	109590	157.8
2.32	179.7	1344	80650	116.1	2.82	245.6	1837	110210	158.7
2.33	180.9	1354	81210	116.9	2.83	247.0	1848	110840	159.6
2.34	182.2	1363	81770	117.8	2.84	248.4	1858	111470	160.5
2.35	183.4	1372	82330	118.6	2.85	249.8	1868	112090	161.4
2.36	184.7	1382	82890	119.4	2.86	251.2	1879	112720	162.3
2.37	185.9	1391	83450	120.2	2.87	252.6	1890	113360	163.2
2.38	187.2	1400	84020	121.0	2.88	254.0	1900	113990	164.2
2.39	188.5	1410	84580	121.8	2.89	255.4	1911	114620	165.1
2.40	189.7	1419	85150	122.6	2.90	256.8	1921	115260	166.0
2.41	191.0	1429	85720	123.4	2.91	258.2	1932	115890	166.9
2.42	192.3	1438	86290	124.3	2.92	259.7	1942	116530	167.8
2.43	193.5	1448	86860	125.1	2.93	261.1	1953	117170	168.7
2.44	194.8	1457	87430	125.9	2.94	262.5	1964	117810	169.7
2.45	196.1	1467	88000	126.7	2.95	263.9	1974	118450	170.6
2.46	197.4	1477	88580	127.6	2.96	265.4	1985	119100	171.5
2.47	198.7	1486	89160	128.4	2.97	266.8	1996	119740	172.4
2.48	199.9	1496	89730	129.2	2.98	268.2	2007	120390	173.4
2.49	201.2	1505	90310	130.1	2.99	269.7	2018	121030	174.3
2.50	202.5	1515	90890	130.9	3.00	271.1	2028	121680	175.2

12

Chapter
13

Palmer-Bowlus
flume
(manufactured by
Plasti-Fab, Inc.)
discharge tables

This chapter contains discharge (flow rate vs head) tables for Palmer-Bowlus flumes (manufactured by Plasti-Fab, Inc.) Note that all of the tabular data is for free flow.

Palmer-Bowlus flumes (manufactured by Plasti-Fab)

13-1: 4 in. Palmer-Bowlus Flume

13-2: 6 in. Palmer-Bowlus Flume

13-3: 8 in. Palmer-Bowlus Flume

13-4: 10 in. Palmer-Bowlus Flume

13-5: 12 in. Palmer-Bowlus Flume

13-6: 15 in. Palmer-Bowlus Flume

13-7: 18 in. Palmer-Bowlus Flume

13-8: 21 in. Palmer-Bowlus Flume

13-9: 24 in. Palmer-Bowlus Flume

13-10: 27 in. Palmer-Bowlus Flume

13-11: 30 in. Palmer-Bowlus Flume

13

Note: The discharges of the flumes are listed in four different units:

CFS—cubic feet per second,　　　GPS—gallons per second,

GPM—gallons per minute,　　　MGD—million gallons per day.

The source of data used to develop each table is listed on the table.

* All Palmer-Bowlus flume data, © Copyright Plasti-Fab, Inc., Tualatin, Oregon

13-1: 4 in. Palmer-Bowlus Flume Discharge Table

Manufactured by Plasti-Fab, Inc. (Data from Plasti-Fab, Inc.)
Formulas: GPS = CFS x 7.481

Head Feet	CFS	GPS	GPM	MGD	Head Feet	CFS	GPS	GPM	MGD
0.01					0.14	0.0392	0.2933	17.57	0.0253
0.02	0.0013	0.0097	0.5627	0.0008	0.15	0.0447	0.3344	20.08	0.0289
0.03	0.0026	0.0195	1.179	0.0017	0.16	0.0508	0.3800	22.78	0.0327
0.04	0.0043	0.0322	1.937	0.0028	0.17	0.0572	0.4279	25.67	0.0369
0.05	0.0063	0.0471	2.833	0.0041	0.18	0.0641	0.4795	28.76	0.0413
0.06	0.0086	0.0643	3.865	0.0056	0.19	0.0714	0.5341	32.03	0.0460
0.07	0.0112	0.0838	5.036	0.0072	0.20	0.0790	0.5910	35.46	0.0510
0.08	0.0141	0.1055	6.347	0.0091	0.21	0.0870	0.6508	39.05	0.0561
0.09	0.0174	0.1302	7.805	0.0112	0.22	0.0953	0.7129	42.76	0.0615
0.10	0.0210	0.1571	9.417	0.0135	0.23	0.1038	0.7765	46.58	0.0670
0.11	0.0249	0.1863	11.19	0.0161	0.24	0.1125	0.8416	50.48	0.0726
0.12	0.0293	0.2192	13.14	0.0189	0.25	0.1213	0.9074	54.45	0.0783
0.13	0.0340	0.2544	15.26	0.0219					

13-2: 6 in. Palmer-Bowlus Flume Discharge Table

Manufactured by Plasti-Fab, Inc. (Data from Plasti-Fab, Inc.)
Formulas: GPS = CFS x 7.481

Head Feet	CFS	GPS	GPM	MGD	Head Feet	CFS	GPS	GPM	MGD
0.01					0.19	0.0898	0.6718	40.31	0.0580
0.02					0.20	0.0989	0.7399	44.39	0.0638
0.03	0.0037	0.0277	1.677	0.0024	0.21	0.1085	0.8117	48.70	0.0700
0.04	0.0061	0.0456	2.719	0.0039	0.22	0.1186	0.8872	53.24	0.0765
0.05	0.0088	0.0658	3.963	0.0057	0.23	0.1293	0.9673	58.03	0.0834
0.06	0.0120	0.0898	5.398	0.0078	0.24	0.1405	1.051	63.07	0.0907
0.07	0.0156	0.1167	7.016	0.0101	0.25	0.1523	1.139	68.35	0.0982
0.08	0.0196	0.1466	8.811	0.0127	0.26	0.1646	1.231	73.86	0.1062
0.09	0.0240	0.1795	10.78	0.0155	0.27	0.1774	1.327	79.61	0.1144
0.10	0.0288	0.2155	12.91	0.0186	0.28	0.1907	1.427	85.59	0.1230
0.11	0.0339	0.2536	15.22	0.0219	0.29	0.2045	1.530	91.78	0.1319
0.12	0.0394	0.2948	17.70	0.0254	0.30	0.2187	1.636	98.17	0.1411
0.13	0.0453	0.3389	20.35	0.0293	0.31	0.2334	1.746	104.7	0.1506
0.14	0.0517	0.3868	23.18	0.0333	0.32	0.2484	1.858	111.5	0.1602
0.15	0.0584	0.4369	26.20	0.0377	0.33	0.2637	1.973	118.3	0.1701
0.16	0.0656	0.4908	29.42	0.0423	0.34	0.2793	2.089	125.3	0.1802
0.17	0.0732	0.5476	32.84	0.0472	0.35	0.2951	2.208	132.4	0.1904
0.18	0.0813	0.6082	36.47	0.0524					

13

Manufactured by Plasti-Fab, Inc. (Data from Plasti-Fab, Inc.)
Formulas: GPS = CFS x 7.481

Head Feet	CFS	GPS	GPM	MGD	Head Feet	CFS	GPS	GPM	MGD
0.01					0.26	0.1942	1.453	87.18	0.1253
0.02					0.27	0.2086	1.561	93.61	0.1346
0.03	0.0044	0.0329	1.986	0.0029	0.28	0.2235	1.672	100.3	0.1442
0.04	0.0076	0.0569	3.425	0.0049	0.29	0.2391	1.789	107.3	0.1542
0.05	0.0113	0.0845	5.076	0.0073	0.30	0.2553	1.910	114.6	0.1647
0.06	0.0155	0.1160	6.936	0.0100	0.31	0.2720	2.035	122.1	0.1755
0.07	0.0201	0.1504	9.000	0.0129	0.32	0.2895	2.166	129.9	0.1867
0.08	0.0251	0.1878	11.26	0.0162	0.33	0.3075	2.300	138.0	0.1984
0.09	0.0306	0.2289	13.73	0.0197	0.34	0.3261	2.440	146.4	0.2104
0.10	0.0365	0.2731	16.39	0.0236	0.35	0.3454	2.584	155.0	0.2228
0.11	0.0429	0.3209	19.24	0.0277	0.36	0.3652	2.732	163.9	0.2356
0.12	0.0497	0.3718	22.29	0.0320	0.37	0.3856	2.885	173.1	0.2488
0.13	0.0569	0.4257	25.53	0.0367	0.38	0.4066	3.042	182.5	0.2623
0.14	0.0646	0.4833	28.97	0.0416	0.39	0.4281	3.203	192.1	0.2762
0.15	0.0727	0.5439	32.61	0.0469	0.40	0.4500	3.366	202.0	0.2903
0.16	0.0812	0.6075	36.45	0.0524	0.41	0.4725	3.535	212.1	0.3048
0.17	0.0902	0.6748	40.50	0.0582	0.42	0.4954	3.706	222.3	0.3196
0.18	0.0997	0.7459	44.76	0.0643	0.43	0.5187	3.880	232.8	0.3346
0.19	0.1097	0.8207	49.24	0.0708	0.44	0.5423	4.057	243.4	0.3499
0.20	0.1202	0.8992	53.94	0.0775	0.45	0.5663	4.236	254.2	0.3654
0.21	0.1312	0.9815	58.87	0.0846	0.46	0.5906	4.418	265.1	0.3810
0.22	0.1427	1.068	64.04	0.0921	0.47	0.6151	4.602	276.1	0.3968
0.23	0.1547	1.157	69.44	0.0998	0.48	0.6399	4.787	287.2	0.4128
0.24	0.1673	1.252	75.10	0.1080	0.49	0.6648	4.973	298.4	0.4289
0.25	0.1805	1.350	81.01	0.1165	0.50	0.6900	5.162	309.6	0.4451

13

13-4: 10 in. Palmer-Bowlus Flume Discharge Table

Manufactured by Plasti-Fab, Inc. (Data from Plasti-Fab, Inc.)
Formulas: GPS = CFS x 7.481

Head Feet	CFS	GPS	GPM	MGD	Head Feet	CFS	GPS	GPM	MGD
0.01					0.31	0.3083	2.306	138.3	0.1989
0.02					0.32	0.3272	2.448	146.9	0.2111
0.03					0.33	0.3469	2.595	155.7	0.2238
0.04	0.0092	0.0688	4.141	0.0060	0.34	0.3673	2.748	164.8	0.2370
0.05	0.0137	0.1025	6.170	0.0089	0.35	0.3884	2.906	174.3	0.2506
0.06	0.0188	0.1406	8.454	0.0122	0.36	0.4102	3.069	184.1	0.2647
0.07	0.0245	0.1833	10.98	0.0158	0.37	0.4328	3.238	194.2	0.2792
0.08	0.0306	0.2289	13.74	0.0197	0.38	0.4560	3.411	204.7	0.2942
0.09	0.0373	0.2790	16.72	0.0240	0.39	0.4800	3.591	215.4	0.3097
0.10	0.0444	0.3322	19.92	0.0286	0.40	0.5047	3.776	226.5	0.3256
0.11	0.0520	0.3890	23.34	0.0335	0.41	0.5302	3.966	237.9	0.3420
0.12	0.0601	0.4496	26.96	0.0388	0.42	0.5563	4.162	249.7	0.3589
0.13	0.0686	0.5132	30.79	0.0443	0.43	0.5831	4.362	261.7	0.3762
0.14	0.0776	0.5805	34.82	0.0501	0.44	0.6106	4.568	274.0	0.3939
0.15	0.0870	0.6508	39.05	0.0561	0.45	0.6387	4.778	286.7	0.4121
0.16	0.0969	0.7249	43.50	0.0625	0.46	0.6675	4.994	299.6	0.4306
0.17	0.1073	0.8027	48.15	0.0692	0.47	0.6968	5.213	312.7	0.4496
0.18	0.1181	0.8835	53.02	0.0762	0.48	0.7268	5.437	326.2	0.4689
0.19	0.1294	0.9680	58.10	0.0835	0.49	0.7573	5.665	339.9	0.4886
0.20	0.1413	1.057	63.40	0.0911	0.50	0.7883	5.897	353.8	0.5086
0.21	0.1536	1.149	68.93	0.0991	0.51	0.8197	6.132	367.9	0.5289
0.22	0.1664	1.245	74.69	0.1074	0.52	0.8517	6.372	382.2	0.5495
0.23	0.1798	1.345	80.70	0.1160	0.53	0.8840	6.613	396.7	0.5703
0.24	0.1937	1.449	86.95	0.1250	0.54	0.9167	6.858	411.4	0.5914
0.25	0.2083	1.558	93.46	0.1344	0.55	0.9498	7.105	426.3	0.6128
0.26	0.2233	1.671	100.2	0.1441	0.56	0.9832	7.355	441.2	0.6343
0.27	0.2390	1.788	107.3	0.1542	0.57	1.017	7.607	456.4	0.6560
0.28	0.2554	1.911	114.6	0.1648	0.58	1.051	7.860	471.6	0.6779
0.29	0.2723	2.037	122.2	0.1757	0.59	1.085	8.116	486.9	0.6999
0.30	0.2900	2.169	130.1	0.1871	0.60	1.119	8.373	502.3	0.7221

13

13-5: 12 in. Palmer-Bowlus Flume Discharge Table

Manufactured by Plasti-Fab, Inc. (Data from Plasti-Fab, Inc.)
Formulas: GPS = CFS x 7.481

Head Feet	CFS	GPS	GPM	MGD	Head Feet	CFS	GPS	GPM	MGD
0.01					0.36	0.4631	3.464	207.8	0.2988
0.02					0.37	0.4871	3.644	218.6	0.3143
0.03					0.38	0.5119	3.830	229.7	0.3302
0.04					0.39	0.5373	4.020	241.2	0.3467
0.05	0.0164	0.1227	7.346	0.0106	0.40	0.5635	4.216	252.9	0.3636
0.06	0.0221	0.1653	9.897	0.0142	0.41	0.5905	4.418	265.0	0.3809
0.07	0.0284	0.2125	12.75	0.0183	0.42	0.6181	4.624	277.4	0.3988
0.08	0.0354	0.2648	15.89	0.0228	0.43	0.6466	4.837	290.2	0.4171
0.09	0.0430	0.3217	19.30	0.0278	0.44	0.6757	5.055	303.3	0.4360
0.10	0.0512	0.3830	23.00	0.0331	0.45	0.7057	5.279	316.7	0.4553
0.11	0.0601	0.4496	26.96	0.0388	0.46	0.7364	5.509	330.5	0.4751
0.12	0.0695	0.5199	31.18	0.0448	0.47	0.7679	5.745	344.6	0.4954
0.13	0.0795	0.5947	35.66	0.0513	0.48	0.8001	5.986	359.1	0.5162
0.14	0.0900	0.6733	40.39	0.0581	0.49	0.8331	6.232	373.9	0.5375
0.15	0.1011	0.7563	45.36	0.0652	0.50	0.8668	6.485	389.0	0.5593
0.16	0.1127	0.8431	50.59	0.0727	0.51	0.9014	6.743	404.5	0.5815
0.17	0.1249	0.9344	56.05	0.0806	0.52	0.9366	7.007	420.4	0.6043
0.18	0.1376	1.029	61.76	0.0888	0.53	0.9726	7.276	436.5	0.6275
0.19	0.1508	1.128	67.70	0.0973	0.54	1.009	7.551	453.0	0.6512
0.20	0.1646	1.231	73.89	0.1062	0.55	1.047	7.830	469.8	0.6753
0.21	0.1790	1.339	80.32	0.1155	0.56	1.085	8.115	486.9	0.6999
0.22	0.1938	1.450	86.99	0.1250	0.57	1.123	8.405	504.2	0.7249
0.23	0.2092	1.565	93.90	0.1350	0.58	1.163	8.700	521.9	0.7503
0.24	0.2252	1.685	101.1	0.1453	0.59	1.203	9.000	539.9	0.7761
0.25	0.2417	1.808	108.5	0.1559	0.60	1.244	9.303	558.1	0.8023
0.26	0.2588	1.936	116.2	0.1670	0.61	1.285	9.612	576.6	0.8289
0.27	0.2765	2.068	124.1	0.1784	0.62	1.327	9.924	595.3	0.8558
0.28	0.2947	2.205	132.3	0.1901	0.63	1.369	10.24	614.3	0.8831
0.29	0.3135	2.345	140.7	0.2023	0.64	1.411	10.56	633.5	0.9106
0.30	0.3330	2.491	149.4	0.2148	0.65	1.455	10.88	652.9	0.9385
0.31	0.3531	2.642	158.4	0.2278	0.66	1.498	11.21	672.4	0.9666
0.32	0.3737	2.796	167.7	0.2411	0.67	1.542	11.54	692.2	0.9950
0.33	0.3951	2.956	177.3	0.2549	0.68	1.587	11.87	712.1	1.024
0.34	0.4171	3.120	187.2	0.2691	0.69	1.631	12.20	732.1	1.052
0.35	0.4398	3.290	197.4	0.2837	0.70	1.676	12.54	752.4	1.081

13

Manufactured by Plasti-Fab, Inc. (Data from Plasti-Fab, Inc.)
Formulas: GPS = CFS x 7.481

Head Feet	CFS	GPS	GPM	MGD	Head Feet	CFS	GPS	GPM	MGD
0.01					0.46	0.8441	0.8441	378.8	0.5446
0.02					0.47	0.8783	0.8783	394.2	0.5667
0.03					0.48	0.9133	0.9133	409.9	0.5892
0.04					0.49	0.9492	0.9492	426.0	0.6124
0.04					0.50	0.9858	0.9858	442.4	0.6360
0.06	0.0269	0.0269	12.08	0.0174	0.51	1.023	1.023	459.2	0.6602
0.07	0.0348	0.0348	15.61	0.0224	0.52	1.062	1.062	476.4	0.6849
0.08	0.0433	0.0433	19.45	0.0280	0.53	1.101	1.101	494.0	0.7101
0.09	0.0526	0.0526	23.60	0.0339	0.54	1.141	1.141	511.9	0.7359
0.10	0.0625	0.0625	28.05	0.0403	0.55	1.181	1.181	530.2	0.7622
0.11	0.0731	0.0731	32.79	0.0471	0.56	1.223	1.223	549.0	0.7891
0.12	0.0843	0.0843	37.84	0.0544	0.57	1.266	1.266	568.1	0.8166
0.13	0.0962	0.0962	43.18	0.0621	0.58	1.309	1.309	587.5	0.8446
0.14	0.1088	0.1088	48.81	0.0702	0.59	1.353	1.353	607.4	0.8732
0.15	0.1220	0.1220	54.73	0.0787	0.60	1.399	1.399	627.7	0.9023
0.16	0.1358	0.1358	60.94	0.0876	0.61	1.445	1.445	648.4	0.9321
0.17	0.1502	0.1502	67.43	0.0969	0.62	1.492	1.492	669.4	0.9623
0.18	0.1653	0.1653	74.20	0.1067	0.63	1.539	1.539	690.9	0.9931
0.19	0.1811	0.1811	81.26	0.1168	0.64	1.588	1.588	712.7	1.024
0.20	0.1974	0.1974	88.59	0.1274	0.65	1.637	1.637	734.9	1.056
0.21	0.2144	0.2144	96.20	0.1383	0.66	1.688	1.688	757.5	1.089
0.22	0.2319	0.2319	104.1	0.1496	0.67	1.739	1.739	780.4	1.122
0.23	0.2501	0.2501	112.3	0.1614	0.68	1.791	1.791	803.7	1.155
0.24	0.2689	0.2689	120.7	0.1735	0.69	1.843	1.843	827.4	1.189
0.25	0.2883	0.2883	129.4	0.1860	0.70	1.897	1.897	851.4	1.224
0.26	0.3083	0.3083	138.4	0.1989	0.71	1.951	1.951	875.7	1.259
0.27	0.3289	0.3289	147.6	0.2122	0.72	2.006	2.006	900.4	1.294
0.28	0.3502	0.3502	157.2	0.2259	0.73	2.062	2.062	925.3	1.330
0.29	0.3720	0.3720	167.0	0.2400	0.74	2.118	2.118	950.6	1.367
0.30	0.3945	0.3945	177.1	0.2545	0.75	2.175	2.175	976.2	1.403
0.31	0.4176	0.4176	187.4	0.2694	0.76	2.233	2.233	1002	1.440
0.32	0.4413	0.4413	198.1	0.2847	0.77	2.291	2.291	1028	1.478
0.33	0.4657	0.4657	209.0	0.3005	0.78	2.349	2.349	1054	1.516
0.34	0.4907	0.4907	220.2	0.3166	0.79	2.409	2.409	1081	1.554
0.35	0.5164	0.5164	231.7	0.3331	0.80	2.468	2.468	1108	1.592
0.36	0.5427	0.5427	243.6	0.3501	0.81	2.528	2.528	1135	1.631
0.37	0.5696	0.5696	255.7	0.3675	0.82	2.589	2.589	1162	1.670
0.38	0.5973	0.5973	268.1	0.3854	0.83	2.650	2.650	1189	1.710
0.39	0.6256	0.6256	280.8	0.4036	0.84	2.711	2.711	1217	1.749
0.40	0.6547	0.6547	293.8	0.4224	0.85	2.773	2.773	1245	1.789
0.41	0.6844	0.6844	307.2	0.4415	0.86	2.835	2.835	1272	1.829
0.42	0.7149	0.7149	320.8	0.4612	0.87	2.897	2.897	1300	1.869
0.43	0.7460	0.7460	334.8	0.4813	0.88	2.960	2.960	1328	1.909
0.44	0.7780	0.7780	349.1	0.5019	0.89	3.023	3.023	1357	1.950
0.45	0.8106	0.8106	363.8	0.5230	0.90	3.086	3.086	1385	1.991

13

13-7: 18 in. Palmer-Bowlus Flume Discharge Table
Manufactured by Plasti-Fab, Inc. (Data from Plasti-Fab, Inc.)
Formulas: GPS = CFS x 7.481

Head Feet	CFS	GPS	GPM	MGD	Head Feet	CFS	GPS	GPM	MGD
0.01					0.54	1.278	9.561	573.6	0.8246
0.02					0.55	1.322	9.888	593.2	0.8527
0.03					0.56	1.366	10.22	613.1	0.8814
0.04					0.57	1.411	10.56	633.5	0.9106
0.05					0.58	1.458	10.91	654.2	0.9405
0.06					0.59	1.505	11.26	675.4	0.9709
0.07					0.60	1.553	11.62	697.0	1.002
0.08	0.0505	0.3778	22.66	0.0326	0.61	1.602	11.98	718.9	1.034
0.09	0.0604	0.4519	27.11	0.0390	0.62	1.652	12.36	741.3	1.066
0.10	0.0713	0.5334	32.01	0.0460	0.63	1.703	12.74	764.1	1.099
0.11	0.0832	0.6224	37.33	0.0537	0.64	1.754	13.12	787.4	1.132
0.12	0.0960	0.7182	43.07	0.0619	0.65	1.807	13.52	811.0	1.166
0.13	0.1096	0.8199	49.20	0.0707	0.66	1.861	13.92	835.1	1.200
0.14	0.1242	0.9291	55.73	0.0801	0.67	1.915	14.33	859.7	1.236
0.15	0.1395	1.044	62.63	0.0900	0.68	1.971	14.75	884.6	1.272
0.16	0.1557	1.165	69.89	0.1005	0.69	2.028	15.17	910.0	1.308
0.17	0.1727	1.292	77.50	0.1114	0.70	2.085	15.60	935.8	1.345
0.18	0.1904	1.424	85.46	0.1229	0.71	2.144	16.04	962.1	1.383
0.19	0.2089	1.563	93.76	0.1348	0.72	2.203	16.48	988.8	1.421
0.20	0.2281	1.706	102.4	0.1472	0.73	2.264	16.93	1016	1.460
0.21	0.2480	1.855	111.3	0.1600	0.74	2.325	17.39	1043	1.500
0.22	0.2687	2.010	120.6	0.1733	0.75	2.387	17.86	1071	1.540
0.23	0.2900	2.169	130.1	0.1871	0.76	2.450	18.33	1100	1.581
0.24	0.3119	2.333	140.0	0.2013	0.77	2.515	18.81	1129	1.622
0.25	0.3346	2.503	150.2	0.2159	0.78	2.580	19.30	1158	1.664
0.26	0.3579	2.677	160.6	0.2309	0.79	2.646	19.79	1188	1.707
0.27	0.3818	2.856	171.3	0.2463	0.80	2.713	20.29	1218	1.750
0.28	0.4064	3.040	182.4	0.2622	0.81	2.781	20.80	1248	1.794
0.29	0.4316	3.229	193.7	0.2784	0.82	2.849	21.31	1279	1.838
0.30	0.4574	3.422	205.3	0.2951	0.83	2.919	21.83	1310	1.883
0.31	0.4839	3.620	217.2	0.3122	0.84	2.989	22.36	1342	1.928
0.32	0.5110	3.823	229.3	0.3297	0.85	3.060	22.89	1373	1.974
0.33	0.5387	4.030	241.8	0.3475	0.86	3.132	23.43	1406	2.021
0.34	0.5670	4.242	254.5	0.3658	0.87	3.205	23.98	1438	2.068
0.35	0.5960	4.459	267.5	0.3845	0.88	3.278	24.52	1471	2.115
0.36	0.6256	4.680	280.8	0.4036	0.89	3.352	25.08	1505	2.163
0.37	0.6559	4.907	294.4	0.4232	0.90	3.427	25.64	1538	2.211
0.38	0.6868	5.138	308.2	0.4431	0.91	3.503	26.20	1572	2.260
0.39	0.7184	5.374	322.4	0.4635	0.92	3.579	26.77	1606	2.309
0.40	0.7506	5.615	336.9	0.4843	0.93	3.655	27.35	1641	2.358
0.41	0.7835	5.861	351.6	0.5055	0.94	3.733	27.93	1675	2.408
0.42	0.8171	6.113	366.7	0.5272	0.95	3.811	28.51	1710	2.458
0.43	0.8514	6.369	382.1	0.5493	0.96	3.889	29.09	1745	2.509
0.44	0.8864	6.631	397.8	0.5719	0.97	3.968	29.68	1781	2.560
0.45	0.9221	6.898	413.9	0.5949	0.98	4.047	30.28	1816	2.611
0.46	0.9586	7.171	430.2	0.6184	0.99	4.127	30.87	1852	2.663
0.47	0.9958	7.450	446.9	0.6424	1.00	4.207	31.47	1888	2.714
0.48	1.034	7.733	463.9	0.6669	1.01	4.288	32.08	1924	2.766
0.49	1.073	8.023	481.3	0.6919	1.02	4.369	32.68	1961	2.819
0.50	1.112	8.319	499.0	0.7174	1.03	4.450	33.29	1997	2.871
0.51	1.152	8.620	517.1	0.7434	1.04	4.532	33.91	2034	2.924
0.52	1.193	8.928	535.6	0.7699	1.05	4.614	34.52	2071	2.977
0.53	1.235	9.241	554.4	0.7970					

13

Manufactured by Plasti-Fab, Inc. (Data from Plasti-Fab, Inc.)
Formulas: GPS = CFS x 7.481

Head Feet	CFS	GPS	GPM	MGD	Head Feet	CFS	GPS	GPM	MGD
0.01					0.51	1.283	9.595	575.6	0.8275
0.02					0.52	1.327	9.930	595.7	0.8564
0.03					0.53	1.373	10.27	616.2	0.8858
0.04					0.54	1.419	10.62	637.1	0.9158
0.05					0.55	1.467	10.97	658.3	0.9464
0.06					0.56	1.515	11.33	679.9	0.9774
0.07					0.57	1.564	11.70	701.9	1.009
0.08					0.58	1.614	12.07	724.3	1.041
0.09	0.0669	0.5005	30.03	0.0432	0.59	1.665	12.45	747.1	1.074
0.10	0.0812	0.6075	36.46	0.0524	0.60	1.716	12.84	770.3	1.107
0.11	0.0963	0.7204	43.23	0.0622	0.61	1.769	13.23	793.9	1.141
0.12	0.1122	0.8394	50.34	0.0724	0.62	1.822	13.63	817.9	1.176
0.13	0.1287	0.9628	57.77	0.0830	0.63	1.877	14.04	842.3	1.211
0.14	0.1460	1.092	65.52	0.0942	0.64	1.932	14.45	867.1	1.246
0.15	0.1640	1.227	73.60	0.1058	0.65	1.988	14.87	892.3	1.283
0.16	0.1827	1.367	82.00	0.1179	0.66	2.045	15.30	917.9	1.319
0.17	0.2021	1.512	90.72	0.1304	0.67	2.103	15.74	944.0	1.357
0.18	0.2223	1.663	99.75	0.1434	0.68	2.162	16.18	970.5	1.395
0.19	0.2431	1.819	109.1	0.1568	0.69	2.222	16.63	997.4	1.434
0.20	0.2646	1.979	118.8	0.1707	0.70	2.283	17.08	1025	1.473
0.21	0.2869	2.146	128.8	0.1851	0.71	2.345	17.54	1053	1.513
0.22	0.3098	2.318	139.0	0.1999	0.72	2.408	18.01	1081	1.554
0.23	0.3334	2.494	149.6	0.2151	0.73	2.472	18.49	1109	1.595
0.24	0.3577	2.676	160.6	0.2308	0.74	2.537	18.98	1139	1.637
0.25	0.3827	2.863	171.8	0.2469	0.75	2.603	19.47	1168	1.679
0.26	0.4084	3.055	183.3	0.2635	0.76	2.669	19.97	1198	1.722
0.27	0.4348	3.253	195.2	0.2805	0.77	2.737	20.48	1229	1.766
0.28	0.4619	3.455	207.3	0.2980	0.78	2.806	20.99	1259	1.810
0.29	0.4897	3.663	219.8	0.3159	0.79	2.876	21.51	1291	1.855
0.30	0.5181	3.876	232.5	0.3343	0.80	2.947	22.04	1323	1.901
0.31	0.5473	4.094	245.6	0.3531	0.81	3.018	22.58	1355	1.947
0.32	0.5772	4.318	259.0	0.3724	0.82	3.091	23.13	1387	1.994
0.33	0.6077	4.546	272.7	0.3921	0.83	3.165	23.68	1421	2.042
0.34	0.6390	4.780	286.8	0.4122	0.84	3.240	24.24	1454	2.090
0.35	0.6709	5.019	301.1	0.4329	0.85	3.316	24.80	1488	2.139
0.36	0.7036	5.264	315.8	0.4539	0.86	3.393	25.38	1523	2.189
0.37	0.7370	5.513	330.8	0.4755	0.87	3.470	25.96	1558	2.239
0.38	0.7711	5.769	346.1	0.4975	0.88	3.549	26.55	1593	2.290
0.39	0.8059	6.029	361.7	0.5200	0.89	3.629	27.15	1629	2.341
0.40	0.8415	6.295	377.7	0.5429	0.90	3.710	27.75	1665	2.393
0.41	0.8778	6.567	393.9	0.5663	0.91	3.791	28.36	1702	2.446
0.42	0.9148	6.844	410.6	0.5902	0.92	3.874	28.98	1739	2.499
0.43	0.9526	7.126	427.5	0.6146	0.93	3.958	29.61	1776	2.553
0.44	0.9911	7.414	444.8	0.6394	0.94	4.042	30.24	1814	2.608
0.45	1.030	7.708	462.5	0.6648	0.95	4.128	30.88	1853	2.663
0.46	1.071	8.008	480.4	0.6906	0.96	4.214	31.52	1891	2.719
0.47	1.111	8.314	498.8	0.7170	0.97	4.301	32.18	1930	2.775
0.48	1.153	8.625	517.4	0.7438	0.98	4.389	32.84	1970	2.832
0.49	1.195	8.943	536.5	0.7712	0.99	4.479	33.50	2010	2.889
0.50	1.239	9.266	555.9	0.7991	1.00	4.569	34.18	2050	2.947

13

Manufactured by Plasti-Fab, Inc. (Data from Plasti-Fab, Inc.)
Formulas: GPS = CFS x 7.481

Head Feet	CFS	GPS	GPM	MGD	Head Feet	CFS	GPS	GPM	MGD
1.01	4.659	34.86	2091	3.006	1.14	5.909	44.20	2652	3.812
1.02	4.751	35.54	2132	3.065	1.15	6.009	44.96	2697	3.877
1.03	4.843	36.23	2174	3.125	1.16	6.111	45.71	2742	3.942
1.04	4.937	36.93	2216	3.185	1.17	6.212	46.47	2788	4.008
1.05	5.031	37.63	2258	3.246	1.18	6.315	47.24	2834	4.074
1.06	5.125	38.34	2300	3.307	1.19	6.417	48.01	2880	4.140
1.07	5.221	39.06	2343	3.368	1.20	6.521	48.78	2926	4.207
1.08	5.317	39.78	2386	3.430	1.21	6.624	49.55	2973	4.274
1.09	5.414	40.50	2430	3.493	1.22	6.728	50.33	3020	4.341
1.10	5.512	41.23	2474	3.556	1.23	6.833	51.11	3066	4.408
1.11	5.610	41.97	2518.	3.619	1.24	6.937	51.90	3114	4.476
1.12	5.709	42.71	2562	3.683	1.25	7.043	52.68	3161	4.544
1.13	5.809	43.45	2607	3.748					

13

13-9: 24 in. Palmer-Bowlus Flume Discharge Table

Manufactured by Plasti-Fab, Inc. (Data from Plasti-Fab, Inc.)
Formulas: GPS = CFS x 7.481

Head Feet	CFS	GPS	GPM	MGD	Head Feet	CFS	GPS	GPM	MGD
0.01					0.51	1.419	10.62	636.9	0.9155
0.02					0.52	1.468	10.98	658.7	0.9469
0.03					0.53	1.517	11.35	680.8	0.9787
0.04					0.54	1.567	11.72	703.4	1.011
0.05					0.55	1.618	12.11	726.2	1.044
0.06					0.56	1.670	12.49	749.5	1.077
0.07					0.57	1.723	12.89	773.1	1.111
0.08					0.58	1.776	13.29	797.1	1.146
0.09					0.59	1.830	13.69	821.5	1.181
0.10	0.0958	0.7167	43.00	0.0618	0.60	1.886	14.11	846.3	1.216
0.11	0.1114	0.8334	49.99	0.0719	0.61	1.942	14.53	871.4	1.253
0.12	0.1279	0.9568	57.41	0.0825	0.62	1.999	14.95	897.0	1.290
0.13	0.1454	1.088	65.27	0.0938	0.63	2.057	15.38	923.0	1.327
0.14	0.1639	1.226	73.54	0.1057	0.64	2.115	15.82	949.3	1.365
0.15	0.1832	1.371	82.24	0.1182	0.65	2.175	16.27	976.1	1.403
0.16	0.2035	1.522	91.34	0.1313	0.66	2.235	16.72	1003	1.442
0.17	0.2247	1.681	100.8	0.1450	0.67	2.297	17.18	1031	1.482
0.18	0.2468	1.846	110.8	0.1592	0.68	2.359	17.65	1059	1.522
0.19	0.2697	2.018	121.0	0.1740	0.69	2.423	18.12	1087	1.563
0.20	0.2935	2.196	131.7	0.1894	0.70	2.487	18.61	1116	1.605
0.21	0.3182	2.380	142.8	0.2053	0.71	2.552	19.09	1146	1.647
0.22	0.3436	2.570	154.2	0.2217	0.72	2.619	19.59	1175	1.689
0.23	0.3699	2.767	166.0	0.2387	0.73	2.686	20.09	1205	1.733
0.24	0.3971	2.971	178.2	0.2562	0.74	2.754	20.60	1236	1.777
0.25	0.4250	3.179	190.7	0.2742	0.75	2.823	21.12	1267	1.821
0.26	0.4537	3.394	203.6	0.2927	0.76	2.893	21.65	1299	1.867
0.27	0.4832	3.615	216.9	0.3117	0.77	2.965	22.18	1331	1.913
0.28	0.5135	3.841	230.5	0.3313	0.78	3.037	22.72	1363	1.959
0.29	0.5446	4.074	244.4	0.3513	0.79	3.110	23.27	1396	2.007
0.30	0.5764	4.312	258.7	0.3719	0.80	3.185	23.82	1429	2.055
0.31	0.6090	4.556	273.3	0.3929	0.81	3.260	24.39	1463	2.103
0.32	0.6424	4.806	288.3	0.4144	0.82	3.337	24.96	1497	2.153
0.33	0.6765	5.061	303.6	0.4364	0.83	3.414	25.54	1532	2.203
0.34	0.7113	5.321	319.3	0.4589	0.84	3.493	26.13	1567	2.253
0.35	0.7470	5.588	335.2	0.4819	0.85	3.572	26.72	1603	2.305
0.36	0.7833	5.860	351.6	0.5054	0.86	3.653	27.33	1639	2.357
0.37	0.8204	6.137	368.2	0.5293	0.87	3.735	27.94	1676	2.409
0.38	0.8583	6.421	385.2	0.5537	0.88	3.817	28.56	1713	2.463
0.39	0.8969	6.710	402.5	0.5786	0.89	3.901	29.19	1751	2.517
0.40	0.9362	7.004	420.2	0.6040	0.90	3.986	29.82	1789	2.572
0.41	0.9763	7.304	438.2	0.6299	0.91	4.072	30.47	1828	2.627
0.42	1.017	7.610	456.5	0.6562	0.92	4.160	31.12	1867	2.684
0.43	1.059	7.921	475.2	0.6831	0.93	4.248	31.78	1907	2.741
0.44	1.101	8.237	494.2	0.7104	0.94	4.337	32.45	1947	2.798
0.45	1.144	8.560	513.5	0.7382	0.95	4.428	33.12	1987	2.857
0.46	1.188	8.888	533.2	0.7665	0.96	4.519	33.81	2028	2.916
0.47	1.233	9.223	553.3	0.7953	0.97	4.612	34.50	2070	2.975
0.48	1.278	9.562	573.6	0.8246	0.98	4.706	35.20	2112	3.036
0.49	1.324	9.908	594.4	0.8544	0.99	4.800	35.91	2154	3.097
0.50	1.371	10.26	615.5	0.8847	1.00	4.896	36.63	2197	3.159

13

13-9: 24 in. Palmer-Bowlus Flume
Discharge Table *(Continued)*

Manufactured by Plasti-Fab, Inc. (Data from Plasti-Fab, Inc.)
Formulas: GPS = CFS x 7.481

Head Feet	CFS	GPS	GPM	MGD	Head Feet	CFS	GPS	GPM	MGD
1.01	4.993	37.35	2241	3.221	1.21	7.139	53.41	3204	4.606
1.02	5.091	38.09	2285	3.285	1.22	7.256	54.28	3256	4.681
1.03	5.190	38.83	2329	3.348	1.23	7.373	55.16	3309	4.757
1.04	5.290	39.58	2374	3.413	1.24	7.491	56.04	3362	4.833
1.05	5.391	40.33	2420	3.478	1.25	7.610	56.93	3415	4.910
1.06	5.493	41.10	2465	3.544	1.26	7.730	57.83	3469	4.987
1.07	5.596	41.87	2512	3.611	1.27	7.850	58.73	3523	5.064
1.08	5.700	42.65	2558	3.678	1.28	7.971	59.63	3577	5.143
1.09	5.806	43.43	2606	3.746	1.29	8.092	60.54	3632	5.221
1.10	5.912	44.23	2653	3.814	1.30	8.214	61.45	3687	5.300
1.11	6.019	45.03	2701	3.883	1.31	8.337	62.37	3742	5.379
1.12	6.127	45.83	2750	3.953	1.32	8.461	63.29	3797	5.458
1.13	6.236	46.65	2799	4.023	1.33	8.585	64.22	3853	5.538
1.14	6.346	47.47	2848	4.094	1.34	8.709	65.15	3909	5.619
1.15	6.456	48.30	2898	4.165	1.35	8.834	66.09	3965	5.699
1.16	6.568	49.14	2948	4.237	1.36	8.959	67.02	4021	5.780
1.17	6.681	49.98	2998	4.310	1.37	9.085	67.97	4077	5.861
1.18	6.794	50.83	3049	4.383	1.38	9.211	68.91	4134	5.943
1.19	6.908	51.68	3100	4.457	1.39	9.338	69.86	4191	6.025
1.20	7.023	52.54	3152	4.531	1.40	9.465	70.81	4248	6.107

13

13-10: 27 in. Palmer-Bowlus Flume Discharge Table

Manufactured by Plasti-Fab, Inc. (Data from Plasti-Fab, Inc.)
Formulas: GPS = CFS x 7.481

Head Feet	CFS	GPS	GPM	MGD	Head Feet	CFS	GPS	GPM	MGD
0.01					0.51	1.555	11.63	697.8	1.003
0.02					0.52	1.607	12.03	721.4	1.037
0.03					0.53	1.661	12.43	745.4	1.072
0.04					0.54	1.715	12.83	769.8	1.107
0.05					0.55	1.770	13.24	794.5	1.142
0.06					0.56	1.826	13.66	819.6	1.178
0.07			.		0.57	1.883	14.09	845.1	1.215
0.08					0.58	1.941	14.52	871.0	1.252
0.09					0.59	1.999	14.96	897.2	1.290
0.10					0.60	2.058	15.40	923.8	1.328
0.11	0.1257	0.9404	56.42	0.0811	0.61	2.119	15.85	950.8	1.367
0.12	0.1434	1.073	64.35	0.0925	0.62	2.180	16.31	978.2	1.406
0.13	0.1621	1.213	72.77	0.1046	0.63	2.241	16.77	1006	1.446
0.14	0.1820	1.362	81.67	0.1174	0.64	2.304	17.24	1034	1.487
0.15	0.2029	1.518	91.05	0.1309	0.65	2.368	17.71	1063	1.528
0.16	0.2248	1.682	100.9	0.1450	0.66	2.432	18.20	1092	1.569
0.17	0.2478	1.854	111.2	0.1599	0.67	2.498	18.69	1121	1.611
0.18	0.2717	2.033	122.0	0.1753	0.68	2.564	19.18	1151	1.654
0.19	0.2967	2.220	133.2	0.1914	0.69	2.631	19.69	1181	1.698
0.20	0.3226	2.413	144.8	0.2082	0.70	2.700	20.20	1212	1.742
0.21	0.3495	2.615	156.9	0.2255	0.71	2.769	20.71	1243	1.786
0.22	0.3774	2.823	169.4	0.2435	0.72	2.839	21.24	1274	1.831
0.23	0.4062	3.039	182.3	0.2620	0.73	2.910	21.77	1306	1.877
0.24	0.4359	3.261	195.6	0.2812	0.74	2.982	22.31	1338	1.924
0.25	0.4665	3.490	209.3	0.3010	0.75	3.055	22.85	1371	1.971
0.26	0.4980	3.726	223.5	0.3213	0.76	3.129	23.41	1404	2.019
0.27	0.5304	3.968	238.0	0.3422	0.77	3.204	23.97	1438	2.067
0.28	0.5636	4.216	252.9	0.3636	0.78	3.280	24.54	1472	2.116
0.29	0.5977	4.471	268.3	0.3856	0.79	3.357	25.11	1507	2.166
0.30	0.6327	4.733	284.0	0.4082	0.80	3.435	25.69	1542	2.216
0.31	0.6685	5.001	300.0	0.4313	0.81	3.514	26.29	1577	2.267
0.32	0.7052	5.276	316.5	0.4550	0.82	3.594	26.89	1613	2.319
0.33	0.7427	5.556	333.3	0.4792	0.83	3.675	27.49	1649	2.371
0.34	0.7810	5.843	350.5	0.5039	0.84	3.757	28.11	1686	2.424
0.35	0.8201	6.135	368.1	0.5291	0.85	3.840	28.73	1724	2.478
0.36	0.8601	6.434	386.0	0.5549	0.86	3.925	29.36	1761	2.532
0.37	0.9008	6.739	404.3	0.5812	0.87	4.010	30.00	1800	2.587
0.38	0.9424	7.050	422.9	0.6080	0.88	4.097	30.65	1839	2.643
0.39	0.9847	7.367	441.9	0.6353	0.89	4.184	31.30	1878	2.700
0.40	1.028	7.690	461.3	0.6632	0.90	4.273	31.96	1918	2.757
0.41	1.072	8.018	481.0	0.6915	0.91	4.363	32.64	1958	2.815
0.42	1.117	8.353	501.1	0.7204	0.92	4.454	33.32	1999	2.873
0.43	1.162	8.694	521.5	0.7497	0.93	4.546	34.01	2040	2.933
0.44	1.208	9.040	542.3	0.7796	0.94	4.639	34.70	2082	2.993
0.45	1.256	9.392	563.5	0.8100	0.95	4.733	35.41	2124	3.054
0.46	1.303	9.751	585.0	0.8409	0.96	4.829	36.12	2167	3.115
0.47	1.352	10.12	606.8	0.8723	0.97	4.925	36.84	2210	3.178
0.48	1.402	10.49	629.0	0.9042	0.98	5.023	37.58	2254	3.240
0.49	1.452	10.86	651.6	0.9367	0.99	5.122	38.32	2299	3.304
0.50	1.503	11.24	674.5	0.9696	1.00	5.222	39.06	2344	3.369

13-10: 27 in. Palmer-Bowlus Flume Discharge Table *(Continued)*

Manufactured by Plasti-Fab, Inc. (Data from Plasti-Fab, Inc.)

Formulas: GPS = CFS x 7.481

Head Feet	CFS	GPS	GPM	MGD	Head Feet	CFS	GPS	GPM	MGD
1.01	5.323	39.82	2389	3.434	1.31	8.882	66.45	3986	5.730
1.02	5.425	40.59	2435	3.500	1.32	9.017	67.45	4047	5.817
1.03	5.529	41.36	2481	3.567	1.33	9.152	68.47	4108	5.905
1.04	5.633	42.14	2528	3.634	1.34	9.289	69.49	4169	5.993
1.05	5.739	42.93	2576	3.703	1.35	9.426	70.52	4231	6.082
1.06	5.846	43.74	2624	3.772	1.36	9.565	71.55	4293	6.171
1.07	5.954	44.54	2672	3.841	1.37	9.704	72.59	4355	6.261
1.08	6.064	45.36	2721	3.912	1.38	9.844	73.64	4418	6.351
1.09	6.174	46.19	2771	3.983	1.39	9.984	74.69	4481	6.442
1.10	6.286	47.02	2821	4.055	1.40	10.13	75.75	4545	6.533
1.11	6.398	47.87	2872	4.128	1.41	10.27	76.81	4608	6.625
1.12	6.512	48.72	2923	4.201	1.42	10.41	77.88	4673	6.717
1.13	6.627	49.58	2974	4.276	1.43	10.55	78.96	4737	6.809
1.14	6.743	50.45	3026	4.351	1.44	10.70	80.04	4802	6.903
1.15	6.861	51.32	3079	4.426	1.45	10.84	81.12	4867	6.996
1.16	6.979	52.21	3132	4.503	1.46	10.99	82.22	4932	7.090
1.17	7.098	53.10	3186	4.580	1.47	11.14	83.31	4998	7.185
1.18	7.219	54.01	3240	4.657	1.48	11.28	84.41	5064	7.279
1.19	7.341	54.92	3295	4.736	1.49	11.43	85.51	5130	7.375
1.20	7.463	55.83	3350	4.815	1.50	11.58	86.62	5196	7.470
1.21	7.587	56.76	3405	4.895	1.51	11.73	87.73	5263	7.566
1.22	7.712	57.69	3461	4.976	1.52	11.88	88.84	5330	7.662
1.23	7.838	58.64	3518	5.057	1.53	12.03	89.97	5397	7.759
1.24	7.965	59.59	3575	5.139	1.54	12.18	91.09	5465	7.856
1.25	8.093	60.54	3632	5.221	1.55	12.33	92.22	5532	7.953
1.26	8.222	61.51	3690	5.305	1.56	12.48	93.35	5600	8.050
1.27	8.352	62.48	3749	5.388	1.57	12.63	94.48	5668	8.148
1.28	8.483	63.46	3807	5.473	1.58	12.78	95.61	5736	8.246
1.29	8.615	64.45	3867	5.558	1.59	12.93	96.75	5805	8.344
1.30	8.748	65.44	3926	5.644	1.60	13.09	97.90	5873	8.443

13

13-11: 30 in. Palmer-Bowlus Flume Discharge Table

Manufactured by Plasti-Fab, Inc. (Data from Plasti-Fab, Inc.)
Formulas: GPS = CFS x 7.481

Head Feet	CFS	GPS	GPM	MGD	Head Feet	CFS	GPS	GPM	MGD
0.01					0.51	1.688	12.63	757.8	1.089
0.02					0.52	1.744	13.05	782.8	1.125
0.03					0.53	1.801	13.47	808.2	1.162
0.04					0.54	1.858	13.90	833.9	1.199
0.05					0.55	1.916	14.34	860.1	1.236
0.06					0.56	1.976	14.78	886.6	1.274
0.07					0.57	2.036	15.23	913.6	1.313
0.08					0.58	2.096	15.68	940.9	1.353
0.09					0.59	2.158	16.15	968.7	1.393
0.10					0.60	2.221	16.62	996.9	1.433
0.11					0.61	2.285	17.09	1026	1.474
0.12					0.62	2.349	17.58	1055	1.516
0.13	0.1309	0.9793	58.75	0.0844	0.63	2.415	18.07	1084	1.558
0.14	0.1599	1.196	71.77	0.1032	0.64	2.482	18.56	1114	1.601
0.15	0.1895	1.418	85.05	0.1223	0.65	2.549	19.07	1144	1.645
0.16	0.2196	1.643	98.57	0.1417	0.66	2.618	19.58	1175	1.689
0.17	0.2503	1.872	112.3	0.1615	0.67	2.687	20.10	1206	1.734
0.18	0.2816	2.107	126.4	0.1817	0.68	2.757	20.63	1238	1.779
0.19	0.3134	2.345	140.7	0.2022	0.69	2.829	21.16	1270	1.825
0.20	0.3459	2.588	155.2	0.2231	0.70	2.901	21.70	1302	1.872
0.21	0.3789	2.835	170.1	0.2444	0.71	2.974	22.25	1335	1.919
0.22	0.4125	3.086	185.1	0.2661	0.72	3.049	22.81	1368	1.967
0.23	0.4468	3.343	200.5	0.2882	0.73	3.124	23.37	1402	2.016
0.24	0.4816	3.603	216.2	0.3107	0.74	3.201	23.94	1437	2.065
0.25	0.5171	3.868	232.1	0.3336	0.75	3.278	24.52	1471	2.115
0.26	0.5533	4.139	248.3	0.3570	0.76	3.357	25.11	1507	2.166
0.27	0.5901	4.415	264.8	0.3807	0.77	3.436	25.71	1542	2.217
0.28	0.6275	4.694	281.6	0.4048	0.78	3.517	26.31	1578	2.269
0.29	0.6656	4.979	298.7	0.4294	0.79	3.598	26.92	1615	2.321
0.30	0.7044	5.270	316.1	0.4544	0.80	3.681	27.54	1652	2.375
0.31	0.7438	5.564	333.8	0.4799	0.81	3.765	28.16	1690	2.429
0.32	0.7840	5.865	351.9	0.5058	0.82	3.850	28.80	1728	2.484
0.33	0.8248	6.170	370.2	0.5321	0.83	3.935	29.44	1766	2.539
0.34	0.8664	6.482	388.8	0.5589	0.84	4.022	30.09	1805	2.595
0.35	0.9086	6.797	407.8	0.5862	0.85	4.110	30.75	1845	2.652
0.36	0.9516	7.119	427.1	0.6139	0.86	4.200	31.42	1885	2.709
0.37	0.9953	7.446	446.7	0.6421	0.87	4.290	32.09	1925	2.768
0.38	1.040	7.778	466.6	0.6708	0.88	4.381	32.78	1966	2.827
0.39	1.085	8.116	486.9	0.7000	0.89	4.474	33.47	2008	2.886
0.40	1.131	8.460	507.5	0.7296	0.90	4.567	34.17	2050	2.947
0.41	1.178	8.810	528.5	0.7597	0.91	4.662	34.87	2092	3.008
0.42	1.225	9.165	549.8	0.7904	0.92	4.758	35.59	2135	3.069
0.43	1.273	9.526	571.5	0.8215	0.93	4.854	36.32	2179	3.132
0.44	1.322	9.893	593.5	0.8532	0.94	4.953	37.05	2223	3.195
0.45	1.372	10.27	615.9	0.8853	0.95	5.052	37.79	2267	3.259
0.46	1.423	10.64	638.6	0.9180	0.96	5.152	38.54	2312	3.324
0.47	1.474	11.03	661.7	0.9512	0.97	5.253	39.30	2358	3.389
0.48	1.527	11.42	685.2	0.9849	0.98	5.356	40.07	2404	3.455
0.49	1.580	11.82	709.0	1.019	0.99	5.460	40.84	2450	3.522
0.50	1.634	12.22	733.2	1.054	1.00	5.565	41.63	2497	3.590

13

13-11: 30 in. Palmer-Bowlus Flume Discharge Table (Continued)

Manufactured by Plasti-Fab, Inc. (Data from Plasti-Fab, Inc.)

Formulas: GPS = CFS x 7.481

Head Feet	CFS	GPS	GPM	MGD	Head Feet	CFS	GPS	GPM	MGD
1.01	5.671	42.42	2545	3.659	1.39	10.55	78.93	4735	6.807
1.02	5.778	43.22	2593	3.728	1.40	10.70	80.05	4803	6.904
1.03	5.886	44.03	2642	3.798	1.41	10.85	81.18	4870	7.001
1.04	5.996	44.85	2691	3.868	1.42	11.00	82.32	4939	7.099
1.05	6.106	45.68	2741	3.940	1.43	11.16	83.47	5007	7.198
1.06	6.218	46.52	2791	4.012	1.44	11.31	84.62	5076	7.297
1.07	6.331	47.36	2841	4.085	1.45	11.47	85.78	5146	7.397
1.08	6.445	48.22	2893	4.158	1.46	11.62	86.94	5216	7.498
1.09	6.561	49.08	2944	4.233	1.47	11.78	88.12	5287	7.599
1.10	6.677	49.95	2997	4.308	1.48	11.94	89.30	5357	7.701
1.11	6.795	50.83	3049	4.384	1.49	12.10	90.49	5429	7.804
1.12	6.913	51.72	3103	4.460	1.50	12.26	91.69	5501	7.907
1.13	7.033	52.62	3157	4.538	1.51	12.42	92.89	5573	8.011
1.14	7.154	53.52	3211	4.616	1.52	12.58	94.10	5645	8.115
1.15	7.277	54.44	3266	4.695	1.53	12.74	95.32	5718	8.220
1.16	7.400	55.36	3321	4.774	1.54	12.90	96.54	5792	8.325
1.17	7.525	56.29	3377	4.855	1.55	13.07	97.77	5865	8.432
1.18	7.650	57.23	3434	4.936	1.56	13.23	99.00	5940	8.538
1.19	7.777	58.18	3490	5.018	1.57	13.40	100.2	6014	8.645
1.20	7.905	59.14	3548	5.100	1.58	13.57	101.5	6089	8.753
1.21	8.034	60.11	3606	5.184	1.59	13.73	102.8	6164	8.861
1.22	8.165	61.08	3664	5.268	1.60	13.90	104.0	6240	8.970
1.23	8.296	62.06	3723	5.352	1.61	14.07	105.3	6316	9.079
1.24	8.429	63.06	3783	5.438	1.62	14.24	106.6	6392	9.189
1.25	8.562	64.06	3843	5.524	1.63	14.41	107.8	6469	9.299
1.26	8.697	65.06	3903	5.611	1.64	14.59	109.1	6546	9.410
1.27	8.833	66.08	3964	5.699	1.65	14.76	110.4	6623	9.521
1.28	8.970	67.11	4026	5.787	1.66	14.93	111.7	6701	9.633
1.29	9.109	68.14	4088	5.877	1.67	15.10	113.0	6779	9.745
1.30	9.248	69.18	4150	5.966	1.68	15.28	114.3	6857	9.857
1.31	9.388	70.23	4214	6.057	1.69	15.45	115.6	6936	9.970
1.32	9.530	71.29	4277	6.148	1.70	15.63	116.9	7015	10.08
1.33	9.672	72.36	4341	6.240	1.71	15.81	118.2	7094	10.20
1.34	9.816	73.43	4406	6.333	1.72	15.98	119.6	7173	10.31
1.35	9.961	74.52	4471	6.426	1.73	16.16	120.9	7253	10.43
1.36	10.11	75.61	4536	6.521	1.74	16.34	122.2	7333	10.54
1.37	10.25	76.71	4602	6.615	1.75	16.52	123.6	7413	10.66
1.38	10.40	77.82	4668	6.711					

13

Chapter

14

H flume discharge tables

This chapter contains discharge (flow rate vs head) tables for H flumes. Note that all of the tabular data is for free flow.

Note also that discharges are listed for heads which are below the minimum recommended operating head of the flume in question. Discharge for these heads outside the normal operating range are listed for reference only; it should not be implied that the primary device is intended to be used in these regions. Refer to Chapter 4 for minimum and maximum recommended heads.

H flumes

14-1: $^1/_2$ ft. H Flume

14-2: $^3/_4$ ft. H Flume

14-3: 1 ft. H Flume

14-4: 1 $^1/_2$ ft. H Flume

14-5: 2 ft. H Flume

14-6: 2 $^1/_2$ ft. H Flume

14-7: 3 ft. H Flume

14-8: 4 $^1/_2$ ft. H Flume

14

Note: The discharges of the flumes are listed in four different units:

CFS—cubic feet per second,   GPS—gallons per second,

GPM—gallons per minute,   MGD—million gallons per day.

The source of data used to develop each table is listed on the table.

14-1: ¹/₂ ft. H Flume Discharge Table

Source: U.S.D.A. Handbook No. 224

Formulas: GPS = CFS x 7.481   GPM = CFS x 448.8
MGD = CFS x 0.6463

Head Feet	CFS	GPS	GPM	MGD	Head Feet	CFS	GPS	GPM	MGD
0.01	0.0002	0.0015	0.0898	0.0001	0.26	0.0767	0.5738	34.42	0.0496
0.02	0.0004	0.0030	0.1795	0.0003	0.27	0.0834	0.6239	37.43	0.0539
0.03	0.0009	0.0067	0.4039	0.0006	0.28	0.0905	0.6770	40.62	0.0585
0.04	0.0016	0.0120	0.7181	0.0010	0.29	0.0979	0.7324	43.94	0.0633
0.05	0.0024	0.0180	1.077	0.0016	0.30	0.1057	0.7907	47.44	0.0683
0.06	0.0035	0.0262	1.571	0.0023	0.31	0.1139	0.8521	51.12	0.0736
0.07	0.0047	0.0352	2.109	0.0030	0.32	0.1224	0.9157	54.93	0.0791
0.08	0.0063	0.0471	2.827	0.0041	0.33	0.1314	0.9830	58.97	0.0849
0.09	0.0080	0.0598	3.590	0.0052	0.34	0.1407	1.053	63.15	0.0909
0.10	0.0101	0.0756	4.533	0.0065	0.35	0.1505	1.126	67.54	0.0973
0.11	0.0122	0.0913	5.475	0.0079	0.36	0.1607	1.202	72.12	0.1039
0.12	0.0146	0.1092	6.552	0.0094	0.37	0.1713	1.281	76.88	0.1107
0.13	0.0173	0.1294	7.764	0.0112	0.38	0.1823	1.364	81.82	0.1178
0.14	0.0202	0.1511	9.066	0.0131	0.39	0.1938	1.450	86.98	0.1253
0.15	0.0233	0.1743	10.46	0.0151	0.40	0.2050	1.534	92.00	0.1325
0.16	0.0267	0.1997	11.98	0.0173	0.41	0.2170	1.623	97.39	0.1402
0.17	0.0304	0.2274	13.64	0.0196	0.42	0.2300	1.721	103.2	0.1486
0.18	0.0343	0.2566	15.39	0.0222	0.43	0.2440	1.825	109.5	0.1577
0.19	0.0385	0.2880	17.28	0.0249	0.44	0.2570	1.923	115.3	0.1661
0.20	0.0431	0.3224	19.34	0.0279	0.45	0.2710	2.027	121.6	0.1751
0.21	0.0479	0.3583	21.50	0.0310	0.46	0.2850	2.132	127.9	0.1842
0.22	0.0530	0.3965	23.79	0.0343	0.47	0.3000	2.244	134.6	0.1939
0.23	0.0585	0.4376	26.25	0.0378	0.48	0.3150	2.357	141.4	0.2036
0.24	0.0643	0.4810	28.86	0.0416	0.49	0.3310	2.476	148.6	0.2139
0.25	0.0704	0.5267	31.60	0.0455	0.50	0.3470	2.596	155.7	0.2243

14

14-2: ³/₄ ft. H Flume Discharge Table

Source: U.S.D.A. Handbook No. 224

Formulas: GPS = CFS x 7.481   GPM = CFS x 448.8

MGD = CFS x 0.6463

Head Feet	CFS	GPS	GPM	MGD	Head Feet	CFS	GPS	GPM	MGD
0.01	0.0003	0.0022	0.1346	0.0002	0.39	0.2110	1.578	94.70	0.1364
0.02	0.0006	0.0045	0.2693	0.0004	0.40	0.2240	1.676	100.5	0.1448
0.03	0.0013	0.0097	0.5834	0.0008	0.41	0.2370	1.773	106.4	0.1532
0.04	0.0022	0.0165	0.9874	0.0014	0.42	0.2500	1.870	112.2	0.1616
0.05	0.0032	0.0239	1.436	0.0021	0.43	0.2630	1.968	118.0	0.1700
0.06	0.0046	0.0344	2.064	0.0030	0.44	0.2770	2.072	124.3	0.1790
0.07	0.0061	0.0456	2.738	0.0039	0.45	0.2910	2.177	130.6	0.1881
0.08	0.0080	0.0598	3.590	0.0052	0.46	0.3060	2.289	137.3	0.1978
0.09	0.0101	0.0756	4.533	0.0065	0.47	0.3210	2.401	144.1	0.2075
0.10	0.0126	0.0943	5.655	0.0081	0.48	0.3370	2.521	151.2	0.2178
0.11	0.0151	0.1130	6.777	0.0098	0.49	0.3530	2.641	158.4	0.2281
0.12	0.0179	0.1339	8.034	0.0116	0.50	0.3700	2.768	166.1	0.2391
0.13	0.0210	0.1571	9.425	0.0136	0.51	0.3880	2.903	174.1	0.2508
0.14	0.0242	0.1810	10.86	0.0156	0.52	0.4060	3.037	182.2	0.2624
0.15	0.0278	0.2080	12.48	0.0180	0.53	0.4240	3.172	190.3	0.2740
0.16	0.0317	0.2371	14.23	0.0205	0.54	0.4430	3.314	198.8	0.2863
0.17	0.0358	0.2678	16.07	0.0231	0.55	0.4620	3.456	207.3	0.2986
0.18	0.0403	0.3015	18.09	0.0260	0.56	0.4820	3.606	216.3	0.3115
0.19	0.0451	0.3374	20.24	0.0291	0.57	0.5020	3.755	225.3	0.3244
0.20	0.0501	0.3748	22.48	0.0324	0.58	0.5230	3.913	234.7	0.3380
0.21	0.0555	0.4152	24.91	0.0359	0.59	0.5440	4.070	244.1	0.3516
0.22	0.0612	0.4578	27.47	0.0396	0.60	0.5660	4.234	254.0	0.3658
0.23	0.0672	0.5027	30.16	0.0434	0.61	0.5880	4.399	263.9	0.3800
0.24	0.0735	0.5499	32.99	0.0475	0.62	0.6110	4.571	274.2	0.3949
0.25	0.0802	0.6000	35.99	0.0518	0.63	0.6350	4.750	285.0	0.4104
0.26	0.0872	0.6523	39.14	0.0564	0.64	0.6590	4.930	295.8	0.4259
0.27	0.0946	0.7077	42.46	0.0611	0.65	0.6830	5.110	306.5	0.4414
0.28	0.1023	0.7653	45.91	0.0661	0.66	0.7080	5.297	317.8	0.4576
0.29	0.1104	0.8259	49.55	0.0714	0.67	0.7340	5.491	329.4	0.4744
0.30	0.1190	0.8902	53.41	0.0769	0.68	0.7600	5.686	341.1	0.4912
0.31	0.1280	0.9576	57.45	0.0827	0.69	0.7860	5.880	352.8	0.5080
0.32	0.1370	1.0249	61.49	0.0885	0.70	0.8130	6.082	364.9	0.5254
0.33	0.1460	1.0922	65.52	0.0944	0.71	0.8410	6.292	377.4	0.5435
0.34	0.1560	1.167	70.01	0.1008	0.72	0.8690	6.501	390.0	0.5616
0.35	0.1670	1.249	74.95	0.1079	0.73	0.8980	6.718	403.0	0.5804
0.36	0.1770	1.324	79.44	0.1144	0.74	0.9270	6.935	416.0	0.5991
0.37	0.1880	1.406	84.37	0.1215	0.75	0.9570	7.159	429.5	0.6185
0.38	0.1990	1.489	89.31	0.1286					

14

14-3: 1 ft. H Flume Discharge Table

Source: U.S.D.A. Handbook No. 224

Formulas: GPS = CFS x 7.481   GPM = CFS x 448.8
          MGD = CFS x 0.6463

Head Feet	CFS	GPS	GPM	MGD	Head Feet	CFS	GPS	GPM	MGD
0.01	0.0001	0.0007	0.0449	0.0001	0.51	0.4160	3.112	186.7	0.2689
0.02	0.0007	0.0052	0.3142	0.0005	0.52	0.4340	3.247	194.8	0.2805
0.03	0.0017	0.0127	0.7630	0.0011	0.53	0.4530	3.389	203.3	0.2928
0.04	0.0027	0.0202	1.212	0.0017	0.54	0.4720	3.531	211.8	0.3051
0.05	0.0040	0.0299	1.795	0.0026	0.55	0.4920	3.681	220.8	0.3180
0.06	0.0056	0.0419	2.513	0.0036	0.56	0.5120	3.830	229.8	0.3309
0.07	0.0075	0.0561	3.366	0.0048	0.57	0.5330	3.987	239.2	0.3445
0.08	0.0097	0.0726	4.353	0.0063	0.58	0.5540	4.144	248.6	0.3581
0.09	0.0122	0.0913	5.475	0.0079	0.59	0.5760	4.309	258.5	0.3723
0.10	0.0150	0.1122	6.732	0.0097	0.60	0.5980	4.474	268.4	0.3865
0.11	0.0179	0.1339	8.034	0.0116	0.61	0.6210	4.646	278.7	0.4014
0.12	0.0211	0.1578	9.470	0.0136	0.62	0.6440	4.818	289.0	0.4162
0.13	0.0246	0.1840	11.04	0.0159	0.63	0.6680	4.997	299.8	0.4317
0.14	0.0284	0.2125	12.75	0.0184	0.64	0.6920	5.177	310.6	0.4472
0.15	0.0324	0.2424	14.54	0.0209	0.65	0.7170	5.364	321.8	0.4634
0.16	0.0367	0.2746	16.47	0.0237	0.66	0.7430	5.558	333.5	0.4802
0.17	0.0413	0.3090	18.54	0.0267	0.67	0.7690	5.753	345.1	0.4970
0.18	0.0462	0.3456	20.73	0.0299	0.68	0.7960	5.955	357.2	0.5145
0.19	0.0515	0.3853	23.11	0.0333	0.69	0.8230	6.157	369.4	0.5319
0.20	0.0571	0.4272	25.63	0.0369	0.70	0.8150	6.097	365.8	0.5267
0.21	0.0630	0.4713	28.27	0.0407	0.71	0.8800	6.583	394.9	0.5687
0.22	0.0692	0.5177	31.06	0.0447	0.72	0.9090	6.800	408.0	0.5875
0.23	0.0758	0.5671	34.02	0.0490	0.73	0.9390	7.025	421.4	0.6069
0.24	0.0827	0.6187	37.12	0.0534	0.74	0.9690	7.249	434.9	0.6263
0.25	0.0900	0.6733	40.39	0.0582	0.75	1.000	7.481	448.8	0.6463
0.26	0.0976	0.7301	43.80	0.0631	0.76	1.031	7.713	462.7	0.6663
0.27	0.1055	0.7892	47.35	0.0682	0.77	1.063	7.952	477.1	0.6870
0.28	0.1138	0.8513	51.07	0.0735	0.78	1.096	8.199	491.9	0.7083
0.29	0.1226	0.9172	55.02	0.0792	0.79	1.129	8.446	506.7	0.7297
0.30	0.1320	0.9875	59.24	0.0853	0.80	1.160	8.678	520.6	0.7497
0.31	0.1410	1.055	63.28	0.0911	0.81	1.200	8.977	538.6	0.7756
0.32	0.1510	1.130	67.77	0.0976	0.82	1.230	9.202	552.0	0.7949
0.33	0.1610	1.204	72.26	0.1041	0.83	1.270	9.501	570.0	0.8208
0.34	0.1720	1.287	77.19	0.1112	0.84	1.300	9.725	583.4	0.8402
0.35	0.1830	1.369	82.13	0.1183	0.85	1.340	10.02	601.4	0.8660
0.36	0.1940	1.451	87.07	0.1254	0.86	1.380	10.32	619.3	0.8919
0.37	0.2060	1.541	92.45	0.1331	0.87	1.410	10.55	632.8	0.9113
0.38	0.2180	1.631	97.84	0.1409	0.88	1.450	10.85	650.8	0.9371
0.39	0.2310	1.728	103.7	0.1493	0.89	1.490	11.15	668.7	0.9630
0.40	0.2440	1.825	109.5	0.1577	0.90	1.530	11.45	686.7	0.9888
0.41	0.2570	1.923	115.3	0.1661	0.91	1.570	11.75	704.6	1.015
0.42	0.2710	2.027	121.6	0.1751	0.92	1.610	12.04	722.6	1.041
0.43	0.2850	2.132	127.9	0.1842	0.93	1.660	12.42	745.0	1.073
0.44	0.3000	2.244	134.6	0.1939	0.94	1.700	12.72	763.0	1.099
0.45	0.3150	2.357	141.4	0.2036	0.95	1.740	13.02	780.9	1.125
0.46	0.3310	2.476	148.6	0.2139	0.96	1.780	13.32	798.9	1.150
0.47	0.3470	2.596	155.7	0.2243	0.97	1.830	13.69	821.3	1.183
0.48	0.3640	2.723	163.4	0.2353	0.98	1.870	13.99	839.3	1.209
0.49	0.3810	2.850	171.0	0.2462	0.99	1.920	14.36	861.7	1.241
0.50	0.3980	2.977	178.6	0.2572	1.00	1.970	14.74	884.1	1.273

14

14-4: 1 1/2 ft. H Flume Discharge Table

Source: U.S.D.A. Handbook No. 224

Formulas: GPS = CFS x 7.481   GPM = CFS x 448.8
MGD = CFS x 0.6463

Head Feet	CFS	GPS	GPM	MGD	Head Feet	CFS	GPS	GPM	MGD
0.01	0.0004	0.0030	0.1795	0.0003	0.51	0.4730	3.539	212.3	0.3057
0.02	0.0011	0.0082	0.4937	0.0007	0.52	0.4930	3.688	221.3	0.3186
0.03	0.0023	0.0172	1.032	0.0015	0.53	0.5140	3.845	230.7	0.3322
0.04	0.0039	0.0292	1.750	0.0025	0.54	0.5350	4.002	240.1	0.3458
0.05	0.0057	0.0426	2.558	0.0037	0.55	0.5570	4.167	250.0	0.3600
0.06	0.0078	0.0584	3.501	0.0050	0.56	0.5790	4.331	259.9	0.3742
0.07	0.0103	0.0771	4.623	0.0067	0.57	0.6010	4.496	269.7	0.3884
0.08	0.0131	0.0980	5.879	0.0085	0.58	0.6240	4.668	280.1	0.4033
0.09	0.0164	0.1227	7.360	0.0106	0.59	0.6480	4.848	290.8	0.4188
0.10	0.0200	0.1496	8.976	0.0129	0.60	0.6720	5.027	301.6	0.4343
0.11	0.0237	0.1773	10.64	0.0153	0.61	0.6970	5.214	312.8	0.4505
0.12	0.0276	0.2065	12.39	0.0178	0.62	0.7220	5.401	324.0	0.4666
0.13	0.0319	0.2386	14.32	0.0206	0.63	0.7470	5.588	335.3	0.4828
0.14	0.0365	0.2731	16.38	0.0236	0.64	0.7730	5.783	346.9	0.4996
0.15	0.0414	0.3097	18.58	0.0268	0.65	0.8000	5.985	359.0	0.5170
0.16	0.0467	0.3494	20.96	0.0302	0.66	0.8270	6.187	371.2	0.5345
0.17	0.0523	0.3913	23.47	0.0338	0.67	0.8550	6.396	383.7	0.5526
0.18	0.0582	0.4354	26.12	0.0376	0.68	0.8830	6.606	396.3	0.5707
0.19	0.0645	0.4825	28.95	0.0417	0.69	0.9120	6.823	409.3	0.5894
0.20	0.0711	0.5319	31.91	0.0460	0.70	0.9420	7.047	422.8	0.6088
0.21	0.0780	0.5835	35.01	0.0504	0.71	0.9720	7.272	436.2	0.6282
0.22	0.0854	0.6389	38.33	0.0552	0.72	1.002	7.496	449.7	0.6476
0.23	0.0931	0.6965	41.78	0.0602	0.73	1.033	7.728	463.6	0.6676
0.24	0.1011	0.7563	45.37	0.0653	0.74	1.065	7.967	478.0	0.6883
0.25	0.1095	0.8192	49.14	0.0708	0.75	1.097	8.207	492.3	0.7090
0.26	0.1183	0.8850	53.09	0.0765	0.76	1.130	8.454	507.1	0.7303
0.27	0.1275	0.9538	57.22	0.0824	0.77	1.163	8.700	522.0	0.7516
0.28	0.1371	1.026	61.53	0.0886	0.78	1.197	8.955	537.2	0.7736
0.29	0.1470	1.100	65.97	0.0950	0.79	1.231	9.209	552.5	0.7956
0.30	0.1570	1.175	70.46	0.1015	0.80	1.270	9.501	570.0	0.8208
0.31	0.1680	1.257	75.40	0.1086	0.81	1.300	9.725	583.4	0.8402
0.32	0.1790	1.339	80.34	0.1157	0.82	1.340	10.02	601.4	0.8660
0.33	0.1910	1.429	85.72	0.1234	0.83	1.380	10.32	619.3	0.8919
0.34	0.2030	1.519	91.11	0.1312	0.84	1.410	10.55	632.8	0.9113
0.35	0.2150	1.608	96.49	0.1390	0.85	1.450	10.85	650.8	0.9371
0.36	0.2280	1.706	102.3	0.1474	0.86	1.490	11.15	668.7	0.9630
0.37	0.2410	1.803	108.2	0.1558	0.87	1.530	11.45	686.7	0.9888
0.38	0.2550	1.908	114.4	0.1648	0.88	1.570	11.75	704.6	1.015
0.39	0.2690	2.012	120.7	0.1739	0.89	1.610	12.04	722.6	1.041
0.40	0.2830	2.117	127.0	0.1829	0.90	1.650	12.34	740.5	1.066
0.41	0.2980	2.229	133.7	0.1926	0.91	1.690	12.64	758.5	1.092
0.42	0.3140	2.349	140.9	0.2029	0.92	1.730	12.94	776.4	1.118
0.43	0.3300	2.469	148.1	0.2133	0.93	1.780	13.32	798.9	1.150
0.44	0.3460	2.588	155.3	0.2236	0.94	1.820	13.62	816.8	1.176
0.45	0.3630	2.716	162.9	0.2346	0.95	1.860	13.91	834.8	1.202
0.46	0.3800	2.843	170.5	0.2456	0.96	1.910	14.29	857.2	1.234
0.47	0.3980	2.977	178.6	0.2572	0.97	1.950	14.59	875.2	1.260
0.48	0.4160	3.112	186.7	0.2689	0.98	2.000	14.96	897.6	1.293
0.49	0.4350	3.254	195.2	0.2811	0.99	2.050	15.34	920.0	1.325
0.50	0.4540	3.396	203.8	0.2934	1.00	2.090	15.64	938.0	1.351

14

Source: U.S.D.A. Handbook No. 224
Formulas: GPS = CFS x 7.481   GPM = CFS x 448.8
MGD = CFS x 0.6463

Head Feet	CFS	GPS	GPM	MGD	Head Feet	CFS	GPS	GPM	MGD
1.01	2.140	16.01	960.4	1.3831	1.26	3.590	26.86	1611	2.320
1.02	2.190	16.38	982.9	1.4154	1.27	3.660	27.38	1643	2.366
1.03	2.240	16.76	1005	1.4477	1.28	3.730	27.90	1674	2.411
1.04	2.300	17.21	1032	1.4865	1.29	3.800	28.43	1705	2.456
1.05	2.350	17.58	1055	1.5188	1.30	3.870	28.95	1737	2.501
1.06	2.400	17.95	1077	1.5511	1.31	3.940	29.48	1768	2.546
1.07	2.450	18.33	1100	1.5834	1.32	4.010	30.00	1800	2.592
1.08	2.500	18.70	1122	1.6158	1.33	4.080	30.52	1831	2.637
1.09	2.560	19.15	1149	1.6545	1.34	4.150	31.05	1863	2.682
1.10	2.610	19.53	1171	1.6868	1.35	4.220	31.57	1894	2.727
1.11	2.670	19.97	1198	1.7256	1.36	4.300	32.17	1930	2.779
1.12	2.730	20.42	1225	1.7644	1.37	4.370	32.69	1961	2.824
1.13	2.780	20.80	1248	1.7967	1.38	4.450	33.29	1997	2.876
1.14	2.840	21.25	1275	1.8355	1.39	4.520	33.81	2029	2.921
1.15	2.900	21.69	1302	1.8743	1.40	4.600	34.41	2064	2.973
1.16	2.960	22.14	1328	1.9130	1.41	4.680	35.01	2100	3.025
1.17	3.020	22.59	1355	1.9518	1.42	4.760	35.61	2136	3.076
1.18	3.080	23.04	1382	1.9906	1.43	4.840	36.21	2172	3.128
1.19	3.140	23.49	1409	2.0294	1.44	4.920	36.81	2208	3.180
1.20	3.200	23.94	1436	2.0682	1.45	5.000	37.41	2244	3.232
1.21	3.270	24.46	1468	2.1134	1.46	5.080	38.00	2280	3.283
1.22	3.330	24.91	1495	2.1522	1.47	5.160	38.60	2316	3.335
1.23	3.390	25.36	1521	2.1910	1.48	5.240	39.20	2352	3.387
1.24	3.460	25.88	1553	2.2362	1.49	5.330	39.87	2392	3.445
1.25	3.520	26.33	1580	2.2750	1.50	5.420	40.55	2432	3.503

14

14-5: 2 ft. H Flume Discharge Table

Source: U.S.D.A. Handbook No. 224

Formulas: GPS = CFS x 7.481 GPM = CFS x 448.8
MGD = CFS x 0.6463

Head Feet	CFS	GPS	GPM	MGD	Head Feet	CFS	GPS	GPM	MGD
0.01	0.0005	0.0037	0.2244	0.0003	0.51	0.5300	3.965	237.9	0.3425
0.02	0.0014	0.0105	0.6283	0.0009	0.52	0.5520	4.130	247.7	0.3568
0.03	0.0031	0.0232	1.391	0.0020	0.53	0.5740	4.294	257.6	0.3710
0.04	0.0050	0.0374	2.244	0.0032	0.54	0.5970	4.466	267.9	0.3858
0.05	0.0073	0.0546	3.276	0.0047	0.55	0.6200	4.638	278.3	0.4007
0.06	0.0100	0.0748	4.488	0.0065	0.56	0.6440	4.818	289.0	0.4162
0.07	0.0130	0.0973	5.834	0.0084	0.57	0.6680	4.997	299.8	0.4317
0.08	0.0166	0.1242	7.450	0.0107	0.58	0.6930	5.184	311.0	0.4479
0.09	0.0205	0.1534	9.200	0.0132	0.59	0.7190	5.379	322.7	0.4647
0.10	0.0248	0.1855	11.13	0.0160	0.60	0.7450	5.573	334.4	0.4815
0.11	0.0293	0.2192	13.15	0.0189	0.61	0.7710	5.768	346.0	0.4983
0.12	0.0341	0.2551	15.30	0.0220	0.62	0.7980	5.970	358.1	0.5157
0.13	0.0392	0.2933	17.59	0.0253	0.63	0.8260	6.179	370.7	0.5338
0.14	0.0447	0.3344	20.06	0.0289	0.64	0.8540	6.389	383.3	0.5519
0.15	0.0505	0.3778	22.66	0.0326	0.65	0.8820	6.598	395.8	0.5700
0.16	0.0567	0.4242	25.45	0.0366	0.66	0.9110	6.815	408.9	0.5888
0.17	0.0632	0.4728	28.36	0.0408	0.67	0.9410	7.040	422.3	0.6082
0.18	0.0701	0.5244	31.46	0.0453	0.68	0.9710	7.264	435.8	0.6276
0.19	0.0774	0.5790	34.74	0.0500	0.69	1.002	7.496	449.7	0.6476
0.20	0.0850	0.6359	38.15	0.0549	0.70	1.030	7.705	462.3	0.6657
0.21	0.0930	0.6957	41.74	0.0601	0.71	1.070	8.005	480.2	0.6915
0.22	0.1015	0.7593	45.55	0.0656	0.72	1.100	8.229	493.7	0.7109
0.23	0.1103	0.8252	49.50	0.0713	0.73	1.130	8.454	507.1	0.7303
0.24	0.1195	0.8940	53.63	0.0772	0.74	1.160	8.678	520.6	0.7497
0.25	0.1290	0.9650	57.90	0.0834	0.75	1.200	8.977	538.6	0.7756
0.26	0.1390	1.040	62.38	0.0898	0.76	1.230	9.202	552.0	0.7949
0.27	0.1494	1.118	67.05	0.0966	0.77	1.270	9.501	570.0	0.8208
0.28	0.1602	1.198	71.90	0.1035	0.78	1.300	9.725	583.4	0.8402
0.29	0.1714	1.282	76.92	0.1108	0.79	1.340	10.02	601.4	0.8660
0.30	0.1830	1.369	82.13	0.1183	0.80	1.380	10.32	619.3	0.8919
0.31	0.1950	1.459	87.52	0.1260	0.81	1.420	10.62	637.3	0.9177
0.32	0.2070	1.549	92.90	0.1338	0.82	1.460	10.92	655.2	0.9436
0.33	0.2200	1.646	98.74	0.1422	0.83	1.490	11.15	668.7	0.9630
0.34	0.2340	1.751	105.0	0.1512	0.84	1.530	11.45	686.7	0.9888
0.35	0.2480	1.855	111.3	0.1603	0.85	1.570	11.75	704.6	1.015
0.36	0.2620	1.960	117.6	0.1693	0.86	1.620	12.12	727.1	1.047
0.37	0.2760	2.065	123.9	0.1784	0.87	1.660	12.42	745.0	1.073
0.38	0.2910	2.177	130.6	0.1881	0.88	1.700	12.72	763.0	1.099
0.39	0.3070	2.297	137.8	0.1984	0.89	1.740	13.02	780.9	1.125
0.40	0.3230	2.416	145.0	0.2088	0.90	1.780	13.32	798.9	1.150
0.41	0.3390	2.536	152.1	0.2191	0.91	1.830	13.69	821.3	1.183
0.42	0.3560	2.663	159.8	0.2301	0.92	1.870	13.99	839.3	1.209
0.43	0.3740	2.798	167.9	0.2417	0.93	1.920	14.36	861.7	1.241
0.44	0.3920	2.933	175.9	0.2533	0.94	1.960	14.66	879.6	1.267
0.45	0.4100	3.067	184.0	0.2650	0.95	2.010	15.04	902.1	1.299
0.46	0.4290	3.209	192.5	0.2773	0.96	2.060	15.41	924.5	1.331
0.47	0.4480	3.351	201.1	0.2895	0.97	2.100	15.71	942.5	1.357
0.48	0.4680	3.501	210.0	0.3025	0.98	2.150	16.08	964.9	1.390
0.49	0.4880	3.651	219.0	0.3154	0.99	2.200	16.46	987.4	1.422
0.50	0.5090	3.808	228.4	0.3290	1.00	2.250	16.83	1010	1.454

14

14-5: 2 ft. H Flume Discharge Table *(Continued)*

Source: U.S.D.A. Handbook No. 224
Formulas: GPS = CFS x 7.481
MGD = CFS x 0.6463

Head Feet	CFS	GPS	GPM	MGD	Head Feet	CFS	GPS	GPM	MGD
1.01	2.300	17.21	1032	1.486	1.51	5.740	42.94	2576	3.710
1.02	2.350	17.58	1055	1.519	1.52	5.830	43.61	2617	3.768
1.03	2.400	17.95	1077	1.551	1.53	8.920	66.73	4003	5.765
1.04	2.450	18.33	1100	1.583	1.54	6.010	44.96	2697	3.884
1.05	2.510	18.78	1126	1.622	1.55	6.110	45.71	2742	3.949
1.06	2.560	19.15	1149	1.655	1.56	6.200	46.38	2783	4.007
1.07	2.620	19.60	1176	1.693	1.57	6.290	47.06	2823	4.065
1.08	2.670	19.97	1198	1.726	1.58	6.380	47.73	2863	4.123
1.09	2.730	20.42	1225	1.764	1.59	6.480	48.48	2908	4.188
1.10	2.780	20.80	1248	1.797	1.60	6.580	49.22	2953	4.253
1.11	2.840	21.25	1275	1.835	1.61	6.670	49.90	2993	4.311
1.12	2.900	21.69	1302	1.874	1.62	6.770	50.65	3038	4.375
1.13	2.960	22.14	1328	1.913	1.63	6.870	51.39	3083	4.440
1.14	3.020	22.59	1355	1.952	1.64	6.970	52.14	3128	4.505
1.15	3.080	23.04	1382	1.991	1.65	7.070	52.89	3173	4.569
1.16	3.140	23.49	1409	2.029	1.66	7.170	53.64	3218	4.634
1.17	3.200	23.94	1436	2.068	1.67	7.270	54.39	3263	4.699
1.18	3.260	24.39	1463	2.107	1.68	7.370	55.13	3308	4.763
1.19	3.320	24.84	1490	2.146	1.69	7.470	55.88	3353	4.828
1.20	3.380	25.29	1517	2.184	1.70	7.580	56.71	3402	4.899
1.21	3.450	25.81	1548	2.230	1.71	7.680	57.45	3447	4.964
1.22	3.510	26.26	1575	2.269	1.72	7.790	58.28	3496	5.035
1.23	3.580	26.78	1607	2.314	1.73	7.900	59.10	3546	5.106
1.24	3.650	27.31	1638	2.359	1.74	8.000	59.85	3590	5.170
1.25	3.710	27.75	1665	2.398	1.75	8.110	60.67	3640	5.241
1.26	3.780	28.28	1696	2.443	1.76	8.220	61.49	3689	5.313
1.27	3.850	28.80	1728	2.488	1.77	8.330	62.32	3739	5.384
1.28	3.920	29.33	1759	2.533	1.78	8.440	63.14	3788	5.455
1.29	3.990	29.85	1791	2.579	1.79	8.560	64.04	3842	5.532
1.30	4.060	30.37	1822	2.624	1.80	8.670	64.86	3891	5.603
1.31	4.130	30.90	1854	2.669	1.81	8.780	65.68	3940	5.675
1.32	4.200	31.42	1885	2.714	1.82	8.900	66.58	3994	5.752
1.33	4.280	32.02	1921	2.766	1.83	9.010	67.40	4044	5.823
1.34	4.350	32.54	1952	2.811	1.84	9.130	68.30	4098	5.901
1.35	4.430	33.14	1988	2.863	1.85	9.240	69.12	4147	5.972
1.36	4.500	33.66	2020	2.908	1.86	9.360	70.02	4201	6.049
1.37	4.580	34.26	2056	2.960	1.87	9.480	70.92	4255	6.127
1.38	4.660	34.86	2091	3.012	1.88	9.600	71.82	4308	6.204
1.39	4.740	35.46	2127	3.063	1.89	9.720	72.72	4362	6.282
1.40	4.820	36.06	2163	3.115	1.90	9.850	73.69	4421	6.366
1.41	4.900	36.66	2199ʼ	3.167	1.91	9.970	74.59	4475	6.444
1.42	4.980	37.26	2235	3.219	1.92	10.09	75.48	4528	6.521
1.43	5.060	37.85	2271	3.270	1.93	10.21	76.38	4582	6.599
1.44	5.140	38.45	2307	3.322	1.94	10.34	77.35	4641	6.683
1.45	5.230	39.13	2347	3.380	1.95	10.47	78.33	4699	6.767
1.46	5.310	39.72	2383	3.432	1.96	10.60	79.30	4757	6.851
1.47	5.400	40.40	2424	3.490	1.97	10.72	80.20	4811	6.928
1.48	5.480	41.00	2459	3.542	1.98	10.85	81.17	4869	7.012
1.49	5.570	41.67	2500	3.600	1.99	10.98	82.14	4928	7.096
1.50	5.650	42.27	2536	3.652	2.00	11.10	83.04	4982	7.174

14

14-6: 2 ¹/₂ ft. H Flume Discharge Table

Source: U.S.D.A. Handbook No. 224
Formulas: GPS = CFS x 7.481   GPM = CFS x 448.8
MGD = CFS x 0.6463

Head Feet	CFS	GPS	GPM	MGD	Head Feet	CFS	GPS	GPM	MGD
0.01	0.0007	0.0052	0.3142	0.0005	0.51	0.5870	4.391	263.4	0.3794
0.02	0.0018	0.0135	0.8078	0.0012	0.52	0.6110	4.571	274.2	0.3949
0.03	0.0038	0.0284	1.705	0.0025	0.53	0.6350	4.750	285.0	0.4104
0.04	0.0061	0.0456	2.738	0.0039	0.54	0.6590	4.930	295.8	0.4259
0.05	0.0089	0.0666	3.994	0.0058	0.55	0.6840	5.117	307.0	0.4421
0.06	0.0121	0.0905	5.430	0.0078	0.56	0.7100	5.312	318.6	0.4589
0.07	0.0158	0.1182	7.091	0.0102	0.57	0.7360	5.506	330.3	0.4757
0.08	0.0200	0.1496	8.976	0.0129	0.58	0.7630	5.708	342.4	0.4931
0.09	0.0247	0.1848	11.09	0.0160	0.59	0.7900	5.910	354.6	0.5106
0.10	0.0298	0.2229	13.37	0.0193	0.60	0.8180	6.119	367.1	0.5287
0.11	0.0350	0.2618	15.71	0.0226	0.61	0.8460	6.329	379.7	0.5468
0.12	0.0406	0.3037	18.22	0.0262	0.62	0.8750	6.546	392.7	0.5655
0.13	0.0465	0.3479	20.87	0.0301	0.63	0.9040	6.763	405.7	0.5843
0.14	0.0528	0.3950	23.70	0.0341	0.64	0.9340	6.987	419.2	0.6036
0.15	0.0595	0.4451	26.70	0.0385	0.65	0.9650	7.219	433.1	0.6237
0.16	0.0666	0.4982	29.89	0.0430	0.66	0.9960	7.451	447.0	0.6437
0.17	0.0741	0.5543	33.26	0.0479	0.67	1.027	7.683	460.9	0.6638
0.18	0.0820	0.6134	36.80	0.0530	0.68	1.059	7.922	475.3	0.6844
0.19	0.0903	0.6755	40.53	0.0584	0.69	1.092	8.169	490.1	0.7058
0.20	0.0990	0.7406	44.43	0.0640	0.70	1.130	8.454	507.1	0.7303
0.21	0.1081	0.8087	48.52	0.0699	0.71	1.160	8.678	520.6	0.7497
0.22	0.1176	0.8798	52.78	0.0760	0.72	1.190	8.902	534.1	0.7691
0.23	0.1275	0.9538	57.22	0.0824	0.73	1.230	9.202	552.0	0.7949
0.24	0.1379	1.032	61.89	0.0891	0.74	1.270	9.501	570.0	0.8208
0.25	0.1486	1.112	66.69	0.0960	0.75	1.300	9.725	583.4	0.8402
0.26	0.1597	1.195	71.67	0.1032	0.76	1.340	10.02	601.4	0.8660
0.27	0.1713	1.281	76.88	0.1107	0.77	1.380	10.32	619.3	0.8919
0.28	0.1834	1.372	82.31	0.1185	0.78	1.410	10.55	632.8	0.9113
0.29	0.1960	1.466	87.96	0.1267	0.79	1.450	10.85	650.8	0.9371
0.30	0.2090	1.564	93.80	0.1351	0.80	1.490	11.15	668.7	0.9630
0.31	0.2220	1.661	99.63	0.1435	0.81	1.530	11.45	686.7	0.9888
0.32	0.2360	1.766	105.9	0.1525	0.82	1.570	11.75	704.6	1.015
0.33	0.2500	1.870	112.2	0.1616	0.83	1.610	12.04	722.6	1.041
0.34	0.2650	1.982	118.9	0.1713	0.84	1.650	12.34	740.5	1.066
0.35	0.2800	2.095	125.7	0.1810	0.85	1.700	12.72	763.0	1.099
0.36	0.2960	2.214	132.8	0.1913	0.86	1.740	13.02	780.9	1.125
0.37	0.3120	2.334	140.0	0.2016	0.87	1.780	13.32	798.9	1.150
0.38	0.3280	2.454	147.2	0.2120	0.88	1.830	13.69	821.3	1.183
0.39	0.3450	2.581	154.8	0.2230	0.89	1.870	13.99	839.3	1.209
0.40	0.3630	2.716	162.9	0.2346	0.90	1.920	14.36	861.7	1.241
0.41	0.3810	2.850	171.0	0.2462	0.91	1.960	14.66	879.6	1.267
0.42	0.3990	2.985	179.1	0.2579	0.92	2.010	15.04	902.1	1.299
0.43	0.4180	3.127	187.6	0.2702	0.93	2.060	15.41	924.5	1.331
0.44	0.4370	3.269	196.1	0.2824	0.94	2.110	15.78	947.0	1.364
0.45	0.4570	3.419	205.1	0.2954	0.95	2.160	16.16	969.4	1.396
0.46	0.4780	3.576	214.5	0.3089	0.96	2.210	16.53	991.8	1.428
0.47	0.4990	3.733	224.0	0.3225	0.97	2.260	16.91	1014	1.461
0.48	0.5200	3.890	233.4	0.3361	0.98	2.310	17.28	1037	1.493
0.49	0.5420	4.055	243.2	0.3503	0.99	2.360	17.66	1059	1.525
0.50	0.5640	4.219	253.1	0.3645	1.00	2.410	18.03	1082	1.558

14

Source: U.S.D.A. Handbook No. 224
Formulas: GPS = CFS x 7.481
MGD = CFS x 0.6463

Head Feet	CFS	GPS	GPM	MGD	Head Feet	CFS	GPS	GPM	MGD
1.01	2.460	18.40	1104	1.590	1.51	6.000	44.89	2693	3.878
1.02	2.510	18.78	1126	1.622	1.52	6.090	45.56	2733	3.936
1.03	2.570	19.23	1153	1.661	1.53	6.180	46.23	2774	3.994
1.04	2.620	19.60	1176	1.693	1.54	6.270	46.91	2814	4.052
1.05	2.680	20.05	1203	1.732	1.55	6.370	47.65	2859	4.117
1.06	2.740	20.50	1230	1.771	1.56	6.460	48.33	2899	4.175
1.07	2.790	20.87	1252	1.803	1.57	6.550	49.00	2940	4.233
1.08	2.850	21.32	1279	1.842	1.58	6.650	49.75	2985	4.298
1.09	2.910	21.77	1306	1.881	1.59	6.750	50.50	3029	4.363
1.10	2.970	22.22	1333	1.920	1.60	6.840	51.17	3070	4.421
1.11	3.030	22.67	1360	1.958	1.61	6.940	51.92	3115	4.485
1.12	3.090	23.12	1387	1.997	1.62	7.040	52.67	3160	4.550
1.13	3.150	23.57	1414	2.036	1.63	7.140	53.41	3204	4.615
1.14	3.210	24.01	1441	2.075	1.64	7.240	54.16	3249	4.679
1.15	3.270	24.46	1468	2.113	1.65	7.340	54.91	3294	4.744
1.16	3.330	24.91	1495	2.152	1.66	7.450	55.73	3344	4.815
1.17	3.400	25.44	1526	2.197	1.67	7.550	56.48	3388	4.880
1.18	3.460	25.88	1553	2.236	1.68	7.660	57.30	3438	4.951
1.19	3.530	26.41	1584	2.281	1.69	7.760	58.05	3483	5.015
1.20	3.590	26.86	1611	2.320	1.70	7.860	58.80	3528	5.080
1.21	3.660	27.38	1643	2.365	1.71	7.970	59.62	3577	5.151
1.22	3.730	27.90	1674	2.411	1.72	8.080	60.45	3626	5.222
1.23	3.800	28.43	1705	2.456	1.73	8.190	61.27	3676	5.293
1.24	3.860	28.88	1732	2.495	1.74	8.300	62.09	3725	5.364
1.25	3.930	29.40	1764	2.540	1.75	8.410	62.92	3774	5.435
1.26	4.000	29.92	1795	2.585	1.76	8.530	63.81	3828	5.513
1.27	4.070	30.45	1827	2.630	1.77	8.640	64.64	3878	5.584
1.28	4.150	31.05	1863	2.682	1.78	8.750	65.46	3927	5.655
1.29	4.220	31.57	1894	2.727	1.79	8.870	66.36	3981	5.733
1.30	4.290	32.09	1925	2.773	1.80	8.980	67.18	4030	5.804
1.31	4.370	32.69	1961	2.824	1.81	9.100	68.08	4084	5.881
1.32	4.440	33.22	1993	2.870	1.82	9.220	68.97	4138	5.959
1.33	4.520	33.81	2029	2.921	1.83	9.340	69.87	4192	6.036
1.34	4.590	34.34	2060	2.967	1.84	9.450	70.70	4241	6.108
1.35	4.670	34.94	2096	3.018	1.85	9.570	71.59	4295	6.185
1.36	4.750	35.53	2132	3.070	1.86	9.700	72.57	4353	6.269
1.37	4.820	36.06	2163	3.115	1.87	9.820	73.46	4407	6.347
1.38	4.900	36.66	2199	3.167	1.88	9.940	74.36	4461	6.424
1.39	4.980	37.26	2235	3.219	1.89	10.06	75.26	4515	6.502
1.40	5.060	37.85	2271	3.270	1.90	10.20	76.31	4578	6.592
1.41	5.150	38.53	2311	3.328	1.91	10.30	77.05	4623	6.657
1.42	5.230	39.13	2347	3.380	1.92	10.40	77.80	4668	6.722
1.43	5.310	39.72	2383	3.432	1.93	10.60	79.30	4757	6.851
1.44	5.390	40.32	2419	3.484	1.94	10.70	80.05	4802	6.915
1.45	5.480	41.00	2459	3.542	1.95	10.80	80.79	4847	6.980
1.46	5.560	41.59	2495	3.593	1.96	11.00	82.29	4937	7.109
1.47	5.650	42.27	2536	3.652	1.97	11.10	83.04	4982	7.174
1.48	5.740	42.94	2576	3.710	1.98	11.20	83.79	5027	7.239
1.49	5.820	43.54	2612	3.761	1.99	11.40	85.28	5116	7.368
1.50	5.910	44.21	2652	3.820	2.00	11.50	86.03	5161	7.432

14

14-6: 2 ¹/₂ ft. H Flume Discharge Table *(Continued)*

Source: U.S.D.A. Handbook No. 224
Formulas: GPS = CFS x 7.481   GPM = CFS x 448.8
MGD = CFS x 0.6463

Head Feet	CFS	GPS	GPM	MGD	Head Feet	CFS	GPS	GPM	MGD
2.01	11.60	86.78	5206	7.497	2.26	15.30	114.5	6867	9.888
2.02	11.80	88.28	5296	7.626	2.27	15.50	116.0	6956	10.02
2.03	11.90	89.02	5341	7.691	2.28	15.60	116.7	7001	10.08
2.04	12.00	89.77	5386	7.756	2.29	15.80	118.2	7091	10.21
2.05	12.20	91.27	5475	7.885	2.30	16.00	119.7	7181	10.34
2.06	12.30	92.02	5520	7.949	2.31	16.10	120.4	7226	10.41
2.07	12.50	93.51	5610	8.079	2.32	16.30	121.9	7315	10.53
2.08	12.60	94.26	5655	8.143	2.33	16.40	122.7	7360	10.60
2.09	12.70	95.01	5700	8.208	2.34	16.60	124.2	7450	10.73
2.10	12.90	96.50	5790	8.337	2.35	16.80	125.7	7540	10.86
2.11	13.00	97.25	5834	8.402	2.36	17.00	127.2	7630	10.99
2.12	13.20	98.75	5924	8.531	2.37	17.10	127.9	7674	11.05
2.13	13.30	99.50	5969	8.596	2.38	17.30	129.4	7764	11.18
2.14	13.50	101.0	6059	8.725	2.39	17.50	130.9	7854	11.31
2.15	13.60	101.7	6104	8.790	2.40	17.60	131.7	7899	11.37
2.16	13.80	103.2	6193	8.919	2.41	17.80	133.2	7989	11.50
2.17	13.90	104.0	6238	8.984	2.42	18.00	134.7	8078	11.63
2.18	14.10	105.5	6328	9.113	2.43	18.20	136.2	8168	11.76
2.19	14.20	106.2	6373	9.177	2.44	18.30	136.9	8213	11.83
2.20	14.40	107.7	6463	9.307	2.45	18.50	138.4	8303	11.96
2.21	14.50	108.5	6508	9.371	2.46	18.70	139.9	8393	12.09
2.22	14.70	110.0	6597	9.501	2.47	18.90	141.4	8482	12.22
2.23	14.80	110.7	6642	9.565	2.48	19.10	142.9	8572	12.34
2.24	15.00	112.2	6732	9.694	2.49	19.20	143.6	8617	12.41
2.25	15.10	113.0	6777	9.759	2.50	19.40	145.1	8707	12.54

14

14-7: 3 ft. H Flume Discharge Table

Source: U.S.D.A. Handbook No. 224
Formulas: GPS = CFS x 7.481   GPM = CFS x 448.8
          MGD = CFS x 0.6463

Head Feet	CFS	GPS	GPM	MGD	Head Feet	CFS	GPS	GPM	MGD
0.01	0.0010	0.0075	0.4488	0.0006	0.51	0.6440	4.818	289.0	0.4162
0.02	0.0021	0.0157	0.9425	0.0014	0.52	0.6690	5.005	300.2	0.4324
0.03	0.0045	0.0337	2.020	0.0029	0.53	0.6950	5.199	311.9	0.4492
0.04	0.0073	0.0546	3.276	0.0047	0.54	0.7210	5.394	323.6	0.4660
0.05	0.0105	0.0786	4.712	0.0068	0.55	0.7480	5.596	335.7	0.4834
0.06	0.0143	0.1070	6.418	0.0092	0.56	0.7750	5.798	347.8	0.5009
0.07	0.0186	0.1391	8.348	0.0120	0.57	0.8030	6.007	360.4	0.5190
0.08	0.0234	0.1751	10.50	0.0151	0.58	0.8320	6.224	373.4	0.5377
0.09	0.0288	0.2155	12.93	0.0186	0.59	0.8610	6.441	386.4	0.5565
0.10	0.0347	0.2596	15.57	0.0224	0.60	0.8900	6.658	399.4	0.5752
0.11	0.0407	0.3045	18.27	0.0263	0.61	0.9200	6.883	412.9	0.5946
0.12	0.0471	0.3524	21.14	0.0304	0.62	0.9510	7.114	426.8	0.6146
0.13	0.0538	0.4025	24.15	0.0348	0.63	0.9820	7.346	440.7	0.6347
0.14	0.0610	0.4563	27.38	0.0394	0.64	1.014	7.586	455.1	0.6553
0.15	0.0686	0.5132	30.79	0.0443	0.65	1.047	7.833	469.9	0.6767
0.16	0.0766	0.5730	34.38	0.0495	0.66	1.080	8.079	484.7	0.6980
0.17	0.0851	0.6366	38.19	0.0550	0.67	1.113	8.326	499.5	0.7193
0.18	0.0939	0.7025	42.14	0.0607	0.68	1.147	8.581	514.8	0.7413
0.19	0.1032	0.7720	46.32	0.0667	0.69	1.182	8.843	530.5	0.7639
0.20	0.1130	0.8454	50.71	0.0730	0.70	1.220	9.127	547.5	0.7885
0.21	0.1230	0.9202	55.20	0.0795	0.71	1.250	9.351	561.0	0.8079
0.22	0.1340	1.002	60.14	0.0866	0.72	1.290	9.650	579.0	0.8337
0.23	0.1450	1.085	65.08	0.0937	0.73	1.330	9.950	596.9	0.8596
0.24	0.1560	1.167	70.01	0.1008	0.74	1.360	10.17	610.4	0.8790
0.25	0.1680	1.257	75.40	0.1086	0.75	1.400	10.47	628.3	0.9048
0.26	0.1800	1.347	80.78	0.1163	0.76	1.440	10.77	646.3	0.9307
0.27	0.1930	1.444	86.62	0.1247	0.77	1.480	11.07	664.2	0.9565
0.28	0.2070	1.549	92.90	0.1338	0.78	1.520	11.37	682.2	0.9824
0.29	0.2200	1.646	98.74	0.1422	0.79	1.560	11.67	700.1	1.008
0.30	0.2340	1.751	105.0	0.1512	0.80	1.600	11.97	718.1	1.034
0.31	0.2490	1.863	111.8	0.1609	0.81	1.650	12.34	740.5	1.066
0.32	0.2640	1.975	118.5	0.1706	0.82	1.690	12.64	758.5	1.092
0.33	0.2800	2.095	125.7	0.1810	0.83	1.730	12.94	776.4	1.118
0.34	0.2960	2.214	132.8	0.1913	0.84	1.780	13.32	798.9	1.150
0.35	0.3120	2.334	140.0	0.2016	0.85	1.820	13.62	816.8	1.176
0.36	0.3290	2.461	147.7	0.2126	0.86	1.860	13.91	834.8	1.202
0.37	0.3470	2.596	155.7	0.2243	0.87	1.910	14.29	857.2	1.234
0.38	0.3650	2.731	163.8	0.2359	0.88	1.960	14.66	879.6	1.267
0.39	0.3830	2.865	171.9	0.2475	0.89	2.000	14.96	897.6	1.293
0.40	0.4020	3.007	180.4	0.2598	0.90	2.050	15.34	920.0	1.325
0.41	0.4210	3.150	188.9	0.2721	0.91	2.100	15.71	942.5	1.357
0.42	0.4410	3.299	197.9	0.2850	0.92	2.150	16.08	964.9	1.390
0.43	0.4620	3.456	207.3	0.2986	0.93	2.200	16.46	987.4	1.422
0.44	0.4830	3.613	216.8	0.3122	0.94	2.250	16.83	1010	1.454
0.45	0.5040	3.770	226.2	0.3257	0.95	2.300	17.21	1032	1.486
0.46	0.5260	3.935	236.1	0.3400	0.96	2.350	17.58	1055	1.519
0.47	0.5490	4.107	246.4	0.3548	0.97	2.410	18.03	1082	1.558
0.48	0.5720	4.279	256.7	0.3697	0.98	2.460	18.40	1104	1.590
0.49	0.5960	4.459	267.5	0.3852	0.99	2.510	18.78	1126	1.622
0.50	0.6200	4.638	278.3	0.4007	1.00	2.570	19.23	1153	1.661

14

14-7: 3 ft. H Flume Discharge Table (Continued)

Source: U.S.D.A. Handbook No. 224
Formulas: GPS = CFS x 7.481
MGD = CFS x 0.6463

Head Feet	CFS	GPS	GPM	MGD	Head Feet	CFS	GPS	GPM	MGD
1.01	2.620	19.60	1176	1.693	1.51	6.300	47.13	2827	4.072
1.02	2.680	20.05	1203	1.732	1.52	6.390	47.80	2868	4.130
1.03	2.730	20.42	1225	1.764	1.53	6.480	48.48	2908	4.188
1.04	2.790	20.87	1252	1.803	1.54	6.580	49.22	2953	4.253
1.05	2.850	21.32	1279	1.842	1.55	6.670	49.90	2993	4.311
1.06	2.910	21.77	1306	1.881	1.56	6.770	50.65	3038	4.375
1.07	2.970	22.22	1333	1.920	1.57	6.870	51.39	3083	4.440
1.08	3.030	22.67	1360	1.958	1.58	6.960	52.07	3124	4.498
1.09	3.090	23.12	1387	1.997	1.59	7.060	52.82	3169	4.563
1.10	3.150	23.57	1414	2.036	1.60	7.160	53.56	3213	4.628
1.11	3.210	24.01	1441	2.075	1.61	7.260	54.31	3258	4.692
1.12	3.270	24.46	1468	2.113	1.62	7.360	55.06	3303	4.757
1.13	3.340	24.99	1499	2.159	1.63	7.470	55.88	3353	4.828
1.14	3.400	25.44	1526	2.197	1.64	7.570	56.63	3397	4.892
1.15	3.460	25.88	1553	2.236	1.65	7.670	57.38	3442	4.957
1.16	3.530	26.41	1584	2.281	1.66	7.780	58.20	3492	5.028
1.17	3.600	26.93	1616	2.327	1.67	7.880	58.95	3537	5.093
1.18	3.660	27.38	1643	2.365	1.68	7.990	59.77	3586	5.164
1.19	3.730	27.90	1674	2.411	1.69	8.100	60.60	3635	5.235
1.20	3.800	28.43	1705	2.456	1.70	8.200	61.34	3680	5.300
1.21	3.870	28.95	1737	2.501	1.71	8.310	62.17	3730	5.371
1.22	3.940	29.48	1768	2.546	1.72	8.420	62.99	3779	5.442
1.23	4.010	30.00	1800	2.592	1.73	8.530	63.81	3828	5.513
1.24	4.080	30.52	1831	2.637	1.74	8.640	64.64	3878	5.584
1.25	4.150	31.05	1863	2.682	1.75	8.750	65.46	3927	5.655
1.26	4.230	31.64	1898	2.734	1.76	8.870	66.36	3981	5.733
1.27	4.300	32.17	1930	2.779	1.77	8.980	67.18	4030	5.804
1.28	4.370	32.69	1961	2.824	1.78	9.100	68.08	4084	5.881
1.29	4.450	33.29	1997	2.876	1.79	9.210	68.90	4133	5.952
1.30	4.530	33.89	2033	2.928	1.80	9.330	69.80	4187	6.030
1.31	4.600	34.41	2064	2.973	1.81	9.450	70.70	4241	6.108
1.32	4.680	35.01	2100	3.025	1.82	9.560	71.52	4291	6.179
1.33	4.760	35.61	2136	3.076	1.83	9.680	72.42	4344	6.256
1.34	4.840	36.21	2172	3.128	1.84	9.800	73.31	4398	6.334
1.35	4.920	36.81	2208	3.180	1.85	9.920	74.21	4452	6.411
1.36	5.000	37.41	2244	3.232	1.86	10.05	75.18	4510	6.495
1.37	5.080	38.00	2280	3.283	1.87	10.17	76.08	4564	6.573
1.38	5.160	38.60	2316	3.335	1.88	10.29	76.98	4618	6.650
1.39	5.240	39.20	2352	3.387	1.89	10.41	77.88	4672	6.728
1.40	5.330	39.87	2392	3.445	1.90	10.50	78.55	4712	6.786
1.41	5.410	40.47	2428	3.496	1.91	10.70	80.05	4802	6.915
1.42	5.500	41.15	2468	3.555	1.92	10.80	80.79	4847	6.980
1.43	5.580	41.74	2504	3.606	1.93	10.90	81.54	4892	7.045
1.44	5.670	42.42	2545	3.665	1.94	11.00	82.29	4937	7.109
1.45	5.760	43.09	2585	3.723	1.95	11.20	83.79	5027	7.239
1.46	5.840	43.69	2621	3.774	1.96	11.30	84.54	5071	7.303
1.47	5.930	44.36	2661	3.833	1.97	11.40	85.28	5116	7.368
1.48	6.020	45.04	2702	3.891	1.98	11.60	86.78	5206	7.497
1.49	6.110	45.71	2742	3.949	1.99	11.70	87.53	5251	7.562
1.50	6.200	46.38	2783	4.007	2.00	11.90	89.02	5341	7.691

14

14-7: 3 ft. H Flume Discharge Table *(Continued)*

Source: U.S.D.A. Handbook No. 224
Formulas: GPS = CFS x 7.481   GPM = CFS x 448.8
MGD = CFS x 0.6463

Head Feet	CFS	GPS	GPM	MGD	Head Feet	CFS	GPS	GPM	MGD
2.01	12.00	89.77	5386	7.756	2.51	20.10	150.4	9021	12.99
2.02	12.10	90.52	5430	7.820	2.52	20.30	151.9	9111	13.12
2.03	12.30	92.02	5520	7.949	2.53	20.50	153.4	9200	13.25
2.04	12.40	92.76	5565	8.014	2.54	20.70	154.9	9290	13.38
2.05	12.60	94.26	5655	8.143	2.55	20.90	156.4	9380	13.51
2.06	12.70	95.01	5700	8.208	2.56	21.10	157.8	9470	13.64
2.07	12.80	95.76	5745	8.273	2.57	21.30	159.3	9559	13.77
2.08	13.00	97.25	5834	8.402	2.58	21.50	160.8	9649	13.90
2.09	13.10	98.00	5879	8.467	2.59	21.70	162.3	9739	14.02
2.10	13.30	99.50	5969	8.596	2.60	21.90	163.8	9829	14.15
2.11	13.40	100.2	6014	8.660	2.61	22.10	165.3	9918	14.28
2.12	13.60	101.7	6104	8.790	2.62	22.30	166.8	10010	14.41
2.13	13.70	102.5	6149	8.854	2.63	22.50	168.3	10100	14.54
2.14	13.90	104.0	6238	8.984	2.64	22.70	169.8	10190	14.67
2.15	14.00	104.7	6283	9.048	2.65	22.90	171.3	10280	14.80
2.16	14.20	106.2	6373	9.177	2.66	23.10	172.8	10370	14.93
2.17	14.30	107.0	6418	9.242	2.67	23.30	174.3	10460	15.06
2.18	14.50	108.5	6508	9.371	2.68	23.50	175.8	10550	15.19
2.19	14.60	109.2	6552	9.436	2.69	23.70	177.3	10640	15.32
2.20	14.80	110.7	6642	9.565	2.70	23.90	178.8	10730	15.45
2.21	14.90	111.5	6687	9.630	2.71	24.10	180.3	10820	15.58
2.22	15.10	113.0	6777	9.759	2.72	24.30	181.8	10910	15.71
2.23	15.30	114.5	6867	9.888	2.73	24.50	183.3	11000	15.83
2.24	15.40	115.2	6912	9.953	2.74	24.70	184.8	11090	15.96
2.25	15.60	116.7	7001	10.08	2.75	24.90	186.3	11180	16.09
2.26	15.70	117.5	7046	10.15	2.76	25.20	188.5	11310	16.29
2.27	15.90	118.9	7136	10.28	2.77	25.40	190.0	11400	16.42
2.28	16.10	120.4	7226	10.41	2.78	25.60	191.5	11490	16.55
2.29	16.20	121.2	7271	10.47	2.79	25.80	193.0	11580	16.67
2.30	16.40	122.7	7360	10.60	2.80	26.00	194.5	11670	16.80
2.31	16.60	124.2	7450	10.73	2.81	26.20	196.0	11760	16.93
2.32	16.70	124.9	7495	10.79	2.82	26.50	198.2	11890	17.13
2.33	16.90	126.4	7585	10.92	2.83	26.70	199.7	11980	17.26
2.34	17.10	127.9	7674	11.05	2.84	26.90	201.2	12070	17.39
2.35	17.20	128.7	7719	11.12	2.85	27.10	202.7	12160	17.51
2.36	17.40	130.2	7809	11.25	2.86	27.40	205.0	12300	17.71
2.37	17.60	131.7	7899	11.37	2.87	27.60	206.5	12390	17.84
2.38	17.80	133.2	7989	11.50	2.88	27.80	208.0	12480	17.97
2.39	17.90	133.9	8034	11.57	2.89	28.00	209.5	12570	18.10
2.40	18.10	135.4	8123	11.70	2.90	28.30	211.7	12700	18.29
2.41	18.30	136.9	8213	11.83	2.91	28.50	213.2	12790	18.42
2.42	18.50	138.4	8303	11.96	2.92	28.70	214.7	12880	18.55
2.43	18.70	139.9	8393	12.09	2.93	28.90	216.2	12970	18.68
2.44	18.80	140.6	8437	12.15	2.94	29.20	218.4	13110	18.87
2.45	19.00	142.1	8527	12.28	2.95	29.40	219.9	13200	19.00
2.46	19.20	143.6	8617	12.41	2.96	29.70	222.2	13330	19.20
2.47	19.40	145.1	8707	12.54	2.97	29.90	223.7	13420	19.32
2.48	19.60	146.6	8796	12.67	2.98	30.10	225.2	13510	19.45
2.49	19.80	148.1	8886	12.80	2.99	30.40	227.4	13640	19.65
2.50	19.90	148.9	8931	12.86	3.00	30.70	229.7	13780	19.84

14

14-8: 4 1/2 ft. H Flume Discharge Table

Source: U.S.D.A. Handbook No. 224
Formulas: GPS = CFS x 7.481   GPM = CFS x 448.8
MGD = CFS x 0.6463

Head Feet	CFS	GPS	GPM	MGD	Head Feet	CFS	GPS	GPM	MGD
0.01	0.0025	0.0187	1.122	0.0016	0.51	0.8150	6.097	365.8	0.5267
0.02	0.0031	0.0232	1.391	0.0020	0.52	0.8450	6.321	379.2	0.5461
0.03	0.0066	0.0494	2.962	0.0043	0.53	0.8760	6.553	393.1	0.5662
0.04	0.0106	0.0793	4.757	0.0069	0.54	0.9070	6.785	407.1	0.5862
0.05	0.0154	0.1152	6.912	0.0100	0.55	0.9390	7.025	421.4	0.6069
0.06	0.0208	0.1556	9.335	0.0134	0.56	0.9720	7.272	436.2	0.6282
0.07	0.0269	0.2012	12.07	0.0174	0.57	1.005	7.518	451.0	0.6495
0.08	0.0337	0.2521	15.12	0.0218	0.58	1.039	7.773	466.3	0.6715
0.09	0.0413	0.3090	18.54	0.0267	0.59	1.073	8.027	481.6	0.6935
0.10	0.0496	0.3711	22.26	0.0321	0.60	1.110	8.304	498.2	0.7174
0.11	0.0578	0.4324	25.94	0.0374	0.61	1.140	8.528	511.6	0.7368
0.12	0.0666	0.4982	29.89	0.0430	0.62	1.180	8.828	529.6	0.7626
0.13	0.0758	0.5671	34.02	0.0490	0.63	1.122	8.394	503.6	0.7251
0.14	0.0855	0.6396	38.37	0.0553	0.64	1.250	9.351	561.0	0.8079
0.15	0.0959	0.7174	43.04	0.0620	0.65	1.290	9.650	579.0	0.8337
0.16	0.1067	0.7982	47.89	0.0690	0.66	1.330	9.950	596.9	0.8596
0.17	0.1180	0.8828	52.96	0.0763	0.67	1.380	10.32	619.3	0.8919
0.18	0.1298	0.9710	58.25	0.0839	0.68	1.410	10.55	632.8	0.9113
0.19	0.1420	1.062	63.73	0.0918	0.69	1.450	10.85	650.8	0.9371
0.20	0.1550	1.160	69.56	0.1002	0.70	1.490	11.15	668.7	0.9630
0.21	0.1680	1.257	75.40	0.1086	0.71	1.530	11.45	686.7	0.9888
0.22	0.1820	1.362	81.68	0.1176	0.72	1.580	11.82	709.1	1.021
0.23	0.1960	1.466	87.96	0.1267	0.73	1.620	12.12	727.1	1.047
0.24	0.2110	1.578	94.70	0.1364	0.74	1.660	12.42	745.0	1.073
0.25	0.2260	1.691	101.4	0.1461	0.75	1.710	12.79	767.4	1.105
0.26	0.2420	1.810	108.6	0.1564	0.76	1.750	13.09	785.4	1.131
0.27	0.2590	1.938	116.2	0.1674	0.77	1.800	13.47	807.8	1.163
0.28	0.2760	2.065	123.9	0.1784	0.78	1.840	13.77	825.8	1.189
0.29	0.2930	2.192	131.5	0.1894	0.79	1.890	14.14	848.2	1.222
0.30	0.3110	2.327	139.6	0.2010	0.80	1.940	14.51	870.7	1.254
0.31	0.3300	2.469	148.1	0.2133	0.81	1.990	14.89	893.1	1.286
0.32	0.3490	2.611	156.6	0.2256	0.82	2.040	15.26	915.6	1.318
0.33	0.3680	2.753	165.2	0.2378	0.83	2.090	15.64	938.0	1.351
0.34	0.3880	2.903	174.1	0.2508	0.84	2.140	16.01	960.4	1.383
0.35	0.4090	3.060	183.6	0.2643	0.85	2.190	16.38	982.9	1.415
0.36	0.4300	3.217	193.0	0.2779	0.86	2.240	16.76	1005	1.448
0.37	0.4520	3.381	202.9	0.2921	0.87	2.290	17.13	1028	1.480
0.38	0.4740	3.546	212.7	0.3063	0.88	2.350	17.58	1055	1.519
0.39	0.4970	3.718	223.1	0.3212	0.89	2.400	17.95	1077	1.551
0.40	0.5200	3.890	233.4	0.3361	0.90	2.450	18.33	1100	1.583
0.41	0.5440	4.070	244.1	0.3516	0.91	2.510	18.78	1126	1.622
0.42	0.5690	4.257	255.4	0.3677	0.92	2.560	19.15	1149	1.655
0.43	0.5940	4.444	266.6	0.3839	0.93	2.620	19.60	1176	1.693
0.44	0.6200	4.638	278.3	0.4007	0.94	2.680	20.05	1203	1.732
0.45	0.6460	4.833	289.9	0.4175	0.95	2.740	20.50	1230	1.771
0.46	0.6730	5.035	302.0	0.4350	0.96	2.790	20.87	1252	1.803
0.47	0.7000	5.237	314.2	0.4524	0.97	2.850	21.32	1279	1.842
0.48	0.7280	5.446	326.7	0.4705	0.98	2.910	21.77	1306	1.881
0.49	0.7560	5.656	339.3	0.4886	0.99	2.980	22.29	1337	1.926
0.50	0.7850	5.873	352.3	0.5073	1.00	3.040	22.74	1364	1.965

14

Source: U.S.D.A. Handbook No. 224
Formulas: GPS = CFS x 7.481   GPM = CFS x 448.8
           MGD = CFS x 0.6463

Head Feet	CFS	GPS	GPM	MGD	Head Feet	CFS	GPS	GPM	MGD
1.01	3.100	23.19	1391	2.004	1.51	7.170	53.64	3218	4.634
1.02	3.160	23.64	1418	2.042	1.52	7.270	54.39	3263	4.699
1.03	3.220	24.09	1445	2.081	1.53	7.370	55.13	3308	4.763
1.04	3.290	24.61	1477	2.126	1.54	7.480	55.96	3357	4.834
1.05	3.350	25.06	1503	2.165	1.55	7.590	56.78	3406	4.905
1.06	3.420	25.59	1535	2.210	1.56	7.690	57.53	3451	4.970
1.07	3.490	26.11	1566	2.256	1.57	7.800	58.35	3501	5.041
1.08	3.550	26.56	1593	2.294	1.58	7.900	59.10	3546	5.106
1.09	3.620	27.08	1625	2.340	1.59	8.010	59.92	3595	5.177
1.10	3.690	27.60	1656	2.385	1.60	8.120	60.75	3644	5.248
1.11	3.760	28.13	1687	2.430	1.61	8.230	61.57	3694	5.319
1.12	3.830	28.65	1719	2.475	1.62	8.340	62.39	3743	5.390
1.13	3.900	29.18	1750	2.521	1.63	7.450	55.73	3344	4.815
1.14	3.970	29.70	1782	2.566	1.64	8.560	64.04	3842	5.532
1.15	4.040	30.22	1813	2.611	1.65	8.680	64.94	3896	5.610
1.16	4.120	30.82	1849	2.663	1.66	8.790	65.76	3945	5.681
1.17	4.190	31.35	1880	2.708	1.67	8.900	66.58	3994	5.752
1.18	4.270	31.94	1916	2.760	1.68	9.020	67.48	4048	5.830
1.19	4.340	32.47	1948	2.805	1.69	9.140	68.38	4102	5.907
1.20	4.420	33.07	1984	2.857	1.70	9.250	69.20	4151	5.978
1.21	4.500	33.66	2020	2.908	1.71	9.370	70.10	4205	6.056
1.22	4.580	34.26	2056	2.960	1.72	9.490	70.99	4259	6.133
1.23	4.650	34.79	2087	3.005	1.73	9.610	71.89	4313	6.211
1.24	4.730	35.39	2123	3.057	1.74	9.730	72.79	4367	6.288
1.25	4.810	35.98	2159	3.109	1.75	9.850	73.69	4421	6.366
1.26	4.890	36.58	2195	3.160	1.76	9.980	74.66	4479	6.450
1.27	4.980	37.26	2235	3.219	1.77	10.10	75.56	4533	6.528
1.28	5.060	37.85	2271	3.270	1.78	10.22	76.46	4587	6.605
1.29	5.140	38.45	2307	3.322	1.79	10.35	77.43	4645	6.689
1.30	5.220	39.05	2343	3.374	1.80	10.50	78.55	4712	6.786
1.31	5.310	39.72	2383	3.432	1.81	10.60	79.30	4757	6.851
1.32	5.390	40.32	2419	3.484	1.82	10.70	80.05	4802	6.915
1.33	5.480	41.00	2459	3.542	1.83	10.80	80.79	4847	6.980
1.34	5.570	41.67	2500	3.600	1.84	11.00	82.29	4937	7.109
1.35	5.660	42.34	2540	3.658	1.85	11.10	83.04	4982	7.174
1.36	5.740	42.94	2576	3.710	1.86	11.20	83.79	5027	7.239
1.37	5.830	43.61	2617	3.768	1.87	11.40	85.28	5116	7.368
1.38	5.920	44.29	2657	3.826	1.88	11.50	86.03	5161	7.432
1.39	6.020	45.04	2702	3.891	1.89	11.60	86.78	5206	7.497
1.40	6.110	45.71	2742	3.949	1.90	11.80	88.28	5296	7.626
1.41	6.200	46.38	2783	4.007	1.91	11.90	89.02	5341	7.691
1.42	6.290	47.06	2823	4.065	1.92	12.00	89.77	5386	7.756
1.43	6.390	47.80	2868	4.130	1.93	12.20	91.27	5475	7.885
1.44	6.480	48.48	2908	4.188	1.94	12.30	92.02	5520	7.949
1.45	6.580	49.22	2953	4.253	1.95	12.50	93.51	5610	8.079
1.46	6.680	49.97	2998	4.317	1.96	12.60	94.26	5655	8.143
1.47	6.770	50.65	3038	4.375	1.97	12.80	95.76	5745	8.273
1.48	6.870	51.39	3083	4.440	1.98	12.90	96.50	5790	8.337
1.49	6.970	52.14	3128	4.505	1.99	13.00	97.25	5834	8.402
1.50	7.070	52.89	3173	4.569	2.00	13.20	98.75	5924	8.531

Source: U.S.D.A. Handbook No. 224
Formulas: GPS = CFS x 7.481   GPM = CFS x 448.8
MGD = CFS x 0.6463

Head Feet	CFS	GPS	GPM	MGD	Head Feet	CFS	GPS	GPM	MGD
2.01	13.30	99.50	5969	8.596	2.51	21.80	163.1	9784	14.09
2.02	13.50	101.0	6059	8.725	2.52	22.00	164.6	9874	14.22
2.03	13.60	101.7	6104	8.790	2.53	22.20	166.1	9963	14.35
2.04	13.70	102.5	6149	8.854	2.54	22.40	167.6	10050	14.48
2.05	13.90	104.0	6238	8.984	2.55	22.60	169.1	10140	14.61
2.06	14.10	105.5	6328	9.113	2.56	22.80	170.6	10230	14.74
2.07	14.20	106.2	6373	9.177	2.57	23.00	172.1	10320	14.86
2.08	14.40	107.7	6463	9.307	2.58	23.20	173.6	10410	14.99
2.09	14.50	108.5	6508	9.371	2.59	23.40	175.1	10500	15.12
2.10	14.70	110.0	6597	9.501	2.60	23.60	176.6	10590	15.25
2.11	14.80	110.7	6642	9.565	2.61	23.80	178.0	10680	15.38
2.12	15.00	112.2	6732	9.694	2.62	24.00	179.5	10770	15.51
2.13	15.20	113.7	6822	9.824	2.63	24.20	181.0	10860	15.64
2.14	15.30	114.5	6867	9.888	2.64	24.40	182.5	10950	15.77
2.15	15.50	116.0	6956	10.02	2.65	24.60	184.0	11040	15.90
2.16	15.60	116.7	7001	10.08	2.66	24.90	186.3	11180	16.09
2.17	15.80	118.2	7091	10.21	2.67	25.10	187.8	11270	16.22
2.18	15.90	118.9	7136	10.28	2.68	25.30	189.3	11360	16.35
2.19	16.10	120.4	7226	10.41	2.69	25.50	190.8	11440	16.48
2.20	16.30	121.9	7315	10.53	2.70	25.70	192.3	11530	16.61
2.21	16.40	122.7	7360	10.60	2.71	25.90	193.8	11620	16.74
2.22	16.60	124.2	7450	10.73	2.72	26.10	195.3	11710	16.87
2.23	16.80	125.7	7540	10.86	2.73	26.40	197.5	11850	17.06
2.24	16.90	126.4	7585	10.92	2.74	26.60	199.0	11940	17.19
2.25	17.10	127.9	7674	11.05	2.75	26.80	200.5	12030	17.32
2.26	17.30	129.4	7764	11.18	2.76	27.00	202.0	12120	17.45
2.27	17.40	130.2	7809	11.25	2.77	27.20	203.5	12210	17.58
2.28	17.60	131.7	7899	11.37	2.78	27.40	205.0	12300	17.71
2.29	17.80	133.2	7989	11.50	2.79	27.70	207.2	12430	17.90
2.30	18.00	134.7	8078	11.63	2.80	27.90	208.7	12520	18.03
2.31	18.10	135.4	8123	11.70	2.81	28.10	210.2	12610	18.16
2.32	18.30	136.9	8213	11.83	2.82	28.40	212.5	12750	18.35
2.33	18.50	138.4	8303	11.96	2.83	28.60	214.0	12840	18.48
2.34	18.70	139.9	8393	12.09	2.84	28.80	215.5	12930	18.61
2.35	18.80	140.6	8437	12.15	2.85	29.00	216.9	13020	18.74
2.36	19.00	142.1	8527	12.28	2.86	29.30	219.2	13150	18.94
2.37	19.20	143.6	8617	12.41	2.87	29.50	220.7	13240	19.07
2.38	19.40	145.1	8707	12.54	2.88	29.70	222.2	13330	19.20
2.39	19.60	146.6	8796	12.67	2.89	30.00	224.4	13460	19.39
2.40	19.70	147.4	8841	12.73	2.90	30.20	225.9	13550	19.52
2.41	19.90	148.9	8931	12.86	2.91	30.40	227.4	13640	19.65
2.42	20.10	150.4	9021	12.99	2.92	30.70	229.7	13780	19.84
2.43	20.30	151.9	9111	13.12	2.93	30.90	231.2	13870	19.97
2.44	20.50	153.4	9200	13.25	2.94	31.20	233.4	14000	20.16
2.45	20.70	154.9	9290	13.38	2.95	31.40	234.9	14090	20.29
2.46	20.90	156.4	9380	13.51	2.96	31.70	237.1	14230	20.49
2.47	21.00	157.1	9425	13.57	2.97	31.90	238.6	14320	20.62
2.48	21.20	158.6	9515	13.70	2.98	32.20	240.9	14450	20.81
2.49	21.40	160.1	9604	13.83	2.99	32.40	242.4	14540	20.94
2.50	21.60	161.6	9694	13.96	3.00	32.70	244.6	14680	21.13

14

Source: U.S.D.A. Handbook No. 224
Formulas: GPS = CFS x 7.481   GPM = CFS x 448.8
MGD = CFS x 0.6463

Head Feet	CFS	GPS	GPM	MGD	Head Feet	CFS	GPS	GPM	MGD
3.01	32.90	246.1	14770	21.26	3.51	47.10	352.4	21140	30.44
3.02	33.20	248.4	14900	21.46	3.52	47.40	354.6	21270	30.63
3.03	33.40	249.9	14990	21.59	3.53	47.70	356.8	21410	30.83
3.04	33.70	252.1	15130	21.78	3.54	48.00	359.1	21540	31.02
3.05	33.90	253.6	15210	21.91	3.55	48.30	361.3	21680	31.22
3.06	34.20	255.9	15350	22.10	3.56	48.60	363.6	21810	31.41
3.07	34.40	257.3	15440	22.23	3.57	49.00	366.6	21990	31.67
3.08	34.70	259.6	15570	22.43	3.58	49.30	368.8	22130	31.86
3.09	35.00	261.8	15710	22.62	3.59	49.60	371.1	22260	32.06
3.10	35.20	263.3	15800	22.75	3.60	49.90	373.3	22400	32.25
3.11	35.50	265.6	15930	22.94	3.61	50.30	376.3	22580	32.51
3.12	35.80	267.8	16070	23.14	3.62	50.60	378.5	22710	32.70
3.13	36.00	269.3	16160	23.27	3.63	50.90	380.8	22840	32.90
3.14	36.30	271.6	16290	23.46	3.64	51.20	383.0	22980	33.09
3.15	36.60	273.8	16430	23.65	3.65	51.60	386.0	23160	33.35
3.16	36.80	275.3	16520	23.78	3.66	51.90	388.3	23290	33.54
3.17	37.10	277.5	16650	23.98	3.67	52.20	390.5	23430	33.74
3.18	37.40	279.8	16790	24.17	3.68	52.60	393.5	23610	34.00
3.19	37.70	282.0	16920	24.37	3.69	52.90	395.7	23740	34.19
3.20	37.90	283.5	17010	24.49	3.70	53.20	398.0	23880	34.38
3.21	38.20	285.8	17140	24.69	3.71	53.60	401.0	24060	34.64
3.22	38.50	288.0	17280	24.88	3.72	53.90	403.2	24190	34.84
3.23	38.80	290.3	17410	25.08	3.73	54.30	406.2	24370	35.09
3.24	39.00	291.8	17500	25.21	3.74	54.60	408.5	24500	35.29
3.25	39.30	294.0	17640	25.40	3.75	54.90	410.7	24640	35.48
3.26	39.60	296.2	17770	25.59	3.76	55.30	413.7	24820	35.74
3.27	39.90	298.5	17910	25.79	3.77	55.60	415.9	24950	35.93
3.28	40.20	300.7	18040	25.98	3.78	56.00	418.9	25130	36.19
3.29	40.50	303.0	18180	26.18	3.79	56.30	421.2	25270	36.39
3.30	40.80	305.2	18310	26.37	3.80	56.70	424.2	25450	36.65
3.31	41.20	308.2	18490	26.63	3.81	57.00	426.4	25580	36.84
3.32	41.30	309.0	18540	26.69	3.82	57.40	429.4	25760	37.10
3.33	41.60	311.2	18670	26.89	3.83	57.70	431.7	25900	37.29
3.34	41.90	313.5	18810	27.08	3.84	58.10	434.6	26080	37.55
3.35	42.20	315.7	18940	27.27	3.85	58.40	436.9	26210	37.74
3.36	42.50	317.9	19070	27.47	3.86	58.80	439.9	26390	38.00
3.37	42.80	320.2	19210	27.66	3.87	59.20	442.9	26570	38.26
3.38	43.10	322.4	19340	27.86	3.88	59.50	445.1	26700	38.45
3.39	43.40	324.7	19480	28.05	3.89	59.90	448.1	26880	38.71
3.40	43.70	326.9	19610	28.24	3.90	60.20	450.4	27020	38.91
3.41	44.00	329.2	19750	28.44	3.91	60.60	453.3	27200	39.17
3.42	44.30	331.4	19880	28.63	3.92	61.00	456.3	27380	39.42
3.43	44.60	333.7	20020	28.82	3.93	61.30	458.6	27510	39.62
3.44	44.90	335.9	20150	29.02	3.94	61.70	461.6	27690	39.88
3.45	45.20	338.1	20290	29.21	3.95	62.10	464.6	27870	40.14
3.46	45.50	340.4	20420	29.41	3.96	62.40	466.8	28010	40.33
3.47	45.80	342.6	20560	29.60	3.97	62.80	469.8	28190	40.59
3.48	46.10	344.9	20690	29.79	3.98	63.20	472.8	28360	40.85
3.49	46.40	347.1	20820	29.99	3.99	63.60	475.8	28540	41.10
3.50	46.80	350.1	21000	30.25	4.00	63.90	478.0	28680	41.30

14

14-8: 4 ¹/₂ ft. H Flume Discharge Table (Continued)

Source: U.S.D.A. Handbook No. 224
Formulas: GPS = CFS x 7.481   GPM = CFS x 448.8
MGD = CFS x 0.6463

Head Feet	CFS	GPS	GPM	MGD	Head Feet	CFS	GPS	GPM	MGD
4.01	64.30	481.0	28860	41.56	4.26	74.20	555.1	33300	47.96
4.02	64.70	484.0	29040	41.82	4.27	74.60	558.1	33480	48.21
4.03	65.10	487.0	29220	42.07	4.28	75.00	561.1	33660	48.47
4.04	65.40	489.3	29350	42.27	4.29	75.40	564.1	33840	48.73
4.05	65.80	492.2	29530	42.53	4.30	75.80	567.1	34020	48.99
4.06	66.20	495.2	29710	42.79	4.31	76.20	570.1	34200	49.25
4.07	66.60	498.2	29890	43.04	4.32	76.60	573.0	34380	49.51
4.08	67.00	501.2	30070	43.30	4.33	77.10	576.8	34600	49.83
4.09	67.40	504.2	30250	43.56	4.34	77.50	579.8	34780	50.09
4.10	67.80	507.2	30430	43.82	4.35	77.90	582.8	34960	50.35
4.11	68.20	510.2	30610	44.08	4.36	78.30	585.8	35140	50.61
4.12	68.50	512.4	30740	44.27	4.37	78.80	589.5	35370	50.93
4.13	68.90	515.4	30920	44.53	4.38	79.20	592.5	35550	51.19
4.14	69.30	518.4	31100	44.79	4.39	79.60	595.5	35720	51.45
4.15	69.70	521.4	31280	45.05	4.40	80.00	598.5	35900	51.70
4.16	70.10	524.4	31460	45.31	4.41	80.50	602.2	36130	52.03
4.17	70.50	527.4	31640	45.56	4.42	80.90	605.2	36310	52.29
4.18	70.90	530.4	31820	45.82	4.43	81.30	608.2	36490	52.54
4.19	71.30	533.4	32000	46.08	4.44	81.80	611.9	36710	52.87
4.20	71.70	536.4	32180	46.34	4.45	82.20	614.9	36890	53.13
4.21	72.10	539.4	32360	46.60	4.46	82.60	617.9	37070	53.38
4.22	72.50	542.4	32540	46.86	4.47	83.10	621.7	37300	53.71
4.23	72.90	545.4	32720	47.12	4.48	83.50	624.7	37480	53.97
4.24	73.30	548.4	32900	47.37	4.49	84.00	628.4	37700	54.29
4.25	73.80	552.1	33120	47.70	4.50	84.50	632.1	37920	54.61

14

Chapter

15

Leopold-Lagco flume discharge tables

This chapter contains discharge (flow rate vs head) tables for Leopold-Lagco flumes. Note that all of the tabular data is for free flow.

Leopold-Lagco flumes

15-1: 4 in. Leopold-Lagco Flume

15-2: 6 in. Leopold-Lagco Flume

15-3: 8 in. Leopold-Lagco Flume

15-4: 10 in. Leopold-Lagco Flume

15-5: 12 in. Leopold-Lagco Flume

15-6: 15 in. Leopold-Lagco Flume

15-7: 18 in. Leopold-Lagco Flume

15-8: 21 in. Leopold-Lagco Flume

15-9: 24 in. Leopold-Lagco Flume

15-10: 30 in. Leopold-Lagco Flume

15

Note: The discharges of the various weirs and flumes are listed in four different units:

CFS—cubic feet per second   GPS—gallons per second

GPM—gallons per minute   MGD—million gallons per day.

The equation used to develop each table is listed on the table.

15-1: 4 In. Leopold-Lagco Flume Discharge Table

Formulas: $CFS = 0.8448H^{1.547}$ $GPS = CFS \times 7.481$
$GPM = CFS \times 448.8$ $MGD = CFS \times 0.6463$

Head Feet	CFS	GPS	GPM	MGD	Head Feet	CFS	GPS	GPM	MGD
0.01	0.0007	0.0051	0.3054	0.0004	0.13	0.0360	0.2691	16.15	0.0233
0.02	0.0020	0.0149	0.8923	0.0013	0.14	0.0403	0.3018	18.11	0.0261
0.03	0.0037	0.0278	1.671	0.0024	0.15	0.0449	0.3358	20.15	0.0290
0.04	0.0058	0.0435	2.607	0.0038	0.16	0.0496	0.3711	22.26	0.0321
0.05	0.0082	0.0614	3.682	0.0053	0.17	0.0545	0.4076	24.45	0.0352
0.06	0.0109	0.0814	4.882	0.0070	0.18	0.0595	0.4453	26.71	0.0385
0.07	0.0138	0.1033	6.197	0.0089	0.19	0.0647	0.4841	29.04	0.0418
0.08	0.0170	0.1270	7.619	0.0110	0.20	0.0701	0.5241	31.44	0.0453
0.09	0.0204	0.1524	9.142	0.0132	0.21	0.0755	0.5652	33.91	0.0488
0.10	0.0240	0.1794	10.76	0.0155	0.22	0.0812	0.6074	36.44	0.0525
0.11	0.0278	0.2078	12.47	0.0180	0.23	0.0870	0.6506	39.03	0.0562
0.12	0.0318	0.2378	14.27	0.0205	0.24	0.0929	0.6949	41.69	0.0600

15-2: 6 in. Leopold-Lagco Flume Discharge Table

Formulas: $CFS = 1.243H^{1.547}$ $GPS = CFS \times 7.481$
$GPM = CFS \times 448.8$ $MGD = CFS \times 0.6463$

Head Feet	CFS	GPS	GPM	MGD	Head Feet	CFS	GPS	GPM	MGD
0.01	0.0010	0.0075	0.4493	0.0006	0.19	0.0952	0.7123	42.73	0.0615
0.02	0.0029	0.0219	1.313	0.0019	0.20	0.1031	0.7711	46.26	0.0666
0.03	0.0055	0.0410	2.458	0.0035	0.21	0.1112	0.8316	49.89	0.0718
0.04	0.0085	0.0639	3.836	0.0055	0.22	0.1195	0.8936	53.61	0.0772
0.05	0.0121	0.0903	5.418	0.0078	0.23	0.1280	0.9572	57.43	0.0827
0.06	0.0160	0.1197	7.183	0.0103	0.24	0.1367	1.022	61.34	0.0883
0.07	0.0203	0.1520	9.118	0.0131	0.25	0.1456	1.089	65.33	0.0941
0.08	0.0250	0.1869	11.21	0.0161	0.26	0.1547	1.157	69.42	0.1000
0.09	0.0300	0.2242	13.45	0.0194	0.27	0.1640	1.227	73.59	0.1060
0.10	0.0353	0.2639	15.83	0.0228	0.28	0.1735	1.298	77.85	0.1121
0.11	0.0409	0.3058	18.35	0.0264	0.29	0.1831	1.370	82.20	0.1184
0.12	0.0468	0.3499	20.99	0.0302	0.30	0.1930	1.444	86.62	0.1247
0.13	0.0529	0.3960	23.76	0.0342	0.31	0.2031	1.519	91.13	0.1312
0.14	0.0594	0.4441	26.64	0.0384	0.32	0.2133	1.596	95.72	0.1378
0.15	0.0661	0.4941	29.64	0.0427	0.33	0.2237	1.673	100.4	0.1446
0.16	0.0730	0.5460	32.76	0.0472	0.34	0.2342	1.752	105.1	0.1514
0.17	0.0802	0.5997	35.98	0.0518	0.35	0.2450	1.833	110.0	0.1583
0.18	0.0876	0.6551	39.30	0.0566					

15

15-3: 8 in. Leopold-Lagco Flume Discharge Table

Formulas: CFS = 1.636H$^{1.547}$ GPS = CFS x 7.481

          GPM = CFS x 448.8   MGD = CFS x 0.6463

Head Feet	CFS	GPS	GPM	MGD	Head Feet	CFS	GPS	GPM	MGD
0.01	0.0013	0.0099	0.591	0.0009	0.24	0.1799	1.346	80.73	0.1163
0.02	0.0039	0.0288	1.728	0.0025	0.25	0.1916	1.433	85.99	0.1238
0.03	0.0072	0.0539	3.236	0.0047	0.26	0.2036	1.523	91.37	0.1316
0.04	0.0113	0.0842	5.049	0.0073	0.27	0.2158	1.615	96.86	0.1395
0.05	0.0159	0.1189	7.131	0.0103	0.28	0.2283	1.708	102.5	0.1476
0.06	0.0211	0.1576	9.454	0.0136	0.29	0.2411	1.803	108.2	0.1558
0.07	0.0267	0.2000	12.00	0.0173	0.30	0.2540	1.900	114.0	0.1642
0.08	0.0329	0.2459	14.75	0.0212	0.31	0.2673	1.999	119.9	0.1727
0.09	0.0394	0.2951	17.70	0.0255	0.32	0.2807	2.100	126.0	0.1814
0.10	0.0464	0.3473	20.84	0.0300	0.33	0.2944	2.202	132.1	0.1903
0.11	0.0538	0.4025	24.15	0.0348	0.34	0.3083	2.306	138.4	0.1993
0.12	0.0616	0.4605	27.63	0.0398	0.35	0.3224	2.412	144.7	0.2084
0.13	0.0697	0.5212	31.27	0.0450	0.36	0.3368	2.520	151.2	0.2177
0.14	0.0781	0.5845	35.07	0.0505	0.37	0.3514	2.629	157.7	0.2271
0.15	0.0869	0.6504	39.02	0.0562	0.38	0.3662	2.739	164.3	0.2367
0.16	0.0961	0.7186	43.11	0.0621	0.39	0.3812	2.852	171.1	0.2464
0.17	0.1055	0.7893	47.35	0.0682	0.40	0.3964	2.966	177.9	0.2562
0.18	0.1153	0.8623	51.73	0.0745	0.41	0.4119	3.081	184.8	0.2662
0.19	0.1253	0.9375	56.24	0.0810	0.42	0.4275	3.198	191.9	0.2763
0.20	0.1357	1.015	60.89	0.0877	0.43	0.4434	3.317	199.0	0.2865
0.21	0.1463	1.095	65.66	0.0946	0.44	0.4594	3.437	206.2	0.2969
0.22	0.1572	1.176	70.56	0.1016	0.45	0.4757	3.558	213.5	0.3074
0.23	0.1684	1.260	75.58	0.1088					

15

15-4: 10 in. Leopold-Lagco Flume Discharge Table

Formulas: $CFS = 2.023H^{1.547}$ $\quad GPS = CFS \times 7.481$
$\qquad\qquad GPM = CFS \times 448.8 \quad MGD = CFS \times 0.6463$

Head Feet	CFS	GPS	GPM	MGD	Head Feet	CFS	GPS	GPM	MGD
0.01	0.0016	0.0122	0.731	0.0011	0.31	0.3305	2.472	148.3	0.2136
0.02	0.0048	0.0356	2.137	0.0031	0.32	0.3471	2.597	155.8	0.2243
0.03	0.0089	0.0667	4.001	0.0058	0.33	0.3640	2.723	163.4	0.2353
0.04	0.0139	0.1041	6.244	0.0090	0.34	0.3812	2.852	171.1	0.2464
0.05	0.0196	0.1470	8.818	0.0127	0.35	0.3987	2.983	178.9	0.2577
0.06	0.0260	0.1949	11.69	0.0168	0.36	0.4165	3.116	186.9	0.2692
0.07	0.0331	0.2474	14.84	0.0214	0.37	0.4345	3.251	195.0	0.2808
0.08	0.0407	0.3041	18.24	0.0263	0.38	0.4528	3.388	203.2	0.2927
0.09	0.0488	0.3649	21.89	0.0315	0.39	0.4714	3.526	211.6	0.3047
0.10	0.0574	0.4295	25.77	0.0371	0.40	0.4902	3.667	220.0	0.3168
0.11	0.0665	0.4977	29.86	0.0430	0.41	0.5093	3.810	228.6	0.3292
0.12	0.0761	0.5694	34.16	0.0492	0.42	0.5286	3.955	237.3	0.3417
0.13	0.0862	0.6445	38.67	0.0557	0.43	0.5482	4.101	246.1	0.3543
0.14	0.0966	0.7228	43.36	0.0624	0.44	0.5681	4.250	255.0	0.3672
0.15	0.1075	0.8042	48.25	0.0695	0.45	0.5882	4.400	264.0	0.3801
0.16	0.1188	0.8886	53.31	0.0768	0.46	0.6085	4.552	273.1	0.3933
0.17	0.1305	0.9760	58.55	0.0843	0.47	0.6291	4.706	282.3	0.4066
0.18	0.1425	1.066	63.97	0.0921	0.48	0.6499	4.862	291.7	0.4201
0.19	0.1550	1.159	69.55	0.1002	0.49	0.6710	5.020	301.1	0.4337
0.20	0.1678	1.255	75.29	0.1084	0.50	0.6923	5.179	310.7	0.4474
0.21	0.1809	1.353	81.19	0.1169	0.51	0.7138	5.340	320.4	0.4614
0.22	0.1944	1.454	87.25	0.1256	0.52	0.7356	5.503	330.1	0.4754
0.23	0.2083	1.558	93.46	0.1346	0.53	0.7576	5.668	340.0	0.4896
0.24	0.2224	1.664	99.82	0.1438	0.54	0.7798	5.834	350.0	0.5040
0.25	0.2369	1.772	106.3	0.1531	0.55	0.8023	6.002	360.1	0.5185
0.26	0.2517	1.883	113.0	0.1627	0.56	0.8250	6.172	370.3	0.5332
0.27	0.2669	1.997	119.8	0.1725	0.57	0.8479	6.343	380.5	0.5480
0.28	0.2823	2.112	126.7	0.1825	0.58	0.8710	6.516	390.9	0.5629
0.29	0.2981	2.230	133.8	0.1926	0.59	0.8943	6.691	401.4	0.5780
0.30	0.3141	2.350	141.0	0.2030	0.60	0.9179	6.867	412.0	0.5932

15

15-5: 12 in. Leopold-Lagco Flume Discharge Table

Formulas: $CFS = 2.407H^{1.547}$ $GPS = CFS \times 7.481$
$GPM = CFS \times 448.8$ $MGD = CFS \times 0.6463$

Head Feet	CFS	GPS	GPM	MGD	Head Feet	CFS	GPS	GPM	MGD
0.01	0.0019	0.0145	0.870	0.0013	0.36	0.4955	3.707	222.4	0.3203
0.02	0.0057	0.0424	2.542	0.0037	0.37	0.5170	3.868	232.0	0.3341
0.03	0.0106	0.0793	4.760	0.0069	0.38	0.5388	4.031	241.8	0.3482
0.04	0.0166	0.1238	7.429	0.0107	0.39	0.5609	4.196	251.7	0.3625
0.05	0.0234	0.1749	10.49	0.0151	0.40	0.5833	4.363	261.8	0.3770
0.06	0.0310	0.2319	13.91	0.0200	0.41	0.6060	4.533	272.0	0.3916
0.07	0.0393	0.2943	17.66	0.0254	0.42	0.6290	4.705	282.3	0.4065
0.08	0.0484	0.3618	21.71	0.0313	0.43	0.6523	4.880	292.8	0.4216
0.09	0.0580	0.4342	26.05	0.0375	0.44	0.6759	5.057	303.4	0.4368
0.10	0.0683	0.5110	30.66	0.0441	0.45	0.6998	5.235	314.1	0.4523
0.11	0.0792	0.5922	35.53	0.0512	0.46	0.7240	5.417	324.9	0.4679
0.12	0.0906	0.6775	40.65	0.0585	0.47	0.7485	5.600	335.9	0.4838
0.13	0.1025	0.7668	46.00	0.0662	0.48	0.7733	5.785	347.1	0.4998
0.14	0.1150	0.8600	51.59	0.0743	0.49	0.7984	5.973	358.3	0.5160
0.15	0.1279	0.9569	57.40	0.0827	0.50	0.8237	6.162	369.7	0.5324
0.16	0.1413	1.057	63.43	0.0913	0.51	0.8494	6.354	381.2	0.5489
0.17	0.1552	1.161	69.67	0.1003	0.52	0.8753	6.548	392.8	0.5657
0.18	0.1696	1.269	76.11	0.1096	0.53	0.9014	6.744	404.6	0.5826
0.19	0.1844	1.379	82.75	0.1192	0.54	0.9279	6.941	416.4	0.5997
0.20	0.1996	1.493	89.58	0.1290	0.55	0.9546	7.141	428.4	0.6170
0.21	0.2153	1.610	96.61	0.1391	0.56	0.9816	7.343	440.5	0.6344
0.22	0.2313	1.730	103.8	0.1495	0.57	1.009	7.547	452.8	0.6520
0.23	0.2478	1.854	111.2	0.1601	0.58	1.036	7.753	465.1	0.6698
0.24	0.2646	1.980	118.8	0.1710	0.59	1.064	7.961	477.6	0.6877
0.25	0.2819	2.109	126.5	0.1822	0.60	1.092	8.170	490.1	0.7058
0.26	0.2995	2.241	134.4	0.1936	0.61	1.120	8.382	502.8	0.7241
0.27	0.3175	2.376	142.5	0.2052	0.62	1.149	8.595	515.7	0.7426
0.28	0.3359	2.513	150.8	0.2171	0.63	1.178	8.811	528.6	0.7612
0.29	0.3547	2.653	159.2	0.2292	0.64	1.207	9.028	541.6	0.7800
0.30	0.3738	2.796	167.7	0.2416	0.65	1.236	9.247	554.8	0.7989
0.31	0.3932	2.942	176.5	0.2541	0.66	1.266	9.468	568.0	0.8180
0.32	0.4130	3.090	185.4	0.2669	0.67	1.295	9.691	581.4	0.8372
0.33	0.4331	3.240	194.4	0.2799	0.68	1.325	9.916	594.9	0.8566
0.34	0.4536	3.393	203.6	0.2932	0.69	1.356	10.14	608.5	0.8762
0.35	0.4744	3.549	212.9	0.3066	0.70	1.386	10.37	622.2	0.8959

15

15-6: 15 in. Leopold-Lagco Flume Discharge Table

Formulas: CFS = $2.977H^{1.547}$ GPS = CFS x 7.481
GPM = CFS x 448.8   MGD = CFS x 0.6463

Head Feet	CFS	GPS	GPM	MGD	Head Feet	CFS	GPS	GPM	MGD
0.01	0.0024	0.0179	1.076	0.0015	0.46	0.8955	6.699	401.9	0.5788
0.02	0.0070	0.0524	3.144	0.0045	0.47	0.9258	6.926	415.5	0.5983
0.03	0.0131	0.0981	5.888	0.0085	0.48	0.9564	7.155	429.3	0.6181
0.04	0.0205	0.1532	9.188	0.0132	0.49	0.9874	7.387	443.2	0.6382
0.05	0.0289	0.2163	12.98	0.0187	0.50	1.019	7.622	457.2	0.6584
0.06	0.0383	0.2868	17.20	0.0248	0.51	1.050	7.859	471.5	0.6789
0.07	0.0487	0.3640	21.84	0.0314	0.52	1.083	8.098	485.8	0.6996
0.08	0.0598	0.4475	26.85	0.0387	0.53	1.115	8.341	500.4	0.7206
0.09	0.0718	0.5370	32.21	0.0464	0.54	1.148	8.585	515.0	0.7417
0.10	0.0845	0.6320	37.92	0.0546	0.55	1.181	8.832	529.9	0.7631
0.11	0.0979	0.7324	43.94	0.0633	0.56	1.214	9.082	544.9	0.7846
0.12	0.1120	0.8380	50.27	0.0724	0.57	1.248	9.334	560.0	0.8064
0.13	0.1268	0.9484	56.90	0.0819	0.58	1.282	9.589	575.2	0.8284
0.14	0.1422	1.064	63.81	0.0919	0.59	1.316	9.846	590.7	0.8506
0.15	0.1582	1.183	71.00	0.1022	0.60	1.351	10.11	606.2	0.8730
0.16	0.1748	1.308	78.45	0.1130	0.61	1.386	10.37	621.9	0.8956
0.17	0.1920	1.436	86.17	0.1241	0.62	1.421	10.63	637.8	0.9184
0.18	0.2097	1.569	94.13	0.1356	0.63	1.457	10.90	653.7	0.9414
0.19	0.2280	1.706	102.3	0.1474	0.64	1.493	11.17	669.9	0.9647
0.20	0.2469	1.847	110.8	0.1596	0.65	1.529	11.44	686.1	0.9881
0.21	0.2662	1.992	119.5	0.1721	0.66	1.565	11.71	702.5	1.012
0.22	0.2861	2.140	128.4	0.1849	0.67	1.602	11.99	719.1	1.036
0.23	0.3065	2.293	137.5	0.1981	0.68	1.639	12.26	735.7	1.060
0.24	0.3273	2.449	146.9	0.2115	0.69	1.677	12.54	752.5	1.084
0.25	0.3487	2.608	156.5	0.2253	0.70	1.715	12.83	769.5	1.108
0.26	0.3705	2.771	166.3	0.2394	0.71	1.753	13.11	786.6	1.133
0.27	0.3927	2.938	176.3	0.2538	0.72	1.791	13.40	803.8	1.157
0.28	0.4155	3.108	186.5	0.2685	0.73	1.830	13.69	821.1	1.182
0.29	0.4386	3.281	196.9	0.2835	0.74	1.868	13.98	838.6	1.208
0.30	0.4623	3.458	207.5	0.2988	0.75	1.908	14.27	856.2	1.233
0.31	0.4863	3.638	218.3	0.3143	0.76	1.947	14.57	873.9	1.258
0.32	0.5108	3.821	229.2	0.3301	0.77	1.987	14.86	891.7	1.284
0.33	0.5357	4.008	240.4	0.3462	0.78	2.027	15.16	909.7	1.310
0.34	0.5610	4.197	251.8	0.3626	0.79	2.067	15.47	927.8	1.336
0.35	0.5867	4.389	263.3	0.3792	0.80	2.108	15.77	946.0	1.362
0.36	0.6129	4.585	275.1	0.3961	0.81	2.149	16.08	964.4	1.389
0.37	0.6394	4.784	287.0	0.4133	0.82	2.190	16.38	982.9	1.415
0.38	0.6664	4.985	299.1	0.4307	0.83	2.231	16.69	1001	1.442
0.39	0.6937	5.189	311.3	0.4483	0.84	2.273	17.01	1020	1.469
0.40	0.7214	5.397	323.8	0.4662	0.85	2.315	17.32	1039	1.496
0.41	0.7495	5.607	336.4	0.4844	0.86	2.357	17.64	1058	1.524
0.42	0.7779	5.820	349.1	0.5028	0.87	2.400	17.95	1077	1.551
0.43	0.8068	6.036	362.1	0.5214	0.88	2.443	18.27	1096	1.579
0.44	0.8360	6.254	375.2	0.5403	0.89	2.486	18.60	1116	1.607
0.45	0.8656	6.475	388.5	0.5594	0.90	2.529	18.92	1135	1.635

15

15-7: 18 in. Leopold-Lagco Flume Discharge Table

Formulas: $CFS = 2.977H^{1.547}$ $GPS = CFS \times 7.481$
$GPM = CFS \times 448.8$ $MGD = CFS \times 0.6463$

Head Feet	CFS	GPS	GPM	MGD	Head Feet	CFS	GPS	GPM	MGD
0.01	0.0028	0.0212	1.274	0.0018	0.46	1.060	7.930	475.7	0.6851
0.02	0.0083	0.0620	3.722	0.0054	0.47	1.096	8.198	491.8	0.7083
0.03	0.0155	0.1162	6.969	0.0100	0.48	1.132	8.470	508.1	0.7317
0.04	0.0242	0.1813	10.88	0.0157	0.49	1.169	8.744	524.6	0.7554
0.05	0.0342	0.2560	15.36	0.0221	0.50	1.206	9.022	541.2	0.7794
0.06	0.0454	0.3395	20.37	0.0293	0.51	1.244	9.303	558.1	0.8037
0.07	0.0576	0.4309	25.85	0.0372	0.52	1.281	9.586	575.1	0.8282
0.08	0.0708	0.5298	31.78	0.0458	0.53	1.320	9.873	592.3	0.8530
0.09	0.0850	0.6356	38.13	0.0549	0.54	1.358	10.16	609.7	0.8780
0.10	0.1000	0.7482	44.88	0.0646	0.55	1.398	10.46	627.2	0.9033
0.11	0.1159	0.8670	52.01	0.0749	0.56	1.437	10.75	645.0	0.9288
0.12	0.1326	0.9919	59.51	0.0857	0.57	1.477	11.05	662.9	0.9546
0.13	0.1501	1.123	67.35	0.0970	0.58	1.517	11.35	680.9	0.9806
0.14	0.1683	1.259	75.54	0.1088	0.59	1.558	11.65	699.2	1.007
0.15	0.1873	1.401	84.04	0.1210	0.60	1.599	11.96	717.6	1.033
0.16	0.2069	1.548	92.87	0.1337	0.61	1.640	12.27	736.2	1.060
0.17	0.2273	1.700	102.0	0.1469	0.62	1.682	12.58	755.0	1.087
0.18	0.2483	1.857	111.4	0.1605	0.63	1.724	12.90	773.9	1.114
0.19	0.2699	2.019	121.1	0.1745	0.64	1.767	13.22	793.0	1.142
0.20	0.2922	2.186	131.2	0.1889	0.65	1.810	13.54	812.2	1.170
0.21	0.3151	2.358	141.4	0.2037	0.66	1.853	13.86	831.6	1.198
0.22	0.3387	2.534	152.0	0.2189	0.67	1.897	14.19	851.2	1.226
0.23	0.3628	2.714	162.8	0.2345	0.68	1.941	14.52	870.9	1.254
0.24	0.3875	2.899	173.9	0.2504	0.69	1.985	14.85	890.8	1.283
0.25	0.4127	3.088	185.2	0.2667	0.70	2.030	15.18	910.9	1.312
0.26	0.4385	3.281	196.8	0.2834	0.71	2.075	15.52	931.1	1.341
0.27	0.4649	3.478	208.6	0.3005	0.72	2.120	15.86	951.4	1.370
0.28	0.4918	3.679	220.7	0.3179	0.73	2.166	16.20	972.0	1.400
0.29	0.5192	3.884	233.0	0.3356	0.74	2.212	16.55	992.6	1.429
0.30	0.5472	4.094	245.6	0.3537	0.75	2.258	16.89	1013	1.459
0.31	0.5757	4.307	258.4	0.3721	0.76	2.305	17.24	1034	1.490
0.32	0.6046	4.523	271.4	0.3908	0.77	2.352	17.60	1056	1.520
0.33	0.6341	4.744	284.6	0.4098	0.78	2.399	17.95	1077	1.551
0.34	0.6641	4.968	298.0	0.4292	0.79	2.447	18.31	1098	1.582
0.35	0.6946	5.196	311.7	0.4489	0.80	2.495	18.67	1120	1.613
0.36	0.7255	5.427	325.6	0.4689	0.81	2.544	19.03	1142	1.644
0.37	0.7569	5.662	339.7	0.4892	0.82	2.592	19.39	1163	1.675
0.38	0.7888	5.901	354.0	0.5098	0.83	2.641	19.76	1186	1.707
0.39	0.8211	6.143	368.5	0.5307	0.84	2.691	20.13	1208	1.739
0.40	0.8539	6.388	383.2	0.5519	0.85	2.741	20.50	1230	1.771
0.41	0.8872	6.637	398.2	0.5734	0.86	2.791	20.88	1252	1.804
0.42	0.9209	6.889	413.3	0.5952	0.87	2.841	21.25	1275	1.836
0.43	0.9550	7.144	428.6	0.6172	0.88	2.892	21.63	1298	1.869
0.44	0.9896	7.403	444.1	0.6396	0.89	2.943	22.01	1321	1.902
0.45	1.025	7.665	459.8	0.6622	0.90	2.994	22.40	1344	1.935

15

15-7: 18 in. Leopold-Lagco Flume
Discharge Table *(Continued)*

Formulas: CFS = $2.977H^{1.547}$ GPS = CFS x 7.481
GPM = CFS x 448.8 MGD = CFS x 0.6463

Head Feet	CFS	GPS	GPM	MGD	Head Feet	CFS	GPS	GPM	MGD
0.91	3.046	22.78	1367	1.968	0.99	3.470	25.96	1557	2.242
0.92	3.098	23.17	1390	2.002	1.00	3.524	26.36	1582	2.278
0.93	3.150	23.56	1414	2.036	1.01	3.579	26.77	1606	2.313
0.94	3.202	23.96	1437	2.070	1.02	3.634	27.18	1631	2.348
0.95	3.255	24.35	1461	2.104	1.03	3.689	27.60	1656	2.384
0.96	3.308	24.75	1485	2.138	1.04	3.744	28.01	1681	2.420
0.97	3.362	25.15	1509	2.173	1.05	3.800	28.43	1706	2.456
0.98	3.416	25.55	1533	2.207					

15

15-8: 21 in. Leopold-Lagco Flume Discharge Table

Formulas: $CFS = 4.103H^{1.547}$ $\quad GPS = CFS \times 7.481$

$\qquad\quad GPM = CFS \times 448.8 \quad MGD = CFS \times 0.6463$

Head Feet	CFS	GPS	GPM	MGD	Head Feet	CFS	GPS	GPM	MGD
0.01	0.0033	0.0247	1.483	0.0021	0.51	1.448	10.83	649.8	0.9357
0.02	0.0097	0.0722	4.334	0.0062	0.52	1.492	11.16	669.6	0.9643
0.03	0.0181	0.1353	8.114	0.0117	0.53	1.537	11.50	689.6	0.9931
0.04	0.0282	0.2111	12.66	0.0182	0.54	1.582	11.83	709.9	1.022
0.05	0.0398	0.2981	17.88	0.0258	0.55	1.627	12.17	730.3	1.052
0.06	0.0528	0.3952	23.71	0.0341	0.56	1.673	12.52	750.9	1.081
0.07	0.0671	0.5017	30.10	0.0433	0.57	1.720	12.86	771.8	1.111
0.08	0.0824	0.6168	37.00	0.0533	0.58	1.767	13.22	792.8	1.142
0.09	0.0989	0.7401	44.40	0.0639	0.59	1.814	13.57	814.1	1.172
0.10	0.1164	0.8711	52.26	0.0753	0.60	1.862	13.93	835.5	1.203
0.11	0.1349	1.009	60.56	0.0872	0.61	1.910	14.29	857.2	1.234
0.12	0.1544	1.155	69.29	0.0998	0.62	1.959	14.65	879.0	1.266
0.13	0.1747	1.307	78.42	0.1129	0.63	2.008	15.02	901.0	1.298
0.14	0.1960	1.466	87.95	0.1266	0.64	2.057	15.39	923.2	1.330
0.15	0.2180	1.631	97.85	0.1409	0.65	2.107	15.76	945.7	1.362
0.16	0.2409	1.802	108.1	0.1557	0.66	2.157	16.14	968.3	1.394
0.17	0.2646	1.980	118.8	0.1710	0.67	2.208	16.52	991.0	1.427
0.18	0.2891	2.163	129.7	0.1868	0.68	2.259	16.90	1014	1.460
0.19	0.3143	2.351	141.1	0.2031	0.69	2.311	17.29	1037	1.494
0.20	0.3402	2.545	152.7	0.2199	0.70	2.363	17.68	1061	1.527
0.21	0.3669	2.745	164.7	0.2371	0.71	2.415	18.07	1084	1.561
0.22	0.3943	2.950	177.0	0.2548	0.72	2.468	18.47	1108	1.595
0.23	0.4224	3.160	189.6	0.2730	0.73	2.522	18.86	1132	1.630
0.24	0.4511	3.375	202.5	0.2916	0.74	2.575	19.26	1156	1.664
0.25	0.4805	3.595	215.7	0.3106	0.75	2.629	19.67	1180	1.699
0.26	0.5106	3.820	229.1	0.3300	0.76	2.684	20.08	1204	1.734
0.27	0.5413	4.049	242.9	0.3498	0.77	2.738	20.49	1229	1.770
0.28	0.5726	4.284	257.0	0.3701	0.78	2.794	20.90	1254	1.806
0.29	0.6045	4.523	271.3	0.3907	0.79	2.849	21.32	1279	1.841
0.30	0.6371	4.766	285.9	0.4118	0.80	2.905	21.73	1304	1.878
0.31	0.6703	5.014	300.8	0.4332	0.81	2.962	22.16	1329	1.914
0.32	0.7040	5.267	316.0	0.4550	0.82	3.018	22.58	1355	1.951
0.33	0.7383	5.523	331.4	0.4772	0.83	3.075	23.01	1380	1.988
0.34	0.7732	5.784	347.0	0.4997	0.84	3.133	23.44	1406	2.025
0.35	0.8087	6.050	362.9	0.5226	0.85	3.191	23.87	1432	2.062
0.36	0.8447	6.319	379.1	0.5459	0.86	3.249	24.31	1458	2.100
0.37	0.8813	6.593	395.5	0.5696	0.87	3.308	24.75	1485	2.138
0.38	0.9184	6.870	412.2	0.5936	0.88	3.367	25.19	1511	2.176
0.39	0.9560	7.152	429.1	0.6179	0.89	3.426	25.63	1538	2.214
0.40	0.9942	7.438	446.2	0.6426	0.90	3.486	26.08	1564	2.253
0.41	1.033	7.727	463.6	0.6676	0.91	3.546	26.53	1591	2.292
0.42	1.072	8.021	481.2	0.6930	0.92	3.606	26.98	1619	2.331
0.43	1.112	8.318	499.0	0.7186	0.93	3.667	27.43	1646	2.370
0.44	1.152	8.620	517.1	0.7447	0.94	3.728	27.89	1673	2.410
0.45	1.193	8.924	535.4	0.7710	0.95	3.790	28.35	1701	2.449
0.46	1.234	9.233	553.9	0.7977	0.96	3.852	28.82	1729	2.489
0.47	1.276	9.545	572.7	0.8247	0.97	3.914	29.28	1757	2.530
0.48	1.318	9.861	591.6	0.8520	0.98	3.977	29.75	1785	2.570
0.49	1.361	10.18	610.8	0.8796	0.99	4.040	30.22	1813	2.611
0.50	1.404	10.50	630.2	0.9075	1.00	4.103	30.69	1841	2.652

15-8: 21 in. Leopold-Lagco Flume Discharge Table *(Continued)*

Formulas: CFS $= 4.103H^{1.547}$ GPS = CFS x 7.481
GPM = CFS x 448.8   MGD = CFS x 0.6463

Head Feet	CFS	GPS	GPM	MGD	Head Feet	CFS	GPS	GPM	MGD
1.01	4.167	31.17	1870	2.693	1.14	5.025	37.59	2255	3.248
1.02	4.231	31.65	1899	2.734	1.15	5.093	38.10	2286	3.292
1.03	4.295	32.13	1928	2.776	1.16	5.162	38.62	2317	3.336
1.04	4.360	32.61	1957	2.818	1.17	5.231	39.13	2348	3.381
1.05	4.425	33.10	1986	2.860	1.18	5.300	39.65	2379	3.426
1.06	4.490	33.59	2015	2.902	1.19	5.370	40.17	2410	3.471
1.07	4.556	34.08	2045	2.944	1.20	5.440	40.70	2441	3.516
1.08	4.622	34.58	2074	2.987	1.21	5.510	41.22	2473	3.561
1.09	4.688	35.07	2104	3.030	1.22	5.581	41.75	2505	3.607
1.10	4.755	35.57	2134	3.073	1.23	5.652	42.28	2537	3.653
1.11	4.822	36.07	2164	3.116	1.24	5.723	42.81	2568	3.699
1.12	4.889	36.58	2194	3.160	1.25	5.795	43.35	2601	3.745
1.13	4.957	37.08	2225	3.204					

15

15-9: 24 in. Leopold-Lagco Flume Discharge Table

Formulas: CFS = $4.660H^{1.547}$ GPS = CFS x 7.481
GPM = CFS x 448.8   MGD = CFS x 0.6463

Head Feet	CFS	GPS	GPM	MGD	Head Feet	CFS	GPS	GPM	MGD
0.01	0.0038	0.0281	1.684	0.0024	0.51	1.644	12.30	738.0	1.063
0.02	0.0110	0.0820	4.922	0.0071	0.52	1.695	12.68	760.5	1.095
0.03	0.0205	0.1536	9.216	0.0133	0.53	1.745	13.06	783.2	1.128
0.04	0.0320	0.2397	14.38	0.0207	0.54	1.796	13.44	806.2	1.161
0.05	0.0453	0.3386	20.31	0.0293	0.55	1.848	13.83	829.4	1.194
0.06	0.0600	0.4489	26.93	0.0388	0.56	1.900	14.22	852.9	1.228
0.07	0.0762	0.5698	34.18	0.0492	0.57	1.953	14.61	876.6	1.262
0.08	0.0936	0.7005	42.03	0.0605	0.58	2.006	15.01	900.5	1.297
0.09	0.1124	0.8405	50.43	0.0726	0.59	2.060	15.41	924.6	1.331
0.10	0.1322	0.9893	59.35	0.0855	0.60	2.114	15.82	948.9	1.367
0.11	0.1533	1.147	68.78	0.0991	0.61	2.169	16.23	973.5	1.402
0.12	0.1753	1.312	78.69	0.1133	0.62	2.224	16.64	998.3	1.438
0.13	0.1985	1.485	89.07	0.1283	0.63	2.280	17.06	1023	1.474
0.14	0.2226	1.665	99.88	0.1438	0.64	2.336	17.48	1049	1.510
0.15	0.2476	1.853	111.1	0.1600	0.65	2.393	17.90	1074	1.547
0.16	0.2736	2.047	122.8	0.1768	0.66	2.450	18.33	1100	1.584
0.17	0.3005	2.248	134.9	0.1942	0.67	2.508	18.76	1126	1.621
0.18	0.3283	2.456	147.3	0.2122	0.68	2.566	19.20	1152	1.658
0.19	0.3570	2.670	160.2	0.2307	0.69	2.625	19.64	1178	1.696
0.20	0.3864	2.891	173.4	0.2498	0.70	2.684	20.08	1204	1.735
0.21	0.4167	3.118	187.0	0.2693	0.71	2.743	20.52	1231	1.773
0.22	0.4478	3.350	201.0	0.2894	0.72	2.803	20.97	1258	1.812
0.23	0.4797	3.589	215.3	0.3100	0.73	2.864	21.42	1285	1.851
0.24	0.5124	3.833	229.9	0.3311	0.74	2.925	21.88	1313	1.890
0.25	0.5458	4.083	244.9	0.3527	0.75	2.986	22.34	1340	1.930
0.26	0.5799	4.338	260.3	0.3748	0.76	3.048	22.80	1368	1.970
0.27	0.6148	4.599	275.9	0.3973	0.77	3.110	23.27	1396	2.010
0.28	0.6503	4.865	291.9	0.4203	0.78	3.173	23.74	1424	2.051
0.29	0.6866	5.137	308.2	0.4438	0.79	3.236	24.21	1452	2.091
0.30	0.7236	5.413	324.7	0.4677	0.80	3.300	24.68	1481	2.133
0.31	0.7612	5.695	341.6	0.4920	0.81	3.364	25.16	1510	2.174
0.32	0.7996	5.982	358.8	0.5168	0.82	3.428	25.65	1539	2.216
0.33	0.8385	6.273	376.3	0.5420	0.83	3.493	26.13	1568	2.258
0.34	0.8782	6.570	394.1	0.5676	0.84	3.558	26.62	1597	2.300
0.35	0.9185	6.871	412.2	0.5936	0.85	3.624	27.11	1626	2.342
0.36	0.9594	7.177	430.6	0.6200	0.86	3.690	27.61	1656	2.385
0.37	1.001	7.488	449.2	0.6469	0.87	3.757	28.10	1686	2.428
0.38	1.043	7.803	468.1	0.6741	0.88	3.824	28.61	1716	2.471
0.39	1.086	8.123	487.3	0.7018	0.89	3.891	29.11	1746	2.515
0.40	1.129	8.448	506.8	0.7298	0.90	3.959	29.62	1777	2.559
0.41	1.173	8.777	526.5	0.7582	0.91	4.027	30.13	1807	2.603
0.42	1.218	9.110	546.5	0.7870	0.92	4.096	30.64	1838	2.647
0.43	1.263	9.448	566.8	0.8162	0.93	4.165	31.16	1869	2.692
0.44	1.309	9.790	587.3	0.8457	0.94	4.235	31.68	1900	2.737
0.45	1.355	10.14	608.1	0.8757	0.95	4.305	32.20	1932	2.782
0.46	1.402	10.49	629.1	0.9060	0.96	4.375	32.73	1963	2.827
0.47	1.449	10.84	650.4	0.9366	0.97	4.446	33.26	1995	2.873
0.48	1.497	11.20	671.9	0.9676	0.98	4.517	33.79	2027	2.919
0.49	1.546	11.56	693.7	0.9990	0.99	4.588	34.32	2059	2.965
0.50	1.595	11.93	715.7	1.031	1.00	4.660	34.86	2091	3.012

15

Formulas: CFS $= 4.660H^{1.547}$ GPS = CFS x 7.481
GPM = CFS x 448.8 MGD = CFS x 0.6463

Head Feet	CFS	GPS	GPM	MGD	Head Feet	CFS	GPS	GPM	MGD
1.01	4.732	35.40	2124	3.058	1.21	6.258	46.82	2809	4.045
1.02	4.805	35.95	2156	3.105	1.22	6.338	47.42	2845	4.097
1.03	4.878	36.49	2189	3.153	1.23	6.419	48.02	2881	4.149
1.04	4.951	37.04	2222	3.200	1.24	6.500	48.63	2917	4.201
1.05	5.025	37.59	2255	3.248	1.25	6.581	49.23	2954	4.253
1.06	5.100	38.15	2289	3.296	1.26	6.663	49.84	2990	4.306
1.07	5.174	38.71	2322	3.344	1.27	6.745	50.46	3027	4.359
1.08	5.249	39.27	2356	3.393	1.28	6.827	51.07	3064	4.412
1.09	5.325	39.83	2390	3.441	1.29	6.910	51.69	3101	4.466
1.10	5.400	40.40	2424	3.490	1.30	6.993	52.31	3138	4.520
1.11	5.476	40.97	2458	3.539	1.31	7.076	52.94	3176	4.573
1.12	5.553	41.54	2492	3.589	1.32	7.160	53.56	3213	4.628
1.13	5.630	42.12	2527	3.639	1.33	7.244	54.19	3251	4.682
1.14	5.707	42.70	2561	3.689	1.34	7.329	54.82	3289	4.736
1.15	5.785	43.28	2596	3.739	1.35	7.413	55.46	3327	4.791
1.16	5.863	43.86	2631	3.789	1.36	7.498	56.10	3365	4.846
1.17	5.941	44.45	2666	3.840	1.37	7.584	56.74	3404	4.901
1.18	6.020	45.03	2702	3.891	1.38	7.670	57.38	3442	4.957
1.19	6.099	45.63	2737	3.942	1.39	7.756	58.02	3481	5.013
1.20	6.178	46.22	2773	3.993	1.40	7.842	58.67	3520	5.069

15

15-10: 30 in. Leopold-Lagco Flume Discharge Table

Formulas: $CFS = 5.764H^{1.547}$ $\quad GPS = CFS \times 7.481$
$\qquad\qquad GPM = CFS \times 448.8 \quad MGD = CFS \times 0.6463$

Head Feet	CFS	GPS	GPM	MGD	Head Feet	CFS	GPS	GPM	MGD
0.01	0.0046	0.0347	2.083	0.0030	0.51	2.034	15.22	912.8	1.315
0.02	0.0136	0.1015	6.088	0.0088	0.52	2.096	15.68	940.7	1.355
0.03	0.0254	0.1900	11.40	0.0164	0.53	2.159	16.15	968.8	1.395
0.04	0.0396	0.2965	17.79	0.0256	0.54	2.222	16.62	997.2	1.436
0.05	0.0560	0.4188	25.12	0.0362	0.55	2.286	17.10	1026	1.477
0.06	0.0742	0.5552	33.31	0.0480	0.56	2.351	17.58	1055	1.519
0.07	0.0942	0.7048	42.28	0.0609	0.57	2.416	18.07	1084	1.561
0.08	0.1158	0.8665	51.98	0.0749	0.58	2.482	18.57	1114	1.604
0.09	0.1390	1.040	62.37	0.0898	0.59	2.548	19.06	1144	1.647
0.10	0.1636	1.224	73.41	0.1057	0.60	2.615	19.57	1174	1.690
0.11	0.1896	1.418	85.08	0.1225	0.61	2.683	20.07	1204	1.734
0.12	0.2169	1.622	97.34	0.1402	0.62	2.751	20.58	1235	1.778
0.13	0.2455	1.836	110.2	0.1586	0.63	2.820	21.10	1266	1.823
0.14	0.2753	2.059	123.5	0.1779	0.64	2.890	21.62	1297	1.868
0.15	0.3063	2.291	137.5	0.1980	0.65	2.960	22.14	1328	1.913
0.16	0.3385	2.532	151.9	0.2187	0.66	3.031	22.67	1360	1.959
0.17	0.3717	2.781	166.8	0.2402	0.67	3.102	23.21	1392	2.005
0.18	0.4061	3.038	182.3	0.2625	0.68	3.174	23.75	1425	2.051
0.19	0.4415	3.303	198.2	0.2854	0.69	3.247	24.29	1457	2.098
0.20	0.4780	3.576	214.5	0.3089	0.70	3.320	24.83	1490	2.145
0.21	0.5155	3.856	231.3	0.3331	0.71	3.393	25.39	1523	2.193
0.22	0.5539	4.144	248.6	0.3580	0.72	3.468	25.94	1556	2.241
0.23	0.5934	4.439	266.3	0.3835	0.73	3.542	26.50	1590	2.289
0.24	0.6337	4.741	284.4	0.4096	0.74	3.618	27.06	1624	2.338
0.25	0.6751	5.050	303.0	0.4363	0.75	3.694	27.63	1658	2.387
0.26	0.7173	5.366	321.9	0.4636	0.76	3.770	28.20	1692	2.437
0.27	0.7604	5.689	341.3	0.4914	0.77	3.847	28.78	1727	2.486
0.28	0.8044	6.018	361.0	0.5199	0.78	3.925	29.36	1761	2.536
0.29	0.8493	6.354	381.2	0.5489	0.79	4.003	29.94	1796	2.587
0.30	0.8950	6.696	401.7	0.5784	0.80	4.081	30.53	1832	2.638
0.31	0.9416	7.044	422.6	0.6085	0.81	4.161	31.13	1867	2.689
0.32	0.9890	7.399	443.9	0.6392	0.82	4.240	31.72	1903	2.740
0.33	1.037	7.759	465.5	0.6703	0.83	4.321	32.32	1939	2.792
0.34	1.086	8.126	487.5	0.7020	0.84	4.401	32.93	1975	2.845
0.35	1.136	8.499	509.9	0.7342	0.85	4.483	33.53	2012	2.897
0.36	1.187	8.877	532.6	0.7669	0.86	4.564	34.15	2049	2.950
0.37	1.238	9.262	555.6	0.8001	0.87	4.647	34.76	2086	3.003
0.38	1.290	9.652	579.0	0.8338	0.88	4.730	35.38	2123	3.057
0.39	1.343	10.05	602.8	0.8680	0.89	4.813	36.01	2160	3.111
0.40	1.397	10.45	626.8	0.9027	0.90	4.897	36.64	2198	3.165
0.41	1.451	10.86	651.3	0.9379	0.91	4.982	37.27	2236	3.220
0.42	1.506	11.27	676.0	0.9735	0.92	5.066	37.90	2274	3.274
0.43	1.562	11.69	701.1	1.010	0.93	5.152	38.54	2312	3.330
0.44	1.619	12.11	726.4	1.046	0.94	5.238	39.18	2351	3.385
0.45	1.676	12.54	752.1	1.083	0.95	5.324	39.83	2390	3.441
0.46	1.734	12.97	778.1	1.121	0.96	5.411	40.48	2429	3.497
0.47	1.793	13.41	804.5	1.158	0.97	5.499	41.14	2468	3.554
0.48	1.852	13.85	831.1	1.197	0.98	5.587	41.79	2507	3.611
0.49	1.912	14.30	858.0	1.236	0.99	5.675	42.46	2547	3.668
0.50	1.973	14.76	885.3	1.275	1.00	5.764	43.12	2587	3.725

15

15-10: 30 in. Leopold-Lagco Flume Discharge Table (Continued)

Formulas: CFS = $5.764H^{1.547}$ GPS = CFS x 7.481
GPM = CFS x 448.8   MGD = CFS x 0.6463

Head Feet	CFS	GPS	GPM	MGD	Head Feet	CFS	GPS	GPM	MGD
1.01	5.853	43.79	2627	3.783	1.39	9.593	71.77	4305	6.200
1.02	5.943	44.46	2667	3.841	1.40	9.700	72.57	4353	6.269
1.03	6.034	45.14	2708	3.900	1.41	9.808	73.37	4402	6.339
1.04	6.125	45.82	2749	3.958	1.42	9.915	74.18	4450	6.408
1.05	6.216	46.50	2790	4.017	1.43	10.02	74.99	4499	6.478
1.06	6.308	47.19	2831	4.077	1.44	10.13	75.80	4547	6.549
1.07	6.400	47.88	2872	4.136	1.45	10.24	76.62	4596	6.619
1.08	6.493	48.57	2914	4.196	1.46	10.35	77.44	4645	6.690
1.09	6.586	49.27	2956	4.257	1.47	10.46	78.26	4695	6.761
1.10	6.680	49.97	2998	4.317	1.48	10.57	79.08	4744	6.832
1.11	6.774	50.68	3040	4.378	1.49	10.68	79.91	4794	6.904
1.12	6.869	51.38	3083	4.439	1.50	10.79	80.74	4844	6.975
1.13	6.964	52.09	3125	4.501	1.51	10.90	81.58	4894	7.048
1.14	7.059	52.81	3168	4.562	1.52	11.02	82.41	4944	7.120
1.15	7.155	53.53	3211	4.624	1.53	11.13	83.25	4995	7.192
1.16	7.252	54.25	3255	4.687	1.54	11.24	84.10	5045	7.265
1.17	7.349	54.98	3298	4.749	1.55	11.35	84.94	5096	7.338
1.18	7.446	55.70	3342	4.812	1.56	11.47	85.79	5147	7.412
1.19	7.544	56.44	3386	4.876	1.57	11.58	86.64	5198	7.485
1.20	7.642	57.17	3430	4.939	1.58	11.70	87.50	5249	7.559
1.21	7.741	57.91	3474	5.003	1.59	11.81	88.36	5301	7.633
1.22	7.840	58.65	3519	5.067	1.60	11.93	89.22	5352	7.708
1.23	7.940	59.40	3563	5.131	1.61	12.04	90.08	5404	7.782
1.24	8.040	60.15	3608	5.196	1.62	12.16	90.95	5456	7.857
1.25	8.140	60.90	3653	5.261	1.63	12.27	91.82	5508	7.933
1.26	8.241	61.65	3699	5.326	1.64	12.39	92.69	5561	8.008
1.27	8.343	62.41	3744	5.392	1.65	12.51	93.57	5613	8.084
1.28	8.445	63.17	3790	5.458	1.66	12.62	94.45	5666	8.160
1.29	8.547	63.94	3836	5.524	1.67	12.74	95.33	5719	8.236
1.30	8.650	64.71	3882	5.590	1.68	12.86	96.21	5772	8.312
1.31	8.753	65.48	3928	5.657	1.69	12.98	97.10	5825	8.389
1.32	8.856	66.25	3975	5.724	1.70	13.10	97.99	5879	8.466
1.33	8.960	67.03	4021	5.791	1.71	13.22	98.88	5932	8.543
1.34	9.065	67.81	4068	5.859	1.72	13.34	99.78	5986	8.620
1.35	9.170	68.60	4115	5.926	1.73	13.46	100.7	6040	8.698
1.36	9.275	69.39	4163	5.994	1.74	13.58	101.6	6094	8.776
1.37	9.381	70.18	4210	6.063	1.75	13.70	102.5	6148	8.854
1.38	9.487	70.97	4258	6.131					

15

Chapter

16

Trapezoidal
flume
discharge
tables

This chapter contains discharge (flow rate vs head) tables for Trapezoidal flumes. Note that all of the tabular data is for free flow.

Trapezoidal flumes
(manufactured by Plasti-Fab)

16-1: 12 in. 45° SRCRC Trapezoidal Flume

16-2: Large 60° V Trapezoidal Flume

16-3: 2 in. 45° WSC Trapezoidal Flume

Note: The discharges of the flumes are listed in four different units:

    CFS—cubic feet per second,   GPS—gallons per second,

    GPM—gallons per minute,   MGD—million gallons per day.

The source of data used to develop each table is listed on the table.

16

16-1: 12 in. 45° SRCRC Trapezoidal Flume Discharge Table

Manufactured by Plasti-Fab, Inc. (Data from Plasti-Fab, Inc.)
Formulas: GPS = CFS x 7.481   GPM = CFS x 448.8
MGD = CFS x 0.6463

Head Feet	CFS	GPS	GPM	MGD	Head Feet	CFS	GPS	GPM	MGD
0.01					0.51	0.8800	6.583	394.9	0.5687
0.02					0.52	0.9200	6.883	412.9	0.5946
0.03					0.53	0.9500	7.107	426.4	0.6140
0.04					0.54	0.9900	7.406	444.3	0.6398
0.05					0.55	1.030	7.705	462.3	0.6657
0.06					0.56	1.070	8.005	480.2	0.6915
0.07					0.57	1.110	8.304	498.2	0.7174
0.08					0.58	1.160	8.678	520.6	0.7497
0.09					0.59	1.200	8.977	538.6	0.7756
0.10					0.60	1.240	9.276	556.5	0.8014
0.11					0.61	1.290	9.650	579.0	0.8337
0.12					0.62	1.340	10.02	601.4	0.8660
0.13					0.63	1.380	10.32	619.3	0.8919
0.14					0.64	1.430	10.70	641.8	0.9242
0.15					0.65	1.480	11.07	664.2	0.9565
0.16					0.66	1.530	11.45	686.7	0.9888
0.17					0.67	1.580	11.82	709.1	1.021
0.18					0.68	1.640	12.27	736.0	1.060
0.19					0.69	1.690	12.64	758.5	1.092
0.20	0.1600	1.197	71.81	0.1034	0.70	1.740	13.02	780.9	1.125
0.21	0.1800	1.347	80.78	0.1163	0.71	1.800	13.47	807.8	1.163
0.22	0.1900	1.421	85.27	0.1228	0.72	1.860	13.91	834.8	1.202
0.23	0.2000	1.496	89.76	0.1293	0.73	1.920	14.36	861.7	1.241
0.24	0.2200	1.646	98.74	0.1422	0.74	1.970	14.74	884.1	1.273
0.25	0.2300	1.721	103.2	0.1486	0.75	2.030	15.19	911.1	1.312
0.26	0.2400	1.795	107.7	0.1551	0.76	2.100	15.71	942.5	1.357
0.27	0.2600	1.945	116.7	0.1680	0.77	2.160	16.16	969.4	1.396
0.28	0.2800	2.095	125.7	0.1810	0.78	2.220	16.61	996.3	1.435
0.29	0.3000	2.244	134.6	0.1939	0.79	2.290	17.13	1028	1.480
0.30	0.3100	2.319	139.1	0.2004	0.80	2.350	17.58	1055	1.519
0.31	0.3300	2.469	148.1	0.2133	0.81	2.420	18.10	1086	1.564
0.32	0.3500	2.618	157.1	0.2262	0.82	2.490	18.63	1118	1.609
0.33	0.3700	2.768	166.1	0.2391	0.83	2.560	19.15	1149	1.655
0.34	0.3900	2.918	175.0	0.2521	0.84	2.630	19.68	1180	1.700
0.35	0.4200	3.142	188.5	0.2714	0.85	2.700	20.20	1212	1.745
0.36	0.4400	3.292	197.5	0.2844	0.86	2.770	20.72	1243	1.790
0.37	0.4600	3.441	206.4	0.2973	0.87	2.840	21.25	1275	1.835
0.38	0.4800	3.591	215.4	0.3102	0.88	2.920	21.84	1310	1.887
0.39	0.5100	3.815	228.9	0.3296	0.89	3.000	22.44	1346	1.939
0.40	0.5400	4.040	242.4	0.3490	0.90	3.070	22.97	1378	1.984
0.41	0.5600	4.189	251.3	0.3619	0.91	3.150	23.57	1414	2.036
0.42	0.5900	4.414	264.8	0.3813	0.92	3.230	24.16	1450	2.088
0.43	0.6200	4.638	278.3	0.4007	0.93	3.310	24.76	1486	2.139
0.44	0.6500	4.863	291.7	0.4201	0.94	3.390	25.36	1521	2.191
0.45	0.6800	5.087	305.2	0.4395	0.95	3.480	26.03	1562	2.249
0.46	0.7100	5.312	318.6	0.4589	0.96	3.560	26.63	1598	2.301
0.47	0.7400	5.536	332.1	0.4783	0.97	3.650	27.31	1638	2.359
0.48	0.7800	5.835	350.1	0.5041	0.98	3.740	27.98	1679	2.417
0.49	0.8100	6.060	363.5	0.5235	0.99	3.820	28.58	1714	2.469
0.50	0.8400	6.284	377.0	0.5429	1.00	3.910	29.25	1755	2.527

16

Manufactured by Plasti-Fab, Inc. (Data from Plasti-Fab, Inc.)

Formulas: GPS = CFS x 7.481   GPM = CFS x 448.8

MGD = CFS x 0.6463

Head Feet	CFS	GPS	GPM	MGD	Head Feet	CFS	GPS	GPM	MGD
1.01	4.000	29.92	1795	2.585	1.16	5.520	41.30	2477	3.568
1.02	4.100	30.67	1840	2.650	1.17	5.630	42.12	2527	3.639
1.03	4.190	31.35	1880	2.708	1.18	5.750	43.02	2581	3.716
1.04	4.280	32.02	1921	2.766	1.19	5.860	43.84	2630	3.787
1.05	4.380	32.77	1966	2.831	1.20	5.980	44.74	2684	3.865
1.06	4.480	33.51	2011	2.895	1.21	6.100	45.63	2738	3.942
1.07	4.580	34.26	2056	2.960	1.22	6.210	46.46	2787	4.014
1.08	4.680	35.01	2100	3.025	1.23	6.330	47.35	2841	4.091
1.09	4.780	35.76	2145	3.089	1.24	6.460	48.33	2899	4.175
1.10	4.880	36.51	2190	3.154	1.25	6.580	49.22	2953	4.253
1.11	4.980	37.26	2235	3.219	1.26	6.700	50.12	3007	4.330
1.12	5.090	38.08	2284	3.290	1.27	6.830	51.10	3065	4.414
1.13	5.200	38.90	2334	3.361	1.28	6.960	52.07	3124	4.498
1.14	5.300	39.65	2379	3.425	1.29	7.080	52.97	3178	4.576
1.15	5.410	40.47	2428	3.496					

16

16-2: Large 60° V Trapezoidal Flume Discharge Table

Manufactured by Plasti-Fab, Inc. (Data from Plasti-Fab, Inc.)

Formulas: GPS = CFS x 7.481   GPM = CFS x 448.8
MGD = CFS x 0.6463

Head Feet	CFS	GPS	GPM	MGD	Head Feet	CFS	GPS	GPM	MGD
0.01					0.24	0.0390	0.2918	17.50	0.0252
0.02					0.25	0.0430	0.3217	19.30	0.0278
0.03					0.26	0.0480	0.3591	21.54	0.0310
0.04					0.27	0.0530	0.3965	23.79	0.0343
0.05					0.28	0.0580	0.4339	26.03	0.0375
0.06					0.29	0.0640	0.4788	28.72	0.0414
0.07					0.30	0.0690	0.5162	30.97	0.0446
0.08					0.31	0.0760	0.5686	34.11	0.0491
0.09					0.32	0.0820	0.6134	36.80	0.0530
0.10					0.33	0.0890	0.6658	39.94	0.0575
0.11					0.34	0.0960	0.7182	43.08	0.0620
0.12					0.35	0.1030	0.7705	46.23	0.0666
0.13					0.36	0.1110	0.8304	49.82	0.0717
0.14	0.0100	0.0748	4.488	0.0065	0.37	0.1190	0.8902	53.41	0.0769
0.15	0.0120	0.0898	5.386	0.0078	0.38	0.1280	0.9576	57.45	0.0827
0.16	0.0140	0.1047	6.283	0.0090	0.39	0.1370	1.025	61.49	0.0885
0.17	0.0160	0.1197	7.181	0.0103	0.40	0.1460	1.092	65.52	0.0944
0.18	0.0190	0.1421	8.527	0.0123	0.41	0.1550	1.160	69.56	0.1002
0.19	0.0210	0.1571	9.425	0.0136	0.42	0.1650	1.234	74.05	0.1066
0.20	0.0240	0.1795	10.77	0.0155	0.43	0.1760	1.317	78.99	0.1137
0.21	0.0280	0.2095	12.57	0.0181	0.44	0.1860	1.391	83.48	0.1202
0.22	0.0310	0.2319	13.91	0.0200	0.45	0.1980	1.481	88.86	0.1280
0.23	0.0350	0.2618	15.71	0.0226					

16

Manufactured by Plasti-Fab, Inc. (Data from Plasti-Fab, Inc.)
Formulas: GPS = CFS x 7.481   GPM = CFS x 448.8
MGD = CFS x 0.6463

Head Feet	CFS	GPS	GPM	MGD	Head Feet	CFS	GPS	GPM	MGD
0.01					0.40	0.3990	2.985	179.1	0.2579
0.02					0.41	0.4220	3.157	189.4	0.2727
0.03					0.42	0.4450	3.329	199.7	0.2876
0.04					0.43	0.4700	3.516	210.9	0.3038
0.05					0.44	0.4950	3.703	222.2	0.3199
0.06					0.45	0.5210	3.898	233.8	0.3367
0.07					0.46	0.5470	4.092	245.5	0.3535
0.08					0.47	0.5750	4.302	258.1	0.3716
0.09					0.48	0.6030	4.511	270.6	0.3897
0.10	0.0230	0.172	10.32	0.0149	0.49	0.6320	4.728	283.6	0.4085
0.11	0.0280	0.209	12.57	0.0181	0.50	0.6620	4.952	297.1	0.4279
0.12	0.0330	0.247	14.81	0.0213	0.51	0.6930	5.184	311.0	0.4479
0.13	0.0380	0.284	17.05	0.0246	0.52	0.7250	5.424	325.4	0.4686
0.14	0.0440	0.329	19.75	0.0284	0.53	0.7570	5.663	339.7	0.4892
0.15	0.0510	0.382	22.89	0.0330	0.54	0.7910	5.917	355.0	0.5112
0.16	0.0580	0.434	26.03	0.0375	0.55	0.8250	6.172	370.3	0.5332
0.17	0.0650	0.486	29.17	0.0420	0.56	0.8600	6.434	386.0	0.5558
0.18	0.0730	0.546	32.76	0.0472	0.57	0.8960	6.703	402.1	0.5791
0.19	0.0810	0.606	36.35	0.0524	0.58	0.9330	6.980	418.7	0.6030
0.20	0.0900	0.673	40.39	0.0582	0.59	0.9710	7.264	435.8	0.6276
0.21	0.1000	0.748	44.88	0.0646	0.60	1.010	7.556	453.3	0.6528
0.22	0.1100	0.823	49.37	0.0711	0.61	1.050	7.855	471.2	0.6786
0.23	0.1210	0.905	54.30	0.0782	0.62	1.090	8.154	489.2	0.7045
0.24	0.1320	0.987	59.24	0.0853	0.63	1.130	8.454	507.1	0.7303
0.25	0.1440	1.077	64.63	0.0931	0.64	1.170	8.753	525.1	0.7562
0.26	0.1560	1.167	70.01	0.1008	0.65	1.220	9.127	547.5	0.7885
0.27	0.1690	1.264	75.85	0.1092	0.66	1.260	9.426	565.5	0.8143
0.28	0.1830	1.369	82.13	0.1183	0.67	1.310	9.800	587.9	0.8467
0.29	0.1970	1.474	88.41	0.1273	0.68	1.360	10.17	610.4	0.8790
0.30	0.2120	1.586	95.15	0.1370	0.69	1.400	10.47	628.3	0.9048
0.31	0.2280	1.706	102.3	0.1474	0.70	1.450	10.85	650.8	0.9371
0.32	0.2440	1.825	109.5	0.1577	0.71	1.500	11.22	673.2	0.9694
0.33	0.2610	1.953	117.1	0.1687	0.72	1.550	11.60	695.6	1.002
0.34	0.2780	2.080	124.8	0.1797	0.73	1.600	11.97	718.1	1.034
0.35	0.2970	2.222	133.3	0.1920	0.74	1.660	12.42	745.0	1.073
0.36	0.3160	2.364	141.8	0.2042	0.75	1.710	12.79	767.4	1.105
0.37	0.3360	2.514	150.8	0.2172	0.76	1.770	13.24	794.4	1.144
0.38	0.3560	2.663	159.8	0.2301	0.77	1.820	13.62	816.8	1.176
0.39	0.3770	2.820	169.2	0.2437					

16

Chapter

17

Conversion
tables

Overview

- *This chapter contains conversion tables*
- *found useful in flow measurement work.*
- *The tables contain volumetric, flow rate*
- *and length conversion.*

Conversion tables

17

Table 17-1: Volumetric Conversion Factors

Note: Gallons are U.S. Gallons

To convert	Into	Multiply by
Acre Feet	Cubic Feet	4.356×10^4
	Cubic Meters	1.233×10^3
	Gallons	3.259×10^5
	Liters	1.233×10^6
	Million Gallons	0.3260
Cubic Feet	Acre Feet	2.296×10^{-5}
	Cubic Meters	0.02832
	Gallons	7.481
	Liters	28.32
	Million Gallons	7.481×10^{-6}
Cubic Meters	Acre Feet	8.107×10^{-4}
	Cubic Feet	35.31
	Gallons	264.2
	Liters	10^3
	Million Gallons	2.642×10^{-4}
Gallons	Acre Feet	3.069×10^{-6}
	Cubic Feet	0.1337
	Cubic Meters	3.785×10^{-3}
	Liters	3.785
	Million Gallons	10^{-6}
Liters	Acre Feet	8.107×10^{-7}
	Cubic Feet	0.03531
	Cubic Meters	10^{-3}
	Gallons	0.2642
	Million Gallons	2.644×10^{-7}
Million Gallons	Acre Feet	3.068
	Cubic Feet	1.337×10^5
	Cubic Meters	3.785×10^3
	Gallons	10^6
	Liters	3.785×10^6

17

Table 17-2: Flow Rate Conversion Factors

Note: Gallons are U.S. Gallons

To convert	Into	Multiply by
Acre ft. per day	Cubic ft. per day	4.356×10^4
	Cubic ft. per sec.	0.5042
	Cubic meters per day	1.233×10^3
	Cubic meters per sec.	0.01428
	Gallons per sec.	3.771
	Gallons per min.	226.3
	Liters per sec.	14.28
	Million gallons per day	0.3258
Cubic ft. per day	Acre ft. per day	2.296×10^{-5}
	Cubic ft. per sec.	1.157×10^{-5}
	Cubic meters per day	0.02832
	Cubic meters per sec.	3.278×10^{-7}
	Gallons per sec.	8.658×10^{-5}
	Gallons per min.	5.195×10^{-3}
	Liters per sec.	3.278×10^{-4}
	Million gallons per day	7.481×10^{-6}
Cubic ft. per sec.	Acre ft. per day	1.984
	Cubic ft. per day	8.640×10^4
	Cubic meters per day	2.447×10^3
	Cubic meters per sec.	0.0283
	Gallons per sec.	7.481
	Gallons per min.	448.8
	Liters per sec.	28.32
	Million gallons per day	0.6463
Cubic meters per day	Acre ft. per day	8.106×10^{-4}
	Cubic ft. per day	35.31
	Cubic ft. per sec.	4.088×10^{-4}
	Cubic meters per sec.	1.157×10^{-5}
	Gallons per sec.	3.057×10^{-3}
	Gallons per min.	0.1835
	Liters per sec.	0.0116
	Million gallons per day	2.642×10^{-4}

17

Table 17-2: Flow Rate Conversion Factors *(Continued)*

Note: Gallons are U.S. Gallons

To convert	Into	Multiply by
Cubic meters per sec.	Acre ft. per day	70.04
	Cubic ft. per day	3.051×10^6
	Cubic ft. per sec.	35.31
	Cubic meters per day	8.640×10^4
	Gallons per sec.	264.2
	Gallons per min.	1.585×10^4
	Liters per sec.	10^3
	Million gallons per day	22.82
Gallons per sec.	Acre ft. per day	0.2652
	Cubic ft. per day	1.155×10^4
	Cubic ft. per sec.	0.1337
	Cubic meters per day	327.1
	Cubic meters per sec.	3.78×10^{-3}
	Gallons per min.	60
	Liters per sec.	3.785
	Million gallons per day	0.0864
Gallons per min.	Acre ft. per day	4.42×10^{-3}
	Cubic ft. per day	192.5
	Cubic ft. per sec.	2.23×10^{-3}
	Cubic meters per day	5.451
	Cubic meters per sec.	6.309×10^{-5}
	Gallons per sec.	0.01667
	Liters per sec.	0.0631
	Million gallons per day	1.44×10^{-3}
Liters per sec.	Acre ft. per day	0.0700
	Cubic ft. per day	3.051×10^3
	Cubic ft. per sec.	0.0353
	Cubic meters per day	86.4
	Cubic meters per sec.	10^{-3}
	Gallons per min.	15.85
	Gallons per sec.	0.2643
	Million gallons per day	0.02282

17

Table 17-2: Flow Rate Conversion Factors *(Continued)*

Note: Gallons are U.S. Gallons

To convert	Into	Multiply by
Million gallons per day	Acre ft. per day	3.069
	Cubic ft. per day	1.337×10^5
	Cubic ft. per sec.	1.548
	Cubic meters per day	3.785×10^3
	Cubic meters per sec.	4.381×10^{-2}
	Gallons per min.	694.4
	Gallons per sec.	11.57
	Liters per sec.	43.82

17

Table 17-3: Length Conversion Factors

Fractions in inches	Decimals of a foot	Millimeters
1/16	0.0052	1.585
1/8	0.0104	3.770
3/16	0.0156	4.755
1/4	0.0208	6.340
5/16	0.0260	7.925
3/8	0.0313	9.541
7/16	0.0365	11.125
1/2	0.0417	12.710
9/16	0.0469	14.295
5/8	0.0521	15.880
11/16	0.0573	17.465
3/4	0.0625	19.050
13/16	0.0677	20.635
7/8	0.0729	22.220
15/16	0.0781	23.805
1	0.0833	25.390
1 1/16	0.0885	26.975
1 1/8	0.0938	28.590
1 3/16	0.0990	30.175
1 1/4	0.1042	31.760
1 5/16	0.1094	33.345
1 3/8	0.1146	34.930
1 7/16	0.1198	36.515
1 1/2	0.1250	38.100
1 9/16	0.1302	39.685
1 5/8	0.1354	41.270
1 11/16	0.1406	42.855
1 3/4	0.1458	44.440
1 13/16	0.1510	46.025
1 7/8	0.1563	47.640
1 15/16	0.1615	49.225
2	0.1667	50.810
2 1/16	0.1719	52.395
2 1/8	0.1771	53.980
2 3/16	0.1823	55.565
2 1/4	0.1875	57.150
2 5/16	0.1927	58.735

17

Table 17-3: Length Conversion Factors (*Continued*)

Fractions in inches	Decimals of a foot	Millimeters
2 3/8	0.1979	60.320
2 7/16	0.2031	61.905
2 1/2	0.2083	63.490
2 9/16	0.2135	65.075
2 5/8	0.2188	66.690
2 11/16	0.2240	68.275
2 3/4	0.2292	69.860
2 13/16	0.2344	71.445
2 7/8	0.2396	73.030
2 15/16	0.2448	74.615
3	0.2500	76.200
3 1/16	0.2552	77.785
3 1/8	0.2604	79.370
3 3/16	0.2656	80.955
3 1/4	0.2708	82.540
3 5/16	0.2760	84.125
3 3/8	0.2813	85.740
3 7/16	0.2865	87.325
3 1/2	0.2917	88.910
3 9/16	0.2969	90.495
3 5/8	0.3021	92.080
3 11/16	0.3073	93.665
3 3/4	0.3125	95.250
3 13/16	0.3177	96.835
3 7/8	0.3229	98.420
3 15/16	0.3281	100.005
4	0.3333	101.590
4 1/16	0.3385	103.175
4 1/8	0.3438	104.790
4 3/16	0.3490	106.375
4 1/4	0.3542	107.960
4 5/16	0.3594	109.545
4 3/8	0.3646	111.130
4 7/16	0.3698	112.715
4 1/2	0.3750	114.300
4 9/16	0.3802	115.885
4 5/8	0.3854	117.470

17

Table 17-3: Length Conversion Factors (*Continued*)

Fractions in inches	Decimals of a foot	Millimeters
4 11/16	0.3906	119.055
4 3/4	0.3958	120.640
4 13/16	0.4010	122.225
4 7/8	0.4063	123.840
4 15/16	0.4115	125.425
5	0.4167	127.010
5 1/6	0.4219	128.595
5 1/8	0.4271	130.180
5 3/16	0.4323	131.765
5 1/4	0.4375	133.350
5 5/16	0.4427	134.935
5 3/8	0.4479	136.520
5 7/16	0.4531	138.105
5 1/2	0.4583	139.690
5 9/16	0.4635	141.275
5 5/8	0.4688	142.890
5 11/16	0.4740	144.475
5 3/4	0.4792	146.060
5 13/16	0.4844	147.645
5 7/8	0.4896	149.230
5 15/16	0.4948	150.815
6	0.5000	152.400
6 1/16	0.5052	153.985
6 1/8	0.5104	155.570
6 3/16	0.5156	157.155
6 1/4	0.5208	158.740
6 5/16	0.5260	160.325
6 3/8	0.5313	161.940
6 7/16	0.5365	163.525
6 1/2	0.5417	165.110
6 9/16	0.5469	166.695
6 5/8	0.5521	168.280
6 11/16	0.5573	169.865
6 3/4	0.5625	171.450
6 13/16	0.5677	173.035
6 7/8	0.5729	174.620
6 15/16	0.5781	176.205

17

Table 17-3: Length Conversion Factors *(Continued)*

Fractions in inches	Decimals of a foot	Millimeters
7	0.5833	177.790
7 1/16	0.5885	179.375
7 1/8	0.5938	180.790
7 3/16	0.5990	182.575
7 1/4	0.6042	184.160
7 5/16	0.6094	185.745
7 3/8	0.6146	187.330
7 7/16	0.6198	188.915
7 1/2	0.6250	190.500
7 9/16	0.6302	192.085
7 5/8	0.6354	193.670
7 11/16	0.6406	195.255
7 3/4	0.6458	196.840
7 13/16	0.6510	198.425
7 7/8	0.6563	200.040
7 15/16	0.6615	201.625
8	0.6667	203.210
8 1/16	0.6719	204.795
8 1/8	0.6771	206.380
8 3/16	0.6823	207.965
8 1/4	0.6875	209.550
8 5/16	0.6927	211.135
8 3/8	0.6979	212.720
8 7/16	0.7031	214.305
8 1/2	0.7083	215.890
8 9/16	0.7135	217.475
8 5/8	0.7188	219.090
8 11/16	0.7240	220.675
8 3/4	0.7292	222.260
8 13/16	0.7344	223.845
8 7/8	0.7396	225.430
8 15/16	0.7448	227.015
9	0.7500	228.600
9 1/16	0.7552	230.185
9 1/8	0.7604	231.720
9 3/16	0.7656	233.355
9 1/4	0.7708	234.940

17

Table 17-3: Length Conversion Factors (*Continued*)

Fractions in inches	Decimals of a foot	Millimeters
9 5/16	0.7760	236.525
9 3/8	0.7813	238.140
9 7/16	0.7865	239.725
9 1/2	0.7917	241.310
9 9/16	0.7969	242.895
9 5/8	0.8021	244.480
9 11/16	0.8073	246.065
9 3/4	0.8125	247.650
9 13/16	0.8177	249.235
9 7/8	0.8229	250.820
9 15/16	0.8281	252.405
10	0.8333	253.990
10 1/16	0.8385	255.575
10 1/8	0.8438	259.190
10 3/16	0.8490	258.775
10 1/4	0.8542	260.360
10 5/16	0.8594	261.945
10 3/8	0.8646	263.530
10 7/16	0.8698	265.115
10 1/2	0.8750	266.700
10 9/16	0.8802	268.285
10 5/8	0.8854	269.870
10 11/16	0.8906	271.455
10 3/4	0.8958	273.040
10 13/16	0.9010	274.625
10 7/8	0.9063	276.240
10 15/16	0.9115	277.825
11	0.9167	279.410
11 1/16	0.9219	280.995
11 1/8	0.9271	282.580
11 3/16	0.9323	284.165
11 1/4	0.9375	285.750
11 5/16	0.9427	287.335
11 3/8	0.9479	288.920
11 7/16	0.9531	290.505
11 1/2	0.9583	292.090
11 9/16	0.9635	293.675

17

Table 17-3: Length Conversion Factors *(Continued)*

Fractions in inches	Decimals of a foot	Millimeters
11 5/8	0.9688	295.290
11 11/16	0.9740	296.875
11 3/4	0.9792	298.460
11 13/16	0.9844	300.045
11 7/8	0.9896	301.630
11 15/16	0.9948	303.215
12	1.0000	304.800

17

Index

Additional copies of the *Isco Open Channel Flow Measurement Handbook* are available for $19.95 per copy. Please send payment along with your request to:

Isco Handbook
P.O. Box 82531
Lincoln, NE 68501-2531

To receive complete information and pricing on Isco Wastewater Samplers and Open Channel Flow Measuring instruments, fill out and mail the attached postage paid postcard, or phone Isco toll free at (800) 228-4373. In Alaska, Nebraska, and outside the U.S.A. phone (402) 474-2233.

☑ **I want more information.**

Please send me additional information on Isco:

❏ Portable Wastewater Samplers
❏ Refrigerated Wastewater Samplers
❏ Open Channel Flow Meters
❏ Well Sampling Equipment
❏ Leasing Isco Equipment
❏ Other_____

My need is:

❏ Immediate. Have a representative contact me. My telephone number is
(_____) _____
❏ Future application.
❏ Information only.

Name _____

Organization _____

Phone (_____) _____

Address _____

City _____ State ___ Zip _____